WITHDRAWN

Educational Charters
and Documents
598 to 1909

Educational Charters and Documents
598 to 1909

BY
ARTHUR F. *Francis* LEACH

AMS PRESS
NEW YORK

Reprinted from the edition of 1911, Cambridge
First AMS EDITION published 1971
Manufactured in the United States of America

International Standard Book Number: 0-404-03893-X

Library of Congress Catalog Number: 76-137263

LA
631
L5
1971

AMS PRESS INC.
NEW YORK, N.Y. 10003

TABLE OF CONTENTS

	PAGE
INTRODUCTION	ix
Dunwich (?) and Canterbury Schools. 631	2
Teaching of Archbishop Theodore. 668	2
Song Schools at Canterbury, York and Rochester. 633–668	6
Some pupils of Theodore and Hadrian. 693–709	6
Aldhelm's Studies. c. 680	8
Alcuin on York School. 732–786	10
Grammar, Song and Writing Schools separated. 796	18
Alcuin on Hexham School. c. 797	20
Canon Law orders bishops to provide Grammar Schools. 826	20
State of Education in England. 871–893	22
Education of Alfred and his children according to Asser. c. 1001	24
King Edgar's Educational Canons. c. 960	34
Educational Canons of 994 (?)	36
Abbot Aelfric's Colloquy edited by Aelfric Bata	36
Aelfric's English-Latin Grammar	48
King Canute founds Public Schools and Exhibitions. c. 1020	52
A Scholar's Rank. 1029–60	52
Waltham Holy Cross School. 1060–1177	54
Warwick School *temp.* Edward the Confessor	58
Dunwich School granted to Eye Priory. 1076–1083	58
Lanfranc's Constitutions. c. 1075	60
Pontefract School. 1075–1087	66
Hastings Grammar and Song Schools before 1090	68
York School. 1075–1090	70
Salisbury School in the Institution of St Osmund. 1091	72
Christ Church (Hants) School. 1100	74
Gloucester School. c. 1100	76
Beverley Grammar-Schoolmaster in love. c. 1100	76

Table of Contents

	PAGE
St Albans and Dunstable Schools. c. 1100	78
St Paul's School. c. 1111	80
Thetford School restored to secular government. c. 1114	82
London Schools in Thomas-à-Becket's boyhood. 1118	82
Appointment of Master of St Paul's School. c. 1125	86
Warwick School contested between two Collegiate Churches. 1123	86
Monopoly of St Paul's School enforced by excommunication. c. 1138	90
Huntingdon School granted to Huntingdon Priory. 1127	92
Dunstable School granted to Dunstable Priory. 1131	92
Reading School placed under Reading Abbey between 1125 and 1139	94
Gloucester School granted to Llanthony Abbey. 1137	94
Synod of Westminster forbids hiring out Schools. 1138	96
Endowment of Salisbury School. 1139	96
Bristol School under the Kalendars' Gild. c. 1141	98
The Origin of Oxford University. c. 1133–1150	100
Grant of Derby School to Darley Abbey confirmed. c. 1155	108
Grant to Derby School of School and Boarding-house. c. 1160	110
Winchester School dispute appealed to Pope. c. 1159	112
Bedford School transferred from secular to regular Canons. c. 1160	116
Alexander Neckham's education at St Albans School and Paris University. 1167–1173	116
Pope Alexander III forbids fees for licences to teach. 1160–1172	118
Exhibitioner at Northampton School. 1176–8	120
The Lateran Council orders Cathedral Schools to be free. 1179	122
Exhibitions of Durham Schoolboys in the Cathedral Priory Almonry. 1190–1230	124
York School separately endowed. 1180–1191	126
Bury St Edmunds School endowed. 1180–1198	128
St Albans and Dunstable Schools. c. 1183	132
Royal Exhibitioners at Oxford. c. 1200	134
Mathematics at Oxford. c. 1200	136

Table of Contents

	PAGE
Council of London forbids fees for licences to teach. 1200	138
Priests' Schools in Council of Westminster. 1200	138
A Royal Exhibitioner at Winchester. 1205	140
Secession of Oxford scholars to Cambridge and Reading. 1209	140
All Cathedrals to keep Grammar and Theological schools. 1215	142
University students excused from residence on benefices. 1219	144
Beneficed clergy ordered to attend schools. 1219–1225	146
Cambridge University first mentioned. 1231	148
Marlborough Schoolmaster acts as judge in ecclesiastical case. 1232	152
Northampton Vicar ordered to attend Northampton School. 1230	154
University scholars at Northampton and Salisbury. 1238.	154
Newark Grammar School and Chancellor of Southwell Minster. 1238	156
Grammar and Logic Schools connected with Southwell Minster. 1248	158
Northampton University encouraged and suppressed. 1261–1265	158
The earliest University College in England at Salisbury. 1262	164
Jurisdiction over University scholars at Salisbury. 1278	168
Foundation of Merton College at Malden, Surrey. 1264.	170
Re-foundation of Merton College at Oxford. 1274	180
Oxford Grammar School Statutes. 13th century	186
Oxford Curriculum for B.A. degree. 1267	190
Foundation of Gloucester College, Oxford, for Benedictine monks. 1275–1287	196
Rights of Grammar-Schoolmaster, and Chancellor of Cambridge, and Archdeacon of Ely. 1276	202
Merton College Grammar School accounts. 1277–1310 .	210
Foundation of Peterhouse, the first Cambridge College. 1280–1285	222
Norwich Schoolmaster appointed by Archbishop of Canterbury. 1288	232

Table of Contents

	PAGE
Canterbury Schoolmaster's power of excommunication. 1291	232
Holy-water-carrying, a form of school exhibition. 1295	232
Limited monopoly of Nottingham School. 1289	234
Gilbertine College at Stamford. 1303	236
Monopoly of Lincoln Song School. 1305	236
Canterbury Schoolmaster appointed by Archbishop. 1306	238
St Mary-le-Bow Schoolmaster appointed by the Dean of Arches. 1309	238
St Albans School Statutes. 1309	240
Canterbury Schoolmaster's jurisdiction exercised. 1311–1323	252
Council of Vienne orders teaching of Hebrew, Greek, Arabic and Chaldee. 1311	268
Manumission of an Oxford M.A. 1312	270
Right of Beverley choristers to free admission to Grammar School. 1312	270
Warwick Grammar and Song School Statutes. 1316(?)	272
Assertion of priority of Oxford to Paris University. 1317–1322	276
Six Lincolnshire Grammar Schools. 1329	280
Secession from Oxford University to Stamford. 1334–5	282
Papal Statutes for education of Benedictine monks. 1335	288
Creation of Bachelors in Beverley Grammar School. 1338	294
St Albans Almonry School Statutes. c. 1330	296
Merton Grammar School accounts. 1347–1395	298
Westminster Almonry School accounts. 1335–1540	306
Bishop of Exeter attacks the teaching of the classics. 1357	314
Kingston-on-Thames Public School. 1364	318
Winchester College Foundation Deed. 1382	320
A Lollard School or Conventicle. 1382	328
Wotton-under-Edge Grammar School Foundation deed. 1384	330
English schoolboys begin to translate Latin into English instead of French. 1327–1349	340
Grammar and Song Schools combined at Northallerton. 1385	342

Table of Contents

	PAGE
Chaucer's Oxford Scholar and Song School. 1388	344
Higham Ferrers Schoolmaster also Mayor. 1391	348
New College, Oxford, Statutes. 1400	348
Higham Ferrers Schoolmaster appointed by King. 1400	372
Lollard keepers of Schools or Conventicles to be burnt. 1400	374
Stratford-on-Avon Gild Grammar School. 1402–1482	376
Statute of Apprentices not to apply to school. 1405–6	386
Lincoln City or Cathedral Grammar School and new Choristers' Grammar School. 1407–9	386
Schoolmasters not to teach Sacraments. 1408	394
Supporters of Lollard Schools or Conventicles to be arrested. 1414	394
Cornhill Grammar School royal exhibitioner. 1419	396
Teaching of English law, French and Letter-writing at Oxford. 1432	396
Sevenoaks Grammar School foundation. 1432	398
God's House, Cambridge, for training Grammar Schoolmasters. 1439	402
Eton College Foundation Charter. 1440	404
Eton College Monopoly for 10 miles round. 1446	412
Cambridge Grammar School absorbed in King's College. 1440	414
Farthinghoe Free School under Mercers' Company. 1443	414
London Schools increased. 1446–7	416
Appeal to Lords and Commons for Oxford University Library. 1447–50	420
Ipswich Grammar School fees. 1477–1482	422
Rotherham Free Schools of Grammar, Song and Writing. 1483	422
Aldwincle Spelling and Reading School. 1489	434
King's Hall, Cambridge, Free Lectures. 1492	436
Macclesfield Free Grammar School founded by ex-Lord Mayor. 1503	436
Priests forbidden to teach at Bridgenorth. 1503	439
Westminster Monks' lack of learning. 1504	439
Giggleswick Grammar School founded with Building Lease. 1507	441

Table of Contents

	PAGE
Canterbury Monks' ignorance of grammar. 1511	444
Educational Canons of Convocation. 1529	444
Winchester and Eton Time-tables. 1530	448
Canterbury Cathedral Grammar School re-founded. 1541	452
Educational Injunctions of Edward VI. 1547	472
School provisions of the Chantries Act. 1547	472
Continuance of Chantry Schools in Cornwall. 1548	475
Sherborne School re-founded as Free Grammar School of King Edward VI. 1550	478
Cardinal Pole's Educational Articles. 1558	494
Queen Elizabeth's Educational Injunctions. 1559	494
Westminster School Statutes on re-foundation. 1560	496
Recusant Schoolmasters. 1580	524
Bury St Edmunds Schoolmaster dismissed. 1581	526
Penalties for unlicensed schools. 1603–4	528
Exeter Cathedral Grammar School monopoly defended by Bishop. 1624–5	528
Hoole's Grammar School Curriculum. 1637–1660	530
Advancement of Education during Commonwealth and Protectorate. 1643–1660	534
Charity School Movement. 1699–1718	539
Act to prevent Dissenters and Non-jurors from teaching. 1713	542
National Schools Trust Deed. 1870–1902	544
British Schools Trust Deed. 1870–1902	547
Bradford Grammar School Scheme made by Commissioners under the Endowed Schools Act 1869. 1871	548
Andover Grammar School. Amending Scheme made by Board of Education under the Charitable Trusts Acts 1853 to 1894. 1909	560
INDEX	571

INTRODUCTION

THIS book aims at doing, so far as the scantier space allows, for the educational history of England what Bishop Stubbs' *Select Charters* did for its constitutional history. It sets out the text of the salient documents relating to the origin and development of educational institutions.

Educational charters, being largely both legal and ecclesiastical, tend to combine the prolixity of the preacher with the verbosity of the conveyancer. Hence, few of them can be presented at full length. As the chief object of the work is to show the origins of educational institutions, which are in many cases centuries earlier than hitherto supposed, the earlier bulk much more largely than the later documents.

In nothing, not even in religion, has the innate conservatism of the human race been more marked than in education. It is hardly an exaggeration to say that the subjects and the methods of education remained the same from the days of Quintilian to the days of Arnold, from the first century to the mid-nineteenth century of the Christian era.

The history of English education begins with the coming of Christianity. But the education introduced by Augustine of Canterbury was identical in means and methods with that of Augustine of Hippo. The conversion of the English caused the establishment in Canterbury of a school on the model of the Grammar and Rhetoric Schools of Rome, themselves the reproduction of the Grammar and Rhetoric Schools of Alexandria and of Athens.

This is brought home to us by the first document in the text, an extract from Bede's *Ecclesiastical History*. It relates how in a year, fixed to 631, Sigebert, king of the East English, with the assistance of bishop Felix, who came from

Canterbury, provided masters and ushers after the Canterbury (or Kentish) fashion, and set up a school in which boys might be taught grammar. For so the word *litteris*, commonly translated *letters*, a translation which gives an erroneous impression either of a mere A B C school, or of a school of *belles-lettres*, is properly and accurately translated. The term *ludus literarius*, a translation of the Greek grammar school, first appears in Plautus *c.* 210 B.C. Suetonius, *c.* 120 A.D., specifically states in his book, *On Famous Schoolmasters*, that the grammar masters were at first called *literati*, a translation of the Greek *grammatici*, a term which by his time had superseded it. At all epochs the term *ludus literarius* or *schola literarum*, or *literae* simply, was used as a literary equivalent to the usual grammar school or grammar, and at all epochs too, grammar meant and included, not merely grammatical learning, but the learning to speak and write Latin and the study of the matter as well as the language of classical authors, especially the poets.

Grammar Schools and Rhetoric Schools were spread all over the Roman Empire. For centuries after the introduction of Christianity, eminent Christians like St Jerome and St Augustine, the latter himself a schoolmaster, were bred in pagan literature, and under heathen teachers. When these schools, which from the days of the Antonines were public schools, gave place to church schools is not, probably cannot be, precisely ascertained. Gregory of Tours is perhaps the earliest celebrity who, though he was a master of the classical learning of the age, is said to have been brought up, not in a public school, but by two bishops, *c.* 520. Though in France the bishops appear to have obtained long before the control of the schools, a letter of Pope Gregory (*Ep*. xi. 54), addressed to Desiderius, bishop of Vienne in 595, is probably the first actual evidence of a bishop himself teaching school. 'As we cannot relate without shame it has come to our knowledge that your brotherhood teaches grammar to certain persons, which we take all the worse as it converts what we formerly said in your praise to lamentation and woe, since the praise of Christ cannot

lie in one mouth with the praise of Jupiter. Consider yourself what a crime it is for bishops to recite what would be improper in a religiously-minded layman.' These words are an adaptation of a phrase of St Jerome. They refer to the fact that the Grammar Schools still brought up their pupils on the classical authors, and especially to the famous line in Virgil's *Eclogues*, which always remained one of the chief of school books, *Ab Jove principium Musae, Jovis omnia plena*. This letter brings us close to Canterbury School, for it was a letter of introduction of Lawrence the priest and Mellitus the monk, who were returning from Rome to Canterbury with a new batch of clerks and monks.

As Sigebert was assisted by bishop Felix, the first bishop of East Anglia, and his see was at Dunwich, his school has been rightly inferred to have been in the same place; and Dunwich has been often dubbed in consequence the cradle of English learning. It is strange that the fact was overlooked that, as Dunwich took its masters from Canterbury, the earliest English school must be sought, not in Dunwich, but in Canterbury.

Now if Canterbury had a school which was a model in 631, who is likely to have founded it but its first missionary and archbishop, Augustine? We know that in the next century when the English Winfrid became, under the name of Boniface, the first missionary and archbishop of the Germans, he set up schools as an essential part of a missionary establishment, just as missionaries everywhere do to-day. We cannot therefore be wrong in asserting that the Canterbury School was founded at or about the same time as the church of Canterbury, namely, in 598, when king Ethelbert was baptized and 'did not defer giving his teachers a settled residence in his metropolis of Canterbury with such possessions as were necessary for their subsistence.' Here Augustine lived according to the express directions of Pope Gregory not like a monk in a cloister, but as a bishop with his clerks, preaching, that is, and teaching, as well as praying and singing the services.

This brings us to one of the fundamental facts which receives

continuous illustration in our documents, that in England from the first, education was the creature of religion, the school was an adjunct of the church, and the schoolmaster was an ecclesiastical officer. For close on eleven hundred years, from 598 to 1670, all educational institutions were under exclusively ecclesiastical control. The law of education was a branch of the canon law. The church courts had exclusive jurisdiction over schools and universities and colleges, and until 1540 all schoolmasters and scholars were clerks, or clerics or clergy, and in orders, though not necessarily holy orders.

Our next document shows us this very plainly. Bede's account of the coming of the Greek archbishop, Theodore, and his colleague, the abbot Hadrian, in 668 and of the archbishop's visitation of all England and his acceptance as Primate by all the kingdoms of the Heptarchy, round which he went preaching and teaching, has been misinterpreted into an account of the foundation of Canterbury School and of schools elsewhere. What it does show is that the introduction of Greek in addition to Latin gave an impetus to English learning which made English scholars the first in the world, and conduced to the production of Bede, himself the sanest of historians for 800 years. Bede, in his account of Paulinus, the apostle of the North, shows us also that side by side with the Grammar School arose the Song School, which has been often confused with it, but was from the beginning quite distinct, and though it sometimes encroached on the sphere of the Grammar School, and in smaller places was combined with it, always had a different function. Canterbury supplied York with its Song School on the Roman, i.e. Gregorian, model, as it did Dunwich with its Grammar school model. Bede vaunts the learning of the pupils of Theodore and Hadrian, who knew Greek and Latin as well as English.

In the next generation, Aldhelm appears to have owed his learning to Winchester, not to Canterbury, and to Irish rather than Roman sources. The dates and facts of the life of this scion of the West Saxon royal house make it impossible for him

to have been a pupil, as sometimes claimed, of abbot Hadrian, while his Brito-Irish teacher Maidulf seems to be evolved from Bede's place-name for Malmesbury. In a letter to his former chief, Haeddi, bishop of Winchester, excusing himself from a visit to join in the Christmas dances, Aldhelm sets out a marvellous programme of studies. It includes Roman law, prosody, even to the niceties of brachy- and hypercatalectics, astronomy, and the most laborious of all studies, arithmetic, in which, 'by the special grace of God,' he has at last understood 'the most difficult of all things, fractions.' Leaping a generation and passing from Wessex to Northumbria, we come to Alcuin's poem 'On the Bishops and Saints of the Church of York,' one of the most illuminating documents in the history of education. A false monastic educational genealogy has been concocted, making Bede the pupil of archbishop Theodore, archbishop Egbert of York of Bede, Alcuin of Egbert, and Rabanus Maurus and a host of Franco-German monks of Alcuin. Alcuin's own poem snaps the chain at the second link. Egbert was not a pupil of Bede, of whom he was the superior and patron, and was a secular, not a monk. Nor was Egbert the master of Alcuin, but of Ethelbert or Albert, who succeeded him in the archbishopric. Albert was also emphatically a secular and no monk, and a teacher so famous that foreign potentates tried in vain to lure him away from England as Alcuin was afterwards lured by Charlemagne. He it was who was Alcuin's master.

The truth is that, except for perhaps a century and a half in Ireland and such scattered parts of England and France as in the 7th and 8th centuries fell under Irish influence, the monasteries were never schools nor the monks educators, except of their own younger brethren. Their own rules forbade them to be so. Bede particularly mentions that when, *c.* 648, the little English boys and some older were taught by Scots (i.e. Irish) it was the regular, i.e. monkish, discipline they learnt. The Cathedral and Collegiate churches, in which schools were an essential and important part of the foundation, were the

centres of education. The clerks, later called canons, who
taught the schools, were the educators and promoters of
education. Alcuin's poem shows us that at York the curriculum
was encyclopaedic. Grammar and rhetoric came first, but
were followed by law, music, mathematics comprising astronomy,
arithmetic and geometry; the science of the calendar; and finally
theology. It was a boarding school. 'Whatever youths he saw of
conspicuous intelligence he joined to himself, he taught, he fed,
he loved.' Architecture also seems to have been included, as,
with his two favourite pupils, of whom Alcuin was one, Albert
built a new cathedral with 30 side-altars and chapels round it.
When Albert died the mastership of the school was separated
from the archbishopric, Eanbald taking the latter, while Alcuin
succeeded to the 'school, the master's chair and the books,' a
catalogue of which is given. In it the grammarians vie with
the theologians in number, while the classical authors, Virgil,
Lucan, Statius, Cicero, Pliny, Aristotle, are rivalled by the
Christian poets Sedulius and Juvencus, and others. It is
pleasing to note that Bede and Aldhelm were already numbered
among the classics. When Alcuin went over to teach the
Palace School of Charlemagne, his letters show him still interested in the promotion of English education at Lichfield under
Offa, at Canterbury, and at Hexham, as well as in his own old
school at York. In the last he recommends a division of
labour, the separation of the Song and Writing School from
the Grammar School, under different masters. We last see
him about the year 804 when retired to become abbot of Tours
sending for some of his books at York to scatter the perfumes
of English learning on the banks of the Loire.

A canon of Pope Eugenius made in 826 enforced as law
what was already established by custom, the duty of bishops to
act as inspectors of schools with the Pope as President of a
European Board of Education.

Our next document, if it is to be taken literally, shows a sad
falling off in England since the days of Alcuin. In the preface
to his translation of Pope Gregory the Great's *Pastoral Care*,

Alfred the Great draws a depressing contrast between 'the good old days' when foreigners came to England in search of education and learning, and his own day when England had to get learning from abroad. We cannot but think that he is guilty of rhetorical exaggeration when he says that he could not recall anyone south of the Thames who could understand the services in English. However, he ends his preface with the hope that if peace is preserved, every English freeman's son will learn to read English, while those who wish to continue in learning, and go to the higher ranks or orders, will also learn Latin. If the canons of Edgar imputed to the year 960 are to be trusted as to date and to being a true representation of the state of England at the time and are not merely repetition of old canons, this hope had been more than realized.

Not only suspect but self-convicted as to its real date and authenticity is the Life of Alfred purporting to be by Asser. In it two miracles are recorded in regard to the education of Alfred. The first enabled him to read Saxon as a little boy at his mother's knee, pleased at a pretty picture-book, by the simple process of taking the book out of the room to a master, getting him to read it aloud, and coming back able to read it to his mother. The other is even more marvellous. For he learnt to construe Latin, we are told, not merely in a single day but during the time which it took the biographer to write down a single Latin passage in the hero's note-book. The first miracle has long been shown to be impossible. At the time when it is said to have occurred, when Alfred was 12 years old, in 861 or 862, he had no mother. His stepmother, a Frankish girl, Judith, had been married to Alfred's father in 855, when she was 13 years old. In 859, when Alfred's father died, she married Alfred's brother, who is depicted as looking at the pretty picture-book with him. No earlier date can be assigned for the incident, as Alfred was sent to Rome in 853, when four years old. The other miracle is self-contradicted. For while chapter 22 represents Alfred as 'illiterate,' i.e. ignorant of

Latin only to his 12th year or more, chapter 25 says that 'to the present day,' i.e. 887, and, 'I believe to the day of his death,' he insatiably desired to learn Latin but never did, and chapter 87 relates the miraculous learning in a day. All three accounts cannot be true. Probably none are true, and Alfred began Latin as a little boy at Rome. These and other contradictions have been sought to be explained as being due to the Life being an unfinished draft. Such a defence is a plea of guilty. The only MS. of Asser ever known is admitted to have been written about 100 years after Alfred's death. That a hagiographer should have written three different versions of his hero's education and learning in a draft romance is a rational explanation. That a contemporary should do so of the hero with whom he lived in daily intercourse, speaking of things within his own knowledge, is merely impossible.

While therefore we cannot consider Asser's Life as evidence of the state of education in the 9th century it is highly interesting as evidence of what an early 11th century writer thought possible. It shows at all events that English mothers of the 11th century taught their children, even royal children, to read English poetry, and that it was customary for English kings and nobles to send their sons to the Grammar School with ordinary freemen, to learn Latin and fit them for judicial business, or for clerical work in the modern as well as the medieval sense.

The two school-books of Aelfric, the *Colloquy* and the *Grammar*, show that Alfred's ideal was realized in the 11th century. It is now well established that Aelfric is not the archbishop of Canterbury of that name, but a scholar and clerk of Winchester, who became abbot of Evesham, and devoted himself as a sort of medieval Bohn to the translation of Latin works into English. The *Colloquy* is fixed to the year 995. If it really represents English schools at the time it shows an amazing diffusion of education among all classes, boys in all the different occupations, ploughboy, gamekeeper, hawker, baker, smith, merchant, learning Latin of a secular master side by side with a young monk. It may be that it is only a trans-

lation of some older Latin original of the days of the Roman Public School. The opening sentences, which assume the incessant use of flogging as a means of instilling learning into the youthful mind, are characteristic proof of the Rule of the Rod which prevailed in all schools from the date of the Mimes of Herondas at Alexandria, *c.* B.C. 270, to the days of *Tom Brown's Schooldays*, A.D. 1850.

Aelfric's *Grammar*, however, proves the existence of a considerable amount of learning and demand for education. It is taken chiefly from the *Ars Major* of Priscian, a great work in 18 books, by a Constantinople Grammar Schoolmaster at the beginning of the 6th century. That book was itself chiefly a translation—the extant MSS. of which descend from one made in 526-7—from the Greek of Apollonius of Alexandria, written three centuries before. Aelfric's *Grammar* postulates a previous acquaintance with Donatus, whose *Ars Minor* or Short Treatise on the Parts of Speech, was written by Aelius Donatus, a schoolmaster at Rome, in the latter half of the 4th century. Donatus was the teacher of Hieronymus (St Jerome) who preserves his famous *mot*, 'Pereant qui ante nos nostra dixerunt.' A 'Donat' became a term for a first text-book in any subject, and a knowledge of 'old Donatus' was demanded by William of Wykeham as a condition precedent to admission to his college at Winchester.

It is remarkable that Aelfric's *Grammar* assumes not only that boys are learning Latin but girls also, his example to illustrate that the gerundive in *-do* does not vary in gender, being 'ipsa monialis vigilat docendo puellas,' 'the nun is awake teaching maiden-children,' and 'a man and a woman are taught by reading.' Now it is certain from the letters of Boniface of Mainz to the friends he left behind in England that princesses and high-born abbesses and nuns were educated. Several of them send him Latin verses of their own composition for correction, and he asks them in return for learned books and discusses points of scholarship with them. It is almost equally certain that after the Conquest this had ceased.

Whereas the monks were addressed in Latin the nuns were invariably addressed in the vernacular. Even as late as the 13th century, when archbishop Peckham wrote to rebuke the nuns of Godstow for their familiarity with Oxford undergraduates, he wrote in French; and from the reign of Henry VI onwards nuns were addressed not in Latin but English.

It is interesting to see the Danish conqueror, Canute, depicted by an 11th century chronicler going about as a sort of Charity Commissioner, settling educational endowments in the chief centres of population and establishing exhibitions, not only for freemen, but freedmen's sons. The curious document called 'Ranks,' attributed to Canute's time, lends some credit to this account, as scholars are especially mentioned as receiving worship (*weorthscipe*), or honour, according to their proficiency.

The two last of our documents referring to pre-Conquest times bear witness at least to the existence of flourishing Grammar Schools attached to two great collegiate churches of secular canons.

The last of the English kings, more Dane than English, Harold, when he was still only earl, enlarged the church of the Holy Cross of Waltham into a college for a dean and 12 canons. The dean was English, but the second dignitary of the church, the schoolmaster, Master Athelard, was sought for abroad, not in Normandy or France, but in the Teutonic lands, a native of Liège. The reason for this was, perhaps, rather a reactionary one, namely, that the Teutonic churches still combined the grammar school and singing school in one, and that the discipline was severe. The 'Child Master,' one of the canons, was sent to Hastings under the banner of the founder, and brought back his body to burial at Waltham. An interesting account of the school in *c.* 1100 is given by one of the last of the secular canons, who were turned out by Henry II about 1170 for the crime of luxury, that is marriage, when he converted the church into a priory of regular canons in vicarious atonement for the death of Thomas à Becket.

The school attached to the collegiate church in Warwick

Castle, which we may fairly attribute to the foundation of Ethelfleda, lady of the Mercians, daughter of Alfred, appears in a writ of Henry I, confirming to the original mother church of All Saints 'the school of Warwick as it was in the days of King Edward,' the Confessor, against the Norman earl who sought to transfer it to the rival church of St Mary's. The dispute was eventually settled by a union of the two churches, the school of All Saints' being transferred from the castle to St Mary's in the town in 1123.

The Norman Conquest had little direct effect on the schools, though it no doubt at first cut off the supply of scholars, and substituted French for English as the vernacular into which Latin was translated, and made all the Old English translations and school-books obsolete. The cathedrals and collegiate churches which kept the schools, remained. At York, which had suffered most from Norman fury, the first Norman archbishop, Thomas of Bayeux, appointed in 1072, though he found the whole place depopulated and ravaged, yet found 'of the seven canons (for there were no more) only three among the ruins of the burnt city and cathedral; the rest being dead or fled through fear.' He re-roofed the church, collected and restored the canons, and increased their number, placing them under a Provost. 'But a few years later,' about 1090, he substituted a Dean for a Provost and established a treasurer and precentor; 'the school-master (Magister Scolarum) he had already established.' As it is in the highest degree improbable that the school had ever ceased except during William's devastation, this must mean that he had restored the master, as the second person in the church. The new constitution of four principal persons or dignitaries, dean or provost, precentor, schoolmaster, or, as he was later called, chancellor, treasurer or sacrist, in which the schoolmaster sank to the third place, became the normal one in all the English cathedrals, which had not passed into monkish control, and of the ancient collegiate churches like Beverley. It appears most clearly in the *Institution of St Osmund*, or foundation statutes of the first bishop of

Salisbury. While the precentor ruled the choir in singing, and the treasurer presided over its lights and ornaments, the chancellor presided over the teaching of the school and the correction of the books;—the reading presumably, not the singing books. It is the duty of the chief of the school (*archiscola*) to hear and determine the lessons, carry the seal, and compose letters and deeds and mark the readers on the table (the orders of the day), while the precentor marks the singers on the table. The use of the word 'chancellor' suggests that the *Institution* is not in its original state but brought up to date in the late 12th or beginning of the 13th century. For, in a later document of the reign of Stephen, we find the schoolmaster of Salisbury still called by that name. At York, the schoolmaster was still so called at the end of the 12th century, as he was also at St Paul's until the year 1205.

At St Paul's we see the schoolmaster given an official residence and the duties of librarian as well as schoolmaster in a document of about 1111. A later document, of about 1127, giving the appointment and further endowment of his successor, has the interest attaching to its being the oldest appointment of an English schoolmaster actually extant. A similar interest attaches to the writ in which Henry of Blois, bishop of Winchester, as acting bishop of London, from 1138 to 1140, threatens the thunders of the church by excommunication to put down rival masters, and enforces the monopoly of teaching and granting licences to teach of the schoolmaster of St Paul's. Twenty years later, the same bishop was concerned in a similar contest for monopoly at Winchester. An appeal was taken to the famous John of Salisbury as 'Official' of Canterbury and was sent on by him to the Pope. The requirement of a licence from the Ordinary (i.e. generally the bishop) before any kind of teaching could be given prevailed down to 1670, and for grammar still prevails, except in cases in which schemes made under the Endowed Schools Act, 1869, have deprived him of his power.

At Canterbury, the new Norman archbishop, Lanfranc, no Norman but an Italian, had himself been a schoolmaster before

he became an abbot, and was one of the greatest doctors of the age. He, too, published new constitutions for his cathedral, but as it was in the hands of monks, the *Constitutions of Lanfranc* are purely monastic. Though boys are mentioned, they are only the oblates, or boys 'offered' as infants or little children on the altar and sworn to monkhood when old enough. An elderly monk was assigned as a master to every two oblates, who were carefully kept from contact with the monks and each other. The only reference to instruction is contained in the direction that they should read a little when they first go in the cloister in the morning. They seem to have been taught little but the Rule of the order. The same applies to the novices, brought in from the world at a later age. The School of Canterbury, the Grammar School, was outside the monastery and had nothing to do with the monks, and does not therefore appear at all in these *Constitutions*. It remained, as was the case in all the monastic cathedrals, under the exclusive and immediate control of the archbishop or bishop, who himself appointed the master, as may be seen from examples given at Canterbury, Worcester and Norwich; which could be extended to Winchester, Carlisle and Ely, and elsewhere.

At the end of the 11th and the beginning of the 12th century, a movement towards monasticism took place, which threatened to extrude the secular clergy altogether from the cathedrals and collegiate churches in favour of monks. Opinion was not all one way. Some bishops, like Walkelin of Winchester, and many laymen were in favour of the secular clergy. There was at first a certain movement for the establishment of new collegiate churches or the consolidation of old ones, especially in the castles. Thus we find Ilbert of Lacy founding the collegiate church of St Clement in Pontefract castle, and confirming or giving to it the school of Kirby-Pontefract, *c.* 1075; while at the other end of the kingdom, Robert, count of Eu, in founding the collegiate church of St Mary in the castle of Hastings, or perhaps dividing into separate prebends what had been a college of clerks living on common estates, made one canon *ex-officio* master of the Grammar School, and

another of the Song School. In both cases, we learn of this from a confirmation by their grandsons.

The monastic movement appears in the documents which show the schools already transferred to the control of the monastery, as at St Albans where we hear of the abbot appointing the master c. 1100; at Thetford in 1114 as being re-transferred from monastic to secular control; and as being transferred from secular to regular control at Huntingdon in 1127; Dunstable, 1131; Reading, c. 1135; Gloucester, c. 1137; Derby, c. 1150; Bedford, c. 1160. These are only isolated instances of what was going on all over the country, the documents relating to which do not happen to have been preserved or yet produced.

A similar movement, which proceeded to greater lengths, was going on in the transfer of hospitals for the sick, infirm and poor. The movement bid fair to run the course it did in the Greek church and transfer the bishoprics, and all higher posts in the church and education to the monks, leaving only poor married priests to do the isolated work of the parishes. Two things stayed the plague. The secular clergy gave way to the monastic *furore* so far as to forswear matrimony, while in the sphere of education the rise of universities restored to seculars a corporate organization. In England, the Council of 1150 finally accepted the principle of the celibacy of the secular clergy, while from 1130 onwards Oxford University was becoming one of the strongest bodies in the country.

The account given by FitzStephen in his *Life of Becket* of the schools of London in Becket's boyhood, where the monopoly of the schoolmaster of St Paul's and his two colleagues was broken for anyone famous in philosophy, and the rivalry of the schools in organized debates and disputations shows that a university was in the air there also. In modern times a university tends to mean a corporate body with the power of granting degrees, or titles of honour which are certificates of proficiency, attained by a course of training in a certain number of subjects by pupils older than school-age. The word 'university' means simply a corporation. Just as corporation has

Universities xxiii

become the more or less exclusive term for a municipal corporation, and company for a trading corporation, so university became the distinctive term for an educational corporation of teachers and pupils in the higher faculties. Attempts have been made by a German friar, Denifle, to establish that a university was no university without incorporation by the Pope. But this is to fasten the ideas and the laws of the 14th on the institutions of the 12th century. The earliest universities were not made by Pope or Prince, Parliament or Privy Council. They grew. They were voluntary congregations of learners to listen to popular teachers in the subjects of law, physic and divinity: and more like University Extension movements than any other modern institution. The Pope was introduced because these voluntary congregations of clerics wanted to escape from the interference of the ordinary clerical authorities of the places in which they met. The real name of the university was a *studium generale* or common or public school. The term 'university' was not used till more than a century after the universities were established; at first in the form of 'university,' i.e. corporation, 'of scholars,' or 'masters and scholars,' in 1219 at Paris, in 1245 at Oxford. The local term 'University of Paris' does not appear before 1262, nor that of 'University of Oxford' before 1274.

The *jus ubique docendi*, or right of a master in one university to teach anywhere without fresh noviciate or licence, was only invented and fostered in Paris in 1291, and was only asked for Oxford, in a document here printed, in 1317. Degrees were then already becoming titles of honour rather than what they were at first, licences to teach. The 'Origin of Oxford' is to be found in the contemporaneous teaching in the higher faculties recorded between 1130 and 1135, of Robert the Chicken, afterwards chancellor of Rome, in divinity, Robert of Cricklade, afterwards prior of St Frideswide's, now Christ Church, Oxford, in arts, and Theobald of Étampes, who, while lecturing to from 60 to 100 scholars, was consulted by the archbishop of York on points of canon law. The civil law was taken up in 1149 when

Vacarius came from Lombardy, probably from Bologna University, to lecture on it. We may infer from the teachers named the existence of other teachers who remain unnamed.

Want of space has kept out two documents on which Dr Rashdall has based the hypothesis of a later origin of Oxford in a migration of English scholars from Paris in 1167. As these documents contain no mention of Paris, Oxford, or students, they have no real claim to inclusion. Both were proclamations of Henry II, one forbidding any ecclesiastic, regular or secular, from going between England and France without a passport, another ordering all clerks who held English benefices to return to them without delay on pain of deprivation. Both were aimed at Becket, the first to prevent adherents joining him in his exile in France, the second to deprive him of the assistance of the Italian and French clerks beneficed in England. University students were not as a rule beneficed. As Dr Rashdall himself in a note does 'not assert that the connexion of the migration,' which itself is not even shown to have existed, 'with Oxford is direct or immediate,' *cadit quaestio*. It is more historical to seek the origin of Oxford in a proved congregation of masters and scholars in 1130–49 than in a hypothetical migration of 1167.

That the university was in full bloom in 1189 is admitted on all hands. In that year it is recorded that Gerald of Wales read his Irish travels at Oxford where the clergy in England chiefly flourished and excelled in clerkship, and entertained on three successive days (1) the poor, (2) the doctors and chief scholars, and (3) the rest of the scholars, knights and burgesses. So that while St Thomas of Canterbury (Becket) and Alexander Neckham went to the University of Paris and the Warrens of St Albans to that of Salerno, St Edmund of Abingdon, who became archbishop of Canterbury in 1228, was purely English bred, being a boy in the grammar school at Oxford, then an M.A., and before he passed on to become a D.D. was student and lecturer in mathematics there. Whether the royal exhibitioners at Oxford in 1195 and at Northampton in 1175

were university students or grammar school boys does not appear. The one at Winchester in 1205 must be the latter.

The rise of the universities, chiefly in theological studies, seems to have inspired the bishops to attempt something of the same sort each in his own cathedral, and we find the Pope ordering in 1179 a chair of theology to be established at each 'metropolis,' or archiepiscopal see. The schoolmaster at York was accordingly specially endowed and given the title of chancellor *c.* 1198, and the same thing happened at St Paul's in 1198-1205.

The 13th century witnessed considerable developments of education, especially of the university type.

The Council of Westminster in 1200 renewed the prohibition of the Lateran Council of 1179, against exacting fees for licences to teach, and revived once more on paper, as Theodulph of Orleans had done in 797, the old canons of the 6th Council of Constantinople in 692, as to every priest sending his relations to the cathedral schools free and himself keeping a school for children under seven in his own house.

The next decade witnessed the establishment of Cambridge University and attempts at universities at Reading, Salisbury and Northampton. In 1209 two clerks, i.e. scholars, at Oxford, were hung for the murder of a woman by their chamber-fellow who had run away. 'Whereon 3000 clerks'—the number is medieval—'both masters and scholars, left Oxford, so that not one of the whole university remained. Some of them devoted themselves to the study of the liberal arts at Cambridge, others at Reading.'

Whether Cambridge owed its origin entirely to this secession from Oxford may be doubted. Probably there was already a tendency for scholars to congregate there. But certain it is that while nothing is heard of its schools before 1209, by 1231 it has blossomed into a university with a chancellor of its own. For Henry III issued to the sheriff of Cambridge in 1231 a mandate (addressed in almost exactly the same terms to the sheriff of Oxford) directing him to arrest any criminous clerks who would not submit to the correction of the chancellor and

masters, and put them in prison or expel them from the town. At the same time the mayor and bailiffs were ordered to let their houses to scholars at reasonable rents, to be assessed by two masters and two burgesses. The only difference observable between the elder university and the younger is that, while at Oxford the sheriff is to arrest on the direct orders of the chancellor, at Cambridge the chancellor has to inform the bishop of Ely, who is to give the order to the sheriff.

The importance now attached to proper education of the clergy is shown by some documents selected from many others in the bishop of Lincoln's Register, the earliest episcopal register yet published, ordering clerks admitted to livings to attend schools, sometimes the local school at Northampton or Lincoln, sometimes the university. A number of documents are given tending to show the ubiquity of schools, often through the schoolmaster being employed as a papal delegate to act as judge in some local ecclesiastical case, appealed to the Pope. Thus we find schools at Leicester, Marlborough, Newark and Southwell.

In 1238 a fight at Oxford with the servants of the Cardinal Legate Otho resulted in a new secession, this time to Northampton and Salisbury. Some twenty years later, we find a university at Northampton flourishing on secessions from Cambridge as well as Oxford, and, encouraged at first by the king, finally forcibly suppressed in 1265.

The second half of the 13th century marked a new educational development, the creation of university colleges. The social impulse which made scholars join their forces to establish hostels under principals of their own choosing, led the rich and charitable to do the same by endowments, given not to corporations existing for other purposes, like hospitals, as had been done from 1180, but to bodies of scholars and teachers themselves. The university college was only a collegiate church founded *ad studendum et orandum* instead of *ad orandum et studendum*. The first was probably the far-famed college of the Sorbonne at Paris, which afterwards nearly devoured the university itself, founded in 1256-7 by Robert

of Sorbonne, a canon of Paris, for 16 students of theology under himself as principal. The word college, a Roman law term for a gild or corporation, was not used in the foundation, and indeed, had not then been revived. The institution was called the 'House of the Scholars of Robert of Sorbonne.' Within five years it was imitated in England. But, surprising as it may seem, and the fact seems to have been wholly forgotten until brought to light in connection with the history of Winchester College, the first university college in England was not at Oxford or Cambridge, but at Salisbury. This was the 'House of the Valley Scholars of the Blessed Nicholas' founded near the hospital of St Nicholas by Giles of Bridport, bishop of Salisbury, in 1262.

The Valley Scholars were a religious order in France founded by an English master of Paris University who abandoned logic for theology and life about town for monastic solitude. It very soon, however, set up a branch monastery, which was practically a college, for members of the Order at Paris itself. The Salisbury College does not seem to have had any connection with the Order except in its name. It was for secular clerks, a warden, two chaplains, and 20 poor, needy, well-behaved and teachable scholars studying Scripture and the liberal arts. Two years later, in 1264, Walter of Merton, ex-chancellor of England, founded the 'House of the Scholars of Merton' on his manor of Maldon near Merton in Surrey, with a warden and two ministers of the altar, who were to live there and manage the property and pay the proceeds to 20 scholars living in the schools at Oxford, 'or elsewhere where a university may chance to flourish.' The scholars were in the first place to be chosen from his own relations, because he changed the succession due to them by the laws of England to their right to maintenance in the house, if capable and desirous of proficiency in learning.

In 1269 a second university college at Salisbury, the 'House of the Scholars of St Edmund,' was founded by bishop de la Wyle for 13 students in theology, and a new church was

built and annexed to the Provostry of the college, placed by it. Probably influenced by this example, in 1274, Merton, having moved his whole establishment to Oxford, enlarged the endowment, annexed St John's church to it, and made it in fact a collegiate church with the fellows as canons, and directed that the number should be increased as the revenues grew. He also provided for a grammar school attached, with a grammar master to teach 13 boys of his own relations or founder's kin, who were afterwards to be elected scholars. He now provided an elaborate code of statutes which has formed the model and nucleus of all subsequent college statutes.

The accounts of the Merton Grammar School boys with their master of Glomery, a term which is a corruption of the word grammar, and was hitherto supposed to be peculiar to Cambridge, and tuition fees of 4*d.* a quarter, are the earliest school bills extant. Multiplying the value of money by 40, even 13*s.* 4*d.* a term was not an expensive education.

In 1275 the Benedictine monks followed the seculars' example and set up a college at Oxford, established by the grant of Gloucester, now Worcester, College, by a near relation of the bishop of Worcester. The Cistercian monks were also provided with a college, afterwards known as Rewley Abbey, at Oxford, in 1280. Cambridge was not far behind. In 1280 Hugh of Balsham, bishop of Ely, turned out the secular brethren of St John's Hospital at Cambridge (now St John's College), and put in their places scholars 'to live together and study in the University of Cambridge according to the rule of the scholars of Oxford who are called Merton's.' But the remaining brethren of St John's were regulars of the order of Augustine, and it was always found impossible for seculars and regulars to live together in harmony. Quarrels ensuing, in 1285 the bishop moved the scholars to some hostels or inns by St Peter's church at the other end of the town outside Trumpington gate, which belonged to the hospital, and annexed the church to the inns. The 'House of the Scholars of the Bishops of Ely' thus became known, and is still known, as Peterhouse.

The university curriculum and the school curriculum of the day are fully set out in the Oxford statutes of 1267 for the Bachelor's degree and the Grammar Schools. The triangular contest between the Chancellor of Cambridge, the master of glomery or grammar, and the archdeacon of Ely for jurisdiction over various kinds of scholars in 1276 is interesting.

The opening of the 14th century is characterized by a wealth of educational documents. This is due, not so much to new educational developments, as to the fact that the registers of bishops and ecclesiastical bodies now began to be kept in book-form instead of in rolls, and so were less easily lost. As in the 12th century so now, the established grammar school or song school, as the case might be, of the cathedral or collegiate church, or where the cathedral was monastic, the school of the bishop, asserted by the power of excommunication its right to an unassailed monopoly of teaching, and of payment for teaching, in a given area of their jurisdiction. The schoolmaster of Canterbury occupied the most exalted position in this regard, being able himself to excommunicate the offender instead of as at most places having to invoke his ecclesiastical superiors to do it for him. This position was that of the Chancellor of Oxford University, and he owed it no doubt to his holding office direct from the archbishop, there being no chapter to which the government of the school was deputed, just as the Oxford Chancellor owed his to a similar cause.

The collection of school statutes of the early 14th century is highly illuminating. At St Albans we find a body of Bachelors in the school, who apparently got their degree there, for which they underwent a sort of examination, having to write an essay in prose and make verses on a given theme, a proverb selected by the master, and pay fees of not less than 6*d.* in the shape of an offering on the Sunday after St Nicholas' day, 6 Dec., the day of the boy-bishop; and give the usual feast or drinking. In Beverley grammar school also Bachelors

existed. A dispute in 1338 as to the fees in the shape of gloves to be given to the chapter officials on the occasion was settled by the chapter deciding that the custom of giving a pair to each of eight officials headed by the chapter clerk was legally binding, and directing that it should be enforced by excommunication, if necessary. The fact that at St Albans anyone assaulting the schoolmaster or attempting any wrong against him was, while excommunicated, (which in such case he was *ipso facto*) to receive salutary discipline in the school from all the bachelors, rather points to the derivation of their name from *baculus*, a club or stick: as if, like the prefects at Winchester, they wielded some sort of weapon like a ground-ash, used for purposes of discipline. The *ostiarius* in this school, who sat by the door and gave leave out of school, seems like the *ostiarius* at Winchester to have been a prefect and not an usher or under-master, as he had to take delinquents to the vice-monitor for chastisement. Vice-monitor was the title of the under-master at Canterbury and in the Oxford grammar schools. The statutes made for the grammar and music schools of Warwick in 1316 show that already the eternal difficulty of preventing a lower grade school from trying to trespass on the province of a higher grade school, especially when both are under one governing body, had made itself felt. The music master in this case had been teaching the Donatists, that is, those beginning to learn grammar in their Donat, or *Ars minor* of Donatus, on the parts of speech. These are now naturally adjudged to belong to the grammar school, while the music school is restricted to teaching reading out of the psalter, which was a natural preliminary to singing it, and to its proper work of playing music and singing.

In the university sphere the early 14th century was full of life and progress. The Council of Vienne held under Clement V in 1311 paid no small attention to education. One of its most important efforts was the direction that at the papal court, and at the universities of Paris, Oxford, Bologna and Salamanca—they are named in this order—two

masters should be established in each of the languages of Hebrew, Greek, Arabic and Chaldee, and to translate books from those languages into Latin. The expressed object was to produce learned missionaries.

The pay of these Professors of Oriental languages was to be provided by a tax on religious houses and the clergy. A mandate of the bishop of Winchester in February, 1321, informs us that at the Parliament held in 1320 the convocation of Canterbury had ordered a levy of a farthing in the pound on all ecclesiastical possessions for the pay of a convert teaching Hebrew and Greek at Oxford. The chamberlain of Worcester Cathedral Priory accounts in the year 1321-2 for 12*d.* to the 'master of the Greeks at Oxford,' and at Westminster a receipt is extant for payment in 1325 'for the expenses of the masters lecturing in the Hebrew, Arabic and Chaldean languages in the university.' A genuine effort was therefore made. How long it lasted in England is not clear. As late as 1420 the University of Paris asked Henry V of England for 50 francs for a converted Jew, Master Paul of Good Faith (de Bonne Foy, and de Bona Fide), who taught Hebrew there.

A renewed outburst of college foundations was perhaps due also to the influence of the Council of Vienne. The King's Hall, 1310 to 1316, and Michael House, Cambridge, 1324, both now swallowed up in Trinity College; Oriel, Oxford, 1324; Clare Hall, Cambridge, 1326, the first in which the scholars are spoken of as a collegium; Queen's, Oxford, 1340; the House of the Scholars of Valence-Marie, now prosaically called Pembroke College, Cambridge, 1347; Gonville Hall, now Gonville and Caius College, Cambridge, 1348; the College of the Scholars of the Holy Trinity of Norwich, i.e. Trinity Hall, Cambridge, 1350; Corpus Christi College, Cambridge, 1352, form a series of educational foundations to which no parallel can be found again before the Victorian era.

The monasteries took a new educational departure, almost by accident. The great extension of the cult of the Virgin was

accompanied by the introduction of choristers to sing the anthems in her honour in the Lady Chapel. These choristers were housed in the almonry, or house of the officer called the almoner, the distributor of the alms or charity of the monastery. As this took the form of an indiscriminate distribution of doles, chiefly of broken meats from the table of the monks, at the outer gate of the monastery, the almonry was always found by this gate. The first use of the almonry for boys was at Canterbury in 1320, where the ordinance of a chantry for the soul of Edward I provided that 'no scholar shall be taken into the almonry unless he can read and sing in the chapel and is 10 years old.' At first, and perhaps always, the boys attended the ordinary grammar school, where there was one. For though we find in 1364 an almonry schoolmaster who left Canterbury without notice to go to the 'public school' at Kingston, he is said to have been pedagogue, not magister. At York in 1535 it was reported that the 50 almonry boys maintained at St Mary's Abbey, York, then attended the cathedral, or city grammar school. At St Albans it is specifically stated that the almoner paid the grammar schoolmaster for teaching the almonry boys. At Westminster, on the other hand, where, so far as we know, there was no public grammar school, the almoner's accounts first show boys in the almonry in a payment for clothing them in 1355. A master for them appears in 1367 and he is first called grammar master and schoolmaster in 1386–7. A century later, when there were 24 boys, a teacher of singing boys distinct from the grammar school boys is ranked as a servant. When Henry VIII converted the dissolved abbey into a cathedral, the two sets of boys were represented by the grammar scholars, now raised to 40, with a master and usher, and the choristers fixed at 10, under a song master. In most monasteries, the almonry boys as a rule did not exceed 13 in number and were often less. But the almonries provided altogether education for a large number, say 1500, of charity boys, who would not otherwise have enjoyed the benefits of the grammar schools.

The demonstration of Pope Clement in favour of the reform and education of the monks was renewed by Pope Benedict XII in 1335. Elaborate statutes were issued for the reform of the Benedictine monks, followed a year or two later by identical provisions, *mutatis mutandis*, for the Augustinian canons. Every monastery was to keep a master to teach the monks 'the primitive sciences,' which are explained as being 'grammar, logic and philosophy.' This master might be a secular, but it was also expressly provided that seculars should not be admitted to be taught with the regulars. It was further provided that one out of every 20 monks, or 5 per cent., should be sent on to the universities, half to learn theology, half to learn canon law—which latter study had been expressly forbidden to monks by Pope Honorius III a century before. Though stringent penalties were enacted, the whole southern province in England did not manage to keep 60 monks all told at Gloucester College. The full number at Durham College, founded by bishop Hatfield in 1380, was only eight. A Benedictine college was founded at Cambridge in 1427, but it was very small. The monasteries could not become homes of learning. Perhaps the most striking evidence of their lack of it is the foundation of Henry VII at Westminster in 1504 for sending three monks to Oxford, to become B.D. or D.D., so as to be fit to become chantry priests to pray for his soul in the Lady Chapel, now known as Henry VII's Chapel, and the complaint of archbishop Warham at his visitation of Canterbury in 1511 of the monks' gross ignorance of the services and the absence of a teacher of grammar.

The still fluid and voluntary character of universities received a striking illustration in 1334–5 in the secession of the northern masters and scholars after assaults, for which they could obtain no redress from gown or town, chancellor or mayor, to Stamford. After appeals and counter-appeals, the Stamford schism was finally suppressed by the royal order after some two years' troubled existence in July 1335, when 17 M.A.'s, 1 Bachelor, 6 rectors and vicars of Stamford, and

14 students were driven out by the eschaetor. That so small a number of seceders should strike terror in the university and leave their impress for 200 years in an oath not to lecture or attend lectures at Stamford may give pause to the reckless assertions made as to the numbers attending the medieval universities.

The Black Death of 1349, followed as it was by the Secunda Pestis of 1361 and a third plague in 1367, profoundly affected the universities and schools. The foundation of new colleges was absolutely stopped. None were founded at Cambridge between 1352, when Corpus Christi College was founded expressly to repair the ravages created by the Plague of 1349, and God's House in 1439. At Oxford none were founded between 1340 and 1379. The flow of scholars was seriously diminished. Perhaps the most striking testimony to this is the appointment of the master of York grammar school in 1368, when the chapter departed in terms from the 'ancient custom' of at least 150 years, of appointing for three or four years only, and 'on account of the rarity of M.A.'s' appointed one 'until he obtains an ecclesiastical benefice.' The person appointed was still master in 1380, when he was admitted a freeman of the city.

It was therefore no rhetorical phrase repeating an obsolete formula, but sober fact, which made William of Wykeham give as a reason for his great foundations, 'to cure the common disease of the clerical army, which we have seen grievously wounded by lack of clerks, due to plagues, wars and other miseries.' Probably from the time he became bishop, certainly from 1373, Wykeham maintained a boarding grammar school at Winchester for 70 boys, and the same number in the higher faculties at Oxford, except in 1376–7, when his revenues were sequestrated. In 1379 he permanently founded 'Seint Marie College of Wynchestre' at Oxford, and in 1382 'Seint Marie College by Wynchestre.' Statutes were given to each at the time, but the final edition made in 1400 is alone extant. Both colleges were undoubtedly modelled on Merton College and

on the royal college of Navarre at Paris, founded by Joan, queen of France and Navarre, in 1304, for 70 scholars in grammar, arts and theology. Both models were improved on.

The French queen had assigned separate buildings for 20 grammar scholars within the precinct of the college: and this was then perhaps the most flourishing part of the establishment, being crowded with paying scholars or commoners, who flooded over into adjoining houses. Wykeham made his grammar scholars as numerous as his university scholars, and established them as a separate college with separate endowments, not as a part of the college, though under its visitatorial authority, nor even at Oxford, but at Winchester, where he himself had been at school. As in the Navarre College, the grammar scholars were to be promoted in their turn to be artist scholars when they left Winchester for Oxford. The breath of the Renaissance is already felt in the much larger proportions which the grammar and artist scholars bear to the theologians, and in the assignment of 20 out of the 70 fellowships to canon and civil law, two to astronomy and two to medicine; so that rather more than a third of the whole number of fellows, and more than half of the graduate fellows, were set free from theology. The expressed object of the whole college, however, was as usual declared in words borrowed from the canon law, that 'the holy scripture or page, mother and mistress of all the other sciences, may spread its tents more freely and more than the rest.' All the scholars or fellows, from the smallest boy at Winchester to the senior doctor of divinity at New College, were, in the words alike of Joan of Navarre and William of Wykeham, 'scholars clerks,' clerks who studied in the schools, and at the age of fifteen took the clerical tonsure. The elaborate, not to say wordy, statutes of New College superseded the statutes of Merton as the model for college statutes up to the Reformation; alike at Oxford and Cambridge, at Eton and at Rotherham. Those of Eton and King's and of Magdalen, Oxford, are indeed mere transcripts, *mutatis mutandis.*

The earliest chantry grammar school, the statutes of which

have descended to us, was founded two years later than Winchester, in 1384, by a woman, Katharine lady Berkeley—the still flourishing school, though sadly robbed of its endowments, of Wotton-under-Edge. Wotton was, however, only a small country town, and the foundation consisted only of a master and two 'scholars clerks.' The scholars were to be a sort of pupil-teachers and assist in teaching all 'scholars whatsoever, howsoever and whencesoever coming for instruction in the art of grammar, without exacting, claiming or taking any advantage or gain for their labour by way of stipend or salary' other than the revenues of the foundation.

Apropos of the position of these country grammar schoolmasters, it may be proved that it was by no means a low one. The master of Higham Ferrers school, which no doubt educated, before he went to Winchester, archbishop Chicheley, who incorporated the school in the college which he founded there in 1425, was mayor of the town in 1391, and used to alternate in office with Chicheley's father. An appointment of one of his successors is interesting, as being made by Henry IV as duke of Lancaster, and therefore lord of Higham Ferrers, immediately after his accession to the throne, and as being in French, instead of Latin. This is rather remarkable as we learn from Higden's complaint in 1327 that English boys had to translate their Latin into French, while his translator in 1385, a fellow of Exeter College, tells us that since the first death, i.e. 1349, John Cornwall, a master of grammar, who appears in the accounts of Merton College as teaching the schoolboys there, made the boys in the grammar school construe into English instead of French. 'So that now, A.D. 1385, in all the grammar schools children leave French and construe and learn in English.'

One of the earliest results of this change must have been Chaucer, who, being a Londoner's son, was, we may suppose, bred at St Paul's School. His picture of the 'litel clergeon,' the *clericulus* or young clerk, is the most informing document we have on the song school of the day. For such and not

a grammar school, as the last learned clerk who has written on it (Dr Carleton Brown, Chaucer Society, 2nd Series, No. 45) tries to show, was the 'litel scole' that stood at the end of the Jewry, in 'a city of Asie,' which may be located as London or Lincoln. As if to leave no doubt about the status of this school, Chaucer tells us precisely that the 'doctrine' in it was 'to sing and to read.' Even the elder boy who learnt to sing the antiphons to the Virgin could not construe them; 'I learn song, I know but small grammar.' Had he learnt grammar the grammar master would have protested, as at Warwick and Walden, at his province being trenched upon.

Equally illuminating on the real relations to education of the secular clerk and the regular orders respectively is Chaucer's contrast of the quiet and book-loving clerk of Oxenford, ever ready both to learn and teach, with the roystering cloister-monk, who took good care never to be found in the cloister and regarded reading as mere madness, and with the fat and wanton friar, who lisped, like the lady's man of all ages.

Owing to the contempt poured by Erasmus, Colet and other 16th century writers on their more immediate predecessors, which has been accentuated by the *odium theologicum* of the Reformers for the reactionaries of their own day, the 15th century has commonly been decried as a period of decadence. So far as education is concerned, our documents lend no colour to this view. A great development of educational foundations took place, alike in the re-endowment and enlargement of old schools and the erection of new schools and colleges. The history of Stratford-on-Avon Grammar School, which, from being the school in which Shakespeare must have acquired his little Latin and less Greek, must always be of abounding interest, is typical. The accounts of the Stratford Gild show it growing from an unendowed fee-school, carried on in a deserted house down in the 'old town' under John 'Scolemayster' in 1402, to a fine new school house, still subsisting, built in 1420 in the new residential and commercial

quarter by the Gild Hall, with a large endowment given in
1487. The chief object of the endowment was to make the
school free. The master was 'to teach grammar freely to all
scholars coming to him in the said town, taking nothing of the
scholars for their teaching.'

Throughout the century a similar desire to spread education,
and that generally free education, is shown. A notable instance appears in the Statute of Apprentices in 1406. While
the unfortunate labourers on the land were forbidden to raise
their children in life by apprenticing them to trades and
manufactures in the towns unless they owned land worth
£1 a year—not less than £30 a year now—an express
exception was made, that any man or woman of any estate
should be free to send his son or daughter to learn literature,
i.e. Latin, at any school they pleased. In 1407 we find the
Dean and Chapter of Lincoln raising their choristers' school
into a separate and rival school from the old cathedral and
City Grammar School, undoubtedly as a free school, whereas
the old school was a fee school. In 1432 William Sevenoaks,
later corrupted to Snooks, a member of the Grocers' Company,
and citizen of London, founded a Free Grammar School at
Sevenoaks, with the remarkable provision that the master
'shall by no means be in holy orders *(infra sacros ordines
minime constitutus).*' Another London citizen, a member of
the Mercers' Company, John Abbot, founded a school for
the 'little ones' (*parvuli*) at Farthinghoe in Northamptonshire and made the Mercers' Company its Governors in 1443,
67 years before the supposed advanced Renaissance and
16th century innovation of Dean Colet in making the Mercers'
Company trustees of the re-founded St Paul's School. In
1503 Sir John Percyvale, Merchant Taylor and Lord Mayor,
founded his Free Grammar School at Macclesfield for gentlemen's sons and other good men's sons thereabouts. In 1502
the corporation of Bridgenorth set up a 'comyn' or public
school and forbad any priest to keep a school, save one child
to help him to say mass, on pain of the formidable fine of £1.

The most famous of all schools, St Mary's College of Eton by Windsor, the royal foundation of Henry VI, was founded as a Free Grammar School. The charter of 11 Oct. 1440 provided for 25 poor and needy scholars to learn grammar, 25 almsmen and a master or informator to teach the scholars, 'and all others whatsoever and whencesoever of our realm of England coming to the said college, the rudiments of grammar gratis, without exacting money or anything else.' As Chicheley's school-college at Higham Ferrers, founded 1425, had no organic connection with his University College of All Souls, founded 1434, so Eton had no organic connection with the other royal college of St Nicholas founded by Henry at Cambridge for a Provost and 12 scholars. Subsequent enlargements assimilated the two colleges in size and relation to Winchester and New College. A curious addition was the royal writ purporting to give Eton a monopoly of grammar school education for 10 miles round.

While the spirit of progress was on the whole in the ascendant, the spirit of reaction was in power. Under archbishop Arundel, a fierce persecutor of the Lollards, Convocation in 1408 forbad any Master of Arts or Grammar who taught school to meddle with the Catholic faith or the sacraments or allow the scholars to dispute—the usual method of teaching anything—on the subject. In the Statute of Lollards in 1414, Parliament gave Justices of the Peace power to enquire into and arrest teachers of Lollard schools. It is doubtful whether by schools in this statute real schools were meant or whether, as in the case of the Jewish 'scolae,' which were synagogues, the word is not used as a synonym for conventicle or propagandist meeting-house. The only actual record I have been able to find of such a 'school' is at St John the Baptist's chapel just outside Leicester, which 'school' certainly appears to mean 'conventicle.' So the later charter of Eton in 1443 protests that it is intended for 'the extirpation of the heresies and errors which perturb the peace of Kingdom and Universities'; while, a little later, the

members had to swear not to 'favour the opinions, damned errors or heresies of John Wycklyfe, Reginald Peacock or any other heretic, as long as he lives in this world, under pain of perjury and expulsion *ipso facto.*'

An extension of the principle of free education to a college lectureship is to be seen in the will of Robert Bellamy, fellow of the King's Hall, Cambridge, in 1492. This precedent was followed in the establishment of University Professorships by the Lady Margaret, mother of Henry VII, in 1504, and by Henry VIII in the next generation.

In the sphere of university education generally the 15th century was a progressive age. New subjects clamoured for recognition. At Oxford in 1432 we find that there were students of the combined subjects of English law and the French language, the latter because the Law Courts and the Law Reports still clung to it. The University gave them the cold shoulder by relegating them to the state of 'cursory' instead of 'ordinary' lectures, i.e. afternoon instead of the morning, a precedent which was followed in the old schools, as regards 'modern subjects,' down to 1850. Two letters of the University at this date bear their striking testimony against those who assert that the upper classes did not frequent the University and that the schools were only filled with children of the chorister or charity boy type. For as in writing to Lord Say, whose son, or near relation, William Say, was at Winchester and New College, Chancellor of Oxford, and Dean of St Paul's, they remind him that his family frequented Oxford, so they remind the Commons that 'many of your own issue and also kinsmen have, are now, and shall be in time coming,' advanced with the ripe fruit of 'cunning' in our mother, the University.

At Cambridge, a quite new development took place. William Bingham, a London parson, asked in 1439 for a licence to found the first Secondary Training College, to train masters for Grammar Schools. He gives striking evidence of the decay of the unendowed schools, saying that in going from

Hampton—presumably Hampton-on-Thames—to Ripon via Coventry he had found no less than 70 schools, which formerly flourished, shut up; which he attributes to the lack of endowment for grammar at the University. Obtaining his licence, he duly founded God's House. The progressive spirit of the age is marked in the reasons assigned in the charter for the importance of grammar. It is no longer merely the necessary gateway to theology but it gives 'an understanding of Latin necessary for dealing with the laws and other difficult business of the realm and also for mutual communication and conversation with strangers and foreigners.'

The 15th century saw also a considerable development of free tuition and endowments for the lower branches of education. The most striking example of this is the College of Jesus at Rotherham near Sheffield, founded by Archbishop Rotherham, an ex-Chancellor, and one of the first scholars of King's College, in 1480, modelled apparently on the College of Acaster, not far from York, founded by Bishop Stillingfleet, an ex-Lord Chancellor, about 1460. Each of these Colleges consisted of a Provost and three Fellows, the Provost to preach, the three Fellows to teach. Two were to be masters of three several Free Schools, the usual grammar school, and song school. The third school 'to teche to write and all such thing as belonged to scrivener craft,' as Stillingfleet expressed it, or 'the art of writing and reckoning (computandi),' as Rotherham put it, was a novelty. The reason for it; viz. because that country 'produced many youths endowed with light and sharpness of ability, who do not all want to attain the dignity and elevation of the priesthood, that these may be better fitted for the mechanical arts and other concerns of this world,' is quite in the Humanist vein. Of an even more elementary type was the chantry school of William Chamber of Aldwincle in Northamptonshire, founded 8 Nov. 1489, to pray for his soul and for teaching gratis six boys in spelling and reading (*syllabicacione et lectura*). A curious attempt to combine the grammar and elementary school was that at Newland in

Gloucestershire, founded by Robert Gryndour c. 1480, for a priest and one scholar, a pupil-teacher under him, to teach in the chantry or school-house 'a grammar school half-free, that is to say, to take of scholars learning grammar 8*d*. the quarter and of others learning to read 4*d*. the quarter.' A similar tariff was imposed at Ipswich in 1477. The grammarians were charged 10*d*., while 'psalterians' were charged 8*d*. and 'primarians,' those learning the primer, 6*d*. a quarter.

The first part of the 16th century merely carried on the movement already begun for the development of free education by endowments. But a rather remarkable origin for a school is that of Giggleswick in Yorkshire. James Carr or Ker, priest, on 12 Nov. 1507, obtained from Durham Cathedral Priory a building lease for 79 years of half an acre of land by the church-garth of Giggleswick, whereon to build a grammar school, apparently as a private adventure school. Later he seems to have endowed it as a Chantry of the Rood with school attached. The augmented St Paul's School rebuilt by Colet in 1508–10, refounded and re-endowed in 1510–12, with statutes which in their existing form were given in 1518, in which for the first time Greek is mentioned as desirable, 'if it can be gotten,' has been often heralded as a great advance in education. But in truth it was rather reactionary, as Colet wanted the boys to obtain the 'veray Roman tongue of Tully' by studying not the classics but Juvencus and Sedulius and the other Low Latin Christian poets who versified the Gospels and the Acts of the Apostles, whom archbishop Albert had collected for York school over 700 years before. It is to be regretted that his picturesque attack on what he calls 'blotterature rather than literature' is crowded out, as well as bishop Oldham's statutes for Manchester School in 1525 and Wolsey's striking curriculum of 1527 for his ephemeral college at Ipswich. The latter shows the true Renaissance spirit in its insistency on classical authors.

The beginning of the revolution called the Reformation in the Parliament of 1529, which asserted the royal supremacy

The New Cathedral Schools, 1540

and uniformity in matters ecclesiastical, was accompanied with a similar assertion by Convocation in matters educational by the establishment of a single authorized grammar to be put forth by the archbishop, four bishops and four abbots.

The abolition of the greater monasteries ten years later resulted in a considerable educational development, in the foundation of 13 grammar schools as part of the cathedrals 'of the new foundation,' in which after 600 years the monks who had turned out the canons were now in turn turned out to make room for canons. In all the new cathedrals established in 1540, including Westminster but excepting Winchester, 'because of that noble school of Wykeham's foundation,' a grammar school with a master and usher, paid on the highest scale of the day, was included. In all except Bristol, Gloucester, and perhaps Carlisle and Norwich, there was added a boarding-school on the model of Winchester in which a number of scholars, varying from 50 at Canterbury and 40 at Westminster to 18 at Durham, were lodged, boarded, gowned and taught at the expense of the cathedral foundation. A song school under a separate master for choristers varying in number from 12 to six was also established. The head or high master, archididascalus, a new-fangled phrase, took rank and pay as in the old secular cathedrals immediately after the canons and before the minor canons or vicars choral. Besides the scholars on the foundation the schools were open to all who chose to come to learn grammar. Though none of these schools were wholly new, yet Henry VIII, both in their foundation and in those of other collegiate churches and schools, erected on the dissolution of other monasteries and churches, enlarged and enriched them, so that they greatly advanced education.

The first Acts of Edward VI promised distinctly well for education. In the Injunctions issued in 1547 all chantry priests were directed to exercise themselves in teaching youth. Thus by a stroke of the pen all the chantries were on paper converted into educational endowments. The Act for the

dissolution of colleges, chantries, gilds and brotherhoods of the following year, 1548, promised the 'change and amendment of the same to good and godly uses as in erecting of grammar schools, and the further augmenting of the Universities.' But while it abolished them all at one fell swoop it left their 'amendment' to a separate commission. Also, while it reserved grammar schools where the first foundation expressly provided for them, it ignored those the endowments of which had in fact been applied for education, and struck a deadly blow at elementary education by ignoring the Song Schools. The endowments of all the 300 or more grammar schools maintained by collegiate churches and chantries were confiscated and mostly sold. Interim orders continuing the schoolmasters at a pay equivalent to their net receipts from the confiscated endowments were made pending 'further order,' which in the vast majority of cases never came. In the distant county of Cornwall, where, say the commissioners, 'God knows the people be very ignoraunt,' and therefore the more in need of schools, six schools were continued, the endowment of that of Week St Mary, a boarding school foundation not 40 years old, being transferred to and fused with that of Launceston. In no single case in this county was the 'further order' ever made. The lamentable result is shown in the report of the Endowed Schools Commissioners in 1868, when only Truro was really a Grammar School, and that has since collapsed.

The 'further order' came only where local pressure through powerful patrons at court prevailed. Three, Berkhampstead, St Albans and Stamford, were at once refounded by Act of Parliament. A Professor of English History, Mr A. W. Pollard, cited these Acts in *England under Protector Somerset* as disposing of the assertion made in *English Schools at the Reformation* that no new schools were founded by Edward VI. But unfortunately the Professor had not read the Acts; for they recited at length the previous foundations in the case of Berkhampstead and Stamford. St Albans, as

we have seen, existed at least as early as 1100, and the Act of 1549 in that case did not refound the school but only granted licence to Richard Boreman, the ex-abbot, to found it, and it was not actually refounded till 1553 under a new power granted by letters patent to the corporation of St Albans. Several schools were refounded by letters patent as part of the refoundation as municipal corporations of some of the dissolved gilds, as at Saffron Walden and Morpeth. The earliest instance of the typical Edward VI Free Grammar School under a grant to a body of Governors created *ad hoc* is that of Sherborne, Dorset, on 13 May 1550. The endowment granted consisted of two whole chantry endowments and scraps of three others scattered about in the neighbourhood. The first account of the Governors after the re-foundation shows the kind of loss inflicted on the schools, which were deprived of their lands and confined to a fixed salary. While the rents of the lands granted came to £21. 5s. 10d. one-third more was received in fines for renewal of leases. As the years went on the fines and the rents grew almost every year. All this increment was lost to those schools which were not refounded. The whole number of refoundations by patent of Edward VI seems to have been 30.

The return of the Catholics to power meant little loss to the schools. In his last convocation Cardinal Pole prescribed that every cathedral church should maintain 60 scholars. When the monks were restored to Westminster Abbey the school was allowed to remain. Queen Elizabeth in her first year revived the Injunctions of Edward VI for the maintenance of scholars by the well-beneficed clergy. But there is no evidence of their being carried out. Westminster was in 1560 restored as a collegiate church with an elaborate code of statutes in which the school was given far more space and importance than ever before. These statutes take the boys through the whole day, from their being roused by the cry of 'Surgite' 'Get up' at 5 a.m. to their prayers on going to bed at night, two in a bed. These are the first statutes in which Hebrew is

required of the Head Master in addition to Latin and Greek, a requirement after this frequently found in school statutes to the last quarter of the 17th century. That it was no empty flourish is clear from the evidence by Charles Hoole as to the proficiency in oriental languages at Westminster in the time of Dr Busby a century afterwards. They are also the first and perhaps the only school statutes to prescribe a play. As we saw at St Albans in 1100 the production of a play was already a schoolmaster's function. Indeed the modern drama largely owed its origin to such plays and to the Christmas performances connected with the ceremonial of the Boy-Bishop. But this is the only school in which a play was statutory, and so the famous Westminster Play was preserved for us.

In 1580 the Papal outburst against the Queen caused antiseptic measures to be taken on the other side. We find at Bury St Edmunds the Lord Treasurer Burghley himself ordering the Governors to turn out a master who was not 'of so good choyce' for 'soundness in religion' as he ought to have been. Twenty years later, the Gunpowder Plot produced a renewal of the requirement of licence from the Ordinary for teaching school and an increase of the penalties. As late as 1624 we find at Exeter the bishop able to stop the erection of a rival to the ancient Grammar School which the city wanted to set up. In the end however he and the chapter were defeated and letters patent obtained for establishing a new school in St John's Hospital, which eventually swallowed up the old one.

A large number of new schools were founded in the reign of Elizabeth, many of them obtaining the title of 'Free Grammar School of Queen Elizabeth.' But the endowments were provided not by her but by private founders, many of them by subscription. In the latter part of her reign a considerable number of Elementary Schools, some free, some not, were founded, such as that at Henley-in-Arden in Warwickshire by George Whately of Stratford-on-Avon by deed of 28 Sept. 1586, for instructing in reading, writing and

arithmetic, 30 children. In James I's reign such schools were founded in increasing numbers. Nicholas Latham, rector of Barnwell in Northamptonshire, founded no less than four such schools by one deed in 1620 for teaching children to read. Space forbids specimens.

The 'Great Rebellion' and its child the Commonwealth so far from being, as many writers on school and educational history have supposed, adverse to education or hostile to schools were just the reverse.

Even while the struggle was still going on the Committee for Plundered Ministers looked after schoolmasters. The care taken may be gauged by the frequent references back to the local committee in the case of Canterbury. At Bury St Edmunds on the other hand the master was dismissed for 'malignancy' displayed in action. When Deans and Chapters were abolished by Act of Parliament on 30 April 1649, an express clause continued 'all the revenues...which before 1 Dec. 1641 had been or ought to have been paid for the maintenance of any Grammar School or Scholars.' The Trustees in whom the 'spiritual' possessions—tithes and the like—of the chapters were vested not only maintained all but augmented many of the Schools, as the case of Salisbury shows. Parliament also created new schools.

Under two Acts for the Propagation of the Gospel, one in the four Northern Counties, the other in Wales, passed on 1 March and 2 Feb. 1650 respectively, Commissions were appointed to augment livings and increase education out of the Crown and Cathedral lands. Numerous new schools were created under these Acts, as examples of which those for Caren in Wales and Sunderland in Durham are selected. The latter is noticeable for being a new departure, the first attempt, so far as is known, at a maritime school 'to teach children to write and instruct them in arithmetique to fitt them for the sea or other necessary callings.' The famous Mathematical School at Christ's Hospital, and at Rochester were adaptations of this Parliamentary innovation.

The year 1655 is distinguished for the first endowed school founded for girls as well as boys. It was built and endowed by deed of 10 March 1654-5 of Sir Francis Nethersole, knight, at Polesworth in Warwickshire. It was not however a mixed school, but 'dual,' the building being divided, the boys under a master learning to read and write, the girls to read and work with the needle.

In the sphere of university education, the same augmentation of the old and creation of new institutions were found. When the Chapters were abolished, £2000 a year was reserved for the augmentation of the universities and applied partly in increasing the pay of Heads of Houses, as in the specimens given of St John's and Emmanuel at Cambridge; and also in professorships, especially a mathematical professorship at Cambridge. The erection of Durham College out of Cathedral revenues and its proposed conversion into a university anticipated by nearly 200 years what was eventually done by the Dean and Chapter themselves too late. All these new schools and augmentations were swept away at the Restoration. Not only institutionally did education flourish during the Commonwealth but in method and curriculum also. Charles Hoole's 'New Discovery of the Old Art of Teaching School' might appear a mere dream were it not recorded as fact and supported by Milton's *Tractate on Education* and his practice.

The Commonwealth was the era of the development of Private Schools, set up, especially in London, by schoolmasters on both sides driven out of their places. Stephens, expelled as we saw from Bury St Edmunds Grammar School, set up a private school there, and was so successful that when things had settled down the Governors were fain to reinstate him in the Grammar School. Education had to thank the abolition of the Bishops and Chapters and their coercive and restrictive powers for this. The Restoration had its educational victims, notably the Head Master of Eton, Singleton, who fled to London and set up a school in St Mary Axe where he is said to have had 300 boys. The Restoration Parliament in the

Act of Uniformity required subscription to the Articles, and licences from the Ordinary for all schoolmasters. As late as 1713 all schoolmasters who frequented conventicles, or even services according to the Church of England where the Queen was not prayed for, were disabled from keeping a school; thus keeping out with even hand the low church dissenter and the high church non-juror. But in this Act for the first time an exception appears for teachers of 'reading, writing and arithmetick, or any fact of mathematical learning only so far as' it 'relates to Navigation or any mechanical Art only...and shall be taught in the English tongue.' This was due to the action of the Courts, which had, in ignorance or defiance of history, ruled out of the bishop's jurisdiction all schools but grammar schools. Hence a great development of private schools which nominally confined themselves to mathematics and other modern subjects.

In the last month of the last year of the 17th century, the first systematic effort was made to spread elementary instruction among the poorest classes, by what were known as Charity Schools. Subscriptions for them were set on foot by a circular issued in December 1699 by the new Society for the Promotion of Christian Knowledge, founded a year or two before. The success of the movement was immediate and extraordinary. By May 1705, 36 schools had been founded in London and 10 miles round, which by 1718 had grown to 1378 schools with 28,610 children, boys and girls, besides those in 241 other schools in which the numbers were not stated. They aimed at being a sort of lower Christ's Hospital, the children being clothed in gray, or green or yellow 'Blue coat' dress. The movement might have been more prolonged and successful if too much insistence had not been placed on the Church catechism and the power of the parson. Though dissenters subscribed largely, they were allowed no voice in management. A century later two rival bodies, the undenominational British and Foreign School Society, first founded as the Royal Lancasterian Institution in 1808, and

the strictly Church National Society inaugurated in 1811, began another organised movement for spreading elementary education broadcast. Rival sects still dispute to whom the movement was really due—Joseph Lancaster who started a school in the Borough Road in 1801 and published his book on Improvements in Education in 1803, or the Rev. Andrew Bell who introduced in a single school, in 1798, the method he had practised in Madras in an orphan asylum there. The main points of each were the same, to broaden education by cheapening it, through large classes, learning mainly by repetition in chorus, taught by pupil teachers. Between the two Societies 1,520 schools for about 200,000 children had been established by 1820. The year after the Reform Act of 1832 a grant in aid was made by Parliament in the shape of £20,000 to build school houses, and in 1836 the first Schools Sites Act, to empower tenants for life and other limited owners to give or sell sites for schools, was passed. Under these Acts most of the 8,281 elementary schools existing in 1870 and of the 5,000 voluntary schools since built, were founded.

While Elementary schools were yearly improving both in quantity and quality, Secondary schools were in a state of deplorable decadence. Except for the schools which came to be known *par excellence* as Public Schools, the Grammar Schools nearly everywhere decayed. The restriction of the term Public Schools to a select few of the aristocratic Boarding Schools is quite modern. Public Schools are, as we have seen, spoken of in the days of Canute, by Abbot Samson writing *c*. 1170, and Kingston Grammar School is so called in 1364. The synonymous terms General and Common are more often used in the 14th to the 16th centuries, when the term Public came into vogue. These greater Public Schools took the cream of the upper classes, while the Private Schools, which professed at least to give commercial education and to teach modern subjects, carried off the middle classes. Many died away into bad elementary schools, or perished altogether.

But decadence does not lend itself to documentary illustration.

For similar reasons the 18th and early 19th century history of the Universities, where a similar decay had set in, is left unillustrated, together with that of the revival under the Universities Commission in 1854. For the Schools some attempt at revival began with the Grammar Schools Act in 1848. But effective progress only took place after the Public Schools Act, 1862, and the Endowed Schools Act, 1869, the Commissioners appointed under which possessed such nominally extensive powers that it was said they could convert a Church of England Grammar School for boys in Cornwall into a Mohammedan Elementary School for girls in Northumberland.

Their scheme for Bradford Grammar School is taken as a specimen of their handiwork. Though adding no endowment, it resulted in changing a school of 58 boys getting a poor classical education into two schools of 550 boys and 300 girls receiving the best education of the day, classical and other. Yet a political reaction in 1875 caused the destruction of the Endowed Schools Commissioners and a transfer of their powers to the Charity Commission. A further transfer of the same powers took place under the Act of 1899 to the Board of Education, who, as may be seen from one of their latest schemes, that for Andover Grammar School, still follow the model set in 1872. The chief difference is that the curriculum of instruction is no longer defined by a detailed list of subjects but comprised in the formula 'such subjects as are usually taught in Secondary Schools.' Thus the school legislator of the last days of Edward VII follows his predecessors in the days of Edward VI and Edward III with their simple formula of a Grammar School.

Rigorous restriction of space has prevented any inclusion of documents to illustrate the development of elementary education, the rise of technical education with its novel schools and colleges, the organization of the education of

girls and women, and, most remarkable development of all, the new University Colleges and Universities, in which the United Kingdom bids fair to rival the outcrop of Universities in Germany in the 15th century.

These things are a matter of common knowledge, and perhaps do not require records at present. This book will, it is hoped, at least set the early history of our educational institutions once for all on a solid basis of historical documents.

EDUCATIONAL CHARTERS

Foundation of East Anglian Grammar School, on the Model of Canterbury School. 631.

[Bede, *Hist. Eccl.* III. 18, ed. C. Plummer, 1896.]

His temporibus regno Orientalium Anglorum, post Erpualdum Redualdi successorem, Sigberct frater eius praefuit, homo bonus ac religiosus; qui dudum in Gallia, dum inimicitias Redualdi fugiens exularet, lauacrum baptismi percepit, et patriam reuersus, ubi regno potitus est, mox ea, quae in Galliis bene disposita uidit, imitari cupiens, instituit scolam, in qua pueri litteris erudirentur; iuuante se episcopo Felice, quem de Cantia acceperat, eisque pedagogos ac magistros iuxta morem Cantuariorum praebente.

The Teaching of Archbishop Theodore and Abbot Hadrian. 668.

[*Ib.* IV. 1.]

Erat autem in monasterio Niridano, quod est non longe a Neapoli Campaniae, abbas Hadrianus, uir natione Afir, sacris litteris diligenter inbutus, monasterialibus simul et ecclesiasticis disciplinis institutus, Grecae pariter et Latinae linguae peritissimus....

Erat ipso tempore Romae monachus Hadriano notus, nomine Theodorus, natus Tarso Ciliciae, uir et saeculari et diuina litteratura, et Grece instructus et Latine, probus moribus, et aetate uenerandus, id est annos habens aetatis lx et vi. Hunc offerens Hadrianus pontifici, ut episcopus ordinaretur, obtinuit.

Foundation of East Anglian Grammar School, on the Model of Canterbury School. 631.

At this time, after Redwald's successor Erpwald, his brother Sigebert presided over the kingdom of the East Angles, a good and religious man; who some time before, while in exile in Gaul, flying from the enmity of Redwald, received baptism. After his return home, as soon as he obtained the throne, wishing to imitate what he had seen well ordered among the Gauls, he set up a school in which boys might be taught grammar. He was assisted therein by bishop Felix, who came to him from Kent, and provided them with pedagogues and masters after the fashion of the Canterbury men.

The Teaching of Archbishop Theodore and Abbot Hadrian. 668.

Now there was in the monastery of Niridanum, which is not far from Naples in Campania, abbot Hadrian, an African by birth, well learned in sacred literature, and versed in both monastic and ecclesiastical discipline, and highly skilled in the Greek equally with the Latin tongue....

There was at the same time at Rome a monk known to Hadrian, whose name was Theodore, born at Tarsus in Cilicia, a man instructed in secular and divine literature both Greek and Latin; of approved character and venerable age, that is, about 66 years old. Hadrian suggested him to the Pope to be ordained bishop, and the suggestion was adopted.

[*Ib.* IV. 2.]

Ut Theodoro cuncta peragrante, Anglorum ecclesiae cum catholica ueritate, litterarum quoque sanctarum coeperint studiis inbui.

Peruenit autem Theodorus ad ecclesiam suam secundo postquam consecratus est anno, sub die VI Kalendarum Iuniarum, dominica, et fecit in ea annos XX et unum, menses III, dies XXVI. Moxque peragrata insula tota, quaquauersum Anglorum gentes morabantur, nam et libentissime ab omnibus suscipiebatur, atque audiebatur, rectum uiuendi ordinem, ritum celebrandi paschae canonicum, per omnia comitante et cooperante Hadriano disseminabat. Isque primus erat in archiepiscopis, cui omnis Anglorum ecclesia manus dare consentiret. Et quia litteris sacris simul et saecularibus, ut diximus, abundanter ambo erant instructi, congregata discipulorum caterua, scientiae salutaris cotidie flumina inrigandis eorum cordibus emanabant; ita ut etiam metricae artis, astronomiae, et arithmeticae ecclesiasticae disciplinam inter sacrorum apicum uolumina suis auditoribus contraderent. Indicio est, quod usque hodie supersunt de eorum discipulis, qui Latinam Grecamque linguam aeque ut propriam, in qua nati sunt, norunt. Neque umquam prorsus, ex quo Brittaniam petierunt Angli, feliciora fuere tempora; dum et fortissimos Christianosque habentes reges cunctis barbaris nationibus essent terrori, et omnium uota ad nuper audita caelestis regni gaudia penderent, et quicumque lectionibus sacris cuperent erudiri, haberent in promtu magistros, qui docerent.

Sed et sonos cantandi in ecclesia, quos eatenus in Cantia tantum nouerant, ab hoc tempore per omnes Anglorum ecclesias discere coeperunt; primusque, excepto Iacobo, de quo supra diximus, cantandi magister Nordanhymbrorum ecclesiis Aeddi cognomento Stephanus fuit, inuitatus de Cantia a reuerentissimo uiro Uilfrido, qui primus inter episcopos, qui de Anglorum gente essent, catholicum uiuendi morem ecclesiis Anglorum tradere didicit.

How through Theodore's travelling everywhere, the churches of the English began to be steeped both in catholic truth and the study of holy writ.

Theodore then arrived at his church in the second year after his consecration, on Sunday, 27 May, and lived in it 21 years, 3 months and 26 days. He soon travelled through the whole island, wherever it was inhabited by the English race. For he was willingly received and listened to by everyone, and everywhere in the company and with the assistance of Hadrian he sowed the right rule of life, the canonical rite for the celebration of Easter. And he was the first of the archbishops to whom the whole English church consented to do fealty. And because, as we have said, both were abundantly learned both in sacred and profane literature, rivers of saving knowledge daily flowed from them to irrigate the hearts of the band of pupils whom they brought together, insomuch that they passed on to their hearers the knowledge even of the art of metre, of astronomy and of ecclesiastical arithmetic, together with the volumes of the sacred text. A proof of this is that even to-day [*c.* A.D. 731] some of their pupils are still living, who know the Latin and Greek languages as well as their native tongue. Never since the English came to Britain were there happier times than these, in which, under brave and Christian kings, they were a terror to all barbarian tribes, when the aspirations of all hung on the lately revealed joys of the kingdom of heaven, and everyone who wished to become learned in holy writ, had masters at hand to teach him.

Besides, they thenceforth began to learn in all the churches of the English the notes of ecclesiastical chants, which hitherto they had only known in Kent. The first singing master (except James whom we mentioned above) in the Northumbrian churches was Stephen Aeddi, who was invited from Kent by the venerable Wilfrid, who was the first among the bishops of English birth to teach the catholic method of life to the churches of the English.

Song Schools at Canterbury, York and Rochester.

[*Ib.* II. 20.]

Reliquerat autem in ecclesia sua Eboraci Iacobum diaconum, uirum utique ecclesiasticum et sanctum....Qui, quoniam cantandi in ecclesia erat peritissimus, recuperata postmodum pace in prouincia, et crescente numero fidelium, etiam magister ecclesiasticae contionis iuxta morem Romanorum siue Cantuariorum multis coepit existere.

[*Ib.* IV. 2.]

Et ipse [Theodore] ueniens mox in ciuitate Hrofi...ordinauit uirum magis ecclesiasticis disciplinis institutum,...cui nomen erat Putta; maxime autem modulandi in ecclesia more Romanorum, quem a discipulis beati papae Gregorii didicerat, peritum.

Some Pupils of Theodore and Hadrian. 693–709.

[*Ib.* V. 8.]

Qui [Berctuald archiepiscopus] inter multos, quos ordinauit antistites, etiam Gebmundo Hrofensis ecclesiae praesule defuncto, Tobiam pro illo consecrauit, uirum Latina, Greca, et Saxonica lingua atque eruditione multipliciter instructum.

[*Ib.* V. 20.]

Ut religioso abbati Hadriano, Albinus...successerit.

Anno quinto Osredi regis, reuerentissimus pater Hadrianus abbas, cooperator in uerbo Dei Theodori beatae memoriae

Song Schools at Canterbury, York and Rochester.

Paulinus when he fled from Northumbria to Kent [in 633] had left in his church of York, James the deacon, a man who while an ecclesiastic [i.e. a secular cleric] was also a saint.... When peace was restored in the province [Northumbria] and the number of the faithful increased, he acted as master to many in church chanting after the Rome or Canterbury fashion.

And he coming soon to the city of Rochester,...ordained a man well informed in ecclesiastical learning,...named Putta; he was especially skilled in the art of church chanting, which he had learnt from the pupils of the blessed Pope Gregory.

Some Pupils of Theodore and Hadrian. 693–709.

Archbishop Bertwald ordained many bishops, and when Gebmund, prelate of the church of Rochester, died, consecrated Tobias in his place, a man of manifold erudition in the Latin, Greek, and Saxon languages and learning.

How Albinus succeeded the religious abbot Hadrian.
In the 5th year of king Osred, the most reverend father abbot Hadrian, fellow-worker in the word of God with bishop

episcopi, defunctus est....Cuius doctrinae simul et Theodori inter alia testimonium perhibet, quod Albinus discipulus eius, qui monasterio ipsius in regimine successit, in tantum studiis scripturarum institutus est, ut Grecam quidem linguam non parua ex parte, Latinam uero non minus quam Anglorum, quae sibi naturalis est, nouerit.

Aldhelm's Studies, c. 680.

[Aldhelmi *Opera*, ed. Dr Giles, p. 96.]

Epistola ad Heddam episcopum.

Domino reverendissimo, omnique virtutum conamine venerando, et post Deum peculiari patrono, supplex almitatis vestrae vernaculus, in Domino salutem.

Fateor, o beatissime Presul, me dudum decrevisse, si rerum ratio ac temporum volitans vicissitudo pateretur, vicinam optati Natalis Domini solemnitatem, ibidem in consortio fratrum tripudians celebrare; et postmodum vita comite vestra caritatis affabili praesencia frui. Sed, quia diversis impedimentorum obstaculis retardati, quemadmodum lator praesentium viva voce plenius promulgabit, illud perficere nequivimus; idcirco difficultatis veniam precor impendite. Neque enim parva temporum intervalla in hoc lectionis studio protelanda sunt ei duntaxat, qui, sagacitate legendi succensus, legum Romanorum iura medullitus rimabitur, et cuncta Jurisconsultorum secreta ex intimis praecordiis scrutabitur: et quod his multo arctius ac perplexius est, centena scilicet metrorum genera pedestri regula discernere, et admista cantilenae modulamina recto syllabarum tramite lustrare. Cuius rei studiosis lectoribus tanto inextricabilior obscuritas praetenditur, quanto rarior Doctorum numerositas reperitur. Sed de his prolixo ambitu verborum disputare epistolaris angustia minime sinit, quomodo videlicet ipsius metricae artis clandestina instrumenta literis, syllabis, pedibus, poeticis figuris, versibus, tonis, temporibusque conglomerantur: poetica quoque septenae divisionis

Theodore of blessed memory, died. Among other proofs of his learning and that of Theodore is this, that his pupil Albinus, who succeeded him in the rule of the monastery, was so advanced in the study of literature, that he had no small knowledge of the Greek language and knew the Latin language as well as that of the English, which was his native tongue.

Aldhelm's Studies, c. 680.

Letter to bishop Haeddi.

To the most reverend lord, venerable for all the virtues, your excellency's suppliant slave, health in the Lord.

I confess, most blessed prelate, that I long ago determined, if the course of events and the flying chances of time would allow it, to celebrate the coming solemnity of the Lord's birthday dancing there with the brethren, and afterwards if life remained to enjoy the affable company of your grace. But being kept back by divers obstacles, as the bearer will tell you more fully, *viva voce*, I was unable to do so. So I pray pardon my troublesomeness. For indeed no small time must be spent in the study of reading, especially by one who, inflamed by the desire of knowledge, wishes at the same time to explore Roman law to the marrow, and examine in the most intimate fashion all the mysteries of the Roman lawyers; and what is much more difficult and perplexing, to digest the hundred kinds of metres into prose rules, and illustrate the mixed modulations of song in the straight path of syllables. And in this subject the obscurity is so much the harder for the studious reader to penetrate because of the small number of teachers to be found.

But the restricted space of a letter does not permit of a long dissertation on this matter: how, for instance, the secret instruments of the art of metre are collected in letters, syllables, feet, poetical figures, verses, accents, and quantities; how the art of prosody too, is divided into a seven-fold division, the

disciplina, hoc est acephalos, lagaros, protilos, cum ceteris qualiter varietur; qui versus monoschemi, qui penteschemi, qui decaschemi, certa pedum mensura trutinentur: et qua ratione catalectici, brachycatalectici seu hypercatalectici versus, sagaci argumentacione cognoscantur. Haec, ut reor, et his similia, brevis temporis intercapedine momentaneoque ictu apprehendi nequaquam possunt.

De ratione vero calculationis quid commemorandum? cum tanta supputationis imminens desperatio colla mentis oppresserit, ut omnem praeteritum lectionis laborem parvi penderem, cuius me pridem secreta cubicula nosse credideram; et ut sententia beati Hieronymi utar, qui mihi prius videbar sciolus, rursus cepi esse discipulus, dum se occasio obtulit, sicque tandem superna gracia fretus, difficillima rerum argumenta et calculi supputationes, quas partes numeri appellant, lectionis instantia reperi. Porro de Zodiaco et duodecim Signorum, quae vertigine coeli volvuntur, ratione ideo tacendum arbitror; ne res opaca et profunda, quae longa explanandarum rerum ratione indiget, si vili interpretationis serie propalata fuerit, infametur et vilescat: praesertim cum Astrologicae artis peritia, et perplexa horoscopi computatio, elucubrata doctioris indagacione egeat.

Haec idcirco, carissime pater, cursim pedetentim perstrinximus non garrulo verbositatis strepitu illecti, sed ut scias, tanta rerum arcana examussim non posse intelligi, nisi frequens et prolixa meditatio fuerit adhibita.

Alcuin on St Peter's School, York. 732–786.

[Transcribed from lost MS. in monastery of St Theodoric in 1690, printed in *Hist. of Church of York* (Rolls Series, No. 71), by James Raine, 1879, p. 390: see A. F. Leach, *Early Yorkshire Schools*, I. 4.]

De Pontificibus et Sanctis Ecclesiae Eboracensis Carmen.

De quo plura vetat narrari Musa recurrens
Carminis ad finem; propriique ad gesta magistri,
Qui post Egbertum venerandae insignia sedis
Suscepit sapiens Aelbertus nomine dictus.

Aldhelm learns fractions

headless hexameter, the weak line, and the rest; how the balance of verse is weighed by a certain measure in single lines, or stanzas of 5 or 10 lines; and on what principles the catalectic, brachycatalectic or hypercatalectic verses are recognized by clever proof. All this methinks and other like learning cannot be grasped in a mere interval of time and a momentary application.

As to the principles of arithmetic what shall be said? when the despair of doing sums oppressed my mind so that all the previous labour spent on learning, whose most secret chamber I thought I knew already, seemed nothing, and to use Jerome's expression I who before thought myself a past master began again to be a pupil, until the difficulty solved itself, and at last, by God's grace, I grasped after incessant study the most difficult of all things, what they call fractions. As to the Zodiac and its twelve signs, which circle in the height of heaven, I think it better to say nothing, lest any matter so obscure and deep, which needs a long and reasoned exposition, should be made to seem cheap and worthless by a perfunctory explanation.

All this, my dearest father, I have touched on lightly and by the way, not for the sake of talking but to show you that the mysteries of things cannot be understood without long and frequent study.

Alcuin on St Peter's School, York. 732–786.

Of whom [Archbishop Egbert] the Muse forbids me to say more, passing on to the end of the poem, and to the deeds of my own master, Albert [Aethelbert] the wise, who took the insignia of the venerable see after Egbert.

Vir bonus et justus, largus, pius atque benignus;
Catholicae fidei fautor, praeceptor, amator;
Ecclesiae rector, doctor, defensor, alumnus.
De quo versifico paulo plus pergere gressu
Euboricae mecum libeat tibi, quaeso, juventus,
Hic quia saepe tuos perfudit nectare sensus,
Mellifluo dulces eructans pectore succos.
Quem mox a primis ratio pulcherrima cunis
Corripuit rerum, summamque vehebat in arcem
Doctrinae, pandens illi secreta sophiae.
Hic fuit ergo satis claris genitoribus ortus,
Ex quorum cura studiis mox traditur almis
Atque monasterio puerilibus inditur annis,
Sensibus ut fragilis sacris adolesceret aetas.
De puero nec cassa fuit spes tanta parentum.
Jam puer egregius crescebat corpore quantum,
Ingenio tantum librorum proficiebat.
Tunc pius et prudens doctor simul atque sacerdos,
Pontificique comes Ecgbert conjunctus adhaesit,
Cui quoque sanguineo fuerat jam jure propinquus,
A quo defensor clero decernitur omni,
Et simul Euborica praefertur in urbe magister.
Ille ubi diversis sitientia corda fluentis
Doctrinae, et vario studiorum rore rigabat:
His dans grammaticae rationis gnariter artes,
Illis rhetoricae infundens refluamina linguae;
Illos juridica curavit cote polire,
Illos Aonio docuit concinnere cantu,
Castalida instituens alios resonare cicuta,
Et juga Parnassi lyricis percurrere plantis.
Ast alios fecit praefatus nosse magister
Harmoniam coeli, solis, lunaeque labores,
Quinque poli zonas, errantia sidera septem,
Astrorum leges, ortus simul atque recessus,
Aerios motus, pelagi terraeque tremorem,
Naturas hominum, pecudum, volucrumque ferarum,
Diversas numeri species variasque figuras;
Paschalique dedit sollemnia certa recursu,
Maxime scripturae pandens mysteria sacrae,
Nam rudis et veteris legis patefecit abyssum.

A good man and just, broad, pious and kind; supporter, teacher and lover of the Catholic faith; ruler, doctor, defender, and pupil of the Church.

Bide with me for a while, I pray ye, youth of York, while I proceed with poetic steps to treat of him, because here he often drenched your senses with nectar, pouring forth sweet juices from his honey-flowing bosom. Fairest Philosophy took him from his very cradle and bore him to the topmost towers of learning, opening to him the hidden things of wisdom. He was born of ancestors of sufficient note, by whose care he was soon sent to kindly school, and entered at the Minster in his early years, that his tender age might grow up with holy understanding. Nor was his parents' hope in vain; even as a boy as he grew in body so he became proficient in the understanding of books.

Then pious and wise, teacher at once and priest, he was made a colleague of Bishop Egbert, to whom he was nearly allied by right of blood. By him he is made advocate of the clergy, and at the same time is preferred as master in the city of York.

There he moistened thirsty hearts with diverse streams of teaching and the varied dews of learning, giving to these the art of the science of grammar, pouring on those the rivers of rhetoric. Some he polished on the whetstone of law, some he taught to sing together in Aeonian chant, making others play on the flute of Castaly, and run with the feet of lyric poets over the hills of Parnassus. Others the said master made to know the harmony of heaven, the labours of sun and moon, the five belts of the sky, the seven planets, the laws of the fixed stars, their rising and setting, the movements of the air, the quaking of sea and earth, the nature of men, cattle, birds and beasts, the divers kinds of numbers and various shapes. He gave certainty to the solemnity of Easter's return; above all, opening the mysteries of holy writ and disclosing the abysses of the rude

Indolis egregiae juvenes quoscunque videbat,
Hos sibi conjunxit, docuit, nutrivit, amavit;
Quapropter plures per sacra volumina doctor
Discipulos habuit, diversis artibus auctos.
Non semel externas peregrino tramite terras
Jam peragravit ovans, sophiae deductus amore,
Si quid forte novi librorum seu studiorum,
Quod secum feriet, terris reperiret in illis.
Hic quoque Romuleam venit devotus ad urbem,
Dives amore Dei, late loca sancta peragrans.
Inde domum rediens, a regibus atque tribunis
Doctor honorifice summus susceptus ubique est,
Utpote quem magni reges retinere volebant,
Qui sua rura fluens Divino rore rigaret.
Ad sibi sed properans praefinita facta magister,
Dispensante Deo patriae prodesse redibat.
Nam proprias postquam fuerat delatus in oras,
Mox pastoralem compulsus sumere curam,
Efficitur summus populo rogitante sacerdos,...
Sed neque decrevit curarum pondera propter,
Scripturas fervens industria prisca legendi:
Factus utrumque, sagax doctor pius atque sacerdos;...
Namque ubi bellipotens sumpsit baptismatis undam
Edvin rex, praesul grandem construxerat aram,
Texit et argento, gemmis simul undique et auro,
Atque dicavit eam Sancti sub nonine Pauli,
Doctoris mundi, nimium quem doctor amabat.

   Ergo ministrator clarissimus ordine sacro,
Praesul perfectus meritis plenusque dierum,
Tradidit Eanbaldo dilecto laetus alumno
Pontificale decus, sibimet secreta petivit
Septa, Deo soli quo jam servire vacaret.
Tradidit ast alio caras super omnia gazas
Librorum nato, patri qui semper adhaesit,
Doctrinae sitiens haurire fluenta suetus:
Cujus si curas proprium cognoscere nomen,

Alcuin on York School

and ancient law. Whatever youths he saw of conspicuous intelligence, those he joined to himself, he taught, he fed, he loved; and so the teacher had many disciples in the sacred volumes, advanced in various arts. Soon he went in triumph abroad, led by the love of wisdom, to see if he could find in other lands anything novel in books or schools, which he could bring home with him. He went also devoutly to the city of Romulus, rich in God's love, wandering far and wide through the holy places. Then returning home, he was received everywhere by kings and princes as a prince of doctors, whom great kings tried to keep that he might irrigate their lands with learning. But the master hurrying to his appointed work, returned home to his fatherland by God's ordinance. For no sooner had he been borne to his own shores, than he was compelled to take on him the pastoral care, and made high priest at the people's demand.

But his old fervent industry for reading the Scriptures was not diminished by the weight of his cares, and he was made both a wise doctor and a pious priest.

As prelate he built a great altar where king Edwin had received baptism, covered it in all parts with silver, gold and precious stones and dedicated it to Paul, the doctor of the world, whom as a doctor he especially loved.

Then the illustrious minister in holy orders, the prelate, perfect in good works and full of days, gladly handed over to his beloved disciple Eanbald the episcopal ornaments, while he sought for himself a sequestered cloister in which to devote himself wholly to God's service. But he gave the dearer treasures of his books to the other son, who was always close to his father's side, thirsting to drink the floods of learning. His name, if you care to know it, these verses on the face of them

Fronte sua statim praesentia carmina prodent.
His divisit opes diversis sortibus; illi
Ecclesiae regimen, thesauros, rura, talenta:
Huic sophiae specimen, studium, sedemque, librosque,
Undique quos clarus collegerat ante magister,
Egregias condens uno sub culmine gazas.
Illic invenies veterum vestigia patrum,
Quidquid habet pro se Latio Romanus in orbe,
Graecia vel quidquid transmisit clara Latinis,
Hebraicus vel quod populus bibit imbre superno,
Africa lucifluo vel quidquid lumine sparsit.
Quod pater Hieronymus, quod sensit Hilarius, atque
Ambrosius praesul, simul Augustinus, et ipse
Sanctus Athanasius, quod Orosius edit avitus:
Quidquid Gregorius summus docet, et Leo papa;
Basilius quidquid, Fulgentius atque, coruscant
Cassiodorus item, Chrysostomus atque Johannes.
Quidquid et Athelmus docuit, quid Beda magister,
Quae Victorinus scripsere Boetius atque;
Historici veteres, Pompeius, Plinius, ipse
Acer Aristoteles, rhetor quoque Tullius ingens;
Quid quoque Sedulius, vel quid canit ipse Juvencus,
Alcimus et Clemens, Prosper, Paulinus, Arator;
Quid Fortunatus, vel quid Lactantius edunt,
Quae Maro Virgilius, Statius, Lucanus et auctor,
Artis grammaticae vel quid scripsere magistri,
Quid Probus atque Focas, Donatus, Priscianusve,
Servius, Euticius, Pompeius, Comminianus.
Invenies alios perplures, lector, ibidem
Egregios studiis, arte et sermone magistros,
Plurima qui claro scripsere volumina sensu;
Nomina sed quorum praesenti in carmine scribi
Longius est visum, quam plectri postulet usus.

will at once betray. Between them he divided his wealth of different kinds: to the one, the rule of the church, the ornaments, the lands, the money; to the other, the sphere of wisdom, the school, the master's chair, the books, which the illustrious master had collected from all sides, piling up glorious treasures under one roof.

There you will find the footsteps of the old fathers, whatever the Roman has of himself in the sphere of Latin, or which famous Greece passed on to the Latins, or which the Hebrew race drinks from the showers above, or Africa has spread abroad with light-giving lamp.

What father Jerome, what Hilarius, bishop Ambrose, Augustine, Saint Athanasius felt, what old Orosius published, whatever the chief doctor Gregory teaches and Pope Leo, what Basil and Fulgentius, while Cassiodorus, Chrysostom and John also shine. Whatever Aldhelm taught and Bede the Master, what Victorinus and Boethius wrote; the ancient historians, Pompeius, Pliny, keen Aristotle himself and the mighty orator Tully. What also Sedulius, and Juvencus himself sings, Alcimus and Clemens, Prosper, Paulinus, Arator; what Fortunatus and Lactantius produce; what Virgilius Maro, Statius and Lucan the historian, what too the masters of the art of grammar have written, Probus and Phocas, Donatus, Priscian, Servius, Euticius, Pompeius, Comminianus. You will find there, reader, many other masters eminent in the schools, in art, and in oratory, who have written many a volume of sound sense, the writing of whose names in verse would take longer than the usage of the bow allows.

Ex-Schoolmaster Alcuin recommends Eanbald II, Archbishop of York, to separate the Grammar, Song and Writing Schools. 796.

[Alcuini Epistolae 72, ed. Jaffé, *Bib. Rer. Germ.* 1873, p. 331.]

Dilectissimo in Christo filio Eanbaldo Archiepiscopo devotus per omnia pater Albinus, salutem.

Laus et gloria Domino Deo Omnipotenti, qui dies meos in prosperitate bona conservavit, ut in filii mei karissimi exaltatione gauderem, et aliquem, ego ultimus ecclesiae vernaculus, ejus donante gratia, qui est omnium bonorum largitor, erudirem ex filiis meis, qui dignus haberetur dispensator esse mysteriorum Christi, et laborare vice mea in ecclesia, ubi ego nutritus et eruditus fueram, et praeesse thesauris sapientiae, in quibus me magister meus dilectus Helbrechtus Archiepiscopus heredem reliquit.

. . . .

Praevideat sancta sollertia tua magistros pueris et clero; separentur separatim orae illorum, qui libros legant, qui cantilenae inserviant, qui scribendi studio deputentur. Habeas et singulis his ordinibus magistros suos, ne vacantes otio vagi discurrant per loca, et inanes exerceant ludos, vel aliis mancipentur ineptiis. Haec omnia et solertissima, fili karissime, tua consideret providentia, quatenus in sede principali gentis nostrae totius bonitatis et eruditionis fons inveniatur; et ex eo sitiens viator vel ecclesiasticae disciplinae amator, quidquid desiderat anima sua, haurire valeat....

Consideret quoque tua diligentissima in eleemosynis pietas ubi xenodochia, id est, Hospitalia, fieri jubeas, in quibus sit quotidiana pauperum et peregrinorum susceptio, et ex vestris substanciis habeant solatia.

Ex-Schoolmaster Alcuin recommends Eanbald II, Archbishop of York, to separate the Grammar, Song and Writing Schools. 796.

To his most beloved son in Christ, Archbishop Eanbald, his devoted father Albinus, greeting.

Praise and glory to the Lord God Almighty who has preserved my days in good prosperity, so that I might rejoice in the elevation of my dearest son, and that I, the lowest slave of the church, should have educated one of my sons, who, by the grace of Him who is the giver of all good, is thought worthy to be the dispenser of the mysteries of Christ and to labour in my stead in the church where I was brought up and taught, and to preside over the treasures of wisdom, the inheritance of which my beloved master Archbishop Albert left to me.

. . . .

Your holy wisdom should provide masters for the boys, and the clerks. Let there be separate spheres for those who read books, who serve singing, who are assigned to the writing school. Have special masters for each of these classes, lest having leisure time they wander about the place and practice empty games or be employed in other futilities. Let your most wise prudence, my most beloved son, consider all this, so that a well of all goodness and learning may be found in the principal seat of our nation, from which the thirsty traveller or the lover of church learning, may draw whatever his soul desires.

Let your most diligent piety also consider where to order inns, that is hospitals, to be erected in which the poor and the traveller may be received daily and be relieved at your expense.

Alcuin on Hexham School. c. 797.

[*Ib.* 88, p. 374.]

Praecipuae dignitatis pastori Aedilbercto episcopo et omni congregationi in ecclesia sancti Andreae Deo servientium Alchuinus, vestrae clientellus caritatis, in Christo, salutem....
Maneat vero in vobis lumen scientiae....
Pueros adolescentesque diligenter librorum scientiam ad viam Dei docete, ut digni vestri honoris fiant successores, etiam et intercessores pro vobis....Qui non seminat, non metet; et qui non discit, non docet. Et talis locus sine doctoribus aut non aut vix salvus fieri poterit. Magna est elimosina, pauperem cibo pascere corporali; sed maior est, animam doctrina spirituali satiare esurientem. Sicut pastor providus gregi suo optima praevidere pascua curat, ita doctor bonus suis subiectis perpetuae pascua vitae omni studio procurare debet. Nam multiplicatio gregis, gloria est pastoris; et multitudo sapientium, sanitas est orbis. Scio vos, sanctissimi patres, haec optime scire et voluntarie implere.

Canonical Duty of Bishops to maintain Schools. 826.

[Decreti Prima Pars, Dist. XXXVII. c. 12. *C. Jur. Canon.*, ed. Leipzig, 1879. A. F. Leach, *Early Yorkshire Schools*, I. 1.]

Magistros et doctores Episcopi congruis locis constituant.

Item ex sinodo Eugenii Papae [II. c. 34] 826.

De quibusdam locis ad nos refertur, neque magistros, neque curam inveniri pro studio literarum. Idcirco ab universis episcopis subjectis plebibus, et aliis locis, in quibus necessitas occurret, omnino cura et diligentia habeatur [*sic*], ut magistri et doctores constituantur, qui studia literarum liberaliumque artium dogmata assidue doceant, quia in his maxime divina manifestantur atque declarantur mandata.

Alcuin on Hexham School. c. 797.

To the pastor of chief dignity, Ethelbert bishop, and all the congregation serving God in the church of St Andrew, Alcuin, client of your love, greeting in Christ....

May the light of learning remain among you....Teach the boys and young men diligently the learning of books in the way of God, that they may become worthy successors in your honours and intercessors for you....He who does not sow neither shall he reap, and he who does not learn cannot teach. And such a place without teachers shall not, or hardly, be saved. It is a great work of charity to feed the poor with food for the body, but a greater to fill the hungry soul with spiritual learning. As a careful shepherd provides the best pasture for his flock, so a good teacher should with all his zeal provide for his subjects the pasture of eternal life. For the increase of the flock is the glory of the shepherd, and the multitude of learned men is the safety of the world. I know that you, most holy fathers, know this well and will willingly carry it out.

Canonical Duty of Bishops to maintain Schools. 826.

Bishops should establish masters and teachers in fit places.

From the Council of Pope Eugenius.

Complaints have been made that in some places no masters nor endowment for a Grammar School is found. Therefore all bishops shall bestow all care and diligence, both for their subjects and for other places in which it shall be found necessary, to establish masters and teachers who shall assiduously teach grammar schools and the principles of the liberal arts, because in these chiefly the commandments of God are manifested and declared.

Notationes correctorum.

In indice etiam synodi a Gregorio VII Romae habitae talis cujusdam capitis haec ponitur summa: 'Ut omnes episcopi artes literarum in suis ecclesiis docere faciant.'

State of Education in England in 871 and c. 893.

[Pref. to King Alfred's Translation of Gregory's Pastoral Care, MS. Bodl. Hatton 20; ed. H. Sweet, E. E. T. Soc. 1871.]

Aelfred kyning hateth gretan Waerferth biscep his wordum luflice ond freondlice; ond the cythan hate thaet me com swithe oft on gemynd, hwelce wiotan iu waeron giond Angelcynn, aegther ge godcundra hada ge worul[d]cundra...ond eac tha godcundan hadas hu giorne hie waeron aegther ge ymb lare ge ymb liornunga, ge ymb ealle tha thiowotdomas the hie Gode [don] scoldon; ond hu man utanbordes wisdom ond lare hieder on lond sohte, on hu we hie nu sceoldon ute begietan gif we hie habban sceoldon. Swae claene hio waes othfeallenu on Angelcynne thaet swithe feawa waeron behionan Humbre the hiora theninga cuthen understondan on Englisc, oththe furthum an aerendgewrit of Laedene on Englisc areccean; ond ic wene thaet[te] noht monige begiondan Humbre naeren. Swae feawa hiora waeron thaet ic furthum anne anlepne ne maeg gethencean be suthan Temese tha tha ic to rice feng. Gode aelmihtegum sie thonc thaet[te] we nu aenigne onstal habbath lareowa....Da ic that this eall gemunde tha gemunde ic eac hu ic geseah, aerthemthe hit eall forhergod waere ond forbaerned, hu tha ciricean giond eall Angelcynn stodon mathma ond boca gefyldae ond eac micel men[i]geo Godes thiowa, ond tha swithe lytle fiorme thara boca wiston, forthaemthe hie hiora nan wuht ongiotan ne meahton forthaemthe hie naeron on hiora agen gethiode awritene.

Forthy me thyncth betre, gif iow swae thyncth, thaet we eac sumae bec, tha the niedbethearfosta sien eallum monnum to wiotonne, thaet we tha on thaet gethiode wenden the we ealle

Notes by correctors [a committee of revisers of Corpus Juris in 1566].

Also in the index of the synod held at Rome by Gregory VII (1073-85) there is this heading of a chapter: 'That all bishops cause the art of grammar to be taught in their churches.'

State of Education in England in 871 *and c.* 893.

King Alfred bids greet bishop Waerferth with his words lovingly and with friendship; and I let it be known to them that it has very often come into my mind, what wise men there formerly were throughout the English nation, both of sacred and secular orders...and also the sacred orders how zealous they were both in teaching and learning, and in all the services they owed to God; and how foreigners came to this land in search of wisdom and learning, and how we should now have to get them from abroad if we would have them. So general was its decay among the English people that there were very few on this side of the Humber who could understand their services in English, or translate a letter from Latin into English; and I believe that there were not many beyond the Humber. There were so few of them that I cannot remember a single one south of the Thames when I came to the throne. Thanks be to God Almighty that we have any teachers among us now....When I considered all this I remembered also how I saw, before it had been all ravaged and burnt, how the churches throughout the whole of England stood filled with treasures and books, and there was also a great multitude of God's servants, but they had very little knowledge of the books, for they could not understand anything of them, because they were not written in their own language.

Therefore I think it is better, if you think so too, that we also should translate some of the books, which are most useful for all men to know, into the language which we can all under-

gecnawan maegen, ond ge don swae we swithe eathe magon mid Godes fultume, gif we tha stilnesse habbath, thaet[te] eall sio gioguth the nu is on Angelcynne friora monna, thara the tha speda haebben thaet hie thaem befeolan maegen, sien to liornunga othfaeste, tha hwile the hie to nanre otherre note ne maegen, oth thone first the hie wel cunnen Englisc gewrit araedan: laere mon siththan furthur on Laedengethiode tha the mon furthor laeran wille ond to hieran hade don wille. Tha ic tha gemunde hu sio lar Laedengethiodes aer thissum afeallen waes giond Angelcynn, ond theah monige cuthon Englisc gewrit araedan, tha ongan ic ongemang othrum mislicum ond manigfealdum bisgum thisses kynerices tha boc wendan on Englisc the is genemned on Laeden Pastoralis, ond on Englisc Hierdeboc, hwilum word be worde, hwilum andgit of andgi[e]te, swae swae ic hie geliornode aet Plegmunde minum aercebiscepe ond aet Assere minum biscepe ond aet Grimbolde minum maesseprioste ond aet Iohanne minum maessepreoste. Siththan ic hie tha geliornod haefde, swae swae ic hie forstod, ond swae ic hie andgitfullicost areccean meahte, ic hie on Englisc awende; ond to aelcum biscepstole on minum rice wille ane onsendan; ond on aelcre bith an aestel, se bith on fiftegum mancessa. Ond ic bebiode on Godes naman thaet nan mon thone aestel from thaere bec ne do, ne tha boc from thaem mynstre.

The Education of Alfred the Great, c. 860 and 887, as told by the pseudo-Asser. [c. 1001.]

[Asserius, *de Rebus Gestis Aelfredi*, ed. W. H. Stevenson, 1904, p. 18.]

21. Anno Dominicae Incarnationis DCCCLXVI, nativitatis autem Aelfredi regis decimo octavo....

22. Cui ab incunabulis ante omnia et cum omnibus praesentis vitae studiis, sapientiae desiderium cum nobilitate generis, nobilis mentis ingenium supplevit; sed, proh dolor! indigna suorum parentum et nutritorum incuria usque ad

stand, and should do as we very easily can with God's help if we have peace, that all the youth of our English freemen, who are rich enough to be able to devote themselves to it, should be set to learning, as long as they are not fit for any other occupation, until they are well able to read English writing: and further let those afterwards learn Latin who will continue in learning, and go to a higher rank. When I remembered how the knowledge of Latin had formerly decayed among the English, and yet many could read English writing, I began, among other various and manifold troubles of this kingdom, to translate into English the book which is called in Latin Pastoralis, and in English The Herd's Book, sometimes word for word and sometimes meaning for meaning, as I had learnt it from Plegmund my archbishop, and Asser my bishop, and Grimbold my mass-priest, and John my mass-priest. And when I had learnt it to the best of my ability, and as I could most clearly interpret it, I translated it into English; and I will send a copy to every bishopric in my kingdom; with a clasp on each worth fifty mancuses. And I forbid in God's name anyone to take the clasp from the book or the book from the minster.

The Education of Alfred the Great, c. 860 and 887, as told by the pseudo-Asser. [*c.* 1001.]

21. In the year of the Incarnation of the Lord 866, and of the birth of King Alfred the 18th....

22. From the cradle before everything and notwithstanding all the distractions of daily life, the love of knowledge next only to the nobility of his nature gave its bent to his noble mind; but, sad to say, through the discreditable neglect of his parents and

duodecimum aetatis annum, aut eo amplius, illiteratus permansit. Sed Saxonica poemata die noctuque solers auditor, relatu aliorum saepissime audiens, docibilis memoriter retinebat. In omni venatoria arte industrius venator incessabiliter laborat non in vanum; nam incomparabilis omnibus peritia et felicitate in illa arte, sicut et in ceteris omnibus Dei donis, fuit, sicut et nos saepissime vidimus.

23. Cum ergo quodam die mater sua sibi et fratribus suis quendam Saxonicum poematicae artis librum, quem in manu habebat, ostenderet, ait: 'Quisquis vestrum discere citius istum codicem possit, dabo illi illum.' Qua voce, immo divina inspiratione, instinctus [Aelfredus], et pulchritudine principalis litterae illius libri illectus, ita matri respondens, et fratres suos aetate, quamvis non gratia, seniores anticipans, inquit: 'Verene dabis istum librum uni ex nobis, scilicet illi, qui citissime intelligere et recitare eum ante te possit?' Ad haec illa, arridens et gaudens atque affirmans: 'Dabo,' infit, 'illi.' Tunc ille statim tollens librum de manu sua, magistrum adiit et legit. Quo lecto, matri retulit et recitavit.

24. Post haec cursum diurnum, id est celebrationes horarum, ac deinde psalmos quosdam et orationes multas [didicit]; quos in uno libro congregatos in sinu suo die noctuque, sicut ipsi vidimus, secum inseparabiliter, orationis gratia, inter omnia praesentis vitae curricula ubique circumducebat. Sed, proh dolor! quod maxime desiderabat, liberalem scilicet artem, desiderio suo non suppetebat, eo quod, ut loquebatur, illo tempore lectores boni in toto regno Occidentalium Saxonum non erant.

25. Quod maximum inter omnia praesentis vitae suae impedimenta et dispendia crebris querelis et intimis cordis sui suspiriis fieri affirmabat: id est, eo quod illo tempore, quando aetatem et licentiam atque suppetentiam discendi habebat, magistros non habuerat; quando vero et aetate erat provectior et incessabilius die noctuque, immo omnibus istius insulae medicis incognitis infirmitatibus, internisque atque externis regiae potestatis sollicitudinibus, necnon et paganorum

tutors he remained unable to read till his twelfth year or later. But being a diligent listener night and day to Saxon poems, and often hearing others recite them, and having a good memory, he learnt them by heart. In every branch of venery being an industrious hunter he worked incessantly and not in vain; for he was of incomparable skill and luck in that craft, as in all the rest of God's gifts, as I myself have often seen.

23. Once upon a time then his mother showed him and his brothers a book of Saxon poetry, which she had in her hand, and said, 'I will give this book to whichever of you can learn it quickest.' Excited by these words, or rather by the inspiration of God, and the attraction of the beauty of the capital letter, Alfred anticipated his brothers, his seniors in age though not in grace, and said in answer to his mother, 'Will you really give this book to the one of us who is quickest in understanding it and reading it to you?' And she, smiling and delighted, repeated, 'I will give it to that one.' Then he immediately took the book from her hand and went to a master and read it; and when he had read it, brought it back and read it aloud to his mother.

24. Afterwards he learnt the daily course, that is, the hours, and some psalms and many prayers, and he collected them in a book which, as I myself saw, he carried about with him in his bosom day and night, wherever he went, among all the changes and chances of this life, for his prayers. But alas, his desire for the liberal art [i.e. grammar] which he most wanted he could not satisfy, because, as he used to say, there were not at that time any good teachers in the whole realm of Wessex.

25. And he used frequently to complain with deep sighs that among all the annoyances and difficulties of this present life the greatest was that, when he was of an age and had time and leisure for learning, he had no masters; while when he was advanced in age he was so incessantly preoccupied, or rather overwhelmed, day and night, by an illness unknown to all the doctors in the island, and by the foreign and internal

terra marique infestationibus occupatus, immo etiam perturbatus, magistros et scriptores aliquantula ex parte habebat, legere ut non poterat. Sed tamen inter praesentis vitae impedimenta ab infantia usque ad praesentem diem [et, ut credo, usque ad obitum vitae suae], in eodem insaturabili desiderio, sicut nec ante destituit, ita nec etiam adhuc inhiare desinit.

84. Anno Dominicae Incarnationis DCCCLXXXVII, natiuitatis autem Elfridi regis trigesimo anno.

87. Eodem quoque anno saepe memoratus Aelfred, Angulsaxonum rex, divino instinctu legere et interpretari simul uno eodemque die primitus inchoavit. Sed, ut apertius ignorantibus pateat, causam huius tardae inchoationis expedire curabo.

[Here follows a long story as to how Alfred one day produced a book which he always carried in his bosom and asked Asser to write down in it a passage he had quoted. Asser could not find a vacant space, so wrote it down at the beginning of a new book with three or four other passages.]

89. Nam primo illo testimonio scripto, confestim legere et in Saxonica lingua interpretari, atque inde perplures instituere studuit....

Hic aut aliter, quamvis dissimili modo, in regia potestate sanctae rudimenta scripturae, divinitus instinctus, praesumpsit incipere in venerabili Martini solemnitate. Quos flosculos undecunque collectos a quibuslibet magistris discere et in corpore unius libelli, mixtim quamvis, sicut tunc suppetebat, redigere, usque adeo protelavit, quousque propemodum ad magnitudinem unius psalterii perveniret. Quem enchiridion suum, id est manualem librum, nominari voluit, eo quod ad manum illum die noctuque solertissime habebat; in quo non mediocre, sicut tunc aiebat, habebat solatium.

cares of a kingdom and the attacks of the heathen by land and sea, that though he had to some extent teachers and writers he could not learn. But nevertheless in all the difficulties of life, from his infancy to this day (and as I believe to the day of his death), as he never desisted from his insatiable wish to learn, so even still he does not cease to yearn for it.

84. In the year of our Lord's Incarnation 887, and in the 30th year of the birth of King Alfred.

87. In the same year the often-mentioned Alfred, king of the Anglo-Saxons, by divine inspiration first began to read and construe on one and the same day. That this may be plainer to the uninitiated, I will try to explain the reason of this late beginning.

89. As soon as the first passage was written he began at once to read and construe it into English, and then was eager to set down more [so that he resembled the happy thief on the cross who first began to learn the rudiments of the Christian faith on the gallows].

At this or another time, though in a different way, while enjoying royal power, by divine inspiration he began the rudiments of Holy Scripture on the venerable feast of St Martin. And these flowers collected from all quarters and all sorts of masters he used to learn and enter in a little book, without any order, just as they occurred to him; and he enlarged it to such a degree that it almost attained the size of a psalter. This he called his enchiridion or hand-book, because he always had it at hand by day and night; and in it he had, as he used to say, no small solace.

The Education of Alfred's Children.

75. Nati sunt ergo ei filii et filiae de supradicta coniuge sua, [scilicet] Æthelflaed primogenita, post quam Eadwerd, deinde Æthelgeofu, postea Ælfthryth, deinde Æthelweard natus est....

Æthelweard, omnibus iunior, ludis literariae disciplinae, divino consilio et admirabili regis providencia, cum omnibus pene totius regionis nobilibus infantibus et eciam multis ignobilibus, sub diligenti magistrorum cura traditus est. In qua scola utriusque linguae libri, Latine scilicet et Saxonice, assidue legebantur, scriptioni quoque vacabant, ita, ut antequam aptas humanis artibus vires haberent, venatoria scilicet et ceteris artibus, quae nobilibus conveniunt, in liberalibus artibus studiosi et ingeniosi viderentur. Eadwerd et Ælfthryth semper in curto regio nutriti cum magna nutritorum et nutricum diligencia, immo cum magno omnium amore, et ad omnes indigenas et alienigenas humilitate, affabilitate et eciam lenitate, et cum magna patris subiectione huc usque perseverant. Nec eciam illi sine liberali disciplina inter cetera praesentis vitae studia, quae nobilibus conveniunt, otiose et incuriose [vivere] permittuntur, nam et psalmos et Saxonicos libros et maxime Saxonica carmina studiose didicere, et frequentissime libris utuntur.

Alfred's Palace School.

76. Filios quoque eorum, qui in regali familia nutriebantur, non minus propriis diligens, omnibus bonis moribus instituere et literis imbuere solus die noctuque inter cetera non desinebat. Sed quasi nullam in his omnibus consolationem haberet, et nullam aliam intrinsecus et extrinsecus perturbationem pateretur, ita tamen cotidiana et nocturna anxius tristitia ad Dominum et ad omnes, qui sibi familiari dilectione adsciti forent, quere-

The Education of Alfred's Children.

75. There were born to him then sons and daughters from his aforesaid wife, namely, Ethelfled the first-born, after her Edward, next Ethelgifu, afterwards Elfthryth, next Ethelward was born....

Ethelward the youngest of all, by God's advice and the admirable prudence of the king, was sent to the Grammar School, with the children of almost all the nobility of the country, and many also who were not noble, under the diligent care of masters. In that school, books in both languages, namely, Latin and Saxon, were diligently read. They also had leisure for writing, so that before they had strength for manly arts, namely hunting and such pursuits as befit gentlemen, they were seen to be studious and clever in the liberal arts. Edward and Elfthryth were bred in the king's court with great care on the part of their male and female tutors, nay with great love from all, and they persevere even till now in humility, affability and also gentleness to all natives and foreigners, and great obedience to their father. Nor are even they suffered to pass their time idly and unprofitably among the other pursuits of this life, such as befit gentlemen, without liberal teaching. For they studiously learnt the Psalms and Saxon books, especially Saxon poems, and very often they use books.

Alfred's Palace School.

76. The sons, too, of those who were brought up in the royal family, he loved not less than his own, and never ceased day or night amid all his other business, alone and by himself, to institute them in all good conduct and imbue them with learning. Yet he had little consolation in all this, and as though he underwent no other opposition either at home or from abroad, was so vexed by sadness day and night that he complained to the Lord and to all, who were admitted to familiar

laretur, et assiduo gemebat suspirio, eo quod Deus Omnipotens eum expertem divinae sapientiae et liberalium artium fecisset: in hoc pium et opinatissimum atque opulentissimum Salomonem Hebraeorum regem aequiparans....Coadiutores bonae meditationis suae, qui eum in desiderata sapientia adiuvare possent, quo ad concupita perveniret, quandocunque posset, acquireret; qui subinde—velut apis prudentissima,—mentis oculos longum dirigit, quaerens extrinsecus quod intrinsecus non habebat, id est in proprio regno suo....

Quorum omnium doctrina et sapientia regis indesinenter desiderium crescebat et implebatur. Nam die noctuque, quandocunque aliquam licentiam haberet, libros ante se recitare talibus imperabat—non enim unquam sine aliquo eorum se esse pateretur—quapropter pene omnium librorum notitiam habebat, quamvis per se ipsum aliquid adhuc de libris intelligere non posset. Non enim adhuc aliquid legere inceperat.

102. ...tertiam scholae, quam ex multis suae propriae gentis nobilibus et etiam pueris ignobilibus studiosissime congregaverat.

106. ...omnia pene totius suae regionis iudicia, quae in absentia tua fiebant, sagaciter investigabat, qualia fierent, iusta aut etiam iniusta....Denique si illi iudices profiterentur propterea se talia ita iudicasse, eo quod nihil rectius de his rebus scire poterant, tunc ille...aut terrenarum potestatum ministeria, quae habetis, illico dimittatis, aut sapientiae studiis multo devotius docere ut studeatis, impero....ita ut mirum in modum illiterati ab infantia comites pene omnes, praepositi ac ministri literatoriae arti studerent, malentes insuetam disciplinam quam laboriose discere, quam potestatum ministeria dimittere. Sed si aliquis

intercourse with him, continually lamenting that God Almighty had made him ignorant of divine wisdom and the liberal arts; being in this like the pious and famous and rich king Solomon.... He got however from wherever he could assistants in his good purpose, to help him towards the wisdom he wanted, until he attained his desire; and then, like the busy bee, turned the eyes of his mind afar, seeking from abroad what he had not at home, that is, in his own kingdom.

[He then mentions four Mercians: Wilfrith bishop of Worcester, Plegmund archbishop of Canterbury, Aethelstan and Werwulf priests and chaplains.]

By whose learning and wisdom the king's desire was at once increased and satisfied. For by day and night, whenever he had any leave, he ordered such persons to read books to him; for he never allowed himself to be without one of them—by which means he had [some] knowledge of nearly all books, although by himself he could not as yet understand anything of these books. For he had not yet begun to read anything. [A long, inconsistent and incomprehensible account of Asser's coming is given, followed under the year 887 by the account already given of Alfred's learning to read Latin in one day.]

102. [Alfred had divided his income into two halves, one for secular purposes; the second he divided into four parts, one for the poor, two for two monasteries he founded], the third for the school which he had with great zeal collected from many noble boys, and also boys who were not noble, of his own nation.

106. He always examined the judgments of his judges, given in his absence, as to their legality or illegality....If the judges alleged that they had given such and such a judgment because they knew no better about that matter, he would say, I order you either to give up the local jurisdiction you have or give much more attention to the learned studies.... So that in a marvellous manner nearly all the earls, the bailiffs and thanes who had been illiterate from infancy, studied the art of grammar, preferring to learn an unaccustomed learning than to resign their office and power. But

litteralibus studiis aut pro senio vel etiam pro nimia inusitati ingenii tarditate proficere non valeret, suum, si haberet, filium, aut etiam aliquem propinquum suum, vel etiam, si aliter non habeat, suum proprium hominem, liberum vel servum, quem ad lectionem longe ante promoverat, libros ante se die nocteque, quandocunque unquam ullam haberet licentiam, Saxonicos imperabat recitare. Et suspirantes nimium intima mente dolebant, eo quod in iuventute sua talibus studiis non studuerant, felices arbitrantes huius temporis iuvenes, qui liberalibus artibus feliciter erudiri poterant, se vero infelices existimantes, qui nec hoc in iuventute didicerant, nec etiam in senectute, quamvis inhianter desiderarent, poterant discere. Sed hanc senum iuvenumque in discendis literis solertiam ad praefati regis notitiam explicavimus.

King Edgar's Canons. c. 960.

[*Anc. Laws* (Rec. Com.), ed. B. Thorpe, 1831, p. 396.]

10. And we lærath thæt ænig preost ne underfó othres scolere, but on thæs leafe the he ær folgode.

11. And we lærath thæt preosta gehwilc toeacan lare leornige hand-cræft georne.

12. And we lærath thæt ænig gelæred preost ne scænde thone sam-læredan, ac gebete hine gif he bet cunne.

17. And we lærath thæt ælc cristen man his bearn to cristendome geornlice wænige and him Pater noster and Credon tæce.

22. And we lærath thæt ælc man leornige that he cunne Pater noster and Credon be them the he wille on gehalgodan legere licgan, oththe husles wurthe beon. Fortham he ne bith wel cristen the thæt geleornian nele; ne he nah mid rihte othres mannes to onfonne æt fulluhte, ne æt biscopes handa rede thæt ne cann: ær he hit geleornige.

51. And we lærath thæt preostas geoguthe geornlice læran, and to cræftan teon thæt hi ciric-fultum habban.

if any of them could not get on in his study of literature through age or the stupidity of an unused intellect, he ordered his son if he had one, or other near relation, or if there was no one else his freeman or slave, whom he had long before advanced to reading, to read aloud Saxon books to him, day and night, whenever he had any leave. And they used to sigh and lament in the recesses of their minds, that in their youth they had not devoted themselves to such studies, thinking the youth of this time happy, in being happily able to learn the liberal arts, and themselves unhappy, in that they had not learnt this in their youth, and that in their old age, though they vehemently wanted to, they could not learn. But this zeal of old and young to learn letters we have explained to the aforesaid king's knowledge.

King Edgar's Canons. c. 960.

10. And we enjoin that no priest receive another's scholar without the leave of him whom he formerly followed.

11. And we enjoin that every priest in addition to lore, do diligently learn a handicraft.

12. And we enjoin that no learned priest put to shame the half-learned, but amend him, if he know better.

17. And that every Christian man zealously accustom his children to Christianity and teach them the Pater Noster and Creed.

22. And we enjoin that every man learn so that he know the Pater Noster and Creed, if he wish to lie in a hallowed grave, or to be worthy of housel; because he is not truly a Christian who will not learn them, nor may he who knows them not receive another man at baptism, nor at the bishop's hand, ere he learn them.

51. And we enjoin that priests diligently teach youth, and educate them in crafts that they may have ecclesiastical support.

Council of 994 (?).

[Wilkins, *Concil.* I. 270, from MS. C.C.C.C. s. xviii.]

Liber legum ecclesiasticarum.

xix. De scholis in ecclesiis.

Si quis presbyter velit nepotem suum vel quendam consanguineum virum erudiendum mittere ad ecclesias quae nobis ad gubernandum concreditae sunt, concedimus ei hoc libentissime.

xx. Ut presbyteri per villas scholas habeant et gratis parvulos doceant.

Presbyteri semper debent in domibus suis ludimagistrorum scholas habere, et si quis devotus parvulos suos eis ad instructionem concedere velit illos quam libentissime suscipere et benigne docere debent. Cogitare debetis quod scriptum sit quod 'qui docti sunt fulgebunt sicut splendor coeli' et quod 'qui multos ad justitiam erudiverunt et docuerunt splendebunt sicut stellae in aeternum.' Attamen non debent pro instructione eorum aliquid a consanguineis expectare nisi quod propria voluntate facere voluerint.

Aelfric's Colloquy. 1005.

[Wright's *Anglo-Saxon Vocabularies*, I. 89. From Cott. Tib. A. III. f. 28.]

Hanc sententiam Latini sermonis olim Aelfricus abbas composuit, qui meus fuit magister, sed tamen ego Aelfric Bata multas postea huic addidi appendices.

we cildra biddath the eala lareow thæt thu tæce us
D. Nos pueri rogamus te, magister, ut doceas nos
sprecan [rihte] for tham ungelærede we syndon and gewæmmodlice
loqui recte quia idiote sumus et corrupte
we sprecath
loquimur.

hwæt wille ge sprecan
M. Quid uultis loqui?

Council of 994 (?).

Book of Ecclesiastical Laws.

xix. Of schools in churches.

If any priest wish to send his nephew or other kinsman to be taught to the churches which are entrusted to our governance, we willingly grant him this.

xx. That priests shall keep schools in the villages and teach small boys freely.

Priests ought always to have schools of schoolmasters in their houses, and if any of the faithful wish to give his little ones to learning they ought willingly to receive them and teach them for nothing. You should think that it has been written [Dan. xii. 3] 'The learned shall shine as the brightness of the firmament' and that 'those who have educated and taught many to righteousness shall shine as the stars for ever.' But they ought not to expect anything from their relations except what they wish to do of their own accord.

Aelfric's Colloquy. 1005.

This dialogue in Latin was composed by Abbot Aelfric, who was my master; but I Aelfric Bata afterwards made many additions to it.

Boys. Master, we children ask you to teach us to speak correctly for we are unlearned and speak corruptly.

Master. What do you want to say?

	hwæt rece we hwæt we sprecan buton hit riht spræc
D.	Quid curamus quid loquamur, nisi recta locutio

sy and behefe næs idel oththe fracod
sit, et utilis, non anilis, aut turpis?

	wille [ge beon] beswungen on leornunge
M.	Uultis flagellari in discendo?

	leofre ys us beon beswungen for lare thænne
D.	Carius est nobis flagellari pro doctrina, quam

hit ne cunnan ac we witan the bilewitne wesan and nellan
nescire; sed scimus te mansuetum esse, et nolle

onbelæden swincgla us buton thu bi to-genydd fram us
inferre plagas nobis, nisi cogaris a nobis.

	ic axle the hwæt sprycst thu hwæt hæfst thu
M.	Interrogo te quid mihi loqueris? Quid habes

weorkes
operis?

	ic eom geanwyrde monuc and ic sincge ælce dæg
D.	Professus sum monachum, et psallam omni die

seofon tida mid gebrothrum and ic eom bysgod [on rædinga]
septem sinaxes cum fratribus, et occupatus sum lectionibus

and on sange ac theah hwæthere ic wolde betwenan leornian
et cantu; sed tamen uellem interim discere

sprecan on Leden gereorde
sermocinari Latina lingua.

	hwæt cunnon thas thine geferan
M.	Quid sciunt isti tui socii?

	sume synt yrthlincgas sume scephyrdas sume oxanhyrdas
D.	Alii sunt aratores, alii opiliones, quidam bubulci,

sume eac swylce huntan sume fisceras sume fugeleras
quidam etiam uenatores, alii piscatores, alii aucupes,

sume cypmenn sume scewyrhtan sealteras
quidam mercatores, quidam sutores, quidam salinatores,

bæceras
quidam pistores loci.

B.   What do we care what we say so long as we speak correctly and say what is useful, not old-womanish or improper?

M.   Will you be flogged while learning?

B.   We would rather be flogged while learning than remain ignorant; but we know that you will be kind to us and not flog us unless you are obliged.

M.   I ask you what you were saying to me. What work have you?

1st Boy.   I am a professed monk and I sing seven times a day with the brethren and I am busy with reading and singing; and meanwhile I want to learn to speak Latin.

M.   What do these companions of yours know?

1st Boy.   Some are ploughmen, others shepherds, some are cowherds, some too are hunters, some are fishermen, some hawkers, some merchants, some shoemakers, some salters, some bakers of the place.

        hwæt sægest thu yrthlingc   hu   begæst thu weorc
M. Quid dicis tu, arator, quomodo exerces opus

thin
tuum?

       eala leof hlaford thearle ic deorfe ic ga ut on dægræd
A. O mi domine, nimium laboro; exeo diluculo,

thywende oxon to felda and iugie hig to syl nys hyt
minando boues ad campum et iungo eos ad aratrum; non est

swa stearc winter thæt ic durre lutian æt ham for ege
tam aspera hiemps ut audeam latere domi pre timore

hlafordes mines ac geiukodan oxan and gefæstnodon sceare
domini mei; sed iunctis bobus, et confirmato uomere

and cultre mid thære syl ælce dæg ic sceal erian fulne
et cultro aratro, omni die debeo arare integrum

æcer oththe mare
agrum, aut plus.

       hæfst thu ænigne geferan
M. Habes aliquem socium?

       ic hæbbe sumne cnapan thywende oxan mid
A. Habeo quendam puerum minantem boues cum

gadisene the eac swilce nu has ys for cylde and
stimulo, qui etiam modo raucus est, pre frigore et

hreame
clamatione.

       hwæt mare dest thu on dæg
M. Quid amplius facis in die?

       gewyslice thænne mare ic do ic sceal fyllan binnan
A. Certe adhuc plus facio. Debeo implere presepia

oxan mid hig and wæterian hig and scearn heora beran ut
boum feno, et adaquare eos, et fimum eorum portare foras.

       hig hig micel gedeorf ys hyt
M. O, O, magnus labor est!

       ge leof micel gedeorf hit ys fortham ic neom freoh
A. Etiam, magnus labor est, quia non sum liber.

Aelfric's Colloquy

M. What do you say, ploughboy, how do you do your work?

P. Oh, sir, I work very hard. I go out at dawn to drive the oxen to the field, and yoke them to the plough; however hard the winter I dare not stay at home for fear of my master; and having yoked the oxen and made the plough-share and coulter fast to the plough, every day I have to plough a whole acre or more.

M. Have you anyone with you?

P. I have a boy to drive the oxen with the goad, and he is now hoarse with cold and shouting.

M. What more do you do in the day?

P. A great deal more. I have to fill the oxen's bins with hay, and give them water, and carry the dung outside.

M. Oh, it is hard work.

P. Yes, it is hard work, because I am not free.
[So they go through all the other occupations. At the end there is a discussion who does the best work and which is the

[p. 100] *se getheahtend sægth eala geferan and gode wyrhtan*
Consiliarius dicit: O socii et boni operarii,

uton towurpon hwætlicor thas geflitu and sy sibb and
dissoluamus citius has contentiones et sit pax et

gethwærnyss betweoh us and framige urum gehwylcum othron
concordia inter nos, et prosit unusquisque alteri

on cræfte hys and gedwærian symble mid tham yrthlinge
arte sua, et conueniamus semper apud aratorem,

thær we bicleofan us and foddor horsum urum habbath
ubi uictum nobis et pabula equis nostris habemus;

and this getheaht ic sylle eallum wyrhtum thæt anra gehwylc
et hoc consilium do omnibus operariis, ut unusquisque

cræft his geornlice begange fortham se the cræft his
artem suam diligenter exerceat; quia qui artem suam

forlæt he byth forlæten fram tham cræfte swa hwæðer
dimiserit, ipse dimittatur ab arte. Siue

thu sy swa mæsseprest swa munuc swa ceorl swa kempa
sis sacerdos siue monachus, seu laicus, seu miles,

bega oththe behwyrf the sylfne on thisum and beo thæt thu eart
exerce temet ipsum in hoc; et esto quod es,

fortham micel hynd and sceamu hyt is menn nelle
quia magnum dampnum et uerecundia est homini nolle

wesan thæt thæt he ys and thæt the he wesan sceal
esse quod est et quod esse debet.

   eala cild hu eow licath theos spæc
M. O pueri, quomodo uobis placet ista locutio?

   wel heo licath us ac thearle deoplice
D. Bene quidem placet nobis, sed ualde profunde

sprycst and ofer mæthe ure thu forthtyht spræce ac
loqueris, et ultra etatem nostram protrahis sermonem; sed

Aelfric's Colloquy

most useful, and a counsellor is called in to decide the question. He decides that divine service comes first, but among secular crafts agriculture, because it feeds all. Then the smith and the wheelwright point out that the ploughman is no use without the plough which they make.]

The counsellor says: Oh, all you good fellows and good workers, let us end this dispute and have peace and harmony among us, and let each help the other by his craft, and let us all meet at the ploughman's, where we find food for ourselves and fodder for our horses. And this is the advice I give all workmen, that each of them should do his work as well as he can, as the man who neglects his work is dismissed from his work. Whether you are a priest or a monk, a layman or a soldier, apply yourself to that, and be what you are, as it is a great loss and shame for a man not to be what he is and what he ought to be.

M. Now, children, how do you like this speech?

B. We like it very much, but what you say is too deep for us, and is beyond our age. But talk to us in a way we can

  sprec us æfter urum andgyte thæt we magon
loquere nobis juxta nostrum intellectum, ut possimus

understandan tha thing the thu sprecst
 intelligere que loqueris?

   ic ahsige eow forhwi swa geornlice leornia ge
M. Interrogo uos cur tam diligenter discitis.

   fortham we nellath wesan swa stunte nytenu tha
D. Quia nolumus esse sicut bruta animalia, quae

nan thing witath buton gærs and wæter
 nihil sciunt nisi herbam et aquam.

  ac sprec us æfter uron gewunon næs swa deoplice
  sed loquere nobis nostro more, non tam profunde.

   and ic do æal swa ge biddath thu cnapa hwæt
M. Et ego faciam sicut rogatis. Tu, puer, quid

dydest [to] dæg
 fecisti hodie?

   manega thingc ic dyde on thisse niht tha tha cnyll
D. Multas res feci. Hac nocte quando signum

ic gehyrde ic aras on minon bedde and eode to cyrcean and
 audiui, surrexi de lectulo et exiui ad ecclesiam et

sang uhtsang mid gebrothrum æfter tha we sungon be
cantaui nocturnam cum fratribus; deinde cantauimus de

eallum halgum and dægredlice lofsanges æfter thysum prim
omnibus sanctis et matutinales laudes; post haec, primam,

and seofon seolmas mid letanian and capitol mæssan syththan
 et vii. psalmos, cum letaniis, et primam missam; deinde

undertide and dydon mæssa be dæge æfter thisum we sungan
 tertiam, et fecimus missam de die; post haec cantauimus

middæg and æton and druncon and slepon and
sextam, et manducauimus et bibimus, et dormiuimus, et

 eft we arison and sungon non and nu we synd
iterum surreximus, et cantauimus nonam, et modo sumus

her ætforan the gearuwe gehyran hwæt thu us secge
hic coram te, parati audire quid nobis dixeris.

   hwænne wylle ge syngan æfen oththe nihtsangc
M. Quando uultis cantare uesperum aut completorium?

follow so that we may understand what you are talking about.

M. Well, I ask you why you are learning so diligently?

B. Because we do not want to be like beasts, who know nothing but grass and water.

[The master then goes off into a disquisition whether they want to be worldly wise, full of craft, or otherwise. They complain again that he is too deep for them.]

But talk to us so that we can understand, not so profoundly.

M. Well, I will do what you ask. You, boy, what did you do to-day?

B. I did many things. At night when I heard the bell, I got out of bed and went to church and sang the nocturne with the brethren. Then we sang the martyrology and lauds; after that, prime and the seven psalms with litanies and first mass; next tierce, and did the mass of the day; after that we sang sext, and ate and drank and slept; and then we got up again and sang nones, and now here we are before you ready to listen to what you tell us.

M. When will you sing vespers or compline?

       thonne hyt tima byth
D. Quando tempus erit.

       wære thu todæg beswuncgen
M. Fuisti hodie uerberatus?

       ic næs fortham wærlice ic me heold
D. Non fui, quia caute me tenui.

       and hu thine geferan.
M. Et quomodo tui socii?

       hwæt me ahsast be tham ic ne deor yppan the
D. Quid me interrogas de hoc? Non audeo pandere tibi
digla ure anra gehwylc wat gif he beswuncgen wæs
secreta nostra. Unusquisque scit si flagellatus erat
oththe na
an non.

       hwær slæpst
M. Ubi dormis?

       on slæpern mid gebrothrum
D. In dormitorio cum fratribus.

       hwa awecth the to uhtsancge
M. Quis excitat te ad nocturnos?

       hwilon ic gehyre cnyll and ic erise hwilon
D. Aliquando audio signum, et surgo; aliquando
lareow min awecth me stithlice mid gyrde
magister meus excitat me duriter cum uirga.

       eala ge [gode] cildra and wynsume leorneras eow manath
M. O probi pueri, et uenusti mathites, uos hortatur
eower lareow thæt ge hyrsumian godcundum larum and
uester eruditor ut pareatis diuinis disciplinis et
thæt ge healdan eow sylfe ænlice on ælcere stowe gath
obseruetis uosmet eleganter ubique locorum. Inceditis
theawlice thonne ge gehyran cyricean bellan and
morigerate, cum auscultaueritis ecclesie campanas et
gath into cyrcean and abugath eadmodlice to halgum
ingredimini in orationem, et inclinate suppliciter ad almas
wefodum and standath theawlice and singað anmodlice
aras, et state disciplinabiliter et concinite unanimiter

B. When it's time.

M. Were you flogged to-day?

B. I was not, because I was very careful.

M. And how about the others?

B. Why do you ask me that? I daren't tell you our secrets. Each one knows whether he was flogged or not.

M. Where do you sleep?

B. In the dormitory with the brethren.

M. Who calls you to nocturnes?

B. Sometimes I hear the bell, and get up; sometimes my master wakes me with a ground-ash.

M. All you good children and clever scholars, your teacher exhorts you to keep the commandments of God, and behave properly everywhere. Walk quietly when you hear the church bells and go into church, and bow to the holy altars, and stand quietly and sing in unison, and ask pardon for your sins, and go out again without playing, to the cloister or to school.

and gebiddath for eowrum synnum and gath ut butan
et interuenite pro uestris erratibus, et egredimini sine
hygeleaste to claustre oththe to leorninge
scirilitate in claustrum uel in gimnasium.

The first English-Latin Grammar.

[Aelfric's *Grammar and Glossary*, ed. Julius Zupitza, Berlin, 1880, p. 1.]

Incipit Praefatio huius libri.

Ego Aelfricus, ut minus sapiens, has excerptiones de Prisciano minore uel majore uobis puerulis tenellis ad uestram linguam transferre studui, quatinus perlectis octo partibus Donati in isto libello, potestis utramque linguam, uidelicet latinam et anglicam, uestrae teneritudini inserere interim, usque quo ad perfectiora perueniatis studia. Noui namque multos me reprehensuros, quod talibus studiis meum ingenium occupare uoluissem, scilicet grammaticam artem ad anglicam linguam uertendo. Sed ego deputo hanc lectionem inscientibus puerulis, non senibus, optandam fore. Scio multimodis uerba posse interpretari, sed ego simplicem interpretationem sequor fastidii uitandi causa. Si alicui tamen displicuerit, nostram interpretationem dicat, quomodo uult: nos contenti sumus, sicut didicimus in scola Adelwoldi, uenerabilis praesulis, qui multos ad bonum imbuit. Sciendum tamen, quod ars grammatica multis in locis non facile anglicae linguae capit interpretationem, sicut de pedibus uel metris, de quibus hic reticemus; sed aestimamus ad inchoationem tamen hanc interpretationem paruulis prodesse posse, sicut iam diximus. Miror ualde, quare multi corripiunt sillabas in prosa, quae in metro breues sunt, cum prosa absoluta sit a lege metri; sicut pronuntiant pater brittonice et malus et similia, quae in metro habentur breues. Mihi tamen uidetur melius inuocare deum patrem honorifice producta sillaba, quam brittonice corripere, quia nec deus arti grammaticae subiciendus est. Valete, o pueruli, in domino.

The first English-Latin Grammar.

Here begins the Preface of this book.

I Aelfric, as not being very learned, have taken pains to translate these extracts from the larger and smaller Priscian for you tender children into your own language, so that when you have gone through Donatus on the Parts of Speech, you may be able to instil both languages, Latin and English, into your youthful minds, by this little book, until you reach more advanced studies. I am aware that many will blame me, for being willing to devote my mind to such a pursuit as to turn 'The Art of Grammar' into English. But I destine this lesson-book for little boys who know nothing, not for their elders. I know that words can be construed in many different ways, but to avoid raising difficulties I follow the simplest meaning. If anyone is offended at it he can call it my construction, if he pleases. I am content to do it, as I learnt it in the school of the venerable prelate Ethelwold, who taught many the elements to good purpose. It must be remembered however that in many places 'The Art of Grammar' cannot easily be turned into English, as in the part about metres and feet, of which I say nothing here. But I think that for a beginning this translation may help little boys, as I have already said. I often wonder indeed why many people pronounce syllables short in prose which are short in verse, seeing that prose is not governed by the laws of metre. Thus they pronounce pater pătter like the Britons, and malus măllus and the like. But in my opinion it is better to invoke God the Father 'Deus pāter,' giving Him honour by making the syllable long than by making it short like the Britons, for God ought not to be subject to the rules of grammar. Farewell, little boys, in the Lord.

Praefatio de partibus Orationis.

p. 8. Partes orationis sunt octo eahta daelas synd ledenspraece: Nomen, pronomen, verbum, adverbium, participium, coniunctio, praepositio, interiectio. Nomen is nama, mid tham we nemnath ealle thing aegther ge synderlice ge gemaenelice. Synderlice be agenum naman: Eadgarus, Athelwoldus; gemaenelice: rex cyning, episcopus bisceop. Pronomen is thaes naman speliend, se spelath thone naman, thaet thu ne thurfe tuwa hine nemnan, gif thu cwest nu: hwa laerde the? thonne cwethe ic: Dunstan; hwa hadode the? he me hadode: thonne stent se he on his naman stede and spelath hine. Eft, gif thu axast: quis hoc fecit? hwa dyde this? thonne cwest thu: ego hoc feci ic dyde this.

p. 151. Gerundia vel participalia verba sunt haec: docendi, docendo, docendum, doctum, doctu. Tempus est docendi tima hyt ys to taecenne. Docendo loquor, taecende ic sprece. Docendum est mihi, me ys to taecenne. Habes pueros ad docendum, haefst thu cild to laerenne. Uis doctum ire, wylt thu gan taecan? Doctu veni, fram lare ic com. Thas word magon to eallum hadum and to eallum tidum and to aegthrum getele and to aelcum cynne. Multum ipse laborat docendo pueros; swithe he swincth taecende tham cildum. Ipsa monialis vigilat docendo puellas, seo mynecene wacath taecende tham maedencildum. Legendo docetur vir et legendo docetur mulier.

Preface to the Parts of Speech.

p. 8. The parts of speech are eight. There are eight parts of speech in Latin: Noun, pronoun, verb, adverb, participle, conjunction, preposition, interjection. The noun is a name, with it we name everything either by a proper name or a common name. These are proper names, Edgar, Ethelwold: common names, king, bishop. A pronoun is the substitute for a noun. It represents the name so that you need not name it twice. If you ask Who taught you? Then I say, Dunstan. Who ordained you? He ordained me. Then the 'he' stands in the place of his name and represents him. Again, if you ask, Who did this? Then you answer, I did this.

p. 151. These are gerunds or participial words: of teaching, by teaching, to be taught, to teach, in teaching. It is time to teach. I speak while teaching. I have to teach. You have boys to teach. Will you go and teach? I come from teaching. These words may apply to all persons and to all times, and to both numbers and to each sex. He works hard at teaching boys. The nun is awake teaching little girls. A man is taught by reading and a woman is taught by reading.

King Canute founds Public Schools and gives Exhibitions to Poor Boys. c. 1020.

[*Mem. of Bury St Edmunds* (Rolls Series), by Herman, I. 46–7. From Cott. Tib. B. II. f. 25.]

Quo tempore hereditarius Sweyn, Chnut dictus nomine... invisens Sanctum Edmundum...actu regali xeniavit locum donis....Nec pretereundum silentio hic rex bonus quid elemosine fecerit modo, videlicet, sicubi monasteria vel castella nominata petiit, clericali et monastico ordini ex suo sumptu pueros docendos tradidit, non quos invenerat de libertinis, verum ex elegantioribus de paupertinis, quosdam etiam sic incedens regio more liberos dabat propria manu.

[*Ib.* 126, by Samson, afterwards abbot.]

Hic [Canutus] ergo tam pius, tam benignus, tam religionis amator fuisse memoratur, ut per urbes et oppida, publicas instituens scolas, magistris deputatis elegantes boneque spei pueros, necnon servorum filios manumissos, litteris traderet imbuendos, de ratione fiscali sumptibus constitutis.

The Rank of a Scholar. c. 1029–60.

[F. Liebermann, *Die Gesetze der Angelsachsen*, from MS. C.C.C.C. 201, A.D. 1050–80.]

Be wergildum and be gethingthum.

Hwilum wæs [in Engla lagum] thæt leod and lagu for be gethingthum and tha wæron theodwitan wurthscipes wurthe, ælc be his mæthe, ge eorl ge ceorl, ge thegen ge theoden.

King Canute founds Public Schools and gives Exhibitions to Poor Boys. c. 1020.

At which time Sweyn's heir, called Canute...visiting St Edmund...with kingly act endowed the place with gifts.... Nor must we pass over in silence what this good king did by way of charity, namely, whenever he went to any famous monastery or borough he sent there at his own expense boys to be taught for the clerical or monastic order, not only those whom he found among freemen but also the cleverer of the poor, and with his own hand in kingly munificence he also in his progress gave some freemen's children.

Canute then is related to have been so pious, so charitable, so great a lover of religion that he established public schools in the cities and boroughs and appointed masters to them, and sent to them to be taught grammar not only noble boys of good promise, but also the freed sons of slaves, charging the expense on the royal purse.

The Rank of a Scholar. c. 1029–60.

Of wergilds and ranks.

It was once among the laws of the English that people and their laws went according to their ranks, and then were the wise men of the nation honoured each according to his quality, earl and churl, servant and master.

[*Quadripartitus*, A.D. 1114.]

De veteri consuetudine promotionum.

Aliquando fuit in Anglorum laga, quod populus et leges consilio regebantur; et tunc erant sapientes populi magni prorsus nominis et pretii, comes et villanus, tainus et alii, singuli pro modo suo.

[7] And gif leornere wære the thurh lare gethuge, thæt he had hæfde and thenode Criste, wære se siththan mæthe and munde swa micelre wyrthe, swa thonne tham hade gebirede and rihte, gif he hine heolde swa swa he scolde.

Et si scolaris profecisset in doctrina cur ad sacros ordines pertransiret et Christo domino ministraret, erat denique dignitatis et pacis dignus quanta pertinebat super illud, nisi foris faceret cur ipsius ordinis officio non uteretur.

Waltham Holy Cross College School, 1060–1177. *The Foundation by Earl Harold, 3 May*, 1060.

[*Tractatus de inventione Sante Crucis*, ed. W. Stubbs, 1861, from Cotton MS. Julius D. 6 (*c.* 1180) and Harl. 3776.]

p. 15. Duobus igitur predictis clericis quos instituerat Toui le prude in ecclesia Walthamensi uir ille strenuus comes Haraldus xj sociauit alios uiros prudentes, literatos, selectos a communibus, inter precipuos terre diligenter exquisitos; inter quos Theutonicum quendam diuino munere et inexperato sibi collatum, Magistrum Athelardum, Leodicensem genere, Trajectensem studii disciplina, quatenus leges instituta et consuetudines, tam in ecclesiasticis quam in secularibus ecclesiarum in quibus educatus fuerat, in ecclesia Walthamensi constitueret, quum multorum relatione didicerat ordinatissima distinctione regi Theutonicorum ecclesias; ut, si quid dignum ultione uel correptione inter clericos oriretur a Decano ecclesie siue ab ipso Magistro Athelardo, excessus acri uerbo, enormitates flagello, immania etiam peccata ipsius prebende priuatione, multarentur. Quod et predecessorum nostrorum temporibus inoleuisse et

Of the ancient custom of precedence.

It was an ancient law of the English that the people and customs were held in honour, and by the Witan was given to each according to his measure, to count and villein, thane and others, each according to his measure.

[7] And if a scholar became so proficient in learning that he had been ordained and served Christ, he was then thought worthy of such honour and peace as belonged and appertained to his order, if he behaved as he should.

And if a scholar had become proficient in learning and so had attained holy orders and ministered to Christ the lord, he was then worthy of such dignity and peace as belonged thereto, unless he forfeited the use of the duties of his order.

Waltham Holy Cross College School, 1060– 1177. *The Foundation by Earl Harold*, 3 *May*, 1060.

p. 15. With the two clerks therefore whom Tovi the proud had instituted in the church of Waltham that great man Earl Harold associated 11 others, wise, learned, selected from the commons or carefully chosen from the highest in the land. Among them was a certain Dutchman who came to him by a divine and unexpected gift, Master Athelard, born at Liége, brought up in the school of Utrecht, that he might establish in Waltham church the laws, statutes and customs, both in ecclesiastical and in secular matters, of the churches in which he had been educated, since he [Harold] had heard from many people that the Dutch churches were governed by most carefully devised rules. So if anything needing punishment or rebuke arose among the clerks it was punished by the Dean or Master Athelard himself, mere excess by a sharp word, breaches of order by the birch, and serious offences even by deprivation of the prebend. There is no doubt that what had been prac-

usque ad tempora pueritie nostre perdurasse non ambigimus. His autem xii clericis perhibetur comes ille Wlwinum Decanum prefecisse, uirum religiosum, moribus illustrem, doctrina literali uenustum, speciali castitatis prerogatiua fulgentem, qui cum Magistro Athelardo ecclesie statum ita distinctum ordinauerunt.

Unicuique assignata est portio sua in prebendam, ut, deductis expensis que fratrum uictualibus exhibere debebant, quod residuum erat in proprios usus, loco prebende cederet....

Uiso autem hoc infausto auspicio multo dolore correpti duos fratres de ecclesia precipuos et maiores natu Osegodum Cnoppe et Ailricum childemaister in comitatu Regis miserunt ad prelium ut cognitis rei euentibus de corpore regis et suorum ecclesie deuotorum curam agerent, et si fortuna sic darent cadauera reportarent.

p. 35, c. 25. Quam ordinate se habebant canonici in primis.

Puer ego quinque annorum uidi usque ad presentia tempora multa, canonicus constitutus in ecclesia S. Crucis a bone memorie Ernulpho, Decano, assensu et donatione uenerabilis Domine Adalize Regine, cuius tunc donationis erant prebende, et ad prima litterarum rudimenta traditus Magistro Petro, filio Magistri Athelardi, institutoris et ordinatoris presentis ecclesie. Fons enim uberrima discipulis doctrine tunc scaturiebat ab ipso Petro, secundum modum Teutonicorum, non enim obstantibus lectionibus uel litteris et uersibus componendis minus addiscebatur et frequentabatur in ecclesia cantus. Et ordinatissima distinctio puerilis habitudinis ita ut, more religiosorum fratrum, honeste et non sine grauitate incederent, starent, legerent et cantarent, et quicquid ad gradum chori uel in ipso choro cantare oportebat, corde tenus, unus uel duo uel plures, absque libri solatio cantarent et psallerent. In choro constituti non respiciebat puer alterum, nisi forte ex obliquo tamen raro, nec faceret ei uerbum unum : non discurrebant per chorum nisi quibus fuisset iniunctum a magistro, pro coppis aut pro libris transferendis uel aliis

tised under my predecessors lasted to the time when I was a boy. Over these 12 clerks the Earl is said to have set Wulwin as Dean, a religious man, illustrious for his character, well known for his literary learning, and conspicuous for the special prerogative of chastity, and he and Master Athelard established the constitution of the church.

Each was assigned his portion as a prebend, so that after deducting the expenses due for the maintenance of the brethren in living, the residue went to their own use by way of a prebend.

Deeply grieved at this inauspicious omen they sent the two principal and senior brethren of the church, Osgood Cnoppe and Ailric the master of the boys, with the King [Harold] to the battle, to learn the result and look after the person of the king and of those devoted to the church, and if fate so decreed to bring back their bodies.

p. 35, c. 25.   How orderly the canons behaved at first.

I from a boy of five years old to the present time have seen many things, being made a canon in the Holy Cross Church by Dean Ernulf of good memory, with the assent and on the presentation of the lady Adaliza the Queen, in whose gift the prebends were, and for the first rudiments of learning sent to Master Peter, son of Master Athelard, the organizer and founder of the present church. A most copious spring of learning and instruction flowed from that Peter, after the Dutch fashion, for besides reading and the composition of letters and verses, singing was no less learnt and practised in the church; and a well ordered difference from the usual habit of boys was that they walked, stood, read and chanted, like brethren in religion, and whatever had to be sung at the steps of the choir or in the choir itself they sang and chanted by heart, one or two or more together, without the help of a book. One boy never looked at another, when they were in their places in choir, except sideways and that very seldom, and they never spoke a word to one another; they never walked about the choir to carry copes or books or for any other reason, unless sent on an errand by the master,

quibuslibet causis, manentes in choro. Sicut processione procedentes a scola intrant chorum, sic exeuntes intrant scolas, ad modum canonicorum de nocte surgentium.

p. 10, c. 11. Sanguinem hunc de silice elicitum...nos uidere et in capsa argentea repositum, miseratione diuina meruimus, quos a teneris annis educauit ecclesia Walthamiensis 53 annis, et in gremio suo literalibus instruxit disciplinis. Me miserum! quod datum est uidere in hac uita quod separer ab uberibus uite mee.

Confirmation by Henry I of Warwick School as it was in the Days of Edward the Confessor.

[A. F. Leach, *History of Warwick School and College*, 5, from Chartul. St Mary's, Warwick, *Q. R. Eccl.* Misc. Bks. 22.]

Confirmacio Henrici Regis de consuetudinibus et iudicio ferri et aque et scolis Warr[wici].

H. Rex Angl[orum], T. episcopo Wigornie et R. episcopo de Cestra, et comiti Rogero et Galfrido de Clinton et Omnibus Baronibus de Warwicscira, salutem.

Preci[pi]o quod ecclesia Omnium Sanctorum de Warrewic habeat omnes consuetudines suas et iudicia ferri et aque ita bene et iuste sicut solebat habere tempore Edwardi regis et patris et fratris mei, et scolas similiter habeat.

Teste, Episcopo Lincoln. apud Wudestocam.

Grant of Dunwich School to the Priory of Eye. Between 1076 and 1083.

[A. F. Leach, *V. C. H. Suffolk*, II. 303. Dugd. *Mon.* III. 405 from Reg. Eye, then in possession of Thomas Deye.]

Carta Roberti Malet Fundatoris Ecclesiae Conventualis de Eya.

...Ego Robertus Malet assensu domini mei Willielmi regis Angliae pro anima ipsius et uxoris ejus Matildis reginae, pro

remaining in the choir. As if walking in procession from school they go to choir, and on leaving the choir go to school, like canons getting up in the night [for service].

p. 10, c. 11. This blood struck from the flint...and placed in a silver shrine, I by the mercy of God gained a sight of, for I was brought up from tender years in Waltham church for 53 years, and in its bosom instructed in grammar learning. Unhappy me! to whom it has happened to see myself in this life torn from the breasts which gave me life.

Confirmation by Henry I of Warwick School as it was in the Days of Edward the Confessor.

King Henry's confirmation of the customs and ordeal of iron and water and the school of Warwick.

Henry, King of the English, to T., Bishop of Worcester, and R., Bishop of Chester, and Earl Roger and Geoffrey of Clinton and all the barons of Warwickshire, greeting.

I command that the Church of All Saints, Warwick, have all its customs and the ordeals of iron and water, as well and lawfully as they used to have them in the time of King Edward, and of my father and brother, and have the School in like manner.

Witness the Bishop of Lincoln at Woodstock.

Grant of Dunwich School to the Priory of Eye. Between 1076 and 1083.

Charter of Robert Malet, founder of the conventual church of Eye.

...I, Robert Malet, with the assent of my lord William, King of the English, for his soul and that of his wife queen Matilda,

memetipso, et pro animabus patris mei Willielmi Malet et matris meae Hesiliae, et pro animabus omnium antecessorum et parentum meorum, ad usus monachorum apud Eyam monasterium construo, et monachorum conventum in eo pono.

At ut ipsi Deo libere et quiete servire possint eidem monasterio, de meis propriis terris, ecclesiis, et decimis, ad eorum sustentamentum confero, praesentis scripti attestatione confirmo. Imprimis ecclesiam Eye, quae in honore Sancti Petri fundata est, concedo cum omnibus terris et decimis eidem pertinentibus....

Do eis etiam decimam fori Eye et omnes ecclesias de Donevico quae factae sunt et faciendae; necnon et decimam totius villae, tam in denariis quam in allecibus, et unam feriam...Scholas etiam ejusdem villae....

The Oblates and Novices School at Canterbury.
c. 1075.

[Wilkins, *Concilia*, I. 3, 55 seq.]

Constitutiones Lanfranci.

Offerendus puer, facta sibi prius corona, manibus portans hostiam, et calicem cum vino, sicut mos est, post evangelium sacerdoti, qui missam celebrat, a parentibus offeratur. Qua oblatione a sacerdote suscepta, involvant praedicti parentes manus pueri in palla, qua altare coopertum est, et cujus pars anterius pendet, et tunc suscipiat eum abbas: quo facto, praefati parentes...statim promittant quod...susceptum ordinem puer nunquam relinquat....Hanc promissionem prius scriptam coram testibus verbis ibi prius edicant, et postea super altare ponant.

for myself, and for the souls of my father William Malet and my mother Hesilia, and for the souls of all my predecessors and relations, construct a monastery for the use of monks at Eye and place a convent of monks in it.

And that they may freely and quietly serve God, I confer on the same monastery and by the witness of this present writing confirm for their maintenance out of my own lands, churches and tithes; first I grant the church of Eye which is founded in honour of St Peter with all lands and tithes to the same belonging....

I give them also the tithe of the market of Eye and all the churches of Dunwich built or to be built, also the tithe of the whole town, both in money and herrings and a fair....The school also of the same town....

The Oblates and Novices School at Canterbury.
c. 1075.

Lanfranc's Constitutions.

When a boy is to be offered [i.e. made an oblate], let a round tonsure be made on his head, and carrying the host in his hands and the cup with the wine, as the custom is, let him be offered by his parents after the Gospel to the priest who celebrates mass. When the priest has accepted the offering, the aforesaid parents should wrap the boy's hands in the pall with which the altar is covered and part of which hangs down in front, and then the abbot should receive him. After which the said parents...should immediately promise that...the boy will never leave the order he has accepted....This promise they should make beforehand in writing in the presence of witnesses and afterwards place it on the altar.

[Continuation of Lanfranc's Constitutions, from page 60.]

Tali hora prior mane ad excitandos fratres sonitum debet facere, ut pueri, factis solutis orationibus, in claustro valeant legere. Qui cum legere inchoant, alte quamdiu legant, separati abinvicem ita sedeant, ut alter alterum nec manibus, nec vestibus contingere possit. Infans infanti non signo innuere, non verbo aliquid dicere, nisi vidente atque audiente magistro, praesumat; non de loco, in quo sedet, sine praecepto vel licentia surgat. Quocunque pergunt infantes, unus magister inter duos infantes sit. Transeuntes ante fratres inclinent fratribus, et fratres eis sedentes tantum. Duobus una laterna sufficiat; si tres fuerint, tertius alteram portet; si plures fuerint, hoc ordine disponantur. In nullius manum aliquid dent; de nullius manu aliquid accipiant, nisi abbatis, prioris majoris, magistri eorum, et hoc non ubique, sed in congruis locis, ubi aliter esse non possit, aut non debeant. Cantor quoque, cum in scholis eorum est, potest librum, in quo cantari, aut legi debet, dare eis, et accipere ab eis. Ad altare si serviunt, dant etiam ibi et accipiunt, sicut ordines eorum exposcunt. In capitulo suo vapulent, sicut majores in majori capitulo. Confessuri ad abbatem, vel ad priorem vadant, vel ad eos, quos specialiter in capitulo designaverit abbas. Dum confitetur unus, sedeat alter in suppedaneo, magistro eorum extra capitulum sedente in proximo. Si post versum, qui ante cibum dicitur, ingrediuntur refectorium, vel post 'Gloriam' primi psalmi ad horas intrent chorum, ipsi quidem ad loca sua vadant, solito more inclinent, magister vero eorum ad loca, quae tardantibus instituta sunt, eat: puero, qui ante mensam abbatis servit, abstinentia cibi, vel potus sine ejus praecepto minime injungatur. Quodsi praecipienti eo injungitur, aut ei indulgeatur, aut interim

The prior ought to make a noise to waken the brethren at such hour in the morning as the boys when they have said their several prayers can see to read in the cloister, and when they begin to read let them for some time read aloud, sitting separate from each other, so that one cannot touch another with his hands or clothes. No child shall dare to make a sign or say a word to another except in the sight and hearing of the master; nor get up from the place in which he sits unless told or given leave to do so. Wherever the children go there should be a master between every two of them. When they pass in front of the brethren they should bow to them, and the brethren remaining seated should do the same. One lantern should serve for two; if there are three, the third should carry a second lantern; if there are more, the same arrangement should be observed. They should not put anything into anyone's hand or take anything from anyone's hand, except in the case of the abbot, the senior prior, or their own master, and that not everywhere but only in proper places, where it cannot or ought not to be otherwise. The precentor, too, when he is in their school may give or take from them a book from which to sing or read. If they are serving at the altar, too, they can give or take as their orders require. They should be flogged in a chapter of their own, as their elders are in the great chapter. When they go to confession they should go to the abbot or prior or those specially assigned for the purpose by the abbot. While one confesses another should sit on the steps, and the master should sit close by outside the chapter-house. If they go into the refectory after the verse which is said before food, or into choir at the hours after the Gloria of the first psalm, they are to go to their places and bow as usual, while their master is to go to the place set apart for those who are tardy: but the boy who waits at the abbot's table is not to have any abstinence from food or drink imposed on him except by the abbot's orders. But if by his orders it is imposed, either he

a mensa abbatis removeatur. In choro, praesente abbate, nisi praecepto ejus nullus eos percutiat, nullus exire faciat. Absente eo, cantor de iis, quae sui officii sunt, eos castiget ; prior vero de caeteris, in quibus se leviter habent. Ubicumque sint, praeter personas superius designatas, nullus eis signum faciat, nullus arrideat.

In scholam eorum nullus ingrediatur, nullus cum eis alicubi loquatur, nisi sibi ab abbate, vel priore ingrediendi, vel loquendi licentia concedatur. Meridianis horis in lectis suis nunquam legant, nihil aliud ibi agant, sed cooperti tantum quiescant. Unus super alios magistros sit magister eorum maturus et discretus, qui auditis clamoribus, culpas delinquentium moderata discretione sciat vel punire, vel indulgere ; collocatis in lectis suis assistant magistri, dum sint cooperti, in nocte cum accensis candelis.

Juvenes tam nutriti quam de seculo venientes, qui magistris custodiendi commendantur, in multis sicut infantes, de quibus superius dictum est, custodiantur ; remoti, ut supra, a seinvicem sedeant ; extra locum custodiae suae sine custode nusquam procedant ; duo et duo laternas ferant ; abbati, vel priori et nulli alii, nisi specialiter designatum sit, confessiones suas faciant. Meridianis horis in lectis suis non debent legere, non scribere, non quippiam operis facere ; sed cooperti tantum quiescere ; lectos suos ante, vel inter lectos magistrorum habere ; si necesse habent surgere, prius magistros excitent, et postea accensa laterna, si nox est, ad necessitates suas explendas cum magistris ambulent. Praeter abbatem, priorem, magistrosque eorum, nulli liberum sit in loco custodiae eorum deputato sedere, nec verbo, nec signo aliquid eis innotescere, nisi accepta licentia abbate, vel priore ; quae licentia cum conceditur, magister sedere debet inter juvenem et eum qui juveni loquitur ; juvenis cum juvene non loquatur, nisi audiente, et intelligente magistro, quid

must be pardoned or he must be removed from the abbot's table. In choir, if the abbot is there, no one may strike them, no one order them out except by his direction. When he is away, the precentor may chastise them for things to do with his office, and the prior for other things, in which they behave childishly. Wherever they are, no one except the persons above-mentioned may make signs to them, no one may smile at them.

No one shall go into their school, no one shall speak to them anywhere, unless leave to go in or to talk to them has been given by the abbot or prior. They are never to read or do anything else in bed at midday but to cover themselves up and keep quiet. A monk of more than ordinary gravity and discretion shall be master over the other masters, one who may know how, when he has heard any charge against them, to inflict punishment in moderation on those who are at fault or to let them off. When they go to bed the masters shall stand by them at night with lighted candles until they are covered up.

Young men, whether those who have been brought up in the monastery or those coming in from the outside world, who are given in charge to masters, shall be looked after in most things as is before provided with regard to the boys. They shall, as is above said, sit separate from each other; shall never leave the place in which they are kept, except with the monk who has charge of them; shall carry lanterns in pairs; and shall make confession to no one but the abbot or prior, unless by special arrangement. At the midday rest they shall not read or write, or do any work; but cover themselves up and keep quiet; they shall have their beds before or between their masters' beds. If they have to get up, they shall first wake their master, then light a lantern, if it is night, and go to the Necessarium with their master. No one shall be allowed to sit in the place assigned to them except the abbot, the prior and their masters; nor make any communication to them by words or signs, except with the leave of the abbot or prior; and when leave is given the master ought to sit between the youth and the one who is talking to him. No youth is to talk to another, except

utrinque dicatur. Magistri inter eos sedeant, vel ante illos, sic ut eos, cum volunt, conspicere valeant. Cum dormitum vadunt, tamdiu stent ante ipsos magistri, usque dum ipsi juvenes in lectis suis jaceant cooperti : si nox est, cum candelis accensis assistant.

In monasterio, capitulo, refectorio, processione mixti sint senioribus, non observato, si necesse sit, ordine conversionis eorum. Si ad mensam legunt, vel de coquina serviunt, surgentibus a mensa fratribus cum eis ad monasterium vadant, et dicto 'Et ne nos,' cum custodibus ad refectorium revertantur: duo simul, aut plures, si fieri possit, de conventu non remaneant: quodsi paucitas majorum, et pluralitas juvenum aliter agendum coegerit, sufficientes eis custodes deputentur: porro si custodia illa juvenum, quae in nonnullis coenobiis tenetur, magis placet, ut videlicet in diversis, ac separatis abinvicem locis, per claustrum sedeant, singuli singulos, aut plures, si tanta copia est, custodes habeant, singuli singulos laternas in nocte ferant. Custos juvenem non relinquat nisi commendatum alicui fratri, in quo, et de quo bene confidat. Omnis denique custodia ei adhibeatur, quae superius descripta est.

Kirby-Pontefract School given to St Clement's Collegiate Church. Between 1075 and 1087.

[Printed in A. F. Leach's *Early Yorkshire Schools* (*Yorks. Archaeol. Journ.*, Rec. Ser. 1903), II. 1.]

Quando Ilbertus de Laceo in honorem Dei et Sancte Marie et Omnium Sanctorum ecclesiam beati Clementis in castello suo, pro salute Willelmi regis majoris, Willelmi filii ejus et filiorum ipsorum, et pro animabus predecessorum et pro animabus uxoris et filiorum suorum, et pro salute omnium fidelium vivorum et mortuorum, in tempore principis supradicti fundavit, donavit et confirmavit eidem ecclesie plenarie decime sue duas partes de dominico suo, videlicet in Camasella....

so that the master may hear and understand what is said by both of them. The masters ought to sit between them or in front of them, so as to be able to see them, if they want to. When they go to bed the masters ought to stand in front of them until they lie down and are covered over, and at night, with lighted candles.

In the monastery, in chapter, refectory and processions they are to be mixed up with the elder monks, and, if necessary, without regard to the order of their admission. If they read at table, or are serving in the kitchen, when the brethren get up from table they shall go with them into the monastery, and when 'And lead us not into temptation' has been said shall return with their keepers to the refectory. No two or more of the convent shall stay with them, if possible; but if the scarcity of older monks or the greater numbers of the young ones require it, a sufficient number shall be assigned to take charge of them. But if the method of taking care of the youths which prevails in some monasteries is preferred, that, namely, they shall sit singly in different and separate places about the cloister, each custodian shall have his separate charge, one or more together, if their number is so great as to demand it, and each singly shall carry a lantern at night. A custodian shall never leave his charge, without confiding him to another of the brethren in whom he has full confidence. In a word all the care shall be shown him as above described.

Kirby-Pontefract School given to St Clement's Collegiate Church. Between 1075 and 1087..

When Ilbert of Lacy founded the church of St Clement in his castle in honour of God and St Mary and All Saints for the health of King William the elder, William his son and their sons, and for the souls of his ancestors and for the souls of his wife and sons, and for the health of all the faithful living and dead in the time of the said prince, he fully granted and confirmed to the same church two-thirds of the tithe of his demesne, viz. in Campsall...[a long list of places follows].

Harum rerum omnium supradictarum tenuit Ranulphus, Grammaticus dimidiam partem cum octo bovatis terre in Darthingtona ad servicium ecclesie et dimidiam commune contra Ranulphum Grammaticum, et Godefridum presbiterum....

Et pater meus Robertus de Laceo dedit ibi...Barones eiusdem castellarie....

Hec autem beneficia confirmavit authoritate Thome senioris archiepiscopi, dedicavit ipsam ecclesiam, cum scolis de Kirkby et Pontisfracti.

Et sicut antecessores mei has donaciones et confirmaciones statuerunt in suis temporibus; ita ego Ilbertus concedo et confirmo eas cum auctoritate Turstini archiepiscopi.

Hastings Grammar and Song Schools before 1090.

[P. R. O. Anc. Deeds, D. 1073.]

Transcriptum carte de fundacione prebendarum.

Henricus, divina consciente clemencia Comes Augi, omnibus primatibus suis et omnibus suis subditis et omnibus suis hominibus tam Francis quam Anglis, salutem....

R. Comes Augi fundator et edificator Ecclesie Sancte Marie de Hastings dedit et dimisit Gymmingo habendam in prebendam capellam de Berchingis et decimam eiusdem loci ...unam mansuram in castello et alteram in Baillio ad pontem....

In prebendam Ausch ecclesiam de Turok et terram eidem ecclesie pertinentem...et unam mansuram in Estehow et in castello unam....

Ad prebendam Auch pertinet regimen scole gramatice et ad prebendam Wymingi regimen scole cantus.

Hi sunt testes, clerici, Hugo Decanus, Willelmus filius Mazel et multi alii.

Of all the aforesaid property Randolph the Grammarian held half with eight ox-gangs of land in Darthington to the service of the church and half the common opposite Randolph the Grammarian and Godfrey the priest....

And my father Robert of Lacy gave there....The barons of the same castle-ward gave....

All these grants he confirmed by the authority of archbishop Thomas I, and dedicated the same church with the school of Kirby and Pomfret.

And as my ancestors established these grants and confirmations in their time, so I, Ilbert, grant and confirm them with the authority of Archbishop Thurstan.

Hastings Grammar and Song Schools before 1090.

Copy of charter of foundation of the prebends.

Henry, by the consent of the clemency of God, Count of Eu, to all his superiors and all his subjects and all his men both French and English, health....

Robert, Count of Eu, founder and builder of the church of St Mary of Hastings, gave and demised to Gymming to hold as a prebend the chapel of Barking and the tithe of the same place...a mansion in the castle and another in the Bailey at the bridge...[Three more prebends are set out.]

To Ausch[er] for a prebend the church of Thurrock and the land to the same church belonging...a mansion in Easthow and one in the castle...[Four more prebends are set out and certain possessions common to all the prebendaries.]

To Auscher's prebend belongs the keeping of the grammar school and to Wyming's prebend the keeping of the song school.

These are witnesses, the clerks, Hugh the dean, William, son of Mazel, and many others.

York School. 1075—1090.

[A. F. Leach, *Early Yorkshire Schools*, I. 10, from Hugh the Chanter, *Hist. Ch. of York* (Rolls Series), II. 107.]

De archiepiscopo [Thomas I] breviter recapitulare volo. Quando archiepiscopatum suscepit, cuncta hostili vastatione depopulata et vastata invenit: de septem canonicis (non enim plures fuerant) tres in civitate et ecclesia combusta et destructa reperit. Reliqui vel mortui vel metu et desolatione erant exulati. Ecclesias vero re-coopertas, et juxta facultatem suam restructas, canonicis quos invenerat restituit: dispersos revocavit; ad Deo serviendum et ecclesie aliquos addidit: refectorium refecit et dormitorium: prepositum constituit, qui ceteris preesset, et eos procuraret: villas aliquas et terras et ecclesias dedit, et ab aliis ablatas reddidit; plurima de suo proprio canonicis necessaria administrabat; archidiaconos quoque sapientes et industrios per diocesim divisit. Annis pluribus canonicis communiter sic vescentibus, consilio quorundam placuit archiepiscopo de terra S. Petri, que multum adhuc vasta erant, singulis prebendas partiri; ita ut canonicorum numerus crescere posset, et quisque, sicut per se partem suam studiosius et edificaret et excoleret.

Quod et sic factum est. Tunc enim statuit decanum, thesaurarium, cantorem, dans cuique dignè et ecclesie et suo et personarum honorem: magistrum scolarum jam antea statuerat....

[Archbishop Thomas II, educated in York School *c.* 1075, succeeded Gerard A.D. 1108.] Erat enim apud nos sub patruo suo amabili et amicabili educatus, et decenter eruditus.

York School. 1075—1090.

Of archbishop [Thomas I] I wish to shortly sum up. When he received the archbishopric he found the whole place depopulated and ravaged by invasion; of the seven canons (for there were no more) he found three among the burnt ruins of the city and church. The rest were dead or driven into exile in fear and despair. He re-roofed the church, and to the extent of his means rebuilt it, and restored it to the canons whom he found; and summoned back those who were dispersed; adding some for the service of God and the church. He re-erected the refectory and dormitory; and established a provost to preside over the rest and provide for them. He gave them some manors and lands and churches, and recovered those which had been taken away by others. Most of the wants of the canons he met out of his own revenues. He divided the diocese among wise and industrious archdeacons. After the canons had thus lived in common for some years, the archbishop determined on the advice of certain persons to divide St Peter's land, much of which was still lying waste, into separate prebends; so that the number of canons might be increased, and that each of them might be the more eager to build and bring into cultivation his own share.

And this was done. Then, too, he established a dean, a treasurer and a precentor, giving each what was fitting for the honour of the church and himself and the person. The schoolmaster he had established before this....

[Archbishop Thomas II, educated in York School *c.* 1075, succeeded Gerard A.D. 1108.] For he was brought up among us and properly educated under his loveable and friendly uncle.

Salisbury School in the Foundation Statutes of the Cathedral. 1091.

[W. H. Frere, *The Use of Sarum* (1898), 259, from Registrum Osmundi, f. 24.]

Institucio Osmundi.

Hee sunt dignitates et consuetudines Sarum ecclesie quas ego Osmundus episcopus eiusdem ecclesie in nomine sancte trinitatis, anno ab Incarnatione Domini MXCI, institui simul et concessi personis et canonicis eiusdem ecclesie, participato dominorum archiepiscopi et aliorum coepiscoporum nostrorum consilio, quorum nomina subscripta sunt, et domini Regis Willelmi interueniente assensu. Videlicet, ut decanus et cantor, cancellarius et thesaurarius residentes sint assidue in ecclesia Sarum, remota omni excusationis specie....Canonicos nichil potest excusare quin et ipsi residentes sint in ecclesia Sarum, nisi causa scholarum et seruitium domini Regis, qui unum habere potest in capella sua, et archiepiscopus unum, et episcopus tres.

Decanus omnibus canonicis et omnibus uicariis preest quoad regimen animarum et correccionem morum.

Cantor debet chorum regere quoad cantum, et potest cantus eleuare et deponere.

Thesaurarius in conseruandis thesauris et ornamentis, et in administrandis luminaribus preeminet. Similiter cancellarius in scolis regendis et in libris corrigendis.

Archidiaconi in sollicitudine parrochiarum, et in cura pollent animarum.

Decanus, et cantor, thesaurarius, et cancellarius, duplicem percipiunt communam. Reliqui canonici simplicem.

Subdecanus a decano archidiaconatum urbis et suburbii, succentor a cantore que ad cantariam pertinent, possideant. Si decanus defuerit ecclesie, subdecanus uices eius impleat. Succentor similiter et cantoris.

Salisbury School in the Foundation Statutes of the Cathedral. 1091.

The Institution of Osmund.

These are the dignities and customs of the church of Salisbury, which I, Osmund, bishop of that church, in the name of the Holy Trinity, in the year of our Lord 1091, established and granted to the persons and canons of the same church, with the advice of the lords, the archbishop and other my co-bishops whose names are subscribed, and with the assent of the lord King William; namely, that Dean and Chanter, Chancellor and Treasurer shall be continually resident in the church at Salisbury, without any kind of excuse....Nothing can excuse the canons from being personally resident in the church of Salisbury, except attendance at the schools and the service of the lord King, who can have one in his chapel, and the archbishop one, and the bishop three.

The dean presides over all canons and vicars [choral] as regards the cure of souls and correction of conduct.

The precentor ought to rule the choir as to chanting and can raise or lower the chant.

The treasurer is pre-eminent in keeping the treasures and ornaments and managing the lights. In like manner the chancellor in ruling the school and correcting the books.

The archdeacons excel in the superintendence of parishes and the cure of souls.

Dean and precentor, treasurer and chancellor, receive double, the rest of the canons single commons.

The sub-dean holds from the dean the archdeaconry of the city and suburbs, the succentor from the precentor all that pertains to the singing. If the dean is away from the church the sub-dean fills his place, and the succentor in like manner the precentor's.

Archischola debet lectiones ascultare et terminare, et sigillum ecclesie portare, literas et cartas componere, et in tabula lectores notare, et cantor similiter cantatores....

Confirmation, c. 1108, of School to Dean and Chapter of Christ Church, Hants, as in 1100.

[A. F. Leach, *V. C. H. Hants*, II. 251, Cott. Tib. D. VI. f. 13 a. Printed *Mon.* VI. 304.]

Carta Baldwini de Redveriis senioris, Comitis Devonie, de antiquis libertatibus.

Baldewinus de Redveriis omnibus hominibus Francis et Anglis ceterisque Christi fidelibus ad quos presens scriptum pervenerit universis, salutem.

Sciatis me pro Dei amore et pro salute anime mee et pro animabus omnium tam antecessorum quam successorum et amicorum meorum, concessisse et presenti carta mea confirmasse Hyllario, Decano, et ceteris omnibus in Christi Ecclesia de Twinham Deo servientibus et servituris, omnes tam ecclesiasticas possessiones quam seculares tenuras et omnia quecunque illorum sunt et esse debent super feudum meum de quibus saisiata est ecclesia...in liberam, puram et perpetuam elemosinam perpetuo plene possideant, sicut melius, plenius, et liberius possunt possideri, ut dignitatem suam plenam et omnes suas liberas consuetudines in omnibus rebus honorifice habeant, sicut antiquitus semper habere solebant; ville scilicet ipsius scolam, suam liberam curiam, cum soc et sac...sicut rex Henricus patri meo Ricardo de Redveriis plenius et liberius habere concessit, quando ei primum hereditario iure habendum totum contulit feudum, ipsam videlicet Christescherchiam de Twinham cum omnibus suis pertinenciis, in qua Deo serviunt... [a long list of churches and other property]; quia hec omnia cum eorum pertinenciis ante me, testibus multis, habuerunt, libere et quiete de me et de heredibus meis tenenda et integra habenda sibi et successoribus suis concessi, presenti carta mea, et sigillo meo confirmavi.

The schoolmaster ought to hear and determine the lessons, and carry the church seal, compose letters and deeds and mark the readers on the table, and the precentor in like manner the singers....

Confirmation, c. 1108, of School to Dean and Chapter of Christ Church, Hants, as in 1100.

Charter of Baldwin of Redvers the elder, Earl of Devon, of the ancient liberties.

Baldwin of Redvers to all his men, French and English, and all the rest of the faithful of Christ to whom the present writing shall come, greeting.

Know that I, for the love of God and the health of my soul and for the souls of all my ancestors, successors and friends, have granted and by this my present deed confirmed to Hilary the Dean and to all others serving or to serve God in Christ Church of Twyneham, that they may for ever fully possess all ecclesiastical possessions and secular holdings and everything which is theirs or ought to be, on my fee of which the church is seised...in free, pure and perpetual alms as they can best, most fully and most freely be held, so that they may honourably have their full dignity and all their free customs in all things, as anciently they have been accustomed to have them; namely, the school of the same town, their free court with soc and sac... as King Henry most fully and freely granted them to my father, Richard of Redvers, when he first transferred the whole fee to him to hold by hereditary right, namely, Christ Church of Twyneham itself with all its appurtenances, in which they serve God...because they held all these things with their appurtenances before me, according to many witnesses, I have granted to have and to hold freely and quietly of me and my heirs to them and their successors, and by this present charter and my seal confirmed.

Confirmation of Grant of Gloucester School to St Oswald's Church. *c.* 1100.

[Cal. Pat. 12 Ric. II, pt ii. m. 10.]

Henricus, rex Anglorum et dux Normannorum, omnibus suis fidelibus Francis et Anglis, salutem.

Sciatis me confirmasse scolas tocius Gloucestrie ecclesie Sancti Oswaldi de Gloucestria capelle mee, quas episcopi Wigornienses Sansonus et ceteri predicte ecclesie dederunt et carte sue testimonio confirmaverunt. Valete.

Beverley Grammar-Schoolmaster in Love. *c.* 1100.

[A. F. Leach, *Early Yorkshire Schools*, 180 c, from B. M. Faust., B. IV. 156. *Hist. Ch. of York* (Rolls Series), I. 281.]

Miracula Sancti Johannis.

De multis, igitur, unum producamus in medium prefati pontificis ope mirabiliter a demoniace perversionis artibus liberatum ; et quod ab ejus ore veredico sepius accepimus, ad laudem Dei Omnipotentis, et ad memoriam Sancti Sui, reducere satagamus.

Scolasticus quidam ejusdem temporis intervallo Beverlacum petiit, cupiens ibidem, quoniam locus ille clericorum abundabat copia, scolastice discipline studium regere ; qui unanimi devocione a prelatis ejusdem ecclesie susceptus est. Hinc quoniam litteratoria pollebat disciplina, hinc quia morum honestate nobilitabatur, placuit mox omnibus illius conversacio, quoniam humilis et benigna ; placuit artis pericia, quoniam dulci et sollicita exercitacione et jocunda severitate condita. Regebat assidue scolarum frequenciam exterius, et chori curam moderabatur concorditer interius, in utroque non segnis provisor, sed officialis egregius.

Injecit enim juvenis ille oculos in cujusdam formose virginis faciem, mox et eam cepit juvenili dilectione concupiscere ;

Confirmation of Grant of Gloucester School to St Oswald's Church. c. 1100.

Henry, king of the English and duke of the Normans, to all his faithful subjects, French and English, health.

Know ye that I have confirmed to the church of St Oswald of Gloucester, my chapel, the schools of all Gloucester which the bishops of Worcester, Samson and the rest, gave to the aforesaid church and confirmed by the evidence of their deeds. Farewell.

Beverley Grammar-Schoolmaster in Love.
c. 1100.

Miracles of St John of Beverley.

Of many therefore we will produce one who by the help of the aforesaid prelate was miraculously delivered from the craft of demoniacal perversion, and endeavour to reproduce to the praise of God Almighty and the memory of his saint the tale as we have often heard it from his truthful mouth.

A certain scholar came to Beverley at that time, wishing, as the place was full of clerks, to keep school there; and was received by the prelates of the church with unanimous approval. As on the one hand he was full of learning, and on the other was of a noble character, his conduct was favourably regarded by all, being at once modest and kindly. His skill in his profession also pleased, made up as it was of care in teaching and pleasantness in severity. Outside the church he taught a crowded school diligently; inside he governed the choir harmoniously, in both no lazy prebendary, but an active official.

But the young master cast his eyes on a pretty girl and he at once began to long for her with youthful affection. The

crevit quotidie male cepta suggestio. Cepit illico rigor discipline scolastice mollescere, fervorque studii literalis tepescere; putaresque hominem non minima infirmitate languentem, cujus pallor et feda macies juvenilem dehonestaverat faciem.

Divino itaque commonitus instinctu, interius, exteriusque non mediocriter egrotans, ad potentis medici suffragium, quasi ad asylum confugit, beatissimum videlicet Johannem; et ut commodius virum Dei exoraret, post peractam matutinalis officii psalmodiam, more solito discedente clero, in choro solus remansit. Projecit se illico coram altari, velut aquam misericordi Deo effudit animam suam.

Finitis itaque precibus et singultibus lachrymosis, cum ab oracione surrexisset, mirabile dictu! a languoribus et demoniace decepcionis, quibus opprimebatur, laqueis dissolutus: nulla in medium mora, Divinum sensit juvamen. Convaluit egrotus, de celo suscepta medela, sanctissimi Johannis solita subveniente gracia. Refriguit mox calor pestilens...Mirabantur qui aderant tam subite melioracionis medelam.

St Albans and Dunstable Schools in the 12th Century.

[From A. F. Leach, *V. C. H. Herts*, II. 47. *Gesta Abbatum Monasterii Sancti Albani* (Rolls Series), I. 72–3.]

Gaufridus Abbas.

...Iste de Cenomannia, unde oriundus erat, venit, vocatus ab Abbate Ricardo, dum adhuc secularis esset, ut scolam apud Sanctum Albanum regeret. Et cum venisset, concessa fuit scola alii magistro, quia non venit tempestive. Legit igitur apud Dunestapliam, expectans scolam Sancti Albani, sibi repromissam; ubi quemdam ludum de Sancta Katerina—quem Miracula vulgariter appellamus—fecit. Ad que decoranda, petiit a Sacrista Sancti Albani, ut sibi cape chorales accommodarentur, et obtinuit. Et fuit ludus ille de Sancta Katerina.

ill conceived idea increased daily. From that moment the rigour of scholastic discipline began to slacken, and the fervour of literary studies to cool; and you would have thought the man was stricken by a severe disease, so did pallor and emaciation destroy the youthful beauty of his face.

But warned by a divine instinct within and being outwardly no little ill, he fled, as to an asylum, to the prayers of the powerful physician, the most blessed John; and the better to pray to the man of God, after the psalms were finished at matins, after the choir had departed as usual, he remained behind alone in the choir. He threw himself down before the altar, and poured out his soul like water before the merciful God.

When he got up, having finished his prayers and stopped his tears, wonderful to relate, he was freed from languor and the snares of the deceits of the devil in which he had been caught; and without a moment's delay felt the help of God. The sick man was healed, receiving medicine from heaven through the intervention of the wonted grace of the most holy John. Soon the pestilent fever abated....Those present were astonished at the sudden cure.

St Albans and Dunstable Schools in the 12th Century.

Abbot Geoffrey.

...He came from Maine, where he was born, being summoned by Abbot Richard while he was still a secular, to keep the school at St Albans. And when he arrived the school had been granted to another master, as he had not come when he was expected. He taught therefore at Dunstable while waiting for St Alban's school which was again promised him, where he made a play of St Katharine—what we commonly call a Miracle Play. To set it off he asked and obtained from the Sacrist of St Albans the loan of some choir copes. And that play was of Saint Katharine.

De Capa Sancte Katerine.

Casu igitur, nocte sequenti, accensa est domus Magistri Gaufridi, et combusta est domus, cum libris suis et capis memoratis. Nesciens igitur quomodo hoc damnum Deo et Sancto Albano restauraret, seipsum reddidit in holocaustum Deo, assumens habitum religionis in Domo Sancti Albani. Et hec fuit causa, quare tantum habuit diligentie, ut capas chorales in eisdem, postea in Abbatem promotus, faceret preciosas.

Confirmation to the Schoolmaster of St Paul's, London, of House and Librarianship, ex-officio.

[A. F. Leach, 'St Paul's School before and after Colet,' *Journ. of Education*, June 1909, and *Archæol.* 62, pt i. p. 211. Mun. St Paul's, Lib. A. f. xxviii.]

De Magistro Scolarum et de Cancellario vij Littere, j.

R. Dei gracia Londoniensis ecclesie minister, W. Decano totique fratrum conuentui, salutem et paternam benediccionem.

Noueritis filii mei karissimi uestra dileccio me Hugoni, Magistro Scolarum, ex Magisterii dignitate, suisque eiusdem dignitatis successoribus stabilisse firmiter Magistri Durandi stacionem in angulo turris, uidelicet ubi Decanus Willelmus meo illum collocauit imperio inter Robertum de Auco et Odonem. Concedo eciam illi scolarumque priuilegio nostre ecclesie omnium librorum custodiam. Volo igitur, et tibi, Decane, precipio ut illos omnes in conspectu fratrum in quodam cirographo ascriptos, cuius scilicet altera pars in thesauro custodiatur, alteram sibi retineat, ei commendes, et de hac custodia eum seisias, diligenter et sub anathemate inuestigans si aliqui librorum tam secularium quam diuinorum extra missi per aliquem fuerint; quod si fuerint, sub obediencia precipio ut retromittantur.

Fac eciam illi habere claues armariorum (*sic*) iuxta altare, que ad illud opus fieri imperaui.

NOTA. Magistrum Scolarum debere custodiam librorum almariis habere.

Of St Katharine's Cope.

The following night Master Geoffrey's house was accidentally set on fire; and was burnt, with his books and the copes. So not knowing how to repair the loss to God and St Albans, he offered up himself as a burnt offering to God, taking the religious habit in St Alban's house. And this was the reason why, after he was promoted to be abbot [in 1119], he was so diligent in making precious choir copes in it.

Confirmation to the Schoolmaster of St Paul's, London, of House and Librarianship, ex-officio.

Seven letters of the Schoolmaster and Chancellor. No. 1.

R[ichard de Belmeis], by the grace of God minister of the Church of London, to W[illiam] dean and all the assembly of brethren, greeting and paternal blessing.

Know ye beloved, my dearest sons, that I have confirmed to Hugh the schoolmaster, in right of the dignity of his mastership, and to his successors in the same dignity, the station of Master Durand in the angle of the tower, namely, where Dean William placed him by my orders between Robert of Eu and Odo. I grant him also and to the privilege of the school the custody of all the books of our church. I will therefore and command you, Dean, to give him charge of them all when written in an indenture before the brethren, one part of which shall be safeguarded in the Treasury, and the other shall be kept by him, and give him seisin of their custody, making diligent inquiry under pain of excommunication whether any of the books, either secular or theological, have been taken out by anyone; and if there have been, I order them in virtue of their obedience to be returned.

Let him also have the keys of the cupboards by the altar, which I ordered to be made for the purpose.

NOTE. The schoolmaster ought to have the custody of the books in the cupboards.

Restoration of Thetford School to the Dean of Thetford.

[A. F. Leach, *V. C. H. Suffolk*, II. 303. Anstruther's *Epistolae Herberti Lozinge* XXXII.]

Herbertus episcopus fratribus et filiis apud Tedford. Sciatis me reddidisse Bundo Decano scolas suas apud Tedford sicut unquam melius et integrius habuit; et precipio ut alie scole non habeantur ibi, nisi sue vel quas ipse permiserit.

London Schools in 1118.

[FitzStephen, *Life of Thomas à Becket* (Rolls Series, 1877), III. 3, 97.]

De Fontibus.

Sunt etiam circa Londoniam ab aquilone suburbani fontes praecipui, aqua dulci, salubri, perspicua et 'per claros rivo trepidante lapillos'; inter quos Fons Sacer, Fons Clericorum, Fons sancti Clementis, nominatiores habentur, et adeuntur celebriore accessu et majore frequentia scholarium, et urbanae juventutis in serotinis aestivis ad auram exeuntis. Urbs sane bona, si bonum habeat dominum.

De Scholis.

In Londoniis tres principales ecclesiae scholas celebres habent de privilegio et antiqua dignitate. Plerumque tamen favore personali alicujus notorium secundum philosophiam plures ibi scholae admittuntur. Diebus festis ad ecclesias festivas magistri conventus celebrant. Disputant scholares, quidam demonstrative, dialectice alii; hi rotant enthymemata, hi perfectis melius utuntur syllogismis. Quidam ad ostentationem exercentur disputatione, quae est inter colluctantes; alii ad veritatem, ea quae est perfectionis gratia. Sophistae simulatores agmine et inundatione verborum beati judicantur; alii paralogizant. Oratores aliqui quandoque orationibus rhetoricis aliquid dicunt apposite ad persuadendum, curantes artis praecepta servare, et ex contingentibus nihil

Restoration of Thetford School to the Dean of Thetford.

Herbert the bishop to his brethren and sons at Thetford. Know ye that I have given back to Dean Bund his school at Thetford as he ever best and most fully held it, and I order that no other school shall be held there, except his own or any which he shall allow.

London Schools in 1118.

The Wells.

The chief suburban wells near London are on the north, of sweet water, health-giving, clear and 'with stream hurrying over clear pebbles'; among which Holywell, Clerkenwell, St Clement's well, are thought the best known, and are more frequented by the more celebrated of the scholars and youth of the town when they walk out in summer time to take the air. A good city indeed when it has a good lord.

The Schools.

In London the three principal churches have celebrated schools of privilege and ancient dignity. Often, however, through personal favour to some noted philosopher more schools are allowed there. On feast days the masters celebrate assemblies at the churches, *en fête.* The scholars hold disputations, some declaiming, others by way of question and answer. These roll out enthymemes, those use the better form of perfect syllogisms. Some dispute merely for show as they do at collections; others for truth, which is the grace of perfection. The sophists using the Socratic irony are pronounced happy because of the mass and volume of their words; others play upon words. Those learning rhetoric, with rhetorical speeches, speak to the point with a view to persuasion, being careful to observe the precepts of their art, and to leave out

omittere. Pueri diversarum scholarium versibus inter se conrixantur; aut de principiis artis grammaticae, vel regulis praeteritorum vel supinorum, contendunt. Sunt alii qui in epigrammatibus, rhythmis et metris, utuntur vetere illa triviali dicacitate; licentia Fescennina socios suppressis nominibus liberius lacerant; loedorias jaculantur et scommata, salibus Socraticis sociorum, vel forte majorum, vitia tangunt; vel mordacius dente rodunt Theonino audacibus dithyrambis. Auditores,

> multum ridere parati,
> Ingeminant tremulos naso crispante cachinnos.

De Ludis.

Praeterea quotannis, die quae dicitur Carnilevaria, ut a ludis puerorum Londoniae incipiamus (omnes enim pueri fuimus), scholarum singuli pueri suos apportant magistro suo gallos gallinaceos pugnaces, et totum illud antemeridianum datur ludo puerorum vacantium spectare in scholis suorum pugnas gallorum. Post prandium vadit in suburbanam planitiem omnis juventus urbis ad lusum pilae celebrem. Singulorum studiorum scholares suam habent pilam; singulorum officiorum urbis exercitores suam fere singuli. Majores natu, patres, et divites urbis, in equis spectatum veniunt certamina juniorum, et modo suo juvenantur cum juvenibus; et excitari videtur in eis motus caloris naturalis contemplatione tanti motus et participatione gaudiorum adolescentiae liberioris.

Thomas à Becket a Pauline.

[*Ib.* p. 14.]

Puerum eum [Thomam] pater in religiosa domo canonicorum Meritoniae priori Roberto aliquamdiu nutriendum commendaverat.... Annis igitur infantiae, pueritiae et pubertatis simpliciter domi paternae et in scholis urbis decursis, Thomas adolescens factus studuit Parisius.

nothing that belongs to it. The boys of the different schools vie with each other in verses; or dispute on the principles of grammar, or the rules of preterites and supines. Others in epigrams, rhymes and verses, use the old freedom of the highway, with Fescennine licence freely scourge their schoolfellows without mentioning names, hurl abuse and fun at each other, with Socratic wit gird at the failings of their schoolfellows, or even of their elders, or bite them more deeply with the tooth of Theon in audacious dithyrambics. The audience, 'ready for much laughter, wrinkle their noses as they redouble their shaking guffaws.'

Games.

Every year, on the day which is called the Carnival [Shrove Tuesday], to begin with the boys' games [London is a mistake of the MS.] (for we were all boys once), all the boys in each school bring their master their game-cocks, and the whole morning is devoted to the boys' play, they having a holiday to look on at the cock-fights in their schools. In the afternoon the whole youth of the city goes into the suburban level for a solemn game of ball. Each school has its own ball, and nearly all the holders of civic offices also provide one. The grown-up people, the fathers and rich men of the city, come on horseback to look on at the struggles of the young, and in their ways grow young with the young; and the motion of natural heat seems to be excited in them by looking on at so much motion and by sharing in the delight of the freedom of youth.

Thomas à Becket a Pauline.

As a boy his father had committed him [Thomas à Becket] for a little time to Prior Robert to be nursed in the religious house of the canons of Merton...Having passed the years of infancy, boyhood and youth in his father's house, and the school of the city, Thomas, when he became a young man, studied at Paris.

Appointment of Master of St Paul's School.
c. 1125.

[A. F. Leach, *Journ. of Educ.* June 1909, and *Archæol.* 62, pt. i. p. 211, from Mun. St Paul's, A Box, 25 A. No. 1368, and Lib. A. f. xxviii e.]

De Collacione Scolarum.

Ricardus, Dei gracia Londoniensis episcopus, W. Decano totique fratrum conventui, et W. de Occhendona dapifero suo cunctisque suis hominibus salutem et in Christo benedictionem.

Notum vobis facio, karissimi, me concessisse Henrico canonico meo, nutrito Magistri Hugonis, scolas Sancti Pauli ita honorifice sic[ut] unquam melius et honorabilius illa ecclesia habuit, et terram de atrio quam predictus Hugo ad se hospitandum ibi inclusit, et pratum quod eidem Hugoni in Foleham concesseram; scilicet iiij acras, scilicet quicquid est in illo loco a grava usque ad Tamisiam singulis annis, pro xij denariis de recognicione in festo S. Michaelis, et in elemosina decimam de Ilingis et decimam de Madeleia.

Testibus Willelmo de Wintonia, et Willelmo de Occhendona dapifero, et Hugone de Cancerisio. Valete.

Note in Liber A.

NOTA. Magistrum scolarum debere habere iiij acras prati apud Fulham et decimam de Yllinges et de Madeleya.

Grant of Warwick School to St Mary's Church.
1123.

[A. F. Leach, *Hist. of Warwick School and College*, 5, from Chartul. St Mary's, Warwick. Exch. Q. R. Misc. Bks. 22.]

Carta eiusdem [Rogeri Comitis] de scolis Warwici datis ecclesie Sancte Marie.

R. comes de Warewic omnibus suis fidelibus de Warewic, salutem.

Appointment of Master of St Paul's School.
c. 1125.

A Collation of the School.

Richard, by the grace of God bishop of London, to W[illiam] Dean and the whole assembly of brethren, and William of Occhendon his steward and all his men greeting and blessing in Christ.

I make known to you, my dearest, that I have granted to my canon Henry, the nursling of Master Hugh, St Paul's school as honourably as the church ever held it at its best and most honourable wise, and the land of the court which the said Hugh enclosed there to house himself in; and the meadow which I had granted to the same Hugh in Fulham; viz. four acres, namely, whatever there is in that place from the ditch to the Thames for 12*d.* a year recognition at Michaelmas, and as a charity the tithes of Ealing and the tithe of Madeley.

Witness William of Winchester, and William of Occhendon steward, and Hugh of Cancerisio. Farewell.

Note in Liber A.

Note that the schoolmaster ought to have four acres of the meadow at Fulham and the tithes of Ealing and Madeley.

Grant of Warwick School to St Mary's Church.
1123.

Charter of the same Earl Roger of the school of Warwick given to St Mary's church.

R[oger] Earl of Warwick to all his faithful people of Warwick, greeting.

Sciatis me concessisse et dedisse in elemosinam ecclesie Sancte Marie de Warewic scolas ipsius ecclesie Warewic pro me et antecessoribus meis, ut servicium Dei in eadem ecclesia frequentacione scolasticorum emendetur. Precipimus ergo ut quiete et libere teneat eas predicta ecclesia, et ne eas aliquis aliqua violencia surripiat ab ecclesia. Valete.

Testes, Robertus de Novoburgo; G. frater eius; Gundreda comitissa [and nine others named].

Translation of the College of Canons and School of All Saints to St Mary's, Warwick. 1123.

[*Ib.* 32, with photograph.]

Carta eiusdem Domini Rogeri de possessionibus et libertatibus datis et concessis ecclesie Beate Marie Warr. et de translacione Collegii infra castrum ad dictam ecclesiam.

In nomine Sancte et Individue Trinitatis Notum sit omnibus sancte Dei ecclesie filiis presentibus et futuris quatinus ab incarnacione Domini MCXXIII, regnante Henrico Rege, Rogerus comes adeptus consulatum Warewici ibi in honorem Dei et Sancte Dei genitricis Marie et Omnium Sanctorum veneracione, pro anima Willelmi Regis Anglie Expugnatoris eiusque uxoris Regine Matildis et eorum filii Willelmi secundi Regis atque in futura memoria anime H. Regis Willelmi prioris filii et eius uxoris Regine Matilde secunde et pro eorum liberis, et pro recordacione anime Rogeri de Belmund et eius uxoris Aelme, et pro anima Henrici Comitis sui patris, qui prius hoc instituit, et pro recordacione R. comitis Mellent et omnium fidelium defunctorum, disposuit quatenus clerici Ecclesie Sancte Marie de Warewici, et clerici Omnium Sanctorum, que sita est in castello, cum consilio et assensu et devotis peticionibus clericorum

Know that I have granted and given in alms for myself and my ancestors to the church of St Mary of Warwick the school of the same Church of Warwick, that the service of God in the same church may be improved by being frequented by scholars. We order, therefore, that the said church may hold it quietly and freely, and that no one by any violence may take the school from the church. Farewell.

Witnesses, Robert of Newburgh; G[eoffrey] his brother; Countess Gundreda [and nine others named].

Translation of the College of Canons and School of All Saints to St Mary's, Warwick. 1123.

Charter of the same lord Roger of the possessions and liberties given and granted to the church of the Blessed Mary of Warwick and of the transfer of the college in the castle to the said church.

In the name of the Holy and Undivided Trinity be it known to all sons of God's Holy Church present and to come, that in the year from the Incarnation of the Lord, 1123, in the reign of King Henry, Earl Roger, having obtained the Consulship [earldom] of Warwick, there to the honour of God and in reverence to God's holy mother Mary, and All Saints, for the soul of King William, Conqueror of England, and his wife Queen Matilda, and their son King William the Second, and in future memory of the soul of King Henry, William his eldest son and his wife Queen Matilda the Second, and for their children, and in memory of the soul of Roger of Beaumont and his wife Aelma, and for the soul of Earl Henry his father, who first began this, and in memory of R[obert] Count of Mellent and all the faithful departed, arranged that the clerks of the church of St Mary of Warwick and the clerks of All Saints', which was situated in the castle, by the advice and assent and at the devout petition of the clerks of the said

predicte ecclesie Omnium Sanctorum, pariter et Simonis Wigorniensis Episcopi deliberacione, in memorata Ecclesia Sancte Marie omnes pariter canonico more Deo et Sancte Marie diligenter die noctuque servirent, salva integritate prebendarum suarum, ipsi et successores eorum imperpetuum. Et concessit ad eorum victus necessaria hec.

. . . .

Ecclesiam Sancti Nicholai [a long list of churches and lands follows].

Et scolas Warewici et iudicia ferri et aque et duelli et c acras in Cotes et ecclesiam Sancti Jacobi super portam Warewic et terram Wimundi capellani.

Preterea concessit quatinus habeant Decanum et Capitulum et fraternum conventum ipsi clerici in predicta ecclesia Sancte Marie, et ut ita libere et quiete et honorifice omnia et singula obtineant sicut Lincolnienses et Salesberienses et Eboracenses sua ecclesiastica dicuntur obtinere.

Huius rei testes sunt [etc.].

The Monopoly of St Paul's School enforced.
c. 1138.

[A. F. Leach, *Journal of Education*, June 1909, and *Archæol.* 62, pt i., from Mun. St Paul's, A Box 60, 48, and Lib. A. f. xxix.]

De Cancellario.

H[enricus], Dei gracia Wintoniensis ecclesie minister, Capitulo Sancti Pauli et Willelmo archidiacono et ministris suis, salutem.

Precipio uobis per obedientiam, ut, [post] trinam uocationem, sentenciam anatematis in eos proferatis, qui sine licencia Henrici magistri scolarum in tota ciuitate Lundon. regere presumserint, preter eos qui scolas Sancte Marie de Archa et Sancti Martini Magni regunt. Teste magistro Ilario apud Wintoniam.

church of All Saints, and likewise with the deliberation of Simon, Bishop of Worcester, that all they and their successors for ever may serve God and St Mary diligently day and night after the fashion of canons in the aforesaid church of St Mary, keeping the integrity of their prebends. And for the necessaries of living gave them these.

. . . .

The church of St Nicholas [a long list of churches and lands follows].

And the school of Warwick and the ordeals of fire and water and duel, and 100 acres in Cotes and the church of St James above the gate of Warwick and the land of Wimund the chaplain.

Further he granted that the same clerks might have a Dean and Chapter and brotherly assembly in the aforesaid church of St Mary, and might hold them one and all as freely and quietly and honourably as the canons of Lincoln and Salisbury and York are said to hold their ecclesiastical possessions.

Of this matter are witnesses [etc.].

The Monopoly of St Paul's School enforced.
c. 1138.

Of the Chancellor.

Henry [of Blois], by the grace of God minister of the church of Winchester, to the chapter of St Paul's and William archdeacon and his ministers, greeting.

I command you on your obedience that after three warnings you pronounce sentence of anathema on those who, without the licence of Henry, schoolmaster, presume to lecture in the whole city of London, except those who keep the schools of St Mary-le-Bow and St Martin-le-Grand. Witness Master Hillary at Winchester.

Nota quod scole non sunt tenende London. nisi apud Beatum Paulum, exceptis scolis Beate Marie de Arcubus et Sancti Martini Magni.

Grant of Huntingdon School by Henry I to Huntingdon Priory. 1127.

[P. R. O. Cart. antiq. H. No. 8.]

Carta Regis Henrici primi concessiones donatorum recitans et confirmans.

Henricus rex Anglorum episcopo Lincolniensi, comiti Huntedonie et Willelmo de Lovetot et justiciariis et baronibus et vicecomitibus et ministris suis et omnibus de quibus canonici tenent, salutem.

Sciatis me concessisse et presenti carta confirmasse ecclesie Sancte Marie de Huntedone et canonicis ibidem Deo servientibus omnes possessiones suas tam in ecclesiis quam in terris et decimis; et nominatim duas hidas in quibus ipsa ecclesia sita est, liberas et quietas ab omni seculari exaccione, et omnes ecclesias et terras suas infra burgum de Huntedon et extra;...et capellam castelli de Huntedon cum pertinenciis suis et scolam eiusdem ville, ita ut nullus aliquam infra Huntedonsciram absque illorum licencia teneat. Quare volo [etc.].

Testibus Willelmo Cantuarie archiepiscopo, David rege Scotorum, et pluribus aliis.

Grant of Dunstable School to the newly founded Priory there. 1131.

[Charter Roll, 11 Hen. III, pt. 1. m. 27.]

Henricus Rex Dei gracia [etc.]. Inspeximus cartam illustris regis Anglorum Henrici primi in hec verba.

Note that schools are not to be held in London save at St Paul's, except the schools of Blessed Mary of the Arches and St Martin's-le-Grand.

Grant of Huntingdon School by Henry I to Huntingdon Priory. 1127.

Charter of King Henry I reciting and confirming the grants of donors.

Henry, king of the English, to the bishop of Lincoln, the earl of Huntingdon and William of Lovetot and his justices and barons and sheriffs and servants and to all of whom the canons hold, greeting.

Know ye that I have granted and by the present charter confirmed to the church of Saint Mary of Huntingdon and the canons there serving God all their possessions as well in churches as in lands and tithes; namely two hides on which the church itself is situate, free and quit of all secular exaction, and all their churches and lands as well within the borough of Huntingdon as outside;...and the chapel of the castle of Huntingdon with its appurtenances and the school of the same town, so that no one may keep any school in Huntingdonshire without their licence. Wherefore I will [etc.].

Witness William archbishop of Canterbury, David king of Scots, and many others.

Grant of Dunstable School to the newly founded Priory there. 1131.

Henry [III], king, by the grace of God [etc.]. We have inspected a charter of the illustrious king of the English Henry I in these words.

H. rex Anglorum etc. archiepiscopis episcopis etc. salutem.

Noveritis me pro Deo et pro salute mei et domini Willelmi filii mei et Matilde uxoris mee dedisse ecclesie Sancti Petri de Dunstaple quam ego in honore Dei et eiusdem apostoli fundavi et canonicis regularibus ibidem Deo servientibus in perpetuam et liberam elemosinam totum manerium et burgum de Dunstaple cum terris eidem ville pertinentibus, scilicet, quatuor culturas circa villam de Dunstaple, mercatum eiusdem ville et scolas eiusdem ville, cum omnibus libertatibus et liberis consuetudinibus eidem ville pertinentibus.

Testibus Roberto episcopo Hereford. et Simone episcopo Wirecestrie et G[alfrido] cancellario et Roberto de sigillo et N[igello] nepote episcopi, Milone Glocestrie et Humfrido de Bohun [and four others mentioned].

Reading School placed under Reading Abbey. Between 1125 *and* 1139.

[A. F. Leach, *V. C. H. Berks*, II. 245, from Reading Chart., B. M. Harl. 1708, f. 190 b.]

Carta Rogeri Sarisberie episcopi de scolis de Rading.

R. episcopus Sarisberiensis archidiaconis de Berks et omnibus decanis et toti clero de Berks, salutem.

Prohibeo quod nullus regat scolas apud Rading nisi consensu et bona voluntate abbatis et conventus.

Teste A. Th. apud Wintoniam.

Confirmation in 1199 *of Grant of Gloucester School to Llanthony Abbey by Henry II in* 1137.

[A. F. Leach, *V. C. H. Gloucs.* II. 315, from Rot. Chart. p. 7.]

Confirmacio canonicorum de Lantonia de omnibus possessionibus suis.

Johannes Dei gracia [etc.]. Noverit universitas vestra nos pro Dei amore et pro salute anime nostre et antecessorum

Henry, king of the English etc. to archbishops, bishops etc. greeting.

Know ye that I, for God and my health and the health of the lord William, my son, and Matilda my wife, have given to the church of St Peter of Dunstable which I have founded in honour of God and that apostle, and to the canons regular there serving God in perpetual and free alms the whole manor and borough of Dunstable with the lands to the same town belonging, viz. four ploughlands round the town of Dunstable, the market of the same town and the school of the same town, with all liberties and free customs to the same town belonging.

Witness, Robert, bishop of Hereford, and Simon, bishop of Worcester, and G[eoffrey] chancellor, and Robert of the seal, and N[igel] nephew of the bishop, Milo of Gloucester and Humfrey of Bohun [and four others].

Reading School placed under Reading Abbey. Between 1125 and 1139.

Bishop Roger of Salisbury's charter of Reading School.

Roger, bishop of Salisbury, to the archdeacons of Berks and all the [rural] deans and the whole clergy of Berks, greeting.

I forbid anyone to teach school at Reading except with the consent and goodwill of the abbot and convent.

Witness A. Th. at Winchester.

Confirmation in 1199 of Grant of Gloucester School to Llanthony Abbey by Henry II in 1137.

Confirmation to the canons of Llanthony of all their possessions.

John, by the grace of God [etc.]. Know ye all that we, for the love of God and the health of our soul and our ancestors',

nostrorum concessisse et presenti carta nostra confirmasse in perpetuam elemosinam Deo et ecclesie B. Marie et Sancti Johannis Baptiste et canonicis regularibus de Lantonia subscriptas donaciones, que illis racionabiliter facte sunt.

Ex dono Henrici Regis patris nostri capellam intra castellum Glocestrie et scolam unam in eadem villa et medietatem piscarie de Hersepol que est de dominico nostro...

Ex dono Hugonis de Laceio. ...

Hec omnia predicta et alia quecumque eisdem canonicis data sunt racionabiliter vel in futuro dabuntur illis concedimus.

Quare volumus [etc.].

Testibus Simone Bathoniensi episcopo [etc.]. Dat. per manum H. Cantuariensis archiepiscopi, cancellarii nostri, apud Rupem Aurivallis xxx die Julii anno regni nostri primo.

A Synod at Westminster forbids the letting of Schools for hire. 3 Dec. 1138.

[Wilkins, *Concilia*, 1. 415.]

XVII. Sancimus praeterea, ut si magistri scholarum aliis scholas suas pro pretio regendas locaverint, ecclesiasticae vindictae subiaceant.

Salisbury Schoolmaster endowed. 1139.

[*Sar. Ch. and Doc.* (Rolls Series) 8, from Stat. Eccl. Sar. f. 38 b.]

Stephanus rex Anglie Henrico Wintoniensi episcopo et justiciariis et baronibus et omnibus fidelibus suis Francis et Anglis de Wiltescyre, salutem.

Sciatis me dedisse et concessisse in perpetuam elemosinam Deo et ecclesie Saresberiensi ad opus magistri scolarum Saresberie ecclesiam de Odiham cum ecclesiis de Lys et de

have granted and by this our present charter confirmed in perpetual alms to God and the church of the Blessed Mary and Saint John the Baptist and the canons regular of Llanthony the underwritten gifts, which have been reasonably made to them.

Of the gift of King Henry our father the chapel in Gloucester castle and a school in the same town and half the fishery of Horsepool which is in our demesne. ...

Of the gift of Hugh of Lacy...

All these things aforesaid and whatsoever else has been reasonably given or shall in future be so given we grant to them.

Wherefore we will etc. [that they quietly enjoy the same].

Witnesses, Simon, bishop of Bath [etc.]. Given by the hand of H[erbert], archbishop of Canterbury, our chancellor at Roches d'Orivalle 30 July in the first year of our reign.

A Synod at Westminster forbids the letting of Schools for hire. 3 *Dec.* 1138.

17. We decree further that if schoolmasters let their schools for money they shall be subject to ecclesiastical punishment.

Salisbury Schoolmaster endowed. 1139.

Stephen, king of the English, to Henry, bishop of Winchester, and the justices and barons and all his faithful men of Wiltshire, French and English, health.

Know that I have given and granted in perpetual alms to God and the church of Salisbury, for the use of the schoolmaster of Salisbury, the church of Odiham with the churches

Bynthewurthe et cum aliis ecclesiis et capellis sibi pertinentibus.

Quare volo et firmiter precipio quod ipsas bene et in pace et honorifice et libere teneat, sicut Rogerus Saresberiensis episcopus et Ranulphus Dunelmensis episcopus illas unquam melius tenuerint.

Testibus Philippo cancellario [and five others] apud Saresberiam.

Bristol School under the Kalendars' Gild.
c. 1141.

[A. F. Leach, *V. C. H. Gloucestershire*, Schools, II. 355, from Bristol Little Red Book, f. 83 b.]

Nota de Fraternitate Kalendariorum.

Venerabili in Christo patri ac domino Domino Thome Dei gratia Wygornie episcopo sui humiles et devoti Robertus de Hasele, Rector ecclesie de Derham ac Decanus Christianitatis Bristollie, subieccionem omnimodam tanto patri debitam, reverenciam et honorem.

[Recites the bishop's mandate 17 May 1318 repeating one of bishop Walter Giffard, which had not been executed, to inquire into the rights and liberties of the brotherhood; and the holding of an inquisition by which]

Invenimus quod olim dicta Fraternitas vocabatur zilda seu Fraria communitatis cleri et populi Bristolie. Et locus congregacionis fratrum et sororum eiusdem fuit usitatus apud ecclesiam Sancte Trinitatis Bristolie temporibus Aylwardi Mean et Bristoici filii eiusdem, dominorum dicte ville ante conquestum ultimum Anglie; cuius zilde et Frarie principium memoriam hominis excedit.

Post vero conquestum... tempore Domini Henrici filii Matilde Imperatricis, Regis Anglie, quidam Robertus Hardyng, burgensis Bristolie, per consensum dicti Regis Henrici ac Roberti comitis et aliorum quorum tunc intererat, dictam zildam seu Frariam ab ecclesia Sancte Trinitatis in ecclesiam Omnium

of Liss and Bentworth, and the other churches and chapels belonging to it.

Wherefore I will and firmly order that he hold them well and in peace and honourably and freely, as Roger, bishop of Salisbury, and Randolph, bishop of Durham, ever at best held them.

Witness, Philip the chancellor [etc.] at Salisbury.

Bristol School under the Kalendars' Gild.
c. 1141.

Note about the Kalendars' Brotherhood.

To the venerable father and lord in Christ the lord Thomas, by the grace of God bishop of Worcester, his humble and devoted Robert of Haseley, rector of Dereham church, and the Dean of Christianity of Bristol, all subjection, reverence and honour due to so great a father....

We found that once upon a time the said brotherhood was called the gild or brotherhood of the community of the clergy and people of Bristol; and the place of assembly of the brothers and sisters of the same was at Trinity church, Bristol, in the times of Aylward Mean and Bristoic his son, lords of the said town before the last conquest of England; the beginning of which gild and brotherhood passes the memory of man.

After the conquest...in the time of the lord Henry, son of the empress Matilda, king of England, one Robert Hardyng, burgess of Bristol, with the consent of the said king Henry and earl Robert and others interested, translated the said gild or brotherhood from Holy Trinity church to the said All

Sanctorum predictas transtulit, ac scolas Bristollie pro Judaeis et aliis parvulis informandis, sub disposicione dicte frarie stabilivit, et proteccione Maioris Bristollie qui pro tempore fuerit ; ac monasterium Sancti Augustini in suburbio dicte ville fundavit, et ipsam ecclesiam Omnium Sanctorum prefato monasterio appropriari fecit, ac vicarium quemdam de capellanis dicte zilde et frarie eligendum, et per abbatem et conventum monasterii predicti episcopo Wygornie presentandum.

The Beginnings of Oxford University. 1133–49.

The Theological Lectures of Robert Pullein. 1133.

[Oxford Hist. Soc. Collect. II. 159, from Osney Chron. *Ann. Mon.* (Rolls Series), ed. Luard, IV. p. 19.]

MCXXXIII. Magister Robertus Pullein scripturas divinas, quae in Anglia obsoluerant, apud Oxoniam legere coepit, qui postea, cum ex doctrina eius ecclesia tam Anglicana quam Gallicana plurimum profecisset, a Papa Lucio secundo vocatus et in cancellarium sancte Romane ecclesie promotus est.

[*Ib.* 160, from MS. Bodl. 712, f. 275.]

MCXXXIII. Quomodo Robertus cognomento Pullus legit scripturas divinas apud Oxon.

Eodem anno venit Magister Robertus cognomento Pullus de civitate Exonia Oxenfordiam, ibique scripturas divinas, que per idem tempus in Angliam obsolete erant, et scolasticis quippe neglecte fuerant, per quinquennium legit, omnique die dominico verbum Dei populo predicavit. Ex cuius doctrina plurimi profecerunt, qui postea ob eximiam doctrinam et religiosam famam a Papa Lucio vocatus et in cancellarium sancte Romane ecclesie promotus est.

Saints' church, and established a school at Bristol to teach the Jews and other little ones under the government of the said brotherhood and the protection of the Mayor of Bristol for the time being; and founded St Augustine's monastery in the suburbs of the said town and caused All Saints' church to be appropriated to the said monastery, and a vicar to be chosen from the chaplains of the said gild and brotherhood, and presented by the abbot and convent of the said monastery to the bishop of Worcester.

The Beginnings of Oxford University. 1133–49.

The Theological Lectures of Robert Pullein. 1133.

1133. Master Robert Pullein began to lecture at Oxford on the Scriptures, which had gone out of fashion in England. Afterwards when both the English and the French church had greatly profited by his teaching, he was summoned by Pope Lucius II, and promoted to be chancellor of the Holy Roman church.

1133. How Robert, surnamed Chicken, lectured in divinity at Oxford.

The same year came Master Robert, surnamed Chicken, from the city of Exeter to Oxford, and for five years read divinity, which at that time had gone out of fashion in England and had been neglected by schoolmasters, and every Sunday he preached the word of God to the people. Many profited by that teaching of his. And afterwards on account of his excellent teaching and religious reputation he was summoned by Pope Lucius and promoted to be chancellor of the Holy Roman Church.

Mention of Clerks from all over England at Oxford.
c. 1135.

[*Ib.* p. 162, from *Mat. for Life of T. Becket*, ed. Robertson (Rolls Series), II. p. 97.]

[Robert of Cricklade, prior of St Frideswide, Oxford, to Benedict, abbot of Peterborough.]

Testis est mihi populus civitatis nostre, quem [quo modo?] cum in festis diebus, quando loquebar ad eos, excitans eos pro modulo meo ad sectandam viam iustitie, cum interessent eciam clerici diversorum locorum Anglie, pretendebam excusacionem standi pro dolore predicto, et sedens loquebar.

Robert, Prior of St Frideswide's, Oxford, formerly a Scholar and Master of the Schools there. c. 1135.

[*Ib.* 161, from MS. Ball. Coll. CLXVII. f. 177, Prefatiuncula Roberti Prioris Sancte Frideswuth in Librum de Connubio Jacob.]

Domino et amico, vere venerabili fratri, Laurencio monacho, monacho sane non modo habitu et professione verum eciam morum honestate, frater Robertus. Dum adhuc scolaris scolarum insisterem regimini, libellum quem composueram, sed estimo id memoria excidisse tua, tibi transmitti rogasti.

Theobald of Étampes and his Critic on Clerks and Scholars. Between 1119 and 1135.

[*Ib.* 153, from MS. Bodl. 561, f. 61, *Improperium cuiusdam in Monachos.*]

Thurstano, Dei gracia laudabili Eboracensi archiepiscopo, T. Stampensis Magister Oxinfordie. In primis si vales bene, valeo. Deinde prout nostre occurrit memorie diligenter ad interrogata respondeo, quia aliud est ecclesia aliud est monasterium.

Mention of Clerks from all over England at Oxford.
c. 1135.

[Robert of Cricklade, prior of St Frideswide, Oxford, to Benedict, abbot of Peterborough.]

Witness the people of our city, that when I spoke to them, on feast days, urging them after my ability to follow the ways of justice, though the clerks of various places in England were present, I pleaded an excuse for standing because of the pain mentioned, and addressed them sitting.

Robert, Prior of St Frideswide's, Oxford, formerly a
Scholar and Master of the Schools there. c. 1135.

To his lord and friend, the truly venerable brother, Laurence the monk, a monk not only in habit and profession but also in conduct, brother Robert. While I was still a scholar and engaged in teaching school, you asked me to send you a little book I had composed, but I suppose it had escaped your memory.

Theobald of Étampes and his Critic on Clerks and
Scholars. Between 1119 and 1135.

Thomas of Étampes, Master of Oxford, to Thurstan, by the grace of God worthy archbishop of York. And first if you are well so am I. Next to your questions as they occur to me, I answer, that a church is one thing and a monastery another.

Ecclesia namque est convocacio fidelium; monasterium vero locus et carcer damnatorum, id est monachorum, qui se ipsos damnaverunt ut damnacionem evitarent perpetuam. Fructuosius tamen damnantur a se ipsis quam ab alio. Nullus autem monachus dignitatem habet clericalem; quod enim habent capicia in transverso posita, significacio est quia ipsi clerum exuentes iam perdiderunt capita; quia non licet eis populo predicare, vel baptizare, vel penitentem ligare vel solvere, sive cetera talia que dicuntur ad ecclesiam pertinere....

Qui monasticum habitum eligendo, et mundum postponendo, se ipsum damnando dignitate ecclesiastica indignum iudicavit. Quod si monachus sancte ecclesie regimen quandoque sortiatur, hoc non lege ecclesiastica, sed quadam dispensacione voluntaria, et clericorum penuria, fieri comprobatur....

[*Ib.* 156 (and here corrected), from *Rescriptum cuiusdam pro Monachis*, MS. Bodl. 561, f. 62.]

...Monachus, inquit, si quando regimen ecclesie sortiatur, non fit lege ecclesiastica sed quasi dispensacione voluntaria, et clericorum penuria...

O inquam clericorum penuria. O clericorum et canonicorum vindicanda iniuria. Rogo itaque vos, probi scolastici, obsecro vos valentes clerici, contestor vos religiosi canonici, imitamini Christum ducem vestrum, estote patientes, deponite lapides, continete manus, non lapidetur, nec, sicut meruit, miser patiatur. Omnium enim in commune hostis esse probatur. O clericorum penuria. O versipellis vanitas, quid dixisti? Numquid Rome clericorum est penuria? numquid Mediolani? numquid Ticini? numquid Ravenne? O penuria. Numquid Antisiodori? numquid Turonis? numquid Carnoti? numquid Parisius? numquid Andegavis? numquid Rotomagi? numquid Baiocis? O penuria. Numquid Eboraci? numquid Lundonie? numquid Salesberie? numquid Lincolnie? O penuria....

Dicis quia monasteria eo quod a monachis inhabitantur locus et carcer sunt damnatorum, et ideo iure vocantur ancilla; non attendens quia monasteria similiter a clericis sicut a

For a church is an assembly of the faithful, but a monastery is a place and prison of the damned, that is of monks, who have damned themselves to avoid eternal damnation. They are however more profitably damned by themselves than by someone else. Now no monk has the dignity of a clerk, for their wearing their head-coverings crosswise is a sign that they in putting off their clergy have lost their heads; for it is not lawful for them to preach to the people or baptize or bind or absolve a penitent, or do the rest of such things as are stated to be the business of the church....

The man who by choosing the monastic habit and putting the world aside, by thus damning himself has judged himself unworthy of the dignity of an ecclesiastic. And if a monk sometimes obtains the rule of holy church, this is not in accordance with the ecclesiastical law, but is proved to be by a sort of dispensation given at will, and through the want of clerks....

...A monk, he says, if he at any time obtains the rule of the church, does not do so by ecclesiastical law but as it were by a dispensation at will and for want of clerks....

Want of clerks, I say! This is an insult to clerks and canons which calls for vengeance. Now, I ask you, honoured schoolmasters, I beseech you valiant clerks, I call you to witness religious canons, imitate Christ your leader, be patient, put down your stones, hold your hands, let not the wretched man be stoned and suffer as he deserves. For he is shown to be the common enemy of all. Want of clerks! O crafty emptiness, what have you said? Is there a want of clerks at Rome? is there at Milan? at Ticino? at Ravenna? A want! Is there at Auxerre? at Tour? at Chartres? at Paris? at Anjou? at Rouen? at Bayeux? Oh, is there a want of clerks at York? at London? at Salisbury? at Lincoln? A want!...

You say that monasteries, because they are inhabited by monks, are a place and prison of the damned, and therefore rightly called cells; forgetting that minsters [also monasteria

monachis, ut supradictum est, inhabitantur, quemadmodum ecclesia. Quid igitur monasteria Mediolani, Turonis, Carnoti, Lugduni, Catalaune, Pictavis, Rotomagi, Lundonie, Salesberie, Lincolie, Eboraci, que omnia a clericis incoluntur, numquid ancilla iure dicuntur?...Et si vagorum noveras vicia clericorum, debueras tamen honorem deferre timori magistrorum et religioni canonicorum. 'O Coridon, Coridon, que te demencia cepit?' Numquid non sunt ubique terrarum liberales magistri, qui dicuntur et clerici? Tu quoque, nescioquis, nonne magistri vice sexagenos aut centenos, plus minusve, clericos regere diceris, quibus venditor verborum cupidus efficeris, forsitan ut eos incautos nequissime fallas, sicut et ipse falleris? Unde ergo ista tua clericorum penuria? Nam ut de ceteris provinciis sileam, fere totidem aut plures sunt per Galliam et Alemanniam, per Normanniam et Angliam, non solum in urbibus et castellis, verum etiam et in villulis, peritissimi scolarum magistri, quot fiscorum regalium exactores et ministri. Unde ergo clericorum penuria? Quid igitur? Numquid hic sic exensis efficitur ut tales nec clericos nec canonicos appellare dignetur? An potius constat eum contra monachos in ira sic exarsisse, ut quid diceret noluerit previdisse?

Lectures on Roman Law at Oxford. 1149.

[*Ib.* 166, Rob. de Monte, *Chron.*, Pertz, *Script.* VI. p. 476.]

...Magister Vacarius, gente Longobardus, vir honestus et iurisperitus, cum leges Romanas anno ab incarnacione Domini MCXLIX in Anglia discipulos doceret, et multi tam divites quam pauperes ad eum causa discendi confluerent, suggestione pauperum de Codice et Digesta excerptos IX libros composuit, qui sufficiunt ad omnes legum lites que in scolis frequentari solent decidendas, si quis eos perfecte noverit.

in Latin] are inhabited by clerks just as much as by monks, just as the church is. For what of the minsters at Milan, Turin, Chartres, Lyons, Chalons, Poitou, Rouen, London, Salisbury, Lincoln, York, which are all inhabited by clerks? are they, too, properly called cells? And if you were thinking of the vices of wandering clerks, you ought nevertheless to have given due honour to the dreaded masters and religious canons. 'O Corydon, Corydon, what madness has seized thee?' Are there not everywhere on earth masters of the liberal arts, who also are called clerks? You yourself, a nobody, are you not said to have taught as a master 60 or 100 clerks, more or less? Have you not been a greedy seller of words to them, and perhaps have wickedly deceived them in their ignorance, as you have deceived yourself? Where then, I pray, is this want of clerks of yours? For not to mention other parts of the Empire, are there not nearly as many or more skilled schoolmasters in France and Germany, in Normandy and England, not only in boroughs and cities, but even in country towns, as there are tax collectors and magistrates? Where then is your want of clerks? What then? Is he so out of his mind as not to think them worthy to be called clerks or canons? or is it not rather clear that he was so angry with the monks, that he could not think beforehand what he would say.

Lectures on Roman Law at Oxford. 1149.

...Master Vacarius, a Lombard by birth, an upright man and a lawyer, while in 1149 he was teaching Roman law to his pupils, and many, both rich and poor, flocked to learn from him, at the suggestion of his poor pupils, composed nine books extracted from the Code and the Digest, which enable anyone who knows them thoroughly to settle all the points of law which are commonly discussed in the schools.

[*Ib.* 168, from Gervas. Cant., ed. Stubbs (Rolls Series), II. p. 384.]

Indignatus Theodbaldus, et Thome, clerici Londoniensis, industria fretus, egit apud Celestinum papam, qui Innocencio successit, ut amoto Henrico Theodbaldus in Anglia legacione fungeretur. Oriuntur hinc inde discordie graves, lites et appellaciones antea inaudite. Tunc leges et causidici in Angliam primo vocati sunt, quorum primus erat magister Vacarius. Hic in Oxonefordia legem docuit, et apud Romam magister Gracianus et Alexander qui et Rodlandus, in proximo papa futurus, canones compilavit.

Law Lectures of Vacarius stopped. *c.* 1150.

[*Ib.* 165, from John of Salisbury's *Policraticus*, written 1159, VIII. § 22, ed. Giles, vol. IV. p. 357.]

Tempore regis Stephani a regno iusse sunt leges Romane, quas in Britanniam domus venerabilis patris Theobaldi, Britanniarum primatis, asciverat. Ne quis enim libros retineret edicto regio prohibitum est, et Vacario nostro indictum silencium, sed, Deo faciente, eo magis virtus legis invaluit, quo eam amplius nitebatur impietas infirmare.

Confirmation of Derby School to Darley Abbey.
c. 1155.

[A. F. Leach, *V. C. H. Derbyshire*, II. 209, Darley Abbey Chartulary, Cott. MSS. Titus, c. IX. f. 182.]

Confirmacio Walteri Coventrensis Episcopi super diversis donacionibus Canonicis de Derley factis.

W. Dei gracia Cestrensis Episcopus universis Sancte Ecclesie fidelibus, salutem.

Confirmando locum in quo fundata est ecclesia Sancte Marie super Derewent, intimamus vobis ea que canonicis ad opus ecclesie fidelium oblacionibus collata accepimus; scilicet,

[Archbishop] Theobald was indignant, and through the instrumentality of Thomas of London [Becket], a clerk, prevailed on Pope Celestine, Innocent's successor, to remove Henry [de Blois] and let Theobald be legate in England. Thereupon great disputes arose, and suits and appeals before unheard of. Then the Roman law and lawyers were first invited to England, the first of them being Master Vacarius. He taught law in Oxford, while at Rome Master Gratian and Alexander Roland, who was to be the next Pope, compiled the Canons [i.e. the Corpus Juris Canonici].

Law Lectures of Vacarius stopped. *c.* 1150.

In king Stephen's time the Roman law, which the household of the venerable father Theobald, primate of Britain, had brought in, was expelled from the kingdom. A royal edict prohibited anyone keeping books of it and silence was enjoined on our Vacarius, but, by God's grace, the law grew stronger the more irreligion tried to weaken it.

Confirmation of Derby School to Darley Abbey.
c. 1155.

Confirmation by Walter, bishop of Coventry, of sundry gifts made to the canons of Darley.

W[alter] by the grace of God bishop of Chester to all the faithful of holy church, greeting.

Confirming the place in which is founded the church of St Mary on Derwent, we let you know those things which we have heard have been given the canons for the work of the church by the offerings of the faithful; namely, by the gift of Henry,

de dono Henrici Regis Anglorum Derlegam, et locum et fundum ubi predicta ecclesia fundata est.

Et quicquid eis racionabiliter datum est: ex dono Willelmi Barbe Aprilis et meo, scolam de Derbie:...Ex dono Roberti, comitis de Ferrariis, et de concessione Regis Stephani, quia de suo patrimonio est, decimam de tercio denario de Derby... concedo cum ecclesiis Sancti Petri, et Sancti Michaelis, et Sancti Wereburge de Derby....

Concedimus eciam quod predictus Abbas sit Decanus de omnibus ecclesiis que data sunt ecclesie sue in Derbisira: et specialiter eciam de omnibus ecclesiis que sunt in Derbie: et teneat capitulum de clericis secularibus, ut cum ipsis et per ipsos iudicet que secundum canones licet Decanis iudicare....

Et obnixi tam maiores quam minores, tam presentes quam futuros, caritative rogamus hanc predictam ecclesiam religione stabilem, literis decoratam provehant et protegant.

Grant of House in Derby for School and Boarding-House. c. 1160.

[A. F. Leach, *V. C. H. Derbyshire*, II. 213, from Cott. MSS. Titus, c. IX. f. 58.]

Domino suo Henrico Regi Anglie et R. Cestrensi Episcopo et omnibus sancte matris ecclesie filiis Walkelinus de Derbeia et Goda uxor sua, salutem.

Notum sit vobis quod ego Walkelinus et Goda uxor mea dedimus et hac presenti carta nostra confirmavimus Deo et ecclesie Sancte Marie de Derleia et canonicis ibidem Deo servientibus in puram et perpetuam elemosinam pro salute Domini nostri Regis et pro salute animarum nostrarum et antecessorum nostrorum, salvo servicio Regis; scilicet, sex solidis annuatim pro omni servicio....

Totam tenuram quam ego Walkelinus emi de Willelmo de Heriz in molendinis et terris infra burgum et extra, sicut carta ipsius testatur.

king of the English, Darley, and the place and land where the said church is founded.

And whatsoever was reasonably given to them ; by the gift of William of the April beard and myself, the school of Derby ;...by the gift of Robert, earl of Ferrers, and the grant of king Stephen, because it is of his own patrimony, the tithe of the third penny of Derby...I grant with the churches of St Peter and St Michael and St Werburgh of Derby....

We grant also that the aforesaid Abbot shall be dean of all the churches which have been given to his church in Derbyshire, and especially of all the churches in Derby, and may hold a chapter of the secular clerks, that with them and by them he may judge whatever according to canon law deans may judge....

And we earnestly ask and entreat all, as well great as small, those living and those to come, in the name of charity, that they will advance and protect the aforesaid church now established in religion and adorned with learning.

Grant of House in Derby for School and Boarding-House. c. 1160.

To their lord, Henry, king of England, and to Richard, bishop of Chester, and to all the sons of holy mother church, Walkelin of Derby and Goda his wife, greeting.

Be it known to you that I, Walkelin, and Goda my wife, have given and by this our present deed confirmed to God and the church of St Mary of Darley and the canons serving God there in pure and perpetual alms, for the health of our lord the king and for the health of our souls and our ancestors', saving the king's service, namely, 6s. a year for all service....

All that holding which I, Walkelin, bought of William of Heriz, in mills and lands inside the borough and outside, as his deed witnesses.

Dedimus eciam unam seldam mercatoriam et unam bovatam terre quas ego Walkelinus emi de Gutha, et duas acras quas emi de Helga, et unam acram quam emi de Oldrico presbitero, et unam acram et dimidium quas emi de Ricardo Cuinterel, et unam acram quam emi de Eadrico, que est super foveam iudiciariam, et unam acram quam emi de Willelmo iblundo, et unum messuagium quod emi de Roberto filio Wewenild; et unam acram super Capam quam ego Goda emi, et messuagium ubi manemus, quod ego Walkelinus emi de Willelmo Cusin et de Helga, cum omnibus edificiis que in eo sunt, secundum hanc disposicionem; scilicet, quod aula sit in scolam clericorum, et thalami sint in hospicium Magistri et clericorum in perpetuum; ita quod nec Abbas nec Magister nec aliquis accipiat aliquid pro locacione harum domorum, et quod pervenerit de furno sit hospitali canonicorum ad pauperes sustentandos.

Cetera autem edificia sint in usus canonicorum.

Appeal from Court of Arches to the Pope about Winchester School. c. 1159.

[A. F. Leach, *Hist. of Winchester College*, 1899, p. 37; from *Epist. Joh. Saresberiensis*, ed. Dr Giles, No. 19.]

Causa que vertebatur inter magistrum Jordanum Fantasma et magistrum Johannem Joichellum, clericos domini Wintoniensis super Wintoniam, tandem translata est ad audientiam nostram. Auditis ergo allegationibus magistri Jordani, et instrumentis diligenter inspectis, memorato Johanni vestra et nostra auctoritate inhibuimus ne contra voluntatem Jordani scolas regere presumeret in prefata civitate. Die vero sequenti in nostra presentia constiterunt, multa in se proponentes ad invicem: Jordanus siquidem jam dictum Johannem contra religionem fidei in predicta civitate sibi scolas usurpasse, et dampna plurima intulisse dicebat, officio nostro sibi super his satisfieri

Appeal to the Pope about Winchester School

We have also given the merchant's shop and an oxgang of land, which I, Walkelin, bought of Gutha, and two acres which I bought of Helga, and an acre which I bought of Oldric the priest, and one-and-a-half acres which I bought of Richard the girdler, and an acre which I bought of Eadric, which is on the well of justice [the cuckstool pit], and an acre which I bought of William the fair, and a messuage which I bought of Robert, son of Wewenild: and an acre on the sluice which I, Goda, bought, and the messuage in which we live, which I, Walkelin, bought of William Cusin and of Helga, with all the buildings in it, on this trust, that the hall shall be for a school of clerks, and the chambers shall be to house the master and clerks for ever, so that neither the abbot nor the master nor anyone may take anything for leasing the house, and that the proceeds of the oven may be for the canons' hospital to maintain the poor.

The other buildings, however, shall be for the use of the canons.

Appeal from Court of Arches to the Pope about Winchester School. c. 1159.

A case which was argued between Master Jordan the Phantom and Master John Jekyll, clerks of the lord [bishop] of Winchester, at Winchester, was at length transferred to be heard by us. Having heard therefore the allegations of Master Jordan and carefully inspected the documents, we granted by your and our authority an inhibition against the said John, that he should not presume to teach school in the said city without the consent of Jordan. But the next day they appeared before us with many allegations against each other. Jordan said that the said John had against all good faith usurped the school in the city aforesaid and had inflicted much damage on him, and demanded that through our court

postulans. E contra Johannes se judicio sinodi super fidei lesione innocentiam suam purgasse asserebat, et magistrum J., cui similis purgatio adjudicata est, quoniam super fidei lesione similiter fuerat inpetitus, omnino defecisse dicebat, petens ut eum urgeremus vel ad purgationem ex judicio prestandam, vel ad inplendam pactionem que fide interposita dicebatur fuisse roborata. Illis itaque sic altercantibus, Johannes vestram audientiam appellavit, dicens se ostensurum quod sepe dictus Jordanus religionem fidei et sacramenti temeraverat, diem prefigens nativitatem beati Johannis. Cum vero Jordanus prolixitatem temporis causaretur, eo quod ab initio decembris usque ad finem junii terminum prorogasset, eam sepefatus Johannes in festum beati Michaelis protelavit. Nos autem questionem criminum vestre reservantes discretioni, quia de jure scolarum magistri Jordani constabat, communicato fratrum nostrorum Cicestrensis, Herefordensis, Wigorniensis, episcoporum consilio, domino Wintoniensi dedimus in mandatis ne prefatum Jordanum super scolis pateretur a Johanne ulterius fatigari, et, si eum inveniret vestre et nostre auctoritatis contemptorem, ipsum publice denuntiaret anathematis vinculo innodatum. Postmodum vero elapsis paucis diebus, in nostram presentiam redierunt, Jordano veterem querelam innovante. Dicebat enim Johannem post interdictum usurpasse scolas, et in sententiam anathematis incidisse. Johannes vero hoc constantissime inficiatus est, paratus incontinenti, tactis sacrosanctis Ewangeliis, jurare quod post prohibitionem nostram a magisterio destiterat. E contra Jordanus se die prefixa probaturum dicebat, assertione legittimorum testium, quod post edictum magisterium exercuerat; sed Johannes diem recipere recusavit, dicens se jam in procinctu Romani itineris esse. Vos autem auctore Domino litigiis eorum finem debitum imponetis.

he should receive satisfactory damages for this. On the other hand, John asserted that he had in the judgment of the [provincial] synod purged himself of the charge of breach of faith, and said that Master Jordan, who had been ordered a like purgation, since he had likewise been impeached for breach of faith, had wholly failed to do so; and he asked that we should compel him either to the purgation according to the judgment, or to perform the contract which was alleged to have been ratified by the exchange of pledges of good faith. While they were thus disputing, John appealed to your audience, saying he would show that the aforesaid Jordan had defiled the sanctity of faith and oath, naming the 24th June. But when Jordan began to object to the long delay, as he proposed to put the term off from the beginning of December to the end of June, the said John adjourned it to Michaelmas. Thereupon we, reserving for your discretion the investigation of the charges [of breach of faith], as the right of Master Jordan to the school was clear, with the advice of our brethren, the bishops of Chichester, Hereford and Worcester, directed the lord of Winchester not to allow the aforesaid Jordan to be further troubled about the school by John, and, if he should find him [John] guilty of contempt of your and our authority, publicly to proclaim him excommunicate. A few days afterwards, however, they came before us again, Jordan renewing the old plaint. He said that John had usurped the school after an injunction, and had therefore incurred the sentence of excommunication. John, however, persistently denied it, and professed his readiness to take his corporal oath on the holy gospels, that since our prohibition he had desisted from teaching. Against this Jordan said that he would show on a day he named, by the evidence of good witnesses, that he had acted as master since the injunction; but John refused to accept the day fixed, saying he was already getting ready for a journey to Rome. I pray you, by the help of the Lord, put an effectual end to their litigation.

Transfer of Bedford School from the Canons of St Paul's, Bedford, to Newnham Priory. c. 1160.

[A. F. Leach, *V. C. H. Bedfordshire*, II. 152, from Newenham Cart. Harl. MS. 3656, fol. 94 (88 pencil).]

Recognicio quod decime de Hordelhida et scole Bed. sunt de jure ecclesie S. Pauli Bed.

Universis sancte matris ecclesie filiis Nicholaus Archidiaconus Bedfordensis salutem. Noverit universitas vestra quod Capellam Sancte Marie de Bedfordia cum decimis de Hordelhida et scolas Bed. quas ego aliquamdiu assensu concanonicorum meorum in manu habui, confiteor esse de jure et pertinencia ecclesie Sancti Pauli Bed. Et ideo eas Augerio Priori et conventui canonicorum regularium ejusdem ecclesie sponte mea resignavi.

Education of Alexander Neckham, Schoolboy, at St Albans, c. 1167, and Student at Paris, c. 1173.

[A. F. Leach, *V. C. H. Herts*, II.]

Hic locus etatis nostre primordia novit,
    Annos felices leticieque dies.
Hic locus ingenuis pueriles imbuit annos
    Artibus, et nostre laudis origo fuit.

Vix aliquis locus est dicta mihi notior urbe
    Qua modici Pontis parva columna fui.
Hic artes didici docuique fideliter, inde
    Accessit studio leccio sacra meo.
Audivi canones, Hippocratem cum Galieno,
    Jus civile mihi displicuisse negas.

Transfer of Bedford School from the Canons of St Paul's, Bedford, to Newnham Priory. c. 1160.

Recognizance that the tithes of Hordelhide and the school of Bedford belong to St Paul's Church, Bedford.

To all the sons of holy mother church, Nicholas, Archdeacon of Bedford, greeting. Know ye all that the chapel of St Mary of Bedford with the tithes of Hordelhide and Bedford School, which I have held for some time with the consent of my fellow-canons, I confess to be of the right and appurtenant to St Paul's Church, Bedford. And therefore I have voluntarily resigned them to Auger, Prior, and the convent of canons regular of that church.

Education of Alexander Neckham, Schoolboy, at St Albans, c. 1167, *and Student at Paris, c.* 1173.

> St Albans knew me when I was a boy,
> Those years of happiness and days of joy.
> The liberal arts, St Albans taught me then,
> The first beginning of my fame 'mongst men.
>
> Scarce any place is better known than that,
> Where as an arch of Petit-pont I sat.
> There faithfully I learnt and taught the arts,
> While Scripture reading added to my parts;
> Lectures on canon law and medicine,
> On civil law, too, I did not decline.

Canon Law forbids any Charge for Licence to teach. c. 1160.

[A. F. Leach, *Early Yorkshire Schools*, I. from Decretal v. tit. 5, cap. 2, De Magistris.]

Pro licentia docendi nihil exigi debet vel promitti, et exactum restitui et promissum remitti debet; et negligente inferiore praelato ad magistrum constituendum, supplebit hoc superior.

Alexander III, Wintoniensi [Wiennensi?] Episcopo.

Prohibeas attentius de cetero ne in parrochia tua pro licentia docendi aliquos exigatur aliquid aut etiam promittatur. Si 'quid vero postea solutum fuerit vel promissum, remitti promissum facias et restitui appellatione cessante solutum, sciens quod scriptum est 'Gratis accepistis, gratis date.'

Sane si quis occasione hujus prohibitionis distulerit magistros in locis idoneis instituere, tibi liceat de concessione nostra, omni contradictione et appellatione postposita, ibi aliorum instructioni praeficere viros providos, honestos et discretos.

Canon Law overrides Custom to charge Fees for Licences to teach. 1170–2.

[*Ib.* c. 3.]

Pro licentia docendi pecunia exigi non debet, etiamsi hoc habeat consuetudo.

Idem.

Quanto Gallicana ecclesia personarum scientia et honestate praefulget, et cautius nititur evitare quae confundere videantur ecclesiasticam honestatem, tanto vehementiori dignos eos esse animadversione censemus, qui nomen Magistri Scolarum et dignitatem assumunt in ecclesiis vestris, et sine certo pretio ecclesiasticis viris docendi alios licentiam non impendunt.

Quum autem haec prava et enormis consuetudo a cupidi-

Canon Law forbids any Charge for Licence to teach. c. 1160.

For licence to teach nothing shall be exacted or promised; and anything exacted shall be restored and the promise released; and when an inferior authority neglects to appoint a master, the superior shall supply the defect.

Pope Alexander III [1159—1181] to the bishop of Winchester [? Vienne].

Strictly prohibit for the future any exaction or promise of anything from anyone in your diocese for licence to teach. If, however, hereafter anything shall have been paid or promised, you shall cause the promise to be released and that which has been paid to be returned without any appeal; knowing that it was written, 'Freely ye have received, freely give.'

Moreover, if because of this prohibition anyone shall put off instituting masters in proper places, you may, in virtue of our grant, disregarding all opposition or appeal, prefer there for the instruction of others prudent, upright and discreet persons.

Canon Law overrides Custom to charge Fees for Licences to teach. 1170-2.

For licence to teach no money ought to be exacted, even if there is a custom to do so.

The same to the same.

By so much as the church of France is illustrious for the learning and reputation of its dignitaries, and the more carefully it strives to avoid whatever may upset the honour of the church, so much the more do we think worthy of rebuke those who assume the name and dignity of Schoolmaster in your churches, and refuse members of the church licence to teach without fees.

But whereas this bad and illegal custom proceeds from

tatis radice processerit, et decorem ad modum ecclesiasticae honestatis confundat, providendum vobis est et summopere satagendum, ut consuetudo ipsa de ecclesiis vestris penitus extirpetur, quum vobis praecipue et specialiter adscribatur, si quid in ecclesiis eisdem laude dignum inveniatur vel reprehensione notandum.

Nos quoque qui licet immeriti dispensante clementia Conditoris suprema fungimur potestate, tantae cupiditatis et rapacitatis vitium nolentes immendatum relinqui, fraternitati vestrae per apostolica scripta mandamus, quatenus consuetudine ipsa de vestris ecclesiis extirpata, sub anathematis interminatione hoc inhibere curetis, distincte praecipientes, ut, quicumque viri idonei et literati voluerint regere studia literarum, sine molestia et exactione qualibet scholas regere permittantur, ne scientia de cetero pretio videatur exponi, quae singulis gratis debet impendi.

Si qui vero hujusmodi prohibitionis vel praecepti extiterint transgressores, eos auctoritate nostra et vestra officiis et dignitatibus spolietis. Porro si hoc juxta mandatum nostrum corrigere neglexeritis, negligentiam vestram gravem habebimus et molestum [etc.].

Dat. Tusculi XIII Kalendas Novembris.

Northampton School. 1176-8.

[A. F. Leach, *V. C. H. Northants*, II. 234, from Pipe Roll, 22 Hen. II, rot. 4, m. 1; 27 Hen. II, p. 65.]

Vicecomes reddit compotum...in liberacione Johannis clerici A[lianore] Regine Hyspanie, qui moratur in scolis apud Norhamton de tribus septimanis, per breve Regis, vj*s*.

Vicecomes reddit compotum...in liberacione Johannis clerici A., Regine Hyspanie, qui moratur in scolis apud Norhamton, c et iiij*s*.

Exhibition at Northampton School 121

the root of covetousness, and destroys in no small measure the grace of the reputation of the church, you must provide for and with all your power effect the complete extirpation of this custom from your churches, since to you specially and chiefly is ascribed whatever in the same churches may be found either worthy of praise or to be stigmatized with blame.

We too, who, though unworthy, by the dispensing clemency of the Creator exercise supreme power, being unwilling that the sin of such great covetousness and rapacity should be left unamended, command your brotherhood by these apostolic writs that you root out this custom from your churches, and under penalty of excommunication inhibit, plainly ordering that whatever fit and learned persons wish to keep schools of literature shall be allowed to keep schools without any molestation or exaction, lest learning, which ought to be given freely to all, should henceforth seem to be exposed for sale at a price.

If any shall be found transgressing this prohibition or order, you shall deprive them by our and your authority of their offices and dignities. Further, if you shall neglect to correct this according to our mandate, we shall esteem your negligence grievous and injurious [etc.].

Dated at Tusculum 20 October.

Northampton School. 1176–8.

The sheriff renders account...of 6s. the livery of John, clerk of Eleanor, queen of Spain, who is staying at school at Northampton, for three weeks, [ordered] by the king's writ.

The sheriff renders account...for the livery of John, clerk of Eleanor, queen of Spain, who is staying at Northampton at school, 104s.

The Lateran Council orders every Cathedral to provide Free Schools for the Clerks of the Church and Poor. 1179.

[A. F. Leach, *Early Yorkshire Schools*, I. 2, from Decretal V. tit. 5, cap. 1.]

De Magistris.

Et ne aliquid exigatur pro licentia docendi.

Ecclesia cathedralis providere debet magistro de beneficio, qui clericos ejusdem ecclesiae et alios pauperes gratis doceat; et vendens licentiam docendi, aut interdicens idoneum ad docendum, beneficio privetur.

Ex concilio Lateranensi.

Quoniam ecclesia Dei et in his quae spectant ad subsidium corporis, et in iis quae ad profectum proveniunt animarum, indigentibus sicut pia mater providere tenetur, ne pauperibus, qui parentum opibus juvari non possunt, legendi et proficiendi opportunitas subtrahetur, per unamquamque cathedralem ecclesiam magistro, qui clericos ejusdem ecclesiae et scholares pauperes gratis doceat, competens aliquod beneficium praebeatur, quo docentis necessitas sublevetur et discentibus via pateat ad doctrinam.

In aliis quoque restituatur ecclesiis seu monasteriis, si retroactis temporibus aliquid in eis ad hoc fuerit deputatum.

Pro licentia vero docendi nullus omnino pretium exigat, vel, sub obtentu alicujus consuetudinis, ab eis qui docent, aliquid quaerat, nec docere quemquam, qui sit idoneus, petita licentia interdicat. Qui autem contra hoc venire praesumpserit ab ecclesiastico fiat beneficio alienus.

Dignum quippe esse videtur ut in ecclesia Dei fructum sui laboris non habeat, qui cupiditate animi, dum vendit docendi licentiam, ecclesiasticum profectum nititur impedire.

The Lateran Council orders every Cathedral to provide Free Schools for the Clerks of the Church and Poor. 1179.

Of Masters.

And that nothing should be exacted for licence to teach.

A cathedral church ought to provide a master with a benefice, that he may teach the clerks of the church and other poor persons gratis; and the seller of a licence to teach, or preventer of a fit person from teaching, is to be deprived of his benefice.

By the Lateran Council.

Since the church of God, like a loving mother, is bound to provide for the needy both the things which concern the maintenance of the body and which tend to the profit of souls, in order that the poor, who cannot be assisted by their parents' means, may not be deprived of the opportunity of reading and proficiency, in every cathedral church a competent benefice shall be bestowed upon a master who shall teach the clerks of the same church and poor scholars freely, so that both the necessities of the teacher shall be relieved and the way to learning laid open for the learners.

In other churches, too, or monasteries, if anything shall have been in times past assigned for this purpose, it shall be restored.

For a licence to teach no one shall exact money, even if on pretence of any custom he ask anything from those who teach, nor when a licence is asked shall he prevent any one, who is fit, from teaching. Whoever presumes to contravene this shall be put out from any ecclesiastical benefice.

For it seems to be right that none should have the fruits of his labour in the church of God, who in the greediness of his mind, by selling a licence to teach, endeavours to prevent the proficiency of churchmen.

Exhibitions for Durham School in Durham Almonry. *c.* 1190.

[Durham Cathedral Muniments. Liber Elemosinarii, fol. 12 *r.*]

Omnibus Christi fidelibus ad quos presens scriptum pervenerit Magister Simon de Ferlingtone, Archidiaconus Dunelm., salutem in Domino.

Noveritis me dedisse et presenti carta confirmasse Elemosinarie domui Sancti Cuthberti in Dunelmo villam de Kyhou cum pertinenciis, quam emi de Waltero de Monasteriis et heredibus suis, in puram et perpetuam elemosinam, ad sustentacionem trium scolarium de scola Dunelmensi, quos Magister beatim eliget, et cum tabella, in honore Beate Virginis et Sancti Cuthberti confecta, ad Elemosinarium Dunelm. cotidie mittet, qui eis beatim in cibo et potu prospiciet, et in domo Elemosinarie pernoctabunt, et Elemosinarius in lectis eis decenter prospiciet.

Et in hujus rei testimonium presentem cartam sigillo meo roboravi. Hiis testibus, Johanne de Insula, Waltero monacho Dunelm. [etc.].

Compromise between Durham School and Gateshead Hospital. *c.* 1230.

[A. F. Leach, *V. C. H. Durham*, Schools, II. 369, from Durham Cathedral Muniments. Liber Elemosinarii, fol. 12 *v.*]

Ricardus, Dei gracia Dunolmensis episcopus, quondam Salisburiensis episcopus, omnibus Sancte Matris ecclesie filiis, salutem in Domino.

Noverit universitas vestra quod cum aliquando esset convencio inter Priorem et Conventum Dunolm. ex una parte, et Radulfum monachum procuratorem et fratres Hospitalis domus Sancte Trinitatis de Gatisheued ex altera parte, super villa de Kyhou cum pertinenciis, que quondam data fuit Elemosinarie

Exhibitions for Durham School in Durham Almonry. c. 1190.

To all the faithful of Christ to whom this present writing shall come Master Simon of Farlington, archdeacon of Durham, greeting in the Lord.

Know ye that I have given and by the present deed confirmed to the Almonry house of Saint Cuthbert in Durham the manor of Kyo with the appurtenances, which I bought of William de Musters and his heirs in pure and perpetual alms, for the maintenance of three scholars of Durham school, whom the master shall charitably choose and send daily with a tablet [tally?] made in honour of the Blessed Virgin and St Cuthbert to the Almoner of Durham, who shall charitably provide for them food and drink, and they shall pass the night in the almonry house, and the almoner shall provide them properly with beds.

In testimony whereof I have strengthened this deed with my seal. Witness, John de l'Isle, Walter, monk of Durham [etc.].

Compromise between Durham School and Gateshead Hospital. c. 1230.

Richard [le Poer], by the grace of God bishop of Durham, formerly bishop of Salisbury, to all sons of holy mother church, greeting in the Lord.

Know ye all that whereas there was a covenant between the Prior and convent of Durham of the one part, and Ralph a monk the proctor and the brethren of the Hospital of the Holy Trinity of Gateshead of the other part, over the manor of Kyo with its appurtenances, which was formerly given to the

de Durem ad sustentacionem trium clericorum scolarium scolarum Dunolm. liberalium artium, a Magistro Symone de Ferlingtone, et postea ab Henrico fratre suo, qui eandem terram, mortuo fratre suo, Magistro Symone de Ferlingtone, iure hereditario consecutus est in Curia Dunolm., data fuit domui Sancte Trinitatis de Gatisheuid ad sustentacionem trium pauperum et unius capellani, sicut in auctentico Domini episcopi et suo super hoc confectis, plenius continetur; de consensu parcium in hunc modum amicabiliter ordinavimus, scilicet, quod procurator et fratres domus Sancte Trinitatis de Gatisheued dictam villam cum pertinenciis suis a predicto Priore et Conventu Dunolm. tenebunt ad feudalem firmam, reddendo inde annuatim domui elemosinarie ad sustentacionem dictorum clericorum medietatem tocius ville de Kyhou, scilicet, quadraginta solidos, ad duos terminos, scilicet, xx solidos ad festum Sancti Martini in yeme, et xx solidos ad Pentecosten.

Hiis testibus, Magistro Willelmo de Lanum tunc Archidiacono Dunolm., Magistro Helia de Derham, Domino Johanne de Rumeseye, Reginaldo de Calna, Willelmo filio Roberti, militibus, Ada de Merlege, et multis aliis.

Earliest separate Endowment of York School.
c. 1180.

[A. F. Leach, *Early Yorkshire Schools*, I. 13, from Reg. Magn. Alb. III. 3. Raine's *Hist. Ch. of York* (Rolls Series), III. 75.]

R[ogerus], Dei gracia Eboracensis archiepiscopus, H[enrico], decano et capitulo Sancti Petri Eboracensis, salutem.

Donavi ad feodum scole vestre centum solidos per annum, et constituo illos per archidiaconos nostros; ita, viz., de archidiaconatu de Austreing xl*s*., de synodo post Pascha et de Rumpening; de archidiaconatu de Westreing xxx*s*.; et, de archidiaconatu de Notinghamschira, ad festum Sancti Michaelis, xxx*s*.

Almonry of Durham for the maintenance of three clerks, scholars of Durham School in the liberal arts, by Master Symon of Farlington, and afterwards was given by Henry his brother, who obtained the same land on the death of his brother, Master Symon of Farlington, by right of inheritance in the court of Durham, to the House of the Holy Trinity at Gateshead for the maintenance of three poor men and a chaplain, as in a deed of the lord bishop and himself therein made is more fully contained; by consent of the parties we have made a friendly order in this way, namely, that the proctor and brethren of the house of Holy Trinity of Gateshead shall hold the said manor with its appurtenances of the prior and convent of Durham aforesaid in fee farm, rendering therefore yearly to the Almonry house for the maintenance of the said clerks a moiety of the whole manor of Kyo, namely, 40s. at two terms, namely, 20s. at Martinmas in winter, and 20s. at Whitsuntide.

Witness, Master William of Laneham, then archdeacon of Durham, Master Elias of Dereham, Sir John of Romsey, Reginald of Calne, William Fitzrobert, knights, Adam of Morley, and many others.

Earliest separate Endowment of York School.
c. 1180.

Roger, by the grace of God archbishop of York, to Henry, Dean, and the chapter of St Peter's, York, greeting.

I have given to the fee of your school 100s. a year and I establish this through our archdeacons; thus, from the archdeaconry of the East Riding, 40s., from the convocation after Easter and Rome-penny [i.e. Peter's pence]; from the archdeaconry of the West Riding, 30s.; and from the archdeaconry of Nottinghamshire at Michaelmas, 30s.

Confirmation of School Endowment to the Chancellor of York. c. 1191.

[*Ib.*]

G[alfridus], Dei gracia archiepiscopus Eboracensis, Anglie primas, dilectis sibi in Christo omnibus archidiaconis per Eboracensem provinciam constitutis, salutem in Domino.

Mandamus vobis firmiter iniungentes, quatenus de cetero Johanni de Sancto Laurencio, cancellario Eboracensis ecclesie, centum solidos de sinodalibus vestris annuatim, ad duos terminos secundum consuetudinem Eboracensis ecclesie, sine difficultate solvatis, scilicet, ad Pascha l solidos, et ad festum S. Michaelis l*s*. Valete.

Bury S. Edmunds School. 1180 to 1198.

[A. F. Leach, *V. C. H. Suffolk*, Schools, II. from Chron. Jocelyn de Brakelonde (Camden Soc. 1840), p. 3, 32.]

Capellanum quendam, qui eum [Samsonem abbatem] sustinuerat in Scholis Parisiis quaestu aquae benedictae, quando pauper fuerat, mandari fecit; et ei ecclesiasticum beneficium, quo sustentari possit, affectu vicario, contulit.

Magistro Waltero, filio Magistri Willelmi de Dice, petenti caritative vicariam ecclesie de Cheventon respondit : ' Pater tuus Magister Scholarum erat ; et cum pauper clericus eram, concessit mihi introitum scholae suae sine pacto et caritative, et usum discendi ; et ego, causa Dei, concedo tibi quod postulas.'

In villa S. Edmundi domos lapideas emit Abbas, et eas scholarum regimini assignavit, hac occasione, ut pauperes clerici in perpetuum ibi quieti essent de conduccione domus ; ad quam conducendam denarium vel obolum singuli scholares, tam inpotentes quam potentes, bis in anno conferre cogebantur.

Postquam convenit inter Abbatem Samsonem et Robertum de Scalis super medietate advocacionis ecclesiae de Wetterdene,

Confirmation of School Endowment to the Chancellor of York. c. 1191.

Geoffrey, by the grace of God archbishop of York, primate of England, to his beloved in Christ, all the archdeacons established in the province of York, health in the Lord.

We command and firmly enjoin you to pay, for the future, to John of St Lawrence, chancellor of the church of York, 100*s.* from your synodals yearly, at two terms according to the custom of the church of York, without making any difficulties, namely, 50*s.* at Easter and 50*s.* at Michaelmas. Farewell.

Bury S. Edmunds School. 1180 *to* 1198.

[After Samson became abbot *c.* 1182] He caused to be summoned a chaplain who had maintained him in the University of Paris when he was poor, by the sale of holy water, and collated him to an ecclesiastical benefice, which could maintain him as vicar....

When Master Walter, son of Master William of Disse, asked by way of charity for the vicarage of Chevington church, he answered: 'Your father was schoolmaster; and when I was a poor clerk he granted me admission to his school and the means of learning by way of charity and without any payment; so I, for God's sake, grant you what you ask.'

The abbot bought a stone house in the town of St Edmunds, and assigned it for teaching school, for this purpose, that poor clerks should be for ever free of the rent of the house; for the hire of which every scholar, whether able to pay or not, was compelled to pay a penny or a halfpenny twice a year.

After [in 1198] an agreement was made between Abbot Samson and Robert of Scales as to one moiety of the advowson of Wetherden, and the said Robert had recognized the rights

et idem R. recognovisset S. Edmundo et abbati jus suum ; Abbas, nulla conventione prius habita, nullo prius facto promisso, dedit illam ecclesiae medietatem Magistro Rogero de Scalis fratri ejusdem militis, hac conditione, ut annuam pensionem trium marcarum per manum nostri sacristae redderet magistro scolarum, quicumque legeret in villa S. Edmundi.

Hoc autem fecit Abbas memorandae pietatis ductus affectu, et sicut prius emerat domos lapideas ad scolas regendas ut pauperes clerici quieti essent a conductione domus, ita de cetero essent quieti ab omni exactione denariorum, quos magister scholarum, ex consuetudine, exigebat pro eruditione sua. Domino autem Deo volente, et abbate vivente, tota medietas predictae ecclesiae, quae valet, sicut dicitur, centum solidos, ad tales usus converteretur.

[*Ib.* from B. M. Harl. MS. 1005, f. 130.]

Tempore quo Abbas Samson domum scolarum propriis fecit expensis et redditum trium marcarum annuatim reddendarum Magistro Scolarum fecit confirmari, causam sui facti in pleno capitulo ostendit et statuit ; scilicet, ut omnes scolares tam divites quam pauperes ibi essent quieti in perpetuum a conduccione domus, et XL pauperes clerici essent quieti ab omni exaccione versus magistrum propter suam erudicionem. In quorum numero primo debent computari consanguinei monachorum nostrorum dummodo addiscere volunt ; et residuus numerus debet suppleri pro arbitrio magistri scolarum.

Et hac de causa concessum est ut magister semper habeat duos clericos in Elemosinaria comedentes, qui debent tribus terminis anni venire ad scolas magistro incipiente legere, scilicet ad festum Sancti Michaelis, et post Natale Domini et post Pascha ; et eo cessante debent recedere, nisi ante Pascha, quia tunc ibi debent esse usque ad cenam Domini.

Et eadem est consuetudo de ostiario scolarum. Clerici omnes qui comedunt in Elemosinaria quieti debent esse in scolis predicto dicto modo ; sed computari debent in predicto numero ne magister nimis gravetur.

of St Edmund and the abbot; the abbot, without a previous covenant or any promise, gave that half of the church to Master Roger of Scales, the knight's brother, on condition of his paying an annual pension of three marks to our sacrist for the schoolmaster who for the time being taught in the town of St Edmunds.

This the abbot did through gratitude for the kindness above related, and, as he had first bought the stone house for the school, so that poor clerks might be quit of the rent of a house, so now they might be henceforth quit of all payment of fees which the schoolmaster, according to custom, exacted for his teaching. And, by the will of God, in the lifetime of the abbot the whole moiety of the aforesaid church, worth, as it is said, 100s., was converted to these uses.

[The following passages are not given in the Camden Society's volume.]

At the time when Abbot Samson made the schoolhouse at his own expense and caused a rent of three marks a year to be paid to the schoolmaster, he showed the reason for doing so, and established it in full chapter; that all the scholars, both rich and poor, should be quit for ever of hiring the house, and that 40 poor clerks might be free of all fees to the master for their instruction. Among the 40 ought to be first reckoned the relations of our monks so long as they wish to learn, and the remainder ought to be supplied at the discretion of the schoolmaster.

And for this reason the master was allowed always to have two clerks boarded in the almonry, who are bound to attend the school at three terms of the year when the master begins his lectures, viz. at Michaelmas, after Christmas and after Easter; and when his lectures stop they must retire, except before Easter, as then they ought to stay to the Lord's Supper [i.e. Maundy Thursday].

The same custom obtains for the Usher of the School. All the clerks who are boarded in the almonry ought to be free of the school in the same way; but they ought to be reckoned in the aforesaid number, that the master may not be overburdened.

f. 95. 6. Collacio scolarum quibus spectat et qualiter magistri amovendi sive constituendi sint.

f. 97. 6, 7. Collacio quidem scolarum Sancti Edmundi sic pertinet ad Abbatem sicut collacio ecclesiarum in quibus conventus aliquid percipit annuum, et similiter conferri debent prefate scole et prefate ecclesie, scilicet per assensum conventus. Scole vero maneriorum, sicut Mildenhall et de Beccles, juris conferende sunt eorum in quorum vel cujus custodia constituuntur ipsa maneria. Et notandum est hic quod rector scolarum amovendus premuniri debet a datore earum ante Pentecosten. Si vero sponte vult recedere ipse datorem, i.e. abbatem, sacristam, vicarium abbatis et conventus in hoc similiter tenetur premunire.

St Albans and Dunstable Schools. c. 1183.

[A. F. Leach, *V. C. H. Herts*, II.; *Ib.* I. 194, 195, 196.]

De Garino Abbate.

Garinus huic successit, de Cantebrugia stirpe mediocri oriundus. Iste in seculo, ante suscepcionem habitus, magne fame extitit, et celebris nominis, propter honeste vite sue reverenciam, litterature excellentem periciam, et corporalis elegancie pulchritudinem. Hic cum fratre suo, Magistro Mattheo, similibus dotibus, etsi non tantum, insignito, in physica apud Salernum eleganter atque efficaciter erudito, in claustro Sancti Albani habitum religionis suscepit: et infra breve tempus idem Magister Garinus, propter vite excellenciam virtuose, et litterature copiosam periciam, et persone eleganciam, in Priorem electus et creatus est.

Habuerunt eciam hii duo (scilicet, Abbas et Prior), quemdam nepotem, Magistrum, videlicet, Garinum, in Decretis lectorem nominatissimum. Erat enim avunculis suis in venerabili gestu, et vita honesta, et litteratura, consimilis, ut vere nepos talium, immo potius frater, dici mereretur, et agnosci. Hii tres, quanquam seculares, conversacionis honeste et vite

To whom the collation of schools belongs and how masters are to be removed or appointed.

The collation of the school of Bury St Edmunds belongs to the abbot in the same way as the collation of churches out of which the convent receives a yearly payment, and the said school and the said churches ought to be conferred in the same way, namely, with the assent of the convent. But the schools on manors, such as those of Mildenhall and Beccles, are to be conferred in right of those or him in whose custody the manors themselves are. And it is to be observed here that if a schoolmaster is to be removed he ought to be given notice by the grantor before Easter. If a master wishes to retire voluntarily he is bound to give notice to the grantor, i.e. the abbot, sacrist, or deputy of the abbot and convent, in the same way.

St Albans and Dunstable Schools. c. 1183.

Of Abbot Warren.

Warren succeeded him, born at Cambridge of the middle class. In the world, before he took the habit, he was of great repute and celebrity because of the reverence paid to his upright life, his excellence in learning, and his handsome figure. He, with his brother Master Matthew, who was distinguished, though not so much, by similar qualities, and had become a learned and elegant doctor of medicine at Salerno, took the religious habit in St Albans' cloister; and in a short time Master Warren [Matthew], for his virtuous life and his style in literature and elegant person, was elected and created prior.

Moreover these two, the abbot and prior, had a nephew, also named Master Warren, a most distinguished lecturer on canon law. He was like his uncles in his majestic carriage, his upright life and in learning, so that he truly deserved to be called and recognized as their nephew, or rather as their brother. For these three, although they were seculars, deserved

puritate, monachi censeri promeruerunt. Iste Magister Garinus, et frater ejus, Magister Mattheus, et eorum nepos, Magister Garinus, et duo eorum discipuli et socii, Fabianus et Robertus de Salerno, voverunt se fore apud Sanctum Albanum habitum religiosum suscepturos, admoniti visione speciali et spirituali. Omnesque hii votum implererunt, preter Magistrum Garinum, nepotem Abbatis Garini : ille tamen quod habitu omisit, vita honesta complevit. Obiit Magister Mattheus [Garinus], secularis, apud Sanctum Albanum, videlicet, juxta domum Sanctimonialium de Sopwelle.

Hic, de quo sermo fit, Mattheus [Garinus], pluribus annis scolam rexit in burgo Sancti Albani, qua tunc temporis non inveniretur in Anglia scola melior vel fructuosior, aut scolaribus utilior vel copiosior. Quod bene testabatur et sensit Magister Alexander, cognomento 'Nequam,' qui eundem Garinum in scole regimine precesserat. Hic cum temporis anno, scilicet proximo transacto, apud Dunestaple scolam rexisset, vocavit eum Abbas Garinus hiis litteris breviter et jocose scriptis ;—petiverat enim idem Alexander Nequam scolam Sancti Albani instanter ;— 'Si bonus es, venias : si nequam, nequaquam.' Cui tam breviter et jocose rescribens Alexander ait,—'Si velis veniam : sin autem, tu autem' ; acsi diceret ;—'Non multum curo.'

Hic Magister Garinus ad leges et decreta se transtulit ; avunculis suis sibi librorum copiam et alia subsidia fraterno affectu liberaliter ministrantibus.

Exhibition at Oxford for a Hungarian Clerk.
1195–7.

[Pipe Roll, 7 and 8 Ric. I, 10 ; Oxon. *Oxf. Hist. Soc. Collectanea*, II. 184.]

Nicolao, clerico de Hungria, viii^l et xvii^s et viii^d ad sustentandum se in scolis a festo Sancti Michaelis anni preteriti usque ad Pascham per breve Regis.

to be reckoned as monks for the uprightness of their behaviour and purity of their lives. This Master Warren and his brother Matthew and their nephew Master Warren and two of their pupils and companions, Fabian and Robert of Salerno, being warned by a special and spiritual vision, vowed to take the religious habit at St Albans. And they all fulfilled their vow except Master Warren, the nephew of Abbot Warren, and he made up for any deficiency in his habit by the purity of his habits. Master Matthew [Warren] died a secular at St Albans near Sopwell nunnery.

This Matthew [Warren] of whom we are speaking for many years kept the school in the borough of St Albans; and at that time there could scarcely be found a better or more productive school in England, or one more useful to its scholars or more abounding with them. This was fully admitted and perceived by Master Alexander, nicknamed Neckham [in Latin nequam, i.e. wicked], who had preceded this Warren in the mastership of the school. This [Alexander Neckham] after he had for a time, for the year previous, in fact, taught the school at Dunstable, asked urgently for the school at St Albans, and was invited by Abbot Warren in this terse and witty letter, 'If you are good, you may come; if wicked, by no means.' To which Alexander wrote back, equally tersely and wittily, 'If you wish me to come, I will come; if not, you must excuse me' [play on the word veniam], as much as to say 'I don't much care.'

This Master Warren afterwards transferred himself to the civil and canon law, his uncles, in their brotherly affection, liberally supplying him with plenty of books and other assistance.

Exhibition at Oxford for a Hungarian Clerk.
1195–7.

To Nicholas, a clerk of Hungary, £8. 17s. 8d., to maintain himself in the schools from Michaelmas of the past year to Easter by the king's writ.

Nicolao clerico de Hungeria v^s et ix^d de liberacione sua quam habet ex dono Regis, videlicet a die lune proxima ante festum Sancti Andree usque ad Purificacionem per breve Regis; et eidem Nicolao lvi^s et viii^d de liberacione sua a festo Sancti Petri ad Vincula usque ad festum Sancti Michaelis, scilicet dimidiam marcam per ebdomadam per idem breve.

Exhibition at Oxford. 1198–9.

[*Ib.*, Pipe Roll, 10 Ric. I, 10.]

Roberto de Vermeilles x marcas ad sustentacionem suam in scolis, per breve H[uberti] Cantuariensis Archiepiscopi.

Mathematics taught at Oxford, c. 1200.

[*Ib.* 188, from letter of 1243 in Martène, *Thesaur.* III. col. 1839.]

Clementissimo patri suo et domino Innocencio, Dei gracia summo Pontifici, sue sanctitatis grex humilis, Universitas Magistrorum et Scolarium Oxonie commorancium, cum universa multitudine fratrum Predicatorum et Minorum, ceterorumque religiosorum ibidem habitancium, devota pedum oscula cum obediencie humili famulatu.

Quod scimus loquimur, et quod vidimus testamur de conversacione venerabilis patris nostri Edmundi bone memorie, nuper Cantuariensis Archiepiscopi, qui in nostra fuit Universitate non modico tempore discipulus et magister....

Porro transactis fere sex annis, quibus in Artibus rexerat;... ipso adhuc cursim legente arithmeticam quibusdam sociis suis, apparuit ei in somniis pia mater eius, paulo ante defuncta, dicens: 'Fili, quid legis? que sunt ille figure quibus tam studiose intendis?' Quo respondente: 'Talia lego,' ostensis protraccionibus, que in illa solent fieri facultate, illa mox dextram manum eius arripuit, et in illa tres circulos depinxit, in quibus

For Nicholas, a clerk of Hungary, 5s. 9d. for his livery which he has by the king's gift, viz. from Monday before St Andrew's day [30 Nov.] to the Purification [2 Feb.] by the king's writ; and to the same Nicholas 56s. 8d. for his livery from St Peter ad Vincula [1 Aug.] to Michaelmas, viz. half a mark [6s. 8d.] a week by the same writ.

Exhibition at Oxford. 1198–9.

To Robert of Vermeilles 10 marks for his maintenance in the schools by writ of H[ubert], Archbishop of Canterbury.

Mathematics taught at Oxford, c. 1200.

To their most kindly father and lord, Innocent [IV], by the grace of God supreme pontiff, his holiness' humble flock, the University of Masters and Scholars residing at Oxford, with the whole crowd of friars preachers and friars minors and other religious inhabiting there, devoutly kiss his feet as his humble and obedient servants.

We speak what we know and we bear witness to what we have seen of the life of our venerable father Edmund of good memory, late Archbishop of Canterbury, who was in our University no little time as scholar and master....

Further, after nearly six years' regency in arts...while still lecturing cursorily on arithmetic to some of his colleagues, his pious mother, who had died a short while before, appeared to him in a dream, saying, 'Son, what are you reading? what are those figures you are studying so intently?' and when he answered 'Such and such,' showing the processes usual in that faculty, she immediately seized his hand and drew three circles on it, in which

hec tria nomina per ordinem inscripsit: 'Pater, Filius, Spiritus Sanctus,' et hoc facto, sic ait: 'Fili carissime, talibus figuris, et non aliis, de cetero intende.' Quo somnio, quasi per revelacionem edoctus, statim ad studium theologie se transtulit, in quo tam mirabiliter in brevi profecit, quod cito post paucos annos, suadentibus multis, cathedram magistralem ascendit...

The Council of London forbid Fees for Licence to teach. 1200.

[Wilkins, *Concilia*, I. p. 506.]

VIII. Nihil exigendum pro sacramentis administrandis.

Sicut in Lateranensi concilio salubriter a sanctis patribus est provisum, inhibemus ne a personis ecclesiasticis deducendis ad sedem, vel sacerdotibus vel aliis clericis instituendis, aut sepeliendis mortuis, aut benedicendis nubentibus, seu pro chrismate, seu quibuslibet aliis sacramentis aliquid exigatur. Si quis autem contra hoc venire presumpserit, portionem cum Gehazi se noverit habiturum, cuius factum exaccione turpi muneris imitatur. His adiicimus, ne pro licencia celebrandi divina a sacerdotibus, vel docendi a magistris aliquid exigatur; et, si solutum fuerit, repetatur.

Schools at the Council of Westminster. 1200.

[Wilkins, *Concilia*, I. p. 270.]

De scholis in ecclesiis.

XIX. Si quis presbyter velit nepotem suum vel quendam consanguineum suum erudiendum mittere ad ecclesias, quae nobis ad gubernandum concreditae sunt, concedimus ei hoc libentissime.

XX. Ut presbyteri per villas scholas habeant, et gratis parvulos doceant.

she wrote these three names in order, 'Father, Son, Holy Ghost,' and then said, 'Dearest son, henceforth be intent on these figures, not the others.' Thus taught by a dream as if by revelation he at once transferred himself to the study of theology, in which in a short time he made such wonderful progress, that after a very few years, at the persuasion of many, he ascended the doctor's chair.

The Council of London forbid Fees for Licence to teach. 1200.

8. Nothing to be exacted for administering the sacraments.

As it was in the Lateran Council beneficially provided by the holy fathers, we forbid anything to be exacted by ecclesiastical dignitaries for induction or institution of priests or other clerks, for burying the dead, or blessing marriages, or the Chrism or any other sacraments. If, however, anyone presume to contravene this, let him know that he will have his portion with Gehazi, whose deed in the disgraceful exaction of a gift he imitates. To this we add, Let nothing be exacted from priests for a licence to perform divine service or from masters for licence to teach; and if anything has been paid it may be recovered.

Schools at the Council of Westminster. 1200.

Of schools in churches.

19. If any priest wishes to send his nephew or other relation to be taught in the churches, which are entrusted to us to govern, we grant him this most willingly.

20. That priests shall keep schools in their towns and teach little boys gratis.

Presbyteri semper debent in domibus suis ludimagistrorum scholas habere, et si quis devotus [homo] parvulos suos eis ad instructionem concredere velit, illos quam libentissime suscipere et benigne docere debent. Cogitare debetis, quod scriptum sit, quod 'Qui docti sunt, fulgebunt sicut splendor caeli'; et quod 'qui multos ad justitiam erudiverunt et docuerunt, splendebunt sicut stellae in aeternum.' Attamen non debent pro instructione eorum aliquid a consanguineis ipsorum expectare, nisi quod propria voluntate facere voluerint.

A Royal Exhibitioner at Winchester. 1205.

[A. F. Leach, *Hist. Win. Coll.* from Lit. Claus., 6 John (Rec. Com.) 27 b.]

Rex Willelmo de Cornhull.

Mandamus tibi quod Gaufridum latorem presencium scolas apud Wintoniam frequentare facias, ac ei necessaria racionabiliter invenias, et custum quod in eo posueris nobis scire facias et id tibi computabitur.

Teste me ipso apud Londinium 13 Aprilis
per Petrum de Stoks.

Secession from Oxford to Cambridge and Reading.
1209.

[*Chron. Roger of Wendover* (Rolls Series), 84, II. p. 51.]

Per idem tempus clericus quidam, apud Oxoniam liberalibus vacans disciplinis, mulierem quandam casu interfecit, quam cum mortuam deprehendisset, per fugam sibi consuluit. Prefectus autem urbis et multi alii accurrentes, cum mulierem exanimem invenerunt, ceperunt querere homicidam illum in hospicio suo, quod cum tribus sociis suis clericis locaverat, et facti reum non invenientes ceperunt tres socios eius clericos memoratos et de homicidio penitus nescios, et eos in carcerem retruserunt; deinde post dies paucos, rege Anglorum iubente,

Priests ought always to have a school of schoolmasters in their houses, and if any devout person wishes to entrust his little ones to them for instruction, they ought to receive them willingly and teach them kindly. Ye ought to think that it is written, 'The learned shall shine like the brightness of the firmament,' and 'Those who have instructed and taught many to righteousness shall shine like stars for ever.' But they ought not to expect anything from the relations of the boys for their instruction, except what they are willing to do of their own will.

A Royal Exhibitioner at Winchester. 1205.

The King to William of Cornhill.

We command you to cause Geoffrey, the bearer hereof, to attend school at Winchester and find him necessaries on a reasonable scale, and let us know the costs you expend on him and it shall be credited to you.

Witness myself at London, 13 April,
By Peter of the Stocks.

Secession from Oxford to Cambridge and Reading. 1209.

About the same time a clerk, who was studying the liberal arts at Oxford, by accident killed a woman, and when he found she was dead, sought safety in flight. But the bailiff of the town and others who came up and found the woman dead, began to try and find the murderer in his hostel, which he had hired with three other clerks, and not finding the criminal, took his three friends, who knew almost nothing about the murder, and threw them into prison. A few days afterwards,

in contemptum ecclesiastice libertatis, extra villam educti suspendio perierunt. Quod cum factum fuisset, recesserunt ab Oxonia ad tria millia clericorum, tam magistri quam discipuli, ita quod nec unus ex omni universitate remansit; quorum quidam apud Cantabregge, quidam vero apud Radingum, liberalibus studiis vacantes villam Oxonie vacuam reliquerunt.

A Grammar School to be established in every Cathedral and a Theological School in every Archiepiscopal Church. 1215.

[A. F. Leach, *Early Yorkshire Schools*, I. 3. Decretal v., tit. 5.]

In qualibet cathedrali ecclesia, vel alia in facultatibus sufficienti, debet a praelato vel capitulo unus magister eligi, cui reditus unius praebendae debent assignari; in metropolitana vero ecclesia etiam eligi debet theologus. Et si ad grammaticum et theologum non sufficit, provideat ipsi theologo ex reditibus suae ecclesiae, et grammatico faciat provideri in aliqua ecclesiarum suae civitatis vel dioceseos.

Innocentius III in Concilio Generali.

Quia nonnullis propter inopiam, et legendi studium et opportunitas proficiendi subtrahitur, in Lateranensi concilio pia fuit constitutione provisum, ut 'per unamquamque cathedralem...ad doctrinam.'

Verum quoniam in multis ecclesiis id minime observatur, nos, praedictum roborantes statutum, adjicimus, ut non solum in qualibet cathedrali ecclesia sed etiam in aliis, quarum sufficere poterunt facultates, constituatur magister idoneus, a praelato cum capitulo, seu majori et seniore parte capituli eligendus, qui clericos ecclesiarum ipsarum [et aliarum] gratis in grammatica facultate ac aliis instruat juxta posse.

Sane Metropolis Ecclesia theologum nihilominus habeat

on the orders of the king of the English, in contempt of the liberty of the church, they were taken outside the town and hung. On this nearly 3000 clerks, masters and scholars alike, left Oxford, not a single one of the whole University remaining. Some of them went to study the liberal arts at Cambridge, some to Reading, but the town of Oxford was left empty.

A Grammar School to be established in every Cathedral and a Theological School in every Archiepiscopal Church. 1215.

In every cathedral or other church of sufficient means, a master ought to be elected by the prelate or chapter, and the income of a prebend assigned to him, and in every metropolitan church a theologian also ought to be elected. And if the church is not rich enough to provide a grammarian and theologian, it shall provide for the theologian from the revenues of his church, and cause provision to be made for the grammarian in some church of his city or diocese.

Innocent III in the General Council.

Because some are deprived through want of means of the study of learning and of the opportunity of proficiency, it was provided by a pious constitution in the Lateran Council, that 'in every cathedral...to learning.'

And whereas in many churches this is not observed, we, confirming the statute aforesaid, add that not only in every cathedral church, but also in others whose means shall be sufficient, a fit master shall be established to be elected by the prelate and chapter or the greater and wiser part of the chapter, to instruct the clerks of the church and others freely in the faculty of grammar after his ability.

Further, a metropolitical church shall nevertheless have a

qui sacerdotes et alios in sacra pagina doceat et in his praesertim informet,. quae ad curam animarum spectare noscuntur.

Assignetur autem cuilibet magistrorum a capitulo unius praebendae proventus, et pro theologo a metropolitano tantundem ; non quod propter hoc efficiatur canonicus, sed tamdiu reditus ipse percipiat, quamdiu perstiterit in docendo.

Quod si forte de duobus Ecclesia Metropolis gravetur, theologo juxta modum praedictum ipsa provideat, grammatico vero in alia ecclesia suae civitatis sive diocesis quae sufficere valeat, faciat provideri.

Non-residence allowed to beneficed Clergy for Study of Theology at Universities. 1219.

[Decretal v. 5, c. 5.]

Honorius III.

Super speculum Domini licet immeriti constituti....Volumus et mandamus, ut statutum editum in concilio generali de magistris theologis per singulas metropoles statuendis, inviolabiliter observetur, statuentes insuper de consilio fratrum nostrorum ac districte praecipiendo mandantes, ut, quia super hoc propter raritatem magistrorum se possent forsitan aliqui excusare, ab ecclesiarum praelatis et capitulis ad theologicae professionis studium aliqui docibiles destinentur, qui, quum docti fuerint, in Dei ecclesia velut splendor fulgeant firmamenti, ex quibus postmodum copia possit haberi doctorum, qui, velut stellae, in perpetuas aeternitates mansuri ad iustitiam valeant plurimos erudire, quibus, si proprii proventus ecclesiastici non sufficiunt, praedicti necessaria subministrent. Docentes vero in theolo-

theologian to teach the priests and others in the sacred page, and inform them especially in those matters which are recognized as pertaining to the cure of souls.

There shall be assigned to each master by the chapter the revenue of a prebend, and by the metropolitan chapter the same for the theologian; not that he is for this reason to be made a canon, but that he is to receive the income of one so long as he continues teaching.

If, however, the metropolitical church is overburdened by two masters, that church shall provide for a theologian in the way before-mentioned, and shall cause provision to be made for the grammar master in another church of the same city or diocese.

Non-residence allowed to beneficed Clergy for Study of Theology at Universities. 1219.

Honorius III.

Set on the watch-tower of the Lord though unworthy,... we will and command that the statute published in the general council as to masters in theology being established in every mother-church be observed, enacting further, by the advice of our brethren, and strictly enjoining that as through the scarcity of masters some may perhaps excuse themselves from this, then some capable of learning shall be sent by the prelates and chapters of the churches to a school of the theological faculty, so that when they have become learned, they may shine in the church of God like the splendour of the firmament, and from them plenty of doctors may hereafter be created, who, like stars remaining to all eternity, may instruct many in justice, and if their own church revenues do not suffice for them, the said prelates and chapters shall find them what they need. Teachers in the faculty

gica facultate, dum in scholis docuerint, et studentes in ipsa integre per annos quinque, percipiant de licentia sedis apostolicae proventus praebendarum et beneficiorum suorum, non obstante aliqua alia consuetudine vel statuto, quum denario fraudari non debeant in vinea Domini operantes. Hoc autem inconcusse volumus observari, firmiter disponentes, quod feriantur poena debita transgressores.

Datis Viterbii vii Kalendas Decembris pontificatus nostri anno iv.

A Lincolnshire Vicar ordered to attend the Theology School at Lincoln. 1219.

[Ep. Reg. Linc., Rot. Hug. de Wells, III. 101.]

Lincoln : Barton Vicaria.

Radulphus capellanus presentatus per abbatem et conventum de Bardeneia ad perpetuam vicariam ecclesie de Bartona [super Humber], ordinatam auctoritate concilii, facta inquisitione per W. archidiaconum Lincolnie, per quam negotium fuit in expedito, admissus est et in ea canonice vicarius perpetuus institutus....

Injunctum est etiam ipsi vicario ut per biennium apud Lincolniam scolas frequentet et theologiam addiscat, et interim idoneum capellanum in dicta ecclesia de Barton innominet per consilium archidiaconi Lincolnie.

A Parson ordered to attend Grammar School. c. 1225.

[Ep. Reg. Linc., Rot. Hug. de Wells, I. 147.]

Lincoln : Hanewerdhe.

Hugo de Scalleby clericus presentatus per Nigellum Costentin ad ecclesiam de Hanewerdhe, admissus est et in

of theology while teaching in the schools, and those wholly studying in the same faculty for five years, shall receive by licence from the apostolic see the revenues of their prebends and benefices, any custom or statute to the contrary notwithstanding, since those working in the Lord's vineyard ought not to be defrauded of their penny. This we will to be unshakenly observed, firmly directing that transgressors shall be stricken with due penalty.

Dated at Viterbo 25 November, in the 4th year of our bishopric.

A Lincolnshire Vicar ordered to attend the Theology School at Lincoln. 1219.

Lincoln: Barton Vicarage.

Ralph, chaplain, promoted by the abbot and convent of Bardney to the perpetual vicarage of Barton-on-Humber, established by authority of the [Lateran] council, after inquiry by W. Archdeacon of Lincoln, by which the business was expedited, was admitted and canonically instituted in it as perpetual vicar....

The vicar himself was directed to attend the school at Lincoln for two years to learn theology, and meanwhile to appoint a fit chaplain in the said church of Barton with the advice of the Archdeacon of Lincoln.

A Parson ordered to attend Grammar School. *c.* 1225.

Lincoln: [Potter] Hanworth.

Hugh of Scawby, clerk, presented by Nigel Costentin to the church of [Potter] Hanworth, was admitted and canoni-

ea canonice persona institutus, ita quod ad proximos ordines veniat in subdiaconum ordinandus. Propter insufficientem autem ipsius litteraturam injunxit eidem Dominus Episcopus sub periculo beneficii sui ut scolas frequentet. Et mandatum est J. Decano de Wivelinge ut ipsum in corporalem prefate ecclesie possessionem inducat secundum formam premissam, et si scolas non frequentaverit quod illud Domino Episcopo significet.

Earliest Mention of Cambridge University.
1231.

[Cal. Close Rolls, 15 Hen. III, m. 14 d, p. 586.]

Rex vicecomiti Cantebrigie salutem.

Scias quod cum in villa nostra Kantebrigie, ubi convenit multitudo studencium, plures sunt clerici rebelles et incorrigibiles, qui cum delinqunt a cancellario et magistris se corripi nolunt et castigari, et plures malefactores, inter quos quidam sunt sub specie clericali mentientes se esse quod non sunt, a cancellario et magistris scolarum cum delinqunt iuxta morem scolarium se iusticiari non permittunt; pro eorum audacia coercenda et studencium tranquillitate de consilio nostro providimus quod quotiens predicti cancellarius et magistri perpenderint et invenerint inter se huiusmodi clericos rebelles et malefactores, significent illud episcopo, et episcopus postea tibi; ut tu, assumptis tecum quos videris ad hoc assumendos, ad mandatum eiusdem episcopi in propria persona tua accedas usque Cantebrigiam et secundum quod predictus episcopus tibi significabit et predicti cancellarius et magistri tibi dicent, in clericos rebelles et malefactores predictos manum mittas, et ipsos secundum consilium predictorum cancellarii et magistrorum vel ipsos in prisona nostra retineas vel eos a villa de Kantebrigia expelli facias et amoveri.

cally instituted in it as parson, on condition that he comes to the next orders to be ordained subdeacon. But on account of the insufficiency of his grammar, the lord bishop ordered him on pain of loss of his benefice to attend school. And the Dean of Wyville was ordered to induct him into corporal possession of the said church in form aforesaid, and to inform the lord bishop if he does not attend school.

Earliest Mention of Cambridge University.
1231.

The king to the sheriff of Cambridge, greeting.

Know that whereas in our town of Cambridge, where a multitude of students meet, there are divers disorderly and incorrigible clerks who, when they misconduct themselves, refuse to be arrested and punished by the chancellor and masters, and there are divers criminals, among whom are some, in the guise of clerks, pretending to be what they are not, who when they misconduct themselves do not allow themselves to be tried like scholars by the chancellor and schoolmasters; we, with the advice of our council, have provided, for the restraint of their audacity and the peace of the students, that whenever the aforesaid chancellor and masters have examined and found amongst them such disorderly clerks and criminals, they may inform the bishop, and the bishop may inform you; and you, on the orders of the bishop, taking with you such as you shall see fit to take for the purpose, shall yourself go to Cambridge and arrest such of the said disorderly clerks and criminals as the aforesaid bishop shall certify in writing, and the said chancellor and masters shall inform you of by word of mouth, and either keep them in our prison or cause them to be expelled and removed from the town of Cambridge, as the chancellor and masters shall advise you.

Et ideo tibi precipimus quod ad mandatum episcopi Eliensis de predictis clericis rebellibus et malefactoribus prout dicti cancellarius et magistri tibi dicent, in forma predicta provisionem nostram exequaris, ita quod predicti clerici rebelles et malefactores pro defectu coercionis tue occasionem non habeant delinquendi, propter quod decetero ad te nos graviter capere debeamus.

Teste rege apud Oxoniam, iii die Maii.

Rex vicecomiti Cantebrigie salutem.

Quoniam ut audivimus, plures morantur clerici apud Cantebrigiam qui sub nullius magistri scolarum sunt disciplina et tuitione, set potius menciuntur se esse scolares cum non sint, ut tutius et fortius visa ad hoc oportunitate queant malignari; tibi precipimus quod assumptis tecum probis et legalibus hominibus de comitatu tuo, accedas ad villam nostram Cantebrigie et per totam villam illam clamari facias ex parte nostra quod nullus clericus moretur in villa illa qui non sit sub disciplina vel tuitione alicuius magistri scolarum; et si aliqui tales fuerint in villa illa, eam exeant infra xv dies postquam hoc clamatum fuerit; et si ultra terminum illum inventi fuerint in eadem villa huiusmodi clerici, capientur et in prisona nostra mittentur.

Teste ut supra.

Et mandatum est H. Elyensi episcopo quod quotiens cancellarius et magistri scolarum Cantebrigie perpenderint et invenerint inter se huiusmodi clericos rebelles et malefactores et illud eidem episcopo significaverint, ipse vicecomiti Cantebrigie per literas suas istud significet ut assumptis secum etc. ut supra.

Rex maiori et ballivis Cantebrigie salutem.

Satis constat vobis quod apud villam nostram Cantebrigie studendi causa e diversis partibus, tam cismarinis quam transmarinis, scolarium confluit multitudo, quod valde gratum habemus et acceptum, cum exinde toto regno nostro com-

And so we command you that on the orders of the Bishop of Ely you carry out this our provision on the aforesaid disorderly clerks and criminals as the said chancellor and masters shall tell you in form aforesaid, so that the said disorderly clerks and criminals may not, through want of coercion by you, find opportunity of misbehaviour, for which in the future we might have occasion to deal severely with you.

Witness the king at Oxford, 3 May.

The king to the sheriff of Cambridge, greeting.

Since, as we have heard, many clerks are living at Cambridge without being under the discipline or guardianship of any schoolmaster, and further pretend to be scholars when they are not, seeing an opportunity of thus being able to commit crimes in greater safety and with greater ease; we command you that, taking with you good and lawful men of your county, you go to our town of Cambridge, and cause proclamation to be made on our behalf through the whole town that no clerk shall live there who is not under the discipline and guardianship of a master in the school; and that if there are any such in the town they shall leave it within 15 days after this proclamation is made; and if after that time any such clerks shall be found in the same town they shall be taken and sent to our prison.

Witness as before.

And orders were sent to H., Bishop of Ely, that whenever the chancellor and masters of the schools of Cambridge have enquired and found amongst them such disorderly clerks and criminals and have informed the bishop thereof, he shall inform the sheriff of Cambridge thereof by his letters so that taking with him etc. as above.

The king to the mayor and bailiffs of Cambridge, greeting.

You are aware that a multitude of scholars from divers parts, as well from this side the sea as from overseas, meets at our town of Cambridge for study, which we hold a very gratifying and desirable thing, since no small benefit and glory

modum non modicum et honor nobis accrescat; et vos specialiter inter quos personaliter conversantur studentes, non mediocriter gaudere debetis et letari.

Audivimus autem quod in hospiciis vestris locandis tam graves et onerosi estis scolaribus inter vos commorantibus, quod nisi mensurabilius et modestius vos habueritis erga ipsos in hac parte, exaccione vestra faciente, oportebit ipsos villam vestram exire et studio suo relicto a terra nostra recedere, quod nullatenus vellemus.

Et ideo vobis mandamus firmiter iniungentes quatinus, super predictis hospiciis locandis vos mensurantes secundum consuetudinem universitatis, per duos magistros et duos probos et legales homines de villa vestra ad hoc assignandos hospicia predicta taxari, et secundum eorum taxacionem ea locari permittatis, taliter vos gerentes in hac parte, ne, si secus egeritis propter quod ad nos debeat clamor pervenire, ad hoc manum apponere debeamus.

Teste ut supra.

Consimiles literas habet universitas Oxonie directas vicecomiti Oxonie, maiori et ballivis Oxonie, hoc mutato, quod ubi ponitur in primo brevi directo vicecomiti Cantebrigie, 'ad mandatum episcopi Elyensis,' hic ponitur, 'ad mandatum cancellarii et magistrorum Oxonie.' Et ubi ponitur in brevi directo maiori et ballivis Cantebrigie, 'taliter vos gerentes in hac parte,' ponitur hic, 'in hoc et in aliis que predictos scolares contingunt.'

The Master of Marlborough School a Papal Delegate. 11 *June* 1232.

[*Sarum Ch. and Doc.* (Rolls Series), 250.]

Gregorius, episcopus, servus servorum Dei, Dilectis filiis Priori de Sancta Margareta, Decano Christianitatis et Magistro Scolarum de Merleberge, Saresberiensis diocesis, salutem et apostolicam benediccionem.

accrues therefrom to our whole realm; and you, among whom these students personally live, ought especially to be pleased and delighted at it.

We have heard, however, that in letting your houses you make such heavy charges to the scholars living among you, that unless you conduct yourselves with more restraint and moderation towards them in this matter, they will be driven by your exactions to leave your town and, abandoning their studies, leave our country, which we by no means desire.

And therefore we command and firmly enjoin you that in letting the aforesaid houses you follow University custom and allow the said houses to be valued by two masters and two good and lawful men of your town assigned for the purpose, and allow them to be let according to their valuation, so conducting yourselves in this matter that no complaint may reach us through your doing otherwise, which may compel us to interfere.

Witness as above.

The University of Oxford has like letters directed to the sheriff of Oxford, and the mayor and bailiffs of Oxford, with this difference, that where it is put in the first writ directed to the sheriff of Cambridge, 'on the orders of the bishop of Ely,' it is put 'on the orders of the Chancellor and Masters of Oxford.' And where it is put in the writ directed to the mayor and bailiffs of Cambridge, 'so conducting yourselves in this matter,' it is put 'so conducting yourselves in this and other matters which concern the said scholars.'

The Master of Marlborough School a Papal Delegate. 11 *June* 1232.

Gregory, bishop, servant of the servants of God, to his beloved sons the prior of St Margaret, the dean of Christianity and the schoolmaster of Marlborough in the diocese of Salisbury, health and apostolic blessing.

Magister Elia de Derham conquerendo monstravit quod Lucas archidiaconus Surreye et quidam alii Wintoniensis diocesis super decimis ad ecclesiam de Poterne, que prebende sue Sarisberie pertinet, injuriantur eidem.

Ideoque discrecioni vestre per apostolica scripta mandamus quatinus partibus convocatis audiatis causam.

Datis Spoleti iij Idus Junii pontificatus nostri anno vj^{to}.

A Northampton Vicar ordered to attend Northampton School. 1230.

[Ep. Reg. Linc., Rot. Hug. de Wells, II. 171.]

Johannes de Dustone, capellanus, presentatus per priorem et conventum Sancti Andree Northamptonie ad ecclesiam Sancti Bartholomei Northamptonie, facta prius inquisicione per Johannem archidiaconum Northamptonie, per quam etc., ad eandem admissus etc....Injunctum est eciam ipsi Johanni ut scolas Northamptonie frequentet, et addiscat, et hoc anno revoluto redeat archidiacono ostensurus qualiter profecerit in eisdem.

Universities at Northampton and Salisbury. 1238.

[Th. Walsingham, *Ypodigma Neustriae* (Rolls Series), 141.]

Anno 1238 Otho, apostolicae sedis legatus, cum ad abbathiam de Osney juxta Oxon. receptus fuisset, insultum passus a scholaribus ad campanile transfugit. Qui postea Londoniis in scholares Oxonie sententiam excommunicationis fulminavit, studiamque dispersit. Unde factum est ut quidam villam Northamptonie, quidam novam civitatem Sarum ad studium elegerunt.

Master Elias of Dereham complaining has shown us that Luke, archdeacon of Surrey, and others of the diocese of Winchester, do him wrong in the matter of the tithes belonging to the church of Potterne, which belongs to his prebend at Salisbury.

Therefore we commend it to your discretion by apostolic writ that you summon the parties before you and hear the case.

Dated Spoleto 11 June in the 6th year of our bishopric.

A Northampton Vicar ordered to attend Northampton School. 1230.

John of Dustone, chaplain, presented by the prior and convent of St Andrew's, Northampton, to the church of St Bartholomew, Northampton, inquiry having been first made by John, archdeacon of Northampton, by which etc. was admitted to the same etc....And the said John was ordered to attend Northampton School and learn, and that at the end of a year he should return to the archdeacon to show how he had got on in it.

Universities at Northampton and Salisbury. 1238.

In the year 1238, Otto the legate of the apostolic see, was received at Oseney abbey near Oxford, but being assaulted by the scholars took refuge in the bell-tower. Afterwards at London he published sentence of excommunication on the scholars of Oxford and broke up the University. So it came to pass that some chose the town of Northampton, and others the new city of Salisbury for the University.

Newark Grammar School. 1238.

[A. F. Leach, *Mem. of Southwell Minster* (Camden Society, 1891), XLI.-II., from Liber Albus, f. 136.]

Littera de jure presentacionis Scolarum de Newark.

Noverint universi Matris Ecclesie filii ad quorum noticiam presentes littere pervenerint, quod cum lis est mota, auctoritate Domini Pape, inter Stephanum titulo Sancte Marie transtiberine presbyterum cardinalem canonicum Suwell ex una parte, et Priorem et conventum Canonicorum Sancte Katharine ex altera, super collacione scolarum de Newark, tandem dicta lis inter Dominum Abbatem De Rupe procuratorem ipsius Cardinalis in Anglia de consensu capituli Suwell amicabile composicione conquievit in hunc modum, anno scilicet Incarnacionis Dominice millesimo ducentesimo tricesimo octavo; videlicet, quod dicti Prior et conventus clericum ad regimen scolarum predictarum ad instruendum pueros in arte grammatica ydoneum canonico sive custodi dicte prebende quicunque pro tempore fuerit, si canonicus presens non fuerit, quotienscunque eas vacare contigerit in Capitulo Suwell presentabunt. Qui quidem clericus canonico vel custodi dicte prebende et Capitulo obedienciam canonicam jurabit. Si vero dictus clericus in aliquo contra libertates Ecclesie Suwell vel dicte prebende deliquerit, si incorrigibilis existat, et dicti Prior et conventus in corripiendo eum fuerint necligentes super excessibus ipsius corrigendis, recepto prius mandato super hiis a Canonico ipsius prebende sive a Capitulo predicto, per eosdem Priorem et conventum amovebitur, et alius per eosdem loco ipsius presentatus recipietur.

Ut vero hec concessio perpetue firmitatis robur optineat

Newark Grammar School. 1238.

Letter on the right of presentation to Newark School.

Let all sons of mother church to whose knowledge the present letters come, know that when a suit had been brought with the authority of the lord Pope, between Stephen, cardinal priest of the church of St Mary Trastevere, canon of Southwell, of the one part, and the prior and convent of the canons of St Katharine [by Lincoln] of the other, as to the collation of Newark School, at length the said suit was brought to an end by the lord abbot of Roche, the same cardinal's proctor in England, with consent of the chapter of Southwell, by a friendly agreement in this manner, in the year of the Incarnation of the Lord 1238; viz. that the said prior and convent shall in chapter at Southwell present a fit clerk to keep the said school for the instruction of boys in the art of grammar, to the canon, or to the guardian of the said prebend for the time being, if the canon is not present, as often as the school falls vacant; which clerk shall swear canonical obedience to the canon or guardian of the said prebend and to the chapter. If the said clerk shall commit any offence against the liberties of the church of Southwell or of the said prebend, if he is incorrigible, and the said prior and convent shall be negligent in punishing him and correcting his offences, after receiving orders on the matter from the canon of the same prebend or the chapter aforesaid, he shall be removed by the same prior and convent and another presented by them shall be admitted in his stead.

That this grant may obtain the strength of perpetual con-

Capitulum Suwell et predicti Prior et conventus sigilla sua autentica huic scripto hinc inde apposuerunt etc.

[Marginal note in later hand.]

Quia collaciones scolarum grammaticalium per totum Archidiaconatum Notyngham solum et in solidum pertinent ad prebendarium de Normanton in collegiata ecclesia Suthwell ut cancellarium eiusdem ecclesie, et quamvis aliqua pretensa composicio super collacione scolarum grammaticalium ville de Newerk fuerit facta, illa tamen nullius potest existere auctoritatis, ut liquet ex tenore eiusdem, quia peccat in pluribus.

Grammar and Logic Schools at Southwell and on the Prebends of the Canons. 1248.

[A. F. Leach, *Mem. of Southwell Minster*, p. 205, from Chapter Act Book.]

Acta generali convocacione singulorum fratrum et canonicorum Suthwell Ecclesie, die lune proximo post festum Annunciacionis Beate Marie Virginis, incipiente anno Domini millesimo ducentesimo quadragesimo octavo, de communi consilio et unanimi consensu Canonicorum ibimet presencium, et procuratorum Canonicorum absencium.

Ordinatum fuit et statutum....

Item, quod non teneantur Scole de Grammatica vel Logica infra prebendas Canonicorum, nisi secundum consuetudinem Ebor.

Northampton University. 1 *Feb.* 1261— 1 *Feb.* 1265.

[A. F. Leach, *V. C. H. Northants*, II. 234. Pat. 45 Hen. III, m. 17.]

Rex etc. dilectis et fidelibus suis maiori, ballivis et ceteris probis hominibus suis Norhampton, salutem.

Cum quidam magistri et alii scolares proponant in municipio

firmation the chapter of Southwell and the said prior and convent have put their authentic seals to this deed on one side and the other etc.

[Marginal note in later hand.]

Whereas the collations of grammar schools throughout the archdeaconry of Nottingham belong solely and wholly to the prebendary of Normanton in the collegiate church of Southwell as chancellor of the same church, although some alleged agreement may have been made as to the collation to the grammar school of the town of Newark, it cannot be of any authority, as appears from the text of the same, as it is wrong in many points.

Grammar and Logic Schools at Southwell and on the Prebends of the Canons. 1248.

Acts of the general Convocation of all the brethren and canons of the church of Southwell, on Monday after the feast of the Annunciation of the Blessed Virgin Mary, at the beginning of the year of the Lord 1248, by the common counsel and unanimous consent of the canons there present and the proctors of absent canons.

It was ordered and decreed....

Also, that Schools of Grammar or Logic shall not be held in the canons' prebends, except in accordance with the custom of York.

Northampton University. 1 *Feb.* 1261— 1 *Feb.* 1265.

The king etc. to his beloved and faithful the mayor, bailiffs, and his other good men of Northampton, greeting.

Whereas certain masters and others, scholars, propose

vestro morari ad scolasticam disciplinam ibidem excercendam, ut accepimus, nos cultum divinum et regni nostri utilitatem maiorem ex hoc attendentes adventum predictorum scolarium et moram suam ibidem acceptamus, volentes et concedentes quod predicti scolares in municipio predicto sub nostra proteccione et defensione salvo et secure morentur, et ibidem excerceant et faciant ea que ad huiusmodi scolares pertinent. Eo ideo vobis mandamus firmiter precipientes quod ipsos scolares cum ad vos venerint commoraturi in municipio supradicto recommendatos habentes ipsos curialiter recipiatis, et prout statum decet scolasticum manuteneatis; Non inferentes eis aut inferri permittentes impedimentum molestiam aut gravamen.

In cuius rei testimonium etc. Teste rege apud Windes-[oram] primo die Februarii.

Et mandatum est universis magistris et aliis scolaribus venturis ad municipium predictum quod Rex adventum suum in municipium predictum ad scolasticam disciplinam ibidem excercendi affectat, et Rex vult et concedit quod sub sua proteccione et defensione saluo et secure morentur in municipio predicto, et ibidem exerceant et faciant que ad ipsos pertineant. Teste ut supra.

The Oxford Scholars at the Defence of Northampton. 1264.

[Knyghton, *De eventibus Anglie*, II., ed. Twysden, 1652, p. 2448.]

Clerici vero universitatis Oxoniensis, quae quidem universitas jussu baronum ibidem translata fuerat, ipsis ingredientibus et insultantibus majora fecerunt mala quam caeteri barones cum fundis et arcubus et balistis. Habebant enim vexillum per se et in sublime contra regem erectum, unde iratus rex juravit, quod in ingressu suspenderentur omnes. Quo audito raserunt capita multi et fugam qui poterunt velocem inierunt.

Pacificata tamen urbe jussit rex exequi quod juraverat. Et

to live in your borough to pursue school learning there as we are informed, we, expecting therefrom increase of divine worship and the greater advantage of our realm, accept the coming of the aforesaid scholars and their living there, willing and granting that the said scholars may live in the borough aforesaid safely and securely under our protection and defence, and there pursue and do whatever concerns such scholars. Therefore we command you firmly ordering that you hold the scholars when they come to live in the borough aforesaid as recommended by us, and receive them courteously, and maintain them as the estate of scholars demands; not putting nor allowing to be put any impediment, molestation or grievance upon them.

In witness whereof etc. Witness, the king at Windsor, 1 February [1260–1].

And a mandate issued to all the masters and other scholars who were going to the borough aforesaid, that the king favours their coming to the said borough to practice school learning there, and the king wills and grants that they may live safely and securely under his protection and defence in the borough aforesaid, and there practice and do whatever concerns them. Witness as above.

The Oxford Scholars at the Defence of Northampton. 1264.

The clerks of Oxford University, which by the barons' orders had been transferred there, inflicted greater losses on the attacking force which came in through the breach than the rest of the barons, by their slings and bows and balistas. They had their own flag, which they held up on high against the king, which so enraged him that he swore that when he got in he would hang them all. On hearing this many of them shaved their heads and fled as quickly as possible.

When the town was quiet, the king ordered the execution

dixerunt ei, Absit hoc a te, rex, nam filii magnatorum tuorum et caeterorum hominum de regno tuo huc cum universitate tua convenerunt, quos si suspendi feceris seu detruncari, insurgent in te tui qui modo tecum sunt, non permittentes pro posse sanguinem filiorum suorum seu proximorum effundi. Placatusque est rex et contra clericos quievit ira ejus.

Suppression of Northampton University. 1 Feb. 1265.

[Close Roll, 49 Hen. III, m. 10 d.]

Rex maiori et civibus suis Northamptonie, salutem.

Occasione cuiusdam magne contencionis in villa Cantabrigiensi triennio iam elapso suborte nonnulli clericorum tunc ibidem studencium unanimiter ab ipsa villa recessissent, se usque ad villam nostram predictam Northamptonie transferentes et ibidem (studiis inherendo) novam construere Universitatem cupientes: nos illo tempore credentes villam illam ex hoc posse meliorari, et nobis utilitatem non modicam inde provenire, votis dictorum clericorum ad eorum requisicionem annuebamus in hac parte. Nunc autem cum ex relatu multorum fide dignorum veraciter intelleximus quod ex huiusmodi Universitate (si permaneret ibidem) municipium nostrum Oxonie quod ab antiquo creatum est, et a progenitoribus nostris regibus Anglie confirmatum, ac ad commoditatem studencium communiter approbatum, non mediocriter lederetur, quod nulla racione vellemus, maxime cum universis episcopis terre nostre ad honorem Dei et utilitatem ecclesie Anglicane et profectum studencium videatur expedire, quod Universitas amoveatur a villa predicta, sicut per literas suas patentes accepimus. Vobis de consilio magnatum nostrorum firmiter inhibemus ne in villa nostra de cetero aliquam Universitatem esse, nec aliquos studentes ibidem manere permittatis, aliter quam ante creacionem dicte Universitatis fieri consuevit. Teste rege apud Westmonasterium primo die Februarii anno regni quadragesimo nono.

of his oath. But they said to him, 'Far be this from you, king, for the sons of your great men and others of your realm came here with your University, and if you hang or behead them, those who are now on your side will rise against you, as they will not allow the blood of their sons and relations to be shed if they can help it.' So the king was pacified and his anger against the clerks cooled.

Suppression of Northampton University. 1 Feb. 1265.

The king to his mayor and citizens of Northampton, greeting.

On account of a great contest which arose in the town of Cambridge three years ago some of the clerks studying there unanimously left that town and transferred themselves to our said town of Northampton and desired, with a view to adhering to their studies, to establish a new University there: we, believing at the time that town would be benefited by this, and that no small benefit would accrue to us therefrom, assented at their request to the wishes of the said clerks in this behalf. But now, as we are truly informed by the statements of many trustworthy persons that our borough of Oxford, which is of ancient foundation, and was confirmed by our ancestors kings of England, and is commonly commended for its advantage to students, would suffer no little damage from such University, if it remained there, which we by no means wish, and especially as it appears to all the bishops of our realm, as we learn from their letters patent, that it would be for the honour of God, and the benefit of the Church of England, and the advancement of students that the University should be removed from the town aforesaid; we, by the advice of our great men, firmly order that there shall henceforth be no University in our said town, and that you shall not allow any students to remain there otherwise than was customary before the creation of the said University. Witness, the king at Westminster, 1 Feb. in the 49th year of his reign.

The Earliest University College in England at Salisbury. 1262.

[*Sarum Ch. and Doc.* (Rolls Series, No. 9), p. 334, from Mun. Salisbury, Lib. B 404, C 420; Reg. Rubr. 404.]

Carta super ordinatione domus Vallis Scholarium Sarum.

In nomine domini nostri Jesu Christi, Amen. Nos Egidius, Dei patientia Sarum episcopus, ad honorem ejusdem Domini et gloriosae virginis Mariae et beati Nicholai, pro salute animae nostrae et pro animabus benefactorum nostrorum et omnium eorum pro quibus quocunque titulo vel modo sumus astricti, duximus fundare, instituere, aedificare, et construere domum in usum et proprietatem scholarium, quae Vallis Scholarium beati Nicholai vocabitur, in perpetuum, de consensu et assensu domini Roberti decani et capituli Sarum, magistri et fratrum hospitalis beati Nicholai Sarum, in prato juxta ecclesiam cathedralem Sarum et viam regiam ante dictum hospitale, ad perpetuas receptiones, receptationem, et sustentationem unius custodis pro tempore, duorum capellanorum, et viginti pauperum, egenorum, honestorum et docibilium scolarium ibidem Deo et beato Nicholao servientium, et inibi amodo viventium, in divina pagina et liberalibus artibus studentium et proficientium; quem quidem locum cum omnibus pertinentiis suis, pro nobis et successoribus nostris, dictis custodi et successoribus suis, dictis capellanis, et scolaribus successoribusque eorum per dictum custodem qui pro tempore fuerit recipiendis, damus et concedimus, in liberam, puram, et perpetuam elemosinam in perpetuum duraturam; et ipsum locum cum suis ibidem pertinentiis ab omni exactione et censu mundano et ecclesiastico, sectis curiarum et hundredorum, et sequelis quibuscunque, et ab omni seculari servitio et demanda, pro nobis et successoribus nostris in perpetuum constituimus, immunem, liberum et quietum.

The Earliest University College in England at Salisbury. 1262.

Deed of ordinance of the House of the Valley Scholars at Salisbury.

In the name of our Lord Jesus Christ, Amen. We, Giles [of Bridport], by the sufferance of God bishop of Salisbury, to the honour of the same Lord, the glorious Virgin Mary and Blessed Nicholas, for the health of our soul and for the souls of our benefactors and all those for whom we are under whatsoever title or manner bound, have thought fit to found, establish, build and construct a house for the use and ownership of scholars, which shall be called the house of the Valley Scholars of the Blessed Nicholas, for ever, with the consent and assent of Sir Robert, dean, and the chapter of 'Salisbury, of the master and brethren of the Blessed Nicholas' Hospital of Salisbury, in a meadow near the cathedral church of Salisbury and the king's way in front of the said hospital, for the perpetual reception and maintenance of a warden for the time being, two chaplains and 20 poor, needy, well-behaved and teachable scholars serving God and the Blessed Nicholas there, and there living, studying and becoming proficient in the Holy Scriptures and the liberal arts; which place with all its appurtenances we for ourselves and our successors give and grant to the said warden and his successors and the said chaplains and scholars and their successors to be received by the said warden for the time being, in free, pure and perpetual alms to endure for ever; and the same place we with its appurtenances there for ourselves and our successors make immune, free and quit for ever from all exaction and tax, secular or ecclesiastical, from suit of court and hundred, and all their consequences, and from all secular service and demand.

Item, habitis [in]super deliberatione et tractatu diligenti, statuimus, constituimus, et statuendo ordinamus, quod custos praedictae domus, capellanorum et scolarium praedictorum, post cessionem vel decessum domini Johannis de Holteby, canonici Sarum, nunc ejusdem domus custodis, de communi nominatione supradicti solius decani et capituli, et de gremio ejusdem capituli in posterum assumatur, et eorum duntaxat praeficiatur approbatione, assensu, et voluntate; hoc etiam adjecto, quod si eum ex causa viderint ammovendum, causa in communi inter eos absque judiciaria solemnitate examinata et approbata, eundem ammoveant, nullo sibi contra hujus ammotionem ex appellationis beneficio remedio competituro. Et ut cautius in his prospiciatur, statuimus et ordinamus quod idem custos in administrationis susceptione paciscatur et juret se a praedicta ammotionis sententia non appellaturum.

Item, statuimus, constituimus, et statuendo ordinamus, quod idem custos correctionem plenariam habeat tam in temporalibus quam in spiritualibus infra ambitum praedictae domus et ibidem pertinentia, salva gravatis ad eundem decanum duntaxat, et non ultra, appellandi facultate.

Item, statuimus, constituimus, et ordinamus, quod supradicti decanus et capitulum dictae domus sint in perpetuum patroni, et ipsius domus patronatum cum pertinentiis habitis et habendis eisdem decano et capitulo tenore praesentium damus et confirmamus in perpetuum.

Et ut supradictae fundatio, institutio, donationes et concessiones, statuta et ordinationes, ratae et stabiles maneant in perpetuum, tam nos quam praedicti decanus et capitulum, magister et fratres supradicti praesentem scripturam ad perpetuam supradictorum memoriam omnium et singulorum approbationem, sigillorum nostrorum impressionibus roboravimus et confirmavimus.

His testibus: magistro Radulfo de Hegham, cancellario, Radulfo de Eboraco, Rogero de la Grene, archidiacono Wyltes [etc.].

Also, after diligent consultation and consideration we decree, establish and by statute ordain that the warden of the said house, chaplains and scholars aforesaid, after the cession or decease of Sir John of Holtby, canon of Salisbury, now warden of the same house, shall thereafter be chosen by the joint nomination of the dean and chapter only and from the bosom of the same chapter, and be preferred by their sole approval, consent and will; this, too, is to be added, that if they shall see cause for removing him, after the cause has been examined and approved, though without judicial solemnity, by them in common, they may remove him, without any remedy being open to him against such removal by way of appeal. And that greater caution may be exercised in this matter, we decree and ordain that the same warden on taking up the administration shall promise and swear that he will not appeal from the said sentence of removal.

Also we decree and establish and by statute ordain that the same warden shall have full power of correction both in temporal and spiritual matters within the circuit of the same house and its appurtenances, saving to those aggrieved a right of appeal to the same dean only and not further.

Also we decree, establish and ordain that the aforesaid dean and chapter shall be perpetual patrons of the same house, and we give and confirm the patronage of the same house with all that is held or to be held as appurtenant thereto by the tenor of these presents to the same dean and chapter for ever.

And that the aforesaid foundation, institution, gifts and grants, statutes and ordinances may remain ratified and established for ever, we and the aforesaid dean and chapter and the master and brethren before mentioned, have ratified and confirmed this present writing in perpetual remembrance of all and singular the premises by impressions of our seals.

These being witnesses: Master Ralf of Heigham, chancellor, Ralf of York, Roger of the Green, the archdeacon of Wiltshire [etc.].

Dispute as to Jurisdiction of Chancellor and Sub-dean of Salisbury over University Scholars there. 1278.

[H. Rashdall, *Univ. of Europe*, II., pt ii. 765, from Salisbury Lib. Ruber, f. 99.]

De iurisdictione Cancellarii Sarum.

Die mercurii viij Idus Martii anno domini MCC^{mo} septuagesimo viij, cum de iurisdictione inter scolares in Ciuitate Saresberiensi studiorum causa commorantes exercenda inter cancellarium et subdecanum predictos, quorum uterque iurisdictionem ipsam ad suum officium pertinere dicebat, dissentio quedam exorta fuisset, tandem habito super hoc tractatu in capitulo die ipsa de utriusque expresso consensu conuenerunt in hunc modum—uidelicet quod dictus dominus cancellarius, ad cuius officium pertinet scolas regere, inter omnes scolares, cuiuscumque facultatis existant, studiorum causa in ciuitate ipsa commorantes, qui tanquam scolares certi doctoris, cuius scolas frequentant, recommendationem et testimonium habeant, de contencionibus ciuilibus et personalibus que pecuniarum interesse respiciunt, et scolasticis omnibus contractibus et eciam si laicus aliquem huiusmodi scolarium in consimilibus causis impetere uoluerit, cognoscat et diffiniat, et presbyteri ciuitatis decreta et preapta eiusdem cancellarii in hiis exequi teneantur. De aliis uero clericis et qui extra studium certi doctoris scolas minime frequentantes ibidem moram fecerint, et de scolaribus ipsis, si forsan de lapsu carnis seu delicto alio ibidem commisso quod ad correccionem pertineat et salutem respiciat animarum, uocati fuerint, subdecanus ipse, qui est archidiaconus ciuitatis, iurisdiccionem et correccionem habeat, exceptis tamen uicariis et clericis maioris ecclesie tam studentibus quam aliis, in quos decanus cum capitulo et non alius ipso presente, et subdecanus similiter cum capitulo decano absente, secundum hactenus obtentam ecclesie consuetudinem, omnimodam iurisdiccionem et cohercionem exercebunt : ita quod cancellarius ipse per se nullatenus intromittat de eisdem.

Dispute as to Jurisdiction of Chancellor and Subdean of Salisbury over University Scholars there. 1278.

Of the jurisdiction of the Chancellor of Salisbury.

On Wednesday, 8 March 1278, whereas a dispute had arisen between the chancellor and the subdean as to the jurisdiction over the scholars living in Salisbury for the sake of pursuing their studies, each of them saying that the jurisdiction was appurtenant to his office, after debate in the chapter on the matter, an agreement was come to on the same day with the express consent of both parties in these terms; viz. that the said sir chancellor, whose office it is to rule schools, shall have the cognizance and determination of all civil and personal actions which concern any pecuniary interest and all scholastic contracts, even if a layman want to implead any scholar in cases of that kind, between all scholars of whatever faculty they may be, who are living in the same city and have the recommendation and testimonial of a particular doctor, whose school they attend, and the city priests shall be bound to obey the decrees and orders of the chancellor in such matters. But the subdean, who is archdeacon of the city, shall have the jurisdiction over and punishment of other clerks and those outside the University who are living there without attending the school of a particular teacher, and of scholars themselves if they are summoned for fornication or other crime there committed which is a matter of the cure of souls; except, however, the vicars and clerks of the cathedral, both students and others, over whom the dean and chapter and no one else if the dean is present, and the subdean and chapter if the dean is absent, shall, according to the custom of the church heretofore observed, exercise the sole jurisdiction and power of punishment; and the chancellor as such shall not interfere at all with them.

Foundation of the House of Scholars of Merton, at Maldon. 1264.

[*Stat. Coll. Oxford*, I., printed by University Commissioners, 1853.]

In nomine Dei, omnipotentis Patris, et Filii et Spiritus Sancti, in honore ejusdem Sanctae et Individuae Trinitatis et Beatissimae Dei Genetricis Mariae, et Beati Johannis Baptistae Christi praecursoris, atque Sanctorum omnium, ego Walterus de Merton, illustris domini Henrici Regis Angliae, filii Regis Johannis, quondam Cancellarius, tam auctoritate mihi a dicto domino meo Rege concessa, quam ratione juris et potestatis quae mihi in meis maneriis de Maudon et de Farleigh cum eorum pertinentiis competunt, do, assigno et concedo maneria ipsa, cum omnibus pertinentiis suis, quocunque nomine censeri possint, ad fundationem Domus, quam dici volo et nuncupari Domum Scholarium de Merton, quam et ego, in profectum Ecclesiae sanctae Dei, pro salute animae domini mei Regis praedicti et animarum domini Richardi quondam Dunelmensis Episcopi, Richardi quondam Comitis Gloverniae et Hereford, Gilberti, filii ejus, Willelmi de Whatevill et Petri de Codynton, necnon parentum et benefactorum meorum omnium, auctoritate venerabilis patris Johannis Wintoniensis Episcopi loci dioecesani interveniente, necnon et consensu capituli sui, in dicto manerio de Maudon statuo, fundo et stabilio, ad perpetuam sustentationem viginti scholarium in scholis degentium Oxoniae, vel alibi ubi studium vigere contigerit, et ad sustentationem duorum vel trium ministrorum altaris Christi in dicta Domo residentium; sub conditione et modo subscriptis, tam circa scholares quam ministros praedictos, Domino largiente, inposterum observandis.

Circa scholares siquidem praedictos hanc statuo conditionem. Successionem, scilicet quae meis haeredibus, secundum regni consuetudinem, in dictis maneriis debeatur, in profectum Ecclesiae sanctae et nostri generis sempiternum,

Foundation of the House of Scholars of Merton, at Maldon. 1264.

In the name of God, the Almighty Father, and the Son and the Holy Ghost, in honour of the same Holy and Undivided Trinity and of God's most blessed mother Mary, and of the blessed John the Baptist, the forerunner of Christ, and of all Saints, I, Walter of Merton, late chancellor of the illustrious lord Henry, king of England, son of King John, both by the authority granted me by my said lord the king, and by reason of the right and power which belong to me in my manors of Maldon and Farleigh with their appurtenances, give, assign and grant the same manors with all their appurtenances, by whatsoever name they may be called, for the foundation of a house which I wish to be called and named 'The House of Merton's scholars,' which too I, for the profit of the holy church of God, for the health of the soul of my lord the king aforesaid, and of the souls of the lord Richard, late bishop of Durham, of Richard, late earl of Gloucester and Hereford, and Gilbert his son, of William of Whatvill and Peter of Codyngton, also of all my parents and benefactors, with the authority of the venerable father John, bishop of Winchester, the diocesan of the place, and also the consent of his chapter, in the said manor of Maldon, constitute, found, and establish for the perpetual maintenance of 20 scholars living in the schools at Oxford, or elsewhere where a University may happen to flourish, and for the maintenance of two or three ministers of the altar of Christ living in the said house; on the condition and in the manner underwritten, to be hereafter observed, by the largesse of God, as well about the scholars as about the ministers aforesaid.

As to the scholars aforesaid I establish this condition. The succession, which was due to my heirs according to the custom of the realm in the said manors, I, under the eye of God, change for the everlasting profit of holy Church and my

ad laudem nostri conditoris perpetuam, quam in ipso genere augeri et continuari cupio et exopto, sic, Deo inspectore, commuto, ut scholares supradicti de nostra sint parentela, quamdiu honesti et habiles ac proficere volentes in ipsa reperiantur. Ubi autem in ea tales, usque ad complementum numeri supradicti, reperiri non poterunt, alii honesti et habiles, maxime de Wintoniensi dioecesi, loco eorum qui de numero supradicto defuerint, subrogentur.

Habebunt autem singuli scholarium ipsorum annis singulis quadraginta solidos sterlingorum ad minus, vel quinquaginta solidos seu quatuor marcas, si ad hoc res sufficere possit ; quos per manus Custodis ejusdem Domus terminis competentibus recipiant annuatim. In hospitio quoque, quantum sine impedimento suae instructionis fieri poterit, simul habitabunt, indumentis se consimilibus, in signum unitatis ac dilectionis mutuae, vestientes.

Hanc autem sustentationem plene et integre habeant scholares supradicti dum bene et honeste se habuerint : ita quoque quod si eorum aliqui in fata concedant, vel religionis habitum assumant, aut ad aliorum obsequia se transferant, beneficia uberiora sortiantur, a studio recesserint, aut studio pro suo modulo se applicare noluerint, de turpitudine aliqua publice notati fuerint, vel alias minus bene et honeste se habuerint, et de hoc per suos socios sufficienter constare possit, subtrahatur eis sustentatio praedicta, et alii de genere praedicto vel de aliis, ut praedictum est, loco ipsorum libere subrogentur, qui per scholares praedictos sub debito fidelitatis suae nominabuntur de genere praedicto, dum in eo habiles et honesti reperiantur, vel de aliis si in ipso hujusmodi nequeant reperiri.

Et si forte in hujusmodi nominatione minime concordes inveniantur, tunc Cancellarius seu Rector Universitatis ubi ipsos agere contigerit, aut Custos dictae Domus, si Cancellarius aut Rector praedicti id infra mensem efficere non curaverint, illos ad dictam sustentationem admitti decernat, quos per sex

family to the perpetual praise of our founder, which I wish and hope will be increased and continued in the same family, so that the scholars aforesaid shall be of my family, as long as in the same there shall be found men upright and able and desirous of proficiency. But when such cannot be found in it for the completion of the number aforesaid, other honest and able persons, especially from the diocese of Winchester, shall be substituted in the place of those who fall short of the number aforesaid.

Each of the same scholars shall have 40*s.* sterling at least, or 50*s.* or 4 marks [£2. 13*s.* 4*d.*], every year, if there are means to provide this; which they shall receive at proper terms yearly from the warden of the same house. They shall live together in their inn, so far as this can be done without hindrance to their learning, clothing themselves in similar clothes as a mark of their union and mutual affection.

This maintenance the scholars aforesaid shall have fully and wholly as long as they behave themselves well and like gentlemen; on condition, however, that if any of them yield to fate, or take the religious habit, or transfer themselves to other duties, obtain better benefices, depart from the University, or refuse to apply themselves to study after their capacity, are publicly defamed of anything disgraceful, or otherwise behave themselves badly or in an ungentlemanly way, and this can be sufficiently proved by their colleagues, then the aforesaid maintenance shall be taken away from them, and others of the family aforesaid, or of the others, as is aforesaid, shall be freely substituted in their place, being nominated by the scholars aforesaid as their faculty requires from the family aforesaid, so long as able and well-behaved persons can be found in it, or from others if none such can be found in the family.

And if by chance they cannot agree in such nomination, then the chancellor or rector of the University where they may happen to be, or the warden of the said house, if the chancellor or rector aforesaid have not taken care to do it within a month, shall order to be admitted to the said maintenance, those

vel septem de provectioribus et discretioribus scholarium ipsorum, sub debito juramenti eorundem, honestiores intellexerint et habiliores. Illis autem quibus dicta sustentacio ex culpa sua vel ex causis aliis praedictis subtracta fuerit, nulla competat actio contra Custodem Domus supradictae vel alios; dum tamen liqueat quod ex sua culpa aut ex causis aliis praedictis dicta fuerint sustentatione privati.

Si vero parvuli aliqui de parentela praedicta, suis orbati parentibus, aut alias pro exilitate parentum suorum, sustentatione careant dum in puerilibus rudimentis primitus instruantur, tunc Custos ipse, si facultates sufficiant, eos erudiri faciat in Domo praedicta, donec in scholis proficere possint si ad hoc habiles inveniantur; et de illis in subrogationem superius expressam sumantur, qui ad hoc habiles et idonei reperientur.

Annis autem singulis, in festo videlicet Exaltationis Sanctae Crucis, decem vel octo de provectioribus et discretioribus scholarium ipsorum apud Domum supradictam vice omnium conveniant, ibidem per octo dies, si velint, in signum proprietatis et dominii quod eis gratia dictae sustentationis ibi competit, utpote quorum nuncupatione Domus ipsa nomen sortitur, moram facturi. Quibus etiam licebit modis quibus poterunt inquirere diligenter utrum Custos Domus supradictae in administratione rerum et possessionum ejusdem bene se habuerit, honeste et circumspecte; et si aliud reperiatur hoc ei denuntiare ad quem rei hujusmodi correctio pertinebit. Similiter autem, et aliis anni temporibus, si de Custode praedicto sinistrum aliquod audiatur, licebit duobus vel tribus ex dictis scholaribus hujusmodi investigationem ac denuntiationem facere quotiens viderint expedire....

Custos autem dictae Domus et ministri altaris Domini

whom they shall learn from six or seven of the more advanced and discreet of the same scholars under oath to be of the best character and ability. Those from whom the said maintenance is taken away through their own fault or any of the causes before-mentioned, shall have no cause of action against the warden of the house aforesaid or others, as long as it appears that they were deprived of the said maintenance through their own fault or from one of the other causes before-mentioned.

If there are any little boys of the kinship aforesaid, who, through being orphans, or otherwise through the poverty of their parents, are in want of maintenance while they are being instructed in the rudiments of primary education, then the warden himself, if means suffice, shall cause them to be educated in the house aforesaid until they can become proficient in the schools, if they are found fit for this; and those to be substituted as before expressed shall be taken from them, if they shall be found able and fit for it.

Every year, on the Exaltation of the Holy Cross [14 Sept.], ten or eight of the older and more discreet scholars shall, on behalf of them all, meet at the said house, and stay there for eight days, if they wish it, in sign of the property and ownership which belongs to them there for their said maintenance, as it is from them that the house itself obtains its name. They may inquire in all possible ways whether the warden of the house aforesaid has properly conducted the administration of its goods and possessions; and if anything shall be discovered shall report it to him whose business it is to put it right. In like manner if at any other time of the year anything adverse is reported of the warden aforesaid, two or three of the said scholars may make such inquiry and report as often as they shall consider it expedient...

[Provision to be made for the warden when superannuated among the brethren of the house.

Provision for the number of scholars being increased if the revenues increase.]

The warden of the said house and the ministers of the

ibidem commorantes, necnon et scholares ipsi, cum ibi modo et occasione praedictis convenerint, pane et cervisia et uno ferculo carnium seu piscium sibi competente absque murmure sint contenti ; ita tamen quod gratia hospitum aut aliarum necessitatum de dicta domo uberius liceat providendum : tamen dictorum scholarium numerus exinde non minus amplietur; sed respectum semper habeant Custos et fratres ibi commorantes ad fructum ex hujusmodi scholarium exhibitione perpetuis temporibus profuturum, et eam potius augere studeant quam suae voluptati aliquid tribuere, quod eis, quorum sunt procuratores et ministri, ex ordinatione praesenti seu hac institutione debeatur.

Si autem incurabilis sit aegritudo praedicta, per quod scholaris ille in studio vel alibi ad victum suum honeste consequendum sufficere non possit, et ipse de nostro genere existat, tunc gratia successionis meae, quam in scholares praedictos transfundo, ministrentur ei victus et vestitus ad totam vitam suam in Domo supradicta.

Custos vero Domus supradictae, cum ibi ponendus fuerit, nominetur per duodecim provectiores scholarium praedictorum, de consilio fratrum dictae Domus : qui, sub obtentu felicitatis aeternae, omni favore humano postposito, talem studeant nominare qui melior et fidelior in administratione rerum et negotiorum dictae Domus haberi poterit, Domino largiente. Et ipse postmodum Domino Wyntoniensi Episcopo, loci dioecesano qui pro tempore fuerit, per ipsos praesentetur, qui ei custodiam Domus praedictae, si ad hoc idoneus extiterit, committat.

Injungo autem scholaribus praedictis, in virtute Dei et sub obtentu vitae praesentis et futurae, ut cum, praestante Domino, ad uberiorem fortunam devenerint, Domum praedictam in licitis et honestis promovere studeant, ac ejus defensioni, necnon et eorum quae ad eam pertinent, cum opus fuerit, diligenter insistant.

altar of the Lord living there and the scholars themselves, when they shall meet there in the manner and on the occasion mentioned, shall be content with bread and beer and one appropriate dish of flesh or fish, without grumbling; on the understanding, however, that better provision may be made for guests or other necessary reasons; so, however, that the increase in the number of the scholars shall not be thereby lessened. But the warden and brethren living there shall always have regard to the fruit which will always accrue from the maintenance of such scholars, and shall rather be zealous to increase that than to contribute to their own pleasure, as this is due by the present ordinance or institution to them, whose proctors and servants they are.

[A scholar becoming ill during visitation of the house may be kept there for not more than a quarter of a year.]

If, however, his illness is incurable, so that the scholar cannot, at the university or elsewhere, learn an honest living, and he is of my kin, then in recognition of the succession to me which I transform into the scholars aforesaid, food and clothing shall be given him all his life in the house aforesaid.

[Any freeman in Merton's service when he dies unable to earn his living to be also maintained in the house according to his station.]

The warden of the house, when one is to be placed therein, shall be nominated by the twelve seniors of the scholars aforesaid, with the advice of the brethren of the house; and they shall endeavour to nominate, in view of their eternal happiness, putting aside all favour to man, the one who shall be found, by the grace of the Lord, the best and most faithful administrator of the property and business of the said house. And he shall then be presented to the lord bishop of Winchester, the diocesan of the place for the time being, who shall commit to him the guardianship of the house aforesaid, if he shall be fit for it.

[The bishop of Winchester to be patron and protector of the house and scholars.]

I enjoin the scholars aforesaid in virtue of God and having regard to this and the future life, that when, by the aid of the Lord, they have come to ampler fortune, they shall endeavour to promote the house aforesaid in all lawful and honest ways and diligently assist in its defence and that of everything belonging to it, when need shall be.

Domui etiam Sancti Johannis Baptistae de Basingestoke, quam dominus Rex supradictus, in meo territorio et fundo, ad sustentationem ministrorum altaris Christi et pauperum infirmantium, precum mearum instantia, fundavit et stabilivit, obnoxii semper sint et devoti, et eam augeant, secundum quod eis Dominus gratiam inspiraverit ac sibi concesserit facultatem. Domui insuper de Merton, a qua nomen sortiuntur, grati semper sint, et eam utpote hujus operis adjutricem studeant honorare.

Singulis etiam annis semel vel bis, in locis ubi eos agere contigerit, conveniant, et pro suo Fundatore atque aliis suis benefactoribus vivis et defunctis divina celebrari procurent; horumque tenorem, pro memoria et conservatione hujus eleemosinae, ibidem recitari faciant, et suas intentiones in profectum Ecclesiae sacrosanctae dirigant, ac sui Conditoris honorem et nominis sui laudem totis affectibus studeant ampliare...

Illud quoque insuper attendendum est quod si pro dictorum scholarium et fratrum commoditate locus habitationis apud Farleigh, aut alibi in suo territorio, pro situ loci aut causis aliis emergentibus sit competentior, et ad locum hujusmodi ipsi se transferant, vel per alium hujus adjutorem operis transferantur, nihil eis idcirco juris seu possessionis depereat in dictis maneriis seu rebus aliis sibi assignatis, vel deinceps ex pia largitione fidelium assignandis; dum tamen hanc institutionem, tam re quam nomine, teneant et observent, et se suasque possessiones alteri collegio non adjungant.

Ad memoriam rei hujus sempiternam, et ut haec ordinatio et provisio salubris robur obtineant perpetuae firmitatis, sigilla praedictorum domini Henrici Regis et domini Johannis Wyntoniensis Episcopi, necnon et Capituli sui, in sui consensus et approbationis suae testimonium, praesentibus, una cum sigillo meo, apponi procuravi. Datis anno Domini M°CC° sexagesimo quarto.

They shall also always be aiding and devoted to the House of Saint John the Baptist of Basingstoke, which the aforesaid lord the king at my petition founded and established in my domain and property, for the maintenance of ministers of Christ's altar and infirm poor, and shall augment it as the Lord shall inspire them and give them means to do so. To the House of Merton, too, from which they take their name, they shall be ever grateful, and be zealous to honour it as a helper in this work.

Also once or twice in every year they shall meet in the places where they are studying and procure service to be celebrated for their founder and other their benefactors, living and dead; and shall cause the tenor of these presents to be read aloud there in memory and for the preservation of this charity, and shall direct their minds to the profit of the most holy church, and endeavour to enhance the honour of their Creator and the praises of His name with all their strength.

[To do their fealty to the lord of the manor, unless he releases it.]

This also is to be borne in mind, that if, by reason of the site or other causes, a better place for the dwelling of the said scholars and brethren be found at Farleigh or elsewhere on their demesne, and they transfer themselves there or are transferred there by another helper in this work, they shall not therefore lose any right or possession in the said manors or other property assigned to them, or hereafter to be assigned to them by the generosity of the faithful; so long as they keep and observe this foundation in word and deed, and do not annex themselves and their possessions to another college.

In everlasting remembrance of this matter, and that this healthful ordinance and provision may obtain the strength of perpetual confirmation, I have procured the seals of the aforesaid lord King Henry and the lord John, bishop of Winchester, and his chapter, to be affixed, together with my own, to these presents, in witness of their consent and approval. Given A.D. 1264.

Statutes of Merton College in the University of Oxford. 1274.

[*Ib.* I. 23.]

CAP. I. De concessione maneriorum Maldon et Farlegh.

In nomine gloriosissimae et individuae Trinitatis, Patris, et Filii, et Spiritus Sancti. Amen.

Ego, Walterus de Merton, clericus, illustris domini Regis Angliae quondam Cancellarius, de Summi rerum et bonorum Opificis bonitate confisus, ejusdem gratiae qui vota hominum pro sua voluntate ad bonum disponit et dirigit fidenter invisus, animique revolutione saepe sollicitus si quid sui nominis honori retribuam pro hiis quae mihi in hac vita abundanter retribuit, Domum, quam Scholarium de Merton intitulari seu nuncupari volui et mandavi, et quam in meo solo proprio meis laboribus acquisito, videlicet, apud Maldon in comitatu Surriensi, ad perpetuam sustentationem scholarium in scholis degentium, pro salute animae meae [and other souls] ante turbationem in Anglia nuper subortam, fundavi et stabilivi, nunc, pace Angliae reformata ac pristina turbatione sedata, animi stabilitate perpetua approbo, stabilio et confirmo, locumque sibi habitationis et domum Oxoniae, ubi Universitas viget studentium, in meo territorio proprio, ecclesiae Sancti Johannis contermino, concedo et assigno. Quam siquidem Domum scholarium de Merton nuncupari volo, atque in ea scholares perpetuo moraturos esse decerno. Cui siquidem Domui, seu scholaribus in eadem, Altissimo concedente, imperpetuum moraturis, maneria mea de Maldon et de Farlegh cum suis pertinentiis, quae pro ipsorum scholarium et ministrorum altaris, qui in ea residentes erunt, sustentatione perpetua, tempore dictae turbationis contuli, etiam in praesenti, pace regni reformata, concedo, ipsamque collationem spontanea et libera voluntate approbo, ac deliberato judicio ratifico et

Statutes of Merton College in the University of Oxford. 1274.

CHAPTER I. Of the grant of the manors of Maldon and Farleigh.

In the name of the most glorious and undivided Trinity, Father, and Son, and Holy Ghost. Amen.

I, Walter of Merton, clerk, formerly chancellor of the illustrious lord the King of England, trusting in the goodness of the Great Maker of property and possessions, confidently relying on the grace of Him who disposes the desires of men to good and directs them at His will, and after anxiously turning over in my mind what I can contribute to the honour of His name in return for those things which He has abundantly contributed to me in my life, before the disturbances that lately arose in England founded and established a house, which I wished and directed should be entitled or called 'of the Scholars of Merton,' in my own property acquired by my own labours at Maldon in the county of Surrey, for the perpetual maintenance of scholars studying in the schools, for the health of my soul [etc.], now when the peace of England has been re-established and the former disturbances have been quieted, with stable mind I approve, establish and confirm, and grant and assign to them the place of their habitation and house at Oxford, where a university of students flourishes, on my own land adjoining St John's church; which I will shall be called 'the House of the Scholars of Merton' and in it I decree the scholars shall dwell for ever. And to this house, or to the scholars for ever dwelling in the same, by the grant of the Highest, I have transferred my manors of Maldon and Farleigh with their appurtenances, which I gave in the time of disturbance, for the perpetual maintenance of the same scholars and the ministers of the altar who shall reside therein, and now when the peace of the realm has been restored grant and approve, and with deliberate judgment ratify and confirm the

confirmo. Quae etiam maneria dictis scholaribus, una cum aliis per me sibi acquisitis et acquirendis, apud eosdem scholares et fratres perpetuo permanere decerno, sub forma et conditionibus infrascriptis, tam circa personas quam circa regulam eorundem, annuente Domino, futuris temporibus jugiter observandis.

Cap. 2. De legistis et scholaribus in Domo degentibus.

Hanc igitur formam statuo (quam et imperpetuum observandam decerno), ut in ipsa Domo, quae Scholarium de Merton nuncupatur, perpetuo sint scholares literarum studio deputati, qui artium, seu philosophiae, canonum seu theologiae, studio vacare tenebuntur. Quorum pars major artium liberalium et philosophiae studio vacent, donec de sui Custodis et Sociorum arbitrio, tanquam in hiis laudabiliter provecti, ad studium se transferant theologiae. Quatuor autem vel quinque ex sui superioris providentia, quos ipse habiles et ad hoc aptos decreverit, in jure canonico licenter studeant. Cum quibus etiam ipse Superior, ut jura civilia ad tempus audiant, quatenus expedire viderit, poterit dispensare. Sit etiam in ipsa congregatione grammaticus unus qui studio grammaticae totaliter vacet, sibique, de bonis Domus ipsius, librorum copia et alia necessaria ministrentur; et eorum qui studio grammaticae fuerint applicati curam habeat; et ad ipsum etiam provectiores in dubiis suae facultatis habeant absque rubore regressum; sub cujus etiam magisterio scholares ipsi, de quibus et ubi expedire videbitur pro suae promptitudinis commodo, Latino fruantur eloquio seu idiomate vulgari, et ipse pro viribus singulos fideliter instruere teneatur.

Cap. 7. De officio decanorum etc.

De scholaribus autem supradictis aliqui de discretioribus eligantur, qui sub ipso Custode, tanquam ejus coadjutores, minus provectorum curam, qualiter in studio et morum honestate proficiant, agere teneantur. Adeo ut numero cuilibet

same transfer of my own free will. And I decree that these manors with other property acquired or to be acquired by me for them shall always remain with the same scholars and brethren in the form and on the conditions underwritten to be continually observed in time to come, the Lord willing, as well as regards the persons as their rule of life.

CHAPTER 2. Of the lawyers and scholars living in the house.

This form then I constitute and decree to be for ever observed that in this house, called the House of the Scholars of Merton, there shall be for ever scholars devoted to learning, and bound to devote their time to the study of arts, philosophy, canon law or theology. And the greater part of them shall devote themselves to the study of the liberal arts and philosophy, until at the will of the warden and fellows, as being persons who have been laudably proficient in them, they transfer themselves to the study of theology. But four or five of them shall be allowed by the provision of their superior, he declaring that they are able and apt for this, to study canon law. And the same superior may dispense them for a time to hear lectures in civil law if it shall appear expedient. There shall be also in the assembly a grammarian who shall devote his whole time to a grammar school, and books and other necessaries shall be provided for him from the possessions of the house; and he shall have the care of those who are applying themselves to the study of grammar; and even the seniors, if they have any doubts in their own faculties, shall have resort to him without blushing; and under his mastership the scholars themselves, if and when it shall seem to be for the benefit of their own readiness, shall speak Latin or the vulgar idiom [French], and he shall be bound to instruct each of them faithfully to the utmost of his capacity.

CHAPTER 7. Of the deans' duties etc.

Some of the more discreet of the aforesaid scholars shall be elected to take charge, under the warden and as his assistants, of the less advanced as to their progress in learning and

vicenario vel etiam decenario, si necesse fuerit, praesit unus, et iis, dum aliorum curam diligenter expleverint in aliquo, caeteris provideatur uberius, prout videatur honestum. Sit nihilominus in qualibet camera, in qua praefati commanent scholares, unus caeteris maturitate provectior, qui etiam aliis superintendat sociis, et per quem de ipsorum moribus et studiis profectu ipsi Custodi Domus, caeterisque in hujusmodi cura praepositis, ac ipsi congregationi scholarium, si opus fuerit, innotescat.

Cap. 8. De mensa scholarium.

Porro scholares sub ipso Custode et aliis praepositis, vicenariis videlicet et Decanis, in ipsa Domo studendi officio deputati, mensam communem habeant, et etiam habitum conformum quantum possunt.

Cap. 40. De educatione parvulorum etc.

Caeterum, cum successionem quae meis haeredibus seu parentelae meae, secundum regni consuetudinem, in meis feodalibus debeatur, in hanc eleemosynam, Deo inspectore, commutaverim, ut supradictum est, volo et statuo, ut, si parvuli aliqui de parentela praedicta, suis orbati parentibus, aut alias pro exilitate parentum suorum sustentatione careant, dum in puerilibus rudimentis primitus instruantur, tunc Custos ipse eos usque ad tredecim numerum erudiri faciat in Domo praedicta, donec in scholis proficere possint, si ad hoc habiles inveniantur; et de illis, in subrogationem scholarium superius expressam, sumantur qui ad hoc habiles reperientur et idonei.

Et, ne in dicta Domo vel societate praedicta pestis pullulet, quae per carnis illecebras toties vexat incautos, singula praedictae Domus ministeria, ad minus infra septa curiae Domus scholarium necnon et manerii de Maldon, et alibi, quatenus alibi fieri poterit, perpetuis temporibus fiant per mares.

Ad horum autem omnium memoriam et securitatem sempiternam, sigillum serenissimi Principis domini Edwardi Regis

conduct. So that over every twenty, or ten, if necessary, there shall be a president, and more ample provision as appears proper shall be made for them while they diligently fulfil their charge of the rest. Also in each chamber in which the aforesaid scholars live there shall be one more mature than the rest, who shall superintend his fellows, and shall report to the warden of the house himself and the rest of the prepositors having charge and to the assembly of scholars itself, if necessary, on their progress in morals and studies.

CHAPTER 8. Of the scholars' table.

Moreover, the scholars studying in the house shall have a common table under the warden and other prepositors, the twenty-men and deans, and also as far as possible a uniform dress.

CHAPTER 40. Of the education of the boys etc.

But whereas I have exchanged the succession to which my heirs and kindred were entitled in my freehold property by the custom of the realm for this charity, under the eye of God, as is aforesaid, I will and decree that if any little ones of the kindred aforesaid becoming orphans or otherwise through their parents' poverty want maintenance while they are receiving primary instruction in the rudiments, then the warden shall have them educated up to thirteen in number in the house aforesaid, until they can become proficient in the university, if they shall be found to be of ability for it; and from them those who are found able and fit shall be taken to fill the places of the scholars, as above set out.

And lest there should break out in the said house or society, the plague, which through the temptations of the flesh so often vexes the incautious, all service in the said house, at least in the court of the house of the scholars and of the manor of Maldon and elsewhere, as far as may be, shall always be done by males.

In remembrance and everlasting security of all which, the seal of the most serene Prince the lord Edward, the illustrious

Anglorum illustris, in sui consensus et approbationis testimonium, una cum sigillo meo, praesentibus est appensum. Actum mense Augusti, anno Domini 1274.

Oxford Grammar School Statutes. 13th century.

[H. Anstey, *Mun. Acad. Oxon.* II., from Southern Proctor's Book, f. 38 b.]

Antiquae ordinationes pro Magistris in Grammatica, sed non sunt in moderno usu.

Oath of Inceptors.

Item, debent fide media astringi, quum incipiunt, quod observabunt statuta et consuetudines a Domino Cancellario ordinata.

Funerals.

Item, si contingat aliquem eorum in fata discedere, debent omnes Magistri grammaticales illius interesse exequiis et missae in crastino celebrandae pro anima, et praecipue sepulturae: in nocturnis etiam vigiliis debent omnes interesse et psalteria sua devote psallere.

Similiter, et, si fuerit Scholaris alicujus eorum defunctus, omnes Magistri debent interesse exequiis, et praecipue sepulturae illius.

Terminal meetings.

Item, debent convenire in singulis terminis, praecipue in principio et in fine, ad tractandum de iis quae conferunt ad statum suum conservandum, et alias cum necesse fuerit.

Festivals.

Item, cum illi, qui sunt sub una professione, debent eandem regulam observare, provisum est, quod festos dies simul observent, sicut est in kalendario eorum de communi eorum consensu et provisione ordinatum, nisi forte aliquis propter parochiam suam quandoque singulariter cogatur feriare.

King of the English, in witness of his consent and approval, is affixed to these presents together with mine. Done in the month of August, A.D. 1274.

Oxford Grammar School Statutes. 13th century.

Ancient ordinances for masters in grammar, but they are not in use now.

Oath of Inceptors.

Also they ought to be bound by sureties when they incept to observe the statutes and customs ordered by the lord chancellor.

Funerals.

Also, when it happens that any of them depart this life, all the grammar masters ought to be present at his obsequies and at the mass to be celebrated for his soul on the morrow, but especially at his burial: and they ought all to be present at the wake overnight and devoutly sing their psalters.

Likewise, if a scholar of any of them die, all the masters ought to be present at his obsequies, and especially at his burial.

Terminal meetings.

Also they ought to hold meetings every term, chiefly at the beginning and end, to treat of matters relating to the preservation of their estate, and at other times when necessary.

Festivals.

Also, whereas those who are under one profession ought to observe the same rule, it is provided that they keep the same feast days together, as is ordered in their calendar by their common consent and provision, unless it happen that one of them by reason of his diocese be obliged to make holiday by himself.

De modo disputandi in grammatica.

Item, statutum est, quod Magistri scholarum grammaticalium teneantur die Veneris grammaticalia duntaxat disputare.

Quamdiu debuit habere scolas grammaticales.

Item, statutum est, quod nullus Regens in artibus obtineat scholas grammaticales simul ultra triennium.

De rotulo faciendo.

Item, nomina Scholarium grammaticalium notorum et ignotorum [in rotulis magistrorum suorum contineantur, MS. C] in rotulo Magistri regentis in grammatica, cum aliquis talis in hac Universitate fuerit, inscribantur; quem quidem rotulum in suis scholis teneatur Magister quilibet regens illius facultatis in principio cujuslibet termini et etiam posterius omni termino bis publice recitare, ut ad exclusionem falsorum fratrum appareat qui Scholares continui fuerint et veraces. Et caveat bene Magister quicumque facultatis illius, sub poena violationis sacramenti praestiti, ne alicujus nomen scribat in suo rotulo, nec tueatur protegat aut defendat quemcumque pro suo Scholari in morte seu in vita, cujuscunque cogniti vel ignoti, nisi quem sciverit, vel de quo probabilem suspicionem habuerit, quod idem scholas exerceat grammaticales alicujus licentiati per Cancellarium ad docendum publice grammaticam modo debito hactenus consueto. Causam istius constitutionis habet quilibet Magister in suis scholis exponere publice; et etiam quod quicunque extra rotulum inventus fuerit, vel etiam in rotulo suo scholas tamen non frequentans, tam in morte quam in vita tuitionibus carebit atque privilegiis Universitatis istius.

De inrotulatione Scholarium illorum qui non sunt adepti magistralem honorem.

Item, singuli docentes grammaticam publice, quos magistralis status minime decoravit, omnia nomina Scholarium suorum, tam commensalium quam aliorum, Magistro regenti

Of the method of disputations in grammar.

Also it is decreed that grammar-schoolmasters are bound to dispute in grammar only on Fridays.

Of the time for holding grammar schools.

Also it is decreed that no regent in arts may keep a grammar school for longer than three years at one time.

Of making rolls.

Also, the names of grammar scholars, known and unknown, shall be written [in the rolls of their masters] on the roll of the regent master in grammar when there is one in the University; and this roll every regent master in that faculty shall be bound to read publicly twice a term in his school, at the beginning of each term and afterwards, so that, to the exclusion of false brethren, it may appear who are continuous and true scholars. And let every master of that faculty take good care, on pain of the breach of his oath, that he write the name of no one on his roll, nor guard, protect or defend anyone as his scholar, alive or dead, whether he knows him or not, unless he knows or has good reason to think, that he attends the grammar school of some one licensed by the chancellor to teach grammar publicly in the way heretofore usual. Every master must expound publicly in his school the reason of this constitution; and also that anyone who is not found on the roll, or even if on the roll does not attend school, shall, dead or alive, equally go without the protection and privileges of this university.

Of the enrolment of those scholars who have not attained the honour of the mastership.

Also every public teacher of grammar who is not adorned by the status of a master is bound to inform the regent master or masters, if there are more than one, in grammar, of the

in grammatica sive Magistris regentibus, cum plures fuerint, intimare tenentur, atque ut in ejus rotulo sive rotulis eorumdem ad tuitionem dictorum Scholarium inscribantur, debite procurare.

De diligentia Regentis circa alios informatores.

Item, quilibet Regens in grammatica compellere tenetur, quantum in eo est, omnes alios publice docentes grammaticam in ista Universitate, qui honorem non obtineant magistralem, omnia tacta superius, prout ad illorum personas attinet, observare fideliter, quibus etiam omnes alii docentes, ut praemittitur, benigne teneantur in istis omnibus eo debite conformare.

Oxford Curriculum in 1267.

[H. Anstey, *Munimenta Academica Oxon.* I. 34 (Rolls Series), 1868.]

Forma secundum quam Magistri debent admittere determinatores.

Cum videretur expediens et honestum Magistris et Bachilariis Universitatis Oxoniae ut certa forma provideretur, sub qua Bachilarii Artium determinaturi ad determinandum in futurum forent admittendi, provisa erat quaedam ordinatio super praedictis in forma infrascripta; videlicet,

Quod singulis annis, hebdomada quinta praecedente diem cinerum ejusdem anni, in congregatione Magistrorum, quatuor Magistri Artium, duo scilicet boreales et duo australes [vel] a Procuratoribus eligantur, qui, per fidem qua Deo tenentur et Universitati, in praesentia Magistrorum promittent quod nullum indignum ad determinandum secundum formam provisam admittent, qui etiam, quam citius poterint, ad admittendum determinaturos pro se accedant, et, si aliquo modo commode poterint, infra triduum omnino perficiant.

names of all his scholars as well boarders as others, and procure their due insertion on the roll or rolls, for the protection of his said scholars.

Of the regent master's duties as regards other teachers.

Also every regent in grammar is bound, as far as in him lies, to compel all other public teachers of grammar in the university, who have not the honour of the mastership, to observe faithfully all the matters above-mentioned so far as pertains to themselves; while all other teachers are, as is above mentioned, in duty bound to conform to his orders in all such matters.

Oxford Curriculum in 1267.

The order according to which masters ought to admit determiners.

Whereas it seems to the masters and bachelors of the University of Oxford expedient and befitting that a certain rule should be laid down under which bachelors of arts who are about to determine shall in future be admitted to determine, an order was provided in the premises in the form underwritten, viz.:

Every year, in the week before Ash Wednesday, in the congregation of masters, four masters of arts, namely, two northerners and two southerners, shall be chosen by the proctors, and shall promise before the masters, by the fealty by which they are bound to God and the university, not to admit anyone who is not worthy to determine according to the form provided, and also that they will as quickly as possible go and admit those who are going to determine for themselves, and, if they possibly can, finish the whole business within three days.

Coram quibus Magistris cum laudabili testimonio Magistrorum vel Bachilariorum conveniant Bachilarii eodem anno determinaturi, qui, si fuerint pro seipsis determinaturi, jurabunt, tactis sacrosanctis, quod omnes libros veteris logicae ad minus bis audierint, exceptis libris Boethii, quos semel sufficiat audivisse, praeter quartum librum Topicorum Boethii, quem audivisse non astringantur. De nova autem logica librum Priorum Topicorum, Elenchorum, bis; librum autem Posteriorum, saltem una vice jurent se audivisse.

De grammatica autem, De Constructionibus Prisciani bis, Barbarismum Donati semel:

[Vel] tres etiam libros naturales, scilicet librum Physicorum, librum De anima, librum De Generatione et Corruptione, jurent se audivisse.

Et sciendum quod si prius respondent in scholis publice de sophismatibus per annum integre debent respondisse, ita quod nulla pars illius anni in quo de quaestione responderint in dicto anno integro computetur. De una quaestione debent respondisse ad minus in aestate praecedente Quadragesimam in qua sunt determinaturi. Si autem de sophismatibus publice non responderint, omnes libros praedictos jurent se audisse, hoc adjecto, quod bis audierint librum Posteriorum. Debent etiam in audiendo majorem moram fecisse quam si in sophismatibus publice responderunt.

Si autem fuerint aliqui, qui prius pro se non determinaverint et pro aliis voluerint determinare, jurare tenentur quod omnes libros praenominatos modo praedicto audierint, insuper et Prisciani Magnum semel, in suo tempore commode poterant audivisse; tres etiam libros Meteororum omni modo jurent se audivisse.

Magistri etiam vel Bachilarii tale testimonium perhibituri accedant, qui bona fide dicant ipsos in responsionibus secundum modum praedictum probabiliter exercitatos; illos autem, qui prius non determinaverint, laudabiliter studuisse, et quod in

The bachelors who are to determine that year shall come before the said masters with the approved testimony of masters or bachelors and, if they are going to determine for themselves, shall swear on the Gospels that they have gone through all the books of the old Logic in lectures at least twice, except Boethius, for which one hearing is enough, and the Fourth Book of Boethius' Topics, which they are not bound to hear at all; in the new logic, the book of Prior Analytics, Topics, and Fallacies twice; but the book of the Posterior Analytics they shall swear that they have heard at least once.

In Grammar, Priscian's Constructions twice, Donatus' Barbarisms once.

Also in Natural Philosophy three books, viz. the Physics, the De Anima, the Generation and Corruption.

And it is to be understood that if they first answer publicly in the schools, they must have answered in sophistry for a whole year, no part of the year in which they have answered to the question being reckoned in the said whole year. To the question they ought to have answered at least once in the summer before the Lent in which they are going to determine. But if they have not answered in sophistry publicly they shall swear that they have heard all the books aforesaid, with this addition, that they have twice heard the Posterior Analytics. In hearing them also they ought to make a longer stay than if they have publicly answered in sophistry.

If, however, there are any who have not before determined on their own account and want to determine for others, they are bound to swear that they have heard all the before-mentioned books as aforesaid, and besides could have heard in their own time Priscian's Great Grammar once; the three books on Meteors they shall anyhow swear that they have heard.

The masters or bachelors too who are going to give such evidence shall come and say in good faith that the candidates are reasonably exercised in answering as aforesaid; and that those who have not before determined have studied properly,

anno praecedente fuerint in tali statu, quod secundum formam suprascriptam pro se·ipsis laudabiliter poterunt determinasse.

Et sciendum quod si aliqui determinaturi, libros, quos secundum formam suprascriptam bis tenentur audivisse, semel rite audierint et non omnes bis, vel non omnes illos quos secundum formam praedictam semel deberent audivisse, rite audierint, dummodo alios libros qui non sunt de forma rite audierint, qui libri, secundum Magistrorum electorum ad examinationem aestimationem in sacramento suo fidelem, sufficiunt ad faciendum sufficientem compensationem, ad officium determinatorum admittantur, sin autem penitus repellantur.

Haec autem ordinatio provisa erat per decem Magistros electos, Magistro Nicholao de Ewelme, tunc Cancellario, et Magistro Rogero de Plumtone...tunc Procuratoribus Universitatis Oxoniae, die Iovis proximo ante festum S. Matthaei Apostoli, anno Domini millesimo ducentesimo sexagesimo septimo, et confirmata, omnibus contravenientibus excommunicatis ipsam denunciando, atque signo Cancellarii signata, eodem Nicholao remanente Cancellario, et eisdem Procuratoribus, anno Domini millesimo ducentesimo sexagesimo secundo [septimo], in vigilia purificationis Beatae Mariae Virginis.

Item consuetudo est quod determinaturi pro se incipiant infra quatuor dies, ita quod dies lunae primae septimanae quadragesimae sit ultimus dies inceptionis, et tribus ultimis diebus ante cessationem Magistrorum debent terminare, ita quod dies Mercurii sit primus dies terminationis, quibuscunque festis et qualitercunque contingentibus, sive inceptione sive in terminatione.

Curriculum for B.A. Degree

and that in the year before they were in such a stage that they could have properly determined for themselves according to the order aforesaid.

And be it understood that if any of those who are going to determine have properly heard the books, which according to the aforesaid rule they are held to have heard twice, only once and not all twice, or have not heard properly all those which according to the aforesaid rule they ought to have heard once, as long as they have heard other books which are outside the rule, and those books are, in the real opinion upon oath of the masters elected to examine, adequate substitutes, they shall be admitted to the office of determiners, but otherwise shall be utterly refused.

This ordinance was made by ten masters elected for the purpose, Master Nicholas of Ewelme being chancellor, and Master Roger of Plumpton...then proctors of the University of Oxford, on Thursday next before the feast of St Matthew the Apostle A.D. 1267, and confirmed, and all who contravene it denounced excommunicate, and sealed with the chancellor's seal, the same Nicholas remaining chancellor and the same proctors A.D. 1267-8, on the eve of the Purification of the Blessed Virgin Mary [i.e. 1 Feb.].

Also the custom is that those determining for themselves shall incept within four days, so that Monday in the first week of Lent shall be the last day of inception, and ought to determine on the three last days before the masters' vacation, so that Wednesday is the first day of determination, whatever feasts may occur, either in inception or determination.

Foundation of College at Oxford for Benedictine Monks. 1275–87.

[Bodl. MS. 39, p. 58.]

Order of Benedictine Chapter at Reading. 1275.

De studiis.

Et ut in nostra religione refloreat studium ad locum vel ad edificia idonea Oxon. providenda ubi nostri ordinis fratres de diversis monasteriis causa studii transmittendi decenter habitare valeant, unanimiter est statutum quod omnes provincie Cantuarie religionis nostre prelati de omnibus suis spiritualibus et temporalibus bonis de singulis marcis secundum taxacionem quondam domini Norwici, duos denarios conferant isto anno; quod si non fuerint prius requisiti ad tardius in capitulo primo quod erit apud Abindon in crastino Sancti Mathei apostoli Anno gracie 1278, dominis Malmesbury, Gloucestre, Abindon, Abbatibus, qui procuratores huiusmodi negocii deputantur, exsolvent, ab eisdem super hoc quietancias recepturi; annis vero sequentibus de singulis marcis unum denarium contribuent ad predicta loca et deinde in eodem capitulo providenda. Interim autem citius quam possunt sibi provideant de lectore.

The College founded and Gloucester Monks admitted. 1283.

[Hist. Mon. S. Petri Gloucest. (Rolls Series), I. 32.]

Anno domini millesimo ducentesimo octogesimo tertio fundata est domus nostra apud Oxoniam a nobili viro domino Johanne Gyfforde, conventu monachorum Gloucestriae in die Sancti Johannis Evangelistae a venerabili patre domino Reginaldo tunc abbate Gloucestrensi tunc ibidem solenniter introducto domino Johanne Gyfforde praesente ad idem et volente.

Foundation of College at Oxford for Benedictine Monks. 1275–87.

Order of Benedictine Chapter at Reading. 1275.

Of Universities.

And that study may flower again in our religion, it was unanimously decreed, in order to make provision of a place or fit buildings at Oxford where the brethren of our order, to be sent from different monasteries for study, may be able to live properly, that all the prelates of our order in the province of Canterbury shall contribute in that year twopence in every mark of all their spiritual and temporal possessions according to the assessment of the former lord of Norwich; and if this is not asked for before, shall pay it in full at latest in the first chapter which will be held at Abingdon on the day after St Matthew's day, in the year of grace 1278, to the lord abbots of Malmesbury, Gloucester, Abingdon, who are assigned as proctors for this matter, and receive receipts from them; and in following years shall contribute a penny a mark to provide for the said places and other things in the same chapter. Meanwhile they shall provide a lecturer as quickly as possible.

The College founded and Gloucester Monks admitted. 1283.

In the year 1283 our house at Oxford was founded by the nobleman Sir John Giffard, a convent of Gloucester monks being then solemnly inducted there, on St John the Evangelist's day, by the venerable father the lord Reginald, then abbot of Gloucester, in the presence and at the desire of Sir John Giffard.

Bishop Godfrey Giffard of Worcester asks the University to provide a D.D. to teach the Gloucester Monks. 1283.

[A. F. Leach, *V. C. H. Gloucestershire*, II. 338, from Worc. Ep. Reg. Giffard, f. 206.]

Viris venerabilibus et dilectis in Christo Domino...Cancellario et Universitati Magistrorum Oxonii Godefridus, permissione divina minister ecclesie Wigorniensis, salutis plenitudinem et felicitatis eterne.

Summus vicarius Christi in ecclesia Theologie studium censuit ampliandum, ut dilatato tentorii loco funiculos suos faciat longiores, sed ecce eidem Christi vicario specialiter adherentium fratrum Abbathie Beati Petri Gloucestrie nostre diocesis laudabilem et inspiratam a Deo devocionem intelleximus, qui ignoranciam, matrem erroris, deponere, et in luce veritatis incedere iam disponunt, ut in sciencia proficiant ad cumulum meritorum.

Nos igitur tam salubrem intencionem ipsorum quibus possumus auxiliis adjuvantes, vestre universitati preces attentas porrigimus, tota affeccione rogantes quatenus velitis permittere ac concedere quod in domo quam optinent Oxonii ad id idem doctorem in divina pagina sibi habeant intendentem, ut sapienciam sitientibus via pateat ad doctrinam, et ad honorem Dei et ecclesie ipsi docti, demum ad justiciam populos valeant erudire.

Vos in caritate perfecta semper dirigat Altissimus et sue lumine caritatis.

Datis apud Hembure v Idus Aprilis anno supradicto.

Grant of Site for Gloucester (now Worcester) College. 1287.

[A. F. Leach, Gloucester College in *V. C. H. Gloucestershire*, II. 338, from Worc. Ep. Reg., Giffard, f. 429.]

Sciant presentes et futuri quod ego Joannes Giffard dominus de Bremesfeld pro salute anime mee et anime

Bishop Godfrey Giffard of Worcester asks the University to provide a D.D. to teach the Gloucester Monks. 1283.

To the venerable men and beloved in Christ, Sir...Chancellor and the University of Masters of Oxford, Godfrey, by divine permission minister of the church of Worcester, fulness of health and eternal happiness.

The high vicar of Christ in the church thought that the study of theology should be increased, so that by enlargement of the space of its tent it might make its ropes longer, and lo we hear of the laudable and divinely inspired devotion of the brethren of the abbey of St Peter's Gloucester, in our diocese, specially adhering to the same vicar of Christ, who are now disposed to put aside ignorance, the mother of error, and to walk in the light of truth, that they may become proficient in learning to the augmentation of their merits.

We therefore, helping all we can their so healthful purpose, put our earnest prayers before your University, asking you with all affection to permit and grant that in the house they possess in Oxford they may have a doctor in the sacred page to attend them, so that the way of learning may lie open to those thirsting for wisdom, and so at last they themselves becoming learned may be able to instruct the people in righteousness to the honour of God and the church.

May the most Highest always direct you in perfect love and the light of His love.

Dated at Henbury 9 April in the year aforesaid [1283].

Grant of Site for Gloucester (now Worcester) College. 1287.

Know ye present and to come that I John Giffard, lord of Brimsfield, for the health of my soul and the soul of Maud

Matilde Longespee quondam consortis mee et antecessorum et heredum meorum dedi concessi et hac presenti carta mea confirmavi Deo et beate Marie et ecclesie Beatorum Johannis apostoli et evangeliste et Benedicti Abbatis et confessoris Oxonii, et Priori et conventui eiusdem loci, ordinis Sancti Benedicti, et communitati monachorum eiusdem ordinis provincie Cantuarie ibidem causa studii transmissorum seu transmittendorum, sub forma debito modo provisa et statuta per generale capitulum ordinis et provincie predicte Omnes terras et tenementa cum singulis suis pertinenciis que habui in Vico de Stokwelle strete in Suburbio Oxonii, videlicet omnes terras et tenementa que habui de dono et feoffamento fratris Willelmi de Hawvil tunc Prioris sancte domus hospitalis S. Joannis Jerusalem in Anglia et assensu et voluntate omnium fratrum tocius capituli sui, et omnes terras et tenementa que habui ex dono et feoffamento Johannis de Langporte, burgensis Oxonii, et totum illud tenementum quod habui ex dono et feoffamento Eue lotricis, et totum illud tenementum quod habui ex dono et feoffamento Joannis Watson et Ydonee uxoris sue, et totum illud tenementum quod habui ex dono et feoffamento Stephani de Coue[lee] et Alicie uxoris sue ad fundacionem et constitucionem perpetue sustentacionis prioratus et communitatis ordinis predicti ibidem in liberam puram et perpetuam eleemosynam et quietam Habenda et tenenda predictis Priori et Conventui et successoribus suis et communitati predicte...ita quod predicto Priore cedente vel decedente, quilibet Prior succedens electus per Conventum dicti loci mihi et heredibus meis tanquam patrono loci illius presentetur, quem sine difficultate dilacione seu calumnia aliqua recipiemus...In cuius rei testimonium [etc.].

Longsword formerly my wife, and of my ancestors and heirs, have given, granted and by this my deed confirmed to God and the Blessed Mary and the church of the Blessed John the apostle and evangelist and of Benedict the abbot and confessor of Oxford, and to the Prior and Convent of the same place of the order of St Benedict and to the community of the monks of the same order of the Province of Canterbury sent or to be sent there to study, under the form duly provided and decreed by the general chapter of the order and province aforesaid, All the lands and tenements with the appurtenances which I had in Stockwell Street in the suburb of Oxford, namely all the lands and tenements which I had of the gift or feoffment of William of Hawvil, then prior of the holy house of St John of Jerusalem in England, and by the assent and will of all the brethren of his chapter, and all the lands and tenements which I had of the gift and feoffment of John of Langport, burgess of Oxford, and all the tenement which I had of the gift and feoffment of Eve the washerwoman, and all the tenement which I had of the gift and feoffment of John Watson and Idonea his wife, and all that tenement which I had of the gift and feoffment of Stephen of Cowlay and Alice his wife, for the foundation and establishment of the perpetual maintenance of the Prior and Community of the order aforesaid there in free, pure and perpetual and quiet alms, To have and to hold to the aforesaid Prior and Convent and their successors and the community aforesaid...so that when a Prior departs or deceases every succeeding Prior elected by the convent of the said place shall be presented to me and my heirs as patron of that place, and we will receive him without any difficulty, delay or charge. In witness [etc.].

The Jurisdiction of the Grammar-Schoolmaster, Chancellor of Cambridge University, and Archdeacon of Ely, defined. 1276.

[The Archdeacon of Ely's book, Caius Coll. Camb. MS. 204, f. 48, printed in Fuller's *Hist. Univ. Camb.*]

Uniuersis Christi fidelibus presentes literas inspecturis... Hugo, Dei gracia Elyensis episcopus, salutem in Domino.

Ad uniuersitatis uestre noticiam tenore praesencium uolumus peruenire, quod nos affectantes tranquillitatem et pacem Uniuersitatis nostre Cantabrigiensis regencium et scolarium studencium in eadem, uolentesque ut tam archidiaconus noster Elyensis circa sibi subditos quam Cancellarius Uniuersitatis eiusdem circa scolares suos ita iurisdiccionem suam separatim exerceant, ut uterque suo iure contentus non usurpet alienum: ad peticionem et instanciam prefati Archidiaconi nostri, Cancellarii, et Magistrorum Uniuersitatis predictorum (ab utraque parte nobis traditis articulis), ad eternam rei geste memoriam super hiis ordinamus infrascripta.

In primis uolumus et ordinamus quod Magister Glomerie Cantabrigiensis, qui pro tempore fuerit, audiat et decidat [causas] uniuersas glomerellorum ex parte rea existencium, uolentes in hac parte prefatum magistrum eodem priuilegio gaudere quod habent ceteri magistri de scolaribus suis de causis eorum decidendis, ita quod siue sint scolares siue laici qui glomerellos uelint conuenire, uel aliquid ab eis petere, per uiam iudicialis indaginis, hoc faciat coram Magistro Glomerie, ad quem decernimus huiusmodi cause cognicionem spectare pleno iure. Nisi huiusmodi cause cognicio sit de pensionibus domorum per Magistros et Burgenses taxatarum, uel de facinoris enormis euidencia, ubi requiritur incarceracionis pena uel ab Uniuersitate priuacio. In hiis enim casibus et non aliis

The Jurisdiction of the Grammar-Schoolmaster, Chancellor of Cambridge University, and Archdeacon of Ely, defined. 1276.

[The translation is taken from C. H. Cooper, *Annals of Cambridge*, I. 56, 1842, with some amendments.]

To all the faithful in Christ who shall see this letter...Hugh, by the grace of God bishop of Ely, health in the Lord.

We wish that by the tenor of these presents it shall come to the knowledge of all of you, that desiring the tranquillity and peace of our University of Cambridge, and of the regents and scholars, students in the same, and being willing that our archdeacon of Ely shall over his subjects, and that the chancellor of the said university shall over his scholars, severally exercise jurisdiction, so that each being contented with his own rights shall not usurp the other's: at the petition and instance of the aforesaid our archdeacon, of the chancellor and masters of the university (articles on either side having been delivered to us), we thereupon, for the perpetual remembrance of the matter, ordain as follows:

First, we will and ordain that the Master of Glomery [grammar master] at Cambridge for the time being shall hear and decide all suits in which grammar scholars are defendants, willing that in this particular the aforesaid master shall enjoy the same privilege as other masters have with respect to their scholars in deciding their causes, so that whether they be scholars or laymen who wish to convene the grammar boys or demand anything from them by judicial process, they shall do this before the grammar master, to whom we decree that the cognizance of such cause alone in law belongs; unless the cognizance of such cause relate to the rent of houses assessed by the masters and burgesses, or to the evidence of some serious crime, which incurs the penalty of imprisonment, or of deprivation of the privileges of the university. For in these

respondeant glomerelli coram Cancellario cuilibet querelanti, qui iurisdiccionem suam exercet in hiis sicut est alias obseruatum. Si uero magister glomerie cognoscat inter scolarem actorem et glomerellum reum, et contigerit appellari ab interlocutoria uel a diffinitiua sentencia, uolumus et ordinamus quod ad Cancellarium appelletur, qui in ipsa causa appellacionis procedat secundum ordinem obseruatum, cum ab alio magistro regente et de dicta causa sui scolaris cognoscente ab alterutra parcium ad cancellarium appellatur. De causis uero glomerellorum inter se, et laicorum et glomerellorum, Cancellarius in nullo se intermittat, nisi causa sit de pensione domorum taxatarum, uel de enormitate delicti ut superius est expressum.

Et quia in statutis Uniuersitatis uidimus contineri quod duo bedelli Uniuersitatis intersint uirgam deferentes omnibus uesperis, principiis, conuentibus, defunctorum exequiis, et omnibus aliis conuocationibus, nullo alio in preiudicio eorum uirgam delaturo, precipimus quod bedellus glomerie in predictis conuocacionibus et locis coram cancellario et magistris uirgam non deferat. In aliis autem locis quandocunque et ubicunque uoluerit, et maxime pro expedicione sui officii, uirgam libere deferat licenter et quiete.

Et quia in statutis Uniuersitatis eiusdem inter alia continetur, quod familia scolarium, scriptores et alii officia ad usum scolarium tantum deputata exercentes, eadem immunitate et libertate gaudeant qua et scolares, ut coram Archidiacono non respondeant sicuti nec scolares qui sunt eorum domini. Hoc ita tenore presencium declaramus, quod in hoc casu nomine familie solummodo uolumus contineri mancipia scolarium in domibus cum eis commorancia dum personaliter deseruiunt scolaribus antedictis. Item nomine scriptorum et aliorum officia ad usum scolarium tantum deputata exercencium, uolumus intelligi de scriptoribus, illuminatoribus, et stacionariis qui tantum deseruiunt scolaribus, quod sub cancellario respondeant, uxores tamen eorum super crimine adulterii uel alia, cuius cognicio et correccio ad Archidiaconum spectat in casu consimili in personis aliis sibi subditorum diffamate, et

cases and in no others, the grammarians shall answer to any complainant before the chancellor, who exercises his authority in these matters as is elsewhere observed. But if the grammar master takes cognizance of a cause between a scholar as plaintiff, and a grammarian as defendant, and an appeal is made from his interlocutory or definitive sentence, we will and ordain that the appeal shall be made to the chancellor, who shall proceed in the appeal according to the order observed when an appeal is made to the chancellor by either party from another regent master, who has taken cognizance of the suit of his scholar. But the chancellor shall not interfere in any of the suits of grammarians amongst themselves, or between laymen and grammarians, unless the cause concerns the rent of assessed houses or some serious offence as is above expressed.

And whereas we have seen in the statutes of the university, that two bedells of the university should be present, bearing their maces, at all vespers, inceptions, congregations, exequies of the dead, and at all other convocations, no one else being allowed to bear a mace to their prejudice; We order that the grammar bedell shall not bear a mace before the chancellor and masters in the aforesaid convocations and places; but in other places he is licensed to bear a mace, freely and undisturbed, when and wherever he pleases, especially for the execution of his office.

And whereas, in the statutes of the same university, among other things, it is contained that the household servants of the scholars, writers and others exercising offices for the exclusive use of scholars, shall enjoy the same exemptions and liberties as the scholars, so as not to answer before the archdeacon, as neither do the scholars who are their masters; we interpret this by these presents that in this case we will that the term household shall include only the scholars' servants residing in houses with them, and personally serving the aforesaid scholars. Also the term writers and others, exercising offices for the exclusive use of the scholars, we will to be understood of writers, illuminators, and stationers, who serve scholars only, and that they must answer before the chancellor; but their wives, if charged with adultery or any other crime, the cognizance and correction of which pertains to the archdeacon in the case of other persons under his jurisdiction, and the rest of their

reliqua eorum familia ad officium scolarium specialiter non deputata, Archidiacono sint subiecti in omnibus et singulis sicut ceteri alii laici municipii Cantabrigie et tocius nostre diocesis Elyensis.

[Then follows a recital of an ordinance made orally at Barnwell that all parish priests and ministers of parish churches in Cambridge, including chantry priests and chaplains retained by laymen, are under the archdeacon's jurisdiction, even if they casually attend the schools; but if study is their principal object in coming, they are under the chancellor's jurisdiction; and if the reason is in doubt the oath of the person is to determine it. In any case, however, of contract with a scholar, or of default in some scholastic act, they fall under the chancellor's jurisdiction.]

Ad hec inter alia laudabile statutum et salubre a dictis cancellario et magistris editum diligenter inspeximus, ne quis aliquem pro scolare tueatur, qui certum magistrum, infra quindecim dies postquam Uniuersitatem idem scolaris ingressus sit, non habuerit, aut nomen suum infra tempus prelibatum in matricula sui magistri redigi non curauerit, nisi magistri absencia uel iusta rerum occupacio idem impediat. Immo si quis talis sub nomine scolaris latitare inueniatur, uel deiiciatur uel retineatur iuxta regiam libertatem. Et licet quilibet magister, antequam actualiter ad regimen admittatur, statutum huiusmodi fide prestita firmare teneatur, intelleximus tamen quod plures magistri periurii reatum sepius incurrentes contra eiusdem statuti tenorem aliquos ut scolares defendendo, fidem suam nequiter uiolarunt: propter quod uolentes maliciis hominum obuiare, precipimus sub pena excommunicacionis nequis quenquam ut scolarem contra memorati statuti tenorem tueri, uel fauorem sibi ut scolari in aliquo prebere presumat.

Et quia ecclesie nostre dyocesis nobis et archidiacono nostro sunt subiecte, scolares uero Uniuersitatis eiusdem subsunt Cancellario memorato, precipimus et mandamus quod sacerdotes scolares in utriusque presencia uel ipsorum uices

family, not wholly devoted to the service of the scholars, shall be under the archdeacon's jurisdiction in all and singular cases like other lay-persons of the town of Cambridge and our whole diocese of Ely.

[Then follows a recital of an ordinance made orally at Barnwell that all parish priests and ministers of parish churches in Cambridge, including chantry priests and chaplains retained by laymen, are under the archdeacon's jurisdiction, even if they casually attend the schools; but if study is their principal object in coming, they are under the chancellor's jurisdiction; and if the reason is in doubt the oath of the person is to determine it. In any case, however, of contract with a scholar, or of default in some scholastic act, they fall under the chancellor's jurisdiction.]

Moreover, we have diligently inspected amongst other statutes the commendable and beneficial one published by the said chancellor and masters, that no one shall defend as a scholar anyone who has not a definite master within fifteen days after the said scholar has entered the university, or who has not taken care that his name has been within the time aforesaid inserted in his master's register unless the master's absence or legitimate occupation with business prevent the same. Further, if any such person be found concealed under the name of a scholar, he shall be either expelled or detained, according to the king's grant. And although every master before he is actually admitted to be a regent is bound by oath to maintain this statute, we are, however, informed that many masters often incur the guilt of perjury and have wickedly violated their oath by defending some persons, as scholars, contrary to the purport of the said statute: wherefore we, being desirous to obviate the malice of men, enjoin that no one, under pain of excommunication, shall receive anyone as a scholar against the purport of the statute above-mentioned, or shall in any respect show favour to him as a scholar.

And whereas the churches of our diocese are subject to us and to our archdeacon, but the scholars of the same university are subject to the chancellor above-mentioned, we enjoin and order that the priests scholars shall be examined as to their orders in the presence of each of them, or of their deputies,

gerencium super sua ordinacione examinentur, et approbentur uel reprobentur, prout digni uel indigni reperti fuerint.

Et ne ius nostrum negligere uideamur qui alios in sua justicia confouemus, inhibemus sub pena excommunicacionis, quam ueniens in contrarium ipso facto incurrat, ne memorati cancellarius et Uniuersitas diuisim uel coniunctim, clam uel palam aliquid ordinet uel statuat, edita uel statuta huiusmodi obseruet uel seruari faciat, in preiudicium nostre iurisdiccionis seu archidiaconi nostri Elyensis, nobis specialiter inconsultis et non prebentibus assensum huiusmodi statutis uel eciam statuendis: decernimus enim irritum et inane quicquid contra hanc nostram prohibicionem a quoquam ipsorum fuerit attemptatum.

Ad hec quia iurisdiccio dicti Archidiaconi a iurisdiccione prefati Cancellarii tam racione contractuum quam personarum ac eciam causarum liquido est distincta, ac constet vtrumque esse nobis immediate subiectum, nolumus ipsum Archidiaconum uel suam familiam cancellario predicto in aliquo subesse, nec ipsum cancellarium uel suam familiam in aliquo subesse archidiacono memorato. Sed vterque uirtute proprie potestatis suam propriam familiam corrigat, ipsam ad iuris regulas reducendo. Ita quod si necessarium fuerit superioris auxilium in hiis de quibus ecclesia iudicat, ad nos uel ad officialem nostrum recursus habeatur: salua nobis et successoribus nostris potestate addendi, detrahendi, corrigendi, mutandi uel minuendi in posterum sicut nobis et ipsis uisum fuerit expedire.

Data et acta anno Domini MCCLXX sexto apud Dunham in octabis beati Michaelis.

and be approved or rejected according as they have been found competent or incompetent.

And that we may not seem to neglect our own rights whilst confirming the rights of others, we (on pain of excommunication to be *ipso facto* incurred by anyone contravening this) prohibit the aforesaid chancellor and university from ordaining or enacting anything, separately or jointly, secretly or openly, or from observing or causing to be observed, such ordinances or enactments, to the prejudice of our jurisdiction, or of that of our archdeacon of Ely, if our consent has not been specially asked and given to such statutes, enacted or about to be enacted; and we decree that whatever has been attempted by any of them contrary to this our prohibition is of no effect and void.

Moreover, whereas the jurisdiction of the aforesaid archdeacon is clearly distinguished from the jurisdiction of the aforesaid chancellor in the matter of contracts as well as of causes and persons, and it is well established that both are immediately subject to us, we will that the said archdeacon and his household shall not be subject to the aforesaid chancellor in anything, and that the chancellor himself and his household shall not be subject to the aforesaid archdeacon in anything; but each of them by virtue of his own authority shall correct his own household according to the rules of law, so that if the aid of a superior power be required on anything about which the church passes judgment, recourse shall be had to us or to our official; saving to us and our successors, the power of adding, subtracting, correcting, changing, or diminishing this hereafter as shall seem expedient to us and them.

Given and done in the year of the Lord 1276, at Downham, on the octave of Michaelmas.

Admission Oath of Grammar-Schoolmaster.
c. 1276.

[*Ib.* 127.]

Juramentum quod prestabit Magister Glomerye Archidiacono Eliensi et eius ministris in collacione scolarum.

Tu iurabis obedienciam Archidiacono Ecclesie Eliensis et eius ministris nec aliquid contra iurisdiccionem Archidiaconalem per te uel per alium attemptabis uel iuxta posse permittes attemptari.

Jurabis insuper quod onera Scolarum Glomerie Cantabrigie incumbencia iuxta consuetudinem hactenus approbatam pro tempore tuo sine aliqua extorsione a scolaribus scolarum predictarum faciendo fideliter sustinebis. Quod si secus per te uel per alium nomine tuo quicquam attemptatum fuerit, concedis te uirtute iuramenti prestiti ipso facto ab ipsis scolis esse priuatum quousque ab eo cuius interest remedium poteris optinere. Hec omnia promittis te fideliter obseruaturum. Sic Deus te adiuuet etc.

Extracts from Accounts of Merton College Grammar-Schoolboys. 1277-1310.

[Merton College Muniments, 3964 a etc.]

Computus Henrici de Swanebury a domo Scolarium de Merton aput Oxoniam a die Sanctorum Tiburcii et Valeriani ad diem Veneris proximum post festum Sancte Margarete [1277]....

Expense puerorum in custodia Thome de Walingford in communis usque ad festum S. Margarete.—Talliatur in una tallia generali de omnibus expensis eorum usque ad festum Sancti Michaelis.

Admission Oath of Grammar-Schoolmaster.
c. 1276.

Oath to be taken by the grammar master to the archdeacon of Ely and his officers on collation to the school.

You shall swear obedience to the archdeacon of the church of Ely and his officers, and will never attempt anything, by yourself or through another, nor after your power permit any attempt against his archidiaconal jurisdiction.

You shall swear further that you will, during your time, bear faithfully all the charges falling on the Cambridge Grammar School according to the hitherto approved custom, without any extortion from the scholars of the aforesaid school; and if anything shall be otherwise attempted by you or by another in your name, you grant that you are, in virtue of the oath you have taken, *ipso facto* deprived of the same school until you shall have been able to obtain redress from him whose business it is. All this you promise that you will observe faithfully. So help you God etc.

Extracts from Accounts of Merton College Grammar-Schoolboys. 1277–1310.

Account of Henry of Swanbury of the House of the Scholars of Merton at Oxford from the day of SS. Tiburtius and Valerian [14 April] to Friday next after the feast of St Margaret [20 July] [1277]....

Expenses for commons of the boys in the custody of Thomas of Wallingford to the feast of St Margaret.—Tallied in one general tally of all their expenses to Michaelmas.

Idem computat liberatis Thome de Walingford die Veneris proximo post festum sanctorum Tiburcii etc. pro se et W. de Portesmue, Roggero Dodekin, Thoma Dodekin, Iohanne de Chirburn, Iohanne de Harecourt, Nicholao de Littlebyr, Ada de Peteresfeud . . .	v^s.	iiij^d.
Item 2^a septimana	v^s.	iiij^d.
[And so on, the same amount each week for 10 weeks.]		
Item 11^a septimana quia unus Dodekin de villa in media septimana	v^s.	
Eidem Thome de Walingford eunti ad Dominum post computum per preceptum custodis. .		viij^d.
Scilicet in 12 septimana	iiij^s.	viij^d.
,, 13 ,, ...	iiij^s.	viij^d.
,, 14 scilicet die Veneris proximo ante festum Sancte Margarete pro se et W. de Portesmue et R. Dodekin Iohanne de Chirburn Nicholao de Litlebyr	iij^s.	iiij^d.
Summa iij^{li}. xj^s. viij^d.		

Expense in necessariis puerorum in custodia Thome de Walingford usque ad festum Sancte Margarete.

Idem computat liberatis Thome de Walingford pro j lintheamine ad opus Willelmi de Portesmua per preceptum Domini	15$\frac{1}{4}^d$.
Item liberatis eidem die S. Marci Evangeliste ad sotularia Thome Dodekin	4$\frac{1}{2}^d$.
. . . .	
Item liberatis caligis Willelmi de Portesmue vigilia Pentecostes	8^d.
Item in calciamentis Iohannis de Harecourt et calciamentis Thome Dodekin vigilia Sancti Barnabe Apostoli.	23^d.

	s.	d.

The same accounts for [money] delivered to Thomas of Wallingford on Friday next after the feast of SS. Tiburtius [and Valerian] for himself and W. of Portsmouth, Roger Dodkin, Thomas Dodkin, John of Sherborne, John of Harcourt, Nicholas of Littlebury, Adam of Petersfield . . 5 4

Also for the second week 5 4

[And so on, the same amount each week for 10 weeks.]

Also for the eleventh week because one of the Dodkins was away from town in the middle of the week. 5 0

To the same Thomas of Wallingford when he went to the lord [i.e. Walter of Merton, the founder] after the account by order of the warden . 8

Likewise in the 12th week 4 8

„ „ 13th „ 4 8

„ „ 14th, viz. on Friday next before St Margaret's day for himself and W. of Portsmouth and R. Dodkin, John of Sherborne, Nicholas of Littlebury 3 4

Total . . £3 11 8

Expenses for necessaries of the boys in the custody of Thomas of Wallingford till St Margaret's day [20 July].

The same accounts for [money] delivered to Thomas of Wallingford for a sheet for the use of William of Portsmouth by the lord's [Merton's] orders $15\frac{1}{4}$

Also delivered to the same on St Mark the Evangelist's day [25 April] for shoes for Thomas Dodkin . . . . $4\frac{1}{2}$

Also for hose delivered for William of Portsmouth on the vigil of Whitsunday   8

Also for boots of John of Harcourt and the boots of Thomas Dodkin on the vigil of St Barnabas the apostle   23

Merton College Grammar School

	s.	d.
Item Magistro Glomerie pro Iohanne de Harecourt, Iohanne de Chirburn et duobus filiis Willelmi Dodekin et Ada de Peteresfeud . . .		20^d.
Item in conduccione hospicii xii puerorum et magistri eorum pro termino estivali . . .	2	8
Item lotrici et garcioni pro predictis pueris . .		20^d.

Summa 12^s. 11$\frac{3}{4}^d$.

Subwarden's Account. 1300–1.

Computus Magistri Willelmi de Lutegarsal, Vicecustodis, anno regni Regis Edwardi xxix.

[*Ib.* 3964 c.]

Expensis Bereford.

In primis pro uno pari caligarum ad opus eiusdem		5
In cirothecis		2
Item pro una zona ad eundem		2
Item in uno pari cirothecarum emptarum per W. clavigerum in crastino Nativitatis Beate Virginis		1
Item in 1 zona [MS. torn] tunc . . .		2½
Item pro octo ulnis panni ad robam eiusdem .	20	
Item pro tonsura eiusdem panni		3
Item pro furura ad eandem	3	
Item pro sindone serico et ligatura ad eandem .		8
Item in curialitate pro eadem		1
Item in sotularibus eiusdem, viz. quinque paribus a festo Sancti Jacobi usque ad festum S. Andreae...	2	1
Item pro scolagio W. de Ber[eford] pro termino yemali		4
Item pro dica hostiarii		½
Item pro caligis eiusdem contra Natale . .		7

	s.	d.

Also to the Grammar Master for John of Harcourt, John of Sherborne and the two sons of William Dodkin and Adam of Petersfield . . .		20
Also in hire of a house for the 12 boys and their master for the summer term	2	8
Also to the washerwoman and the serving-man for the aforesaid boys		20
Total . . .	12	11¾

Subwarden's Account. 1300–1.

Account of Master William of Ludgershall, Subwarden in the 29th year of the reign of King Edward. [1300–1.]

The Berefords' expenses.

First, for a pair of hose for his use . . .		5
In gloves		2
For a girdle for the same		2
Also in a pair of gloves bought by W. the steward on the morrow of the Nativity of the Blessed Virgin [8 Sept.]		1
Also in a girdle...then		2½
Also for 8 ells of cloth for his gown . .	20	0
Also for shearing the same cloth . . .		3
Also for fur to the same	3	0
Also for a silk hood and binding to the same .		8
Also in gratuity for the same . . .		1
Also in shoes for the same, viz. 5 pairs from St James' [25 July] to St Andrew's day [30 Aug.]	2	1
Also for William of Bereford's schoolage [school fees] for the winter term		4
Also for the usher's fee		½
Also for stockings for the same against Christmas .		7

	s.	d.
Item pro cirothecis eiusdem contra Natale [MS. torn]		
Item pro uno gallo ad opus eiusdem contra carnipriuium		2
Item in unguento ad caput eiusdem		1
Item in uno troco		½
Item in scolagio eiusdem pro termino quadragesimali		4
Item pro dica vicemonitoris		1
Item pro sutura caligarum suarum et pro agulet		½
Item pro cirothecis suis et pilis in vigilia Pentecostes		
Item liberatis pro scolagio [MS. torn]		
Item a festo S. Andreae usque ad festum S. Jacobi pro sotularibus eiusdem, precii paris 5^d. et fuerunt xii paria in toto	5	0

Summa 37^s.... [MS. torn]

Expense nepotum fundatoris.

	s.	d.
In primis liberatis Magistro R. de Scharle pro vii duodenis perchameni ad opus puerorum	2	0
Item pro sotularibus parvi Petri		4
Item pro factura quinque camisarum ad opus eorum		3
Item pro factura duorum capiciorum ad opus Waleys [MS. torn]		1
Item in sotularibus trium puerorum, scilicet, minoris Hodiham, Burton et Roberti de Hodiham		14½
Item pro una libra candelarum pro eisdem die Martis in festo Sancti Martini		2
. . . . . .		
Item pro reparacione sotularium Roberti de Hodiham maioris et pro sotularibus Durrynton		8½
Item pro mutacione manicarum Roberti de Odiham maioris		4
Item eodem tempore liberatis Roberto de Odiham pro stramine ad lectum suum		1^d.
. . . . . .		

	s.	d.
Also for gloves for the same against Christmas		
Also for a cock for his use against the Carnival [Shrove Tuesday]		2
Also in ointment for his head		1
Also for a hoop		½
Also in his schoolage for Lent Term		4
Also for the under-monitor's fee		1
Also for sewing his hose and for an eylet (?)		½
Also for his gloves and balls on the vigil of Whitsunday		—
Also delivered for his schoolage		—
Also from St Andrew's to St James' days for his shoes, at the price of 5*d.* a pair, and there were 12 pairs altogether	5	0
Total	37	0

Expenses of founder's kin.

	s.	d.
In the first place, delivered to Master R. of Scharle for 7 dozen [skins] of parchment for the boys' use	2	0
Also for Peterkin's shoes		4
„ for making 5 shirts for their use		3
„ „ 2 hoods for Wallace's use		1
Also in the shoes of 3 boys, namely, Odiham minor, Burton and Robert of Odiham	1	2½
Also for 1 lb. of candles for the same on Tuesday after Martinmas		2
. . . .		
Also for repairing the shoes of Robert of Odiham major, and for shoes for Durrington		8½
Also for changing the sleeves of Robert of Odiham major		4
Also at the same time delivered to Robert of Odiham for straw for his bed		1
. . . .		

	s.	d.
Item pro scolagio vii puerorum pro termino quadragesimali, scilicet, Iohannis et Roberti de Hodiham, Willelmi Say, Ricardi Maken, Thome de Burton, Iohannis et Willelmi de Berefield	2	4
Item pro dica Vicemonitoris		2
„ pro puero		1
. . . .		
Item in xv ulnis linee tele et dimidia emptis per vices ante festum Beatorum Philippi et Jacobi, precii ulne 3^d.	3	10½
Item venditori pro labore suo		½
. . . .		
Item pro emendacione manicarum Thome de Burton et junioris Say.		4
. . . .		
Item liberatis pro scolagio vj puerorum pro termino estivali, pro puero 4^d.	2	0

Summa 45^s. 3^d.

Expense forinsece.

		s.	d.
Item liberatis ad dicam Beate Katerine			6
„ „ „ Sancti Nicholai			6
„ „ Petro de Clivo pro dica S. Nicholai			½
„ pro exennio misso Iohanni de Pirleye et filiis Edwardi Luvekyn de Kingeston venientibus pro determinacione fratrum suorum cum multis aliis, videlicet sextario vini		1	6
„ in pane			6½
„ dimidio quarterii avene pro eisdem			¾
„ quatuor paribus cirothecarum de coreo ferine emptis ad dandum precepto Custodis cito post Dominicam in albis		1	6
„ iiij pavonibus emptis		6	6

	s.	d.

Also for schoolage of 7 boys for Lent term, namely, John and Robert of Odiham, William Say, Richard Makins, Thomas of Burton, John and William of Berefield 2 4

,, for the under-monitor's fee 2

,, for the boy 1

. . . .

,, in 15½ ells of linen bought at different times before the feast of SS. Philip and James [1 May], price per ell 3*d*. 3 10½

,, to the seller for his trouble . . . . ½

. . . .

,, for mending the sleeves of Thomas of Burton and Say junior 4

. . . .

,, delivered for schoolage of 6 boys for the summer term, for each boy 4*d*. . . . 2 0

Total . . . 45 3

Outside expenses.

Also delivered at St Katherine's offering . . 6

,, ,, St Nicholas' offering . . . 6

,, ,, to Peter of Clive for St Nicholas' offering . . . . . . ½

,, for a present sent to John of Purley and the sons of Edward Lovekin of Kingston coming to their brothers' determination with many others, viz. a quart of wine 1 6

,, in bread 6½

,, half a quarter of oats for the same . . ¾

,, 4 pairs of gloves of doe-skin bought to be given by order of the warden just after Whitsunday 1 6

,, 4 peacocks bought 6 6

Computus de Hakeburne. 34 Ed. I.

Expense puerorum.

	s.	d.
Pro scolagio viij puerorum in termino yemali	3	
Lotrici pro pueris per annum	3	6
Pro scolagio Makenes et Say		6
. . . .		
Radulfo garcioni puerorum per annum	4	6
. . . .		
Pro scolagio vij puerorum in quadragesima	2	11
Pro estate	2	4

Computus. 2 Edward II. 1308–9.

Expensis puerorum.

Iohanni de Mere, Magistro eorum, quando incepit	2	
Pro scolagio ix puerorum pro termino yemali cum dica hostiarii	3	$4\frac{1}{2}$
Pro scolagio octo puerorum in quadragesima	3	4
Pro una olla henea conducta per annum		12
. . . .		
Pro uno Catone		2
Pro tabulis eburneis		$1\frac{1}{2}$
In sotularibus et caligis, stramine et candelis	30	$1\frac{3}{4}$
In scolagio x puerorum in estate	3	4

Summa £7. 0. $20\frac{1}{2}$.

Computus…Vicecustodis. 1309–10.

Expensis Bereford.

In caligis quando ivit domum ad Nativitatem beate Virginis	7
In caligis pro parvo	8
Pro cerico ad robam	4

Expense puerorum.

In stramine empto ad festum beate Frideswyde	4

Hakeburne's account. 1305–6.

The boys' expenses.

	s.	d.
For schoolage of 8 boys in the winter term	3	
To the washerwoman for the boys for a year	3	6
For the schoolage of Makins and Say		6
. . . .		
To Ralph, the boys' servant, for one year	4	6
. . . .		
For schoolage of 7 boys in Lent	2	11
For the summer	2	4

Account. 1308–9.

The boys' expenses.

To John of Mere, their master, when he began	2	0
For schoolage of 9 boys in the winter term with the usher's fee	3	$4\frac{1}{2}$
For schoolage of 8 boys in Lent	3	4
For a brass pot hired for a year		12
. . . .		
For a Cato		2
For ivory tablets		$1\frac{1}{2}$
In shoes and stockings, straw and candles	30	$1\frac{3}{4}$
In schoolage of 10 boys in the summer	3	4
Total	£7 1	$8\frac{1}{2}$

Sub-warden's account. 1309–10.

Expenses of the Berefords.

In hose when he went home on the Nativity of the Blessed Virgin [8 Sept.]		7
In hose for the little one [Bereford jun.]		8
For silk for his gown		4

The boys' expenses.

In straw bought on St Frideswide's Day		4

	s.	d.
Ad Natale pro emendacione communarum		8
In Donato empto		3
In percameno		$3\frac{1}{2}$
Rogero pro sotularibus quando docuit pueros		8
In percameno		$2\frac{1}{4}$
Pro canewacio pro mappa		21^d.
Pro excessibus eorum ebdomada assencionis		$12\frac{1}{4}$
In ebdomada Pentecoste		12
Pro excessibus alterius commune		5
Item pro excessibus		3
Item pro excessibus		3
Pro scolagio septem puerorum per tres terminos	7	10

Computus. 13 Ed. II.

Expensis puerorum aule monialis.

	s.	d.
Item pro pensione aule monialis pro termino yemali	7	8
Item pro scolagio viij puerorum pro termino yemali	2	8

The first Cambridge College, Peterhouse. 1280–5.

Royal Assent to Bishop of Ely placing Scholars in St John's Hospital. 24 Dec. 1280.

[Pat. Roll, 9 Edw. I, m. 28.]

Rex omnibus ad quos etc. salutem.

Rex inclitus Hebree gentis, quem Omnipotens ultra capacitatem comprehensionis intellectus humani prerogativa sapiencie celitus insignivit, promisso sibi a domino munere quod optaret, circumspecte considerans sapienciam terrenis rebus singulis prevalere, ipsam expetiit, prudenter attendens quod illam omnia bona pariter subsequuntur; quapropter decet regiam excellen-

	s.	d.
For improvement of their commons at Christmas .		8
In buying a Donat [Donatus' elementary Latin grammar]		3
In parchment		$3\frac{1}{2}$
To Roger for shoes when he taught the boys .		8
In parchment		$2\frac{1}{4}$
For canvas for a tablecloth		21
For their extras [battels, in later accounts] in Ascension Week		$12\frac{1}{4}$
In Whitsun Week		12
For other extra commons		5
Also for extras		3
Also for extras		3
For schoolage of 7 boys for 3 terms . . .	7	10

Account. 1319–20.

Expenses of the boys of Nun Hall.

Also for the rent of Nun Hall for the winter term .	7	8
Also for schoolage of 8 boys for the winter term .	2	8

The first Cambridge College, Peterhouse. 1280–5.

Royal Assent to Bishop of Ely placing Scholars in St John's Hospital.   24 Dec. 1280.

The king to all to whom etc. greeting.

The famous king of the Hebrew race, whom the Almighty distinguished with the heavenly prerogative of wisdom beyond the capacity of comprehension of the human intellect, being promised by the Lord whatever gift he should desire, carefully considering that wisdom was of most avail in earthly things, asked for wisdom, wisely expecting that all good things would follow thereupon; wherefore it befits the king's excellency con-

ciam exemplis optimis confirmatam, libenter assensum impertiri, ad facta favorabiliter prosequenda, per que viri fiant pro utilitate rei publice sapientes, quorum prudencia regimini regni et sacerdocii provide consulatur, et in huiusmodi studiis doctrina sapiencie iugiter amplietur.

Nos igitur attendentes venerabilem patrem Hugonem Elyensem episcopum proposito laudabili concepisse quod loco fratrum secularium in hospitali suo Sancti Johannis Cantebrigie scolares studiosi subrogentur, qui secundum regulam scolarium Oxoniensium qui de Merton. cognominantur in universitate Cantebrigie studentes per omnia conversentur, perpendentes ex huiusmodi studio per eminenciam sapiencie posse rei publice multa commoda provenire, prefate subrogacioni mutacioni seu translacioni ex ea superscripte faciende nostrum regium prebemus assensum, Nolentes per hoc quod elemosina pauperum ad dictum hospitale confluencium que a sanctis patribus episcopis Elyen. ecclesie est antiquitus consuete, in aliquo defraudetur.

In cuius etc. Teste etc. 24 die Decembris.

Royal Assent to Translation of the Bishop of Ely's Scholars to Peterhouse. 28 May 1285.

[Charter Roll, 13 Edw. I, m. 28.]

Rex archiepiscopis etc., salutem. Inspeximus litteras patentes quas venerabilis pater Hugo Elyens. episcopus fecit Elyensibus Cantebrigge studentibus in hec verba.

Universis presentes litteras visuris vel audituris Hugo permissione divina Elyensis episcopus, salutem in domino sempiternam.

Noverit universitas vestra quod cum nuper per dominum Edwardum dei gracia illustrissimum regem Anglie nobis concessum et permissum fuisset, ut in hospitali nostro Sancti Johannis Cantebrigg ad laudem divinam et eiusdem universitatis

firmed by the best examples, willingly to give his assent to the favourable deeds whereby men may be made wise for the utility of the commonwealth, and by their prudence provident counsel be given for the rule of the realm and of the priesthood, and the science of wisdom be continually increased by such studies.

We therefore, learning that the venerable father Hugh, bishop of Ely, has conceived the laudable design of introducing in the place of the secular brethren of his hospital of St John at Cambridge, scholars in the schools, who are to live together and study in the University of Cambridge, according to the rule of the scholars of Oxford, who are called of Merton, considering that by such study through eminence in wisdom many advantages can accrue to the commonwealth, give our royal assent to the aforesaid substitution, change or transfer being made as above-written, so long as by it the alms of the poor flocking to the said hospital, which was anciently accustomed to be given by the holy fathers, bishops of the church of Ely, be in no wise defrauded.

In witness whereof etc., 24 December.

Royal Assent to Translation of the Bishop of Ely's Scholars to Peterhouse. 28 May 1285.

The king to archbishops etc., greeting. We have inspected the letters patent which the venerable father Hugh, bishop of Ely, made to those of Ely diocese studying at Cambridge in these words.

To all who shall see or hear these present letters Hugh [Balsham], by divine permission, bishop of Ely, eternal health in the Lord.

Know ye all that whereas lately it was granted and allowed us by the lord Edward, by the grace of God most illustrious king of England, that we might cause scholars to be inducted and placed in our hospital of St John at Cambridge, to dwell

incrementum perpetuum scolares faceremus induci et collocari et in ipso hospitali, perpetuo moraturos ac studio sibi congruenti vacaturos; ita tamen quod per huiusmodi ordinacionem nichil attemptaretur per quod elemosina consueta subtraheretur seu caritatis opera pauperibus et infirmis ad dictum hospitale confluentibus ab antiquo impensa minuerentur seu penitus adnichilarentur. Nos huiusmodi regio accedente consensu certum numerum scolarium in dicta domo fecimus induci, certa bona a bonis dicti hospitalis separata ad ipsorum scolarium perpetuam sustentaccionem adquirentes et eisdem assignantes.

Cumque processu temporis inter fratres eiusdem domus et scolares predictos ex variis causis dissensionis materia quampluries oriretur, cuius pretextu difficile seu intollerabile videbatur ut diucius modo prenotato simul commorarentur, ad maiorem ipsorum mutuam benivolenciam et tranquillitatem confovendam ex parte utriusque, nobis humiliter extitit supplicatum ut tam loci quam bonorum sibi communium, si qua essent nobis placeret facere divisionem; pro qua quidem facienda partes pronotate se cum omnibus bonis suis et iuribus quoquo modo adquisitis sponte et pure, omnibus et singulis consencientibus et nullo contradicente, nostre ordinacioni se submiserunt, prout in litteris utriusque partis sigillis communibus earundem signatis et penes nos residentibus luculencius apparet. Nos siquidem attendentes varia incommoda, pariter et pericula, que ex perseverancia huiusmodi communionis possent actualiter pervenire, volentes que, ut decet, potius huiusmodi periclis obviare quam ea que in premissis maiora possent afferre incommoda expectare, auctoritate, qua fungimur in hac parte, necnon et virtute submissionis supradicte, taliter inter partes predictas duximus ordinandum.

In nomine Patris et Filii et Spiritus Sancti, Amen. Nos Hugo, Dei gracia episcopus Elyensis, in primis ordinamus quod scolares nostri, quos scolares episcoporum Elyensium perpetuo volumus nuncupari, a fratribus hospitalis separentur et

in the same hospital for ever, and employ themselves with appropriate study, to the praise of God and the perpetual augmentation of the same university; so, nevertheless, that by such ordinance nothing should be done by which the customary alms should be subtracted, or the works of charity bestowed anciently on the poor and infirm coming to the said hospital should be diminished or brought to nought, We with such royal assent have caused a certain number of scholars to be brought into the said house, and acquired and assigned certain goods separate from those of the said hospital for the perpetual maintenance of the said scholars.

And whereas in process of time from various causes matter of dissension had often arisen between the brethren of the same house and the scholars aforesaid, by reason whereof it seemed difficult or intolerable that they should any longer live together in manner above-mentioned, and we were humbly petitioned by both parties for the better encouragement of mutual good feeling and peace between them, that we would be pleased to effect a division of the place and any property there might be common to them; for the effecting of which division the parties aforesaid, all and each consenting, and no one dissenting, spontaneously and absolutely submitted themselves and all their possessions and rights howsoever acquired to our ordinance, as in the letters of either party sealed with their common seals, and remaining with us, more at large appears. We, therefore, considering the various disadvantages and dangers, which may actually arise from the continuance of such common possession, and desiring, as is proper, rather to prevent such dangers than to wait for events which may bring greater disadvantages, by the authority which we exercise in this behalf and in virtue of the submission aforesaid, have considered that it should be thus ordained between the parties aforesaid.

In the name of the Father, the Son and the Holy Ghost, Amen. We Hugh, by the grace of God bishop of Ely, in the first place ordain that our scholars, whom we will shall for ever be called 'the Bishops' of Ely's scholars,' shall be separated

transferantur ad hospicia iuxta ecclesiam Sancti Petri extra portam de Trumpeton Cantebrigie, et habeant illam ecclesiam cum duobus hospiciis predictis perpetuo, et quod habeant bona infrascripta ad predictam ecclesiam pertinencia, super quibus specialiter nostre ordinacioni predicti fratres se submiserunt, videlicet, decimas garbarum cum alteragio, quas fratres prenominati habere et colligere solebant, et decimas utriusque molendini ad ecclesiam illam spectantes. Et ne per huiusmodi ordinacionem seu alienacionem ipsis fratribus dispendium eveniat, ordinamus insuper, quod predicti fratres habeant de bonis predictis scolaribus per nos dudum assignatis, bona infrascripta, videlicet hospicium contra fratres predicatores et redditum annuum per nos emptum de Isabella Wombe, et domos que fuerunt magistri Roberti Aunger hospitali adiacentes, domos eciam que fuerunt rectoris de Eyworth perpetuo possidenda; nolentes quicquam de bonis alterius partis alteri accrescere, bonis supradictis duntaxat exceptis, sed si qua bona supersint per nos prius adquisita de quibus superius non fit mencio, ea nostre ordinacioni reservamus in futurum.

Partibus igitur memoratis coram nobis comparentibus presentisque ordinacionis tenore coram ipsis recitato pridie Kalendas Aprilis, anno domini 1284, omnes et singuli, tam magister fratrum et fratres ex parte una quam magister scolarium et scolares ex altera, presenti ordinacioni pure et sponte consenserunt et adquiverunt.

Et ad maiorem ipsorum consensus noticiam et dicte ordinacionis nostre perpetuam firmitatem, ut eciam quelibet dissensionis seu contencionis materia inter partes predictas imperpetuum amputetur, presentis ordinacionis nostre tenorem instrumentis ad modum cirographum confectis sigillo nostro consignatis recitari fecimus et conscribi, que penes partes predictas alternatim volumus et precipimus perpetuo remanere, tercio instrumento eiusdem ordinacionis tenorem continente et cirographatim similiter confecto et communi sigillo utriusque partis consignato ad rei geste perpetuam memoriam penes nos nichilominus remanente.

from the brethren of the hospital and translated to the inns by St Peter's church outside Trumpington gate at Cambridge, and shall have that church with the said two inns for ever, and shall have the possessions underwritten belonging to the said church, concerning which the said brethren have specially submitted themselves to our ordinance, viz. the tithes of corn with the altarage, which the said brethren used to have and collect, and the tithes of both mills belonging to the church. And that no loss may fall on the brethren by such ordinance or alienation, we ordain further that the said brethren shall have from the possessions by us formerly assigned to the said scholars, the possessions underwritten, namely, the inn opposite the Friars Preachers and the rent charge bought by us from Isabel Wombe, and the house which belonged to Master Robert Aunger, next the hospital, and the house which was the rector of Eyworth's, to possess for ever. But none of the other possessions of either party shall accrue to the other party, but if there are any possessions beyond those which were formerly acquired by us, of which no mention is made above, we reserve them for our ordinance hereafter.

The said parties therefore appeared before us and the tenor of the present ordinance being read aloud before them, on 1 April 1284, all and every, as well the master of the brethren and the brethren on the one part, and the master of the scholars and the scholars on the other part, absolutely and voluntarily consented and agreed to the present ordinance.

And for better knowledge of their consent and the perpetual confirmation of our said ordinance, and that all cause of dissension or contention between the parties aforesaid may be for ever cut off, we have caused the tenor of our present ordinance to be recited and written in instruments made in manner of an indenture and sealed with our seal, which we will and command shall for ever remain with the parties aforesaid, a third instrument, containing the tenor of the same ordinance and likewise made like an indenture and sealed with the common seal of either party, remaining with us in perpetual remembrance of the matter.

In quorum omnium testimonium sigillum nostrum presentibus est appensum. Datis apud Dunham die et anno supradictis.

Inspeximus eciam quasdam alias litteras patentes quas idem Episcopus fecit eisdem scolaribus in hec verba.

H., Dei gracia Elyensis episcopus, Dilectis in Christo filiis magistro et scolaribus suis Cantebrigie commorantibus, salutem, graciam et benediccionem.

Ecclesiam de Tripelewe nuper vobis et fratribus hospitalis Sancti Johannis Cantibrigie tunc simul commorantibus vestri contemplacione collatam, cum iam ab ipsis fratribus tam corporaliter quam eciam quo ad bona sitis ex causa divisi et seperati ab eis alibi commorantes, vobis solum et successoribus vestris per nos et successores nostros in futurum collocandis ibidem cum pertinenciis suis omnibus ad communem vestram sustentacionem intuitu conferimus caritatis.

In cuius rei testimonium presentes litteras vobis fieri fecimus patentes sigillo nostro consignatas. Datis apud Dodington pridie Kalendas April. A.D. 1284 et Pontificatus nostri anno 27.

Nos autem tenorem predictarum litterarum ratum habentes et gratum, illum pro nobis et heredibus nostris, quantum in nobis est, et tenore presencium acceptamus, prout littere patentes predicte racionabiliter testantur.

Hiis testibus venerabilibus patribus episcopis Bathoniensi et Wellensi et Thoma Menevensi episcopis, Gilberto de Clare comite Gloucestrie et Herefordie, Ricardo de Burgo comite Ultonie, Johanne de Vesey, Ricardo de Bosco et aliis.

Datum per manum nostram apud Westmonasterium 28 die Maii.

In witness whereof our seal is appended to these presents. Dated at Dunham the day and year aforesaid.

We have inspected also certain other letters patent which the same bishop made to the same scholars in these words.

H., by the grace of God bishop of Ely, to his beloved sons in Christ his master and scholars living at Cambridge, health, grace and blessing.

The church of Triplow lately conferred for your benefit on yourselves and the brethren of St John's Hospital of Cambridge when living together, since you are now for certain reasons divided and separated as well in person as in possessions, and living elsewhere than with them, we confer by way of charity on you alone and your successors to be hereafter placed by us and our successors there with all its appurtenances for your common maintenance.

In witness whereof we have made for you these our letters patent sealed with our seal. Dated at Doddington, 31 March 1284, and in the 27th year of our episcopate.

Now we, holding the tenor of the aforesaid letters good and acceptable, for us and our heirs as much as in us lies by tenor of these presents accept it, as the aforesaid letters patent reasonably witness.

These being witnesses, the venerable fathers the bishops of Bath and Wells, and Thomas, bishop of St David's, Gilbert of Clare, earl of Gloucester and Hereford, Richard de Burgh, earl of Ulster, John of Vesey, Richard of the Wood, and others.

Given by our hand at Westminster, 28 May.

Norwich School. 1288.

[Lambeth MSS., Reg. Peckham, f. 38 a.]

Collacio scolarum Norwicensium sede vacante.

xvj Kalendas Novembris apud Croyendon contulit Dominus Magistro Godefrido de Nortona scolas civitatis Norwicensis sede vacante: et habuit dictus Magister G. litteras collacionis et induccionis Officiali Norwicensi.

Confirmation of Jurisdiction of Canterbury Schoolmaster in all Causes affecting his Scholars. 21 March 1291.

[A. F. Leach in *The Guardian*, 19 Jan. 1898, from Canterbury Cath. Mun.]

Frater Johannes, permissione diuina Cantuariensis ecclesie minister humilis, tocius Anglie primas, Dilecto filio Magistro scolarum ciuitatis Cantuariensis, salutem, graciam et benediccionem.

Ut in causis scolarum et scolarium vestrorum cognoscere et iurisdiccionem exercere libere valeatis, prout fieri consueuit ab antiquo vobis cum canonice inhibicionis potestate licenciam concedimus specialem.

Datis apud Wyngham xij Kalendas Aprilis anno Domini millesimo cc nonagesimo primo.

Holy Water Carrying a Form of Exhibition in Winchester Diocese. 1295.

[A. F. Leach, *Hist. Win. Coll.*, 40, from Reg. Pontissera, f. 55.]

Statuta Synodalia.

Item in ecclesiis que scolis civitatis Wynton. vel castrorum nostre diocesis sunt vicine, aqua benedicta portanda solis scolaribus assignetur:

Provideant insuper rectores, vicarii et parochiales presbyteri

Norwich School. 1288.

Collation to Norwich School during the vacancy of the see [of Norwich].

On 17 Oct. at Croydon the lord [archbishop Peckham], during the vacancy of the see, collated Master Godfrey of Norton to the school of the city of Norwich; and the said Master Godfrey had letters of collation and induction from the archbishop addressed to the Official [Principal of the Consistory Court of the bishop] of Norwich.

Confirmation of Jurisdiction of Canterbury Schoolmaster in all Causes affecting his Scholars. 21 *March* 1291.

Friar John, by divine permission humble servant of the church of Canterbury, primate of all England, to his beloved son the master of the school of the city of Canterbury, health, grace and blessing.

We grant you special licence that you may freely take cognizance of and exercise jurisdiction in the causes of your school and scholars, as has been accustomed to be done from ancient time, with power of canonical inhibition.

Given at Wyngham 21 March 1291.

Holy Water Carrying a Form of Exhibition in Winchester Diocese. 1295.

Statutes at Diocesan Council.

Also in the churches near the school of the city of Winchester or other walled cities of our diocese, let scholars only be appointed to carry the holy water.

Moreover, let the rectors, vicars and parish priests take care

quod pueri parochiarum suarum sciant Oracionem Dominicam, Simbolum et Salutacionem Beate Virginis, et recte crucis signaculo se signare.

A laicis eciam iam adultis cum ad confessionem venerint an sciant huiusmodi exquisitius inquiratur, ut si forte eorum non noverint, prout in plerisque accidit, per ipsos presbyteros super hoc informentur.

Inducantur insuper parentes puerorum quod ipsos pueros postquam psalterium legere sciverint cantum addiscant ne postquam forte maiora didicerint ad hoc discendum redire cogantur, vel tanquam huius inscii ad divinum obsequium sint suo perpetuo minus apti.

Rights of Nottingham and Kinoulton Schools.
30 *June* 1289.

[A. F. Leach, *V. C. H. Notts.*, II. 216, from Epis. Reg. York, Romanus, f. 75.]

Lanum. Quod scole non teneantur in parochia de Kynewaldstowe nisi de clericis ejusdem parochie, quod est multum pro magistro Notinghamie.

Magistro scolarum Notinghamie et vicario ecclesie nostre de Knewaldstowe.

Sicut nostra jura nobis volumus servari integra sic aliis in suis juribus per nos nolumus derogari. Decernimus, igitur, quod soli clerici parochie nostre de Kynewaldstowe scolas que in parochia ipsa regi consueverant ab antiquo, si voluerint, exerceant, exclusis a scolis eisdem aliis clericis quibuscumque et foraneis qui in scolis predictis nullatenus admittantur. Per hoc quidem juri ecclesie predicte libere seu capelle nostre prospectum cernimus, et jus tui, magister, quo ad clericos foraneos, tibi est integre reservatum.

In cujus rei testimonium sigillum nostrum presentibus est appensum.

that the boys in their parishes know the Lord's Prayer, the Creed and the Salutation of the Blessed Virgin, and how to cross themselves rightly.

Let inquiry also be made of the grown-up laymen when they come to confession whether they know this exactly, that if by any chance they do not know it, as is very often the case, they may be taught it by the same priests.

Let boys' parents also be induced to let their boys, when they have learnt to read the psalter, learn singing also, so that after they have learnt higher subjects they may not be compelled to return to learn this, nor as being ignorant of this be always less fit for divine service.

Rights of Nottingham and Kinoulton Schools. 30 *June* 1289.

Dated at Laneham. That no school shall be kept in the parish of Kinoulton [Notts.] except for the clerks of the parish; which is much for the master of Nottingham.

To the schoolmaster of Nottingham and the vicar of our church of Kinoulton.

As we wish our rights to be kept in their integrity, so we do not desire ourselves to derogate from the rights of others. We decree therefore that only the clerks of our parish of Kinoulton may, if they wish, attend the school which has been from ancient times customarily kept in that parish, all other clerks and strangers whatsoever being kept out and by no means admitted to the said school. By this we deem that we have regard to the rights of our church or free chapel aforesaid, while as regards clerks from outside [the parish] your rights, master, are wholly preserved to you.

In witness whereof our seal is appended to these presents.

A College of the Gilbertine Order of Sempringham at Stamford. 1303.

[A. F. Leach, *V. C. H. Lincs.* II. 469, from Linc. Ep. Reg., Dalderby, f. 8.]

Johannes permissione divina Lincolniensis Episcopus Priori et Conventui de Sempingham...

Cum Magister Robertus Luterel manerium quod in parochia Sancti Petri Stamfordie habuit vobis contulerit intuitu caritatis, volens ut scolares pro numero conventus vestri augmentando studentes in divina pagina vel philosophia in eodem manerio et unum capellanum secularem vel regularem divina celebraturum in capella Beate Marie infra dictum manerium manuteneatis;

Nos tam pium factum...commendantes licet in dicta capella a multo retroacto tempore cantaria fundata ad maiorem tamen corroboracionem voluntatis Magistri Roberti predicti studienciumque solacium et quietem...licenciam vobis concedimus specialem.

Datis...Buckden iij Novembris 1303.

The Parish Clerks of Lincoln not to teach Song Schools without Licence from the Cathedral Song Schoolmaster. 1305.

[A. F. Leach, *V. C. H. Lincs.* II. 423, from Linc. Chapter Act, Bk. A 2, f. 2.]

Memorandum quod die Sabbati proximo post festum conuersionis S. Pauli fuerunt omnes clerici parochialium ecclesiarum ciuitatis Lincoln. informantes pueros in ecclesiis de cantu siue de musica; quibus presentibus in capitulo coram Magistris R. de Lascy et W. de Thorneton imponentibus eos sic tenuisse scolas adulterinas in preiudicium libertatis matricis ecclesie; qui constanter negabant se nullas scolas in ecclesiis habere, nec pueros de cantu informare; et quia negare non potuerunt quin aliquo tempore talia fecerint, predicti Magistri R. et W. fecerunt eos iurare tactis sacrosanctis euangeliis quod de cetero nullas scolas adulterinas in ecclesiis tenebunt, nec aliquos pueros de cantu siue de musica informabunt, nisi de licencia Magistri scolarum.

A College of the Gilbertine Order of Sempringham at Stamford. 1303.

John, by the sufferance of God, bishop of Lincoln, to the Prior and Convent of Sempringham...

Whereas Master Robert Luttrell has given you in charity a manor which he had in the parish of St Peter's, Stamford, willing that you should maintain scholars to be augmented, according to the number of your convent, studying theology or philosophy in the same manor, and a chaplain secular or regular to celebrate divine service in the Blessed Mary's chapel in the said manor;

We commending so pious a work, although a chantry was founded in the said chapel a long time ago, for the better confirmation of the will of the said Master Robert and the solace and quiet of the students...give you special licence.

Dated...Buckden 3 November 1303.

The Parish Clerks of Lincoln not to teach Song Schools without Licence from the Cathedral Song Schoolmaster. 1305.

Be it remembered that on Saturday next after the feast of the Conversion of St Paul all the parish clerks of the churches of the city of Lincoln were teaching boys in the churches singing or music; and being present in chapter before Masters Robert de Lacy and William of Thornton, who charged them that they had held adulterine schools to the prejudice of the liberty of the mother church, they firmly denied that they were keeping any schools in the churches, or teaching boys singing; but as they could not deny that they had at some time done so, the said Masters Robert and William made them swear, holding the most holy Gospels, that they will not henceforward keep any adulterine schools in the churches, nor teach boys song or music, without licence from the [Song] Schoolmaster.

Appointment of Canterbury Schoolmaster by Archbishop Winchelsea. 11 *April* 1306.

[A. F. Leach in *The Guardian*, 19 Jan. 1898, from Lambeth MSS. Reg. Winchelsea, f. 300 b.]

Robertus etc. Dilecto filio Magistro Ricardo de Maydestane, clerico, salutem.

Regimen scolarum ciuitatis Cantuariensis et ipsas scolas ad nostram meram collacionem spectantes, tibi conferimus intuitu caritatis, et te Rectorem canonice instituimus in eisdem, teque ipsis scolis cum suis iuribus et pertinenciis quibuscunque per nostrum annulum inuestimus.

In cuius rei testimonium sigillum nostrum presentibus est appensum. Datis apud Aldington 3 Idus Aprilis A.D. m°ccc^{mo} sexto consecracionis nostre duodecimo.

Dispute as to Appointment to St Mary-le-Bow Grammar School. 25 *Sept*. 1309.

[Lambeth MSS. Reg. Whittlesey, f. 24 b.]

Pro Magistro Scolarum de Arcubus non amovendo.

R. etc. Dilecto filio...[*sic*] officiali nostro, salutem etc.

Peticio Magistri Johannis, Rectoris scolarum gramaticalium ecclesie Beate Marie de Arcubus Londin., nobis exhibita continebat quod licet regimen scolarum earundem ex collacione dilecti filii Decani ecclesie predicte, ad quem de antiqua approbata et hactenus pacifice observata consuetudine dictarum scolarum ordinacio et disposicio et prefeccio Magistri in eisdem dinoscitur pertinere fuisset et sit legitime assecutus, ipsasque post assecutionem huiusmodi rexerit pacifice et quiete;

Vos tamen immutare consuetudinem huiusmodi satagentes, cuidam Magistro Ricardo Cotoun de facto ipsarum scolarum

Appointment of Canterbury Schoolmaster by Archbishop Winchelsea. 11 *April* 1306.

Robert etc., to his beloved son Master Richard of Maidstone, clerk, health.

We confer on you by way of charity the keeping of the school of the city of Canterbury and the school itself, the collation of which belongs only to us, and we institute you canonically as master in the same, and invest you with the same school and all its rights and appurtenances whatsoever by our ring.

In witness whereof our seal is affixed to these presents. Given at Aldington the 3rd day before the Ides of April, A.D. 1306, in the 12th year of our consecration.

Dispute as to Appointment to St Mary-le-Bow Grammar School. 25 *Sept.* 1309.

Against the removal of the Schoolmaster of the Arches.

Robert [archbishop] etc. to his beloved son...our official, greeting etc.

The petition of Master John, rector of the grammar school of the church of St Mary-le-Bow, London, presented to us contained that although he has lawfully acquired the rectorship of the same school by the collation of [our] beloved son the Dean of the church aforesaid, to whom by ancient approved and hitherto peacefully observed custom the ordering and disposition of the said school and the appointment of the master in the same is recognised to belong, and after such acquisition has peacefully and quietly kept the same;

but you seeking to change such custom have conferred the keeping of the same school in fact on Master Richard Cotton,

regimen contulistis, ipsumque Magistrum Johannem mandastis ab earum regimine amoveri in ipsius Magistri Johannis preiudicium et Decani predicti non modicum et gravamen.

Quocirca vobis firmiter iniungendo mandamus, quatinus si est ita, collacione vestra huiusmodi non obstante, ipsum Magistrum Johannem regimine scolarum predictarum gaudere libere permittatis.

Dat. apud Bysschopebourn vij Kalendas Octobris anno consecrationis xv°.

St Albans School Statutes. 1309.

[A. F. Leach, *V. C. H. Herts*, II. 49, from B. M. Lansd. MS. 375, f. 97, printed Reg. Joh. Whethamstede (Rolls Series), II. 305.]

De Scola Gramaticali.

In Dei nomine, Amen. Universis Sancte Matris Ecclesie filiis per hoc Publicum Instrumentum pateat evidenter, quod anno ab Incarnacione Domini millesimo trecentesimo nono, sexto-decimo Kalendas Octobris, Indiccione septima, in presencia mei, Willelmi Henrici, de Sancto Albano, Sacrosancte Romane Ecclesie et Imperii Pubplici Notarii, in Registro Domini Johannis de Sancta Maria, Comitis Palatini de Lomello, Registrarii, iurium Scolarum Grammaticalium Sancti Albani iudex, in hac parte, ex consuetudine legitime prescripta, competens, presentibus testibus infrascriptis, vocatis ad hoc specialiter, et rogatis, statuta infrascripta predictarum scolarum, non rasa, non abolita, aut in aliqua sua parte viciata, ex unanimi consensu Magistri et omnium Baculariorum, edita eciam et cetera Sigillo Officialitatis Sancti Albani confirmata, feci[t] recitari, et relegi, et in hanc publicam formam redigi.

In Dei nomine, Amen. Prohibet Magister ne aliquis de cetero scolaris scolas ingrediatur, nisi nomen suum in matricula Magistri fuerit insertum. Quod si fecerit, debet expelli, et privilegio scolarum non gaudebit.

Item, prohibet Magister, ne aliquis scolaris de cetero

and have ordered the said Master John to be removed from the rectorship of the same to the no small prejudice and grievance of the same Master John and of the Dean aforesaid.

Wherefore we order firmly enjoining you that, if it be so, notwithstanding your collation, you allow the same Master John freely to enjoy the rectorship of the school aforesaid.

Given at Bishopsbourne 25 Sept. in the 15th year of our consecration.

St Albans School Statutes. 1309.

Of the Grammar School.

In the name of God, Amen. To all the sons of Holy Mother Church be it clearly made known by this Public Instrument that in the year from the Incarnation of the Lord 1309, on 16 September, in the seventh Indiction, in the presence of me, William Henryson of St Albans, notary public of the Holy Roman Church and Empire, Registrar in the registry of Sir John of St Mary, Count Palatine of Lomello, the Judge of the law of the Grammar School of St Albans, competent in this behalf by lawful prescription and custom, in the presence of the witnesses named below, called and invited specially for this purpose, caused to be read the underwritten statutes of the said school, not erased or abolished, or in any part thereof vitiated, by the unanimous consent of the Master and all the Bachelors, published etc. and also confirmed by the seal of the Official of St Albans, and to be re-read and reduced to this public form.

In the name of God, Amen. The Master forbids any scholar henceforth to enter the school, unless his name shall have been entered in the Master's Register. If any do so, he ought to be expelled, and he shall not enjoy the privileges of the school.

Also the Master forbids any scholar henceforth to inflict

molestiam, iniuriam, seu grauamen aliquod, aliquibus, vel alicui, scolaribus, in scolis seu extra, seu laicis vel aliis licenciatis, inferat quoquo modo; quod si fecerit, pro Magistri arbitrio grauiter punietur.

Item, prohibet Magister, ne aliquis scolaris de cetero vaget vel discurrat per vicos et plateas, sine causa racionabili, et iusta: quod si fecerit, debet requiri, et a Magistro ex ordinario punietur.

Item, si ob aliquod delictum, quoquo modo contractum, scolaris rebellis inueniatur, vel alias maliciose se absentauerit, debet in forma iuris citari, et a Magistro canonice corrigi: et si presentiam suam non exhibuerit, per Magistrum bona sua sequestrentur, brachio seculari, si necesse fuerit, ad hoc specialiter conuocato.

Item, prohibet Magister, ne aliquis scolaris, vel alius, cuiuscunque sit condicionis vel status, de cetero arma non ferat in scolis vel extra, in preiudicium Magistri et scolarium, unde pax dictarum scolarum, et tranquillitas, posit [*sic*] perturbari; sub pena excommunicacionis, quam in hiis scriptis proferrimus in eosdem.

Item, prohibet Magister, sub pena excommunicacionis, quam in hiis scriptis proferrimus, ne aliquis de cetero, clericus vel laicus, seu alius bacularius, cuiuscunque fuerit condicionis, seu status, quocunque nomine vel dignitate censeatur, in scolares dicti Magistri, in scolis vel extra, manus violentas iniiciat quoquo modo, vel eosdem defamet, sub pena superius annotata.

Item, si scolaris socium suum, in scolis vel extra, leuiter percusserit, vel rabiando deliquerit, vel strepitum, contra statuta, fecerit, capucium suum per hostiarium capietur, et vice-monitori presentetur, et ab eo castigetur.

Item, statutum est, quod ad hostium hostiarius, siue subhostiarius, continue sedeant, nec duos vel tres scolares simul et semel exire permittant, nisi ex iusta et necessitatis causa: quod si ter moniti fuerint, ut officium suum in omnibus exsequantur, et noluerint, quarto a Magistro priuentur.

in any way molestation, injury or any grievance upon any scholar or scholars, in the school or outside, whether on laymen or on other licenciates. If any do so, he shall be severely punished at the pleasure of the Master.

Also the Master forbids any scholar henceforth to wander or run about the streets and squares without lawful and reasonable cause. If any do, he ought to be sent for, and shall be punished by the Master as Ordinary [judge].

Also, if on account of any default, in whatever way committed, a scholar be found rebellious, or otherwise of malice absent himself, he ought to be cited in form of law and canonically corrected by the Master: and if he shall not present himself, his goods shall be sequestrated by the Master, by means of the secular arm, invoked, if need be, for this special purpose.

Also the Master forbids any scholar, or other, of whatsoever condition or rank he may be, henceforth to bear arms, within the school or without, to the prejudice of the Master and scholars, by means of which the peace and tranquillity of the said school may be disturbed, under penalty of excommunication, which we pronounce by this writing against the same.

Also the Master prohibits henceforth, on pain of excommunication, which in this writing we pronounce, any clerk or layman, bachelor or other, of whatsoever condition or quality he may be, under whatsoever name or dignity he may be classed, to lay violent hands in any way on the scholars of the said Master, within the school or without, or to defame them, under the penalty above stated.

Also, if a scholar within the school or without strike a fellow scholar lightly, or commit some outrage, or make a noise, contrary to the statutes, his hood shall be taken by the ostiarius; and he shall be presented to the vice-monitor, and shall be chastised by him.

Also, it is ordained, that the ostiarius or under-ostiarius shall always sit by the door, and shall not allow two or three scholars to go out at the same time and together, except for lawful and necessary cause. And if after three warnings to do their duty in all things they shall have been unwilling to do it, the fourth time they shall be deprived by the Master.

Item, prohibet Magister, sub pena excommunicacionis, ne bacularii in scola rabiant, vel strepitum faciant, quoquo modo; et si, ter moniti, desistere noluerint, priuentur.

Item, Magister, sub pena excommunicacionis, prohibet, quam in hiis scriptis proferrimus, ne aliquis de cetero locum baculariorum occupet, vel occupare presumat, nisi tales fuerint, qui in Uniuersitate racionabili studuerint, vel de eorum statu legitimis constare poterit documentis.

Item, statutum est, quod si aliquis ad culmen baculariorum ascendere voluerit, a Magistro, qui pro tempore fuerit, prouerbium accipiat, et de eodem versus, litteras, rithmum, componant, et pubplice in scolis conferat (nisi Magister de eiisdem aliquid graciose relaxare voluerit), et sex denarios, aut plus, prout facultates eorum se [habeant], optulerint, ad dicam Sancti Nicholai; alioquin priuilegiis baculariorum non gaudebunt. Potacionibus, et aliis in hoc casu consuetudinibus, in suo robore duraturis.

Item, prohibet Magister, ne aliquis, bacularius vel alius, qualiscunque fuerit, sine licencia ad sedem tenendam in scolis accedat, sub pena excommunicacionis, quam in hiis scriptis proferrimus; nisi prius ab illis quos Magister ad eum examinandum [deputauerit] de regulis gramaticalibus examinatus fuerit, et publice in scolis de eiisdem, et aliis sibi obiiciendis, respondere fuerit paratus, et fecerit.

Item, inhibet Magister, sub pena excommunicacionis maioris, quam in scriptis proferrimus in eodem, ne aliquis, vel aliqui, in Magistros dictarum scolarum manus temerarias iniiciant, vel aliquid mali attemptare presumant; quod si fecerint, durante excommunicacionis sentencia, ab omnibus baculariis disciplinam in scolis accipiant salutarem, nisi prius Deo et Ecclesie satisfactum fuerit.

Item, Magister, qui pro tempore fuerit, si condignam

Also, the Master forbids, under pain of excommunication, the bachelors to rage in school or make a noise in any way; and if, after three warnings, they will not desist, they shall be deprived.

Also, the Master, under pain of excommunication, which we pronounce in this writing, forbids anyone henceforth to take or attempt to take the place of a bachelor, unless he has studied for a reasonable time in a university, or his standing is established by legal evidence.

Also it is decreed that, if anyone desires to rise to the dignity of bachelor, he shall get a proverb from the Master then in office, and shall compose verses, prose or a rhyme on the same, and shall dispute publicly in the school (unless the Master graciously wills to release them from any of these), and he shall offer sixpence, or more, according to his means, to the fee of St Nicholas; otherwise he shall not enjoy the privileges of a bachelor; potations and other customs in this case shall remain in force.

Also, the Master forbids any bachelor, or other of whatsoever quality he may be, to come without licence to take a seat in the school, under the penalty of excommunication, which we pronounce in this writing; unless he shall first have been examined on the rules of grammar by those whom the Master [shall have deputed] to examine him, and shall have been prepared to answer publicly in the school concerning the same and other subjects to be proposed to him, and shall have so done.

Also, the Master forbids, under the penalty of the greater excommunication, which in this writing we pronounce against the same, any person or persons to lay rash hands on the Masters of the said school, or presume to attempt any wrong against them; if any do so, they shall receive during the sentence of their excommunication salutary discipline in the school from all the bachelors, unless satisfaction shall have been previously given to God and the Church.

Also, let the Master, for the time being, if he wishes to

acrimonie ulcionem euitare voluerit, duos de scolis bacularios idoneos et discretos eligat; [et] eiisdem ciste Sancti Nicholai administracionem committat; qui corporale prestabunt sacramentum bonam administracionem, pro voluntate scolarium, facere, et Magistro bonum et fidelem compotum reddere.

Item, statutum est, quod si aliquis scolaris vel mendicans fuerit, de cuius statu Magistro liquere poterit euidenter per probaciones, coram Magistro stans, duodecim cereos de cista Sancti Nicolai, circa funeracionem ac exequias, percipiant: ita tamen, quod predicti duodecim cerei, sine contradiccione alicuius, seu aliquorum, predicto Magistro, vel eius commissario, seu commissariis, reddantur incolumes.

Data apud Sanctum Albanum, presentibus discretis viris, Johanne le Hay de Mideford, Willelmo Suelesho, clericis, Willelmo Battes, Johanne de Locutorio, laicis, testibus ad premissa vocatis, et rogatis.

Subscripcio dicti Instrumenti.

Et ego, Willelmus Henrici antedictus, de Sancto Albano, Lincolniensis diocesis, publicus sacrosancte Romane ecclesie et Imperii auctoritate Notarius, huic conscripcioni predicti tabellionatus officii presens, cum testibus supradictis, interfui, et ea omnia suprascripta, de mandato predicti Magistri Scolarum Gramaticalium de Sancto Albano, fideliter scripsi, et in publicam formam redegi, meoque signo consueto signaui, rogatus, et cetera.

Memorandum, quod die Sabbati proxima ante Festum Sancte Katerine Virginis, undecimo Kalendas Decembris, anno Domini millesimo trecentesimo decimo, in presencia Johannis de Maideford, tunc temporis Rectoris Scolarum Gramaticalium de Sancto Albano, ex unanimi consensu omnium bacularionum et scolarium, fuerat statutum et ordinatum, quod Magister, qui pro tempore fuerit, quolibet anno duas faciet celebrari Missas; unam, videlicet, pro animabus

escape the deserved retribution of sharp censure, choose two fit and discreet bachelors, from the school, and commit to the same the management of St Nicholas' chest; and they shall take a corporal oath to make good administration according to the wishes of the scholars, and to render good and faithful account to the Master.

Also it is decreed, that if there be any scholar, even a beggar, whose status shall clearly appear to the Master by evidence, he shall receive, standing in the presence of the Master, twelve wax candles from St Nicholas' chest, on the occasion of a funeral and obsequies; on condition, however, that the said twelve candles, without hindrance from any person or persons, be returned whole to the aforesaid Master, or his commissary, or commissaries.

Given at St Albans in the presence of the discreet men John le Hay of Mideford, William Silsoe, clerks, William Battes, John of the Parlour, laymen, called and summoned as witnesses to the above.

[Notary's] Subscription to the said Instrument.

And I, the above-named William Harrison, of St Albans, Public Notary of the Diocese of Lincoln, by authority of the Holy Roman Church, present at this writing pertaining to the function of the above-named office, was in company with the aforesaid witnesses, and faithfully wrote all the above writings at the command of the aforesaid Master of the Grammar School of St Albans, and reduced them to public form, and signed them with my accustomed seal, being requested etc.

Be it remembered that on Saturday next before the Feast of St Katharine the Virgin, 25 November, A.D. 1310, in the presence of John of Maideford, then Rector of the Grammar School of St Albans, by the unanimous consent of all the bachelors and scholars it was decreed and ordered that the Master for the time being shall cause two masses to be celebrated every year, viz. they decreed one to be celebrated

Benefactorum defunctorum, in die Sancti Leonardi, cum exequiis nocte precedenti, statuerunt celebrandam ; et aliam in die Sancti Gregorii, Pape, de Sancto Spiritu, pro viuis Benefactoribus celebrandam. Et Magister et omnes bacularii predictis missis interesse debent, et offerant ad easdem, sub pena statuta.

The Abbot's Confirmation of the Statutes.

[*Ib.* f. 99.]

Hugo, permissione diuina, Abbas Monasterii Sancti Albani, omnibus in Christo credentibus, salutem, cum gracia Saluatoris. Cum inspexerimus statuta scolarum nostrarum gramaticalium de Sancto Albano, sigillo officii Archidiaconatus nostri confirmata et cetera, in publicam formam redacta ; volentes igitur scolas, Magistrum, et scolares nostros, foueri, tueri, et defendere, omnia statuta et singula priuilegia predictarum scolarum, in forma iuris concessa, et a quibuscunque rite facta, secundum formam, vim, et effectum utriusque tenoris, quatenus de iure possimus et debemus, ratificamus et confirmamus : predictis statutis adiicientes, Volumus et concedimus quod Magister, qui pro tempore fuerit, omnes scolas adulterinas, infra territorium seu iurisdiccionem nostram, compescat, eneruet, destruat, et euellat ; inhibentes et cetera, sub pena excommunicacionis, ne aliquis, vel aliqui, ad scolas aliquas tenendas, sine voluntate et assensu Magistri scolarum nostrarum gramaticalium, infra predictam iurisdiccionem nostram, accedant, vel tenere presumant ; cui Magistro, qui pro tempore fuerit, omnium predictorum statutorum, et singulorum priuilegiorum, sibi, ut predicitur, concessorum, causarum, contractuum, defamancium, omnium scolarium suorum inquisicionem, citacionem, examinacionem, siue prolacionem, absolutionem, et sentenciarum suarum execucionem, per sigillum officialitatis nostre, committimus, cum coercionis canonice potestate, et concedimus, per presentes. Omnes vero contradictores, et singulos predictis statutis et priuilegiis reclamantes, et contra

for the souls of departed benefactors, on St Leonard's day [6 November], with the office for the dead overnight; and the other, a mass of the Holy Ghost, to be celebrated for living benefactors, on the day of St Gregory the Pope [12 March]; and the Master and all the bachelors ought to be present at the aforesaid masses, and make offerings at the same under the penalty decreed.

The Abbot's Confirmation of the Statutes.

Hugh, by divine permission Abbot of the Monastery of St Albans, to all believers in Christ, greeting, with the Saviour's grace. Whereas we have inspected the statutes of our Grammar School of St Albans, confirmed etc. by the official seal of our Archdeaconry, made in due form; wishing, therefore, to foster, uphold and protect our school, Master, and scholars, we ratify and confirm, as far as rightfully we may and ought, all and singular the statutes and privileges of the said school, granted in form of law, and by whomsoever rightfully made, according to the form, force and effect of the tenor of each of them. Adding to the aforesaid statutes, we will and grant that the Master, for the time being, shall suppress, annul, destroy and eradicate all adulterine schools within our territory or jurisdiction, by inhibiting etc., under pain of excommunication, any person or persons from resorting to or presuming to keep any schools held without the will and assent of the Master of our Grammar School, within our aforesaid jurisdiction. To which Master for the time being, respecting all and singular the aforesaid statutes and privileges, granted to him as aforesaid, and in respect of causes, contracts and defamations of all his scholars, we under the seal of our office commit and grant by these presents the inquisition, citation, examination or adjournment, dismissal and the execution of sentences, together with the power of canonical coercion. And all and singular who oppose and object to the said statutes and privileges, and those

predicta statuta et priuilegia, nostramque confirmacionem, quoquo modo venientes, dum tamen per dictum Magistrum moniti fuerint, extunc auctoritate presentium excommunicamus. In cuius rei testimonium, sigillum nostrum digne duximus apponendum. Datis apud Sanctum Albanum, tercio-decimo Kalendas Julii, anno Domini millesimo trecentesimo decimo.

Confirmation by the Archdeacon of St Albans.

[*Ib.* f. 100.]

Uniuersis Sancte Matris Ecclesie filiis, presentes litteras inspecturis, vel audituris, Frater Johannes Passevant, Monasterii Sancti Albani Archidiaconus, salutem in Domino sempiternam.

Quoniam caritas virtutum omnium mater est, et magistra, sine qua nullum meritum in presenti, vel premium quis assequitur in futuro, tenentur merito tam omnes quam singuli ad caritatis opera promouenda pro viribus asspirare; Inde est quod nos J[ohannes], dictus Archidiaconus, racione preuia, onera Magistri scolarum nostrarum gramaticalium de Sancto Albano intuentes, atque eorum priuilegia et libertates tenues esse et exiles, volumus, quoad possimus, ut inter noua grauamina remedium per nos sentiat innouatum; Dicto eciam Magistro scolarum predictarum Gramaticalium de Sancto Albano, qui pro tempore fuerit, causas et lites scolarium et baculariorum suorum, ac eciam laicorum et aliorum omnium scolaribus dicti Magistri et baculariis iniuriancium, cum eisdem contrahencium, eosdem diffamancium, ac in easdem manus temere violentas iniiciencium, damus, concedimus, et committimus, per presentes.

Item, volumus et concedimus quod Magister qui pro tempore fuerit, omnes beneficiarios iurisdiccionis nostre scolas suas exercere compellat, cum coercionis canonice potestate; inhibentes eciam, sub pena excommunicacionis, quam in hiis scriptis proferrimus in eosdem, ne aliquis, vel aliqui, ad scolas aliquas eregendas vel tenendas, infra predictam iurisdiccionem nostram, sine voluntate et assensu Magistri predictarum scolarum, accedant, vel tenere presumant. Quodsi fecerint,

who in any way contravene the same and our confirmation of them, provided, however, that they shall have been duly warned by the said Master, we excommunicate thenceforth by the authority of these presents. In witness whereof we have deemed it proper that our seal should be affixed. Given at St Albans, 19 June A.D. 1310.

Confirmation by the Archdeacon of St Albans.

To all sons of holy mother church, who shall see or hear these present letters, Brother John Passevant, Archdeacon of the Monastery of St Albans, eternal health in the Lord.

Inasmuch as charity is the mother and mistress of all virtues, without which no one can attain any merit in the present or reward in the future, all and each of us are bound to aspire to promote works of charity according to our ability; hence it is that we, John, the said Archdeacon, after due consideration, seeing the charges on the Master of our Grammar School of St Albans, and that their privileges and liberties are scant and small, will that, to the best of our power, he should feel that with new grievances a new remedy has been provided by us; so we give, grant and commit by these presents to the said Master for the time being of the aforesaid Grammar School of St Albans, the determination of the causes and actions of his scholars and bachelors, and also of laymen and all others doing injury to the scholars and bachelors of the said Master, making contracts with the same, defaming the same, and laying violent hands upon the same.

Also we will and grant that the Master, for the time being, shall compel all beneficed in our jurisdiction to attend school, with power of canonical coercion; inhibiting also, under the penalty of excommunication, which in this writing we pronounce against the same, every person or persons from resorting to or presuming to hold any school, erected or held within our aforesaid jurisdiction without the will and assent of the Master of the aforesaid school. But, if they do so, let the said Master

dictus Magister eosdem [*sic*], sub pena superius annotata, destruat et interrumpat. Cui Magistro, qui pro tempore fuerit, de omnibus priuilegiis, statutis, et libertatibus, predictis scolis concessis, et de omnibus contra predicta venientibus, potestatem inquirendi, citandi, examinandi, corrigendi, et omnia alia faciendi que debito modo terminari debent et possunt, committimus, cum coercionis canonice potestate.

In cuius rei testimonium, sigillum officii Archidiaconatus Sancti Albani digne duximus apponendum. Datis apud Sanctum Albanum, decimo Kalendas Julii, anno Domini millesimo trecentesimo decimo.

[*Ib.* f. 104.]

Memorandum, quod Magister Ricardus de Naundes dedit domum ubi scole tenentur, cum aliis domibus adiacentibus eidem.

Item, Abbates iam defuncti pauperioribus scolarium viginti octo cobas in ebdomada concesserunt, cum mandato, qualibet die scolarum, Magistro, pro arbitrio suo, distribuendas. Dominus Johannes Passevant, Archidiaconus, statuta scolarum, et libertates, contulit.

Item, Johannes Hanle predictis scolis dedit Priscianum magnum. Item, pro Eleemosynariis, qui festum Sancti Nicolai concedebant, celebrant. Item, Dominus Hugo de Euersdone priuilegia, statuta et libertates, predictis scolis concessa, confirmauit.

Jurisdiction of the Schoolmaster of Canterbury in Matters concerning Scholars. 1311–23.

[A. F. Leach, *The Guardian*, 19 Jan. 1898, from Cant. Cath. Mun. x. 4, S. B. 4.]

The Schoolmaster excommunicates Richard Hall for Assault on his Usher.

Reuerende discrecionis viro Domino Decano Cantuariensi Johannes Everard, Rector scolarum ciuitatis Cantuariensis, salutem in auctore salutis.

Quia nos auctoritate nobis commissa Ricardum de Aula de

destroy and break up the same, under the penalty above stated. To which Master, for the time being, we commit, with power of canonical coercion, the power of inquiring, citing, examining, correcting, and of doing all other things which ought and can be duly determined, concerning all privileges, statutes, and liberties granted to the aforesaid school, and concerning all persons who contravene the aforesaid.

In testimony whereof we have deemed it proper to affix the seal of office of the Archdeaconry of St Albans. Given at St Albans, 22 June A.D. 1310.

Be it remembered that Master Richard of Nantes gave the house in which the school is held, with other houses adjacent to the same.

Item, the Abbots now deceased granted to the poorest scholars 28 loaves a week, with a Maundy, on every school day, to be distributed by the Master at his pleasure. Dom John Passevant, Archdeacon, conferred the statutes and liberties of the school.

Likewise, John Hanley gave the large Priscian to the aforesaid school. Likewise, they celebrate for the Almoners who granted the Feast of St Nicholas [6 December]. Likewise, the Lord Hugh of Eversdone confirmed the privileges, statutes and liberties granted to the aforesaid school.

Jurisdiction of the Schoolmaster of Canterbury in Matters concerning Scholars. 1311–23.

The Schoolmaster excommunicates Richard Hall for Assault on his Usher.

To the man of reverend discretion, Sir Dean of Canterbury, John Everard, rector of the school of the city of Canterbury, health in the author of health.

Whereas we, by the authority committed to us, at the

Cantuaria, propter suas multiplicatas et manifestas contumacias ad instanciam Johannis dicti le Plumer, ostiarii nostri et scolaris, coram nobis contractas in scriptis excommunicauimus, iusticia suadente, vos mutue vicissitudinis optentu in iuris subsidium requirimus et rogamus, quatinus ipsum Ricardum sic esse excommunicatum, in singulis ecclesiis vestri decanatus omnibus diebus dominicis et festiuis intra missarum solempnia coram clero et populo publice et solempniter denunciatis seu faciatis per alios denunciari;

Citantes eundem nichilominus peremptorie, quod compareat coram nobis in scolis nostris die Mercurii proxima post festum S. Hilarii proximum venturum prefato Johanni clerico super violenta manuum inieccione et nobis super sibi obiciendis ex officio responsurus, ulteriusque facturus et recepturus quod consonum fuerit racioni.

Quid autem in premissis duxeritis faciendum nos dictis die et loco, si placet, velitis reddere certiores per vestras litteras patentes harum seriem continentes.

Datis Cantuarie 16 Kalendas Januarii A.D. 1311.

Datis per copiam.

H. de Forsham, commissarius Cantuariensis, discreto viro Decano Cantuariensi, salutem in Domino.

Ostenso nobis Registro Magistri Johannis Everard, Rectoris scolarum Cantuariensium, auctoritate priuilegiorum predecessoribus suis et sibi a venerabilibus patribus Archiepiscopis Cantuariensibus concessorum, habito coram ipso contra Ricardum dictum ate Halle de Cantuaria super violencia cuidam Johanni Plomer clerico scolari suo per eundem illata, in eodem vidimus contineri quod prefatus Rector scolarum auctoritate predicta prefatum Ricardum pluries coram ipso citatum et non comparentem, propter suas manifestas et multiplicatas contumacias coram ipso contractas, in scriptis excommunicauit, iusticia suadente; qui nos humiliter requisiuit ut huiusmodi excommunicacionis sentenciam, ut tenemur, execucioni debite demandaremus;

instance of John called the plumber, our usher and scholar, have excommunicated in writing Richard of the Hall, of Canterbury for his multiplied and manifest contumacy shown in our presence, as justice demands, we require and request you in the hope of mutual good offices in support of the law to denounce the same Richard as so excommunicate in every church in your deanery on every Sunday and feast day during the solemnization of mass publicly and solemnly before the clergy and people, or cause him to be so denounced by others;

Citing him peremptorily at the same time to appear before us in our school on Wednesday next after St Hilary's day next to answer to the said John a clerk for a violent assault, and to us for those things we shall object to him *ex officio*, and to do and receive further whatever may be reasonable.

What you shall do in the premisses pray inform me on the said day and place by your letters patent continuing the series hereof.

Dated at Canterbury the 16th day before the Kalends of January [17 December] 1311.

Copy.

H. of Forsham, commissary of Canterbury, to the discreet man the Dean of Canterbury, health in the Lord.

Whereas the process of Master John Everard, rector of Canterbury School, has been shown to us which he held in person under the authority of the privileges granted to him and his predecessors by the venerable fathers, archbishops of Canterbury, against Richard, called at Hall, of Canterbury, on the assault by him on one John Plumber, clerk, his scholar; and whereas we have seen in the same that the aforesaid schoolmaster by the authority aforesaid had several times cited the aforesaid Richard before him, and when he did not appear, had for his manifest and multiplied contumacy excommunicated him in writing, as justice demanded; and whereas he has now humbly requested us to put such sentence of excommunication into execution as we are bound to do;

Nos igitur volentes ipsa priuilegia obseruare, quatenus possimus, ut est iustum, vobis mandamus firmiter iniungentes quatenus ipsum Ricardum sic esse excommunicatum in singulis ecclesiis vestri decanatus exemptis et non exemptis singulis diebus dominicis et festiuis [etc. as above] quousque absolucionis beneficium in forma iuris meruerit optinere; citantes eundem nichilominus peremptorie quod compareat coram nobis in ecclesia Christi Cantuariensi proximo die iuridico post festum Purificacionis B. M. V. proximo venturum super violencia in ecclesia S. Elphegi Cantuariensis, exempta et vacante, per eundem contra libertates ecclesiasticas perpetrata nobis ex officio responsurum et de veritate dicenda, si necesse fuerit, personaliter iuraturum, facturumque ulterius et recepturum quod iusticia suadebit.

Quid autem feceritis in premissis nos dictis die et loco legitime certificetis per vestras patentes litteras harum seriem continentes.

Datis Cantuarie 20 Kalendas Februarii A.D. 1311.

[Endorsed.] Teste P. Besiles de sigillo et voluntate consignantis.

[The Dean of Canterbury refused to act on this mandate on the ground that, though the authority of Archbishop Peckham (above, p. 228) was express, it did not appear how the jurisdiction was to be exercised. So the Commissary summoned a jury of clerics and laymen, who found that for forty years and upwards the schoolmaster had been accustomed to summon delinquents by his Usher (Hostiarius) to appear in the school, and if they did not appear excommunicated them, and the Dean proclaimed the excommunication. But when the Dean after this was about to act the Archdeacon of Canterbury interfered and by his Official stopped him. The matter then went to the Arches Court, and the Archbishop by writ of 18 May 1312, exemplified by the Prior and convent *sede vacante*

We therefore, willing to preserve the same privileges as far as possible, as is right, command you firmly enjoining you to denounce the same Richard as being so excommunicated in every church in your deanery exempt or not exempt on every Sunday and feast day [etc. as above], until he shall deserve to receive the benefit of absolution in form of law; at the same time citing him peremptorily to appear before us in Christ Church, Canterbury, on the next law day after the Purification of the Blessed Virgin Mary [2 Feb.] next for the violence perpetrated by him in the exempt church of St Alphege, Canterbury, when vacant, against the liberties of the church, and to answer to us *ex officio*, and to personally swear, if necessary, to speak the truth and to do and receive further what justice may demand.

Certify us legally what you do in the premises on the said day and place by your letters patent continuing the series of these.

Given at Canterbury the 20th before the Kalends of February [17 January] 1311.

[Endorsed.] Witness, P. Bessils, with the seal and at the wish of the signer.

27 June 1313 (Camb., Univ. Lib. Ee. v. 31), gave effect to its judgment. Though Hall when arrested, and imprisoned as an excommunicate by the Sheriff of Kent, had obtained writs of prohibition and attachment from the Court of King's Bench, he could not sustain them, and eventually submitted and was absolved by William of Ore [Oare], the rector, in St Alphege's church, 5 May 1313. The jurisdiction of the master thus triumphantly established was exercised in the cases following.]

Jurisdiction of Schoolmaster over anyone assaulting Scholars.
1314–5.

Acta in scolis Cantuariensibus coram Magistro Johanne Everard, dictarum scolarum Rectore, die Sabbati proxima post commemoracionem animarum A.D. 1314°.

Vocato ex officio quodam Thoma de Birchwode, scolari dictarum scolarum, super eo quod deliquit multipliciter contra ius scolarum predictarum, viz. vice-monitorem et scolares suos a doctrina communi impediendo, ac eciam super violenta manuum inieccione Magistro Waltero, vice-monitori, facta; quo comparente et iurato fatebatur in dictum W. manus iniecisse violentas: Et quia Rector noluit procedere ex ingnorancia ex officio fecit per quosdam de Baculariis et aliis in scolis existentibus [words interlined illegible] inquisicionem.

Qui quidem iurati dixerunt dictum Thomam Magistrum W. et scolares a doctrina communi impediuisse et in eos manus violentas iniecisse, unde ad instanciam quorumdam assidencium sub spe pacis datus erat sibi dies Jouis proximus sequens etc., ad audiendum punicionem iuxta acta.

Acta in scolis gramaticalibus Cantuariensibus coram nobis Johanne Everard dictarum scolarum Rectore die Lune proximo post festum Inuencionis Sancte Crucis A.D. 1315. Citato ac legitime vocato quodam Rogero le Lymburner super violenta manuum inieccione Willelmo Bor scolari meo facta; et quia sufficienter expectatus, preconizatus, nullo modo comparuit, ideo nos pro huiusmodi contumacia suspendimus ab ingressu ecclesie, et discernimus ipsum iterato fore citandum coram nobis in dictis scolis ad diem Jouis proximo sequentem.

Quo die dictis partibus comparentibus sub spe pacis de consensu parcium datus est eis dies usque ad diem Martis proximum post festum Trinitatis ad faciendum id quod predicitur.

Jurisdiction of Schoolmaster over anyone assaulting Scholars.
1314–5.

Done in Canterbury School before Master John Everard, rector of the said school, on Saturday after All Souls' Day [2 Nov.], 1314.

Thomas of Birchwood, scholar of the said school, being summoned *ex officio* for many delinquencies against the law of the aforesaid school, viz. hindering the vice-monitor and his scholars from their public teaching, and also for a violent assault on Master Walter, the vice-monitor, appeared and was sworn, and confessed that he had violently assaulted the said Walter; and because the Rector would not proceed *ex officio* in ignorance, he caused inquisition to be made by some of the bachelors and others who were in the school.

And they upon their oath said that the said Thomas had impeded Master Walter and the scholars in their public teaching, and had laid violent hands on them; whereupon at the instance of certain persons sitting by, in the hope of peace, a day was assigned him, viz. the Thursday following etc., to hear the punishment according to his acts.

Done in the Grammar School of Canterbury, before us John Everard, rector of the said school, on Monday next after the Invention of the Holy Cross, A.D. 1315. One Roger, the lime burner, was cited and lawfully summoned for a violent assault on William Bor, my scholar; and because, after being sufficiently waited for and proclamation being made for him, he no way appeared there, we therefore for such contumacy suspend him from admission to church, and decree that he shall be again summoned before us in the said school on Thursday next.

On that day the said parties appeared, and in the hope of peace a day was given them by consent of the parties until Tuesday after Trinity Sunday, to do what is aforesaid.

Acta in scolis Cantuariensibus die Lune post festum Sancte Mildrid Virginis.

Vocata quadam Johanna Modi super violencia facta scolari Stephano de Borsted; qua comparente, fatebatur manus iniecisse violentas.

De consensu parcium sub pacis [spe] datus est ei dies Sabbati proximus sequens ad audiendum sentenciam pro commissis.

Jurisdiction of Grammar Schoolmaster over St Martin's School, Canterbury.

[Reg. I. 397 (b)–8, printed in Somner's *Hist. of Canterbury*, ed. 1703, App. No. XXXIII. p. 33.]

Acta et processus super statu scolarum ecclesie Sancti Martini iuxta Cantuariam coram Magistro Roberto de Mallingg generali Commissario Cantuariensi, primo viua voce, et post per specialem commissionem Domini W. Archiepiscopi A.D. 1321 inter Magistrum Radulphum de Waltham, Rectorem scolarum Ciuitatis Cantuariensis et Magistrum Robertum de Henneye, Rectorem ecclesie Sancti Martini iuxta Cantuariam.

Commissio.

Walterus, permissione diuina [etc.], dilecto filio Commissario nostro Cantuariensi, salutem, graciam et benediccionem.

Cum nuper tibi preceperimus viua voce ut in negocio tangente Magistrum Radulphum rectorem scolarum gramaticalium Ciuitatis nostre Cantuariensis et Magistrum Robertum, Rectorem ecclesie Sancti Martini iuxta Cantuariam, ac eiusdem loci rectorem scolarum, ex officio, auctoritate nostra procederes, et inquisita veritate idem negocium debito fine terminares, dictum negocium, de quo miramur, adhuc coram te pendet indecisum.

Quocirca tibi committimus et mandamus quatenus ulterius in dicto negocio auctoritate predicta procedas, et finem sentenciando, preuia racione, celeritate qua poteris, imponere non omittas.

Datis Cantuarie tercio Nonas Januarii A.D. 1321.

Done in Canterbury School, on Monday after St Mildred's Day.

A certain Jane Moody being summoned for violence to a scholar, Stephen of Bourstead, she appeared and confessed she had violently assaulted him.

By consent of the parties in the hope of peace Saturday next was assigned her to hear sentence for her offences.

Jurisdiction of Grammar Schoolmaster over St Martin's School, Canterbury.

Acts and proceedings on the state of the school of St Martin's Church of Canterbury, before Master Robert of Malling, Commissary General of Canterbury, first by word of mouth, and afterwards by special commission of the Lord Walter [Reynolds], archbishop, in the year 1321, between Master Ralph of Waltham, rector of the school of the city of Canterbury, and Master Robert of Henney, rector of St Martin's Church, near Canterbury.

Commission.

Walter, by divine permission [etc.], to his beloved son our Commissary of Canterbury, health, grace, and blessing.

Whereas we lately ordered you *viva voce* to proceed *ex officio* by our authority in the business concerning Master Ralph, rector of the Grammar School of our city of Canterbury, and Master Robert, rector of St Martin's Church by Canterbury, and the rector of the school of the same place, and to inquire into the truth of the same matter and bring it to due conclusion; but the said business we are surprised to find is still pending before you undetermined.

Now, therefore, we commission and command you to proceed further by our authority in the aforesaid matter, and not to neglect to put an end to it by sentence founded on previous consideration as quickly as may be.

Dated at Canterbury, 3 Jan., A.D. 1321.

Inquisicio.

[A jury of nine incumbents and seven laymen.]

Jurati dicunt, quod non debent esse plures gramatici in Scolis Sancti Martini nisi XIII, et hoc se dicunt scire ex relatu bonorum et fide dignorum ab antiquo; et dicunt quod semper consueuit Rector Scolarum Cantuariensium Scolas Sancti Martini, per se vel suos propter numerum scolarium visitare.

Dicunt eciam quod, quando hostiarius vel submonitor scolarum Cantuariensium propter numerum scolarium scolas Sancti Martini visitauit, scolares Sancti Martini absconderunt se usque ad numerum XIII. Et hoc se dicunt scire ex relatu fidedignorum ab antiquo.

De aliis scolaribus in scolis Sancti Martini alphabetum, psalterium et cantum addiscentibus non est certus numerus limitatus, ut dicunt.

Sentencia Diffinitiua.

In Dei nomine, Amen. Cum nuper inter magistrum Radulphum, Rectorem scolarum Ciuitatis Cantuariensis, ad collacionem venerabilis patris Domini W., Dei gracia Cantuariensis Archiepiscopi, totius Anglie Primatis spectancium; et Magistrum Robertum de Henneye, Rectorem ecclesie Sancti Martini iuxta Cantuariam, et eiusdem loci scolarum Rectorem ad dictam Ecclesiam Sancti Martini, de patronatu eiusdem existencium, pertinencium; super eo quod idem Magister Radulphus pretendebat dictum Magistrum scolarum Sancti Martini habere deberet in scolis suis xiij scolares in gramatica erudiendos duntaxat; Idemque magister scolarum S. Martini omnes indistincte ad scolas suas confluentes in preiudicium scolarum ciuitatis predicte et contra consuetudinem admittere, et in suis scolis tenere et docere in gramatica presumpsit, orta fuisset materia questionis;

Tandem dictus venerabilis pater, utriusque loci Patronus et Diocesanus, nobis Commissario suo Cantuariensi generali

Inquisition.

[A jury of nine incumbents and seven laymen.]

The jury say that there ought not to be more than 13 grammar scholars in St Martin's School, and they say that they know this from of old by the relation of good and trustworthy men, and they say that the Rector of Canterbury school has always been accustomed to visit St Martin's School, in person or by his deputies, to ascertain the number of scholars.

They say, further, that when the usher or under-monitor of Canterbury School visited St Martin's School to ascertain the number of scholars, St Martin's scholars hid themselves down to the number of 13, and this they say they know by the evidence of trustworthy persons of old.

As to other scholars in St Martin's School learning the alphabet, psalter and singing there is no limitation of number, as they say.

Definitive Sentence.

In the name of God, Amen. Whereas lately matter of dispute has arisen between Master Ralph, rector of the school of the city of Canterbury, belonging to the collation of the venerable father the Lord W., by the grace of God Archbishop of Canterbury, Primate of all England, and Master Robert of Henney, rector of St Martin's Church by Canterbury, and the rector of the school of the same place belonging to St Martin's Church, and of the patronage of the same, on this that the same Master Ralph alleged that the said schoolmaster of St Martin's ought to have only 13 grammar scholars in his school, and yet the same master of St Martin's School has presumed to admit all without distinction who come to his school, to the prejudice of the school of the city aforesaid and against the custom, and to keep them and teach them grammar in his school;

And whereas the said venerable father, patron and diocesan of both places, has commissioned us his Com-

tam viue vocis oraculo, quam subsequenter litteratorie, huiusmodi questionem seu negocium per viam inquisicionis ex officio commisit fine debito terminandum.

Nos igitur Commissarius predictus magistros utrarumque scolarum predictarum et Rectorem Ecclesie S. Martini predicte coram nobis fecimus euocari, et super dicto negocio per viros fidedignos et clericos specialiter iuratos inquiri fecimus diligenter.

Qua inquisicione facta, pupplicata, et dictis Magistris et Rectori copia decreta, nihil dicto contra inquisicionem vel probato, sed ad audiendum pronunciacionem nostram die eisdem prefixo.

Quia Nos Commissarius antedictus, inuenimus quod magister Scolarum S. Martini xiij scolares duntaxat in gramatica per ipsum scolarum magistrum, quicunque fuerit, docendos habere et tenere ac docere debet ex consuetudine ab antiquo, illam consuetudinem, auctoritate nobis in hac parte commissa, decernimus obseruandam, inhibentes Magistro scolarum S. Martini ne plures scolares ultra numerum predictum in suis scolis in gramatica docendos admittat de cetero, nec consuetudinem predictam infringere presumat quoquo modo.

Ab ista sentencia predictus Magister Robertus appellauit ad sedem Apostolicam, et pro tuicione Curie Cantuariensis.

Appellacio, suggestio et citacio in causa Scolarum
Cantuariensium et Sancti Martini.

Officialis Curie Cantuariensis Discreto viro Magistro Roberto de Mallingg Commissario Cantuariensi generali, Salutem in auctore salutis.

Ex parte magistri Roberti de Henneye, Rectoris ecclesie Sancti Martini Cantuarie, nobis extitit intimatum, quod cum ipse ac precessores seu predecessores sui Rectores in ecclesia predicta omnes et singuli, temporibus suis, a tempore cuius contrarii memoria hominum non existit, fuerint, et adhuc sit idem magister Robertus de Henneye, nomine suo et

missary-General of Canterbury, both by word of mouth and afterwards in writing, to bring to due determination the said question or matter by way of inquisition *ex officio*;

We, therefore, the said Commissary, caused the masters of both the schools aforesaid and the rector of St Martin's Church aforesaid to be summoned before us, and caused diligent inquiry to be made in the said matter by a special jury of trustworthy men and clerks;

And whereas the said inquisition was held and published, and a copy ordered to be delivered to the said masters and rector, and nothing being said or found against the said inquisition, a day was fixed for them to hear our judgment.

Wherefore we, the said Commissary, find that the schoolmaster of St Martin's by ancient custom ought to have, keep and teach 13 scholars only in grammar, to be taught by the schoolmaster for the time being, and that custom, by the authority committed to us in this behalf, we decree shall be observed, inhibiting the schoolmaster of St Martin's from admitting hereafter more scholars than the number aforesaid to be taught grammar in the school and from presuming in any way to infringe the said custom.

From this sentence the aforesaid Master Robert appealed to the apostolic see and for the protection of the Court of Canterbury.

Appeal, suggestion and summons in the case of the Schools of Canterbury and St Martin's.

The Official of the Court of Canterbury to the discreet man Master Robert of Malling, Commissary General of Canterbury, health in the author of health.

On behalf of Master Robert of Henney, rector of St Martin's Church, Canterbury, we have been informed that whereas he and his precessors, or predecessors, rectors in the church aforesaid, all and each in their time, from time whereof the memory of men is not, were, and the same Master Robert

Ecclesie sue predicte, in possessione vel quasi iuris habendi scolas gramaticales in dicta ecclesia S. Martini seu infra septa eiusdem, magistrosque ad informandum et instruendum in arte gramaticali quoscunque illuc ea de causa accedentes ibidem preficiendi seu deputandi, et eos libere admittendi, informandi et instruendi in arte gramaticali predicta.

Ex parte magistri Roberti de Henneye in possessione vel quasi iuris huiusmodi ut premittitur existentis, ac metuentis ex quibusdam causis probabilibus et verisimilibus coniecturis graue sibi et Ecclesie sue predicte circa premissa preiudicium posse generari in futurum, ne quis circa premissa vel eorum aliquid quicquam in ipsius vel Ecclesie sue predicte preiudicium attemptaret, seu faceret aliqualiter attemptari, ad sedem Apostolicam, et pro tuicione Curie Cantuariensis, extitit, ut asseritur, palam et publice ac legitime prouocatum.

Set vos ad instanciam seu procuracionem cuiusdam Radulfi magistrum scolarum Cantuariensium se pretendentis, prouocacione predicta, que vos verisimiliter non latebat non obstante, post et contra eam, predictum magistrum Robertum de Henney quo minus possessione sua huiusmodi libere gaudere potuerit, contra iusticiam molestastis, inquietastis ac multipliciter perturbastis, ac tredecim scolares duntaxat in dictis scolis Ecclesie Sancti Martini et non plures admitti debere minus veraciter pretendentes, cuidam magistro Ioanni de Bucwell, magistro scolarum huiusmodi per dictum magistrum Robertum de Henneye prefecto seu deputato, ne ultra xiij scolares huiusmodi inibi admitteret seu haberet inhibuistis minus iuste, in ipsius magistri Roberti de Henney et ecclesie sue predicte preiudicium, dampnum non modicum et grauamen.

Unde ex parte eiusdem magistri Roberti...

of Henney, still is, in his own name and that of his church aforesaid, in possession or quasi-possession of the right of keeping a grammar school in the said church of St Martin or within its precincts, and of preferring or deputing masters there to teach and instruct, in the art of grammar, all coming there for that purpose, and of freely admitting, teaching and instructing them in the art of grammar aforesaid.

On behalf of Master Robert of Henney, being in possession or quasi-possession of such right as aforesaid, and fearing from certain probable causes and reasonable conjectures that grave prejudice may arise in future to him and his church aforesaid in the premises, lest anyone should attempt or cause to be attempted anything to his prejudice or that of his church aforesaid in any way in the premises or any of them, he openly and publicly and lawfully appealed to the Apostolic See and the protection of the Court of Canterbury.

But you at the instance or procuring of one Ralph, claiming to be master of Canterbury School, notwithstanding the said appeal, of which you were probably not ignorant, after and in spite of it, to prevent the said Robert of Henney from freely enjoying such possession, unlawfully molested, disquieted and many ways disturbed him, and untruly pretending that 13 scholars only and not more ought to be admitted into the said school of St Martin's Church, unlawfully inhibited one Master John of Buckwell, appointed or deputed schoolmaster of the said school by the said Master Robert of Henney, from admitting or having more than 13 such scholars there, to the no small prejudice, loss and damage of the same Master Robert of Henney and his church;

Wherefore, on behalf of the said Master Robert of Henney [an appeal was laid].

[The Commissary was inhibited from proceeding pending the appeal, for which he was to summon the appellant to appear in St Mary Aldermary's Church, London, on the 6th law day after Martinmas (11 Nov.). Dated at London, 21 Oct., 1323. But the appellant not proceeding respondent was dismissed from the examination of the court. On 20 March, 1323-4, Thomas of Cheminster, general examiner of the Court of Canterbury, Commissary of the Official of the same court and of the Dean of the Arches, his Commissary General, informed the Commissary General of Canterbury that he could therefore proceed to execution of his judgment.]

The University of Oxford, etc., directed by the Council of Vienne to establish Masters in Oriental Languages. 1311.

[Clement. *de magistr.* v. 1. i.]

Clemens episcopus servus servorum Dei. Ad perpetuam rei memoriam. Inter sollicitudines....Ideoque illius cuius vicem in terris licet immeriti gerimus, imitantes exemplum, qui ituros per universum mundum ad evangelizandum apostolos in omni linguarum genere fore voluit eruditos, viris catholicis notitiam linguarum habentibus, quibus utuntur infideles precipue, abundare sanctam affectamus ecclesiam, qui infideles ipsos sciant et valeant sacris institutis instruere, christicolarumque collegio per doctrinam christiane fidei ac susceptionem baptismatis aggregare. Ut igitur peritia linguarum huiusmodi possit habiliter per instructionis efficaciam obtineri, hoc sacro approbante Concilio scolas in subscriptarum linguarum generibus, ubicunque Romanam curiam residere contigerit, necnon in Parisiensi, Oxoniensi, Bononiensi et Salamantino studiis, providimus erigendas, statuentes ut in quolibet locorum ipsorum teneantur viri catholici sufficientem habentes hebraice, grece, arabice et chaldaice linguarum notitiam, duo videlicet uniuscuiusque lingue periti, qui scolas regant inibi, et libros de linguis ipsis in latinum fideliter transferentes, alios linguas ipsas sollicite doceant, earumque peritiam studiosa in illos instructione transfundant; ut instructi et edocti sufficienter in linguis huiusmodi fructum speratum, possint Deo auctore producere, fidem propagaturi salubriter in ipsos populos infideles. Quibus equidem in Romana curia legentibus per sedem apostolicam, in studiis vero Parisiensi per regem [regnum] Francie, in Oxoniensi per Anglie, Scotie, Hibernie ac Vallie, in Bononiensi per Italie, in Salamantino per Hispanie prelatos, monasteria, capitula, conventus, collegia, exempta et non exempta, et ecclesiarum rectores in stipendiis competentibus et sumptibus volumus provideri, contributionis onere singulis iuxta facultatum exigentiam imponendo, privilegiis et exemptionibus quibuscunque contrariis nequaquam obstantibus, quibus tamen nolumus quoad alia preiudicium generari.

The University of Oxford, etc., directed by the Council of Vienne to establish Masters in Oriental Languages. 1311.

Bishop Clement, servant of the servants of God. For perpetual remembrance of the matter. Among the anxieties... [pious exordium] and therefore imitating the example of Him whose deputy on earth though unworthy we are, who would that His apostles should be learned in every kind of language and should go through the whole world to preach the Gospel, we desire that holy church should abound with good catholics knowing the languages which infidels chiefly use, so that they may be able to instruct such infidels in the holy institutes, and by teaching them the Christian faith and reception of baptism add them to the college of the worshippers of Christ. In order, therefore, that skill in such tongues may the better be obtained by efficient instruction, we, with the approval of this sacred Council, have provided for the erection of schools in the undermentioned languages wherever the Roman Court resides, and also in the Universities of Paris, Oxford, Bologna and Salamanca, decreeing that in each of these places there shall be kept good catholics having sufficient knowledge of the Hebrew, Greek, Arabic and Chaldee tongues, namely, two learned in each tongue to teach school there, and translate faithfully books in these tongues into Latin, and carefully teach others the same languages, and transfuse into them their learning by zealous teaching; to the end that being sufficiently instructed and learned in such languages they may by God's help bring forth the wished-for fruit and propagate the faith with healing results among the infidel nations. We will that provision of competent stipends and expenses shall be made for such teachers in the Roman Court by the Apostolic See, but in the University of Paris, and that of Oxford, Bologna and Salamanca by the prelates, monasteries, chapters, convents, colleges, exempt or not exempt, and rectors of churches of the kingdoms of France, England, Scotland, Ireland and Wales, Italy, and Spain respectively, a contribution to the charges being imposed on each house according to its means, notwithstanding any privileges and exemptions to the contrary, without prejudice to the same in any other respect.

Manumission of an Oxford M.A. 1312.

[Reg. Palatinum Dunelm. (Rolls Series) p. 97.]

Ricardus [etc.] Dunelmensis episcopus Waltero de Heighington, clerico, nostre diocesis, salutem.

Quia libertatibus iura favent, maxime ut cultus augeatur divinus, tuque in divini cultus augmentum ascribi desideras militie clericali,

Nos...ut ad omnes ordines, vinculo servili, quo nobis astringeris, non obstante, licite valeas promoveri...concedimus facultatem, ob favorem divini cultus pariter et augmentum vinculum predictum et ius dominii in personam tuam nobis competens ex nunc penitus renunciantes.

In cuius rei [etc.]. Dat. apud Stoketon die Sancti Mathei Apostoli A.D. 1312.

Memorandum de eodem

Quod eisdem die et anno habuit Magister Robertus[1] de Heighington, scholaris aule de Merton in Oxonia, quandam litteram libertatis sub eadem forma.

[[1] The editor in the Rolls Series substitutes 'Walterus' for 'Robertus,' the reading of the MS., apparently misled by 'de eodem' into thinking that the second letter of manumission was for the same person, whereas it probably meant the same matter. Master Robert, fellow of Merton, already an M.A., was probably a brother of Walter who remained a simple clerk.]

Contest as to Admission of Choristers to Beverley Grammar School free. 1312.

[A. F. Leach, *Mem. of Beverley Minster*, Surtees Society, No. 98, p. 292.]

De numero puerorum coristarum in scolis.

Item, cum Magister Rogerus de Sutton, Rector Scolarum gramaticalium Beverlacensium, numerum puerorum coristarum ecclesie predicte in scolis predictis addiscencium usque ad numerum septenarium artare voluisset, ac pueros in dicta ecclesia coristas ultra prefatum numerum in scolis predictis addiscentes sibi solvere salarium compellere voluisset, et super

Manumission of an Oxford M.A. 1312.

Richard [of Bury etc.], bishop of Durham, to Walter of Heighington, clerk, of our diocese, greeting.

As the laws favour liberty, especially for the increase of divine worship, and you for the increase of divine worship desire to be enrolled in the clerical army,

We...grant you licence that, notwithstanding the bond of slavery by which you are bound to us, you may be lawfully promoted to all orders, from henceforth renouncing in favour and for the increase of divine worship the bond aforesaid and the right of ownership of your person belonging to us.

In witness [etc.]. Dated at Stockton[-on-Tees], St Matthew's day, A.D. 1312.

Memorandum of the same.

In the same year and on the same day Master Robert of Heighington, scholar of Merton Hall in Oxford, had certain letters of freedom in the same form.

Contest as to Admission of Choristers to Beverley Grammar School free. 1312.

Of the number of chorister boys in the school.

Also, whereas Master Roger of Sutton, rector of Beverley Grammar School, wished to limit the number of chorister boys of the aforesaid church being taught in the said school to the number of seven, and to make the chorister boys of the said church beyond the number aforesaid being taught in the said school pay him fees, and some dissension had arisen

hoc inter ipsum et Succentorem prefate ecclesie esset dissensio aliqualis;

Eodem die, videlicet iij Nonas Maii, presentibus canonicis memoratis, dicti Magister et Succentor coram Capitulo comparuerunt, petentes decretum Capituli in premissis.

Capitulum vero, inquisita plenius veritate de premissis per seniores ecclesie memorate, habentes consideracionem ad antiquas consuetudines ecclesie et scolarum predictarum, decrevit numerum puerorum coristarum in predictis scolis non esse artandum, sed omnes, quotquot fuerint, in ecclesia coriste in scola quieti sint et liberi quoad ipsum Magistrum; et quod ipse Magister, vel aliquis successorum suorum, nomine salarii nihil exigat ab eisdem; verumtamen injunxit Succentori quod in fraudem Magistri Scolarum ad portandum habitum in choro pueros non admittat.

Statutes for Warwick Grammar School and Song School. 1316 (?).

[A. F. Leach, *Hist. of Warwick School*, 66, photograph from Chartulary.]

Statuta.

De Officio Magistri Scolarum Gramaticalium Warr[wici].

Ad perpetuam rei memoriam Nos Robertus de Leicestre Decanus Ecclesie Collegiate Beate Marie Warwicensis de fratrum nostrorum consilio statuimus et ordinamus quod Magister Scolarum Gramaticalium qui pro tempore fuerit circa informacionem et instruccionem scolarium suorum in gramaticalibus diligenter insistat, quodque stallo sibi in ecclesia predicta assignato diebus festorum et in festis ix leccionum cum eundem circa scolares suos informandos vacare non contigerit, diuinis officiis intersit, sextamque leccionem in dictis festis ex officii sui debito in superpellicio vel alio habitu decenti legat.

In festis maioribus capam cericam deferens officium unius

between him and the Succentor of the aforesaid church about it;

On the same day, viz. the 5th of May, in the presence of the canons above-mentioned, the said Master and Succentor appeared before the Chapter, asking for the decree of the Chapter in the matter.

The Chapter having made full inquiry as to the truth of the matter through the senior members of the said church, having regard to the ancient customs of the church and school aforesaid, decreed that the number of choristers in the said school ought not to be limited, but that all who were choristers in the church should be quit and free in the school so far as the Master was concerned; and that neither the Master nor any of his successors should demand anything from them by way of fees; but at the same time they enjoined on the Succentor that he was not to admit any boys to wear the habit in choir so as to defraud the schoolmaster.

Statutes for Warwick Grammar School and Song School. 1316 (?).

Statutes.

The Office of the Master of the Grammar School of Warwick.

For an everlasting remembrance of the matter, we, Robert of Leicester, Dean of the Collegiate Church of the Blessed Mary of Warwick, with the counsel of our brethren, decree and order that the Master of the Grammar School for the time being shall devote himself diligently to the information and instruction of his scholars in grammar; and when not engaged in teaching his scholars, shall be present at divine service in the stall assigned to him in the aforesaid church, on all feast days, and feasts of nine lessons, and shall, as his office obliges him, read the sixth lesson on the said feasts, clad in a surplice or other proper habit.

On greater feasts, he shall wear a silk cope and fill the

de quatuor cantoribus in choro et processione faciat, prout in dicta ecclesia hactenus est optentum. Idemque magister omnibus diebus Sabbati per annum, tempore vacacionis scolarum suarum excepto, in capella Beate Marie dicte ecclesie cum scolaribus suis duos cereos ponderis trium librarum cere semel in anno renouandos processionaliter deferat et in eadem dum missa celebrari contigerit, ardere faciat, quem ad certum habitum de sua propria bursa comparandum in dictam ecclesiam (percipit de communi) constringi nolumus in eadem.

Et ut omnis materia litis et discordie quas hactenus inter dictum magistrum et magistrum scolarum musice didicimus exortas super donatistis et paruulis primas litteras et psalterium addiscentibus imperpetuum conquiescat, facta super hiis debita inquisicione, de fratrum nostrorum consilio, volentes quod magistris ipsis et eorum unicuique ius suum tribuatur et indebite usurpaciones scolarium hinc inde de cetero non fiant, statuimus et inuiolabiliter obseruari precipimus quod magister gramatice qui nunc est, et qui prefici contigerit, donatistas habeat, et deinceps scolares in gramaticalibus seu arte dialectica, si in eadem expertus fuerit, habeat, teneat et informet; magister vero musice primas litteras addiscentes psalterium, musicam et cantum, teneat et informet.

De Officio Magistri Musice.

Item statuimus quod magistrum musice singulis diebus dum missa de Sancta Maria in ipsius capella celebratur intersit cum duobus scolaribus suis, et ibidem ad laudem Virginis Marie musicam usque post Agnus Dei cantet, et capam sericam in choro dicte ecclesie, in processionibus et duplicibus festis maioribus, deferens officium unius cantatoris subportet, et ut superius statutum existit, scolares suos cum omni diligencia quam poterit instruat et informet.

Ad quorum omnium et singulorum obseruacionem magistros predictos quos scolis gramatice ville Warrici seu musice per dicte ecclesie Decanum prefici contigerit, quamque in

office of one of the four precentors in the choir and procession, as has hitherto been usual in the church. And the same master, every Saturday throughout the year, except during school vacations, shall carry in procession with his scholars in the Lady Chapel of the church two wax candles of 3 lbs. weight, to be renewed once a year, and let them burn during the celebration of mass. We by no means wish that he should be bound to provide out of his own purse the habit to be worn in church. He receives it out of the common fund.

And that all material for strife and disagreement, which we learn has hitherto arisen between the master and music schoolmaster over the Donatists and little ones learning their first letters and the psalter, may be put a stop to for ever, after due inquiry in the matter and with the advice of our brethren, and so that the masters and each of them may receive their due, and that undue encroachment of scholars on one side and the other may cease for the future; we decree and direct to be inviolably observed that the present grammar master and his successors shall have the Donatists, and thenceforward have, keep, and teach scholars in grammar or the art of dialectic, if he shall be expert in that art, while the music master shall keep and teach those learning their first letters, the psalter, music and song.

The Office of Music Master.

Also we decree that the music master shall be present at the Lady Mass in the Lady Chapel every day with two of his scholars to sing in praise of the Virgin all the music after the Agnus Dei; while at processions and on the greater double feasts he is to wear a silk cope in the choir of the said church and fill the office of a precentor, and as above stated is to instruct and teach his scholars with all the diligence he may.

We will that the masters aforesaid, who shall be presented by the Dean of the said church to the grammar school of the town of Warwick or the music school, shall on their

eorum admissione sacramento ab eisdem prestito corporali in ipsius ecclesie capitulo una cum sacramento obediencie quod nobis impendere tenentur, volumus onerari, saluo nobis et confratribus nostris in dictis scolis libertatibus priuilegiis et consuetudinibus antiquis.

Quod si premissa vel eorum aliquid predicti Magistri vel eorum alter cessante legitimo impedimento absque licencia speciali dicti Decani, non fecerint seu non obseruauerint, non fecerit seu non obseruauerit, alter eorundem pro periurio et inobediencia eorundem ad arbitrium ipsius Decani grauiter puniatur.

Hiis vero statutis iuramento Magistrorum predictorum firmatis adiiciendo et declarando statuimus eosdem Magistros ad premissa onera non teneri vacacionis scolarum suarum tempore, nisi duntaxat si presentes ipsos in villa Warwici esse contigerit duplicibus festis in dictis vacacionibus, si commode interesse poterunt, officient in ecclesia ante dicta prout superius est expressum.

For Oxford, more ancient than Paris University, the same Rights are asked from the Pope. 26 *Dec.* 1317.

[P. R. O. Rot. Rom. 11 Edw. II, m. 13. Printed in Denifle, *Chart. Univ. Paris*, II. 213.]

Sanctissimo in Christo patri Johanni divina providentia sacrosancte Romane ac universalis ecclesie summo pontifici, Eduardus eadem gratia rex Anglie, dominus Hibernie et dux Aquitanie, devota pedum oscula beatorum.

Inter eximia gratiarum donaria quibus regnum nostrum Anglie manus Altissimi mirifice stabilivit summo meretur attolli preconio et favoris cujuslibet insigniri presidio sublimis illa sapientialis studii dignitas, que in Oxoniensi Universitate continuatis viget successibus et floruit ab antiquo.

Ipsa namque ut mater fecunda prolem innumeram procreare non desinit, cujus scientialis claritas ceteros irradiat et illustrat.

admission take their bodily oath in the Chapter of the church together with their oath of obedience, which they are bound to take to the Dean, to observe all and singular the premises, saving always to the Dean and his brethren their ancient privileges and customs in the said schools.

But if the said masters or either of them shall not do or observe the premises or any of them, in the absence of legitimate impediment or special licence of the Dean, they are to be severely punished for perjury and disobedience at the will of the Dean.

Adding and explaining these statutes confirmed by the oaths of the masters aforesaid, we decree that the same masters are not bound to these duties during school vacations, except that if they are in Warwick on any double feast during such vacations they are to officiate in the church, if conveniently possible, as before expressed.

For Oxford, more ancient than Paris University, the same Rights are asked from the Pope. 26 *Dec.* 1317.

To the most holy father in Christ, John, by divine Providence chief bishop of the most holy Roman and of the universal church, Edward by the same grace King of England, lord of Ireland and duke of Aquitaine, devout kisses on the blessed feet.

Among the chief gifts of grace with which the hand of the Most High has miraculously embellished our realm of England, that illustrious school of learning, which flourishes with continuous success and has flourished from ancient times in the University of Oxford, deserves to be exalted with the highest praise and to be decorated with the assistance of everyone's favour.

For as a fruitful mother it ceases not to bring forth innumerable children, the clearness of whose knowledge sheds its beams and light on all others.

Sane intelleximus hanc dudum a felicis memorie domino Bonifacio papa VIII, predecessore vestro, Universitatibus regni Francie gratiam fuisse concessam, ut omnes qui gradum magistralis honoris in quacunque facultate assecuti fuerint, in iisdem possint ubique terrarum lectiones resumere et easdem continuare pro sue libito voluntatis absque nove examinationis vel approbationis preludiis seu debito iterandi principii aut petende gratie cujuscunque.

Verum quia dubium non est secundum veterum testimonia scripturarum, Gallicanum studium ab Anglicanis nostris originale traxisse principium, constatque talem apostolice dispensationis gratiam in Anglicani studii redundare dispendium, si Universitas nostra Oxoniensis cum predictis Universitatibus regni Francie in libertatibus et scolasticis actibus non concurrat, sanctitati vestre affectuosa instantia supplicamus quatenus ad pacem mutuam inter viros scolasticos nutriendam Universitatem predictam Oxoniensem consimili velitis privilegio decorare.

Nos siquidem gauderemus si in nostri et Universitatis nostre predicte favorem, quod a providentia vestra deposcimus, exaudiretis gratiose, quia valde nobis molestum foret, si tanta Universitas aliqua nostris adversa temporibus pateretur, aut ad insolitam servitutem redigeretur.

Conservet vos Altissimus per tempora prospera et longeva. Teste meipso apud Westmonasterium 16 die Decembris anno regni nostri undecimo.

Oxford University asserts that Paris University was founded by Alcuin, and so later than Oxford. 1322.

[B. M. Çott. Faust. A. V.   Printed in Denifle, *Cart. Univ. Paris*, II. 269.]

Sanctissimo in Christo patri Johanni summo pontifici universitas magistrorum et scolarium studii Oxoniensis....

Intelleximus siquidem quod nuper ad studium Parisiense

the same Privileges as Paris University 279

We learn, indeed, that heretofore the lord Pope Boniface VIII of happy memory, your predecessor, granted this favour to the Universities of the kingdom of France that all who had attained the degree of master in any faculty might resume their lectures in the same anywhere in the world and continue them at their pleasure, without any prelude of new examination or approval or any duty of beginning again or obtaining anyone's leave.

But as there is no doubt that, according to the evidence of ancient writings, the University of Gaul drew its origin from our Englishmen, and it is certain that such a grace of apostolic dispensation redounds to the discredit of the English school if our University of Oxford does not run level with the aforesaid Universities of the kingdom of France in liberties and scholastic acts, we petition your holiness with affectionate insistence that, to nourish peace between scholars, you will decorate the University of Oxford aforesaid with a similar privilege.

We, indeed, should be glad if in favour to us and our University aforesaid you would graciously listen to what we ask of your providence, as it would be very grievous to us if such a University should suffer adversity in our time or be reduced to an unwonted position of servitude.

May the Highest keep you for a long and prosperous time. Witness myself at Westminster 16 December in the 11th year of our reign.

Oxford University asserts that Paris University was founded by Alcuin, and so later than Oxford. 1322.

To the most holy father in Christ, John, the supreme bishop, the University of masters and scholars of the School of Oxford.....

We understand that lately you turned the eyes of pity on the School of Paris and promoted doctors thereof, as well in

misericordes oculos convertistis et ejusdem studii doctores tam philosophos quam theologos ad ecclesiastica beneficia promovistis, et alios quidem immensis honoribus sublimastis, alios vero dedistis pastores et doctores in opere ministerii et in edificationem corporis Christi et consummationem Sanctorum.

Nos autem, pater sanctissime, divina institutione formati audemus dicere, quod nostrum studium Oxoniense illo Parisiensi studio, quamvis excellenter nobili, est quidem antiquius tempore, prius origine et prout credimus non posterius dignitate. Constat namque Albinium philosophum et doctorem catholicum natione Anglum famosissimi principis Caroli Magni magistrum et per eundem Carolum de Anglia accersitum fuisse Parisius studii fundatorem, quod non Anglice, imo Gallice atque Romane historie contestantur.

Six Grammar Schools in Lincolnshire. 1329.

[A. F. Leach, *V. C. H. Lincs.*, II. 449, from Lincoln Chapter Act Book, A. 2, 24, f. 14.]

Memorandum quod Idibus Junii A.D. supradicto reverendi viri et domini Dominus Decanus ecclesie Lincolniensis, Egidius de Redmer et Johannes de Scalleby, canonici ecclesie Lincolniensis vices capituli gerentes et nomine ipsius capituli, in quadam camera bassa sub capella dicti Domini Decani in hospicio eiusdem sedentes, ac inter se de collacione scolarum gramaticalium in comitatu Lincolniensi vacancium, cancellaria dicte Lincolniensis ecclesie vacante et in manu dictorum Dominorum existente, ac de personis ad easdem scolas admittendis inter se tractantes; demum scolas gramaticales de Barton, Willelmo de Gornay; scolas de Partenay, Johanni de Upton; scolas de Grimesby, Willelmo de Coleston; scolas de Horncastre, Johanni de Beverlaco; scolas de Sancto Botulpho, Roberto de Muston; et scolas de Graham Waltero Pigot; clericis, a festo S. Michaelis A.D. 1329 usque ad idem festum

philosophy as in theology, to ecclesiastical benefices, and have exalted some to immeasurable honours, and have given others as pastors and teachers in the work of the ministry to the building up of the body of Christ and the perfecting of the Saints.

Now we too, most holy father, created by the institution of God, venture to say that our School of Oxford is more ancient in time, earlier in origin and, as we believe, not inferior in worth to the School of Paris, most noble as it is. For it is established that Alcuin the philosopher and catholic doctor, an Englishman by birth, the master of the most famous prince Charlemagne and summoned from England by him, was the founder of the School of Paris, as not only English but French and Roman histories testify.

Six Grammar Schools in Lincolnshire. 1329.

Memorandum, that on 13 June, in the year aforesaid [1329], the reverend men and masters, the Lord Dean of the church of Lincoln, and Giles of Redmere, and John of Schalby, Canons of the church of Lincoln, as vicegerents and in the name of the Chapter, sitting in a certain low room below the Lord Dean's Chapel in his house, and discussing the collation of the Grammar Schools in the county of Lincoln which were vacant, the Chancellorship of the said church of Lincoln being vacant and then in their hands, and as to the persons to be admitted to such schools; finally they conferred the Grammar School of Barton on William of Gurney, the school of Partney on John of Upton, the school of Grimsby on William of Coleston, the school of Horncastle on John of Beverley, the school of St Botolph [i.e. Boston] on Robert of Muston, and the school of Grantham on Walter Pigot, clerks, from Michaelmas, 1329, to the same feast in the following

anno revoluto, nomine quo supra, caritatis intuitu contulerunt, ipsos et eorum singulos in corporalem possessionem dictarum scolarum, prout eorum singulos ut premittitur singulariter contulerunt, inducendos fore expressius concedentes.

Et postmodo litteras optinuerunt eorum singuli Decanis locorum predictorum dirigendas et sigillo communi capituli consignatas, mutatis nominibus dictorum magistrorum, sub hac forma;

Antonius, Decanus, et capitulum ecclesie Lincolniensis, Dilecto sibi in Christo, Decano de Candelescheaw, salutem in auctore salutis.

Cum nos ad quos scolarum gramaticalium collacio, racione vacacionis cancellarie ecclesie Lincolniensis predicte in manu nostra existentis, noscitur pertinere, scolas gramaticales de Partenay vacantes magistro Johanni de Upton, clerico, a festo Sancti Michaelis A.D. millesimo ccc^{mo} vicesimo nono usque ad idem festum anno revoluto pro informacione puerorum ipsas scolas frequentare volencium contulerimus intuitu caritatis, vobis mandamus quatinus ipsum Johannem corporalem possessionem dictarum scolarum vice et auctoritate nostra per vos vel alium habere faciatis, hanc nostram collacionem locis et temporibus oportunis publicari prout convenit facientes; et nos de facto vestro, cum requisiti fueritis, apertius certificantes.

Datis Lincolnie Idibus Junii A.D. supradicto.

Secession from Oxford University to Stamford.
1334–5.

[A. F. Leach, *V. C. H. Lincs.*, II. 468.]

University Petition to Queen Philippa, 14 Feb., 1334.

[Royal MS. 12, D. XI. f. 29, printed in Oxford Hist. Soc. *Collectanea*, I. 8.]

A la Reigne Dengleterre de par la univ[ersite].

A sa tresnoble et treshonorable dame, Dame Philippe, par la grace de Dieu Reyne dengleterre, Les soens silui pleist

year, in the above title and by way of charity; expressly granting that they and each of them should be inducted into the bodily possession of the said schools in accordance with their respective collations.

And afterwards each of them obtained letters directed to the [Rural] Deans of the places aforesaid, sealed with the common seal of the Chapter, which, with the change of the names of the masters, were in this form:—

'Anthony, Dean, and the Chapter of the church of Lincoln, to their beloved in Christ, the Dean of Candleshaw, health in the Author of health.

Whereas we, to whom the collation of Grammar Schools is known to belong, by reason of the vacancy of the Chancellorship of the church of Lincoln aforesaid, and its being in our hands, have, by way of charity, conferred the Grammar School of Partney, now vacant, on Master John of Upton, clerk, from Michaelmas, 1329, to the same feast in the following year, for the instruction of boys wishing to attend the school; we command you that you, in our stead and by our authority, either personally or by your agent, cause the same John to have bodily possession of the said school, and cause this our collation to be made public at the proper time and place, as conveniently may be, certifying us openly of what you have done when called upon to do so.

Dated at Lincoln, 13 June aforesaid.'

Secession from Oxford University to Stamford.
1334–5.

University Petition to Queen Philippa, 14 Feb., 1334.

To the Queen of England on behalf of the University.

To the very noble and very honourable lady, Lady Philippa, by the grace of God queen of England, her subjects, if it

subiectz le Chancellier et les Maistres de la Universitee Doxenford, ou treshumbles obeyssances toutes reverences et honeurs. Treshonorable dame, de grantz biens et honneurs qe vus auez souent fet a vostre petite Universite de Oxenford deuotement de queoz vus enmercions....

Et pur ceo dame qaukunes gentz, qe toutz ses honeures ount resceuz entre nus, en destruction quant en eus est de nostre Uniuersite seu sont treez a Estanford, et toutz les iourz treount aultres par leur fauses covines; Vuliez, tresnoble dame, a vostre humble filie per tant conseillier, qe par ses faus fuitz ne soit deseuree ne deuisee, mais par vus maintenue puisse les fuitz de grantz et altres enseignier en bons mours et en sciences, en eiant si le pleist regard de bone gentz et sages, qel ad auant ces heures a grand honeur de vostre Realme norriz par encres de vertuz et entendement de sa juvent tanqe a veilliage, et ne vulliez qe la vile doxenford, qest a nostre Seignur le Roi et a vus, pur honur daultre soit en ceste part desheritee....

Escript le Jour seint Valentin.

The Secessionists petition the King for Protection at Stamford. c. Feb. 1334.

[P.R.O. Anct. Pets. 132, No. 6568.]

Pour ceo que grandes et greueuses descordes ont estez de long temps et unqore sont en le universitie de Oxenford per resone de la grande multitude qil y ad de diuerses gentz, et plusours homicides malfaites roberies et autres mals sanz noumbre ont este fetez illoques, et de iour en autre se fount que Chaunceller od la force de la ville ne le puist chastier ne apeser, et plusours de meistres et de escolers se sont retret et ne osent mes uenir a la ville auantdite per celes enchesons pur dout de mort et perde de lour biens et sont demorantz a Estanford et voulient sil plaist a notre Seignuer le Roi pur seurete de eux et des autres escolers qi ne osent a la dite ville

please her, the Chancellor and Masters of the University of Oxford, all reverence and honour with very humble obedience. Most honourable lady, for the great good and honour that you have often done to your little University of Oxford, for which we devoutly thank you....

And for that, lady, certain persons, who have received all their honours among us, in destruction, as far as in them lies, of our university, have gone to Stamford, and daily attract others there by their false pretences, be pleased, most noble lady, to counsel your humble daughter, so that she may not by her false sons be deprived of work and honour, but, being maintained by you, may teach the sons of great men and others good manners and learning. Have, if it please you, regard to good and wise persons who before now, to the great honour of your kingdom, have been nourished with increase of virtue and understanding from youth to old age; and let not the town of Oxford, which belongs to my lord the king and to you, be disinherited in this behalf for the honour of another....

Written on St Valentine's Day [1334].

The Secessionists petition the King for Protection at Stamford. c. Feb. 1334.

For that great and grievous discords have been for a long time and still are in the University of Oxford, by reason of the great multitude there of different people, and many homicides, crimes, robberies and other evils without number have been done there, and happen from one day to another, which neither the Chancellor nor the force of the town can punish or appease; and many of the masters and scholars have withdrawn themselves, and dare not go to the town aforesaid for such reasons, through fear of death and loss of their property; and are living at Stamford, and wish, if it please our Lord the King, for safety of themselves and the other scholars who dare

de Oxenford aprocher et pur esthauncher les grants mals et
affrais auanditz illoques demorer et estudier, prient les dits
meistres et escolers a notre seigneur le Roy pur dieu et pur
seynte charite qe luy plese de sa bone grace grantier a eux son
real assent a les auoir en sa proteccion pur estauncher touz
les mals auantditz, et en amendement de seynte eglise et de la
clergie de son roialme.

The King orders the Sheriff of Lincolnshire to go to Stamford
and issue Proclamation that no Universities are allowed
except at Oxford and Cambridge.   8 Aug. 1334.

[Close Roll, 8 Edw. III, m. 17 d.]

Rex vicecomiti Lincoln. salutem.

Quia datum est nobis intelligi quod quamplures magistri
et scolares universitatis nostre Oxonie colore quarundam dis-
sensionum in universitate predicta nuper ut dicitur exortarum
et aliis coloribus quesitis se ab eadem universitate retrahentes
apud villam de Stamford se divertere et ibidem studium tenere
ac actus scolasticos excercere presumunt assensu nostro seu
licencia minime requisito, quod si toleraretur non tantum in
nostrum contemptum et dedecus, set eciam in dispersionem
universitatis nostre predicte cederet manifeste ; Nos nolentes
scolas seu studia alibi infra regnum nostrum quam in locis ubi
universitates nunc sunt aliqualiter teneri, tibi precipimus firmiter
iniungentes quod ad predictam villam de Stamford personaliter
accedas, et ibidem ac alibi infra ballivam tuam, ubi expedire
videris, ex parte nostra publice proclamari et inhiberi facias, ne
qui, sub forisfactura omnium que nobis forisfacere poterunt, alibi
quam in universitatibus nostris predictis studium tenere vel actus
scolasticos excercere presumant quoquo modo, et de nominibus
illorum quos post proclamacionem et inhibicionem predictas
inveneris contrarium facientes nobis in Cancellaria nostra
sub sigillo tuo distincte et aperte constare faceretis indilate.

not approach the said town of Oxford, and to staunch the great evils and assaults aforesaid, to stay and study there, the said masters and scholars pray our lord the King, for God and for holy charity, that it may please him of his good grace to grant them his royal assent to take them under his protection, to stop all the evils aforesaid, for the advancement of holy church and of the clergy of his realm.

The King orders the Sheriff of Lincolnshire to go to Stamford and issue Proclamation that no Universities are allowed except at Oxford and Cambridge. 8 Aug. 1334.

The King to the Sheriff of Lincoln, greeting.

Whereas we are informed that many masters and scholars of our University of Oxford, under pretext of certain dissensions lately arisen, as it is said, in the University aforesaid and other colourable pretexts, withdrawing themselves from the same University presume to go to the town of Stamford and there hold school and perform scholastic acts, without our assent or licence, which if it should be tolerated would clearly redound not only to contempt of us and our disgrace, but also to the dispersion of our University aforesaid; We, not wishing that schools or studies should be kept elsewhere within our realm except in the places where Universities are now in some sense held, command you, firmly enjoining you to go in person to the said town of Stamford, and there and elsewhere within your bailiwick where you shall deem it expedient, cause public proclamation and inhibition to be made on our behalf that none presume, on pain of forfeiture of all they can forfeit to us, to hold a University or do scholastic acts in any way elsewhere than in our Universities aforesaid, and you shall without delay certify clearly and openly to us in our Chancery under your seal the names of those whom after such proclamation and inhibition you shall find disobedient.

Volumus enim omnibus et singulis qui de violenciis aut iniuriis apud dictam villam Oxonie illatis coram iusticiariis nostris ibidem ad hoc specialiter deputatis se conqueri voluerint celerem iusticiam exhiberi prout decet.

Teste Rege apud Wyndesore secundo die Augusti per ipsum Regem et concilium.

Consimile breve dirigitur maiori et ballivis ville regis Oxonie mutatis mutandis. Teste ut supra.

[A writ was addressed to the Sheriff of Lincolnshire from Newcastle-on-Tyne on 1 Nov. following, stating that the King heard that both masters and scholars had disobeyed the proclamation, and directing the sheriff to go again and seize all the books and other goods of the disobedient. On 7 Jan. 1335 the King wrote to William Trussel, escheator this side Trent, to go with the sheriff (Pat. 8 Edw. III, m. 28). The sheriff did not go. The Stamford 'clerks' sent another petition in Jan. 1335, saying they were living under the protection of John, Earl of Warren, and asking to be allowed to stay, as people of all kind of occupations (*touz maneres de mestiers*) can dwell

Papal Statutes for Education of Benedictine Monks. 1335.

[B. M. Cott. Faust. VI. (Durham Priory Register).]

Constitutiones Benedicti Pape ejus nomine XII super monachos nigros.

Cap. 7. De studiis.

Quia vero per exercitium lectionis acquiritur scientiae margarita et per studium sacrae paginae ad cognitionem excellentiae divinae familiarius pervenitur, ac per cognitionem humani juris animus rationabilior efficitur, et ad justitiam

For we will that speedy justice shall be done, as is proper, to all and singular who shall before our justices, there specially assigned for that purpose, complain of any violence or wrong done to them in the said town of Oxford.

Witness the King at Windsor, 2 August, by the King and Council.

A like writ is directed to the Mayor and Bailiffs of the King's town of Oxford, *mutatis mutandis*. Witness as above.

in any lordship if they are in the King's allegiance. It was in vain. On 28 March the King wrote to the escheator, as the sheriff would not go, to take down the names of the disobedient. On Wednesday after 25 July, the escheator held an inquisition by a jury, when 17 masters, 5 Stamford clergy, 1 bachelor, and 14 scholars, with Philip, manciple of Brasenose, were found there. As to their goods the jury were in ignorance. They must then have left Stamford, as the episode ends with a letter from Oxford to Cambridge University asking them not to admit as a master there the 'perjured' ringleader, William of Barnby.]

Papal Statutes for Education of Benedictine Monks. 1335.

Statutes of Pope Benedict of that name the Twelfth for the Black Monks.

CHAPTER 7. On Universities.

Because by the practice of reading the pearl of learning is acquired, and by the study of the sacred page we arrive at a more familiar acquaintance with the divine excellence, and through the knowledge of human law the mind is made more

certius informatur, Nos cupientes ut viri ejusdem ordinis seu religionis in agro dominico laborantes in primitivis et deinde in divini et humani canonici videlicet et civilis jurium scientiis instruantur constitutioni Clementis praedecessoris nostri de monachis in scientiis primitivis instruendis infra monasteria quibus degunt editae inhaerentes, illam volumus et praecipimus firmiter observari;

Et nichilominus adjiciendo statuimus et ordinamus ut in quibuslibet ecclesiis cathedralibus et monasticis, prioratibus aut aliis conventualibus et solempnibus locis quibus ad haec suppetunt facultates, ordinis seu religionis hujusmodi, deinceps habeatur magister qui monachos eorum doceat in hujusmodi scientiis primitivis, viz. grammatica, logica et philosophia;

Proviso attentius ut seculares cum ipsis monachis docendi in eisdem ecclesiis, monasteriis, prioratibus et locis aliis nullatenus admittantur.

Qui vero magister si monachus non fuerit ipsius ordinis seu religionis de pane et vino et pittancia providere cotidie sicut uni ex monachis ecclesiarum, monasteriorum, prioratuum et locorum hujusmodi teneantur illi, qui talia tenentur in eis capitulis ecclesiarum, monasteriorum, prioratuum et locorum ipsorum conventibus seu monachis ministrare; Necnon pro vestimentis, calciamentis et salario congrua pensio annua assignetur quae tamen xxti librarum Turorum parvorum summam nequaquam excedat quae de infrascripta communi contributione solvetur, donec pro ea pensionibus monachorum studentium ad generalia seu solempnia studia mittendorum certi et perpetui redditus assignati fuerint, prout infra expressius et plenius continetur.

Si vero in ecclesiis, monasteriis, prioratibus et locis praedictis sit monachus ydoneus ad praedicta, monachus ipse per antistites in cathedralibus ecclesiis, in monasteriis vero et aliis locis praefatis per superiores suos instituere fideliter monachos ipsos in praedictis studiis deputetur, et ad hoc sincere fuerit compellatus; cui scilicet monacho institutori decem librae Turon.

logical and obtains more certain knowledge for doing justice; We, desiring that men of the same [Benedictine] order or vows labouring in the Lord's field may be instructed in the elementary sciences and afterwards in those of God's and man's, that is canon and civil, laws, adhering to the constitution published by our predecessor Clement as to the instruction of monks in the elementary sciences in the monasteries in which they live, will and command that it shall be firmly observed;

And adding thereto, we decree and ordain that in all monastic cathedral churches, priories or other conventual and solemn places of sufficient means belonging to such order or vows, there shall henceforth be kept a master to teach their monks such elementary sciences, viz. grammar, logic and philosophy;

Provided always that seculars shall on no account be admitted to be taught with the monks in the same churches, monasteries, priories or other places.

And this master, if he is not a monk of that order or vows, those in the chapters of the churches, monasteries, priories and places, who are bound to serve with such things their convents or monks, shall be bound to provide with bread and wine and a pittance daily as they are one of the monks of such churches, monasteries, priories and places; also for clothes, shoes and salary a proper yearly pension shall be assigned, not exceeding £20 of small Tours money, which shall be paid out of the common contribution mentioned below, until instead of it certain perpetual rents shall be assigned for the pensions of the student monks to be sent to general or solemn schools, as is more at large and fully contained below.

If, however, there is in the churches, monasteries, priories, and places aforesaid a monk fit for the aforesaid, that monk shall be deputed by the prelates of the cathedral churches and the superiors of the monasteries and other places aforesaid faithfully to instruct the monks in the aforesaid studies, and shall be compelled to do so; and this teaching monk shall have

ultra victum et vestitum pro libris omnimodis vel aliis suis necessitatibus juxta dispositionem antistitis, vel dictorum superiorum, deputetur.

Antistites vero et alii superiores praedicti dictos monachos qui dociles fuerint cum consilio proborum et seniorum ecclesiarum [etc.] eligere teneantur, et ordinare de certo numero eorumdem ac de locis et temporibus, quibus lectionibus, quibusve divinis officiis seu obsequiis aliis opportunis intendant.

Possintque antistites et superiores dictos magistros institutores et instruendos cum consilio proborum et seniorum praedictorum, prout eis visum fuerit expediens, removere et loco eorum alios subrogare.

De studentibus ad generalia studia mittendis.

Caeterum, quia expedire dinoscitur, ut postquam prefati monachi in predictis scienciis primitivis eruditi fuerint ad sacre theologie vel canonum transeant facultates; *Statuimus et ordinamus* ut ecclesie monasteria prioratus et alia loca hujusmodi, singula videlicet eorum, cum suis membris inferius declarandis, de quolibet numero vicenario monachorum unum aptum pro fructu majoris scientie acquirendo ad generalia seu solenia studia mittere teneantur et quemlibet ipsorum mittendorum de infrascripta pensione annua providere. Sic autem hujusmodi numerum vicenarium volumus computari: ut illi dumtaxat monachi numerum ipsum efficiant in hoc casu, qui sunt seu erunt in ecclesiis monasteriis vel locis principalibus, et in locis aliis eisdem ecclesiis monasteriis et locis principalibus subjectis, habentibus octo monachos sive plures; et hii solum cum monachis ecclesiarum monasteriorum et locorum principalium hujusmodi, in computatione ac missione hujusmodi conjungantur....Eligantur quoque ipsi monachi mittendi prout in scientia theologie vel juris canonici, seu magis in unaquaque vel alia ipsorum, aptiores poterunt inveniri : Sic tamen quod si apti reperiantur pro ipso theologie studio ad minus medietas

£10 Tours, besides food and clothing, assigned to him for his books of all kinds and other necessaries according to the arrangement of the prelate or the said superiors.

The prelates and other superiors aforesaid shall be bound to elect, with the advice of the approved and senior monks of the churches [etc.], those monks who appear to be teachable, and to make orders as to the number of them, and as to places and seasons, and what lessons or what divine offices or other suitable services they are to attend.

And the prelates and superiors may remove the said teaching masters and those to be instructed, with the advice of the said approved and senior [monks], as shall seem expedient, and put others in their places.

Of Students to be sent to Universities.

But because it is known to be expedient that when the said monks have been taught the said elementary sciences they should pass on to the faculties of sacred theology or canon law, we decree and order that the cathedral churches, monasteries, priories and other such places, each of them that is with its members mentioned below, shall be bound to send out of every twenty monks one who is fit to acquire the fruit of greater learning to a university, and to provide each one so sent with the yearly pension underwritten. And the number of twenty we will shall be thus reckoned: that those monks only shall make up that number for this purpose, who are or shall be in churches, monasteries or principal places, and in other places subject to the same churches, monasteries, and principal places, having eight monks or more; and these alone are to be reckoned with the monks of such churches, monasteries, and principal places in such reckoning and sending. [Clause as to counting fractions of 20.] These monks shall be elected to be sent according as they are found to be most fit in the science of theology and canon law, or in one or other of them; so, however, that if found fit for the study of theology at least half of those to be sent shall be destined

mittendorum pro ipso theologie studio destinetur: vel saltem quanto plures aptiores potuerint inveniri; ac reliqua medietas eorundem mittendorum ad ipsius juris canonici studium transmittatur....Ita quod in festo Exaltationis Sancte Crucis [14 Sept.] vel circa, ipsi taliter nominati et electi in studio Parisiensi existant qui Parisios fuerint destinandi; in aliis vero studiis in festo beati Luce [18 Oct.] vel circa, infallibiliter sint praesentes.

Creation of Bachelors in Beverley Grammar School. 1338.

[A. F. Leach, *Mem. of Beverley Minster* (Surtees Soc.), No. 108, II. p. 127.]

De cerotecis contribuendis ministris ecclesie.

In Dei nomine. Auditis et intellectis meritis cause seu negocii, que coram nobis, Auditore causarum Venerabilis Capituli ecclesie Sancti Johannis Beverlacensis super prestacione et tradicione cerothecarum ministris ecclesie memorate competencium, a Baculariis de novo creandis in Scolis Gramaticalibus prefate ecclesie tradendarum, ex nostri officii debito vertebatur; videlicet, clerico Capituli et Auditori, unum par, preconi Capituli, unum par; clerico Camerarii; clerico altaris Beate Marie; clerico tabulum in choro conficienti; et tribus sacristis ecclesie sepedicte; cuilibet eorum unum par cerotecarum, ex consuetudine legitima et diutius approbata de jure debitarum;

Verum quia dictam consuetudinem coram nobis legitime esse probatam invenimus, dictam consuetudinem de cetero fideliter perpetuis temporibus in prestacione et solucione hujusmodi cerotecarum firmiter observandam; immo omnes et

to study theology, and as many more as can be found most fit for this; and the other half of those to be sent shall be sent to the study of canon law. [Provisions as to oaths of abbot and eight senior monks to elect the most fit.] So that on 14 September or thereabouts those so nominated and elected who are going to Paris may infallibly be present in the University of Paris; and those in other universities on 18 October or thereabouts. [Provision for the election devolving on the next officer of the monastery if the head fails to have an election ten days before Lady Day. Penalties for breach of the statute to be remitted only by Presidents of the General Chapters of the order. Abbots etc. failing to pay the pensioner within a month to pay double, and if for eight months to be *ipso facto* excommunicated, and if for a year to be *ipso facto* deprived of office and benefice.]

Creation of Bachelors in Beverley Grammar School. 1338.

Of the Gloves to be given to the Ministers of the Church.

In the name of God. Having heard and understood the merits of the cause or matter which was duly argued according to the duty of our office before us, the auditor of the causes of the Venerable Chapter of the church of St John of Beverley, on the presentation and delivery of suitable gloves to the ministers of the said church by the bachelors newly created in the grammar school of the aforesaid church; namely, to the Chapter clerk and auditor, one pair; to the Chapter's summoner, one pair; to the chamberlain's clerk, the clerk of St Mary's altar, the clerk making the table in choir, and to the three [sextons] sacrists of the church aforesaid, to each of them one pair of gloves, rightfully due by lawful and long-approved custom;

Now because we have found the said custom to be proved before us by legal proof, we by way of final judgment declare by this writing that the said custom shall be for ever hereafter faithfully observed in the presentation and payment of such

singulos dictam consuetudinem de cetero infringentes, seu quovismodo violantes in majoris excommunicacionis sentenciam, quater in anno in prefata ecclesia publice et notorie latam ipso facto incidere, sentencialiter et diffinitive pronunciamus in hiis scriptis.

St Albans Almonry Boys' Statutes.

[A. F. Leach, *V. C. H. Herts*, II. 53, from Reg. Whethamstede (Rolls Series), II. 315.]

Ordinacio facta, pro mora pauperum Scolarium in Eleemosynaria Sancti Albani, die Sancti Ambrosii, anno Domini millesimo trecentesimo tricesimo nono et cetera.

In Dei nomine, Amen. Incipit modus vivendi pauperum Scolarum in Elemosinaria.

Primo, admittantur pro mora quinque annorum ad maius, quibus hoc tempus sufficit ad proficiendum in grammaticalibus.

Item, nullus extra Eleemosynariam, sine licencia Sub-Eleemosynarii, sub pena recedendi usque ad reconsiliacionem, se absentet.

Item, quicunque convictus vel notorius incontinens, noctivagus, inquietus, discolus, totaliter expellatur.

Item, admissus statim radat amplam coronam, ad modum choristarum ; et, ut decet clericos, tondeantur.

Item, quilibet dicat cotidie Matutinas de Domina, pro se, et omni die festo septem Psallmos, pro Conventu, et fundatoribus nostris.

The Almoner's Duties, St Albans. c. 1330.

[*Ib.* from B. M. Lansdowne MS. 375.]

Ad Elemosinarium eciam pertinet reparacio Elemosinarie et mansionis eiusdem infra monasterium situate. Reparacio eciam studiorum et domus scolarum grammaticalium in villa Sancti Albani. Straminacio forinceci locutorii. Verum

gloves; and, further, we pronounce that all and each who shall hereafter infringe the said custom or violate it in any way *ipso facto* fall under the sentence of greater excommunication publicly and notoriously proclaimed four times a year in the aforesaid church.

St Albans Almonry Boys' Statutes.

Ordinance made for the residence of the Poor Scholars in the Almonry of St Albans, on St Ambrose Day [4 Apr.], A.D. 1339, et cetera.

In the name of God, Amen. Here begins the manner of life of the Poor Scholars in the Almonry.

First, let them be admitted to live there for a term of five years at the most, to whom this period suffices for becoming proficient in grammar.

Item, no poor scholar shall absent himself from the Almonry without the licence of the sub-almoner, under the penalty of expulsion until reconciliation.

Likewise, whosoever is convicted or notorious for being incontinent, a night walker, noisy, disorderly, shall be wholly expelled.

Likewise, immediately on admission, the scholar shall shave an ample tonsure, after the manner of choristers, and shall cut their hair as becomes clerks.

Likewise, every scholar shall say daily the Matins of Our Lady for himself, and on every festival day the Seven Psalms for the convent and our founders.

The Almoner's Duties, St Albans. c. 1330.

To the almoner also belongs the repair of the Almonry and his house in the monastery. The repair also of the studies [? of the monks in the cloister] and of the grammar school house in the town of St Albans. Provision of straw for the

eciam cum concensu archidiaconi ibidem eidem pertinet de ydoneo magistro gramaticali providere; jura et libertates eidem scole concessa manutenere; 26s. 8d. eidem magistro persolvere pro erudicione puerorum elemosinarie monasterii et aliis consuetudinibus scole annuatim; eosdem eciam pueros ad Elemosinariam recipere, et inde juxta consuetudines eiusdem licite removere, unum vel duos pueros et unum servientem et pagettum ibidem tenere de elemosina ibidem cum victualibus cum ceteris sustentandis providere....

Ad Elemosinarium insuper pertinet ad festum puerorum die Sancti Nicholai 12d. conferre, et Passionistis 12d. pro eorum festis contribuere.

Solet eciam pro honestate, licet non ex debito, mappas et manutergia pro mensa puerorum et serviencium ibidem exhibere....

Monachos eciam ordinandos juxta suum cursum ad ordines conducere et eorum expensas exhibere....

Solet eciam pro expensis et habitibus pauperum clericorum ad religionem reperiendorum ex precepto Domini Abbatis, non tamen ex consuetudine, de suo officio providere.

Solvit insuper Thesaurario conventus 20s. et pro pensione scolarium 26s. 8d.

Hec sunt de albo libro.

Merton Grammar School Accounts.
1347–95.

[Merton Mun. 4105, 4106 b, c, 4109, 4110, 4112.]

1347.

	£	s.	d.
In membrana			13½
In incausto			1
In filo albo et viridi et ceteris pertinenciis ad reparacionem vestium tam arcistarum quam gramaticorum			6

outer parlour. Also, with the consent of the archdeacon, there belongs to him the provision of a fit grammar master; the maintenance of the rights and liberties granted to the same school; payment of 26s. 8d. to the same master for teaching the boys of the almonry of the monastery and other yearly customary payments to the school; the reception of the same boys to the almonry, and their lawful removal thence in accordance with the customs of the same, and keeping of one or two boys and a servant and page there by charity, and finding them there with victuals and other maintenance....

To the almoner also belongs the giving 12d. at the boys' feast on St Nicholas' Day [6 Dec.] and a contribution of 12d. to the Passionists for their feasts.

He usually also, for the sake of good manners, not because he is obliged to do so, maintains table-cloths and napkins for the boys' and servants' table there....

Takes the monks who are to be ordained in their turn to orders, and pays their expenses....

He usually also provides out of his office for the expenses and clothes of poor clerks who are got to enter religion, by the Lord Abbot's command, not however by binding custom.

He also pays the convent treasurer 20s. and 26s. 8d. for the pension of the scholars.

This comes out of the White Book.

Merton Grammar School Accounts.
1347–95.

1347.

	£	s.	d.
In parchment			$13\frac{1}{2}$
In ink			1
In white and green thread and other requirements for mending the clothes both of the artists and of the grammarians			6

	£	s.	d.

Magistro Johanni Cornubiensi pro salario scole in termino quadragesimali 10

Et Hostiario suo 2½

Item Magistro Johanni Cornubiensi pro termino estuali 10

et hostiario suo 2½

Inprimis pro salario vj puerorum gramaticalium modo scribendi prima septimana ante assumpcionem Sancte Marie 10

In secunda septimana pro iv pueris . . . 8

    3th [*sic*]   iv . . . 8

    quarta   iv . . . 8

    quinta   iv . . . 8

    sexta   iv . . . 5

quia unus infirmabatur pro medietate septimane septime pro iij pueris . . . 6

. . . .

In pergameno et incausto 2

. . . .

Pro salario viij gramaticorum, viz. pro singulis 4d.ob in termino 3

. . . .

1347—8.

Item in membranis emptis per vices pro arcistis et gramaticis 3   2

. . . .

Item in debili libro Oracii empto pro pueris . . ½

Item in diversis paribus tabellarum albarum pro gramaticis pro argumentis reportandis . . 2½

Item Magistro Johanni Cornewayle in termino hyemali pro salario domus 12

et suo hostiario 3

Item eidem Johanni pro termino Quadragesimo . 10

Hostiario ad tunc 2½

Item eidem Johanni pro termino estivali . . 12

. . . .

	£	s.	d.
To Master John of Cornwall for rent of the school in Lent term		10	
And to his usher			2½
Also to Master John of Cornwall for the summer term		10	
And to his usher			2½
First for school fees of 6 grammar boys learning writing the first week before the Assumption of St Mary		10	
In the 2nd week for 4 boys		8	
3rd 4		8	
4th 4		8	
5th 4		8	
6th 4		5	
because one was ill for half the 7th week for 3 boys		6	
In parchment and ink		2	
For school fees of 8 grammar boys, namely, for each 4½d. a term		3	

1347—8.

	£	s.	d.
Also in parchment bought at different times for artists and grammarians		3	2
Also in a tattered book of Horace bought for the boys			½
Also in several pairs of white tablets for grammarians for reporting arguments			2½
Also to Master John Cornwall in the winter term for rent of the house		12	
And to his usher			3
Also to the same John for Lent term		10	
To the usher for the same time			2½
Also to the same John for the summer term		12	

Commune Thome Gradone.

	£	s.	d.
In septimana S. Petri ad Vincula			
in communis			ixd
in battelis			jd.ob
In 2 [*sic*] septimana in communis			ixd
battellis			jd.ob
[and so on in each week.]			
et in gramaticis pro sex libris			xijd

Expense Thome Dolling.
1367.

	£	s.	d.
Et magistro suo speciali pro autumpno		2	6
In lumine Sancti Nicholai			2
Item Magistro suo in ordinario		2	
Et pro pencione termino yemali			10
In Magistro suo speciali pro eodem termino		2	6
Item bedello			4
et datis de[termin]atori			8
In papiro			1
Et pro tonsione capitis			½
In oblacionibus			1
Magistro suo speciali pro termino quadragesimali		2	6
Pro pencione camere pro termino quadragesimali		[blank]	
Item in vino collato			6
In cirpis			1
In oblacionibus			½
Pro pencione termino estivali			5
Pro magistro suo speciali		2	6
Item datis Magistro informatori pueros de genere fundatoris		13	4

Necessaria communia.
1386—7.

	£	s.	d.
Pro bedello			8
Solutis gramatico		8	

Thomas Gradone's commons.

	£	s.	d.
In the week of St Peter ad Vincula in commons .			9
in battels .			1½
In 2nd week in commons			9
battels			1½
And for grammarians 6 lbs .			12

Thomas Dolling's expenses.

1367.

	£	s.	d.
And for his special master for the autumn		2	6
In St Nicholas' light .			2
Also to his ordinary master .		2	
And for rent in the winter term .			10
For his special master in the same term		2	6
Also to the beadle			4
And given to the determiner			8
In paper .			1
And for shaving his head [hair cutting or the clerical tonsure?].			½
In offerings.			1
For his special master for Lent term .		2	6
For rent of the room for Lent term .		[blank]	
Also in wine given [viz. at determination] .			6
In rushes .			1
In offerings.			½
For rent in the summer term .			5
For his special master .		2	6
Also given to the Master teaching the Founder's kin boys		13	4

Common necessaries.

1386—7.

	£	s.	d.
For the beadle .			8
Paid to the grammarian .		8	

	£	s.	d.

Pro hostiario 6
Pro gaudiis quando omnes socii aule transiverunt
    ad mayying 2
. . . .
Pro camera pro 2 terminis, yemali et quadragesi-
    mali 4
Item Johanni Olney pro [4?] terminis cum in-
    formaret eosdem ex ordinacione custodis . 6 8

       Expense puerorum de genere Fundatoris.

1393—4.
       Wyard, Thomas.

1° termino 10 4
2°   „ . . . . [illegible]
3°   „ 16 5

   Necessariis.

Pro lumine S. Nicholai 2
Pro salario Magistri pro 3 terminis et pro pensione
    camere 7 6
Pro gaudiis sophisticorum 8
Pro magistro in ordinario 2

   c. 1395.

Pro scolagio eorum 6 8
Pro stramine pro scola 8
In oblacionibus in quadragesima 10
Item die cessacionis in expensis Magistri et re-
    sponsalium 2

Boys' Accounts, 14th century

	£	s.	d.
For the usher			6
For gaudies when all the fellows of the hall went a-maying		2	
. . . .			
For the room for 2 terms, winter and Lent . .		4	
Also to John Olney for [4?] terms when he taught them by the Warden's order . .		6	8

. . . .

Expenses of Founder's kin boys.

1393—4.

Wyard, Thomas.

1st term		10	4
2nd ,, ...		[illegible]	
3rd ,, ...		16	5

Necessaries.

For St Nicholas' light			2
For the Master's salary for 3 terms and for rent of the room		7	6
For the sophists' gaudies			8
For the ordinary Master		2	

c. 1395.

For their schoolage		6	8
For straw for the school			8
In offerings in Lent			10
Also on the breaking-up day in expenses of the Master and respondents		2	

The Almonry School, Westminster.
1335—1540.

[A. F. Leach, *Journ. of Educ.* Jan. 1905, from Westminster Abbey Obedientiaries' Accounts.]

Almoner's Accounts.

	£	s.	d.
1355—6.			
Item Johanni Bokenhull pro vestura puerorum in Elemosynaria		30	
1356—7.			
Fratri Johanni Wallingford pro panno puerorum in Sub-Elemosynaria		8	8
1367—8.			
In panno pro pueris in Elymosinaria		26	8
Et in j roba empta pro Magistro dictorum puerorum cum stipendio suo		26	8
Et solutis ij pauperibus scolaribus euntibus ad Oxoniam		5	0
1370.			
Et liberatis fratri Willelmo Colchester sub-elemosinario pro pueris de Sub-Elemosinaria contra festum Sancti Nicolai		9	0
In panno empto pro pueris de Elemosinaria		46	8
Et in j furrura empta pro Magistro puerorum		2	0
Et in stipendio Magistri puerorum hoc anno		13	4

Accounts of Treasurer of Queen Eleanor's Manors.

1383—4.

Magistro puerorum 6*d.* et xiij pueris 2*s.* 2*d.* . . 2 8

The Almonry School, Westminster.
1335—1540.

Almoner's Accounts.

	£	s.	d.

1355—6.

Also to John Bokenhull for clothing for the boys in the almonry 1 10 0

1356—7.

To brother John Wallingford for cloth for the boys in the under-almonry 8 8

1367—8.

In cloth for the boys in the almonry . . . 1 6 8
And in a gown bought for the said boys' Master with his stipend 1 6 8
Paid to two poor scholars going to Oxford . . 5 0

1370.

And delivered to Brother William Colchester, under-almoner, for the boys of the under-almonry against St Nicholas' day [6 Dec. the Boy-bishop's day]. 9 0
In cloth bought for the boys of the almonry . 2 6 8
And in fur bought for the Master of the boys . 2 0
And in the stipend of the Master of the boys this year 13 4

Accounts of Treasurer of Queen Eleanor's Manors.

1383—4.

To the Master of the boys 6*d*., and to 13 boys 2*s*. 2*d*. 2 8

	£	s.	d.

1385—6.

Magistro puerorum cum xxviij pueris in Elemosinaria unde Magistro pro se 6*d*. . . .   5   2

1386—7.

Magistro grammatice cum xxij pueris . . .   4   2

Almoner's Accounts.

1387.

In panno empto pro Magistro scolarum et pueris
in Sub-Elemosinaria una cum tonsura eiusdem
panni   50

1394—5.

Et Magistro scolarum pro erudicione puerorum
per annum ex certa conuencione . . .   13   4

1395—6.

Et Magistro scolarum pro erudicione puerorum ex
noua conuencione   20   0

1396—7.

Et Magistro scolarum pro erudicione puerorum
per conuencionem, per annum iiij terminis .   26   8

1402—3.

Et Magistro scolarum pro erudicione puerorum .   26   8
Item in pannis emptis pro Magistro scolarum et
pueris, precii panni 33*s*., cum tonsura . .   4   19   0
Et in furrura Magistri   2
Et datis cuidam pauperi scolari studenti Oxonie
precepto Domini Abbatis   1   0   0

1405—6.

Et Magistro scole pro erudicione puerorum hoc
anno   13   4

The Almonry School, Westminster

	£	s.	d.

1385—6.

To the Master of the boys with 28 boys in the almonry, of which to the Master for himself, 6d.   5   2

1386—7.

To the Grammar Master and 22 boys . . .   4   2

Almoner's Accounts.

1387.

For cloth bought for the schoolmaster and boys in the under-almonry, with shearing the same cloth   2   10   0

1394—5.

And to the schoolmaster for teaching the boys for the year under a certain agreement . .   13   4

1395—6.

And to the schoolmaster for teaching the boys, under a new agreement.   1   0   0

1396—7.

And to the schoolmaster for teaching the boys, by agreement for a year for 4 terms . . .   1   6   8

1402—3.

And to the schoolmaster for teaching the boys .   1   6   8
Also in cloth bought for the schoolmaster and boys, price of the cloth 33s., and shearing it .   4   19   0
And in the master's fur   2   0
And given to a poor scholar studying at Oxford by the Lord Abbot's orders   1   0   0

1405—6.

And to the schoolmaster for teaching the boys this year   13   4

	£	s.	d.

Et in iiij pannis dimidio emptis pro Magistro et pueris, precii panni cum tonsura 43*s*. . . 8 12 0
Et in furrura Magistri 1 6

1414—5.

In j carpentario conducto per v dies ad emendandum j groundsell in camera Elemosinarie et ad faciendum latrinam fratrum laicorum, murum scole et j tyle ad ostium, capienti in grosso 2 5
Et j dawbatori cum suo famulo ad emendandum diversos defectus Elemosinarie et in scola per iiij dies 2 0

1421—2.

Custus domorum.

Custus nove domus scolarum cum iiij^{or} cameris et iiij^{or} caminis, in stipendiis carpentariorum, in grosso 6 6 8
[Details of other wages and materials.]
Summa 22 9 9

Sacrist's Account.

1425—6.

De j domo edificata pro cantaria de Knoll nuper dimissa pro 53*s*. nil, quia conceditur Johanni Newborough Magistro scolarum et Margarite uxori eius ad terminum vite eorundem sine aliquo inde reddendo . . . . . —
Et ad solvendum fratri Ricardo Birlyngham Elemosinario pro parte panni puerorum in Sub-Elemosinaria 20

Almoner's Account.

1426—7.

De tenementis in fine grangie iuxta le scole-house ac le Millebank iuxta pratum Elemosinarii . 1 6

	£	s.	d.

And for 4½ pieces of cloth bought for the master and boys, price of the piece with shearing, 43s.   8   12   0

And for fur for the master   1   6

1414—5.

For a carpenter hired for 5 days to mend the groundsill in the almonry chamber and to make a latrine for the lay-brethren, the school wall and a tile for the door, taking altogether .   2   5

And for a dauber with his man to mend divers defects in the almonry and school for 4 days .   2   0

1421—2.
Expenditure on buildings.

Cost of a new schoolhouse with 4 chambers and 4 chimneys, in carpenters' wages, in gross .   6   6   8

[Details of other wages and materials.]

       Total 22   9   9

Sacrist's Account.

1425—6.

Rent for a house built for the Knell chantry, formerly let for 53s., nothing, because it is granted to John Newborough the schoolmaster and Margaret his wife for their lives rent free . . . .   —

And to pay to brother Richard Birlingham, the almoner, for part of the cloth of the boys in the under-almonry 1   0   0

Almoner's Account.

1426—7.

Rent from tenements at the end of the grange next the schoolhouse and the Millbank by the Almoner's meadow   1   6

The Almonry School, Westminster

1446—7.

De tenemento ibidem vocato le Sope-hous, nunc vocato Domus Scolarum, hoc anno nihil . . —

1449—50.

	£	s.	d.
Et solutis Magistro scolarum pro erudicione puerorum hoc anno	1	6	8
Et pro furrura toge predicti Magistri		14	
Et solutis pro panno empto pro pueris Elemosinarie, precii panni cum tonsura 44*s*.	10	3	10

1479—80.

Stipendia famulorum.

Et solutis Willelmo Cornysshe pro erudicione puerorum cantancium pro dimidio anno . 6 8

Expense necessarie.

	£	s.	d.
Et in pannis emptis pro Magistro scolarium et pueris Elemosinarie per annum	7	19	8
Et solutis pro tonsura eiusdem		4	
Et solutis Magistro scolarium pro eorum erudicione		26	8
Et pro furrura dicti Magistri		16	

1507—8.

	£	s.	d.
Et in pannis emptis pro Magistro scolarum et pueris Elemosinarie cum tonsura eorumdem una cum 30*s*. solutis Sub-Elemosinario pro pueris cantantibus	9	6	0
Et solutis Magistro scolarum pro erudicione puerorum gramaticorum		40	

1510—1.

Stipendia famulorum.

Et solutis Jacobo [blank in MS.] pro erudicione puerorum hoc anno 13 4

The Almonry School, Westminster

1446—7.   £ s. d.

Rent from a tenement, there called the Soap-house, now called the School-house, this year nothing   —

1449—50.

And paid to the schoolmaster for teaching the boys, this year 1 6 8
And for fur for the aforesaid master's gown . . 1 2
And paid for the cloth bought for the almony boys, price of the cloth with the shearing 44s. 10 3 10

1479—80.
Wages of servants.

And paid to William Cornish for teaching the singing boys for half a year . . . 6 8

Necessary expenses.

And for cloth bought for the master of the scholars and boys of the almonry for the year . . 7 19 8
And paid for shearing the same 4
And paid to the master of the scholars for their teaching 1 6 8
And for the said master's fur 1 4

1507—8.

And for cloth bought for the schoolmaster and almonry boys, with shearing the same, and 30s. paid to the under-almoner for the singing boys 9 6 0
And paid to the schoolmaster for teaching the grammar boys 2 0 0

1510—1.
Wages of servants.

And paid to James for teaching the [singing] boys this year 13 4

Expense necessarie.	£	s.	d.
Et solutis in pannis pro pueris Elemosinarie . .	8	12	
Et pro tonsura eorumdem, cum pannis pro pueris cantantibus		30	
Et solutis Magistro scolarum pro erudicione puerorum gramaticorum		40	

1539—40.

Stipendia famulorum.

	£	s.	d.
Et solutis Precentori pro cantatoribus secularibus hoc anno		40	
Et solutis Succentori hoc anno		3	4
Et solutis Willelmo Gren pro erudicione puerorum cantancium hoc anno		13	4

Expense necessarie.

	£	s.	d.
Et in pannis pro Magistro scolarum et pueris Elemosinarie, cum tonsura eorumdem [*sic*], una cum 30*s*. solutis Sub-Elemosinario pro pueris cantantibus, hoc anno . . .	10	7	10
Et solutis Magistro scolarum pro erudicione puerorum gramaticorum hoc anno . .		40	

Episcopal Attack on the Classics in the Diocese of Exeter. 1357.

[Reg. Grandisson, ed. F. C. Hingeston-Randolph, II. 1192 (f. 201).]

Mandatum pro pueris informandis.

Johannes etc. dilectis in Christo filiis, singulis Archidiaconis in Ecclesia nostra Cathedrali Exonie, et eorum Officialibus, salutem etc.

Non sine frequenti admiracione ac interiori mentis compassione, ipsimet experti sumus et cotidie experimur apud puerorum et illiteratorum Magistros sive Instructores nostre

The Almonry School, Westminster

Necessary expenses.	£	s.	d.
And paid for cloth for the almonry boys	8	12	0
And for shearing the same, and for cloth for the singing boys	1	10	0
And paid to the schoolmaster for teaching the grammar boys	2	0	0

1539—40.

Servants' wages.	£	s.	d.
And paid the precentor for the lay singers this year	2	0	0
And paid the succentor this year		3	4
And paid William Green for teaching the singing boys this year		13	4

Necessary expenses.	£	s.	d.
And for cloth for the schoolmaster and almonry boys, with shearing the same, and 30s. paid to the under-almoner for the singing boys this year	10	7	10
And paid to the schoolmaster for teaching the grammar boys this year	2	0	0

Episcopal Attack on the Classics in the Diocese of Exeter. 1357.

Mandate as to teaching boys.

John etc. to his beloved sons in Christ, all the archdeacons in our cathedral church of Exeter and their Officials, health etc.

Not without frequent wonder and a feeling of pity have we personally experienced, and daily experience, among the masters or teachers of boys and of the unlearned of our diocese, that

Diocesis, ipsos in Gramatica informantes, modum et ordinem docendi preposteros et minus utiles, immo supersticiosos, Gentilium magis quam Christianorum more, observari, dum ipsi scolares suos, postquam oracionem Dominicam cum salutacione Angelica, et Symbolum, necnon Matutinas et Horas Beate Virginis, et similia que ad Fidem pertinent et anime salutem, legere aut dicere eciam minus perfecte didicerint, absque eo quod quicquam de predictis construere sciant vel intelligere, aut dicciones ibi declinare vel respondere de partibus earundem, ad alios libros magistrales et poeticos aut metricos ad [d]iscendos transire faciunt premature. Unde contigit quod in etate adulta, cotidiana que dicunt aut legunt non intelligant; Fidem, eciam, Catholicam (quod dampnabilius est) propter defectum intelligencie non agnoscant.

Cupientes, igitur, abusum tam nephandum ac fatuum, nimis inolitum per nostram Diocesim, viis et modis quibus possumus extirpare, vobis, et vestrum singulis, committimus et mandamus quatinus vestrum quilibet Magistris seu Instructoribus puerorum quibuscumque, Scolis Gramadicalibus [*sic*] infra fines sui Archidiaconatus presidentibus, auctoritate nostra precipiat et injungat, prout, tenore Presencium, districte precipiendo, injungimus et mandamus quatinus pueros, quos recipiunt in Gramadicalibus imbuendos, non tantum legere aut discere litteraliter, ut hactenus, ut, aliis omnibus omissis, construere et intelligere faciant Oracionem Dominicam cum Salutacione Angelica, Symbolum, et Matutinas, ac Horas de Beata Virgine, et dicciones ibi declinare ac respondere de partibus earundem, antequam eosdem ad alios libros transire permittant. Denunciantes eisdem quod pueros aliquos clericali caractere insignire non intendimus nisi per hunc modum reperti fuerint profecisse.

Datum in manerio nostro de Chuddeleghe, tercio decimo die mensis Februarii A.D. m°ccc°m°lvj^{to} et consecracionis xxx^{mo}.

they, while instructing them in grammar, observe a form and order of teaching which are preposterous and useless, indeed superstitious and more like heathens than Christians, in that as soon as their scholars have learnt to read or say even very imperfectly the Lord's Prayer, with the Hail Mary and the Creed, also Matins and the Hours of the Blessed Virgin, and the like, which are necessary for faith and the safety of their souls, though they do not know how to construe or understand any of the things before-mentioned, or to decline or parse any of the words in them, they make them pass on prematurely to learn other school books of poetry or in metre. And so it happens that when they are grown up they do not understand what they say or read every day; moreover, which is even more damnable, through want of understanding they do not know the catholic faith.

Desiring, therefore, by all the ways and means possible, to root out so dreadful and stupid an abuse which has become too usual in our diocese, we commission and command you and each of you to order and enjoin on all masters or teachers of boys, presiding over Grammar Schools within the boundaries of your archdeaconry, by our authority, as by virtue of these presents we strictly order and enjoin, that they shall not make the boys whom they receive to learn grammar only to read or learn Latin, as hitherto, but leaving everything else make them construe and understand the Lord's Prayer and Ave Maria, the Creed, Matins and Hours of the Blessed Virgin, and decline the words there and parse them before they let them go on to other books. Informing them that we do not intend to mark any boys with the clerical character unless they have by this means been found to have become proficient.

Dated at our manor of Chudleigh 13 Feb. 1356-7, and the 30th year of our consecration.

The Master of the Almonry School, Canterbury, goes to the Public School at Kingston. 1364.

[A. F. Leach, *V. C. H. Surrey*, II. 155, from Canterbury Mun. Reg. L., f. 59 b; printed in *Lit. Cantuar.* (Rolls Series, No. 85), II. 464.]

William of Edyngdon, Bishop of Winchester, to the Prior of Canterbury.

Domine et amice in Christo carissime....Sane, referentibus nobis dilectis filiis parochianis nostris ville de Kyngeston, pridem accepimus, quod ipsi informatore seu magistro puerorum eorundem, et aliorum in dictam villam ubi consueverant scole exerceri confluencium, tediose carentes, cum quodam Hugone de Kyngeston, clerico, de dicta villa oriundo, nuper scolarium in domo Elemosinarie vestre digno, sicut dicitur, petagogo, ut informacioni et doctrine dictorum puerorum et aliorum scolarium in dicta villa intenderet, et scolas publicas gubernaret, primo circiter festum Sancti Michaelis, et postmodum in festo Natalis Domini proximo praeterito, convencionem fecerunt et pactum fidele inierunt, dicti Hugonis fidei dacione vallata; que dictus Hugo, in nostra presencia constitutus et ad sancta Dei evangelia iuratus, publice fatebatur; offerens se premissa omnia fideliter impleturum. Verum cum vester commonachus, Elemosinarius domus vestre predicte, de dicti Hugonis recessu ut accepimus anxius et molestus, quedam eiusdem bona modica arrestaverit seu sequestraverit, et ea detinuerit sequestrata, credens per hoc ipsum Hugonem ad sua obsequia revocare, vestram paternitatem, nomine amicitie de cuius integritate fiduciam indubiam reportamus, requirimus et rogamus, quatinus dictum Elemosinarium salutaribus monicionibus dignemini precipere, ut dicto Hugoni, vel harum baiulo nomine suo, prefata bona restitui et liberari faciat, et eundem Hugonem super non-redditu suo habere velit propensius excusatum; advertentes, si placet, quod de iure creandi sunt de vico populi magistratus, et de eodem loco dandi sunt populi vinitores....

Scriptum apud Essche vij° die mensis Aprilis.

The Master of the Almonry School, Canterbury, goes to the Public School at Kingston. 1364.

William of Edyngdon, Bishop of Winchester, to the Prior of Canterbury.

My lord and dearest friend in Christ....We learnt some time ago, on the report of our beloved sons and parishioners of the town of Kingston, that they to their grief, being without a teacher or master of their boys and others coming to the said town, where a school has been accustomed to be kept, made an agreement and entered into a contract, confirmed by sureties, with one Hugh of Kingston, clerk, born in the said town, lately the worthy pedagogue, as it is said, of the scholars in the house of your Almonry, that he should undertake the instruction and teaching of the said boys and of other scholars in the said town and preside over the Public School there, first about Michaelmas, and again at Christmas last, as the said Hugh, who came before us and was sworn on the Holy Gospels, publicly confessed, offering faithfully to fulfil the same. But your fellow-monk, the Almoner of your house aforesaid, being, as we hear, troubled and annoyed at the said Hugh's leaving, seized or sequestrated some poor goods of his, and keeps them still under sequestration, thinking by these means to recall the said Hugh to his service. In the name of that friendship, in the soundness of which we have undoubting faith, we require and ask your fatherhood, that you would be good enough with salutary warnings to order the said Almoner to restore and deliver the said goods to the said Hugh, or to the bearer of these letters in his name, and that he will hold the said Hugh excused for not returning; seeing, if it please you, that by law magistrates should be created from their own town, and the vinedressers of the people be chosen from the same place....

Written at Esher, 7 April [1364].

Foundation Deed of Winchester College.
20 October 1382.

[A. F. Leach, *Hist. Winchester College*, 66. Photograph from original.]

Uniuersis sancte matris ecclesie filiis ad quos presentes littere nostre peruenerint Willelmus de Wykeham permissione diuina Wyntoniensis episcopus, Salutem in Eo qui est omnium vera salus.

Gloriosissimus et omnipotens deus noster eterni triumphator imperii, qui sua potencia ineffabili et celestis disposicione consilii nos ab utero matris nostre in hanc vallem miserie producere dignatus est miserum atque nudum, Nos eciam licet immeritos qui nonnunquam ponit humiles in sublimi sua prudencia infallibili et gracie ubertate amplis ditauit honoribus et ultra condignum ad gradus et dignitates varios sublimauit; Hec nempe interna meditacione pensantes quoddam collegium perpetuum septuaginta pauperum scolarium clericorum in Theologia canonico et ciuili iuribus et in artibus in Uniuersitate Oxonie studere debencium nuper ereximus ac fundauimus Domino concedente ad laudem gloriam et honorem nominis Crucifixi ac gloriosissime Marie virginis matris sue. Verum quia, prout magistra rerum experiencia edocet manifeste, Gramatica fundamentum ianua et origo omnium liberalium arcium aliarum existit, sine qua artes huiusmodi sciri non possunt nec ad earum prosecucionem quisquam poterit peruenire ; Considerantes preterea quod per litterarum scienciam iusticia colitur et prosperitas humane condicionis augetur quodque nonnulli studentes in scienciis aliis propter defectum bone doctrine sufficientis eciam litterature in Gramatica in deficiendi plerumque incidunt periculum ubi proficiendi posuerant appetitum, Sunt eciam et erunt in posterum ut creditur plerique scolares pauperes disciplinis scolasticis insistentes defectum pecuniarum et indigenciam pacientes quibus ad continuandum et proficiendum in arte gramatica supradicta prope non suppetunt facultates nec suppetent in futurum. Huiusmodi scolaribus

Foundation Deed of Winchester College.
20 October 1382.

To all the sons of holy mother church to whom these our present letters shall come, William of Wykeham, by divine permission bishop of Winchester, health in Him who is the true health of all.

Our most glorious and almighty God, the leader of the triumph of the everlasting empire, who by His ineffable power and the decree of His heavenly council has deigned to bring us miserable and naked from our mother's womb to this vale of misery, who sometimes places the lowly on high, has in His infallible providence and by His overflowing grace enriched us, though unworthy, with ample honours and beyond our deserts raised us to divers degrees and dignities. Weighing these things in our inmost thoughts we, by the Lord's grant, have lately erected and founded a perpetual college of seventy poor scholars, clerks, to study theology, canon and civil law and arts in the University of Oxford, to the praise, glory and honour of the name of the Crucified and the most glorious virgin Mary His mother. But whereas experience, the mistress of all things, plainly teaches that grammar is the foundation, gate and source of all the other liberal arts, without which such arts cannot be known, nor can anyone arrive at practising them; considering moreover that by the knowledge of grammar justice is cultivated and the prosperity of the estate of humanity is increased, and that some students in other sciences, through default of good teaching and sufficient learning in grammar, often fall into the danger of failing where they had set before themselves the desire of success: whereas too there are and will be, it is believed, hereafter many poor scholars intent on school studies suffering from want of money and poverty, whose means barely suffice or will suffice in the future to allow them to continue and profit in the aforesaid art of grammar. For

clericis pauperibus et indigentibus presentibus et futuris, ut litterarum studio im,morari seu vacare ac in facultate et sciencia gramaticali predicta per dei graciam uberius et liberius proficere valeant et ad sciencias seu artes liberales fiant ut expedit aptiores, ad omnium scienciarum facultatum et arcium liberalium titulum ampliandum ac studencium et proficiencium in eisdem quantum in nobis est numerum dilatandum, de facultatibus et bonis nobis a Deo collatis sub forma proponimus infrascripta, diuina nobis assistente clemencia, manus nostras apponere adiutrices et caritatis subsidium impartiri.

Ea propter nos Willelmus de Wykeham, Wintoniensis Episcopus antedictus, diuersa mesuagia terras et pratum cum pertinenciis in Soka Wyntonie nostre Wyntoniensis diocesis et prope ipsam ciuitatem de licencia Illustrissimi Principis et domini nostri Domini Ricardi secundi Regis Anglie et Francie adquisiuimus nobis et successoribus nostris Episcopis Wyntoniensibus videlicet de priore et conuentu sancti Swithuni Wyntoniensis unum mesuagium unam acram terre et dimidiam et tres acras prati cum pertinenciis in Soka Wyntonie et iuxta ciuitatem Wyntonie; De Thoma Tannere de Soka Wyntonie unum mesuagium cum pertinenciis in eadem Soka; et de Thoma Lavyngton unum mesuagium cum pertinenciis in Soka predicta: In et super quibus tribus mesuagiis terra et prato cum pertinenciis sic per nos ut premittitur adquisitis necnon in et super tribus aliis mesuagiis cum pertinenciis in dicta Soka iuxta ciuitatem Wyntonie supradictam, que nos ut parcellam temporalium episcopatus nostri Wyntoniensis tenemus in nomine summe et individue Trinitatis patris et filii et spiritus sancti ad laudem gloriam et honorem nominis Crucifixi, gloriosissime virginis Marie matris eius gloriosorumque patronorum ecclesie nostre Wyntoniensis beatorum apostolorum Petri et Pauli beatorumque Birini, Edde, Swithuni et Athelwoldi eiusdem ecclesie Wyntoniensis confessorum et pontificum, sustentacionemque et exaltacionem fidei Christiane ecclesieque profectum et honorem cultus diuini arciumque scienciarum liberalium et facultatum huiusmodi incrementum, gratum per

Winchester College, 1382

such poor and needy scholars, clerks, present and to come, in order that they may be able to stay or be busy at school, and by the grace of God become more amply and freely proficient in the faculty and science of grammar, and become as is desirable more fit for the sciences or liberal arts, to increase the roll of all the sciences, faculties and liberal arts, and expand as far as in us lies the number of those studying and profiting in them, we propose from the means and goods bestowed on us by God, with the aid of the clemency of God, to hold out helping hands and give the assistance of charity in manner underwritten.

Therefore we, the aforesaid William of Wykeham, bishop of Winchester, having acquired for us and our successors bishops of Winchester divers messuages, lands and a meadow, with their appurtenances, in the soke of Winchester in our diocese of Winchester, and near the city itself, by the licence of our most illustrious prince and lord the Lord Richard the Second, king of England and France, viz., from the prior and convent of St Swithun's, Winchester, a messuage, $1\frac{1}{2}$ acres of land and three acres of meadow, with their appurtenances, in the soke of Winchester, and by the city of Winchester; from Thomas Tanner, of the soke of Winchester, a messuage and appurtenances in the same soke; and from Thomas Lavington a messuage with appurtenances in the soke aforesaid: In and on which three messuages, land and meadow, with their appurtenances so by us acquired as is aforesaid, also in and on three other messuages, with their appurtenances, in the said soke by the city of Winchester aforesaid, which we hold as parcel of the temporalities of our bishopric of Winchester, in the name of the highest and undivided Trinity, Father, Son and Holy Ghost, to the praise, glory and honour of the name of the Crucified and the most glorious virgin Mary His mother and the glorious patrons of our church of Winchester, the blessed apostles Peter and Paul, and the blessed confessors and bishops of the same church of Winchester, Birinus, Hæddi, Swithun and Ethelwold, and for the maintenance and exaltation of the Christian faith and the profit of the church, and for the honour of the worship of God and the increase of the liberal arts,

hoc deo obsequium prestare sperantes, de licencia et auctoritate sedis apostolice, dote per nos primitus assignata iuxta formam litterarum apostolicarum in hac parte concessarum, necnon de licencia dicti domini nostri Regis illustrissimi concurrentibusque omnibus aliis et singulis in ea parte de iure seu alias quomodolibet requisitis quoddam Collegium perpetuum pauperum scolarium clericorum prope ciuitatem Wyntoniensem predictam realiter et effectualiter instituimus fundamus stabilimus ac etiam ordinamus:

Quod quidem collegium consistere volumus inperpetuum atque debet in et de numero septuaginta pauperum et indigencium scolarium clericorum collegialiter viuencium in eodem, studenciumque et proficiscencium in gramaticalibus siue in arte facultate seu sciencia gramaticali per Dei graciam temporibus perpetuis duraturum;

Volentesque institucionem fundacionem et ordinacionem dicti nostri collegii ulterius effectui mancipare magistrum Thomam de Cranle, in theologia bacalaureum, virum prouidum et discretum in spiritualibus et temporalibus circumspectum ac moribus et sciencia approbatum eiusdem nostri collegii preficimus in custodem; septuagintaque pauperes et indigentes scolares clericos in gramaticalibus siue in arte facultate seu sciencia gramaticali studere debentes admittimus ipsosque eidem custodi iungimus; et in eodem nostro collegio realiter ponimus ac eosdem collegialiter aggregamus quorum scolarium clericorum nomina in munimentis dicti nostri collegii plenius sunt scripta; et volentes eidem nostro collegio nomen imponere prout decet ipsum Sancte Marie Collegium, vulgariter Seinte Marie College of Wynchestre, nominamus ac eciam nuncupamus, et illud eodem nomine seu nuncupacione volumus imperpetuum nominari ac eciam nuncupari;

Archamque siue cistam communem dictis custodi et scolaribus clericis in eodem nostro collegio collegialiter ut premittitur aggregatis damus tradimus ac eciam assignamus;

Statuimus eciam ordinamus et volumus quod dicti custos et scolares clerici ac alii futuris temporibus loco ipsorum pro perpetuo in eodem nostro collegio assumendi tanquam persone

sciences and faculties, thereby hoping to do pleasing service to God, by the licence and authority of the apostolic [i.e. papal] see, an endowment being first assigned by us in the form of the apostolic [i.e. papal] letters granted us in this behalf, also by the licence of our said most illustrious lord the King, and with the consent of all and singular other persons whose consent is in that behalf lawfully or otherwise required, actually and effectually institute, found, establish and also ordain a perpetual college of poor scholars clerks by the city of Winchester.

And this college we will and it ought for ever to consist in and of the number of 70 poor and needy scholars clerks living college-wise in the same, studying and becoming proficient in grammaticals or the art faculty or science of grammar, by the grace of God for ever to endure.

And wishing further to give effect to the institution, foundation and ordinance of our said college, we appoint Master Thomas of Cranley, bachelor in theology, a man prudent and discreet in spiritual and circumspect in temporal matters, and of approved life and learning, warden of our same college; and we admit seventy poor and indigent scholars clerks who are to study in grammaticals or the art faculty or science of grammar and join them to the same warden; and we place actually in our same college, and assemble college-wise, the same scholars clerks, whose names are more fully written in the muniments of our said college; and wishing to give a name to the same college, as is proper, we name and also call it 'Sancte Marie Collegium,' in the vulgar tongue 'Seinte Marie College of Wynchestre,' and will that it shall be for ever named and also called by the same name or title.

And we give, deliver and assign a common box or chest to the warden and scholars clerks in our same college college-wise assembled, as is aforesaid;

Also we make a statute, order and will that the said warden and scholars clerks and others in time to come for ever to be admitted in their place in our said college shall associate

collegiales et collegiate simul conuersentur ac in eodem collegialiter stent et viuant;

Scolares insuper predictos presentes et futuros omnes et singulos ac ceteros officiarios et ministros quoscunque eidem nostro collegio necessarios sub custodia disposicione et regimine dicti custodis et successorum suorum custodum qui pro tempore fiunt volumus et disponimus pro perpetuo permanere iuxta statuta et ordinaciones nostri collegii memorati;

Quodque custos et scolares dicti collegii et successores eorundem custodis et scolarium clericorum qui pro tempore fuerint omnes et singuli eciam suis successiuis temporibus omnia et singula statuta et ordinaciones nostras huiusmodi imperpetuum obseruent et teneant inconcusse et ad omnia singula statuta et ordinaciones premissa bene integre et fideliter in omnibus tenenda et inuiolabiliter obseruanda predicti custos et successores sui in eorum profeccione tactis sacrosanctis euangeliis corporale teneantur et prestare debeant iuramentum;

Eisdemque custodi et scolaribus clericis et eorum successoribus imperpetuum in hac nostra primaria fundacione eiusdem collegii nostri damus et concedimus ac presenti carta nostra confirmamus omnia predicta mesuagia terram et pratum cum omnibus suis pertinenciis tenenda et possidenda videlicet communiter et in communi eisdem custodi et scolaribus clericis et successoribus eorundem pro mora et inhabitacione suis in collegio nostro predicto de nobis et successoribus nostris episcopis Wynton. in liberam puram et perpetuam elemosinam imperpetuum libere integre pacifice pariter et quiete;

Tenore tamen presencium ulterius ordinandi et statuendi scolaribus et clericis dicti nostri collegii regulas vite scolastice et arcium scolasticarum direccius, faciendique et edendi statuta et ordinaciones de et super regimine gubernacione ac statu ipsius nostri collegii et personarum eiusdem eisdemque regulis ordinacionibus et statutis addendi et diminuendi ipsaque omnia et singula in parte vel in toto mutandi interpretandi et eciam declarandi nobis dumtaxat potestatem plenam et liberam reseruamus.

Winchester College, 1382

together as colleagues and collegiate persons and in the same college stay and live;

We will and direct moreover that all and singular the said scholars now and to come and all other officers and servants whatsoever necessary for our same college shall for ever remain under the wardenship, direction and rule of the said warden and his successors for the time being, in accordance with the statutes and ordinances of our said college.

And that the warden and scholars of the said college and the successors of the same warden and scholars clerks for the time being, one and all in their successive times, shall for ever observe and keep all and every such our statutes and ordinances unalterably, and the said warden and his successors on their presentation shall be held in duty bound to take their corporal oath with their hands on the most holy Gospels to keep and inviolably observe all and singular the statutes and ordinances aforesaid well wholly and faithfully in all things.

And we give and grant and by this our charter confirm to the same warden and scholars clerks and their successors for ever in this the first foundation of our same college all the aforesaid messuages land and meadow with all their appurtenances, namely to hold and possess as a community and in common to the same warden and scholars clerks and their successors for their dwelling and habitation in our college aforesaid of us and our successors bishops of Winchester in free pure and perpetual alms for ever freely wholly peacefully equally and quietly.

We reserve however by the tenor of these presents to ourselves only full and free power of further ordaining and establishing for the scholars and clerks of our said college rules for the direction of their school life and scholastic arts, and of making and issuing statutes and ordinances of and concerning the rule governance and estate of our college itself and the parsons of the same, and of adding to or taking from the same rules ordinances and statutes, and of changing construing and also declaring the same one and all in whole or in part.

In quorum omnium testimonium atque fidem presentes litteras nostras per notarium publicum infrascriptum scribi et publicari mandauimus nostrique sigilli appensione fecimus communiri. Datis et actis in capella infra manerium nostrum de Suthwerk nostre Wyntoniensis diocesis anno ab Incarnacione domini secundum computacionem ecclesie anglicane millesimo trescentesimo octogesimo secundo, Indiccione sexta, pontificatus sanctissimi in Christo patris et domini nostri domini Urbani diuina prouidencia pape sexti anno quinto, mensis Octobris die vicesima anno regni Regis Ricardi secundi post conquestum sexto, et nostre consecracionis anno sexto decimo: presentibus venerabilibus et discretis viris magistris Johanne de Bloxham, Archidiacono Wyntoniensi, Johanne de Bukyngham Eboracensis, Johanne de Lydford Exoniensis et Johanne de Campeden Suthwellensis ecclesiarum canonicis et aliis testibus ad premissa vocatis specialiter et rogatis.

[The attestation of two notaries follows.]

A Lollard School [?] *or Conventicle.* 1382.

[Chron. H. Knighton (Rolls Series), II. 182.]

Quidam dominus Ricardus Waytestathe, capellanus, et Willelmus Smyth antedictus [ab artificio sic vocatus;...qui... vinum et cervisiam quasi venenum recusavit, nudis pedibus per plures annos incedens, medio tempore abcedarium didicit et manu sua scribere fecit] moram adinvicem traxerunt in quadam capella sancti Johannis Baptistae extra Leycestriam prope mansionem leprosorum ubi caeteri de illa secta saepe convenerunt conventiculaque confecerunt....Ibi enim erat hospitium et diversorium omnium talium adventantium, et ibi habuerunt gingnasium malignorum dogmatum et opinionum et errorum haereticorumque communicationem. Capella quae olim Deo dedicata est jam blasphemis et ecclesiae Christi inimicis atque haereticis receptorium et sedes facta est.

In witness and faith whereof we have directed these our present letters to be written and published by the underwritten notary public and have caused them to be authenticated by appending our seal. Given and done in the chapel in our manor of Southwark in our diocese of Winchester in the year from the Incarnation of the Lord according to the reckoning of the Church of England 1382, in the Sixth Indiction, in the fifth year of the bishopric of the most holy father in Christ and our lord the Lord Urban the sixth by divine providence Pope, on the 20th day of October, in the sixth year of the reign of King Richard the second after the conquest and the sixteenth year of our consecration; in the presence of the venerable and discreet men Masters John of Bloxham, archdeacon of Winchester, John of Buckingham, John of Lydford, and John of Campdon, respectively canons of the churches of York, Exeter and Southwell, and other witnesses specially called and invited to the premises.

[Then follow the attestation clauses of two notaries, filling 27 lines of a printed quarto page.]

A Lollard School [?] *or Conventicle.* 1382.

One Sir Richard Waytestathe, chaplain, and the said William Smith [so called from his craft...who...refused wine and beer as poison, and going barefoot for some years, meanwhile learnt the alphabet and wrote it with his own hand] lived by turns in a chapel of St John the Baptist outside Leicester by the lepers' hospital, where others of that sect often met together and made conventicles....For it was a hospice and inn for all such who came there, and there they had a school of malignant dogmas and opinions and exchange of heretical errors. The chapel once dedicated to God was now made a receptacle and seat for blasphemers and enemies of the church of Christ and heretics.

Foundation of Wotton-under-Edge Free Grammar School. 1384.

[A. F. Leach, *V. C. H. Gloucestershire*, II. 396, from Reg. Ep. Worcester, H. Wakfeld, p. 72.]

Ordinacio domus scolarium de Wotton-sub-Egge.

Carta domine Kitterine de Berkeleye.

Uniuersis Sancte matris ecclesie filiis Katerina, que fui uxor domini Thome de Berkeley nuper domini de Berkeleye, Walterus Burnet, capellanus, Willelmus Pendok, capellanus, salutem in eo qui est omnium vera salus.

Nos dicta Katerina considerantes propensius et attente propositum multorum in gramatica, que est fundamentum omnium arcium liberalium, informari volencium, per penuriam et inopiam indies subtrahi et annullari; ea propter et ad sustentacionem et exaltacionem sancte matris ecclesie, cultusque diuini et aliarum arcium et scienciarum liberaliumque incrementum de bonis nobis a Deo collatis, certa terras et tenementa subscripta, dictos Walterum et Willelmum adquirere procurauimus, sibi et heredibus suis in feodo, ut ipsi quandam domum scolarum in Wotton under Egge de nouo construere et pro inhabitacione siue fundacione, et similiter pro sustentacione, unius magistri et duorum pauperum scolarium artis gramatice ea valeant disponere; qui quidem magister et successores sui gubernabunt et informabunt omnes scolares ad eandem domum siue scolam pro erudicione huiusmodi artis venientes absque aliquo pro labore suo ab eis seu eorum aliquo capiendo.

Nos eciam dicti Walterus et Willelmus salubre propositum et piam intencionem dicte domine Katerine in hac parte in omnibus supplere cupientes, licencia domini regis ac aliorum dominorum quorum interest mediante, in et de quadam placea nostra continente duas acras terre cum pertinenciis in Wotton

Foundation of Wotton-under-Edge Free Grammar School. 1384.

Ordinance of the House of Scholars of Wotton-under-Edge [Gloucestershire].

Deed of Lady Katharine of Berkeley.

To all the sons of holy mother church, I Katharine, who was wife of Sir Thomas of Berkeley, late lord of Berkeley, Walter Burnet, chaplain, William Pendock, chaplain, health in Him who is the true health of all.

We the said Katharine, closely and attentively considering that the purpose of many wishing to be taught grammar, which is the foundation of all the liberal arts, is daily diminished and brought to naught by poverty and want of means, therefore and for the maintenance and exaltation of holy mother church and increase of divine worship and of the other arts and liberal sciences, out of the goods bestowed on us by God, caused the said Walter and William to acquire to them and their heirs in fee the lands and tenements underwritten, that they might newly build a school-house in Wotton-under-Edge for the habitation and foundation and likewise dispose of them for the maintenance of a master and two poor scholars of the art of grammar; which master and his successors shall govern and teach all scholars coming to the same house or school for instruction in such art, without taking anything for their pains from them or any of them.

We too, the said Walter and William, desiring to fulfil the healthful purpose and pious intention of the said Lady Katharine in this behalf in all points, with the licence of the lord king and other lords interested, really and effectively found, constitute, establish and also ordain in and of a certain place of ours containing two acres of land with the appurtenances

under Egge sumptu et prouidencia dicte domine Katerine adquisita de licencia predicta, quandam domum scolarum perpetuam unius magistri et duorum pauperum scolarium clericorum realiter et affectualiter [*sic* for effectualiter] fundamus, constituimus, stabilimus ac eciam ordinamus.

Quam quidem domum scolarium consistere volumus imperpetuum atque debet in et de numero unius magistri et duorum pauperum scolarium clericorum collegialiter viuencium temporibus perpetuis duraturam; Volentesque fundacionem, institucionem et ordinacionem dicte domus ulterius effectui mancipare, Iohannem Stone, presbiterum et magistrum in artibus, virum prouidum et discretum ac moribus et sciencia approbatum, eiusdem domus prefecimus in magistrum ad scolas in eadem ut premittitur regendas siue gubernandas, duosque pauperes et indigentes scolares clericos in dicta arte gramatica proficisci volentes admittimus, ipsosque eidem magistro adiungimus et eadem domo realiter ponimus, ac eosdem collegialiter aggregamus, quorum scolarium clericorum nomina sunt hec, Iohannes Beenleye et Walterus Morkyn.

Statuimus eciam ordinamus et volumus quod dicti magister et scolares clerici ac alii futuris temporibus loco ipsorum pro perpetuo in eadem domo assumendi, tanquam persone collegiales et collegiate simul conuersent ac in eadem collegialiter stent et viuant; scolares insuper predictos, presentes et futuros, possessiones eciam eiusdem domus quascumque tam a nobis in hac nostra primaria fundacione collatas quam similiter a nobis et quibusuis aliis imposterum conferendas, sub custodia disposicione et regimine dicti magistri et successorum suorum magistrorum, qui pro tempore fuerint, volumus et disponimus pro perpetuo permanere iuxta statuta et ordinaciones per dictam dominam Katerinam et nos, dictos Walterum et Willelmum, facienda; que quidem statuta et ordinaciones dicti magistri et scolares et eorum successores successiuis temporibus imperpetuum obseruent et custodiant inconcusse.

Eidemque magistro et scolaribus clericis, et eorum

Wotton-under-Edge Free Grammar School 333

in Wotton-under-Edge acquired by us at the cost and provision of the said Lady Katharine with the licence aforesaid, a perpetual school-house of a master and two poor scholars clerks;

Which house of scholars we will to consist and ought to endure for ever in and of the number of a master and two poor scholars clerks living college-wise therein; and wishing further to give effect to the foundation institution and ordinance of the said house, we have preferred John Stone, priest and master in arts, a prudent and discreet man, approved in character and learning, as master of the same house to teach or govern school in the same as aforesaid, and we now admit two poor and needy scholars clerks wishing to become proficient in the said art of grammar, and join them to the same master and place them in person in the same house and unite them college-wise, the names of which scholars clerks are these, John Beenly and Walter Morkyn.

We decree, too, ordain and will that the said master and scholars clerks and others to be hereafter for ever admitted in the same house in their place shall live together as collegial and collegiate persons, and in the same college shall remain and live; we will and dispose too the scholars aforesaid, present and future, and whatsoever possessions of the same house have been given by us in this our first foundation, as well as those which shall be likewise afterwards conferred by us or anyone else, shall for ever remain under the guardianship, disposition and rule of the said master and his successors, the masters for the time being, according to statutes and ordinances to be made by the said lady Katharine and us the said Walter and William, which the said master and scholars and their successors shall in their successive times for ever unshakenly observe and keep.

And to the same master and scholars clerks and their

successoribus, imperpetuum, in hac nostra primaria fundacione, eiusdem de licencia, damus et concedimus ac presenti carta nostra confirmauimus dictam placeam continentem duas acras terre cum pertinenciis in Wotton under Egge tenendum videlicet communiter et in communi eisdem magistro et scolaribus clericis, et successoribus eorumdem, pro mora et inhabitacione suis in eadem domo imperpetuum possidendum libere integre pacifice pariter et quiete.

Damus eciam eisdem magistro et scolaribus…[grant of property for endowment and warranty of title. Witness clause].

Datis apud Wotton under Egge vicesimo die mensis Octobris anno regni Regis Ricardi secundi octauo.

[Ordinaciones et Statuta.]

In ipsius vero primaria domus fundacione fecimus certas ordinaciones et statuta quas super ipsius regimine imposterum perpetuis temporibus volumus obseruari.

In primis volumus et ordinamus quod dicte domus scolarium magister, quicumque pro tempore fuerit, presbiter sit, et in capella Beate Katerine manerii de Wotton, dummodo ego Katerina predicta vel alii domini vel domine dicti manerii de Wotton presentes fuero vel fuerint aut moram fecero seu fecerint ibidem; et, cum alibi fuero, seu cum fuerit dominus ipsius manerii, in ecclesia parochiali dicte ville idem magister celebrabit imperpetuum pro salubri statu nostro ac predictorum Domini Thome de Berkeley, nunc domini de Berkeley, et Domine Margarete consortis eiusdem, necnon Domini Iohannis de Berkeley, militis, et Elizabethe consortis ipsius, et pro animabus nostris cum ab hac luce migrauerimus, et similiter pro animabus Thome dudum de Berkeley, domini et mariti mei, Katerine predicte, Petri de Veel similiter quondam domini et mariti mei dicte Katerine, Iohannis de Clyuedon, militis, et Emme consortis ipsius, patris et matris meorum dicte Katerine, et omnium progenitorum et parentum dicti domini Thome, nunc domini de Berkeleye, et meorum Katerine predicte, absque aliquo stipendio siue salario a quocumque

Free Grammar School, 1384

successors for ever in this our first foundation by the same licence we give and grant and by this our deed have confirmed the said place containing two acres of land with the appurtenances in Wotton-under-Edge to hold, that is to say, as a common property in common to the same master and scholars clerks and their successors, for their dwelling and living in the same house for ever to possess freely wholly and at the same time peacefully and quietly.

We give also to the same master and scholars...[grant of property for endowment and warranty of title. Witness clause].

Dated at Wotton-under-Edge on the 20th day of the month of October in the eighth year of the reign of King Richard the Second [1384].

[Ordinances and Statutes.]

On the first foundation of the House we have made certain ordinances and statutes for its rule which we will shall be for ever observed.

First we will and ordain that the Master of the said House of Scholars for the time being shall be a priest and shall always celebrate in St Katharine's chapel in the manor-house of Wotton when I the said Katharine or other the lord or lady of the said manor of Wotton shall be there; and when I or the lord of the said manor shall be elsewhere, then in the parish church of the said town, for the healthy estate of us and of the said Sir Thomas of Berkeley, now lord of Berkeley, and the lady Margaret his consort, also for Sir John of Berkeley, knight, and the lady Elizabeth his consort, and for our souls when we shall have passed from this light, and likewise for the souls of Thomas late of Berkeley, lord and husband of me Katharine aforesaid, and of Peter of Veel likewise, formerly the lord and husband of me the said Katharine, of John of Clyvedon knight and Emma his consort, father and mother of me the said Katharine, and of all the progenitors and parents of the said Sir Thomas now lord of Berkeley and of me the aforesaid Katharine, without taking any stipend or salary from anyone besides the rents and

recipiendo preter redditus et prouentus in prima fundacione et dotacione dicte domus scolarum per nos collatos et donatos eidem, vel postea ex donacione fidelium conferendos, vel alio modo licito adquirendos in augmentacionem prouentuum domus antedicte.

[The master to be presented by Lady Berkeley during her life, and afterwards by Sir Thomas Berkeley and his heirs male, whom failing by Sir John Berkeley, her second son, and his heirs male, whom failing by the lord of the manor of Wotton.]

Item, volumus quod magister Iohannes Stone, magister in artibus, ad regimen dicte domus et gubernacionem dictorum scolarium primus magister intitulatus et duo pauperes et indigentes scolares, videlicet Iohannes Beenleye et Walterus Morkyn, in arte gramatica adiscere et proficere volentes dicte domus magistro adiuncti et in eadem domo positi et collegialiter aggregati, et de terris redditibus et aliis prouentibus, quos eis assignauimus et donauimus in dicte domus fundacione pro eorum sustentacione et aliis oneribus incumbentibus, simul stent et in eadem remaneant, ut subicitur, et collegialiter viuant, quodque possessiones dicte domui collate et imposterum conferende sub custodia disposicione et regimine dicti magistri, et successorum suorum dicte domus magistrorum suis temporibus successiuis, imperpetuum permaneant, iuxta statuta et ordinaciones nostras in presenti scriptura inserta, ad que statuta et ordinaciones obseruanda iidem magister et scolares, ipsorumque successores, in admissione eorum corporali iuramento erunt astricti; dictique magistri et eorum successores dictas scolas regent fideliter et utiliter gubernabunt secundum posse suum, scolaresque quoscumque pro erudicione dicte artis gramatice quocumque et undecumque venientes ea de causa benigne recipient, et ipsos in eadem arte debite informabunt, absque aliquo commodo siue lucro pro labore suo nomine stipendii siue salarii exigendo, vendicando vel recipiendo ab eis, de quo poterit argui ambicio magistrorum predictorum.

Volumus insuper et ordinamus quod dicti magister et successores sui a regimine dictarum scolarum non cessabunt,

profits by us bestowed and given to the same in the first foundation and endowment of the said schoolhouse or hereafter to be bestowed by gift of the faithful, or otherwise lawfully acquired in augmentation of the income of the house aforesaid.

[The master to be presented by Lady Berkeley during her life, and afterwards by Sir Thomas Berkeley and his heirs male, whom failing by Sir John Berkeley, her second son, and his heirs male, whom failing by the lord of the manor of Wotton.]

Also we will that Master John Stone, M.A., the first master to be given a title to the rule of the said house and governance of the said scholars, and the two poor and needy scholars, namely, John Beenly and Walter Morkyn, wishing to learn the art of grammar and to become proficient in it, joined to the master of the said house and placed and gathered together college-wise in the said house, shall stay together and remain in the same, as is provided below, and shall live college-wise on the lands, rents and other possessions, which we assigned and gave them on the foundation of the said house for their maintenance and other charges on them, and that the possessions bestowed and hereafter to be bestowed on the said house shall for ever remain under the custody, disposition and control of the said master and his successors, masters of the said house in their time successively, in accordance with our statutes and ordinances contained in this present writing, to the observance of which the same master and scholars and their successors shall on their admission be bound by their corporal oath. And the said masters and their successors shall keep the school faithfully, and usefully govern it after their power, and shall kindly receive all scholars whatsoever, howsoever and whencesoever coming for instruction in the said art of grammar, and duly instruct them in the same art, without exacting, claiming or taking from them any advantage or gain for their labour in the name of stipend or salary, so that the masters aforesaid could be accused of solicitation.

We will also and ordain that the said master and his successors shall not cease from keeping the said school, except

nisi a festo sancti Thome apostoli usque in crastinum Epiphanie, et a dominica in Ramis Palmarum usque ad octauas Pasche, et a vigilia Pentecoste usque in crastinum Sancte Trinitatis, et a festo sancti Petri ad vincula usque in festum exaltacionis Sancte Crucis, pro perpetuo...

[All alienation or diminution of property of the house forbidden except with the consent of the patron in full court of the homage of the lordship, and if made to be void.]

Volumus eciam et ordinamus quod dicti magister et successores sui honeste sint conuersacionis, et quod cure regiminis sui supradicti diligenter intendant, et quod domos, edificia, terras et tenementa, et omnes possessiones eidem domui collatas et conferendas, in statu competenti manutenebunt et sustentabunt, et debitam sustentacionem in esculentis et poculentis dictis duobus scolaribus in dicta domo, ut premittitur, positis et aggregatis, et aliis loco eorum imposterum in eadem admittendis habitacionem et omnia alia necessaria preter vesturam et calciaturam de prouentibus possessionum predictarum inuenient et ministrabunt imperpetuum; residuum vero dictorum prouentuum, ultra sustentacionem magistri domus et dictorum suorum scolarium qui pro tempore fuerint, et similiter ultra manutenenciam et sustentacionem dictarum possessionum aliarumque expensarum debitarum vel honestarum in usum et commodum dicte domus et magistri ipsius conuertentur...

Volumus eciam et ordinamus quod dicti duo scolares in dicta domo nunc positi, ut premittitur, et omnes illi qui loco eorum ibidem imposterum admittentur quos in ipsorum prima admissione etatem decem annorum excedere nolumus, citra autem etatem illam supposita abilitate personarum huiusmodi admissionem eandem interdicere non intendimus, honeste sint conuersacionis scolis intendentes, et magistro suo obedientes, et quod per magistrum qui pro tempore fuerit ad aliqua officia siue ministeria exercenda non ponantur, sed erudicioni et studio continue vacare compellantur. [If disobedient and this proved before patron to be removed.]

Free Grammar School, 1384

from St Thomas' day [21 Dec.] to the morrow of the Epiphany [7 Jan.], and from Palm Sunday to eight days after Easter, and from Saturday before Whitsunday to the day after Trinity Sunday, and from St Peter ad vincula [1 Aug.] to the Exaltation of the Holy Cross [14 Sept.] for ever...

[All alienation or diminution of property of the house forbidden except with the consent of the patron in full court of the homage of the lordship, and if made to be void.]

We will also and ordain that the said master and his successors shall be of good behaviour, and diligently attend to the care of his rule above-mentioned, and shall maintain and sustain the houses buildings lands and tenements and all the possessions bestowed and to be bestowed on the same house in a competent state, and shall for ever find and minister due maintenance in food and drink to the said two scholars placed and assembled in the said house as before-mentioned, and the others hereafter to be admitted in their place, lodging and all other necessaries except clothing and shoes from the revenues of the possessions aforesaid. The residue of the said revenues beyond the maintenance of the master of the house and his said scholars for the time being, and likewise beyond the maintenance and support of the said possessions and other due or proper expenses, shall be commuted to the use and advantage of the said house and the master himself.

[During a vacancy in the mastership the property to be in the custody of the bailiff of the manor of Wotton. Provision for pension of five marks (£3. 6s. 8d.) a year to a master who has to retire through no fault of his own.]

[If the lord of Wotton is a minor the patronage of the school to be exercised by the Abbot of St Augustine's, Bristol.]

We will also and ordain that the said two scholars now placed in the said house, as is before-mentioned, and all those who shall be afterwards admitted there in their place, whose age on their first admission shall not exceed ten years (though we do not intend absolutely to forbid such admission before that age, supposing the persons admitted are of sufficient ability), shall be of good behaviour attending school and obedient to their master, and shall not be set by the master for the time being to do any office or service, but shall be compelled continually to devote their time to learning and study.

Item volumus quid prefati juuenes pauperes duo scolares dicto magistro domus scolarium sic adiuncti ut prefertur postquam in eisdem scolis per sex annos continuos fuerint amoueantur omnino et alii substituantur in locum ipsorum et nominentur per magistrum et admittantur per dominum predictum. Et si quicumque infra dictos sex annos sint indisciplinati et nolint vacare doctrine et post debitam ammonicionem et castigacionem se emendare noluerint per magistrum per superuisum domini vel senescalli sui expellantur et alii subrogentur.

[Master for disobedience to statutes may be removed by the patron after three warnings.]

English Boys translate Latin into French. 1327.

[Higden, *Polychronicon* (Rolls Series, 41), II. 157.]

Angli quoque, quamquam ab initio tripartitam sortirentur linguam austrinam scilicet, mediterraneam et borealem, veluti ex tribus Germaniae populis procedentes, ex commixtione tamen primo cum Danis, deinde cum Normannis, corrupta in multis patria lingua peregrinos jam captant boatus et garritus. Haec quidem nativae linguae corruptio provenit hodie multum ex duobus; quod videlicet pueri in scholis contra morem caeterarum nationum a primo Normannorum adventu, derelicto proprio vulgari, construere Gallice compelluntur; item quod filii nobilium ab ipsis cunabulorum crepundiis ad Gallicum idioma informantur. Quibus profecto rurales homines assimilari volentes, ut per hoc spectabiliores videantur, francigenare satagunt omni nisu.

Also we will that the aforesaid two poor young scholars thus added to the said master of the House of Scholars, as aforesaid, after they have been in the same school for six years continuously shall be wholly removed and others put in their place nominated by the master and admitted by the lord aforesaid; and if any of them within the said six years shall be undisciplined, and shall be unwilling to devote his time to learning, and shall after due warning and chastisement refuse to amend, they shall be expelled by the master under the supervision of the lord or his steward, and others put in their places.

Translation of Latin into English instead of French. 1349.

[Trevisa's translation of Higden's *Polychronicon*.]

Also Englische men, they hadde from the begynnynge thre manere speche, northerne, sowtherne and middel speche in the myddel of the lond, as they come of thre manere peple of Germania. Notheles by comyxtioun and mellynge firste with Danes and afterward with Normans, in meny the contray longage is apayred, and som useth straunge whafferynge, chiterynge, harrynge and garrynge grisbayting. This apayrynge of the burthe of the tunge is bycause of tweie thinges; oon is for children in scole aȝenst the usage and manere of alle othere naciouns beeth compelled for to leue hire owne langage, and for to construe hir lessouns and here thynges in Frensche, and so they have seth the Normans come first in to Engelond. Also gentil men children beeth i-tauȝt to speke Frensche from the tyme that they beeth i-rokked in here cradel and kunneth speke and playe with a childes broche; and vplondisshe men wil likne hym self to gentil men, and fondeth with greet besynesse for to speke Frensce, for to be

Appointment of Master of Song and Grammar School, Northallerton. 15 December 1385.

[A. F. Leach, *Early Yorkshire Schools*, II. 61, from B. M. Cott. Faustin. A. VI. f. (104) 78.]

Robertus Prior Ecclesie Cathedralis Dunelmensis, Ordinarius Spiritualitatis Beati Cuthberti in diocesi Eboracensi, Dilecto nobis in Christo Domino Willelmo de Ledis, capellano, salutem in amplexibus Salvatoris.

Te, ad informandos pueros tam in cantu quam in gramatica, ex laudabili testimonio fidedignorum sufficientem et ydoneum reputantes, Scolas nostras de Allerton, tam cantuales quam gramaticales, prout hactenus conferri consueverunt, tibi conferimus per presentes, intuitu caritatis, Habendas et regendas a dato presencium usque ad terminum trium annorum proximo sequencium, dummodo te bene et honeste habueris, ac circa pueros informandos personaliter diligenciam adhibueris efficacem.

In cuius rei testimonium sigillum nostrum presentibus est appensum.

Datis Dunelmie xv die mensis Decembris A.D. millesimo ccc^{mo} octogesimo quinto.

i-tolde of. This manere was moche i-vsed to for firste deth
and is siththe sumdel i-chaunged; for Iohn Cornwaile, a
maister of grammer, chaunged the lore in gramer scole and
construccioun of Frensche in to Englische; and Richard
Pencriche lerned the manere techynge of hym and othere
men of Pencrich; so that now, the ȝere of oure Lorde a
thowsand thre hundred and foure score and fyve, and of the
secounde kyng Richard after the conquest nyne, in alle the
gramere scoles of Engelond, children leue Frensche and construe and lerne an Englische, and haue therby auauntage in
oon side and disauauntage in another side; here auauntage is,
that they lerne her gramer in lasse tyme than children were
i-woned to doo; disauauntage is that now children of gramer
scole conneth na more Frensche than can hir lift heele, and
that is harme for hem and they schulle passe the see and
trauaille in straunge landes and in many other places. Also
gentil men haue now moche i-left for to teche here children
Frensche.

Appointment of Master of Song and Grammar School, Northallerton. 15 *December* 1385.

Robert Prior of the Cathedral Church of Durham, Ordinary
of the Spiritualities of St Cuthbert in York diocese, to our
beloved in Christ, Sir William of Leeds, chaplain, health in the
embraces of the Saviour.

Considering you on the praiseworthy evidence of trustworthy persons sufficient and fit to teach boys as well song
as grammar, We confer on you by these presents our school
of Allerton, as well of song as of grammar, as they have been
heretofore accustomed to be conferred, by way of charity, To
have and to rule from the date of these presents for the term of
three years next following as long as you behave yourself well
and uprightly, and personally show effective diligence in
teaching boys.

In witness whereof our seal is appended to these presents.
Dated at Durham 15 December, A.D. 1385.

Characteristics of a Monk, a Friar, and an Oxford Scholar. 1388.

[Chaucer's *Canterbury Tales, Prologue,* ed. W. W. Skeat, 1895, p. 420.]

A monk ther was, a fair for the maistrye,
An out-rydere, that lovede venerye;
A manly man, to been an abbot able.
Ful many a deyntee hors hadde he in stable.

. . . .

He yaf nat of that text a pulled hen,
That seith, that hunters been nat holy men;
Ne that a monk, when he is cloisterlees,
Is lykned til a fish that is waterlees;
This is to seyn, a monk out of his cloistre.
But thilke text held he nat worth an oistre;
And I seyde, his opinioun was good.
What sholde he studie, and make himselven wood
Upon a book in cloistre alwey to poure,
Or swinken with his handes, and laboure
As Austin bit? How shal the world be served?
Lat Austin have his swink to him reserved.

. . . .

His botes souple, his hors in greet estat.
Now certeinly he was a fair prelat;
He was nat pale as a for-pyned goost,
A fat swan loved he best of any roost,
His palfrey was as broun as is a berye.

A frere there was, a wantown and a merye,
A limitour, a ful solempne man.
In alle the ordres foure is noon that can
So muche of daliaunce and fair langage.

. . . .

For there he was nat lyk a cloisterer,
With a thredbar cope, as is a poore scoler,
But he was lyk a maister or a pope.
Of double worsted was his semi-cope,
That rounded as a belle out of the presse.
Somwhat he lipsed, for his wantownesse,
To make his English swete upon his tonge.

. . . .

  A clerk ther was of Oxenford also,
That un-to logik hadde longe y-go.
As lene was his hors as is a rake,
And he nas nat right fat, I undertake;
But loked holwe, and ther-to soberly.
Ful thredbar was his overest courtepy;
For he had geten him yet no benefyce,
Ne was so worldly for to have offyce.
For him was lever have at his beddes heed
Twenty bokes, clad in blak or reed,
Of Aristotle and his philosophye,
Than robes riche, or fithele, or gay sautrye.
But al be that he was a philosophre,
Yet hadde he but litel gold in cofre;
But al that he mighte of his freendes hente,
On bokes and on lerninge he it spente,
And bisily gan for the soules preye
Of hem that yaf him wher-with to scoleye.
Of studie took he most care and most hede,
Noght a word spak he more than was nede,
And that was seyd in forme and reverence,
And short and quik, and ful of hy sentence.
Souninge in moral vertu was his speche,
And gladly wolde he lerne, and gladly teche.

A City Song and Reading School. 1388.

[*Ib.*, *The Prioresses Tale*, p. 499.]

Ther' was in Asie, in a greet citee,
Amonges Cristen folk, a Iewerye
. . . .

And thurgh the strete men mighte ryde or wende
For it was free, and open at either ende.
A litel scole of Cristen folk ther stood
Doun at the ferther ende, in which ther were
Children an heep, y-comen of Cristen blood,
That lerned in that scole yeer by yere
Swich maner doctrine as men used there,
This is to seyn, to singen and to rede,
As smale children doon in hir childhede.

Among these children was a widwes sone,
A litel clergeon, seven yeer of age,
That day by day to scole was his wone,
And eek also, wher-as he saugh th' image
Of Cristes moder, hadde he in usage,
As him was taught, to knele adoun and seye
His *Ave Marie*, as he goth by the weye.
. . . .

This litel child, his litel book lerninge,
As he sat in the scole at his prymer,
He *Alma redemptoris* herde singe,
As children lerned hir antiphoner;
And, as he dorste, he drough him ner and ner,
And herkned ay the wordes and the note,
Til he the firste vers coude al by rote.

Noght wiste he what this Latin was to seye,
For he so yong and tendre was of age;
But on a day his felaw gan he preye

T'expounden him this song in his langage,
Or telle him why this song was in usage;
This preyde he him to construe and declare
Ful ofte tyme upon his knowes bare.

His felaw, which that elder was than he,
Answerde him thus: 'This song I have herd seye,
Was maked of our blisful lady free,
Hir to salue, and eek hir for to preye
To been our help and socour whan we deye.
I can no more expounde in this matere;
I lerne song, I can but smal grammere.'

'And is this song maked in reverence
Of Cristes moder?' seyde this innocent;
'Now certes, I wol do my diligence
To conne it al, er Cristemasse is went;
Though that I for my prymer shal be shent,
And shal be beten thryës in an houre,
I wol it conne, our lady for to honoure.'

His felaw taughte him homward prively,
From day to day, til he coude it by rote,
And than he song it wel and boldely
Fro word to word, according with the note;
Twyës a day it passed thurgh his throte,
To scoleward and homward whan he wente;
On Cristes moder set was his entente.

As I have seyd, thurgh-out the Iewerye
This litel child, as he cam to and fro,
Ful merily than wolde he singe, and crye
O Alma redemptoris ever-mo.
The swetnes hath his herte perced so
Of Cristes moder, that, to hir to preye,
He can nat stinte of singing by the weye.

The Schoolmaster of Higham Ferrers is Mayor.
1391.

[A. F. Leach, *V. C. H. Northants*, II. 218, from Higham Ferrers Mun. Court Roll, 14 Ric. II.]

Memo. quod xj die mensis Aprilis anno regni Regis quarto decimo Walter Hontyngdone de Heigham Ferreres remisit relaxavit et omnino imperpetuum quietum clamavit Magistro Henrico Bartone, Scolemayster de eadem, heredibus et assignatis suis, totum ius et clameum quod habuit in toto illo burgagio cum pertinentiis scituato in le Newlond de eadem....

Et propter hoc predictus Walterus suam possessionem per presens habuit in dicto burgagio iure et titulo Margarete uxoris eius...

Examinata vero fuit predicta Margareta per Ricardum Brabasoun et Thomam Raundes clericum burgi de eadem, quibus commissa fuit potestas Maioratus per predictum Henricum quia Maior tunc temporis, causa examinacionis dicte Margarete puplice in predicta curia tenta xxvj° die mensis Maii, ad evitandum cuiuscunque suspicionem.

Statutes of New College, Oxford, and in part of Winchester College. 1400.

[*Statutes of the Colleges of Oxford*, vol. I.]

Liber Statutorum Collegii Beate Marie Wintonie in Oxonia, vulgariter nuncupati New College.

In nomine sancte et indiuidue Trinitatis, Patris, et Filii, et Spiritus Sancti, necnon beatissime Marie Virginis gloriose, omniumque sanctorum Dei. Nos Willelmus de Wicham, permissione diuina Wintoniensis episcopus..., de bonis for-

The Schoolmaster of Higham Ferrers is Mayor.
1391.

Be it remembered that on 11th April, in the 14th year of the king's reign, Walter Huntingdon of Higham Ferrers remitted, released and for ever quit claimed to Master Henry Barton, schoolmaster of the same, his heirs and assigns, all the right and claim which he had in all that burgage with the appurtenances situate in the Newland of the same....

And because of this the aforesaid Walter had possession of the said burgage in right and title of Margaret his wife...

The said Margaret was examined by Richard Brabazon and Thomas Raundes, borough clerk, of the same [town], to whom the Mayor's power had been granted by the said Henry because he himself was Mayor, to take the examination of the said Margaret publicly in the court aforesaid held on 26 May to avoid suspicion on anyone's part.

Statutes of New College, Oxford, and in part of Winchester College. 1400.

Book of the Statutes of the College of the Blessed Mary of Winchester in Oxford, commonly called New College.

In the name of the Holy and Undivided Trinity, Father, Son and Holy Ghost, also of the most blessed Mary the glorious Virgin and of all the Saints of God. We William of Wykeham, by divine sufferance bishop of Winchester..., out of

tune, que nobis in hac vita de sue plenitudinis gracia tribuit abundanter, duo perpetua collegia; unum videlicet collegium perpetuum pauperum et indigencium scolarium clericorum, in studio Uniuersitatis Oxonie, Lincolniensis dioeceseos, in diuersis scienciis et facultatibus studere ac proficere debencium, Seinte Mary College of Wynchestre in Oxenford, vulgariter nuncupatum; et quoddam aliud collegium perpetuum aliorum pauperum et indigencium scolarium clericorum gramaticam addiscere debencium, prope ciuitatem Wintonie, Seinte Mary College of Wynchestre, similiter nuncupatum; ad laudem, gloriam et honorem nominis Crucifixi ac gloriosissime Marie matris eius, sustentacionem et exaltacionem fidei Christiane, Ecclesie sancte profectum, diuini cultus, liberaliumque arcium, scienciarum et facultatum augmentum, auctoritate Apostolica et Regia, ordinauimus, instituimus, fundauimus et stabiliuimus; prout in cartis et litteris nostris patentibus super ordinacionibus, institucionibus ac fundacionibus, collegiorum ipsorum confectis, plenius continetur. Unde nos volentes aliqua, que in presenti nostre occurrunt memorie, facere, statuere ac eciam ordinare, que dicto nostro collegio Oxonie scolaribus clericis, et personis aliis, ac possessionibus et bonis eiusdem collegii, necnon salubri regimini eorundem, necessaria et utilia reputamus, et que doctrinam, incrementum et profectum, ipsorum respicere dignoscuntur, Christi nomine primitus inuocato, ad futuram et perpetuam rei memoriam ad eam procedimus in hunc modum.

Rubrica 1. De totali numero scolarium clericorum, presbyterorum et aliorum ministrorum capelle dicti Collegii Oxonie, et studencium numero particulari in diuersis scienciis et facultatibus in eodem.

Imprimis siquidem, ut sacra Scriptura seu pagina, scienciarum omnium aliarum mater et domina, sua liberius ac pre ceteris dilatet tentoria, et cum ea pacifice militet utriusque iuris, canonici, videlicet, et ciuilis, facultas, nec philosophia desit pro

the goods of fortune, which out of the grace of His fulness He has given us abundantly in this life, have with apostolic and royal authority ordained, instituted, founded and established two everlasting colleges; namely, one everlasting college of poor and needy scholars clerks who are to study and become proficient in divers sciences and faculties in the school of the University of Oxford in the diocese of Lincoln, commonly called Seinte Mary College of Wynchestre in Oxenford; and another everlasting college of other poor and needy scholars clerks who are to study grammar near the city of Winchester, likewise called Seinte Mary College of Wynchestre, to the praise, glory and honour of the name of the Crucified and the most glorious Mary His mother, the maintenance and exaltation of the Christian faith, the profit of Holy Church, the increase of divine worship, and the liberal arts, sciences and faculties, as in our deeds and letters patent made for the ordering, institution and foundation of the same colleges more fully appears. And so we wishing to make establish and also ordain certain things which now occur to us which we think necessary and useful for our said college at Oxford for the scholars clerks and other persons and the possessions and goods of the same college and their healthful regulation, and which are thought to regard their learning, increase and profit, first invoking the name of Christ, for their future and everlasting remembrance proceed thus.

Rubric 1. Of the whole number of the scholars clerks, priests, and other ministers of the chapel of the said college at Oxford, and the particular number of those studying in the same in different sciences and faculties.

In the first place then, that the Holy Writ or page, the mother and mistress of all the other sciences, may more freely and beyond the rest extend its tents, and that the faculty of both laws, namely, canon and civil, may peacefully fight alongside of her, and that philosophy may not be wanting

ceteris imbuendis, prefatum nostrum Oxonie Collegium in et de numero unius Custodis ac septuaginta pauperum indigencium scolarium clericorum, in dictis scienciis et facultatibus studere debencium, subsistere statuimus ac eciam ordinamus, et sic ipsum Collegium de diuersis quas in unum congregabit personis existere dignoscetur, sic in eodem Collegio vigeat per Dei graciam scienciarum diuersitas et eciam facultatum, philosophie scilicet, iurium ciuilis et canonici, et ut precipue feruentius ac frequentius Christus euangelizetur, et fides cultusque diuini nominis augeatur et fortius sustentetur, sacre insuper theologie; ut sic dilatetur laus Dei, gubernetur ecclesia, rigor atque feruor Christiane religionis calescant, sciencie quoque et virtutes amplius conualescant; necnon ut generalem morbum militie clericalis, quam propter paucitatem cleri, ex pestilentiis, guerris et aliis mundi miseriis, contingentem, grauiter vulneratam conspeximus, desolacioni compatientes tam tristi partim alleuare possimus, quem in toto sanare ueraciter non valemus: ad quod reuera pro nostro paruitatis modulo nostros apponimus libenter labores.

Et insuper ut custos, scolares et socii, dicti nostri Collegii; quod ad sui regiminis rectitudinem et munimen, viros diuersarum scienciarum et facultatum, qui collegium ipsum eiusdemque possessiones spirituales ac temporales, libertates et iura, impugnare volentibus resistere sciant et valeant, ex aduerso habere indiget eruditos; et, exercitati iugiter in scienciis et facultatibus supradictis, viros de seipsis continue reperiant circumspectos, prouidos et discretos, ac aliis extraneis verisimiliter diligentiores, fideliores, et eciam promptiores ad conseruandum, tuendum et viriliter defendendum, res et bona, terras, redditus, et possessiones alias spirituales et temporales, libertates et iura quecunque collegii memorati, causas quoque, lites et placita, occasione premissorum emergencia, prosequendum et fideliter defendendum, necnon ad faciendum, procurandum, exercendum et eciam exequendum, omnia alia et singula ipsius Collegii negocia, que pro eius tranquillitate, utilitate, commodo et honore occurrerint, et fuerint facienda; cupientes preterea, quod, sicut prefati

Statutes of New College, Oxford

to give its dye to the rest, we decree and also ordain that our said college at Oxford shall consist in and of the number of one warden and seventy poor needy scholars clerks to study in the said sciences and faculties, and as the college itself will consist of divers persons whom it will collect into one, so in the same college there shall, by God's grace, flourish different sciences and faculties, namely, of philosophy, civil and canon law, and above all that Christ may be preached more fervently and frequently, and that the faith and worship of God's name may be increased and more strongly supported, beyond all of holy theology; that so the praise of God may be spread, the church directed, the strength and fervour of the Christian religion grow hotter, and all knowledge and virtue be increased in strength; also that we may relieve in part, though in truth we cannot wholly cure, that general disease of the clerical army, which we have seen grievously wounded through the want of clergy caused by plagues, wars and other miseries of the world, in compassion for its sad desolation; to this in our small way we willingly spend our labours.

And further that the warden, scholars and fellows of our said college, which, as regards the rights and protection of its rule, needs learned men of divers sciences and faculties who may have the knowledge and ability to resist those wishing to attack the college itself and its spiritual and temporal possessions, liberties and rights, and being themselves continually exercised in the sciences and faculties aforesaid, may find men from their own ranks wise, prudent and discreet and probably more diligent, faithful and ready than others taken from outside to preserve, protect and manfully defend the goods and chattels, lands, revenues and other possessions spiritual and temporal, and all liberties and rights of the said college, and to prosecute and faithfully defend the causes, lawsuits and pleas which may arise in respect of them, and also to do, procure to be done, exercise and execute all the business of the same college, which may be necessary to be done for its tranquillity, use, advantage and honour; desiring, moreover, that as the

scolares clerici, predictis diuersis scienciis et facultatibus intendentes, per collaciones et communicaciones mutuas ubique inueniant quod addiscant, et proficientes continue in eisdem semper fiant, ut conuenit, meliores; sic quoque multitudinis ipsorum ad unum finem tendencium sit semper cor unum et anima una; quodque per ipsorum conuersaciones laudabiles, Deo gratas, eorum corda diuini amoris ignita radiis dileccionis fraterne feruore ac mutue caritatis dulcedine citius ac feruencius copulentur, ut sic, propiciacionis diuine assistente clemencia, dictum nostrum Collegium, tot scienciarum ac facultatum viris preditum et fulcitum, firmius, securius, quietius atque fortius, in pacis pulchritudine feliciter persistere valeat et perpetuo permanere;

Statuimus proinde ut scolarium clericorum predictorum decem iura ciuilia, et alii decem iura canonica audire, et in ipsorum iurium separatim facultatibus cum effectu studere, debeant et eciam teneantur, nisi cum id fieri non poterit propter causas inferius describendas; videlicet, cum de numero in facultate iuris ciuilis sic studencium quis se faciat ad sacerdocium promoueri ante tempus nostris ordinacionibus et statutis inferius limitatum, et sic iura ciuilia publice ulterius audire non valens ad facultatem iuris canonici necessario se diuertere oportebit; vel si quis de ipsa facultate iuris ciuilis existens post lecturam libelli Institucionum completam, antequam in ipsa facultate gradum Doctoratus assumat, ad facultatem iuris canonici, ut in eadem facultate ad sui et dicti Collegii utilitatem pariter et honorem proficiat, effectualiter transferatur; tunc demum in utroque casu predicto prefatum ciuilistarum decennarium numerum minui, dictumque decennarium canonistarum numerum per tres huiusmodi precise personas, simul vel eciam successiue, prout opus fuerit, permittimus augmentari.

Reliquus vero numerus, videlicet quinquaginta, artes, seu philosophiam ac theologiam, particulariter ac diligenter audiant et addiscant. Permittimus nihilominus quod duo ex ipsis

aforesaid scholars clerks, being intent on divers sciences and faculties, may by mutual conferences and communication always find what they wish to learn and always becoming more proficient in the same may become, as is right, better; and so in that large number aiming at one end there may be one heart and one mind, and that by their good lives, pleasing to God, their hearts set on fire by the rays of the divine love may more quickly and fervently be united in the warmth of brotherly love and sweetness of mutual charity, that so, through the clemency of God, our said college, endowed and supported by men of so many sciences and faculties, may more firmly, securely, peacefully and strongly persist and for ever endure in the beauty of peace;

We have therefore decreed that of the scholars clerks aforesaid it shall be the duty of ten, and they shall be bound, to attend lectures on civil law, and another ten on canon law and to study effectively in the three separate law faculties, unless this is impracticable for the reasons stated below; for instance, when any of the number so studying in civil law causes himself to be promoted to priest's orders before the time fixed by our ordinances and statutes, so that he cannot any longer attend public lectures on civil law and must necessarily pass to the faculty of canon law; or, if any of the same faculty of civil law, after he has finished lectures on the Institutes, before he takes his doctor's degree in that faculty, is actually transferred to the faculty of canon law so that he may become proficient in that faculty for the advantage and at the same time the honour of himself and the said college; then in either of such cases we allow the said number of ten civilians to be diminished, and the number of ten canonists to be increased by three such persons, together or at intervals, as may be necessary.

[Similar provision that if the number of canonists is not full the number may be made up with civilians, so long as there are not more than twenty altogether in both laws.]

The rest of the number, namely fifty, shall severally diligently attend lectures in and learn arts, or philosophy and theology. We allow however that two of them may employ themselves

scientie medicine, dum tamen Doctor actualiter regens fuerit in facultate eadem, et alii duo duntaxat sciencie astronomie vacent pariter et intendant.

Nolentes tamen, quod aliquis ad medicine facultatem se conuertat, nisi de voluntate et consensu custodis et decani facultatis theologie, et nisi prius in arcium facultate seu sciencia realiter inceperit, et formam compleuerit in eadem Universitate Oxonie requisitam. Quos sic in facultate medicine studentes, si Doctor in facultate ipsa actualiter regens non fuerit, ad studium theologie conuertere se volumus ac proficere in eodem;

Statuentes preterea ac eciam ordinantes, quod, preter et ultra numerum unius custodis et septuaginta scolarium predictorum, sint semper et continue decem presbyteri et tres clerici stipendiarii capelle predicte ministri, seruientes quotidie in eadem, sufficientis litterature, ac bone condicionis, et conuersacionis honeste, vocem competentem habentes, in lectura et cantu sufficienter instructi; necnon sexdecim pueri scientes competenter legere et cantare, sicut et prout in aliis nostris statutis inferius plenius est expressum.

R. 2. Quales et qui sunt eligendi in [nostrum] Collegium Oxonie supradictum.

Statuimus, ordinamus et volumus, quod in omni eleccione scolarium predictorum futuris temporibus in dictum nostrum Collegium Oxonie facienda, principaliter et ante omnes alios ille ac illi qui sunt vel erunt de consanguinitate nostra et genere, si qui tales sint, dum tamen competenter in gramatica eruditi existant, ubicunque fuerint oriundi seu moram traxerint, per viam specialis prerogatiue in veros et perpetuos socios, absque difficultate qualibet seu aliquo probacionis tempore admittantur, et de bonis communibus dicti nostri Collegii, sicut ceteri veri socii et perpetui eiusdem, honeste et debite sustententur.

Et quia inter opera misericordie Christus precipit pauperes recipere in hospicia..., statuimus, ordinamus et volumus, quod omnes et singuli in Collegium nostrum Oxonie ad annos pro-

and attend to the science of medicine, as long as he shall be an actually regent doctor in that faculty, and two others the science of astronomy only.

We do not wish however that anyone should turn to the faculty of medicine without the will and consent of the warden and the dean of the faculty of theology, and that only if he has first really incepted in the faculty or science of arts, and completed the course prescribed in the University of Oxford. And we wish that these students in the faculty of medicine, unless actually regent doctors in the same faculty, shall pass to the study of theology and become proficient in the same;

Decreeing and also ordaining that above and beyond the number of one warden and seventy scholars aforesaid there shall be always and continuously ten priests and three clerks, paid servants of the chapel aforesaid, daily serving in the same, of sufficient learning and good standing and upright life, having good voices and sufficiently instructed in reading and singing; also sixteen boys sufficiently taught to read and sing, as is below more fully expressed in our other statutes.

Rubric 2.   What sort and who are to be elected into our Oxford College aforesaid.

[According to divine and human law and the custom of the realm the founder's heirs ought to inherit the property which he acquired and of which he has made Christ his heir by giving it to the college. So that if they feel aggrieved in one respect they may be relieved in another, not inflicting on them a double penalty,]

We decree, ordain and will that at every election of the scholars aforesaid to be hereafter held for our college at Oxford, first and before all others that one or those who are or shall be of our blood and family, if any such are competently instructed in grammar, wherever they have been born or lived, by way of special prerogative shall be admitted as true and perpetual fellows without any difficulty and without any period of probation, and be honourably and properly maintained from the common property of our said college, like the rest of the true and perpetual fellows of the same.

And because among the works of mercy Christ enjoins the reception of poor in hospitals...we decree, ordain and will that all who are to be elected into our college at Oxford for years

bacionis eligendi post nostros consanguineos sint pauperes indigentes scolares clerici, primam tonsuram clericalem habentes, bonis moribus ac condicionibus perornati, sufficienterque in gramatica eruditi, et conuersacione honesti, ad studium habiles et idonei et in studio proficere cupientes, in nulla sciencia graduati, alioue collegio collegiati nisi solummodo in collegio nostro prope Wintoniam, iuxta modum et formam inferius describendos: qui, et non alii, in dictum nostrum Collegium eligantur et pro probacionis tempore admittantur.

Item, quia summe affectamus et volumus quod numerus scolarium et sociorum in dicto collegio nostro Oxonie per nos superius institutus plene ac perfecte, per Dei graciam, perpetuis futuris temporibus sit completus; ac considerantes attente quod gramatica, que prima de artibus seu scienciis liberalibus reputatur, fundamentum, ianua et origo, omnium aliarum liberalium arcium ac scienciarum existit, quodque sine ea cetere artes seu sciencie perfecte sciri non possunt, nec ad earum veram cognicionem ac perfeccionem quisquam poterit peruenire; ea propter, diuina fauente clementia, de bonis nobis a Deo collatis, unum aliud collegium prope ciuitatem Wintonie, ut superius memoratur, instituimus, fundauimus et stabiliuimus, in et de numero unius Custodis septuagintaque pauperum indigencium scolarium clericorum, tam de sanguine nostro et genere quam de aliis gramaticam addiscere, et in ipsa arte seu sciencia gramaticali studere et per Dei graciam proficere, debencium in eodem, prout in statutis et ordinacionibus ipsius nostri collegii prope Wintoniam plenius continetur. Cupientesque ut in ipso nostro collegio prope Wintoniam dulcis et suauis doctrine ipsius primitiue sciencie potus reperiatur lacteus,...quodque idem collegium nostrum prope Wintoniam, principium et origo collegii nostri Oxonie predicti, velut hortus irriguus ac vinea pubescens in gemmas ipsum collegium nostrum Oxonie fructifera prole fecundet, flores et fructus mellifluos in vinea Domini Sabaoth per ipsius graciam allaturum;

of probation, next to our kin, shall be poor and needy scholars clerks, having the first clerical tonsure, adorned with good character and behaviour, sufficiently instructed in grammar, upright in conduct, and able and fit for study and desiring to become proficient therein, who have not taken a degree in any science, or been members of any college, other than our college near Winchester, as hereinafter described; and they and no others shall be elected into our said college and admitted for a period of probation.

Also, because we above all desire and wish that the number of scholars and fellows in our said college at Oxford above settled may be full and complete by the grace of God for ever; and considering attentively that grammar, which is reputed to be the first of the liberal arts or sciences, is the foundation, gate and source of all other liberal arts and sciences, and that without it the rest of the arts or sciences cannot be perfectly known, and no one can attain to true or complete knowledge of them; therefore, by the favour of the divine clemency, out of the goods bestowed on us by God, we have instituted, founded and established one other college near the city of Winchester, as above stated, in and of the number of one warden and seventy poor needy scholars clerks, as well of our blood and kin, as of others who are in the same to learn grammar and study and by God's grace become proficient in the same art or science of grammar, as is more fully contained in the statutes and ordinances of our same college near Winchester. And being desirous that in our same college near Winchester the milky drink of sweet and sound learning in this same first science may be found,...and that our same college near Winchester, the reason and source of our college at Oxford, may like a well-watered garden and a budding vine engender a fruitful progeny for our college at Oxford, to bring forth flowers and honeyed fruits in the vineyard of the Lord of Sabaoth by His grace;

Idcirco statuimus, ordinamus et volumus, quod sanguineis nostris deficientibus...primo pauperes scolares clerici de collegio nostro predicto prope Wintoniam qui per annum steterint in eodem, si tot habiles [ad tunc] inibi reperiantur, alioquin illi qui prius fuerant in eodem per annum eruditi, sufficienterque probati, habiles et idonei, secundum condiciones superius et inferius recitatas,...in ipsum collegium nostrum Oxonie eligantur, et ad duos annos probacionis eciam admittantur... volentes tamen quod illi de locis et parochiis in quibus possessiones spirituales et temporales collegiorum nostrorum Oxonie et prope Wintoniam existunt pre ceteris [eligantur]; quibus eciam deficientibus, tunc pauperiores indigentes scolares clerici oriundi de dioecesi Wintonie primo, deinde seriatim de comitatibus Oxonie, Berks, Wilts, Somersett, Bucks, Essex, Middlesex, Dorset, Kant, Sussex, et Cantabrigie, et postea de aliis partibus quibuscunque regni Anglie existentes, cum tamen de dicto collegio nostro prope Wintoniam fuerint, et in eodem per annum eruditi....

Statuentes insuper, quod nullus qui vicesimum etatis sue annum excedit, nec aliquis qui quintumdecimum etatis sue annum non compleuerit, in dictum nostrum collegium Oxonie eligatur nec eciam assumatur; preter illos qui sunt et erunt de nostro sanguine et genere procreati, quos volumus in dictum collegium nostrum Oxonie recipi, dum tamen tricesimum etatis sue annum non excedant, si morigerati et in gramatica eruditi existant.

Statuentes preterea, quod nullus qui morbo incurabili laborauerit, vel qui mutilacionem membrorum enormem et apparentem, seu defectum patitur corporalem vel alium ex suo facto vel culpa prouenientem, propter quem redditur omnino inhabilis ad sacros ordines suspiciendos, in ipsum collegium nostrum Oxonie eligatur seu eciam admittatur.

Item statuimus, ordinamus et volumus, quod nullus habens terras, tenementa, possessiones vel annuos redditus, spirituales aut temporales, quorum redditus et prouentus quinque marcarum sterlingorum valorem annuum excedant, in dictum

Therefore we decree, ordain and will that in default of our next of kin,...first poor scholars clerks of our said college near Winchester of a year's standing in the same, if so many shall then be found fit, otherwise those who have formerly been educated in the same, and are sufficiently approved, able and fit according to the conditions above and below mentioned... shall be elected into our college at Oxford, and admitted to two years' probation in the same,...wishing however that those of the places and parishes in which the spiritual and temporal possessions of our colleges at Oxford and near Winchester are, shall be preferred; and failing them, then the poorer needy scholars clerks born in the diocese of Winchester first, next in order those of the counties of Oxford, Berks, Wilts, Somerset, Bucks, Essex, Middlesex, Dorset, Kent, Sussex, and Cambridge, and afterwards those of any other part of the kingdom of England, as long as they have been in our college near Winchester and educated in the same for a year...

Decreeing moreover that no one who has passed the 20th year of his age or who has not completed his 15th year shall be elected or taken into our college at Oxford; except those who are or shall be begotten of our blood and kin, whom we wish to be admitted into our said college at Oxford, as long as they have not passed the 30th year of their age, if they are of good conduct and learned in grammar.

Decreeing moreover that none who is suffering from an incurable disease, or who is suffering from some great and evident mutilation of limbs or other bodily defect, or any coming from his own act or fault, which renders him wholly incapable of taking holy orders, shall be elected or admitted to our same college at Oxford.

Also we decree, ordain and will that no one having lands, tenements, possessions, or yearly incomes, spiritual or temporal, the rents and profits of which exceed the yearly value of five marks sterling [£3. 6s. 8d.], shall be elected or admitted into

Oxonie collegium eligatur vel eciam admittatur; nostris consanguineis supradictis duntaxat exceptis, quos in dictum nostrum collegium Oxonie recipi volumus et admitti in veros socios, ut prefertur, eciamsi habeant possessiones spirituales aut temporales, quorum redditus et prouentus viginti marcarum sterlingorum supportatis oneribus valorem annuum non excedant.

R. 3. De tempore et modo superuisionis et scrutinii fiendis in collegio nostro prope Wintoniam, et forma eleccionis scolarium de eodem ad collegium Oxonie.

Item statuimus, ordinamus et volumus, quod singulis annis, inter festum Translacionis Sancti Thome Martyris et primum diem mensis Octobris proxime tunc sequentem, custos collegii nostri Oxonie et unus de discretioribus sociis eiusdem collegii, gradu magistratus in facultate philosophie, seu in theologia graduatus, ac unus alius gradu doctoratus aut baccalaureatus in facultate iuris ciuilis aut canonici…sumptibus collegii nostri Oxonie accedant ad collegium nostrum prope Wintoniam, sic quod sex equorum numerum non excedant; et ibidem super regimine ipsius collegii custodis ac magistri in gramatica informatoris, hostiarii sub ipso, scolariumque et aliarum personarum degencium in eodem, ac super informacione doctrine et profectu scolastico scolarium ipsius collegii, et qualiter in victualibus prouideatur eisdem, ac super aliis articulis in statutis eiusdem collegii Wintonie contentis, diligenter inquirant et scrutinium faciant; corrigenda et reformanda eciam in eodem…corrigant et reforment.

Quo quidem superuisionis et scrutinii tempore, volumus quod, si totalis numerus scolarium et sociorum in dicto collegio nostro Oxonie, nostris statutis limitatus, in uno, duobus aut pluribus, eciam quotcunque, fuerit diminutus, tunc superuisores predicti, una cum custode et vicecustode et magistro informatore scolarium eiusdem collegii prope Wintoniam, statim post superuisionem et scrutinium supradicta, pauperes scolares de dicto collegio nostro prope Wintoniam, et, si opus fuerit,

the said college at Oxford; except our kin, whom we will shall be admitted into our said college at Oxford as true fellows, as aforesaid, even if they have spiritual or temporal possessions, the rents and profits of which, all charges borne, do not exceed the yearly value of twenty marks sterling [£13. 6s. 8d.].

Rubric 3. Of the time and manner of the survey and scrutiny to be held in our college near Winchester, and the form of election of scholars from the same to the Oxford college.

Also we decree, ordain and will that every year between the Translation of St Thomas the Martyr [Becket, 7 July] and the first of October following, the warden of our college at Oxford and one of the discreeter fellows of the same college, of the degree of a master in the faculty of philosophy or a graduate in theology, and another of the degree of doctor or bachelor in the faculty of civil or canon law...shall, at the cost of our college at Oxford, go to our college near Winchester, with no more than six horses; and there diligently inquire and hold a scrutiny on the government of the warden of the same college and the master teacher in grammar, the ushers under him, and the scholars and other persons living in the same, and on the teaching and progress in school of the scholars of the same college, and the quality of the food provided for the same, and other articles contained in the statutes of the college at Winchester; and shall correct and reform anything needing correction or reform.

At the time of this survey and scrutiny we will that if the total number of the scholars and fellows in our said college at Oxford fixed in our statutes shall have been diminished by one, two or more, however many, then the surveyors aforesaid, with the warden and subwarden and master teacher of the scholars of the same college near Winchester, immediately after the survey and scrutiny aforesaid, shall diligently and faithfully examine the poor scholars of our said college near Winchester, and, if necessary, those who

alios qui prius fuerant in eodem, diligenter et fideliter examinent super sufficiencia literature in gramatica, condicionibus, moribusque ac qualitatibus superius limitatis: qua examinacione si facta, et habilitate sufficientiaque ipsorum scolarium in premissis omnibus et singulis per communem consensum dictorum examinancium approbatis, de ipsis scolaribus magis idoneos tot eligant dicti examinantes ad dictum collegium nostrum Oxonie quot possunt supplere deficientem numerum in eodem, secundum ordinem personarum et locorum modumque et formam in proximo precedenti statuto plenius recitatos, et eisdem in omnibus observatis.

Quo insuper superuisionis tempore, alii pueri et choriste capelle ibidem, in lectura, plano cantu et antiquo Donato, competenter instructi, et infra etatem nostris statutis limitatam constituti, per dictos examinatores et superuisores examinentur; et qui habiles et idonei reperti fuerint eligantur, de quibus numerus scolarium ibidem tunc deficiens impleatur; ceterorumque puerorum, sic, ut prefertur, instructorum et examinatorum, nomina et cognomina in indenturis predictis scribantur, quos ordine illo quo in indenturis predictis scripti et nominati fuerint in dictum collegium prope Wintoniam per custodem, vel in ipsius absencia vicecustodem, et magistrum informatorem predictos recipi volumus loco scolarium ad collegium nostrum Oxonie, ut premittitur, mittendorum, decedencium, seu alias recedencium ab eodem.

R. 4. Quod collegia predicta iuuent se mutuo in causis et litibus.

Et cum prefata duo nostra collegia, licet locis situata diuersis, ex una stirpe prodeant, originaliterque ab uno fonte procedant, in substancia eciam non discrepent, quorum naturaliter non est diuersus effectus, conuenit, congruit, expedit atque decet, ut qua cognacione vicina congaudent, unius eiusdemque nominis seu vocabuli titulo presignantur, quocies

have been in the same, on the sufficiency of their learning in grammar, their conduct and character and other qualities above defined; and when the examination has been held and the ability and sufficiency of the same scholars in all and every the premises has been approved by the common consent of the said examiners, the said examiners shall elect to our said college at Oxford so many of the most fit of the same scholars as shall be enough to supply the number wanting in the same in the order of persons and places, manner and form, more fully set out in the last preceding statute, the same being in every respect fully observed.

[The Oxford electors to swear to do their duty without fear or favour, prayer or price.]

And further, at the time of the survey, other boys and choristers of the chapel there who are competently instructed in reading, plain song and old Donatus, and within the age limited by our statutes, shall be examined by the said examiners and surveyors; and those who are found able and fit shall be elected, and the number wanting in the scholars there shall be filled up from them; and the names and surnames of the rest of the boys who have been so instructed and examined, as before mentioned, shall be written in the said indentures, and we will that they shall be received into the said college near Winchester by the warden, or in his absence the sub-warden, and master teacher aforesaid, in the order in which they have been written and named in the said indentures, in place of the scholars who are to be sent to our college at Oxford, as before mentioned, or are leaving or otherwise departing from the same.

Rubric 4. That the colleges aforesaid shall mutually help each other in causes and actions.

And since our two colleges aforesaid, though situated in different places, grow from one stem, and originally issue from the same source, and do not differ in substance, and naturally do not produce a different effect, it is convenient, fitting, expedient and becoming that, as they rejoice in near relationship, and are known by one and the same name or title,

opus fuerit mutuis se prosequantur suffragiis, et fauoribus sibi inuicem subueniant opportunis....

R. 5. De iuramento scolarium admittendorum in collegium Oxonie ad annos probacionis.

...Item, quod non ero detractor susurro, seu faciens obloquia, aut prouocans odium, iram, discordias, inuidiam, contumelias, rixas vel iurgia, aut speciales vel precellentes prerogatiuas nobilitatis, generis, scienciarum, facultatum aut diuitiarum, allegans; nec inter socios eorundem collegiorum, aut alios Uniuersitatis Oxonie scolares australes, aquilonares seu boreales, aut scienciarum ad sciencias, facultatum ad facultates, patrie ad patriam, generis ad genus, nobilitatis ad nobilitatem vel ad ignobilitatem, seu alias qualitercunque comparaciones que odiose sunt, in verbo vel in facto, causa commouendi maliciose socios vel scolares, aut sciencias aliquas, faciam quouismodo tacite vel expresse. Item, quod nullas conuenticulas, conspiraciones, confederaciones seu pacciones aliquas, ubicunque infra regnum Anglie vel extra, contra ordinaciones et statuta dicta collegia concernencia, vel contra ipsorum collegiorum statum, commodum et honorem, custodes vel vicecustodes vel aliquem socium eorundem collegiorum, illicite faciam, nec ipsa procurabo seu permittam ab aliis fieri quantum in me fuerit quomodolibet in futurum.

R. 14. De Decanis proficiendis et eorum officio.

Item statuimus, ordinamus et volumus, quod quinque socii nostri collegii predicti, de discretioribus et maturioribus, iuxta discrecionem et arbitrium custodis ac vicecustodis, ac tredecim aliorum seniorum sociorum, quorum tredecim seniorum quinque persone de facultatibus iurium ciuilis et canonici existant, nominentur et eciam assumantur; prouiso quod nullus in decanum iuris ciuilis aut canonici assumatur nisi per tres de quinque iuristis predictis fuerit nominatus. Qui sub dicto custode, tanquam eius coadiutores, scolarium

they should support each other whenever necessary with mutual prayers and exchange opportune favours.

Rubric 5. Of the oath of the scholars to be admitted to years of probation in the college at Oxford.

[To obey the statutes.] Also that I will not be a backbiter, scandal-monger, mischief-maker, or provoker of hatred, anger, quarrels, envy, insults, strife or bickering, or asserter of special or preferable prerogatives of nobility, family, sciences, faculties or riches; and that I will not in any way implied or expressed make any comparisons, which are odious, between the fellows of the same colleges and other scholars of the University of Oxford, southerners or northerners, or of science with science, or faculty with faculty, country with country, family with family, good birth with good birth or for the want of it, or any other comparisons whatsoever, in word or deed, for the sake of malicious disturbance of the fellows or scholars or of any science. Also that I will not unlawfully make any associations, conspiracies, confederacies, or compacts, anywhere in the kingdom of England or outside, against the ordinances and statutes of the said colleges, or against the estate of the colleges themselves, their advantage or honour, the wardens or sub-wardens or any fellow of the same colleges, nor will I procure or permit any such to be made by others so far as in me lies in any way in the future.

Rubric 24. Of the Deans and their duties.

Also we decree, ordain and will that five of the discreeter and more mature fellows of our college aforesaid shall be named and appointed at the discretion and choice of the warden, sub-warden, and thirteen other senior fellows, of which thirteen seniors five persons shall be of the faculties of civil and canon law; provided that no one shall be made dean of civil or canon law unless nominated by three of the five jurists aforesaid. They, under the warden and as his assistants,

et sociorum curam et regimen habeant, qualiter scilicet in studio scolastico et morum honestate proficiant, et eis superintendere, ac eos delinquentes corripere et increpare, ipsorumque transgressiones, excessus, delicta et crimina, custodi et vicecustodi denunciare, et ut ipsi iuxta ordinaciones et statuta nostra corrigantur et puniantur diligenter instare iuxta posse, debeant et eciam teneantur.

Quorum quinque, duo magistri in artibus provectiores et maturiores in theologia minime graduati existant, qui, vel eorum alter, singulis disputacionibus artistarum, tercius vero legista disputacionibus legistarum, quartus eciam canonista in singulis disputacionibus canonistarum, et quintus unus de senioribus in theologia in disputacionibus theologorum, a principio interesse et usque ad finem, impedimento cessante legitimo, exspectare debeant ac eciam teneantur. Quos omnes sic prefectos Decanos volumus nuncupari.

Permittentes quod illi ambo decani facultatum iuris canonici et ciuilis eligi poterint de facultate iuris canonici vel ciuilis, secundum quod eligentibus huiusmodi videbitur melius expedire, ac secundum quod in una facultate vel alia maturiores et discretiores existant.

R. 26. De tempore assumendi gradus in qualibet facultate.

Item statuimus, ordinamus et volumus, ut quilibet socius perpetuus vel scolaris dicti nostri Collegii, ad quamcunque scienciam seu facultatem deputatus, annos in ipsa sciencia seu facultate, iuxta ritum, morem, statuta et consuetudines Uniuersitatis predicte, in huiusmodi sciencia seu facultate necessarios, statutos et haberi consuetos, absque remissione temporis aut complecionis forme, habeat integros et completos, antequam ad statum baccalaureatus in eadem facultate seu sciencia quomodolibet admittatur.

Quibus annis completis, si iudicio custodis [etc.] examinatus, habilis, sufficiens et idoneus, repertus fuerit, statum baccalaureatus assumat, et extunc ad legendum continue, vel

shall have the care and government of the scholars and fellows, as to their proficiency in scholastic studies and good conduct, and shall superintend them and pull them up and rebuke them when in default, and denounce their trespasses, excesses, faults and crimes to the warden and sub-warden, and they shall and shall be bound to insist on their being corrected and punished according to our ordinances and statutes.

Of these five two shall be of the more advanced and mature masters in arts, not graduates in theology, and they or one of them ought and shall be bound to be present at every disputation of artists; the third, a lawyer, at every disputation of lawyers; the fourth, a canonist, at every disputation of canonists; and the fifth, one of the seniors in theology, at every disputation of the theologians, from the beginning to the end, unless there is some lawful impediment. All these prefects we will shall be called deans.

Allowing that both deans of the faculties of canon and civil law may be elected from the faculty of canon or civil law as shall seem most expedient to the electors, and as there may be riper and more discreet persons in the one faculty or the other.

Rubric 26. Of the time of taking degrees in each faculty.

Also we decree, ordain and will that every perpetual fellow or scholar of our said college, to whatever science or faculty he is assigned, shall keep wholly and completely the years in the same science or faculty which according to the practice, custom, statutes and ordinances of the University aforesaid are necessary, statutable and customary in this science or faculty, without any remission of the time or of completion of the course, before he shall be admitted to the degree of bachelor in the same faculty or science.

And when these years are completed, if in the opinion of the warden [etc.] after examination he shall be found able, sufficient and fit, he shall take the bachelor's degree, and shall then at once devote himself to lecture continuously or exercise

actus alios exercendum, in eadem sciencia pro forma baccalaureatus illico se conuertat: et statim, completa forma in dicta Uniuersitate 'statuta et eciam limitata, in quacunque fuerit facultate seu sciencia, et uno anno ultra formam eandem, ad recipiendum et assumendum gradum magistratus seu doctoratus in ipsa sciencia seu facultate...effectualiter sit paratus; et infra annum...incipere realiter teneatur....

Nulla gracia super remissione temporis aut non complecionis forme; preterquam in forma canonistarum, cum quibus dispensari permittimus ut non teneantur iurare se audiuisse decretales complete, ac eciam decretorum doctores non teneantur regere in decretis, et preterquam in forma graduandorum in medicina, ut ipsi videlicet, deficiente Doctore regente in facultate illa, possint uti gratiis concedendis iisdem super non complecione forme in hoc casu alias requisite, dum tamen fraus aut dolus non interueniat in hac parte; qualitercunque ipsis concessa, quomodolibet valitura iisdem: qua, etsi forsan ad instanciam, supplicacionem vel peticionem, quarumcunque personarum, seu alias gratuita, sibi concessa, nullo modo gaudeant vel uti presumant....

Statuentes, insuper, quod quilibet Magister in artibus, postquam in eadem facultate in dicta Uniuersitate tribus annis integris rexerit, anno incepcionis sue, si post festum Pasche inceperit, minime computato, ad facultatem theologie vel astronomie seu medicine illico se conuertere debeat et eciam teneatur, proficiatque et gradus assumat in eadem, prout superius est expressum.

R. 52. De disposicione camerarum.

...Volentes, preterea, quod in superioribus cameris dicti collegii tres socii vel scolares ad minus inuicem collocentur, quatenus numerus sociorum et scolarium collegii sufficit et extendit. In inferioribus autem cameris dicti collegii, quatuor fenestras et quatuor studiorum loca habentibus, sint semper quatuor scolares vel socii collocati; preterquam in illa inferiori camera iuxta cameram in orientali angulo collegii situata, in

other acts proper to the bachelor in the same science according to its course; and shall immediately after he has completed the course decreed and laid down in the said University in whatever shall be his faculty or science, and one year beyond the course prescribed, be ready to receive and take the degree of master or doctor in the same science or faculty, and shall be bound actually to incept in the same science or faculty....

No grace whatsoever for remission of time or non-completion of the course shall be granted which shall in any way be valid for them; except in the course of canonists, whom we permit to have dispensation from being bound to swear that they have heard lectures on the whole Decretals, while doctors of decrees shall not be bound to lecture on decrees; except also in the course for graduates in medicine, that they in the absence of a regent doctor in that faculty may use graces granted them for not completing the course otherwise required, provided that no fraud or deceit be used in the matter. For the rest, even if a grace be granted at the instance, prayer or petition of any person whatsoever, or be granted without asking, they shall no way enjoy the same or venture to make use of it....

We decree, further, that every master of arts, after he has taught in the same faculty in the said University for three whole years, not counting the year of his inception, if he incepted after Easter, ought and shall be bound to devote himself to the faculty of theology or astronomy or medicine, and to become proficient and take degrees in the same, as before-mentioned.

Rubric 52. Of the disposal of chambers.

...Willing, too, that in the upper chambers of the said college three fellows or scholars at most shall be placed together, as far as the number of fellows and scholars of the college suffices and extends. In the lower chambers, however, of the said college, having four windows and four places for study, there shall always be four scholars or fellows placed together; except in the lower chamber next the chamber situate in the east corner of the college, in which three

qua tres tantummodo scolares vel socii habitabunt. Quorum omnium sociorum et scolarium dicti collegii nostri quilibet suum lectum habeat separatim, ac solus sine socio iaceat omnimodo....

Ordinantes, preterea, quod canoniste seu ciuiliste mixtim cum aliis studentibus in facultatibus aliis in prefatis singulis cameris, quatenus ipsorum numerus sufficit et extendit, iuxta disposicionem custodis debite collocentur, ad nutriendum et conseruandum maiorem dileccionem, amiciciam et caritatem, inter eosdem. Quodque in singulis cameris supradictis sit unus socius ceteris maturitate, discrecione ac sciencia, prouectior, qui aliis suis sociis cameralibus studentibus superintendat, et de ipsorum moribus et conuersacione, studiique profectu, custodem, vicecustodem et decanos, de tempore in tempus, quoties causa seu opus fuerit, veraciter certificet et informet,...ut huiusmodi socii et scolares defectum in moribus patientes, negligentes seu in studiis suis desides, castigacionem, correccionem et punicionem, recipiant competentes.

Appointment to Higham Ferrers Grammar School by the King in right of Duchy of Lancaster.
1400.

[A. F. Leach, *V. C. H. Northants*, II. 218, from P. R. O. Duchy Lanc. Misc. Books, XV. 27.]

Henry par le grace de Dieu etc. a tous etc. Sachez nous de notre grace especiale et pur la grande abilite et suffisante discrecion de Gramoir que nous est tesmoignez de la persone de notre bien aime Maistre Robert Orcheorerd de Burton, et pur le bon esploite et profit qil ferra de iour en autre as escolers

scholars or fellows only shall live. All the fellows and scholars of our said college shall have each his own bed separately, and lie alone without a companion always....

Ordaining, moreover, that canonists or civilians shall be duly placed mixed up with the other students in other faculties in each of the said chambers, as far as their number suffices and goes, at the disposition of the warden, so as to nourish and preserve greater affection, friendship and kindness between them. And that in each of the said chambers there shall be one fellow more advanced in age, wisdom and learning than the rest, who shall superintend his chamber-fellows in their studies, and shall truly certify and inform the warden, sub-warden and deans from time to time, as often as may be necessary, of their conduct and behaviour and the progress of their studies...so that such fellows and scholars, if failing in conduct, negligent or idle in their studies, shall receive competent castigation, correction and punishment.

[The rest of the 68 lengthy statutes are taken up with directions as to chapel services (Rubrics 41–46), the management of property (Rubrics 47–51, 53–8), college scrutiny (Rubric 60) as in the Merton statutes, the library (Rubric 61–2) etc. The last rubric, entitled 'End and Conclusion of all the Statutes,' is a somewhat pathetic attempt to secure permanence, by the most stringent oaths and penalties on any one altering them.]

Appointment to Higham Ferrers Grammar School by the King in right of Duchy of Lancaster.
1400.

Henry by the grace of God etc. to all etc. Know ye that we of our special grace, and for the great ability and sufficient knowledge of grammar, evidence of which has been given us, in the person of our well beloved Master Robert Orchard of Burton and for the good achievement and profit that he will make from day to day with the scholars and children wishing to

et enfantz vueillant hanter la faculte de gramoir de soubz sa discipline, a lui avoir octroies les escoiles de gramoir de notre vile de Higham ferrers a avoir et tenir en maniere qil ad este usez devant ces hueres a terme de sa vie, issint quil governe bien et duement en loffice surdit. Pour quoy nous mandons a tous nos leges as queux il appurtient qu au dit Robert en faisante bien et dument le susdit office ils soient aidants favorants et conselantz a tous les foies solanc ce quil leur requerura ou ferra assauoir resonablement de nostre parti. En tesmoignance etc. Don etc.

The Lollards to be burnt for keeping Schools and Conventicles. 1400.

[2 Hen. IV, c. 15. *Stat. of the Realm*, ed. 1816, II. 127.]

...nec de hujusmodi secta nephandisque doctrinis et opinionibus conventiculas aliquas faciat vel scolas teneat vel exerceat quovismodo; ac eciam quod nullus imposterum alicui sic predicanti aut tales vel consimiles conventiculas facienti, seu scolas tenenti vel exercenti, aut talem librum facienti seu scribenti, vel populum sic docenti informanti vel excitanti quomodolibet faveat nec ipsorum aliquem manuteneat aliqualiter vel sustentet.......Et si aliqua persona infra dicta Regnum et Dominia, super dictis nephandis predicacionibus doctrinis opinionibus scolis et informacionibus hereticis et erroneis vel aliqua eorundem, sentencialiter coram loci Diocesano vel Commissariis suis convicta fuerit, et hujusmodi nephandas sectam predicaciones doctrinas opiniones scolas et informaciones debite abjurare recusaverit, aut per loci Diocesanum vel Commissarios suos post abjuracionem per eandem personam factam pronunciata fuerit relapsa......tunc Vicecomes illius loci, et Major et Vicecomites seu Vicecomes aut Major et Ballivi Civitatis Ville vel Burgi ejusdem comitatus,

haunt the faculty of grammar under his teaching, have granted him the Grammar School of our town of Higham Ferrers to have and to hold as has been usual before this time for the term of his life, so long as he governs it well and perfectly in the office aforesaid. Wherefore we command all our lieges to whom it appertains that they will give aid favour and counsel to the said Robert in fulfilling well and duly the said office as often as he shall require them or give reasonable notice thereof on our behalf. In witness etc. Dated etc.

The Lollards to be burnt for keeping Schools and Conventicles. 1400.

[The translation and alternative readings are those given in the *Statutes of the Realm.*]

...None of such sect and wicked doctrines and opinions shall make any conventicles, or in any wise hold or exercise schools; and also that none from henceforth in any wise favour such preacher, or maker of any such or like conventicles, or [person] holding or exercising schools, or making or writing such books, or so teaching, informing, or exciting the people, nor any of them maintain or any wise sustain.......And if any person within the said realm and dominions, upon the said wicked preachings, doctrines, opinions, schools, and heretical and erroneous informations, or any of them, be before the Diocesan of the same place or his Commissaries [sententially convict] convict by sentence, and the same wicked sect, preachings, doctrines and opinions, schools and informations, do refuse duly to abjure, or by the Diocesan of the same place or his Commissaries after abjuration made by the same person be [pronounced fall into relapse]......then the Sheriff of the county of the same place, and Mayor and Sheriffs or Sheriff, or Mayor and Bailiffs of the city, town and borough of the same county next to the same Diocesan or the said Commis-

dicto Diocesano seu dictis Commissariis magis propinqui, in sentenciis per dictum Diocesanum aut Commissarios suos contra personas hujusmodi et ipsarum quamlibet preferendis cum ad hoc per dictum Diocesanum aut Commissarios ejusdem fuerint requisiti, personaliter sint presentes, et personas illas et quamlibet earundem post hujusmodi sentencias prelatas recipiant, et easdem coram populo in eminenti loco comburi faciant.

Stratford-on-Avon Grammar School in the Holy Cross Gild Muniments. 1402–82.

[A. F. Leach, *V. C. H. Warwicks.* II. 329, from Stratford-on-Avon Shakespeare Mun.]

Compotus Johannis Brasyer et Thome Smyth procuratorum Gilde Sancte Crucis Stratford-super-Avene a festo Sancti Michaelis Archangeli anno regni Regis Henrici IV post conquestum tercio, usque eundem festum Sancti Michaelis anno eiusdem regis Henrici quarto [1403].

In primis respondent de...et de vj*s*. viij*d*. receptis de Johanne Scolmayster pro una camera per annum....

Compotus...anno quarto...quinto [1403–4].

Allocaciones de...et de xx*d*. de redditu nove camere in aula quam Johannes Scolemayster tenuit pro j termino.

Compotus Ricardi Fretter et Willelmi Brasier procuratorum Gilde Sancte Crucis, Beate Marie et Sancti Johannis Baptiste de Stratford-super-Avene a crastino Convivii dicte Gilde anno regni regis Henrici quarti quartodecimo usque in crastinum alterius convivii eiusdem Gilde anno regni regis Henrici quinti [1413] post conquestum primo per unum annum integrum.

Allocaciones reddituum...et de iv*s*. de redditu domus Sancte Marie in le Oldetown, quos magister et aldermanni Magistro Scolarum pardonaverunt annuatim quamdiu pueros docere voluerit et scolam in eadem tenere.

saries, shall be personally present in preferring of such sentences [by the same Diocesan or his Commissaries against such persons and every of them], when they by the same Diocesan or his Commissaries shall be required; and they the same persons and every of them, after such sentence promulgate, shall receive, and them before the people in an high place do to be burnt.

Stratford-on-Avon Grammar School in the Holy Cross Gild Muniments. 1402–82.

Account of John the Brazier and Thomas the Smith, proctors of the Holy Cross Gild of Stratford-upon-Avon, from Michaelmas in the third year of Henry IV after the Conquest [1402] to the same feast of Michaelmas in the fourth year of the same king Henry [1403].

First they answer for...and for 6s. 8d. received of John the Schoolmaster for a chamber for the year...

Account...in the fourth to the fifth year [1403–4].

Remissions of...and of 20d. for rent of the new chamber in the hall which John the Schoolmaster held for one term.

Account of Richard the Fretter and William the Brazier, proctors of the Gild of the Holy Cross, Blessed Mary and St John the Baptist of Stratford-upon-Avon, from the day after the dinner of the said Gild in the fourteenth year of Henry IV, to the day after another dinner of the same Gild in the first year of the reign of King Henry the fifth after the Conquest, for a whole year.

Remissions of rents...and of 4s. for rent of St Mary's house in the Oldtown, which the Master and Aldermen forgave the Schoolmaster every year so long as he will teach boys and will keep school in it.

378 *Stratford-on-Avon Latin School building*

[1416–17.] Decasus...et de iv*s.* de tenemento Beate Marie in le Church Stret, quia conceditur Magistro Scolarum per Magistrum et Aldermannos quamdiu scolas in eadem docere voluerit.

Building of Stratford-on-Avon Grammar School. 1426.

[Stratford-on-Avon Mun. Gild Accounts.]

Computus Hugonis Safford Magistri Gilde Sancte Crucis de Stratford, 5–6 Henry VI [1426–27].

Custus de Scolehows.

In meremio empto pro j Scolehows cum j camera desuper inde facienda	xxxiv*s.*
In stipendio Johannis Hesill, magistri carpentarii, existentis ibidem per xxxv dies et dimidiam, capientis per diem vj*d.* ad taxam . .	xvij*s.* vj*d.*
[2 other carpenters and 2 labourers, 1 tiler, 2 plasterers and 1 mason were employed, and 6 cartloads of stones, 15 cartloads of earth and clay for flooring, and 2 cartloads of plaster were used.]	
	Summa x. v. iij*d.* ob.

Schoolmasters Members of Holy Cross Gild. 1453–78.

[Gild Register, f. lxxiij., 32 H. VI.]

Robertus Wyncote, scole mayster de Stratford, receptus est in fraternitatem Gilde et fecit finem pro vj*s.* viij*d.* et x*d.* de lumine.

[f. xcix., 12 Edw. IV. 1472–3.]

Thomas Caunton, monitor Scolarium, et Alicia uxor eius recepti sunt in fraternitatem Gilde; et fecit finem pro 13*s.* 4*d.*

[11, 12 Edw. IV. 1471–2.]

Et de fine Thome Cavnton monitoris Scolarium et Alicie uxoris eius	xiij*s.* iiij*d.*
Idem Magister petit allocari de...solutis ad le Scolemaister pro scriptione unius legende date Capelle Gilde per Johannem Bosbury Capellanum Gilde in parte solucionis maioris summe	viij*s.* iv*d.*

[1416–17.] Decays...and for 4s. for the tenement of the Blessed Mary in Church street, because it is granted to the Schoolmaster by the Master and Aldermen as long as he will keep school in it.

Building of Stratford-on-Avon Grammar School. 1426.

Account of Hugh Safford, Master of the Holy Cross Gild of Stratford. 1426–7.

Costs of the Schoolhouse.

In timber bought to make a Schoolhouse and chamber over it	34s.	
In wages of John Hessle, master carpenter, being there for 35½ days at 6d. a day for the job .	17	6
Total £10	5	3½

Schoolmasters Members of Holy Cross Gild. 1453–78.

Robert Wyncote, schoolmaster of Stratford, was received into the brotherhood of the Gild and paid a fine of 6s. 8d. with 10d. for the light.

Thomas Caunton, monitor of the scholars, and Alice his wife were received into the brotherhood of the Gild and paid a fine of 13s. 4d.

For the fine of Thomas Caunton, monitor of the Scholars, and Alice his wife, 13s. 4d.

The same master seeks allowance for...paid to the Schoolmaster for writing a lesson-book given to the chapel of the Gild by John Bosbury, chaplain of the Gild, in part payment of a larger sum, 8s. 4d.

[f. cvij., 17 Edw. IV. 1477-8.]

Ricardus Fox, Gramatice magister ac eciam Baccularius, nunc temporis de Stratford, receptus est in fraternitate Gilde et fecit finem pro vj*s.* viij*d.*

The Grammar School endowed by Master Thomas Jolyffe, Gild Priest. 1482.

Hec indentura quatripartita facta duodecimo die mensis Februarii anno regni regis Edwardi IV post Conquestum vicesimo primo inter Johannem Stratford capellanum et rectorem ecclesie parochialis de Combarton Magna in Comitatu Wigornie et Thomam Warde de Pyllardyngton in comitatu Warwici, Feoffatos Magistri Thome Jolyffe ex prima parte, et Dominum Johannem Alcoke dei gracia Wigorniensem Episcopum ex parte secunda, ac Magistrum Thomam Balsale clericum ac Gardianum Ecclesie Collegiate de Stratford super Avonam ex parte tercia, et Thomam Clopton Armigerum Magistrum Gilde Sancte Crucis de Stratford predicta, cum assensu et concensu Aldermannorum et Procuratorum eiusdem Gilde ex parte quarta, testatur

Quod cum predictus Thomas Jolyffe ex mera deuocione et ad specialem laudem Dei omnipotentis ac pro salute anime sue et parentum suorum Johannis et Johanne ac pro animabus omnium fratrum et sororum et benefactorum dicte Gilde dederit et concesserit prefate Gilde omnia et singula terras et tenementa sua cum omnibus eorum pertinenciis que vel quas habet in Stratford predicta et Dodwell in comitatu predicto sub forma et condicionibus subsequentibus videlicet,

Quod predictus Thomas Clopton magister dicte Gilde et Aldermanni ac procuratores eiusdem et successores sui invenient unum Presbyterum idoneum et abilem in sciencia ad docendum Gramaticam libere omnibus scolaribus ad scolam in dicta villa sibi venientibus, nichil capiendo de scolaribus pro doctrina sua. Et predictus Presbyter erit unus de quinque presbyteris

1477–8.

Richard Fox, master in grammar, and also Bachelor [of Arts], now of Stratford, was received into the brotherhood of the Gild and paid a fine of 6s. 8d.

The Grammar School endowed by Master Thomas Jolyffe, Gild Priest. 1482.

This Indenture of four parts made 12 Feb. in the 21st year of the reign of King Edward the Fourth after the Conquest between John Stratford, chaplain and rector of the parish church of Great Comberton in the county of Worcester, and Thomas Ward of Pillerton in the county of Warwick, feoffees of Master Thomas Jolyffe, of the first part, and Sir John Alcock, by the grace of God bishop of Worcester, of the second part, and Master Thomas Balsall clerk and warden of the collegiate church of Stratford-upon-Avon of the third part, and Thomas Clopton esquire master of the Gild of the Holy Cross of Stratford aforesaid, with the assent and consent of the Aldermen and Proctors of the same Gild of the fourth part, witnesseth

That whereas the aforesaid Thomas Jolyffe of mere devotion and for the special praise of God Almighty and the health of his soul and the souls of his parents John and Jane and for the souls of all the brethren and sisters and benefactors of the said Gild has given and granted to the said Gild all and singular his lands and tenements with all their appurtenances which he has in Stratford aforesaid and in Dodwell in the county aforesaid in the manner and on the conditions following, namely,

That the aforesaid Thomas Clopton, master of the said Gild, and the Aldermen and proctors of the same and their successors shall find a priest fit and able in the science to teach grammar freely to all scholars coming to him to school in the said town, taking nothing of the scholars for their teaching; and the aforesaid priest shall be one of the

dicte Gilde ad proximam vacacionem quando contigerit vacare, recipiendo autem pro stipendio suo usque ad proximam vacacionem octo libras monete Anglie soluendas per manus dictorum Magistri, Aldermannorum, Procuratorum et successorum suorum ad quattuor anni terminos videlicet ad festa S. Michaelis, Natalis Domini, Annunciacionis Beate Marie Virginis et Natiuitatis Sancti Johannis Baptiste per equales portiones; et post primam vacacionem capiendo decem libras legalis monete Anglie ad terminos predictos per manus supradictorum Magistri Aldermannorum Procuratorum et successorum suorum cum camera infra dictam Gildam cum omnibus et singulis dicte camere pertinenciis.

Proviso semper quod predictus Presbyter siue Magister Gramaticalis fuerit abilis et in sanitate ad docendum; sin autem recipiat annuatim centum solidos et alteros vero centum solidos annuatim soluendos uni alio viro abili in sciencia subtus et vice dicti magistri tociens quociens in posterum contingat sic fieri per superuisum dictorum magistri Thome Balsale Gardiani et Thome Clopton Magistri dicte Gilde ac successorum suorum.

Et predictus Presbyter Gramaticalis, Deo dante, cum fuerit dispositus celebrabit missam in capella dicte Gilde et in diebus festiuis celebrabit missam in ecclesia parochiali de Stratford predicta ad altare Sancti Johannis Baptiste pro bono statu Domini Episcopi Wygorniensis qui pro tempore fuerit et pro animabus predicti Magistri Thome Jolyffe et parentum Johannis et Johanne ac animabus omnium benefactorum dicte Gilde et animabus omnium fidelium defunctorum dicendo ad quamlibet missam pro viuis 'Deus qui caritatis' et pro defunctis 'Inclina Domine' reuertendo se ad populum ante lauatorium misse et dicendo

'Ye shall pray specially for the sowles of Maister Thomas Jolyffe John and Johanne his fadur and modur and the sowles of all brethern and sustern of the seid Gilde and all cristen sowles seyinge of your charite a Paternoster and a Ave.'

Et predictus Magister Gardianus et predictus Thomas

five priests of the said Gild at the next vacancy when one falls vacant, receiving meanwhile for his salary till the next vacancy £8 of money of England to be paid by the hands of the said Master, Aldermen, Proctors and their successors at four terms of the year, viz. Michaelmas, Christmas, Lady Day and Midsummer Day by equal portions; and after the first vacancy taking £10 of lawful money of England at the times aforesaid by the hands of the aforesaid Master, Aldermen, Proctors and their successors with a chamber in the said Gild and all and singular the appurtenances of the said chamber.

Provided always that the said priest or grammar master shall be able and of health to teach; but if not he shall receive £5 a year and the other £5 shall be yearly paid to another man able in learning under and instead of the said master, as often as it shall hereafter happen to be so settled under the supervision of the said Master Thomas Balsall warden and Thomas Clopton master of the said Gild and their successors.

And the grammar priest aforesaid shall, when he shall by God's grace be so disposed, celebrate mass in the chapel of the said Gild, and on feast days shall celebrate mass in the parish church of Stratford aforesaid at the altar of St John the Baptist for the good estate of the lord bishop of Worcester for the time being and the souls of the said Master Thomas Jolyffe and of his parents John and Jane and the souls of all the benefactors of the said Gild and the souls of all the faithful departed, saying at every mass, for the living 'God who art the God of love' and for the departed 'Bow down, O Lord,' turning himself to the people before the lavatory of the mass and saying,

'Ye shall pray specially for the souls of Master Thomas Jolyffe, John and Jane his father and mother, and the souls of all brethren and sisters of the said Gild and all Christian souls saying of your charity a Lord's Prayer and a Salutation of the Virgin.'

And the aforesaid Master Warden and the aforesaid Thomas

Clopton, magister Gilde, et successores sui nominabunt unum presbiterum ad docendum gramaticam tociens quociens vacauerit.

Et predictus Thomas Clopton, magister dicte Gilde et Aldermanni et procuratores eiusdem Gilde et successores sui imperpetuum custodient, seu custodiri imperpetuum facient obitum in vigilia Sancti Bartholomei Apostoli in ecclesia parochiali de Stratford predicta coram altare Sancti Johannis Baptiste cum omnibus presbiteris collegii predicti pro animabus predicti magistri Thome Jolyffe, Johannis ac Johanne parentum suorum et pro animabus omnium fidelium defunctorum. Et in consimili modo predictus Magister Aldermanni procuratores ac successores sui custodient seu custodiri imperpetuum facient obitum pro animabus predictis et pro omnibus animabus fidelibus defunctis in vigilia Sancti Bartholomei predicti infra capellam Gilde predicte cum omnibus presbiteris dicte Gilde.

Et si predicti Thomas Clopton Aldermanni procuratores ac successores sui defecerint et non perimpleuerint omnia et singula premissa per spacium unius anni uno post alium immediate sequente tunc bene licebit prefatis Magistro Thome Balsale clerico ac Gardiano et successoribus suis in omnibus predictis terris et tenementis intrare et ea penes se retinere quousque predicti Thomas Clopton magister gilde predicte ac Aldermanni et procuratores et successores sui inuenient sufficientem securitatem ad omnia premissa perimplenda et si sufficiens securitas huiusmodi ex parte predicti Thome Clopton Magistri Aldermannorum et procuratorum ac successorum suorum inueniri non poterit tunc bene licebit prefato Magistro Thome Balsale Gardiano et successoribus suis Gardianis qui pro tempore erunt in omnibus terris et tenementis supradictis re-intrare et ea gaudere et possidere imperpetuum ad sustentacionem diuersorum choristarum. Et predictus presbiter gramaticalis et scolares bis in septimana videlicet die Mercurii et in die Veneris cantabunt antiphonam de Sancta Maria, et post dictam antiphonam deuote dicendo pro animabus predictis Magistri Thome Jolyffe Johannis et Johanne parentum suorum et pro animabus omnium fidelium defunctorum De profundis.

endowed and made a Free School

Clopton, master of the Gild, and their successors shall name a priest to teach grammar as often as there shall be a vacancy.

And the aforesaid Thomas Clopton, master of the said Gild, and the aldermen and proctors of the same Gild and their successors for ever shall keep, or cause to be kept for ever, an obit on the eve of 24 August in the parish church of Stratford aforesaid before the altar of St John the Baptist with all the priests of the said collegiate church for the souls of the said master Thomas Jolyffe, John and Jane his parents, and for the souls of all the faithful departed. And likewise the aforesaid master, aldermen, proctors and their successors shall keep or cause to be kept for ever an obit for the souls aforesaid and for all faithful souls departed on the eve of 24 August aforesaid in the chapel of the Gild aforesaid with all the priests of the said Gild.

And if the aforesaid Thomas Clopton, aldermen, proctors and their successors shall make default and not fulfil all and singular the premises for the space of a year, one immediately following another, then it shall be lawful for the said Master Thomas Balsall, clerk and warden, and his successors to enter on all the aforesaid lands and tenements and to keep them for themselves until the aforesaid Thomas Clopton, master of the Gild aforesaid, and the aldermen and proctors and their successors shall find sufficient security to fulfil all the premises, and if such sufficient security shall not be able to be found on behalf of the said Thomas Clopton master, the aldermen and proctors and their successors, then it shall be lawful for the said Master Thomas Balsall, warden, and his successors wardens for the time being to re-enter on all the said lands and tenements and enjoy and possess them for ever for the maintenance of divers choristers. And the aforesaid grammar priest and his scholars shall twice a week, viz. on Wednesday and Friday, sing an anthem of St Mary and after the said anthem say devoutly for the aforesaid souls of Master Thomas Jolyffe, John and Jane his parents, and for the souls of all the faithful departed 'Out of the deep.'

In cuius rei testimonium uni parti istarum Indenturarum penes prefatum Johannem Stratford capellanum et Thomam Warde remanenti sigillum commune dicte Gilde est appensum. Dat. apud Stratford predictam in aula Gilde die Lune proximo post festum Translacionis Sancti Thome Martiris, anno regni Regis Edwardi quarti post conquestum vicesimo secundo.

Children may be sent to School notwithstanding Statute of Labourers and Apprentices. 1405–6.

[7 Hen. IV, c. 17, *Stat. of the Realm*, ed. 1816, II. 157.]

Nulle homme ou femme de quele estate ou condicion qil soit, mette son fitz ou file de quele age qil soit de servir come apprentice a nulle mestere nautre laboure dedeinz Citee or Burgh dedeinz le Roialme, sinon qil eit terre ou rent a la value de 20*s*. per an a meins, mes qil soit mys de servir a autiel labour, soit il deinz Citee ou Burgh ou dehors, come ses ditz piere ou miere usent, ou autres labours come leurs estates requiergent, sur peyn denprisonement dun an et de faire fyn et raunceon a la volunte du Roy. Purveux toutesfoitz que chacun homme ou femme de quele estate ou condicion qil soit, soit fraunc de mettre son fitz ou file dapprendre lettereure, a quelconq escole que leur plest deinz le Roialme.

The Choristers' School becomes a rival Grammar School at Lincoln. 1407–9.

[A. F. Leach, *V. C. H. Lincs.* II. 426, from Linc. Chapter Act Book, A. 2, 30.]

Item viij° die Januarii Anno Domini supradicto, conuentum fuit inter canonicos tunc presentes et capitulum facientes, quod coriste ecclesie Lincoln. et eorum commensales descenderent ad scolas gramaticales generales, prout consuetum fuerat temporibus retroactis; Precentore tunc absente, cuius tunc notorium vertebatur interesse.

In witness whereof to one part of these Indentures remaining with the said John Stratford chaplain and Thomas Ward the common seal of the said Gild is appended. Given at Stratford aforesaid in the Gild Hall on Monday next after 7 July in the 22nd year of King Edward IV after the Conquest [1482].

Children may be sent to School notwithstanding Statute of Labourers and Apprentices. 1405–6.

That no man nor woman, of what estate or condition they be, shall put their son or daughter, of whatsoever age he or she be, to serve as apprentice, to no craft nor other labour within any City or Borough in the Realm, except he have land or rent to the value of 20s. by the year at the least, but they shall be put to other labours [to service to such labour be it withyn Citie Burgh or without as his said fader or moder used, or] as their Estates doth require, upon pain of one year's imprisonment, and to make fine and ransom at the king's will. Provided always, that every man or woman, of what estate or condition that he be, shall be free to set their son or daughter to take learning at any manner school that pleaseth them within the Realm.

The Choristers' School becomes a rival Grammar School at Lincoln. 1407–9.

Also on 8 January in the year of the Lord above-mentioned [1406–7] it was agreed between the canons then present and making a chapter, that the choristers of the church of Lincoln and their commoners should go down to the general Grammar School as had been customary in times past: the Precentor being absent, whose interest was notoriously concerned in the matter.

Item xv° die eiusdem mensis Precentor et ceteri canonici tunc presentes voluerunt et consenciebant quod Magister coristarum et eorum Petagogus commensales admittere possit, consanguineos et pueros canonicorum libere informare valeat in scolis Collegii predicti.

Voluerunt tamen quod extraneos pueros a scolis generalibus fugientes, sive fuerint de civitate vel partibus adiacentibus, nullatenus admittat nec informet, set [*sic*] ad scolas generales destinet et remittat. Coriste tamen et eorum commensales tempore honesto, et quando commode poterunt descendere, ad huiusmodi scolas generales declinabunt, quociens et quando Domino Precentori et eorum Informatori videbitur expedire etc.

[*Ib.* and City Register, f. 14.]

[Composicio inter Capitulum ecclesie Lincoln. et Maiorem et ciues ciuitatis Lincoln. pro scola Gramaticali, inuenta per Thomam Grantham.]

[The words in brackets are the reading of the City Register.]

Ordinacio de Scolis Gramaticalibus.

Item eodem die, prehibito [aliquali] tractatu per subdecanum et capitulum ecclesie Lincoln. [Decano eiusdem absente] inter Magistrum Johannem Huntman[e], ecclesie Lincoln. cancellarium, ac Majorem et ciues ciuitatis Lincoln., ex parte una: et Magistrum Johannem Neuport[e], eiusdem ecclesie Precentorem, ex parte altera; de et super regimine Scolarum gramaticalium Coristarum infra clausum ecclesie Lincoln. situatarum, et super admissione et recepcione [tam] scolarium extraneorum et aliorum quam coristarum et eorum commensalium facta per Informatorem et petegogum [*sic*] eorumdem, in derogacionem iuris et regiminis Scolarum Generalium Gramaticalium ciuitatis predicte, per Magistrum Johannem Bracebryg [Brasbryge], Magistrum scolarum generalium [gramaticalium] predictarum [coram eisdem subdecano et capitulo] propositam et pretensam;

Also on the 15th of the same month the Precentor and the rest of the canons then present were desirous and agreed that the master of the choristers and their tutor might admit commoners and teach freely the relations and boys of the canons in the school of the said college.

They would not however let him by any means admit or teach any outside boys who wished to leave the general school, whether they came from the city or from the neighbourhood, but desired that he should order them back to the general school. The choristers, however, and the boarders with them will go to such general school at a proper time and when they conveniently can, as often and at such times as shall seem good to the Precentor and their master etc.

[Agreement between the Chapter of the Church of Lincoln and the Mayor and citizens of the city of Lincoln for the Grammar School, found by Thomas Grantham.]

Ordinance for the Grammar School.

Also the same day [12 Feb. 1406–7] after some treaty through the Subdean and Chapter of Lincoln (the Dean of the same being absent) between Master John Huntman, chancellor of the church of Lincoln, and the mayor and citizens of the city of Lincoln on the one part, and Master John Newport, precentor of the same church, on the other part, on and about the keeping of the Grammar School of the choristers situate in the close of the church of Lincoln and on the admission and reception of outside scholars and others than the choristers and the boarders with them by the Master and Usher of the same in derogation of the rights and governance of the General Grammar School of the city aforesaid, put forward and alleged by Master John Bracebridge, Master of the said General School;

Tandem de consensu et assensu dictorum Dominorum Cancellarii et Precentoris ac Subdecani et capituli, necnon Maioris et ciuium predictorum, tractatus antedictus unanimiter finem habuit, et, prout alias litis huiusmodi materia inter partes predictas suscitata sopita extiterat, in hunc modum capitulariter conquieuit: videlicet,

Quod coristarum Petegogi seu Informatores, vel Magistri eorumdem coristarum, communiter commensales, necnon consanguineos canonicorum et vicariorum dicte ecclesie, eorumue sumptibus et elemosinis degentes vel in eorum familia habitantes, quibuscunque diebus et horis legibilibus, in gramatica absque contradiccione informare valeant libere et quiete, dum tamen predicti Petegogi seu Magistri cum eisdem coristis, eorumque commensalibus ac canonicorum et vicariorum consanguineis, vel in eorum familia et sumptibus, eorumue elemosinis degentibus, cuiusque anni [post] datum presentis composicionis subsequentibus terminis S. Michaelis, Natalis Domini, et Pasche semel ad scolas generales [gramaticales] ecclesie Lincoln. sub regimine proprii Magistri, hora ordinaria et consueta descendere teneantur. Temporibus eciam quibus in dictis scolis generalibus extiterint dicti coriste et alii supradicti erunt sub doctrina et castigacione proprii Magistri, nisi aliud de illius processerit voluntate.

Erunt insuper dicti Informatores seu petegogi coristarum, ac ipsi choriste et eorum commensales et alii supradicti [canonicorum et vicariorum pueri] exempti ab omni punicione, exaccione, et collecte seu salarii solucione, et ceteris oneribus [omnibus] in huiusmodi scolis fieri consuetis, et a compulsione veniendi ad easdem scolas generales ecclesie Lincoln. priuilegiati, nisi illis tribus quarteriis annorum singulorum in quibus dicti coriste et omnes eorum commensales cum aliis prenotatis, hora ordinaria ac consueta, ad scolas generales prescriptas venire tenebuntur, sub forma superius expressata.

[Diffinitum est eciam per nos Subdecanum et capitulum, et parcium predictarum consensu finaliter ordinatum et declaratum quod nulli alii a supradictis; scilicet, coristis,

At length by the consent and assent of the said Chancellor and Precentor and Subdean and Chapter, as well as of the mayor and citizens aforesaid, the discussion before-mentioned was finally and unanimously settled, and as the like controversy had at other times been raised and dropped between the parties, now it was capitularly ended: thus,

That the Ushers or Teachers or Masters of the same choristers might freely and quietly without interference teach grammar to the commoners boarding with them, also the relations of the canons and vicars [choral] of the said church or those living at their expense and on their charity or on their families, on any lawful school-days and school-hours, provided always that the said Ushers or Masters shall be bound once in every year after the date of these presents in the Michaelmas, Christmas and Easter terms following to go down with the same choristers, their commoners and the relations of the canons and vicars and those living in their family or at their expense and on their charity, to the General [Grammar] School of the church of Lincoln under the governance of their own master at the ordinary and usual time. At the time moreover when the said choristers and others above-mentioned shall be in the said general schools they shall be under the teaching and chastisement of the master of that school, unless it shall be arranged otherwise at his wish.

The said Teachers or Ushers of the choristers too, and the choristers themselves and their commoners and other above-mentioned boys of the canons and vicars shall be exempt from all punishment, exaction and payment of collections or fees, and from all other charges customary in such school and privileged from the obligation to go to the said general school of the church of Lincoln, except in the three quarters of each year in which the said choristers and all their commoners and others before-mentioned, shall be bound at the ordinary and customary hour to go to the said general school, as above-mentioned.

[It is also laid down by us the Subdean and chapter aforesaid and finally ordered with the consent of the parties aforesaid and declared, that none others than those above-

eorum commensalibus, canonicorum vel vicariorum consanguineis, vel in eorum familia seu eorum elemosinis vel sumptibus degentibus, ad informacionem seu doctrinam Magistrorum vel Petegorum coristarum, seu inter illos informandi aliqualiter admittantur; set omnes alii in cantariis, vel extra clausum Lincoln. vel infra, aliquo alio loco vel modo quam ut premittitur habitantes et adiscere volentes, sicut antiquitus fieri consueuit, ad scolas generales predictas descendere teneantur; nisi aliud ex Cancellarii ecclesie Lincoln. et Principalis Magistri earumdem Scolarum Generalium processerit voluntate.]

Precedence of the Schoolmaster among the Vicars Choral. 1409.

[Chapter Act Book, A. 2, 30, f. 15 b.]

10mo die mensis Augusti A.D. 1409 Decanus et capitulum ecclesie Lincoln. attendentes quod Henricus Burwasshe, vicarius de maiori forma, et sacrista ecclesie Lincoln., et Johannes Bracebrig, vicarius eiusdem forme, Magister Scolarum ciuitatis Lincolnie, propter dignitatem siue superioritatem officiorum suorum huiusmodi in maiori reuerencia debeant anteferri ceteris vicariis officia non habentibus, unanimiter ordinarunt;

Quod dictus Henricus, Sacrista, et Johannes, Magister Scolarum predictus, in omni processione, loco capitulari, locoue alio, ubi chorus est presens, habeant, et uterque eorum, viz. dictus Henricus Sacrista habeat locum superiorem iuxta Canonicos, ex parte Boriali, et dictus Johannes Magister Scolarum habeat locum superiorem iuxta Canonicos ex parte australi; nisi forte propter paucitatem siue plenitudinem vicariorum in choro, aut propter honorem Sanctorum eos in cantu versiculacionem oporteat intendere, vel eis placuerit, in medio chori iuxta librum cantus cum ceteris consociis suis occupari.

Et quod non intabulentur pro inuitatoriis responsoriis cum suis versibus cantandis, ut vicarii inferiores officia non habentes, nisi paucitas vicariorum id exposcat.

mentioned, namely, the choristers, the commoners with them, the relations of the canons and vicars, or others living in their families or at their expense or on their charity, shall be any way admitted to the teaching or lessons of the Masters or Ushers of the choristers, or to be taught with them, but all others in chantries, whether inside or outside the close of Lincoln, living in any other place or way than as above-mentioned and wanting to be taught shall be bound to go down to the general school as has been anciently the custom, unless some other arrangement is made at the wish of the Chancellor of the church of Lincoln and the Headmaster of the General School.]

Precedence of the Schoolmaster among the Vicars Choral. 1409.

10 Aug. 1409 the Dean and Chapter of the church of Lincoln considering that Henry Borrowash, vicar of the upper form, and Sacrist of the church of Lincoln, and John Bracebridge, vicar of the same form, Master of the school of the city of Lincoln, ought on account of the dignity or superiority of their offices for greater reverence to be given precedence over the rest of the vicars not holding offices, ordered unanimously;

That the said Henry, the Sacrist, and John, the Schoolmaster aforesaid, in every procession, place in chapter, or other place, where the choir is present, shall respectively have, namely the said Henry, the Sacrist, the highest place next the canons, on the North side, and the said John, the Schoolmaster, the highest place next the canons on the South side; unless perhaps through the small or too large number of vicars in choir, or for the honour of the saints, they have to look after the verse in singing, or they wish to be engaged with the rest of their colleagues at the song-book in the middle of the choir.

And they shall not be placed on the Table for singing invitatories or responds and the verses following like the inferior vicars who are not office-holders, unless the scarcity of vicars makes it necessary.

The Sacraments not to be taught by Masters in Arts or Grammar. 1408.

[Wilkins, *Concilia*, III. 317.]

Constitutiones domini Thome Arundel, Cantuariensis Archiepiscopi.

5. Constitutio. Ne magistri in artibus vel grammatica intromittant se de sacramentis pueros suos instruendo.

Similiter quia id quod capit nova testa inveterata sapit, statuimus et ordinamus, quod magistri sive quicunque docentes in artibus, aut grammatica pueros, seu alios quoscunque in primitivis instruentes, de fide catholica, sacramenta altaris, seu aliis sacramentis ecclesie, aut materia aliqua theologica, contra determinata per ecclesiam, se nullatenus intromittant instruendo eosdem; nec de expositione sacre scripture, nisi in exponendo textum, prout antiquitus fieri consuevit; nec permittant scholares suos sive discipulos de fide catholica, seu sacramentis ecclesie publice disputare etiam vel occulte: contrarium autem faciens, ut fautor errorum, et schismatum, per loci ordinarium graviter puniatur.

Statute of Lollards and their Schools. 1414.

[2 Hen. V, Stat. 1. c. 7, *Stat. of Realm*.]

Et outre ceo que les justices du Bank le Roy et Justices du Pees et Justices d'Assises prendre eient pleine poair denquerer de toutz yceux que teignent ascuns errors ou heresies come Lollards, et queux soient lour maintenours recettours fautours susteignours communs escrivers de tieux livres, sibien de lour sermons come de lour escoles, conventicles congregacions et confederacies; et que ceste clause soit mys es Commissions des Justices de la Pees; et si ascuns persones soient enditez dascuns des pointz suisditz eient les ditz Justices poair de agarder vers eux Capias, et soit le Viscount tenuz darrester la persone ou persones ensy endite ou enditez si tost come il les purra trover per luy ou per ses Officiers.

The Sacraments not to be taught by Masters in Arts or Grammar. 1408.

Constitutions of the lord Thomas Arundel, Archbishop of Canterbury.

5. Constitution. That no masters of arts or grammar meddle with the sacraments in instructing their boys.

Likewise because what a cask holds when it is new it tastes of when it is old, we decree and order that no masters or others teaching children in arts or grammar or instructing any others whatsoever in the elementary sciences, in any way meddle in teaching them with the catholic faith, the sacraments of the altar, or other sacraments of the church or any theological matter against what has been determined by the church, nor even in the exposition of holy writ, except by expounding the text as has been anciently accustomed to be done; nor allow their scholars or pupils to dispute about the catholic faith or the sacraments of the church either in public or in private. Whoever does the contrary let him be heavily punished by the ordinary of the place as a supporter of errors and schisms.

Statute of Lollards and their Schools. 1414.

And moreover that the Justices of the King's Bench, and Justices of Peace, and Justices of Assise, have full power to enquire of all of them which hold any errors or heresies, as Lollards, and [which] be their Maintainers, Receivers, Favourers and Sustainers, common writers of such books, as well of [their] Sermons as of their Schools, Conventicles, Congregations, and Confederacies; and that this Clause be put in Commissions of the Justices of the Peace; and if any persons be indicted of any points aforesaid, the said Justices shall have power to award against them a Capias, and the Sheriff shall be bound to arrest the person or persons so indicted as soon as he may them find by him or by his Officers.

Cornhill Grammar School. 1419.

[Issue Rolls (Pells), 7 Hen. V, m. 11, Post festum Trinitatis.]

Rogero Keston magistro scolarum gramaticalium apud Cornehill, London. In denariis sibi liberatis per manus proprias pro tabula doctrina et exhibicione Walteri House in custodia regis racione minoris etatis sue existentis videlicet a festo Sancti Michaelis anno 6 usque 18 diem Julii termino proximo sequente per consideracionem thesaurarii et camerarii de scaccario, £4. 11s. 6½d.

Regulations as to teaching of English Law, French and Letter-Writing at Oxford. 1432.

[W. Anstey, *Mun. Acad. Oxon.* (Rolls Series), I. p. 302.]

Item, cum racioni sit consonum, et in antiquioribus statutis implicitum, scolarem quemcunque artem aliquam addiscentem, nulla existente lectura ordinaria in eadem, ipsius facultatis seu sciencie ordinarium exercere debere, cui ars ipsa quam addiscit maxime vicinatur; verum quia artes scribendi et dictandi loquendique Gallicanum idioma, in quibus nulle ordinarie sunt lecture, magis Grammatice [et] Rhetorice quam aliis scienciis aut facultatibus, tanquam iis subalternate, appropinquant, ordinavit igitur Universitas et decrevit, quod singuli Scolares competenter instructi in Grammatica solummodo, artem scribendi vel dictandi vel loquendi Gallicum, sive cartas aliave huiusmodi scripta componendi, seu curias laicorum tenendi, aut modum placitandi Anglicanum principaliter addiscentes, ordinarias lecciones Artistarum Grammaticam vel Rhetoricam legencium frequentent, iis tanquam propriis Magistris cumulando: sic quod nullus docens aliquam iam dictarum arcium, hora ordinaria facultatis arcium in pleno termino, de aliqua ipsarum quemquam instruat quoquo modo, sintque eciam huiusmodi docentes per Cancellarium, assistentibus Procuratoribus, tales artes ad docendum admissi, et iurati ad pacem, statuta et privilegia, consuetudines, libertates, et alia

Cornhill Grammar School. 1419.

To Roger Keston, master of the Grammar School at Cornhill, London. In cash paid him by my own hands for the board, teaching and maintenance of Walter House, being in the king's guardianship by reason of his minority, namely from Michaelmas 1419 to 18 July in the following term, by order of the Treasurer and Chamberlain of the Exchequer, £4. 11s. 6½d.

Regulations as to teaching of English Law, French and Letter-Writing at Oxford. 1432.

Also whereas it is consonant to reason and implied in the more ancient statutes, that any scholar learning any art, when there is no ordinary lecture in that art, ought to keep an ordinary lecture of that faculty or science which is nearest to the one he is learning; and as the arts of writing and composition and of speaking French, in which there are no ordinary lectures, approach nearest to grammar and rhetoric than to the other sciences or faculties, as being subordinate to them; the University therefore has ordered and decreed that every scholar competently instructed only in grammar, and principally learning the art of writing or composition, or of speaking French, or composing deeds or other writings of that kind, or of keeping lay courts or the mode of holding English pleas, shall attend the ordinary lectures of artists lecturing on grammar or rhetoric, adding them to their own masters; so that no one teaching any of the said arts, may at the ordinary hour of the faculty of arts in full term instruct anyone in any of them in any way; and also that teachers of this kind shall be admitted to teach such arts by the Chancellor with the Proctors as assessors, and sworn to keep unimpaired the peace, statutes and privileges, customs, liberties and all other rights of the University whatsoever; also

Universitatis iura quecunque, illesa observare; necnon cum grammaticis sub supervisione et regimine Magistrorum supervisorum scolarum grammaticalium; atque omnes ipsi simul annuatim, tredecim solidos quatuor denarios solvant Artistis, in recompensam preiudicii per eorum doctrinam Artistis illati, ad cuius summe solucionem quilibet talium docencium, secundum numerum suorum Scolarium, ratum subeat onus, unico vero eorum existente ad dictam summam integre persolvendam nihilominus obligato, prout de summa soluta Artistis per grammaticos est consuetum; proviso semper, quod integra collecta omnium Scolarium facultatis arcium Magistris suis colligere debencium, inter omnes Regentes in artibus lecturam ordinariam in iisdem et philosophiis pro forma inceptorum in eadem facultate equaliter subeuntes, de cetero equaliter dividatum, prout Deus, natura, atque lex manifeste suadent, inter viros eiusdem honoris, paresque omnes, equalia distribui emolumenta.

Foundation of Sevenoaks Grammar School.
4 July 1432.

[P. P. C. 3 Luffenham, 16.]

Willelmus Sevenoks.

In Dei nomine, Amen.

Cum inter cetera pietatis opera, que de fonte caritatis emanantur, intelligere super egenum et pauperem beatum predicitur, hac consideracione inductus Ego Willelmus Sevenoks ciuis et grocerus London compos mentis et sane memorie 4 mensis Julii A.D. 1432 et anno regni Regis Henrici VI post conquestum 10° de omnibus terris et tenementis meis cum waruo adiacente ac edificiis superedificatis et omnibus aliis suis pertinenciis que nuper habui ex dimissione et feoffamento Margerie, que fuit uxor Roberti Walton, in vico de Petywaleys in parochia Omnium Sanctorum de Berkyngchurche prope turrim London, condo facio et ordino presens testamentum meum in hunc modum.

that, together with the grammar-teachers who are under the supervision and governance of the superintendent Masters of the Grammar Schools, all of them together shall yearly pay 13s. 4d. to the artists, in recompense for the prejudice done to the artists by their teaching; to the payment of which sum each of such teachers shall be charged according to the number of his scholars, but if there is only one such teacher he is nevertheless obliged to pay the whole sum, as has been the custom in respect of the sum paid to the artists by the grammar-teachers; provided always, that the whole collection of all the scholars of the faculty of arts who ought to collect for their masters, shall henceforth be equally divided among all the Regent masters in arts keeping an ordinary lecture in arts and the philosophies for the form of inceptors, as God, nature and law clearly teach that among men of the same rank and who are all equal, equal emoluments should be distributed.

Foundation of Sevenoaks Grammar School.
4 July 1432.

William Sevenoaks' Will.

In God's name, Amen.

Whereas among other works of piety which flow from the fountain of charity to think upon the needy and poor is before all called blessed: led by this consideration, I, William Sevenoaks, citizen and grocer of London, being of good understanding and perfect memory, on the fourth day of the month of July A.D. 1432, and in the year of the reign of King Henry the Sixth after the Conquest, the tenth, concerning all my lands and tenements with a wharf adjoining, and the buildings built thereon and all other the appurtenances which I lately have had by the demise and feoffment of Margaret, who was the wife of Robert Walton, in Petty Wales street in the parish of All Saints Barking church, near the Tower of London, do frame make and ordain my present testament in this manner.

In primis lego et commendo animam meam Deo omnipotenti Creatori et Saluatori meo Beateque Marie Virgini matri eius et omnibus sanctis, corpusque meum ad sepeliendum ubi Deus disposuit.

Item, do et lego omnia predicta terras et tenementa cum waruo adiacente [etc.] Domino Johanni Charleton, Rectori ecclesie de Sevenoks in comitatu Kancie, Domino vicario eiusdem ecclesie et custodibus operis eiusdem ecclesie et aliis parochianis ecclesie illius, Habendum et tenendum eis eorumque successoribus, personis, vicariis, custodibus et parochianis eiusdem ecclesie posthac pro tempore futuris omnia predicta terras tenementa [etc.] de capitali domino feodorum illorum per seruicia inde debita et de iure consueta imperpetuum secundum modum et formam et sub condicionibus inferius expressis, scilicet;

Imprimis [to pay an annuity of 20 marks to Margaret Walton for life, and after her death] quod inueniant et sustineant imperpetuum unum Magistrum, virum honestum, in sciencia gramatice sufficienter prouectum et expertum, Bacallarium in Artibus, infra sacros ordines minime constitutum, qui scolas gramaticales in aliqua domo competenti infra dictam villam de Sevenoks cum bonis meis, licencia Regia vel alio modo legitimo iuxta discreciones executorum meorum perquirenda, teneat, pauperes pueros quoscumque erudicionis gracia illuc venientes doceat et informet, nichil participans ab ipsis seu parentibus aut amicis suis pro doctrina vel informacione eorumdem; volo namque quod dicti rector seu vicarius custos et parochiani et successores sui qui pro tempore fuerint de exitibus et reuencionibus omnium terrarum et tenementorum supradictorum cum suis pertinenciis soluant annuatim predicto magistro gramatice, nomine sui salarii siue stipendii pro suo seruicio et labore per ipsum ut premittitur faciendo et exercendo decem marcas sterlingorum ad quatuor anni terminos principales per equales porciones. Preterea volo et ordino quod si quis ac tociens quociens aliquem talem Magistrum seu Doctorem in gramatica decedere, recedere, vel a determinacione huius-

First, I bequeath and commend my soul to God Almighty, my Creator and Saviour, to the Blessed Virgin Mary his mother and all saints, and my body to be buried where God has arranged.

Also, I give and bequeath all my aforesaid lands and tenements with a wharf adjoining and with the buildings thereon built, and all other the appurtenances, unto Mr John Charlton, Rector of Sevenoaks church in the county of Kent, to Master Vicar of the same church, and to the churchwardens of the same church and to other parishioners of that church, To Have and to Hold to them and their successors the Parsons, Vicars, Churchwardens, and Parishioners of the said Church hereafter for the time being all the said lands, tenements [etc.] of the chief Lord of the fees thereof by the services thereof due and of right accustomed, for ever; after the manner and form and under the conditions hereafter expressed, that is to say:

First, [to pay an annuity of 20 marks to Margaret Walton for life, and after her death] do find and maintain for ever one Master, an honest man, sufficiently advanced and expert in the science of grammar, B.A., by no means in holy orders, to keep a Grammar School in some convenient house within the said town of Sevenoaks with my goods, having obtained the licence of the King or by other lawful means according to the discretion of my executors, and to teach and instruct all poor boys whatsoever coming there for the sake of learning, taking nothing of them or their parents or friends for the teaching and instructing them. For I will that the said rector [etc.] and their successors for the time being out of the issues and revenues of all the lands and tenements aforesaid with their appurtenances, do pay yearly to the aforesaid Master of Grammar by way of salary or stipend for his service and labour to be done and exercised as aforesaid, 10 marks sterling at the four principal terms of the year by equal portions. Moreover I will and order that if any, and as often as it happens that any such master or teacher in grammar decease, depart or for the

modi voluntarie per tempus minimum cessare contingat, quod ex tunc infra quarterium anni ad minus proximum sequens unus alius magister huiusmodi, si quis talis interim commode reperiri poterit, per dictum Rectorem seu Vicarium custodes et parochianos et successores suos de nouo eligatur et assumatur inhabitando tenendo scolas et determinando in eadem domo viis modis et formis supradictis.

God's House, a Secondary School Training College at Cambridge. c. June 1439.

[Mun. King's Coll., Cambridge.]

Unto the kyng our souerain lord

Besecheth ful mekely your poure preest and continuell bedeman William Byngham, person of Seint John zacharie of london, vnto your souerain grace to be remembred, how that he hath diuerse tymes sued vnto your Highnesse shewyng and declaryng by bille how gretely the Clergie of this youre Reaume, by the which all wysdom, konnyng, and gouernaunce standeth in, is like to be empeired and febled, by the defaute and lak of Scolemaistres of Gramer, in so moche that as your seyd poure besecher hath founde in W La...de [*sic*] ouer the Est partie of the wey ledying from hamptoñ to Couentre, and so forth no ferther north than Rypoñ, lxx Scoles voide or mo that weren occupied all at ones within 1 yeres passed, bicause that ther is so grete scarstee of maistres of Gramer, whereof as now ben almost none, nor none mowen be hade in your Uniuersitees ouer those that nedes most ben occupied still there: Wherfore please it vnto your most souerain highnesse and plentevous grace to considre how that for all liberall sciences used in your seid universitees certein lyflode is ordeyned and endued, savyng onely for gramer, the which is rote and grounde of all the seid other Sciences, And there upon graciously to graunte licence to your forseid besecher

least time voluntarily cease from such determination, that then within at least the next quarter following another such master, if any such can conveniently be found, be newly elected and chosen by the said rector or vicar, wardens and parishioners and their successors to inhabit and keep school and determine in the same house in ways, manner and form aforesaid.

that he may yeue withouten fyne or fee a mansioñ ycalled Goddishous the which he hath made and edified in your towne of Cambrigge for the free herbigage of poure Scolers of Gramer, and also that he and whatsomeuere other persone or persones to that wele willed and disposed mowen yeue also withouten fyn or fee, lyflode, as londes, tenementes, Rentes, and seruices such as is not holden of you immediately by Knyght service, or advousons of Churches, though thei ben holde of you, or of ony other by knight service, to the value of [blotted and gone] li by yere, or elles to suche yerely value as may please unto your gode Grace, vnto the maister and scolers of Clarehall in your universitee of Cambrigge and to their Successours and also to graunte licence to the same maister and Scolers and their Successours for to resteyne withouten fyn and fee the same Mansioñ, and the seid other londes, tenementes, Rentes and services and advousons to the seid value after the forme of a cedule to this bille annexed, To thentent that the seid Maister and Scolers mowe fynde perpetually in the forseid mansioñ ycalled Goddeshous xxiiii Scolers for to comense in gramer, and a Preest to gouerne them, for reformacion of the said defaute, for the loue of God, and in the wey of Charytee.

[Collated with the original by Dr M. R. James, Provost of King's. The words 'in W La...^{de}' are given as 'now of late' in a 17th century copy in the Baker MSS. (B. M. Add. 5803). This MS. fills the gap as to the limit of the value of lands with £50.]

Foundation of Eton College. 1440–6.

Foundation Charter of 11 Oct. 144-.

[*Rot. Parl.* v. 45.]

Henricus, Dei gracia, rex Anglie et Francie, et dominus Hibernie, omnibus ad quos presentes litere pervenerint, salutem.

Regnans in excelsis triumphans ecclesia, cui presidens est Pater Eternus, cuique ministrant sanctorum agmina, et laudes gloriam angelorum chori decantant, in terris vicariam sibi constituit ecclesiam militantem, quam unigenitus eiusdem Dei filius sic sibi in eterni amoris federe copulavit, ut eam dignaretur sponsam eius dilectissimam nominare, cuique, iuxta dignitatem tanti nominis, tanquam verus et amantissimus sponsus contulit dotes tam amplissimas graciarum, quod omnium in Cristo renascencium mater ac domina vocaretur et esset, habens potestatem in singulos tanquam mater, cunctique fideles ipsam velut matrem et dominam honorarent in obediencia filiali : hac namque digna consideracione diversi retro principes, et perquam maxime nostri progenitores, eandem ecclesiam sacrosanctam summo honore, atque devota veneracione, semper adeo studuerunt excolere, ut preter alia pleraque virtutum opera gloriosa, in eius laudem et sponsi eius gloriam, insignia nonnullis in locis cenobia, basilicas, et alia pia loca, nedum hoc in nostro regno Anglie, verum in exteris quibusdam regionibus, eorum devocio regia fundaret, in possessionum ac rerum affluencia copiosius stabilita : Unde et nos, qui eodem rege regum, per quem omnes regnant reges, disponente, utriusque regni nostri gubernacionem in manus nostras iam suscepimus, ab ipsis mature etatis nostre auspiciis, sedula mentis cogitacione versare coepimus, quomodo qualiterve quali regio munere, iuxta modum devocionis nostre, et nostrorum more maiorum, eidem domine et sanctissime matri nostre congruum facere possemus honorem, in tanti complacenciam sponsi eius; tandemque nobis intima meditacione talia cogitantibus, resedit in corde, ut in honorem ac fulcimentum tante

Foundation of Eton College. 1440–6.

Foundation Charter of 11 Oct. 1440.

Henry, by the grace of God, king of England and France, and lord of Ireland, to all to whom these present letters shall come, health.

The church triumphant reigning on high, over which presides the Eternal Father, and which is served by the ranks of saints, and to the glory of which the choirs of angels sing praises, has established on earth as her vicegerent the church militant, which the only-begotten son of God has so united to himself in the everlasting bonds of love that He has deigned to call her His most beloved spouse, and on her in accordance with the dignity of such a title, as a true and most loving spouse, has conferred such ample dower of grace, that she is called, and is, the mother and mistress of all born again in Christ, having power as a mother over all, while all the faithful honour her in filial obedience as mother and mistress; in due consideration of which divers former princes, and above all our ancestors, were always so zealous to worship the same most holy church with the highest honour and devout reverence, that, besides many other glorious works of virtue, to her praise and the glory of her spouse, their royal devotion founded in no few places noble monasteries, churches and other pious places, not only in this our kingdom of England but also in some foreign realms, copiously endowed with affluence of possessions and property; Wherefore it is that we, who, by the will of the same king of kings by whom all kings reign, have just taken into our hands the governance of both our kingdoms, have from the very beginning of our riper age turned over in earnest thought in our mind how and in what manner and by what royal gift suitable to the measure of our devotion, and following the fashion of our elders, we could do fitting honour to our lady and most holy mother, to the pleasure of her great spouse; and at length, while thinking such things in inmost thought, it became settled in our heart, that we would found a college in the honour and

tamque sanctissime matris, in ecclesia parochiali de Etona iuxta Wyndesoram, que a nostre nativitatis loco non longe remota est, unum collegium fundaremus.

Nolentes igitur tam sanctum nostre cogitacionis spiritum extinguere, ac summopere desiderantes ei per omnia placere, in cuius manu sunt omnium corda principum, quo graciosius illuminet ipse cor nostrum, ut deinceps perfectius in suo beneplacito nostros actus regios dirigamus, ac sic sub eius vexillo in presenti ecclesia militemus, quatinus post hac, cum illa que in coelis est, mereamur eius adiuti gracia feliciter triumphare:

Ad laudem, gloriam, et honorem eiusdem crucifixi, gloriosissime Virginis Marie matris eius, exaltacionem, ac stabilimentum ecclesie sacrosancte, ut predicitur, eius sponse, quoddam collegium, iuxta tenorem presencium regendum et eciam gubernandum, in et de numero unius prepositi, ac decem sacerdotum, quatuor clericorum, et sex puerorum choristarum, inibi divino cultui indies deservire debencium, et viginti et quinque pauperum et indigencium scolarium gramaticam addiscere debencium, ac insuper viginti et quinque pauperum ac debilium virorum, pro salubri statu nostro dum vixerimus, ac anima nostra cum ab hac luce migraverimus, animabusque illustrium principis Henrici patris nostri, nuper Anglie et Francie regis, necnon clarissime memorie domine Katerine, nuper consortis sue, matris nostre, cunctorumque progenitorum nostrorum, ac omnium fidelium defunctorum, debebunt in eodem loco iugiter exorare; necnon unius magistri, sive informatoris in gramatica, qui dictos indigentes scolares, aliosque quoscumque et undecumque de regno nostro Anglie ad dictum collegium confluentes, in rudimentis gramatice gratis, absque pecunie aut alterius rei exaccione, debeat informare;

Quos, prepositum quemcumque pro tempore existentem, sacerdotesque, et clericos, pueros, indigentes scolares, pauperes et magistrum sive informatorem, omnes et singulos successive suis temporibus ibi existentes, iuxta tenorem ordinacionis et statutorum in hac parte edendorum eligi, prefici, institui, regi,

for the support of our great and most holy mother in the parish church of Eton by Windsor, which is not far removed from the place of our birth.

Unwilling therefore that so holy an inspiration of our mind should be extinguished, and above all things desiring to please in all things Him in whose hand are the hearts of all princes, that He might the more graciously illumine our heart, and thenceforth more perfectly direct our royal actions in His good pleasure, and that we might so fight under His banner in this present church that we may deserve by the grace of her help hereafter to triumph happily with the church which is in the heavens;

To the praise, glory and honour of the same Crucified One, to the exaltation of the most glorious Virgin Mary His mother, and the establishment of most holy church, His spouse, as aforesaid, by these presents, with the consent of all whom it may concern, we found, erect and also establish, to endure for all time to come, a college to be ruled and governed according to the tenor of these presents, in and of the number of a Provost and ten priests, four clerks and six chorister boys whose duty it shall be to serve divine worship there daily, and 25 poor and needy scholars whose duty it shall be to learn grammar, and moreover 25 poor and weakly men whose duty it shall be always to pray in the same place for our good estate while we live and for our soul when we have passed from this light, and for the souls of the illustrious prince Henry our father, late king of England and of France, also for the lady Katharine, of most serene memory, his late consort, our mother, and of all our ancestors and of all the faithful departed; also of a master or teacher in grammar, whose duty it shall be to teach the said needy scholars, and all others whatsoever and whencesoever of our realm of England coming to the said college, the rudiments of grammar gratis, without exacting money or anything else;

Which Provost for the time being, priests and clerks, boys, needy scholars, poor men and master or teacher, all and singular for the time being there, we will, according to the tenor of an ordinance and statutes to be issued in this behalf, be elected, preferred, instituted, ruled, directed and governed, corrected,

dirigi, et gubernari, corrigi, puniri, ammoveri, destitui, et privari, volumus, in ecclesia predicta, et in quodam fundo contiguo et adiacente cimiterio eiusdem ecclesie, ex parte boreali eiusdem, continente trescentos pedes in longitudine, et ducentos et sexaginta in latitudine, cuius quidem ecclesie patronatum sive advocacionem ad hos finem et effectum super perquisivimus, tenore presencium, de consensu omnium quorum interest, fundamus, erigimus, ac eciam stabilimus, perpetuis futuris temporibus duraturum: ac Henricum Sever, clericum, prepositum et pro preposito ipsius collegii, necnon Iohannem Kette, clericum, Willelmum Haston et Willelmum Dene, socios sacerdotes, Gilbertum Grefe et Iohannem Moddyng, clericos, et Rogerum Fleknore, Willelmum Kente, Iohannem Helewyn, alias dictum Gray, Henricum Cokkes, pueros choristas, ac Willelmum Stokke et Ricardum Cokkes, scolares indigentes, cum uno magistro sive informatore in gramatica, Iohanne Burdon et Iohanne de Evesham, pauperibus viris, secundum statuta et ordinaciones nostra, et heredum nostrorum regum Anglie, imposterum plenius in hac parte edenda, ut prefertur, regendum, corrigendum, privandum, et ammovendum, preficimus, creamus et eciam ordinamus; salva semper nobis et specialiter reservata libera potestate quamdiu egerimus in humanis, predicto numero, ac ceteris omnibus et singulis premissis, addendi seu detrahendi, ac ea et eorum quodlibet mutandi seu corrigendi, quotiens et quando nobis videbitur expedire. Preterea volumus et concedimus, quod prepositus et socii antedicti, et eorum successores imperpetuum, Prepositus et Collegium Regale Beate Marie de Eton. iuxta Wyndesoram nuncupentur: et quod sint unum corpus in se, et, per nomen et sub nomine Prepositi et Collegii Regalis Beate Marie de Eton. iuxta Wyndesoram, sint persone habiles [to sue and be sued by their corporate name and use a common seal]. Damusque ulterius et concedimus, pro nobis et heredibus nostris, preposito et collegio nostro, ac successoribus suis predictis, patronatum sive advocacionem ecclesie parochialis de Etona predicta; Habendum et tenendum, eisdem preposito et collegio nostro, eorumque successoribus, in perpetuam et

punished, removed, dismissed and deprived, in the said church
and in a certain estate next to and adjoining to the cemetery
of the same church on the north side thereof containing 300 feet
in length and 260 in breadth, the patronage or advowson of
which church also we acquired for this end and purpose; and
we appoint, create and also ordain Henry Sever, clerk, provost,
and as vice-provost of the said college, also John Kette, clerk,
William Haston and William Dene, priest-fellows, Gilbert
Grefe and John Moddyng, clerks, and Roger Fleknore, William
Kent, John Helewyn otherwise called Gray, Henry Cox, chorister
boys, and William Stock and Richard Cox, needy scholars,
with a master or teacher in grammar, John Burdon and John
of Evesham, poor men, to be ruled, corrected, deprived and
removed, according to our statutes and ordinances, and those
of our heirs, kings of England, hereafter more fully to be
issued in this behalf as aforesaid; saving always and specially
reserving to us free power, while we remain among men, of
adding to or subtracting from the aforesaid number and all and
singular other the premises, and of changing or correcting them
or any of them as often as and when it shall seem expedient
to us. Moreover we will and grant that the Provost and
Fellows aforesaid and their successors for ever shall be called
the Provost and College Royal of the Blessed Mary of Eton
by Windsor; and that they shall be one body in themselves,
and by and under the name of the Provost and College Royal
of the Blessed Mary of Eton by Windsor be persons able
[to sue and be sued by their corporate name and to use a
common seal]. We give further and grant for us and our
heirs to our Provost and college and their successors for ever
the patronage or advowson of the parish church of Eton aforesaid To have and to hold to the same our Provost and college
and their successors in pure and perpetual alms for ever; and

puram elemosinam imperpetuum ; ac quod predicti prepositus et collegium nostrum, et eorum successores, possint, cum auctoritate diocesani loci illius, ac assensu et consensu eorum quorum in hac parte interest, eandem ecclesiam modo parochialem erigi, transferri, et commutari in collegiatam, necnon eisdem preposito et collegio nostro appropriari, uniri, annecti, et incorporari facere et procurare ; ac eciam eam sic appropriatam, incorporatam, unitam, et annexam, in usus proprios tenere, sibi et successoribus suis predictis imperpetuum ; eo quod expressa mencio de vicario in ecclesia predicta, de fructubus eiusdem dotando et ordinando, seu de competenti summa inter pauperes parochianos eiusdem ecclesie annuatim distribuenda, iuxta formam statuti inde editi, in presentibus facta non existit, non obstante....

In cuius rei testimonium, has litteras nostras fieri fecimus patentes. Teste me ipso, apud manerium nostrum de Shene, undecimo die Octobris, anno regni nostri decimo nono.

Act of Parliament 20 Hen. VI, A.D. 1442, confirming the Foundation and Endowment of Eton College.

[*Rot. Parl.* v. 45.]

Pro preposito et Collegio Regali Beate Marie de Eton. iuxta Wyndesore.

Item, quedam alia peticio exhibita fuit eidem domino regi, in presenti parliamento, per prefatos communes, pro preposito et Collegio Regali Beate Marie de Eton. iuxta Wyndesore in hec verba :

To the wyse and discrete communes of this present parlement : Please it to youre wise discretions, consideryng the most blissid and gracious disposition of oure most Cristien soveraigne lorde the kynge, in the fundation of his college of Eton, called the Kynges College of oure Lady of Eton beside Wyndesore, to pray oure saide soveraigne lorde, to graunte his lettres patentȝ undre his grete seal, by thadvys and assent of

that the said our Provost and college and their successors may with the authority of the diocesan of that place and the assent and consent of all interested in that behalf make and procure the same church now a parish church to be erected, transferred and changed into a collegiate church, and to be appropriated, united, annexed and incorporated with the same our Provost and college; and also to hold the same so appropriated, incorporated, united, and annexed to their own use for them and their successors for ever, notwithstanding the fact that express mention of a vicar to be ordained in the said church and to be endowed out of its fruits, or of a competent sum to be distributed yearly among the poor parishioners of the same church, according to the form of the statute in that behalf published, is not made in these presents...

[Licence to acquire and hold lands, notwithstanding the Statute of Mortmain, to the value of 1000 marks (£666. 13s. 4d.).]

In witness whereof we have caused these our letters to be made patent. Witness myself in our manor of Sheen 11 Oct. in the 19th year of our reign.

Act of Parliament 20 Hen. VI, A.D. 1442, confirming the Foundation and Endowment of Eton College.

For the Provost and the Kynges College of oure Lady of Eton besyde Windesore.

Also, a certain other petition was exhibited to the same Lord King in this present Parliament by the said Commons in behalf of the Provost and College royal of the Blessed Mary of Eton by Windsor in these words.

the lordes spirituell and temporell in this present parlement assemblid, and by auctoritie of the same parlement, to the provost and the college of the same place, and to theire successours, after the fourme and effect of a cedule to this bille annexed. [The Schedule set out the various grants by Letters Patent in Latin.]

Grant of Monopoly to Eton College for teaching Grammar, and prohibition of other Grammar Schools in Windsor and 10 miles round Eton. 3 June 1446.

[Chancery Warrants, Series I., file 1439.]

Memorandum quod ista billa liberata fuit cancellario Anglie tercio die Junii anno xxiiij° exequenda.

R. H.

Rex etc. salutem. Sciatis quod cum nos in Collegio nostro Regali Beate Marie de Etona iuxta Wyndesoram in comitatu Buckingham inter cetera fundaverimus et pro perpetuis futuris temporibus stabiliverimus septuaginta scolares scienciam gramaticalem addiscere debentes ac sexdecim pueros choristas qui similiter, cum in cantu sufficienter instructi fuerint, gramaticam addiscere debebunt, necnon unum magistrum informatorem in gramatica, ac unum hostiarium, qui prefatos pueros′scolares et choristas necnon quoscumque alios undecumque et de quibuscumque partibus dictum ad collegium eandem scienciam addiscendi gracia confluentes in rudimentis gramatice gratis et absque quavis exactione pecunie seu retribucionis alterius informare debebunt, concessimus preposito et collegio nostro predicto quod ipsi et eorum successores imperpetuum habeant semper infra cepta eiusdem collegii nostri regalis publicas et generales scolas gramaticales, quodque eedem scole sicut omnes tales huius regni nostri scolas gramaticales quascumque excedant in affluencia dotis et precellencia fundacionis, ita in nominis prerogativa omnes alias scolas gramaticales, ut convenit, antecellant, nominenturque proinde generales scole Regis et aliarum omnium scolarum gramaticalium appellentur domina mater et magistra, concessimusque eisdem insuper quod nulli sit licitum cuiuscumque fuerit auctoritatis scolas huiusmodi gramaticales publicas infra villam Wyndesore aut alibi infra spacium decem milliarium Anglicorum a dicto nostro Regali Collegio ullocunque tempore regere, instituere vel fundare presumat. Eo quod expressa mencio de aliis donis et con-

Grant of Monopoly to Eton College for teaching Grammar, and prohibition of other Grammar Schools in Windsor and 10 miles round Eton. 3 June 1446.

Be it remembered that this bill was delivered to the Chancellor of England to be executed 3 June in the 24th year [of Henry VI].

Henry the King.

The King etc. greeting. Know ye that whereas when we amongst other things founded and for all time to come established in our College Royal of the Blessed Mary of Eton by Windsor, in the county of Buckingham, 70 scholars whose duty it is to learn the science of grammar, and 16 choristers whose duty likewise it shall be, when they have been sufficiently instructed in singing, to learn grammar, also a master teacher in grammar and an usher to teach the aforesaid boys, scholars and choristers, and also all others whatsoever, whencesoever and from whatever parts coming to the said college to learn the same science, in the rudiments of grammar freely and without any exaction of money or other contribution, we granted to the Provost and our college aforesaid that they and their successors for ever may always have within the boundaries of the said Royal College a public and general grammar school, and that the same school as it surpasses all other such grammar schools whatsoever of our kingdom in the affluence of its endowment and the pre-excellence of its foundation, so it may excel all other grammar schools, as it ought, in the prerogative of its name, and be named henceforth the King's general school, and be called the lady mother and mistress of all other grammar schools, and have granted to them moreover that it shall not be lawful for anyone, of whatever authority he may be, at any time to presume to keep, set up, or found any such public grammar school in the town of Windsor or elsewhere within the space of 10 English miles from our said Royal College. And this notwithstanding that express mention is not made in these

cessionibus per nos eisdem preposito et collegio ante hec tempora factis in presentibus minime facta existit aut aliquo statuto, actu, sive ordinacione in contrarium facto non obstante.

In cuius etc.

Cambridge Grammar School incorporated in Site of King's College. 16 Nov. 1440.

[King's Coll. Mun. A. 74.]

Sciant presentes et futuri quod ego Johannes Tybbay armiger, frater et heres Thome Tybbay clerici, dedi concessi et hac presenti carta mea confirmaui Johanni ffray Capitali Baroni Scaccarii domini nostri Regis, Magistro Johanni Somerset cancellario eiusdem Scaccarii et Magistro Johanni Langtoñ Cancellario Vniuersitatis Cantebrigie unum tenementum meum vocatum Gramerscole scituatum in vico scolarum Cantebrigie inter tenementum vocatum Artscole ex parte orientali et tenementum nuper Prioris Sancti Johannis Jerusalem in Anglia vocatum Crowched hostell et tenementum Roberti Lincoln' vocatum Arundell ex parte occidentali, et abuttat ad unum caput versus boream super predictum vicum scolarum et ad aliud caput super dictum tenementum dicti Roberti Lincoln' versus austrum Habendum et tenendum predictum tenementum cum pertinenciis predictis Joh. ffray [etc.] heredibus et assignatis suis de capitalibus dominis feodi illius per seruicium inde debitum et de iure consuetum imperpetuum...

In cuius rei testimonium huic presenti carte mee sigillum meum apposui hiis testibus, Thoma Jacob, Maiore ville Cantebr. [etc.].

Date Cantebrigie sextodecimo die mensis Nouembris anno regni Regis Henrici sexti post conquestum decimo nono.

Foundation of Farthinghoe Free School, Northants. 19 June 1443.

[P. P. C. 34 Luffenam, 269.]

Johannes Abbot ciuis ac mercerus ciuitatis London declarauit ultimam voluntatem suam de omnibus terris et

presents of other gifts and grants by us heretofore made to the same Provost and college, and notwithstanding any statute, act or ordinance to the contrary.

In witness etc.

Cambridge Grammar School incorporated in Site of King's College. 16 *Nov.* 1440.

Know present and to come that I, John Tebay, esquire, brother and heir of Thomas Tebay, clerk, have given, granted and by this my deed confirmed to John Fray, chief Baron of the Exchequer of our lord the King, Master John Somerset, Chancellor of the same Exchequer, and Master John Langton, Chancellor of the University of Cambridge, my tenement called Grammar-school, situate in School street, Cambridge, between a tenement called Arts School on the East, and a tenement late of the Prior of St John of Jerusalem in England called Crowched-hostel, and a tenement of Robert of Lincoln called Arundel on the West, and it abuts at one head towards the North on the aforesaid School street and at another head on the tenement of the said Robert of Lincoln towards the South, To have and to hold the said tenement, with its appurtenances to the aforesaid John Fray [etc.] their heirs and assigns of the chief lords of the fee by the service thereof due and of right accustomed for ever...

[Warranty of title. Witness clause.]

Dated at Cambridge 16 November 19 Henry VI.

Foundation of Farthinghoe Free School, Northants. 19 *June* 1443.

John Abbot, citizen and mercer of the city of London, declared his last will of all his lands and tenements, with their

tenementis suis cum pertinenciis tam infra ciuitatem London quam in Farnyngo et Astrop in comitatu Northamptonie, viz. ut Magistri siue Gardiani Mistere Mercerorum London et eiusdem mistere communitas habeant et teneant sibi et successoribus suis imperpetuum omnia illa terras et tenementa sua in Catton Lane sub condicione quod huiusmodi Magistri siue Gardiani et communitas et eorum successores inuenirent annuatim unum capellanum ydoneum et honestum diuina in ecclesia de Farnyngo in comitatu Northamptonie pro anima sua animabusque parentum amicorum et benefactorum suorum et omnium fidelium defunctorum celebraturum imperpetuum ac paruulos parochie ecclesie de Farnyngo predicta libere et quiete docturum et informaturum absque stipendio vel lucro proinde percipiendo;

Prouiso semper quod soluent ipsi Magistri siue Gardiani et communitas et eorum successores annuatim de exitibus reuencionibus et proficuis de eisdem terris et tenementis cum pertinenciis in Catton Lane prouenientibus huiusmodi capellano loco et forma predictis celebranti et docenti nomine salarii sui et stipendii pro predicto diuino seruicio et labore 10 marcas sterlingorum ad quatuor anni terminos principales per equales porciones....

Probatum fuit v die Marcii anno Domini millesimo cccc^{mo} quadragesimo tercio.

The Increase of Schools in London. 1446–7.

[A. F. Leach, 'St Paul's School before Colet,' *Archæol.* LXII. pt. i. 191. P.R.O. Privy Seals, 24 Hen. VI.]

Writ of Privy Seal for two new Grammar Schools in London.
3 May 1446.

Henri by the grace of God King of Engelande and of Fraunce and Lorde of Irlande To oure Chanceller of Engelande greting.

For asmoche as the right reverent fader in God Therche-

Increase of Schools in London

appurtenances, as well in the city of London as in Farthinghoe and Astrop [?], in the county of Northampton, namely, that the masters or wardens of the Mystery of Mercers of London and the commonalty of the same mystery should have and hold to them and their successors for ever all those his lands and tenements in Cat Lane, on condition that such masters or wardens and commonalty and their successors should find yearly a chaplain fit and honest to celebrate divine service in the church of Farthinghoe, in the county of Northampton, for his soul and the souls of his parents, friends and benefactors and all the faithful departed for ever, and to teach and instruct the little ones of the parish of the church of Farthinghoe aforesaid freely and gratis without taking any pay or profit therefor;

Provided always that the said masters or wardens and commonalty and their successors shall pay yearly from the issues, rents and profits arising out of the same lands and tenements and their appurtenances in Cat Lane to such chaplain celebrating and teaching in the place and manner aforesaid, by way of his salary and stipend for the said divine service and labour, ten marks sterling [£6. 13s. 4d.] at the four principal terms of the year by equal portions...

The will was proved 5 March 1443-4.

bisshopp of Canterbury and the reverent fader in God the bisshopp of London considering the greet abusions that have ben of long tyme withinne oure Citee of London that many and divers persones not sufficiently instruct in gramer presumynge to holde commune gramer scoles in greet deceipte aswel unto theire scolers as unto the frendes that fynde theim to scole have of theire greet wysdome sette and ordeigned .v. scoles of gramer and no moo withinne oure said Citee; Oon withinne the chirche yerde of Saint Poule; an other withinne the collegiate Churche of Saint Martin; the thridde in Bowe chirche; the iiij[the] in the chirche of Saint Dunstan in the Est; the .v. in oure hospital of Saint Anthony withinne oure said

Citee. the whiche thei have openly declared suffisantz, as by theire lettres patentes their upon maad it appereth more at large We in consideracion of the premisses have therunto graunted oure Royal wille and assent Wherfore we wol and charge you that here upon ye doo make oure lettres patentes under oure greet seel in due fourme declaring in the same oure said wille and assent, yevyng furthermore in commaundement by the same oure lettres unto alle oure subgittes of oure said Citee that thei nor noon of thaim trouble nor empeche the maistres of the said Scoles in any wyse in this partie. but rather helpe and assiste thaim in asmoche as in thaim is Yeveñ under oure prive seel at Guildeforde the iij^{de} day of May The yere of oure regne. xxiiij.   Langeport.

Memorandum quod sexto die Maij anno vicesimo quarto superscriptum istud breve liberatum fuit Cancellario Anglie exequendum.

Petition for establishing four new Grammar Schools in London, Henry VI. 1447.

[*Rot. Parl.* v. 137.]

To the full worthy and discrete Communes in this present Parlement assemblid; Please it unto the full wyse and discrete Comunes in this present Parliament assemblid to considre, the grete nombre of gramer Scoles, that somtyme were in divers parties of this Realme, beside tho that were in London, and howe fewe ben in thise dayes, and the grete hurt that is caused of this, not oonly in the Spirituell partie of the Chirche, where often tymes it apperith to openly in som persones, with grete shame, but also in Temporell partie, to whom also it is full expedient to have compotent congruite for many causes, as to youre wisedoms apperith. And for asmuche as to the Citee of London is the commune concours of this lond, wherin is grete multitude of younge peple, not oonly borne and brought forthe in the same Citee, but also of many other

Increase of Schools in London

parties of this lond, som for lake of Scole maistres in thier oune Contree, for to be enfourmed of gramer there, and som for the grete almesse of Lordes, Merchauntz and other, the which is in London more plenteously doon, than in many other places of this Reaume, to such pouere Creatures as never shuld have be brought to so greet vertu and connyng as thei have, ne hadde hit ben bi the meane of the almes abovesaid; Wherefore it were expedient, that in London were a sufficeant nombre of Scoles, and good enfourmers in gramer, and not for the singuler availl of ii or iii persones, grevously to hurte the multitude of yonge peple of all this Lond; For where there is grete nombre of Lerners, and fewe Techers, and all the Lerners be compelled to goo to the same fewe Techers, and to noon other, the Maisters wexen riche in money, and the Lerners pouere in connyng, as experience openly shewith, aynst all vertue and ordre of well puplik. And thise premises... and sturen of grete devotion and pitee, Maistre William Lycchefeld, parson of the parich Chirche of all Halowen the more in London; Maister Gilbert, parson of Seint Andrewe in Holbourne subarbs of the saide Citee; Maister John Cote, parson of Seint Petre in Cornhull of London; and John Neell, Maister of the Hous or Hospitall of Seint Thomas of Acres, and parson of Colchirche in London, to compleyne unto you; and for remedie besechyn you to pray the Kyng our Soveraigne Lord, that he bi thadvys and assent of the Lordes Spirituell and Temporell, in this present Parliament assembled, and bi auctorite of the same Parliament, will provide, ordeyne and graunte, to the saide Maistre William, and his successours, that thei, in the seid paressh of all Halowen; to the said Maistre Gilbert, and his successours, that thei in the saied parissh of Seint Andrewe; to the said Maistre John, and his successours, that thei in the said parissh of Seint Petre; and to the said John Maistre, and his successours, that thei within the forsaid parissh of oure Lady of Colchirche, in the whiche the said Hous of Seint Thomas is sette, may ordeyne, create, establish and sette, a persone

sufficiantly lerned in gramer, to hold and exercise a Scole in the same science of gramer, and it there to teche to all that will lerne; And that everiche of the saied Maistre William, Maistre Gilbert, Maistre John, and John Neel Maistre, suche Scole maister so bi him sette, and everiche of theire successours, suche Scole maister bi him, or bi ony of his predecessours so establisshed and sette specially as is above rehercid, may in his owne parich or place remove, and an other in his place substitute and sette, as often as ony of the said persones, or their successours, semith that cause resonable so requireth: and so to doo, iche of the said persones and their successours, as often as it happenyth ony of the said Scoles to be voyde of a Scole Maistre, in ony maner wise; to the honur of God, and encreasyng of vertu.

Responsio.

The Kyng wille, that it be do as it is desired; so that it be doone by thadvyse of the Ordinarie, otherelles of the Archebishope of Canterbury for the tyme beyng.

Oxford University Library. 1447–50.

Appeal to Lord Say and to House of Commons, because the University educates their children and relations, for help to get Duke Humphrey's books. 1447.

[H. Anstey, *Epistolae Academicae Oxon.* I. 261, Oxf. Hist. Soc.]

To the Right noble and oure singuler good lord, the Lord Say, Chamberlayn unto oure soveraigne lord the Kynge.

Ryght noble and our ryght singler lord, we recommend us un to your good lordschip in lowly wyse, wyche Almyghty God preserve and governe longe in welth and prosperite; Besechyng your benyng favoure to oure Universite, and that ye lyk to be good menes to our soveryng lord the Kyng for the buks wyche owr gud lord, the duk of Gloucestre, be for grawntyd to owr said Universite, wan he was last in the same Universite, and

also, as we be sufficiently informyd be wyrschipful and famous men, a lytyl be for he passyd to God he confermyd the same: Consideryng, gracious lord, the gret multitud of scolers and the penury of bokes in the sayd Universite, and that many of your nobyl lynage and kynnesmen hav studyed and schal her after in the saide Universite, to our gret worschip and profete of al the realm. And we schall pray God for yow, for yowr good mediation and instance un to owr Soveryng lord the Kyng in the saide mater: wyche longe mayntene yow in good helth of soule and body.

Writin at Oxon in oure sembly hows, the vi day of April. Yowr poor oratrice, the Universitie of Oxon.

Letter to the House of Commons for similar help. 1450.

[*Ib.* I. 294.]

Right worshipfull syres, grace, pece, and prosperity be to you, to godes Worship and to the gode Welth of the Realme of Englond everduring. Worthy syres, forasmoche that mony of your own Issieu and also kynnesmen hath ben, be now, and shall be in tyme comyng tenderly and bysyly norysshed and avaunced with the rype frute of connyng in oure Moder the Universite of Oxonford; into the glory and the Worship of god in special, and to the mayntenaunce of crysten faith, causyng of wyse menn in the Realme, and to you grete ioy, confort, and eternal mede; that causeth, supporteth, and furthereth suche studiers; Therfore we conceyveth that youre natures and benevolences shuld enjoy with ws of the furtheraunce of the said Universite. And for somoche that oure ryght special lord and myghty Prince the Duke of Gloucestre, late passed out of this worlde,—whos soule god assoyle for his hygh mercy,—not long bifore his decesse, being in oure said Universyte emonge all the Doctours and maisteres of the same sembled togedor, graunted unto us all his latyn bokes, to the lovyng of god, increce of Clergy and connyng menn, to the gode governaunce and prosperite of the Realme of England

withouten ende, bifore all other contreyes or places of the World; the whiche gyfte often tymes aftre, be oure messengeres, and also in his laste testament, as we understande, he conformed, the which bokes we myght, be no maner of laboures, sythen he decessed opteyne; Therfore we besech your sage discreciones, consideryng all this premysses, that ye wyll, at the reverence of god and the instance of oure devote prayers,

Fees at Ipswich Grammar School.
1477 *and* 1482.

[Ipswich Court Book, B. M. MS. Add. 30158, f. 34.]

Ordinacio: Et quod magister scole gramaticalis de cetero habebit jurisdiccionem et gubernacionem omnium scolarium infra libertatem et procinctum istius ville, exceptis petytis vocatis Apesyes et Songe, tantum capiendo pro suo salario de quolibet gramatico saltario et primario secundum taxacionem Domini Episcopi Norwicensis, videlicet pro gramatico xd. quarteragii, saltario viij$d$. et primario vj$d$.

[*Ib.*]

Et quod quilibet burgensis infra villam Gippwici commorans solvat Magistro Gramatico pro puero suo pro quarterio anni, 8d. et non ultra; et quod dictus Magister Gramaticus celebrabit ad totum terminum vite sue pro gilda Corporis Christi.

Foundation of Jesus College, Rotherham, with three Schools of Grammar, Song and Writing.
1 *Feb.* 1483.

[A. F. Leach, *Early Yorks. Schools*, II. 109. From MS. at Sidney Sussex Coll., Cambridge, collated with B. M. Cott. Vitellius, E. x., art. 29, f. 226.]

Universis Sancte Matris ecclesie filiis presentes litteras inspecturis, Thomas, permissione divina, Eboracensis Archie-

to the complesshing of our said ryght special lordes wylle and desire, and of right wesnes to be had in this behalve, ordeyn in suche wyse for us in this present noble parliament that we may reioysse the bokes biforesaid. And so oure lord god inspyre you and governe you to his pleasaunce with helth of soule and body to youre lyves ende,

Writene at Oxonford etc.

Fees at Ipswich Grammar School.
1477 *and* 1482.

1477.

Ordinance. And that the Grammar School-master shall henceforth have the jurisdiction and government of all scholars in the liberty and precinct of this town, except the petties called ABCs and Song, taking only for his fees, from every grammar scholar, psalter scholar and primer scholar according to the scale fixed by the lord Bishop of Norwich, viz. for a grammarian 10*d.*, psalterian 8*d.* and primarian 6*d.* for quarterage.

1482.

And that every burgess, being in the town of Ipswich, shall pay to the Grammar School-master for his son 8*d.* a quarter and not above; and that the said Grammar School-master shall celebrate for the gild of Corpus Christi for the whole term of his life.

Foundation of Jesus College, Rotherham, with three Schools of Grammar, Song and Writing.
1 *Feb.* 1483.

To all the sons of Holy Mother Church who inspect these present letters, Thomas, by divine permission Archbishop of

piscopus, Anglie primas et apostolice sedis Legatus, Salutem in amplexibus Salvatoris.

Quia nos, Archiepiscopus antedictus, perpendentes et considerantes quod in villa de Rotherham nostre Eboracensis diocesis, ubi nati fueramus, et per lavacrum Sancte Regeneracionis renati, ubi eciam nostram impuberem etatem agentes, sine litteris stetimus, stetissemusque sic indocti, illiterati, et rudes ad annos plurimos, nisi quod, gracia Dei, vir in gramatica doctus supervenerit, a quo ut a fonte primo instructi, Deo volente, et, ut credimus, ducatum prestante, pervenimus ad statum in quo nunc sumus, perveneruntque plures alii ad magna.

Proinde gracias Salvatori reddere cupientes, et ne ingrati videamur, beneficiorumque Dei, et unde venimus, arguamur immemores, fontem talem ibidem scaturire facere, Doctorem scilicet gramatice ibidem stabilire decrevimus pro semper;

Secundoque considerantes, quod ad illam ecclesiam multi pertinent parochiani, et quamplures montani ad eam confluunt homines, ut melius diligant Christi religionem, ecclesiamque eius sepius visitent, honorent et diligant, alium in cantu doctum, atque sex choristas, sive capelle pueros, ut divina ibidem honorificentius celebrentur, pro perpetuo duximus stabiliendos;

Tercio que, quia multos, luce et ingenii acumine preditos juvenes profert terra illa, neque omnes volunt sacerdocii dignitatem et altitudinem attingere, ut tales ad artes mechanicas et alia mundum concernencia, magis habilitentur, ordinavimus tercium socium, in arte scribendi et computandi scientem et peritum.

Set quia ars scribendi, musica ipsa simul et gramatica subordinantur legi divine et evangelio, super istos tres socios stabilivimus unum theologum, qui ad minus erit Bacalarius in Theologia, qui Prepositus, pre aliis tribus sociis positus in regimine et policia domus, vocabitur, qui scalam Jacob, Verbum Jesus, viam in celum brevissimam et certissimam in nostra provincia predicare, et Collegium regere, tenebitur.

York, primate of England and legate of the apostolic see, health in the embraces of the Health-giver.

Whereas we, the Archbishop aforesaid, thinking over and considering that in the town of Rotherham of our diocese of York, where we were born and by the bath of holy regeneration re-born, where, too, passing our tender age we remained without letters, and should have so stood untaught, unlettered and rude for many years, if there had not come there by the grace of God a man learned in grammar, from whom as from a spring we drew our first instruction, God willing and as we believe lending His guidance, and so arrived at the state in which we now are, while many others too arrived at great things.

Desiring, therefore, in the first place to render thanks to the Saviour, and that we may not seem ungrateful and be accused of being unmindful of God's benefits and of whence we came, we have determined to make such a spring flow there for ever, in other words to establish a teacher of grammar there;

And in the second place, considering that many parishioners belong to that church and many hill-men flock to it, that they may better love Christ's religion and oftener visit, honour, and love His church, we have thought fit to establish for ever another fellow learned in song and six choristers or children of the chapel, that divine service may be more honourably celebrated;

In the third place, because that county produces many youths endowed with the light and sharpness of ability, who do not all wish to attain the dignity and elevation of the priesthood, that these may be better fitted for the mechanical arts and other concerns of this world, we have ordained a third fellow, learned and skilled in the art of writing and accounts.

But as the art of writing, music, and indeed grammar itself are subordinated to the divine law and the Gospel, above these three fellows we have established a theologian, who shall be at least a Bachelor in Theology, who shall be called Provost or Placed over, because he is placed over the other three fellows in the management and policy of the house; and he shall be bound to preach in my province the ladder of Jacob, the word of Jesus, the shortest and surest way to heaven and to rule the college.

Recolentes jam finaliter, quod Sacerdos fuimus, indignissimus quanquam, nichil eapropter alienum a nobis putemus putabimusque unquam quod ad Sacerdocii pertinet dignitatem, Cantariales eiusdem ecclesie. Sacerdotes qui per antea in diversis locis commensales et pernoctantes, ad eorum et ecclesie scandalum, ocio et inercie dediti fuerunt, ex opere supererogacionis reformare cupientes, ex animo decernimus, decrevimus et volumus istos in nostro perhendinare Collegio, cameras eis assignare et ibidem commensare, eo fine ut in gramatica, musica, cantu, arte scribendi, audiendo bibliam, studendo in libraria, aut aliquid informacionis a Preposito audiendo occupentur ad Dei laudem et eorum salutem animarum.

Ut hec omnia ea propter in uno Jesu et sub uno regimine reducantur et regantur, ad laudem omnipotentis Dei et exaltacionem nominis Jesu Christi, quoddam Collegium perpetuum in villa de Rotherham predicta, ut prefertur, de uno Preposito, predicatore verbi Dei, tribus Sociis in gramatica, cantu et arte scribendi Informatoribus, et sex pueris, ex bonis nobis a Deo collatis, auctoritate nostra ordinaria et metropolitica fundamus creamus, erigimus et stabilimus, Statuentes et ordinantes quod nostrum collegium sub hoc nomine et vocabulo 'Collegium Jesu de Rotherham' de cetero et imperpetuum nuncupari et appellari, Quodque Prepositi et Socii eiusdem Collegii et successores sui Prepositi et Socii Collegii Jesu de Rotherham vocentur et nuncupentur, sintque unum corpus in re et nomine incorporati ac sigillum commune habeant et utantur in omnibus scriptis et litteris causas, negocia et facta eiusdem Collegii concernentibus.

De prefeccione Prepositi.

Statuimus insuper et ordinamus quod Prepositus qualiscunque futurus dicti Collegii nostri sit sacerdos, in sacra theologia Doctor, seu ad minus in eadem Baccalarius Universitatis Cantabrigie, laudabilis vite et bone ac approbate conversacionis et discrecionis, in spiritualibus et temporalibus

Lastly, recalling that I am a priest, though most unworthy, and therefore think, and shall alway think, nothing foreign to me which concerns the dignity of the priesthood, desiring with all my heart as a work of supererogation to reform the chantry priests of the church who, hitherto commoning and lodging in different places, to the scandal of themselves and of the church, have been given over to ease and idleness, we decree and have decreed and will that they shall live in my college, that chambers shall be assigned to them, and that they shall board there, to the end that they may be occupied in grammar, music, singing, the art of writing, in hearing the bible, studying in the library, or obtaining some information from the Provost to the praise of God and health of their souls.

And so that all these things may be brought under and governed in one Jesus and under one rule, to the glory of Almighty God and the exaltation of the name of Jesus Christ, by our ordinary and metropolitical authority we found, create, erect and establish, out of the goods given us by God, a perpetual college in the town of Rotherham aforesaid, of a Provost, a preacher of God's Word, three fellows, teachers of grammar, song, and the art of writing, and six boys, Decreeing and ordering that our college shall for the future and for ever be named and called by this name and title 'the College of Jesus of Rotherham,' And that the Provost and fellows of the same college and their successors shall be named and called 'the Provost and fellows of the college of Jesus of Rotherham,' and may be one body in fact and name incorporated and have and use a common seal in all writings and letters concerning the causes, business and deeds of the same college.

Of the appointment of the Provost.

We decree, moreover, and ordain that every future Provost of our said college shall be a priest, a doctor or at least a bachelor in holy theology of the University of Cambridge, of laudable life and good and approved conduct and discretion, prudent and learned in spiritual and temporal matters, and apt and fit

prudens et circumspectus, et ad huiusmodi officium aptus et idoneus,...per regentes et non regentes Universitatis Cantabrigie, aut maiorem partem eorundem pro tempore existentes, ...in scriptis sub sigillo eiusdem Universitatis nominetur et presentetur.

De Predicacionibus per Prepositum faciendis.

Quem Prepositum sic iuratum volumus et ordinamus predicacioni verbi Dei in diocesi nostra Eboracensi et precipue in villis de Rotherham, Laxton, Almondesbury, ac Eglesfeld et locis adiacentibus eisdem insistere et intendere diligenter cum effectu....

De stipendio Prepositi.

Idemque Prepositus habeat pro stipendio et salario suo annuatim viginti marcas sterlingorum, qua summa in virtute juramenti sui predicti coram sociis, ut prefertur, prestiti se contentum reputabit.

De eleccione trium Sociorum.

Ordinamus insuper, quod socii futuri ad informandum et instruendum in gramatica, cantu et arte scriptoria electi sint, presbiteri, si commode haberi poterint, aut saltem unus eorum secundum discrecionem Prepositi, qui sint bene et sufficienter docti in facultatibus ad eorum officium spectantibus, ac bone conversacionis et honeste, nominandi, eligendi ac assumendi per dictum Prepositum et socios seu saltem, socium seniorem dicti Collegii ad tunc realiter existentem. Quorum

Primum ad hoc magis idoneum et aptum scolares quoscunque gramaticam secundum suum officium ad hoc sibi per Prepositum destinatos volumus informare et instruere per supervisum, discrecionem et industriam eiusdem Prepositi.

Secundum vero quoscunque scolares cantum addiscere cupientes undecunque in regno Anglie, et precipue de diocesi et provincia nostris Eboracensi ad predictum collegium se conferentes et confluentes secundum regulas et instituta artis

for this office...to be named and presented by the regents and non-regents of the University of Cambridge or the majority of them for the time being...in writing under the University seal.

Of the Provost's preaching.

Which Provost so sworn we will and ordain shall be insistent and diligently effectively attend to preaching the word of God in our diocese of York, and especially in the towns of Rotherham, Laxton, Almondbury and Egglesfield, and the places adjacent....

Of the Provost's stipend.

And the same Provost shall have for his stipend and salary 20 marks sterling [£13. 6s. 8d.] a year, and with this sum in virtue of his oath aforesaid taken before the fellows he shall consider himself satisfied.

Of the election of three Fellows.

We ordain, moreover, that the future fellows shall be elected to teach and instruct in grammar, song and scrivener's craft, priests, if such can conveniently be gotten, or at least one of them at the discretion of the Provost, who, being well and adequately learned in the faculties belonging to their office, and of good and upright conduct, shall be nominated, elected and admitted by the said Provost and fellows, or at least the senior fellow of the said college for the time being;

Of whom the first most fit and proper for this we will to teach and instruct in grammar all scholars sent to him by the Provost for this purpose according to his office under the oversight, discretion and labour of the same Provost.

The second we will shall teach all scholars wishing to learn singing, coming and flocking to the said college from anywhere in the kingdom of England, and especially from our diocese and province of York, according to the rules and principles of

musice informare volumus, et presertim in plano et fracto cantu secundum omnes modos et formas eiusdem artis.

Tercium vero in arte scribendi et computandi informatorem.

Qui quidem Informatores huiusmodi scolares ad nostrum collegium confluentes in gramatica cantu et arte scriptoria absque pecunie vel alterius rei cuiuscunque exaccione in certis scolis et domibus infra idem collegium ad huiusmodi usus ordinatis diligenter instruant et informent.

De Salario Sociorum.

Habeat que informator sive instructor in gramatica pro stipendio suo annuatim de bonis et redditibus dicti nostri Collegii decem libras et non ultra:

Et instructor in cantu de eisdem bonis decem marcas et non ultra;

Et instructor in arte scriptoria octo marcas sterlingorum, et non ultra;

solvendas eorum cuilibet per manus Prepositi ad quatuor anni terminos usuales.

De perhendinantibus recipiendis in Collegio.

Et quia hiis diebus sepe oritur scandalum ex cohabitacione clericorum et mulierum, et ex nimia frequentacione earum ad et in domos maxime suspectas virorum laicorum et mulierum, si illuc frequenter accedant, oriri poterit in futurum, ad tollendam igitur huiusmodi infamiam seu scandalum, quantum in nobis est, et ut Capellani et perhendinare volentes in eodem Collegio ocium evitent, et stimulum et calcar ad studium et doctrinam tam ex instruccione gramatice, cantus et artis scriptorie, tam ex lectura et communicacione inter plures simul cohabitantes habeant et accipiant;

Volumus et ordinamus quod liceat dicto Preposito omnes capellanos stipendiarios seu cantaristas in eadem ecclesia de Rotherham ministrantes et celebrantes, et quoscunque alios

the art of music, and especially in plain and broken chant according to all the modes and forms of the same art.

The third [we will to be] a teacher in the art of writing and reckoning.

Which teachers shall diligently instruct and teach such scholars coming to our college in grammar, song and the art of writing without exaction of money or anything else whatsoever in certain schools and houses within the same college assigned for such use.

Of the salary of the Fellows.

And the teacher or instructor in grammar shall have for his stipend yearly from the goods and rents of our said college £10 and not more;

And the instructor in singing from the same goods 10 marks [£6. 13s. 4d.], and not more;

And the instructor in the art of writing 8 marks sterling [£5. 6s. 8d.], and not more;
to be paid to each of them by the hands of the Provost at the four usual terms of the year.

Of receiving commoners in the College.

And whereas in these days scandal often arises from clerks and women living together, and will arise hereafter from too much intercourse with them, and especially in suspect houses of laymen and women, if they frequently go there, To remove this ill-fame and scandal as far as we can, and that the chaplains and others wishing to live in the same college may avoid idleness, and have and feel a stimulus and spur to study and learning both by instruction in grammar, song and the art of writing, as well as by reading and intercourse among many living together;

We will and ordain that the said Provost may receive all the stipendiary chaplains or chantry priests serving and celebrating in Rotherham church, and all other churchmen or

viros ecclesiasticos et scolares presentes et futuros, cuiuscunque fuerint condicionis, dummodo bone fame et honeste conversacionis fuerint, in commensales et perhendinantes ad eius mensam seu aliam quamcunque infra dictum Collegium, ipsorum tamen sumptibus et expensis, recipere, camerasque eis competentes et gratis ad ipsius Prepositi libitum deputare et assignare, dummodo dictis Preposito et Sociis per huiusmodi deputacionem et assignacionem non generetur aliquo modo preiudicium seu aliquod gravamen inducatur.

De eleccione sex puerorum.

Ulterius volumus statuimus et ordinamus quod ultra numerum unius Prepositi et trium sociorum predictorum sex pueri de partibus illis pauperiores et ad doctrinam et virtutes magis idonei et aptiores, et precipue de sanguine nostro et de parochiis de Rotherham et Eglesfeld, per Prepositum assumantur et eligantur in collegium nostrum; quibus ex sumptibus eiusdem collegii in victu et vestitu sufficienter secundum Prepositi discrecionem provideatur, quos instrui et informari volumus ibidem in cantu, gramatica et arte scriptoria ad xviij annum etatis eorundem, nisi prius maturi in sciencia et doctrina inventi fuerint, prout Preposito visum fuerit, de quorum moribus virtute et doctrina eiusdem conscienciam districte oneramus, quos eciam volumus Preposito et Sociis in missis ac illis et aliis commensalibus in mensa et lectura biblie cotidie deservire, et cum iidem pueri annum sue etatis xviij compleverint a collegio amoveantur et alii de pauperioribus vel ceteris, ut predictum est, in loco eorum protinus subrogentur.

De missa Jhesu ac antiphona Beate Marie decantandis.

Volumus insuper ordinamus et statuimus quod magister instructor in cantu ibidem pro tempore existens, et dicti pueri, singulis diebus Veneris imperpetuum ad altare Jesu infra ecclesiam parochialem ad missam de Jesu, et ad vesperam eisdem diebus ibidem imperpetuum, nisi in Sabbatis et vigiliis festorum Beate Marie virginis, antiphonam de Jesu, ac in singulis vigiliis festorum Beate Marie ad vesperam antiphonam de eadem ad altare eiusdem in capella super pontem in dicta villa de Rotherham; necnon singulis diebus Sabbatis per annum ad vesperam imperpetuum, vigiliis Beate Marie non contingentibus, antiphonam de Beata Maria ad altare eiusdem infra dictam ecclesiam devote decantent.

scholars now or in future, of whatever status, as long as they are of good repute and upright behaviour, as commoners and boarders at his or any other table in the said college, at their cost and expense however, and may assign them proper chambers, and if he so wishes, gratis, as long as this does not produce any prejudice or loss.

Of the election of the six boys.

Further we will, decree and ordain that beside the Provost and three fellows aforesaid, six boys, the poorest in those parts, who are most apt and fit for learning and virtue, and by preference those of our kin and of the parishes of Rotherham and Egglesfield, shall be taken and elected by the Provost into our college; and adequate provision shall be made for them at the cost of the said college in food and clothing at the discretion of the Provost; and we wish them to be instructed and taught there in song, grammar and the art of writing till their 18th year, unless they have previously become ripe in learning and knowledge, as seems good to the Provost, whose conscience we charge with strict attention to their conduct, character and learning, and we will that they shall serve the Provost and fellows in masses, and them and the other commoners at table, and in reading the Bible daily; and when these boys have reached the age of 19, they shall be removed from the college, and other poor boys, qualified as aforesaid, shall be forthwith elected in their place.

Of chanting the mass of Jesus and anthem of the Blessed Mary.

We will also, ordain and decree that the master instructor of singing for the time being and the said boys shall every Friday for ever devoutly chant at the Jesus altar in the parish church, at the Jesus mass and at vespers on the same days there for ever, except on Saturdays and vigils of the Blessed Virgin Mary's feasts, the anthem of Jesus, and on every eve of a feast of the Blessed Mary at vespers, an anthem of Our Lady at her altar in the chapel on Rotherham bridge; and every Saturday throughout the year at vespers, when it is not an eve of the Blessed Mary, an anthem of the Blessed Mary at her altar in the said church.

Foundation of a Spelling and Reading School.
8 Nov. 1489.

[A. F. Leach, *V. C. H. Northants*, II. 614, from B. M. Harl. 604, f. 48.]

Fundacio Cantarie de Aldwyncle.

Universis sancte matris ecclesie filiis...Willelmus Chamber de Aldwyncle in comitatu Northamptonie, salutem....

...Universitati vestre notum facio per presentes me... dedisse...Domino Johanni Seliman capellano ad sustentacionem suam et successorum suorum...divina singulis diebus ad altare Sancte Marie Virginis in ecclesia parochiali Omnium Sanctorum...pro singulis animabus prescriptis celebraturo imperpetuum manerium meum de Armeston [and other property].

Ut autem hec ordinacio sit perpetuo duratura volo et ordino quod cantaria predicta Cantaria Willelmi Chamber, Willelmi Aldewyncle et Elizabethe uxoris eorundem pro perpetuo nuncupetur et quod capellanus qui pro tempore fuerit...singulis diebus...missam celebret in altare predicto....

Ad hec volo et ordino quod capellanus predictus pro tempore existens sex pueros de villa de Aldewyncle predicta maxime indigentes per me et Elizabetham uxorem meam dum vixerimus, et post mortem nostram, tres, videlicet, per rectorem ecclesie Sancti Petri de Aldewyncle predicta et alios tres per ipsum capellanum pro tempore existentem nominandos, gratis absque aliqua remuneracione a parentibus vel amicis eorum exigenda seu recipienda instruat et informet in syllabicacione et lectura; qui quidem pueri sic instructi et informati dicent omni nocte in ecclesia Omnium Sanctorum de Aldewyncle predicta ad mandatum capellani predicti pro animabus nostris, necnon animabus omnium fidelium defunctorum psalmum De profundis cum oracionibus Inclina Domine et Fidelium.

Foundation of a Spelling and Reading School.
8 Nov. 1489.

Foundation of Aldwincle Chantry.

To all sons of holy mother church...William Chamber, of Aldwincle, in the county of Northampton, health....

...I make known to you all by these presents that I...have given...to Sir John Seliman, chaplain, for his maintenance and that of his successors...celebrating divine service every day at the altar of St Mary the Virgin, in the parish church of All Saints...for all the souls aforesaid for ever my manor of Armeston [and other property].

That this ordinance may endure for ever I will and ordain that the chantry aforesaid shall be for ever called 'The chantry of William Chamber, William Aldwincle and Elizabeth their wife,' and that the chaplain for the time being shall every day...celebrate mass at the altar aforesaid....

Moreover I will and ordain that the said chaplain for the time being shall teach and instruct, in spelling and reading, six of the poorest boys of the town of Aldwincle aforesaid, to be named by me and my wife Elizabeth while we are alive, and after our death three named by the rector of St Peter's church in Aldwincle aforesaid, and the other three by the chaplain for the time being, freely, without demanding or taking any remuneration from their parents or friends; and the boys, when they have been so instructed and taught, shall say every night in All Saints' church in Aldwincle aforesaid, at the direction of the chaplain aforesaid, for our souls and the souls of all the faithful departed, the psalm 'Out of the deep,' with the prayers 'Incline thine ear' and 'God of the faithful.'

Free Lectures at Cambridge. 8 *Oct.* 1492.

[Surtees Soc. Test. Ebor. IV. 75.]

Will of Robert Bellamy, Master of St Leonard's Hospital, York etc.

Item lego Aule Regie, in qua sum socius, £70, ut Magister et consocii ejus provideant et emant aliquem annuum redditum; cum quo redditu provideatur pro una lectura in jure canonico in dicta aula imperpetuum continuanda.

Et volo quod dicta lectura sit generalis et libera omnibus et singulis consociis in dicta aula studentibus; necnon et aliis clericis pauperibus in Universitate studentibus; non tamen scolaribus qui sufficientem habent exhibitionem ad Universitatem, nisi ex speciali favore illius persone que hujusmodi lecture executionem in se susceperit.

Foundation of Free Grammar School by ex-Lord Mayor. 25 *Jan.* 1503.

[A. F. Leach, *English Schools at the Reformation*, 82, and II. 23–5. Particulars for Schools, Roll 14, and original in possession of Governors.]

To all people to whome this present writyng indented shall come, John Percyvall, Knyght and late Maire of the city of London, sendith greytng in Our Lord God euerlastyng.

Where afore this tyme I, consideryng that in the countie of Chester, and specially aboute the towne of Maxfeld, fast by the which Towne I was borne, God of his habundant grace hath sent and daily sendeth to the Inhabitaunts there copyous plentie of children, to whose lernyng and bryngyng forth in conyng and vertue right fewe Techers and Scolemaisters ben in that contre, wherebye many children for lake of such techyng and draught in conyng fall to Idlenes, and so consequently live disolutely all their dayes, whiche cause with the graciouse mocion of the most Reverende ffader in God and my singler

Free Lectures at Cambridge. 8 Oct. 1492.

Will of Robert Bellamy, Master of St Leonard's Hospital, York etc.

Also I bequeath to the King's Hall, in which I am a fellow, £70, that the master and co-fellows thereof may procure and purchase a yearly rent, and therewith provide for a lecture in Canon Law to be continually kept in the said hall for ever.

And I will that the said lecture shall be public and free to all and every the fellows studying in the said hall; also to other poor clerks studying in the University; not, however, to scholars who have sufficient maintenance at the University, unless by the special favour of the person who takes upon himself the delivery of such lecture.

good Lord Thomas, Archebyshop of Yorke, hath moch stered me of such litle good as God of his grace hath me sent to purvay a preist to syng and pray for me and my freends at Maxfeld aforesaid And there to kepe a Free Gramer Scole for children for euermore....

Wherefore and whereupon I, the said John Percyvall, by this present wrytyng indented, make and declare my wille, as to the disposicion of all the said londs and tenements, as well as x marcs by yere redy purveied as of the said other yerely v marcs, that is to wete of the said hole x li by yere in the maner and fourme hereafter ensuyng, that is to say...the same londs and tenements by good and adequate conveyaunce shall be put in ffeoffement to [17 persons named].

To th' entent that they and their heirs of the issues and profects of all the said londes and tenements shall fynde and susteyne a vertues Preest conyng in Gramer and graduate. The same preest to synge and saye his deuyne seruice dayly, as his disposicion shall be, in the parisshe churche of Maxfeld aforsaid,

praying for my soule and for the soule of Dame Thomasyn my wyf, the soulles also of our Faders Moders benefactors and the soule of Richard Sutton, gentilman, for the good and holsome counsell which he hath given me to the perfourmance of this my will, and for all Cristen soules.

And I woll that the said Preest shall alwey kepe and contynew in the said Town of Maxfeld a Fre Gramer Scole techyng there Gentilmens Sonnes and other godemennes children of the Towne and contre theareabouts, wherby they shall more grow in conyng and vertue to the laude and praise of Almyghtie God and to their owne confort and profett.

And I woll that the said Preest and his scolers with him every evynyng upon feryall or wurchyng dayes shall synge afore some Image of Our Lady in the said Chirch an antempne of our Blessed Lady, and after antempne doon to say the psalm of De profundis with the colletts for my soule and other souls aforesaid. And I woll that the said Preest daily in his Masse after his first lavatory at the South ende of the awter shall turne hym aboute to the people and there say the psalm of the De profundis with the Colletts for my soule and other souls aforesaid.

And that the same preest with his scolers euery yere aboute such tyme of the yere as it shall hap me to decease shall holde and kepe in the chirch of Maxfeld aforsaid myn obyte or annyuersary by note, that is to say, Placebo and Dirige on nyght and Masse of Requyem on the morow folowyng praiyng for my soule and other souls above reherced.

Also I woll that the said Preest shall well ouersee the said scolers and cause theym euery holy day to be at the said chirche there at the tyme of Mateyns, Masse and Evensong, there helpyng to syng and to say their seruices wele and vertuously without jangling or talking or other idell occupacion.

And I woll that the said Preest shall alway be chosen elect and admitted to the same seruice by my feoffees [etc.] and the so chosen and admytted to contynue in the same seruice as

long as he shall be of good and vertuous disposicion and duely kepe his seruice and Gramer Scole as is aforesaid.

[Power to remove him at a quarter's notice, except 'my kynnesman Maister William Bridgys,' who is to hold 'without any expulsion or ammovyng from the same.']

And I woll that all the residue and surplusage of the said yerely £10 above the reparacions of the same londs and tenements and other ordinary and casuall charges of the same And ouer the said yerely 6s. 8d. for the wages of the rent-gaderer shall alwey goo and remayne to the said preest for his yerely salary and wages....

In witnesse of which premyssis to either parte of this my Will endented I have put my seale, Writen the xxv day of January, the yere of Our Lord God m¹ fyve hundreth and two, and the xviij[th] yere of the reigne of King Henry the vij[th].

Priests forbidden to Teach at Bridgenorth. 1503.

[Hist. MS. Com. X. App. IV. 425, from *Great Leet Book*, f. 148.]

Orders made at the Great Court by the 24 Burgesses.
March, 18 H. VII.

That there schall no priste kepe no scole, save oonly oon child to helpe him to sey masse, after that a scole mastur comyth to town, but that every child to resorte to the comyn scole in payne of forfetyng to the chaumber of the towne 20s. of every priste that doth the contrary.

Westminster Monks and their lack of Learning. 16 *July* 1504.

[B. M. MS. Harl. 1498.]

This indenture made betweene the moost Cristen and moste excellent Prince kyng Henry the Seuenth, by the grace of God Kyng of Englande and of France and lord of Irlande,

the xvj daye of July, the nyneteene yere of his moost noble reigne, and John Islipp, Abbot of the monastery of Saynt Petre of Westminster, and the Priour and Couuent of the same monastery, Witnesseth.... [Covenants for chantry of three monks, D.D. or B.D., to sing for the king's soul.]

The Fundacion of the Thre Monks Scolars.

And furthermore forasmuch as the same oure Souuerayne lord the kyng hath by long experience perceyued and often seen that for lakke of grounded lerned men in the lawes of god, vertue emonges religious men is little used, Religion is greatly confounded, and fewe or noo hable persones founde in dyvers houses of Religion, lakking lerned men to be the heddes of the same houses to the high displeasure of god and great subuersion of Religion.

And the same oure souuerayne lord the kyng also perceyuing that by good doctrine and holsome example of Religious men well lerned in the lawes of god, vertue is greatly exalted and Religion duely kept and observed, and where plentye is of sadde and vertuous and well lerned clerks there is good choice of hable heddes and governours;

Therefor oure said souuerayne lord the kyng to the pleasure of god, the encrease of vertue and exaltacion of true Religion willeth and ordeyneth that ouer and aboue the nombre of thre monkes that the said Abbot Prior and Conuent confesse and knowledge that they and thair predecessours have used and ought to fynde to Scoles in the Uniuersite of Oxonford there to studie in the science of Diuinitie,

The said Abbot Prior and Conuent and thair successours shall prouide encrease haue and ·fynde thre moo monkes of the said monastery ouer and aboue the said thre monkes contynually and perpetually to be and contynue Scolers in the said Uniuersite of Oxonford there to studye in the science of Diuinitie, and there contynue in the same till they be Bachelers of Diuinitie and hable by thair contynuance in the same Uniuersitie to be Doctors of Diuinitie. [Stipends £10 a year.]

Howe the Thre Monkes Scolers shalbe called and named.

And that the same monkes shalbe called the Scolers of oure said Souuerayne lord the Kyng, that is to saye, the Scolers of Kyng Henry the vij[th], and accordyng to the said will, mynde and entent of our said Souuerayne lord the Kyng It is couenaunted and agreed betweene the same our Souuerayne lord the Kyng and the said Abbot Prior and Conuent...by these presentes, that they and thair successours...shall, from the date of these presentes, perpetually whill the world shall endure, prouide, fynde and haue in the said Uniuersite, thre monkes of the said monasterye professed, ouer and aboue the noumbre of the said thre monkes that they, afore the makyng of this Indenture, haue vsed, owe and be bounden to fynd, hable in vertue and connyng and of conuenient age to be putte and sette to the said Uniuersite, there to studie and profite in the said science of Diuinite, and shall in the same there contynue tyll they be Bachelers of Diuinite and hable by thair contynuance in the said Uniuersite to be Doctors of Diuinite, and not before that to be taken ne called thes....

[The chantry monks to be chosen from these scholars.]

Foundation of Giggleswick Grammar School by a Building Lease. 12 *Nov.* 1507.

[A. F. Leach, *Early Yorks. Schools*, II. 232, from original in possession of the Governors.]

A Lease by the Prior of Duresme to Sir James Carr, preiste, for the grounde whereon the schoolhouse and schoolehouse yarde air now sett.

This Indentur made the xii day of Novembr the yere of our lorde M[l]Dvii betwix the Right Reverende ffader in Gode, Thomas, prior of Duresme, and convent of the same, on the one partie, and Jamys Karr, preste, on the other partie.

Witnessyth that the forsaide prior and convent of one hole mynde and consent hath graunted, dimised and to ferme lettyn, and by these presentes graunttes and to ferme lattes, to the forsaid Jamys Karr his heires, executors and assignes, half one acre of lande with the appertenance, laitle in the haldyng of Richarde lemyng lyeng neir the church garth of Gyllyswyke in Crawen within the countie of york [boundaries set out].

Also it is agreyd that the said Jamys shall encloise the said half acre and therupon beyld and uphold at hys awne propyr charges and costes, in which beildyng he shall kepe or cause to be kept one gramer Scole, with fre curse and recurse with all maner of caryage necessarye to the same....

To have holde and occupye to the said Jamys his heires and assignes, beyng Scole masters of the said gramer scole, the said half acre of lande with the appurtenance frome the fest of the Invencion of the holy Croce next ensuyng unto the ende and terme of lxxix yeres then next followyng fully to be completyd and expired, yevyng yerlye therfor unto the said prior and convent and ther successors or ther assignes at the fest of Saynct laurence martyr xij*d.* of good and lawfull monye of England as parcell of the rente of the said tenement wherto the said halff acre afforsaid pertenyth and belongyth. [Power of distress if rent unpaid.]

Provided allway that when soever the said Jamys Karr shall change his naturall lyfe, that then it shalbe lawfull, as ofte tymes as it shalbe nedfull, to the vicar of ye churche afforsaid for the tyme beyng and kyrkmasters of the same, heires executors and assignes to the said Jamys jontle, to electe one person beyng within holye orders, to be scole master of the gramer scole afforsaid, whiche so electe, and abled by the Prior of Duresme, shall have occupye and rejoce the said halff acre of land and the hows therapon beildyd with the appurtenaunce, in lyk wyse as the said Jamys occupyed and usyd in hys tyme. Overthis and above, it is covnandyt and agreyd that when so ever it shall pleas the Scolemaster of the said scole for the tym beyng to renewe this leis and dimision at any tyme within the

as Private Adventure School, 1507

yeres above specyfied That then the said Prior and convent shall seall under ther common seall to the said scholemaster a newe Indentur maid in maner and forme afforsaid, no thyng except nor meneshyd, bot as largely as in this said Indentur is specyfied. The said scolemaster paying therfor as oft tymes it shalbe renewed vj$s.$ viij$d.$ for the said Seall.

In witnes wheroff ather partie to other to thes Indentures enterchangeably hath put to ther sealles yevyn the yere and day above said.

Inscription on the Original School. 1512.

[This stone is now in the School Museum.]

Alma dei mater, defende malis Jacobum Car!
Presbiteris, quoque clericulis, domus hec fit in anno
Mil' quin cen' duode'. Jesu nostri miserere!

Senes cum junioribus laudent nomen Domini.

[Kindly mother of God, defend James Ker from ill. For priests and young clerks this house is made in 1512. Jesus, have mercy on us. Old men and children praise the name of the Lord.]

An Early Giggleswick Boarder. c. 1516.

[From Papers of Malham, of Elsack, printed in T. D. Whitaker's *History of Craven* (London, 1805), p. 78.]

Brother,...I am content that James Smith go to Sir James Carr to scoule at Michelmas next comyng, and also I am content ye paye for his bord, which shall be allowed ye ageane. From London the second day of Aprill.

By your Brother, Wm. Malham.

To his Brother, John Malhame.

Canterbury Monks' Ignorance. 1511.

[Brit. Mus. MSS. Arundel 68, f. 69.]

Articuli defectuum detectorum in visitatione facta 9° Sept. A.D. 1511 per Reverendissimum in Christo patrem Willelmum Warham, archiepiscopum.

(5) Item provideatur de aliquo perito instructore gramaticae, qui plane instruat novicios et alios juvenes in gramatica. Nam ex defectu instructionis fit, ut plerique monachi missam celebrantes et alia divina peragentes penitus ignorant quid legunt in maximum scandalum et dedecus tam religionis quam monasterii.

(6) Item provideatur quod novicii et alii monachi non careant deinceps libris.

Reformationes factae tempore ejusdem visitationis.

Quantum ad quintum articulum, de instructore gramaticae providendo ad instruendos minores monachos ad id operis unus de confratribus deputatur: et jamjam cepit exercere, ipsosque indies instruere curat.

Quantum vero ad vj^{tum} articulum, viz. de libris monachorum unicuique rite distribuendis, Ita dispositum est quod precentor ad quem ex officio librorum distributio spectat in ea parte provide invigilabit ut unicuique ut decet et oportunum videbitur libros impartiri faciet.

Educational Canons of Convocation of Canterbury. 1529.

[Wilkins, *Concilia*, III. 722.]

Convocatio praelatorum et cleri provinciae Cant. in ecclesia S. Pauli London., 5 die mensis Novembris inchoata. 1529.

De otio vitando, et honesta clericorum conversatione.

Quia desidia mater est omnium quoddammodo vitiorum hoc sacrum concilium omnibus curatis, rectoribus, vicariis, et cantaristis mandat et praecipit, quod peractis divinis officiis,

Canterbury Monks' Ignorance. 1511.

Articles of the defects detected at the visitation made 9 September 1511 by the most reverend father William Warham, archbishop.

(5) Also a skilled teacher of grammar shall be provided to teach the novices and other youths grammar. For in default of such instruction it happens that most of the monks celebrating mass and performing other divine service are wholly ignorant of what they read to the great scandal and disgrace both of religion in general and the monastery in particular.

(6) Also provision shall be made that the novices and other monks may not henceforth be without books.

Reforms made at the time of the same visitation.

As for the 5th article, about providing a teacher of grammar to instruct the younger monks, one of the brethren is deputed to that work, and has already begun to do it and teaches them daily.

As to the 6th article, namely, as to distributing the books properly to all the monks, arrangements have been made so that the Precentor whose office it is to distribute books shall henceforth take care to cause books to be given to every monk, as shall seem proper and opportune.

Educational Canons of Convocation of Canterbury. 1529.

Convocation of the Prelates and Clergy of the Province of Canterbury in St Paul's Church, London, begun 5 November 1529.

Of avoiding idleness, and the proper behaviour of clerks.

Whereas idleness is in a sense the mother of all vices, this holy council commands and orders all those having cures, rectors, vicars, and chantry priests, that when divine service is

sint deinceps occupati in studiis, orationibus, lectionibus, aut aliis honestis rebus et negotiis, quae suam deceant professionem; videlicet, instruendo pueros in alphabeto, lectura, cantu, aut grammatica; et tribus in hebdomada diebus, tres vel ad minus duas horas in sacrae scripturae, vel alicujus doctoris approbati lectione, cessante legitimo impedimento, se exerceant. De qua re diligenter in suis visitationibus inquirant ordinarii, ut sacerdotes otiosos, et tempus suum male terentes, severe castigent et puniant.

De ludimagistris et uniformi docendi modo.

Quia vetus est adagium: 'Quod nova testa capit, inveterata sapit': et: 'Qualis est moderator in civitate, talis est et populus': hoc sacro approbante concilio, statuimus, quod praeceptores scholarum grammaticalium sint praeter eruditionem, quatenus fieri potest, viri catholici et probi, et ut primum omnium doceant pueros sibi traditos simplicem fidei et agendorum et fugiendorum summam. Et ne pueris rudibus perlegantur opuscula, quae puerorum mores aut fidem videbuntur corruptura, neque ulli alii libri in quibus, quasi per lusum, puerilia ingenia infici possent; et quum vel propter pestem laborantem in locis ubi hujusmodi publicae scholae sunt, aut propter mortem praeceptoris, ut plurimum contingit, quod qui anno aut biennio sub uno praeceptore grammaticam addiscere coepit, illo relicto, cogitur novum adire praeceptorem, apud quem alius est docendi modus, ut pene derisus est apud omnes; atque ita fit, ut rudes adhuc in grammatica magnum ex hoc sentiant in provectione studii detrimentum; ad communem igitur utilitatem totius provinciae Cant. hoc sacro approbante concilio, statuimus, ut post annum a publicatione praesentium unus et uniformis sit docendi modus per totam provinciam Cant. nullus auctor regularum seu praeceptionum grammaticalium pueris in grammatica instituendis ediscendus proponatur, nisi quem archiepiscopus Cantuariensis simul cum quatuor aliis suae provinciae episcopis, quatuor abbatibus, et quatuor archidiaconis in hac synodo deputandis, hoc anno proximo sequenti praescripserunt pueris perlegendum.

done, they shall be employed in study, prayer, lectures or other proper business, becoming their profession; namely, teaching boys the alphabet, reading, singing or grammar; and on three days in the week, for three or at least two hours a day, shall, in the absence of some lawful hindrance, occupy themselves in reading Holy Scripture or some approved doctor. And the ordinaries shall make diligent inquiry about this in their visitations, to the end that they may severely chastise and punish lazy priests, or those who spend their time badly.

Of schoolmasters and a uniform method of teaching.

As it is an old adage 'what the new cask may hold will taste in the old' and 'as the ruler in a city such is the people,' with the approval of this holy council, we ordain, that teachers of grammar schools shall be, as far as possible, besides their learning, men of orthodoxy and reputation, and shall first of all teach the boys entrusted to them a simple summary of the faith and of what to do and to avoid. And that works may not be read by ignorant boys, which seem likely to corrupt their morals or their faith, nor any other books in which, as it were in playing, the boys' minds may be infected; and whereas either through the plague raging in places where public schools are, or through the death of the master, it often happens, that a boy who has begun to learn grammar for a year or two under one teacher, is obliged to leave him and go to a new teacher, who has another method of teaching, so that he is almost laughed at by all; and so it happens that those who are still raw in grammar suffer great loss in the progress of their learning; For the common benefit, therefore, of the whole province of Canterbury, with the approval of this holy council, we ordain, in order that after a year from the date of the publication of these presents, there shall be one uniform method of teaching throughout the whole province of Canterbury, no author of grammar rules or precepts shall be put before boys being taught grammar, except the one which the archbishop of Canterbury with four other bishops of the province, four abbots and four archdeacons to be named at this synod shall next year prescribe for boys to read.

Winchester and Eton Time-Tables. 1530.

[See A. F. Leach, *V. C. H. Hants*, II. 298, and *Bucks*. II. 178. From Mayor's Book, Saffron Walden.]

[These time-tables were sent by the Head Masters of Winchester and Eton to Saffron Walden between 1529 and 1531, the endowment deed of that school in 1525 requiring that it should follow 'the ordre and use of techyng gramer in the scolys of Wynchester and Eton.' Mr T. Wright printed them in 1852 (*Archæologia* XXXIV. 37) as being the Statutes of Saffron Walden School. The names of the masters fix them to Winchester and Eton. Unfortunately the first page of the Winchester curriculum, with the general 'Order' and 'Use' of the VIIth and VIth forms, has disappeared.]

Ovide metamorphoseos the thursday, Salust the fryday, with the vij forme. And at after none renderyng of ther rulys. The saterdaye lyke as the vij forme. The Sonday lykewyse.

The Vth forme.

They have the versyfycall rulys of Sulpice gevyn in ye mornyng of one of the vith forme & this vth forme gevyth rulys to the fowrth; the which be preterita et supina of sulpice. Also iiij verses of ovide Metamorphoseos, the thursday Salust iij fyrst dayes of the weke to be rendered on saterday in the mornyng. The latyne they have with ye fowrthe forme. There constructyons is throwgh owte ye weke unto fryday Vergills Eglogs & an other, tullies epistles they make maters ageynst tewisdaye. The Wedenysday make verses, the thursday epistles. The friday in the mornyng a part of there rulys to be examyned. Att the afternone renderyng of there rulys lernyd that weke. The saterday xij verses to be said withowte boke on the mornyng with the examynatyon of the same with renderyng of there latyns. After none construyth epistles. The Sonday as the other hie formys dothe.

The Fowrthe forme.

After rules & verses geven of the vth forme they hath a verbe providyd ageyne vij of ye Clok when the Scholem^r comyth in. And hase the verbe examyned among them with vulgares

upon the same. And after they write the laten that one of them shall make by ye assygnyng of the master. And the master construyth to them a portyon of Terence. And at after none thei construe it & parce it by the Ussher. And after renderith rules & then there latyn. this contynewith tyll friday then they have a part of there rulys to be examyned. And at after none renderith of ye rulys lernyd that weke. The saterday in the Mornyng xij verses of ovide Metamorphoseos. At after none repetyng & examynyng there terence lernyd before. The sonday with other low holydayes, an englysh of an epistle to be made in latyn dyverse wayes & somtyme Tullies paradoxes to be construyd.

The Thred forme

hath for ther ruls Sulpice genders and his heteroclits declarid every day a portyon of the ussher, and hath throwgh the weke over nyght a verbe set up to be examyned in the mornyng, and makith vulgars upon yt. And after none they have a theme to be made in laten, the which Latyne one of the said forme at the pleasure of the master makith openlie dyverse ways. And after that they write the Masteris owne latyne. For ther constructyons, uponne mondayes and Wedenysdayes, Aesopes fabells, Tuesdayes and Thursdays, Lucyans dialogs. The friday in the mornyng examynation of ther rules. At the after none renderyng, Saterday in the mornyng proper verses of meter of lilies makyng, And after that repetytyon of there latens with the examynatyon of the same. The Sonday a dialoge of lucyane or a fable of Esope to be seid withowt booke and construed.

The seconde Forme

lykewise throwh the weke hath a verbe sett up over nyght, and makith vulgaris on it, and dothe like at laten as the thrid forme. Ther rulys, Parvula of Stanbridge, and ij verses of his vocables. There constructyons Esopes fabuls throwh all the weke, save that on the saterday in the Mornyng they have iiij verses of Cato to be renderid withowte boke with the examynatyon of the same.

The Fyrst forme.

In the mornyng a part of standbridge accidens, and a verbe of the same accidens to be said with owte booke, and

then a laten to be said at the after none; After that repetycyon
of rules. The friday there Comparisons, with the verbe sum.
es. fui. to be said; At the after none repetytyon of there rules.
At Saterday repetytyon of there Cato. The Sonday a fabull
of Aesope.

Also every Forme renderith a fortenyght every quarter for
thyngs lernyd the quarter before.

> By me Johan Twichener, scholem^r.
> By me Thomas Brownyng, ussher.

This ys the order of the same schole [Eton] vsyd by me Richard cox, scholemaster.

They come to schole at vj of the Clok in ye mornyng
they say Deus misereatur with a Colecte; at ix they say de
profundis & go to brekefaste. With in a quarter of an howre
cum ageyne & tary xi & then to dyner, at v to soper, afore an
Antheme & De profundis.

Two prepositors in every forme, whiche doth give in a
schrowe the absents Namys at any lecture & shewith when & at
what tyme, both in the fore none for the tyme paste, & at v.

Also ij prepositors in the body of the Chirche, ij in the
qwere, ffor spekyng of Laten in the thred forme & all other, every
one a custos & in every howse a monytor.

Whan they go home ij. and ij. in order, a monitor to se
that they do soe tyll they come at there hostise dore.

Also prevy monytors how many the Mr wylle.

Prepositors in the feld whan they play, for fyghtyng, rent
clothes, blew eyes, or siche like.

Prepositors for yll kept hedys, unwasshid facys, fowle clothis
& sich other.

Yff there be iiij or v in a howse, monytors for chydyng and
for latyn spekyng.

When any dothe come newe, the master doth inquire fro
whens he comyth, what frendys he hathe, whether there be any
plage, No man gothe owte off the schole, nother home to his
frends with owt ye masters lycence. Yff there be any dullard
the Mr gyvith his frends warnyng and puttyth hym away that
he sclander not the schole.

> By me Richard Cox scholem^r.

Eton Time-Table, 1530

	Mondaye	Tewysdaye	Wedensdaye	Thursdaye	Frydaye	Saterdaye
The Fyrst forme	parte of stanbrid ge accidence eve ry mornyng with the Second, thrid & fowrthe orme. Institutiones parvulorum Voca bula. And also latynes	Idem	Idem	Idem	Quos decet in mensa at the after none & ren deryng of Rules	Quos decet in Mensa at the after none Render Latynys
The seconde Forme	ffabulæ Aesopi, Genera Lilii Latynys fower tymys in the weke	Idem	Idem	Idem	Cato at the after none Render rulys	Cato and at the after none render latynys and vulgares
The thrid Forme	Terence Preterita Lilii Latynys	Idem	Idem	Idem	Most proper Hymmys And at the none rendre rulys	Properest hymys And at the after none ren der latynys And vulgars
The fourthe forme	Terentius, Octo partes Lilii Latyns twies every weke	Idem	Idem	Idem	Vergilii buccolica in the mornyng at the after none render rulys	Vergilii bucc olica at after none rendre latynys & vulgars
The fyfthe forme	Wrytyng of a theme, Salust ius, Versifyeng rulys drawne owte of despau terius other modus consc ribendi epis tolas	The same save they make verses	The same save they make nothyng	Epistole tullii makying of epistles beside Salustius	Vergilii Eneis in the mornyng at the after none renderyng of ruls lernyd the hole weke	Vergilii Eneis repetyng of latyns & vulgars lernyd that weke
The syxte fforme And the seventhe form	Horatius or tullius, mosellanyus fi gures or Copia rerum et verborum of Erasmus	All lyke Monday save they make verses	Like as afore save they make nothyng	Epistole Tullii Making of Epis beside Horatius	Vergilii Eneis in the mornyng At the after none rendrying of ruls lernid the hole weke	Vergilii Eneis repetyng of latyns & vulgars lernyd all ye weke

Every Quarter one fortenyght every forme rendryth all thyngs lernyd that quarter

The Re-foundation of Canterbury Cathedral and Grammar School. 1541.

[Parker MS. Corpus Christi Coll. Camb. 120, f. 15. The words in brackets seem to have been added before the Statutes were actually issued.]

The Incorporation, Statutes and Injunctions of the Cathedral Church of Canterbury.

Henricus Octauus Dei gracia Anglie Francie et Hibernie Rex Fidei defensor ac in terra supremum ecclesie Anglicane et Hibernie caput, Uniuersis sancte matris ecclesie filiis ad quorum noticiam presens scriptum peruenerit, Salutem.

Cum et nobis et regni nostri proceribus uniuersoque senatui quem Parliamentum vocamus visum sit, Deo, ut confidimus, nos huc mouente, monasteria que passim in regno nostro extabant, [tum quia synceram et antiquissimam fidei religionem, spectatissimam vite probitatem, et exquisitam linguarum et scienciarum cognitionem, quarum virtutum laudem in primis monasteriis floruisse constat, eam vero nunc longioris temporis progressu corrupti et deficientes in fedissimam supersticionem turpissimumque vite ocium ac libidinem atque in crassissimam sacrarum litterarum inscitiam commutarunt;] tum propter graues et multiplices illorum enormitates tum ob alias iustas racionabilesque causas supprimere abolere et in [longe] meliores usus conuertere [ad omnipotentis Dei cultum et multo majorem reipublice commodum]; Quapropter nos et diuine voluntate conformius et magis e re christiana esse ducentes, ut ubi ignorancia et supersticio regnabant ibi sincerus Dei cultus vigeat, et sanctum Christi euangelium assidue et pure annuncietur, Et preterea ut ad Christiane fidei ac pietatis incrementum juuentus regni mei in bonis litteris instituatur et pauperes perpetuo sustententur, in ipsorum monasteriorum loco ecclesias ereximus et constituimus. Quarum alias cathedrales, alias collegiatas vocari volumus :

Pro quarum quidem ecclesiarum gubernacione et regimine,

The Re-foundation of Canterbury Cathedral and Grammar School. 1541.

The Incorporation, Statutes and Injunctions of the Cathedral Church of Canterbury.

Henry VIII by the grace of God, king of England, France and Ireland, Defender of the Faith, and on earth supreme head of the Church of England and Ireland, to all the sons of holy mother church to whose notice this present writing shall come, greeting.

Whereas it seemed good to us and the great men of our realm and to all the senate whom we call Parliament, God thereunto as we believe moving us, to suppress and abolish and to convert to far better uses, for the true worship of Almighty God and the far greater benefit of the Commonwealth, the monasteries which existed everywhere in our realm, both because the sincere and most ancient religion, the most admired uprightness of life, and the most profound knowledge of languages and learning, the praise of which virtues it appears flourished in the earliest monasteries, now in the progress of time have become corrupt and deficient, and changed to the foulest superstition and the most disgraceful idleness and lust and the grossest ignorance of Holy Scripture, and because of their grave and manifold enormities, as for other just and reasonable causes; Wherefore we, thinking it more in conformity with the divine will and a more Christian thing that where ignorance and superstition reigned there the true worship of God should flourish and the holy gospel of Christ be assiduously and in purity preached; and further that for the increase of Christian faith and piety the youth of my realm may be instructed in good literature and the poor for ever maintained, we have in place of the same monasteries erected and established churches, some of which we will shall be called cathedrals and others collegiate churches;

For the rule and governance of which churches we have

leges et statuta que sequuntur prescribenda curauimus quibus tam Decani et utriusque ordinis canonici quam ceteri omnes ministri pueri et pauperes qui in ipsis ecclesiis commoraturi sunt pareant et obsequantur eisque ut a nobis conditis et profectis regantur et gubernentur.....

1. De numero integro eorum qui in Ecclesia Cathedrali et Metropolitica Christi Cantuariensi sustentantur.

Inprimis statuimus et ordinamus ut sint perpetuo in dicta ecclesia unus Decanus, 12 Canonici, 6 concionatores, 12 minores Canonici, unus diaconus, unus subdiaconus, 12 clerici laici, unus Magister Choristarum, 10 Choriste, 2 Informatores puerorum in gramatica, quorum unus sit Preceptor, alter sub-Preceptor, 50 pueri in gramatica erudiendi, 12 pauperes de sumptibus dicte ecclesie alendi, 2 virgiferi, 2 subsacriste, 4 ministri in ecclesia qui campanas pulsent et cetera disponant, 2 janitores, qui et barbitonsores erunt, unus obsonator, unus pincerna, et unus subpincerna, unus coquus, unus subcoquus; qui quidem in eadem ecclesia numero prescripto unusquisque in suo ordine juxta statuta et ordinaciones nostras sedulo inseruiant.

26. De choristis et ipsorum [magistro] numero.

Statuimus et ordinamus ut in ecclesia nostra predicta ad electionem et designacionem decani, aut eo absente, vice-decani et capituli, sint decem choriste pueri tenere etatis, et vocibus sonoris, et ad cantandum aptis, choro inseruiant, ministrent et cantent. Ad hos instruendos atque imbuendos tam morum modestia quam canendi peritia, volumus ut per decanum, aut eo absente, vice-decanum et capitulum, preter duodecim clericos ante nominatos, unus eligatur qui sit honeste fame, vite probe, cantandi et organa pulsandi peritus, qui pueris docendis, organis pulsandis in suo tempore, et diuinis officiis cantandis studiose vacabit. Quod si negligens aut in docendo desidiosus inueniatur, post trinam monitionem ab officio deponatur. Qui quidem ad officium fideliter obeundum etiam juramento adigetur.

caused to be drawn up the laws and statutes which follow, which the Deans and the Canons of both orders and all the other ministers, boys and poor who are to dwell in the same churches shall obey and observe, and be ruled and governed by them as being established and made by us...

1. The whole number of those who shall be maintained in the cathedral and metropolitical church of Christ at Canterbury.

First we decree and ordain that there shall be for ever in the said church a Dean, 12 Canons, 6 Preachers, 12 Minor Canons, a deacon, a sub-deacon, 12 lay clerks, a master of the choristers, 10 choristers, two Informators of boys in grammar, of whom one shall be the teacher and the other the under-teacher, 50 boys to be taught grammar, 12 poor to be maintained at the expense of the church, 2 vergers (wand-bearers), 2 sextons (sub-sacrists), 4 servants in the church to ring the bells and arrange other things, two door-keepers who shall be also barbers, a maniciple, a butler and an under-butler, a cook and an under-cook; who shall to the number aforesaid each in his rank sedulously serve in the same church according to our statutes and ordinances.

26. The Choristers and their [Master] number.

We decree and ordain that in our church aforesaid there shall be at the election or nomination of the Dean, or in his absence the Sub-dean, and Chapter, ten choristers, boys of tender age with clear voices and fit for singing, to serve the choir, minister and sing. For their instruction and education, as well in good behaviour as in skill in singing, we will that besides the twelve clerks before-named one shall be elected by the Dean [etc.] and Chapter, of good character, upright life and skilled in singing and playing the organ, to diligently employ himself in teaching the boys, playing the organ at the proper time, and singing divine service. And if he shall be found negligent or idle in teaching he shall after three warnings be deposed from office. And he shall be bound by oath faithfully to discharge his office.

27. De pueris gramaticis et eorum informatoribus.

Ut pietas et bone littere perpetuo in ecclesia nostra suppullulescant, crescant, floreant et suo tempore in gloriam Dei et reipublice commodum et ornamentum fructificent Statuimus et ordinamus ut ad electionem et designacionem Decani, aut eo absente Vicedecani et Capituli, sint perpetuo in ecclesia nostra cathedrali Cantuariensi quinquaginta pueri, pauperes et amicorum ope destituti, de bonis ecclesie nostre alendi, ingeniis (quoad fieri potest) ad discendum natis et aptis.

Quos tamen admitti nolumus in pauperes pueros ecclesie nostre antequam nouerint legere, scribere et mediocriter calluerint prima gramatices rudimenta, idque judicio Decani, aut eo absente Vicedecani et Archididascoli.

Atque hos pueros volumus impensis ecclesie nostre ali donec mediocrem Latine gramatice noticiam adepti fuerint, et Latine loqui, et Latine scribere didicerint. Cui rei dabitur quatuor annorum spacium; aut si ita Decano, aut eo absente Vicedecano et Archididascolo, visum sit ad summum quinque et non amplius.

Volumus autem ut quoties Decanus sacelli nostri regii Decano et capitulo ecclesie nostre Cantuariensis significauerit se e sacello nostro choristam, qui ibidem ad vocis usque defectionem ministrauit missurum ad gramaticam in ecclesia nostra perdiscendam in locum, quem proxime post illam significationem vacare contigerit, choristam illum a Decano sacelle [*sic*] nostre sic nominatum et significatum Decanus et Capitulum eligent et assument absque ulla fraude aut dolo malo.

Volumus preterea ut nullus (nisi sacelle nostre regie aut ecclesie nostre Cantuariensis chorista fuerit) in pauperem discipulum ecclesie nostre eligatur, qui nonum etatis sue annum non compleuerit, vel qui quintumdecimum etatis sue annum excesserit.

Quod si quis puerorum insigni tarditate et hebetudine

27. The Grammar Boys and their Teachers.

That piety and good letters may in our church aforesaid for ever blossom, grow and flower and in their time bear fruit for the glory of God and the advantage and adornment of the commonwealth, we decree and ordain that there shall always be in our cathedral church of Canterbury, elected and nominated by the Dean or in his absence the Sub-dean and Chapter, 50 boys, poor and destitute of the help of their friends, to be maintained out of the possessions of the church, and of native genius as far as may be and apt to learn: whom however we will shall not be admitted as poor boys of our church before they have learnt to read and write and are moderately learned in the first rudiments of grammar, in the judgment of the Dean or in his absence the Sub-dean and the Head Master;

And we will that these boys shall be maintained at the expense of our church until they have obtained a moderate knowledge of Latin grammar and have learnt to speak and to write Latin. The period of four years shall be given to this, or if it shall so seem good to the Dean or in his absence the Sub-dean, and the Head Master, at most five years and not more.

We will also that whenever the Dean of our chapel royal shall signify to the Dean and Chapter of our Church of Canterbury that he is going to send a chorister of our chapel who has served there till he has lost his voice to be taught grammar in our church, the Dean and Chapter shall elect and receive without any fraud or evil craft that chorister so named and certified by the Dean of our chapel into the next place that falls vacant after that signification.

We will further, that none shall be elected a poor pupil of our church who has not completed the ninth year or has passed the fifteenth year of his age, unless he has been a chorister of our chapel royal or of our church of Canterbury.

But if any of the boys is found to be of remarkable slowness

notabilis sit aut natura ab litteris abhorrenti, hunc post multam probationem volumus per Decanum, aut eo absente Vicedecanum, expelli et alio amandari, ne veluti fucus apum mella deuoret; atque hic conscientiam Informatorum oneramus, ut quantammaximum potuerit operam ac diligentiam adhibeant, quo pueri omnes in litteris progrediantur et proficiant; et ne quem puerum tarditatis vicio insigniter notatum inter ceteros diutius inutiliter herere sinant, quin illius nomen statim Decano, aut eo absente Vicedecano, deferant; ut, eo amoto, ad illius locum aptior per Decanum aut eo absente Vicedecanum et Capitulum eligatur.

Statuimus etiam ut per Decanum aut eo absente Vicedecanum et Capitulum, unus eligatur Latine et Grece doctus, bone fame et vite pie, docendi facultate imbutus, qui tam quinquaginta illos ecclesie nostre pueros quam alios quoscunque gramaticam discendi gracia ad scolam nostram confluentes pietate excolat et bonis litteris exornet. Hic in scola nostra primas obtineat et Archididascolus siue Precipuus Informator esto.

Rursum per Decanum aut [etc. as above] volumus unum alterum elegi bone fame et pie vite, Latine doctum, docendique facultate imbutum, qui sub Archididascolo pueros docebit, prima scilicet gramatices rudimenta, et perinde Hipodidascolus siue Secundarius Informator appellabitur.

Hos vero Informatores puerorum volumus ut regulis et docendi ordini, quem Decanus aut [etc. as above] prescribendum duxerint, diligenter ac fideliter obsecundent. Quod si desidiosi aut negligentes aut minus ad docendum apti inueniantur, post trinam monitionem a Decano, aut [etc.] amoueantur et ab officio deponantur. Omnia autem ad functionem suam spectantia sese fideliter prestituros iuramento promittent.

30. De communi mensa omnium ministrorum.

Ut qui una conueniunt, et una Deum laudant in choro una etiam comedant et una Deum laudent in mensa, statuimus et

and stupidity or of a character to which learning is abhorrent, we will that after a long probation he shall be expelled by the Dean, or in his absence the Sub-dean, and another substituted, lest like a drone he should devour the bees' honey; and here we charge the consciences of the masters that they shall bestow the utmost possible labour and pains in making all the boys progress and become proficient in learning; and that they allow no boy who is remarkable for the slowness of his intellect to remain uselessly too long among the rest, but shall report his name at once to the Dean, or in his absence the Sub-dean, so that he may be removed and another more fit be elected in his place by the Dean, or in his absence the Sub-dean and Chapter.

We decree also that the Dean, or in his absence the Sub-dean and Chapter, shall elect one learned in Latin and Greek, of good character and pious life, endowed with the faculty of teaching, to instruct in piety and adorn with good learning those 50 boys of our church and all others whatsoever who come to our school to learn grammar. He shall hold the primacy in our school and be called the Head Master or Chief Teacher.

In the second place we will that the Dean [etc. as above] shall choose another of good character and pious life, learned in Latin and endowed with the faculty of teaching, to teach the boys under the Head Master the first rudiments of grammar and therefore to be called the Lower Master or Second Teacher.

These teachers of the boys we will shall diligently and faithfully follow the rules and order of teaching which the Dean [etc.] shall think fit to prescribe. But if they are idle or negligent or found unfit to teach, they shall after three warnings by the Dean [etc.] be removed and deposed from office. And they shall promise on oath that they will faithfully perform all things belonging to their function.

30. The Common Table of all the Ministers.

That those who meet together and praise God together in choir should also eat together and praise God together at table,

volumus ut tam minores canonici et ministri omnes in choro quam puerorum gramaticorum Informatores, et alii omnes inferiores ecclesie nostre ministri, pueri etiam musicam et gramaticam discentes (si commode fieri potest) in Communi Aula simul comedant et epulentur. In qua quidem Aula Precentor vel, eo absente, primus admissione minor canonicus in superiori mensa primus accumbat: deinde Archididascolus et ceteri minores canonici, Diaconus et Subdiaconus, atque Magister Choristarum. In secundo ordine sedeant duodecim clerici et hipodidascolus. In tercio ordine sedeant pueri gramatici et choriste. In secundo prandio sedeant obsonator, subsacriste, duo virgiferi, quatuor campanarum pulsatores, pincerne, janitores et coquus.

Morum censor in Aula erit Precentor, aut eo absente [etc. as above] qui viros immorigeratos arguet. Pueros autem arguent eciam ipsorum preceptores; ut omnia cum silentio, ordine et decoro agantur in Aula....

Pueris musicam vel gramaticam addiscentibus, victum gratis intra ecclesiam datum habentibus, portionem pecunie pro victu seu commodis suis assignari et tradi permittimus, dummodo hebdomadatim communi sodalium mense juxta Decani et Capituli judicium pecunie aliquid soluant. Statuimus etiam et ordinamus ut Thesaurarius Ecclesie nostre in mensis cujuslibet initio tradat, numeret ac soluat senescallo menstruo pro mensa et communis singulorum communiter vescentium ad hunc, qui sequitur, modum. Nimirum pro vescentibus in primo ordine, id est, pro singulis minoribus canonicis, Diacono et Subdiacono, pro primario Informatore puerorum gramaticorum et pro Magistro Choristarum; per mensem, 6s. Pro mensa et communis communiter vescentium in secundo ordine, nimirum pro clericis et inferiore Informatore puerorum gramaticorum; per mensem 4s. 8d. Pro mensa et communis singulorum communiter vescentium in tercio ordine nimirum pro singulis pueris gramaticis et choristis; per mensem 3s. 4d. Denique pro mensa et communis singulorum qui in secundo prandio sedebunt...per mensem 4s.

we will and decree that both the minor canons and all ministers in the choir, and also the grammar boys' masters and all other inferior ministers of our church, and the boys learning music and grammar shall, if possible, eat and dine together at the same time in a Common Hall. In this Hall the Precentor, or in his absence the first admitted Minor Canon, shall occupy the first seat at the upper table, then the Head Master and other Minor Canons, the Deacon and Sub-deacon and the Master of the Choristers. In the second rank shall sit the 12 clerks and the Under Master. In the third rank shall sit the grammar boys and choristers. At the second dinner shall sit the manciple, the sextons, two vergers, four bellringers, butler, porters and cook.

The Precentor shall be overseer of manners in hall, or in his absence the Senior Minor Canon, and shall rebuke any grown-up person who behaves badly, but the boys shall be rebuked only by their masters, that all may be done in hall in silence and good order....

We allow a portion of the money to be assigned for the food and other necessaries of the boys learning music and grammar who have their living given them gratis in the church to be delivered to them, on condition that they pay weekly something according to the Dean and Chapter's discretion for the common table of their colleagues. We decree and ordain also that the Treasurer of our church shall at the beginning of every month pay the monthly steward for the table and commons of all those dining together after this rate; viz. for those eating in the first rank, that is for each Minor Canon, the Deacon and Sub-deacon, the Head Teacher of the grammar boys and the Master of the Choristers, 6s. a month; for the table and commons of those eating together in the second rank, namely the clerks and Under Teacher of the grammar boys, 4s. 6d. a month; for the table and commons of those eating together in the third rank, namely, for each grammar boy and chorister, 3s. 4d. a month; lastly for the table and commons of those sitting at the second dinner,...4s. a month.

31. De vestibus ministrorum quas liberatas vocant.

[The head master had the same livery as the minor canons, four yards of cloth at 5s. a yard, the choristers' master three yards at 5s., and the under master three yards at 4s. 6d.]

32. De stipendiis ministrorum in ecclesia nostra.

Statuimus et volumus ut ex bonis communibus ecclesie nostre, preter communas et liberatas superius assignatas, soluantur stipendia omnibus ministris ecclesie nostre per manus Thesaurarii singulis anni terminis per equales porciones ad hunc qui sequitur modum, viz.:

	£	s.	d.
Singulis concionatoribus	25	0	0
Minoribus canonicis pro porcione sua	5	2	0
Superiori informatori gramatice	15	2	0
Magistro choristarum	5	7	0
Inferiori informatori gramatice	6	5	10
Singulis clericis	4	5	10
Obsonatori	3	11	4
Cuilibet choriste	1	5	0
,, duorum pincernarum	2	18	0
,, puero gramatice	1	8	4

33. De celebracione Diuinorum.

Statuimus et ordinamus ut Minores Canonici et clerici una cum Diacono et Subdiacono ac Magistro Choristarum diuina officia in choro templi nostri quotidie peragant, secundum morem et ritum aliarum ecclesiarum Cathedralium, ad officia vero noctu decantanda eos obligari nolumus.

Volumus preterea ut uterque Informator gramatice diebus festis choro intersit, insignibus choro conuenientibus indutus; quorum alter sit supra minores canonicos, alter post minores canonicos proximum in choro locum obtineat.

31. The clothing of the ministers which they call liveries.

32. The stipends of the ministers in our church.

[The Dean and Canons had been provided for in a former chapter; the Dean having £56. 13s. 4d. a year stipend and a mark (13s. 4d.) a day when in residence; a Canon £17. 6s. 8d. a year stipend and 1s. 3d. a day when in residence.]

We decree and will that, besides the commons and liveries above assigned, there shall be paid out of the common possessions of our church to all the ministers of our church, by the hands of the treasurer at each term of the year by equal portions, stipends at the following rate, viz.:

	£	s.	d.
To each Preacher	25	0	0
To the Minor Canons for their portion	5	2	0
To the Upper Teacher of Grammar	15	2	0
To the Master of the Choristers	5	7	0
To the Lower Teacher of Grammar	6	5	10
To each clerk	4	5	10
To the manciple	3	11	4
To each Chorister	1	5	0
To each of two Butlers	2	18	0
To each Grammar Boy	1	8	4

33. The celebration of Divine Service.

We decree and ordain that the minor canons and clerks, with the deacon and subdeacon and the master of the choristers, shall daily perform the divine offices in the choir of our temple, after the fashion and rites of other cathedral churches; except that we do not wish them to be bound to sing offices in the night....

We will further that both teachers of grammar shall be present in choir on feast-days clothed in garments befitting the choir; one of them having the seat in choir next above the minor canons, the other next after the minor canons.

Ad hec Pueros Gramaticos, qui sumptibus ecclesie aluntur in festis diebus volumus in habitu competente choro interesse, et officium sibi mandatum a Precentore sedulo facere; nisi alias per Archididascolum amandentur. Quos etiam pueros volumus singulis diebus per annum dum sacra misteria in summa missa peraguntur Corporis Domini eleuationi adesse, ibique morari quoad cantus Agnus Dei perficiatur, ac interim bini et bini dicant ac meditentur Psalmos Miserere mei Deus etc. Deus misereatur nostri etc. orationem Domine Jesu Christe, etc. De profundis clamaui etc. cum oratione Absolue quesumus etc.

[Provision for obit of Henry VIII on the day of his death.]

38. De eleemosinis et in academiis studentibus.

[Provisions for bedesmen and for 24 scholars, 12 at each University. This last provision was repealed in 1545 on surrender to the Crown of some of the cathedral endowment.]

41. De methodo docendi pueros gramaticos.

Que solent esse in edificiorum architecto, ceterisque operum prefectis in urgendo opere, industria ac diligentia: eadem omnino debent esse in Pedagogis, ac tenere pubis Informatoribus, ut inter se amicissime veluti conspirent, contendantque scholasticos sue fidei traditos pietate, ac bonis literis gnauiter imbuere: neque adeo suo studere commodo, aut suo indulgere otio, quam illorum profectui et publice utilitati prospicere, ut suo pulchre officio per omnia respondere videantur. Quod quidem multo felicius prestare poterunt, si, quem prescripsimus, ordinem sedulo conentur imitari.

Omnis scholasticorum numerus in quinque aut sex ordines, seu classes distribuantur. Horum inferiores tres instituat Hipodidascolus: superiores autem Archididascolus instituat.

In scholam nemo admittatur qui non prompte legere quiue orationem Dominicam: salutationem Angelicam: simbolum apostolorum; et decem decalogi precepta vernaculo sermone memoriter non tenuerit; Gramatice omnino rudes, veluti extra ordinem, nominum et verborum accidentia doceantur. Hec cum memoriter habent in primam classem adsumantur.

Moreover we will that the grammar boys who are maintained at the expense of the church shall be present in choir on feast-days, in a proper habit, and diligently do whatever duty is imposed on them by the Precentor; unless they have been otherwise directed by the Head Master. And these boys too we will shall on every day in the year when the sacred mysteries are performed at High Mass be present at the elevation of the body of the Lord, and stay there till the singing of the Agnus Dei is done; and meanwhile, two and two, meditate and say the Psalms 'Have mercy on me, O Lord,' and 'God, have mercy upon us,' and 'O Lord Jesu Christ,' 'Out of the deep I cried,' with the prayer 'Absolve, we beseech thee.'

38. Alms and students in the Universities.

41. The method of teaching the Grammar boys.

[This curriculum is not part of the statutes in the Parker MS., but a separate document. It appears, however, to have been a part of the statutes actually delivered, being embodied in the copy in Bodl. MS.]

The usual qualities which are found in an architect and other overseers of works in pressing on their work, namely, industry and diligence, ought also to be found in pedagogues and teachers of the tender youth, that they may as it were enter into a friendly conspiracy and contention between themselves to imbue thoroughly the scholars committed to their trust with piety and good letters; and not to study their own advantage or indulge their own love of ease so much as to look to their proficiency and the public benefit, so that they may be seen to do their duty fairly in everything. And this they will be able to do much more successfully if they endeavour sedulously to follow the order we have prescribed.

The whole number of the scholars shall be divided into five or six ranks or classes. The Under Master shall teach the three lower, and the Head Master the three upper classes.

No one shall be admitted into the school who cannot read readily, or does not know by heart in the vernacular the Lord's Prayer, the Angelic Salutation, the Apostles' Creed and the Ten Commandments. Those who are wholly ignorant of Grammar shall learn the accidents of nouns and verbs, as it were out of class. When they have learnt these they shall be taken into the First Class.

In prima classe anglica rudimenta ad plenum ediscant: discant et orationis partes congrue connectere: et breuem phrasim anglicanam latinam facere; facilesque aliquas constructiones sensim attingere.

In secunda classe paulo majora audeant: Nominum genera et verborum inflectiones Latine conscriptas probe teneant; Catonis carmina, Aesopi apologos, familiaria aliqua colloquia percurrant.

In tercia vero classe nomina et verba anomala rite variare contendant, ut nusquam nomen aut verbum inueniatur, quod non ad unguem inflectere nouerint. Hic quoque Terencianas commedias, Mantuani eglogas, atque id genus alia sibi faciant familiarissima.

Harum classium curam solicite gerat Hipodidascolus, minutiora illa rudimenta discipulis suis instillando ac inculcando, ut maioribus recipiendis aptos paratosque reddat.

Hipodidascolus mane hora sexta scholam ingrediatur; statimque post fusas ad Deum, quas prescripsimus, preces, aliquam quotidie octo orationis partium memoriter reddere cogat suos scholasticos, donec in singulis fuerint promptissimi. Nec omittat quin altero quouis die sermonem Anglicum, eumque breuem, discipulis dictet, quem illos Latine vertere accurate doceat, libellisque chartaceis sedulo inscribere.

Denique in omnibus que in schola sunt agenda Archididascolo subsit Hipodidascolus, ac pareat; ipsumque de docendi methodo ac ratione consulat; ut ambo in scholasticorum profectum summo studio consentiant. Ambo etiam operam dent ut discipuli apte, ornate et distincte, corporis et oris decore seruato, pronuntiare discant.

In quarta classe doceantur pueri Latinam partium sintaxim prompte callere; exerceanturque in poeticis narrationibus, in familiaribus doctorum virorum epistolis, atque eius generis similibus.

In quinta autem classe memori mente reponant Latine orationis figuras, et canones illos de componendis carminibus factos; simulque assuescant carminibus condendis, et themati-

Curriculum of the Grammar School

In the First Class they shall learn thoroughly by heart the rudiments in English; they shall learn to put together the parts of speech; and to turn a short phrase of English into Latin; and gradually to approach other easy constructions.

In the Second Class they shall learn a little higher; they shall know the genders of nouns and the inflections of verbs written in Latin; they shall run through Cato's verses, Aesop's Fables, and some Familiar Colloquies.

In the Third Class they shall endeavour to make right varyings on the nouns and anomalous verbs, so that no noun or verb may be found anywhere which they do not know how to inflect in every detail. In this form too they shall make Terence's Comedies, Mantuanus' Eclogues, and other things of that sort thoroughly familiar to them.

These classes the Under Master shall take diligent care of, instilling and inculcating the lesser rudiments into his pupils so as to make them fit and prepared to receive higher instruction.

The Under Master shall come into school at 6 a.m., and immediately after saying the prayers to God which we have prescribed, shall make his scholars daily say by heart one of the eight parts of speech until they are ready in each. Nor shall he omit on any other day to dictate to his pupils an English sentence, and that a short one, which he shall teach them to turn exactly into Latin, and to write it carefully in their parchment note-books.

In short, in anything to be done in the school the Under Master shall be subject to and shall obey the Head Master; and shall consult him on the method and plan of teaching; so that they may both agree in their great zeal for the profit of the scholars. Both too shall endeavour to teach their pupils to speak openly, finely and distinctly, keeping due decorum both with their body and their mouth.

In the Fourth Form the boys shall be taught to know the Latin syntax readily; and shall be practised in the stories of poets, and familiar letters of learned men and the like.

In the Fifth Form they shall commit to memory the Figures of Latin Oratory and the rules for making verses; and at the same time shall be practised in making verses and

bus expoliendis; denique versentur in castissimorum Poetarum ac optimorum Historicorum interpretatione.

Postremo in sexta classe imbuantur formulis illis de verborum copia ac rerum ab Erasmo conscriptis, discantque orationem infinitis modis variare, ut vel sic tandem Latine lingue facultatem (quantum pueris satis est) assequantur. Interim Horacium, Ciceronem, ceterosque ejus classis authores degustent. Interim declamatiunculis inter se concertent ut vel contentionis studio docti euadant.

Has precipue classes Latino sermone expolire Archididascolus satagat.

Ante horam diei septimam scholam ingrediatur, ut suo docendi munere gnauiter fungatur. Hic etiam altero quouis die orationem vernaculam latinam facere, eamque in multas formas mutare gregem sibi commissum docere pergat. Preterea totius schole curam sibi commissam intelligat.

Proinde singulis septimanis uniuersum gregem semel, iterum aut tertio inuisat, diligenterque examinet scholasticorum ingenia et in litteris progressum exploret. Quos autem tardos, atque a Musis prorsus alienos etiam omnibus tentatis offenderit, horum amicos fideliter moneat, ne ipsos litteris penitus ineptos frustra tempus producere et aliorum loca occupare patiantur. Ceterum quos aptos et industrios probauerit, hos ter ad minus quotannis in superiores classes surroget, nimirum a prima in secundam, a secunda in tertiam, et sic deinceps, ut quisque dignus habebitur, idque fiat presente et consulto etiam Hipodidascolo de illis, scilicet qui ipsius cure sunt crediti.

Ad hec hora noctis sexta in scholam scholastici reuertantur, et ad septimam usque repetant, ac reddant condiscipulis iis qui iam in litteris maturi erunt, didascolis eciam pluribus presentibus, quecunque per totum diem didicerint.

Quum ludendi facta fuerit copia, una ludant, una iocentur, ne huc illuc errantes, et morum iacturam faciant, et aliarum rerum desiderio a litteris animos sensim alienent, nec ullos iocos exerceant, qui non honestatis speciem pre se ferant, ac omni turpitudine vacent.

Postremo, quicquid vel serio vel ioco tractent, non alio utantur sermone quam Latino vel Greco.

polishing themes; then they shall be versed in translating the chastest Poets and the best Historians.

Lastly, in the Sixth Form they shall be instructed in the formulas of 'Copiousness of Words and Things' written by Erasmus; and learn to make varyings of speech in every mood, so that they may acquire the faculty of speaking Latin, as far as is possible for boys. Meanwhile they shall taste Horace, Cicero and other authors of that class. Meanwhile they shall compete with one another in declamations so that they may leave well learned in the school of argument.

These classes principally the Head Master shall try to polish in Latin.

He shall come into school by 7 o'clock to perform his duty of teaching thoroughly. He too every other day shall make some English sentence into Latin and teach the flock committed to him to change it into many forms. Moreover let him understand that he has charge of the whole school.

So every week he ought to visit the whole flock, once, twice or three times, and diligently test the abilities of the scholars and ascertain their progress in learning. If he shall prove any of them, after testing them in every way, to be slow and wholly strangers to the Muses, he shall faithfully warn their friends not to let them, being wholly unfit for letters, waste their time in vain and fill the places of others. But those he shall find to be fit and industrious he shall, at least three times a year, call up to the higher forms, namely from the first to the second, from the second to the third, and so on as each shall be thought fit. This shall be done in the presence of and after consultation with the Under Master in the case of those who are entrusted to his care.

Moreover at 6 p.m. the scholars shall return to school, and until 7 p.m. shall do their repetition and render to their fellow-pupils who have become ripe in learning, several masters also being present, whatever they have learnt through the day.

When leave to play is given they shall play and sport together, lest, wandering about here and there, they incur some loss of character, and wanting to do other things their minds gradually become estranged from learning. And they shall not practise any games which are not of a gentlemanly appearance and free of all lowness.

Lastly, whatever they are doing in earnest or in play they shall never use any language but Latin or Greek.

Should the poor scholars be gentlemen's sons only?

[John Strype, *Memorials of Thomas Cranmer*, ed. 1694, p. 88, Book I., chap. XXII.; ed. 1840, pp. 126-7. From MSS. Foxe. Harl. 419, f. 115. Camd. Soc. 77, p. 273.]

Anno 1540....This year the Cathedral Church of Canterbury was altered from monks to secular men of the clergy: viz., Prebendaries or Canons, Petticanons, Choristers and Scholars.

At this erection were present Thomas Cranmer, archbishop, the Lord Rich, chancellor of the Court of the Augmentation of the revenues of the Crown; Sir Christopher Hales, Kt, the King's Attorney; Sir Anthony Sentleger, Kt, with divers other Commissioners.

And nominating and electing such convenient and fit persons, as should serve for the furniture of the said Cathedral Church according to the new foundation, it came to pass that when they should elect the children of the Grammar School, there were of the Commissioners more than one or two who would have none admitted but sons or younger brethren of gentlemen. As for other, husbandmen's children, they were more meet, they said, for the plough and to be artificers than to occupy the place of the learned sort. So that they wished none else to be put to school but only gentlemen's children.

Whereunto the...Archbishop...said 'That he thought it not indifferent so to order the matter. For,' said he, 'poor men's children are many times endued with more singular gifts of nature, which are also the gifts of God, as with eloquence, memory, apt pronunciation, sobriety and such like, and also commonly more apt to apply their study than is the gentleman's son delicately educated.'

Hereunto it was on the other part replied that 'it was meet for the ploughman's son to go to plough and the artificer's son to apply the trade of his parent's vocation, and the gentleman's children are meet to have the knowledge of government and rule in the commonwealth; for we have as much need of ploughmen as of any other state; all sorts of men may not go to school.' 'I grant' replied the Archbishop 'much of your

meaning herein, as needful in a commonwealth, but yet to utterly exclude the ploughman's son and the poor man's son from the benefit of learning, as though they were utterly unworthy of having the gifts of the Holy Ghost bestowed upon them as well as upon others is as much as to say that Almighty God should not be at liberty to bestow his great gifts of grace upon any person...the offspring of our best born children should peradventure become most unapt to learn and very dolts, as I myself have seen no small number of them very dull, and without all manner of capacity...To conclude, the poor man's son by painstaking for the most part will be learned, when the gentleman's son will not take the pains to get it...wherefore if the gentleman's son be apt to learning let him be admitted; if not apt, let the poor man's child being apt enter his room.'

Injunctions to Canterbury Cathedral by Archbishop Parker. 1560.

[C. C. C. MS. 120.]

[John Twyne, B.C.L., Oxford, became schoolmaster of the old Archiepiscopal or City School *c.* 1526, and became first master of it when reconstituted as the Cathedral Grammar School in 1541. In 1544 he was Sheriff, in 1554 Mayor of Canterbury. This Injunction seems to have led to his retirement from the mastership in 1561.]

That Mr Twine, their Schoolm^r shall not intermedle with anie publicke office of the incorporation of the Towne or Cittie of Canterberie, but holie with diligence to applie his Schole and Schollers, and that he should utterlie abstaine from riott and dronkynnes, upon paine to be removed from the said rome of Scholem^r or office of teachinge.

Item that the Ussher of the sayd Schole continuallie kepe commons with the Pettie Cannons and behave himself humblie and obedient towarde the Prebendaries of the said Church and others his superiors, upon paine of deprivacion fro his said Usshershippe.

Royal Injunctions of 1547.

[Wilkins, *Concilia*, IV. 3. 5. 8.]

Injunctions given by the most excellent prince Edward VI, in earth under Christ of the Church of England and Ireland, the supreme head. To all and singular his loving subjects, as well of the clergy as of the laity.

And to the intent that learned men may hereafter spring the more, for the execution of the premises, every parson, vicar, clerk, or beneficed man within his deanery, having yearly to dispend in benefices and other promotions of the church £100 shall give competent exhibition to one scholar: and for so many £100 more as he may dispend, to so many scholars more shall he give like exhibition in the University of Oxford or Cambridge, or some grammar-school; which after they have profited in good learning, may be partners of their patrons' cure and charge, as well in preaching, as otherwise, in the execution of their offices, or may (when need shall be) otherwise profit the commonweal with their council and wisdom...

Item, that all chauntery priests shall exercise themselves in teaching youth to read and write, and bring them up in good manners, and other vertuous exercises.

The Chantries Act. 1547.

[1 Edw. VI, c. 14, *Stat. of the Realm*, IV. pt I. 1819, p. 24. See A. F. Leach, *English Schools at the Reformation*, p. 65.]

An Acte wherby certaine Chauntries, Colleges, Free Chapells and the Possessions of the same be given to the King's Majestie.

The King's moste lovinge Subjects the Lords spirituall and temporall and the Commons in this present parliament assembled, consyderinge that a greate parte of Superstition and Errors in Christian Religion hath byn brought into the myndes and estimacion of men, by reasone of the Ignoraunce

of their verie trewe and perfecte salvacion throughe the deathe
of Jesus Christ, and by devising and phantasinge vayne opynions
of Purgatorye and Masses satisfactorye to be done for them
which be departed, the which doctryne and vayn opynion by
nothing more is mayntayned and upholden then by the abuse
of Trentalls, Chauntries and other provisions made for the
contynuance of the saide blyndness and ignoraunce; And
further considering and understanding that the alteracion
chaunge and amendement of the same, and converting to good
and godlie uses, as in erecting of Gramer Scoles to the
educacion of Youthe in vertewe and godlinesse, the further
augmenting of the Universities and better provision for the
poore and nedye, can not in this present parlament be provyded
and convenyentlie doon, nor can not ne ought to anny other
manner parsone be committed then to the King's Highnes,
whose Majestie with and by thadvise of His Highnes moste
prudent Counsaile can and will moste wiseleye and beneficiallye
bothe for the honnor of God and the weale of this his
Majesties Realme order alter converte and dispose the same
[Recital of the Chantries Act, 37 Henry VIII, enabling
Henry VIII during his life to issue commissions and to take
any Colleges, Chantries etc.]. It is now ordeyned and enacted
that all manner of Colleges, Free Chappells and Chauntries,
having being or in esse within 5 yeres next before the firste daye
of this present parlament, which were not in actuall and reall
possession of the saide late King, nor in the actuall and reall
possession of the King our Soveraigne Lorde that now is, nor
excepted in the saide former Acte, And all Mannors...and
other heredytaments and things above mentyoned, given
assigned lymited or appoynted to the fynding of anny preist to
have contynuaunce for ever, and wherewith or whereby anny
preist was susteyned mayntayned or founde, within 5 yeres next
before the first daye of this present parlament, and allso all annuall
rents...bestowed towarde or for the mayntenaunce suppor-
tacion or fynding of anny stipendary Preist intended...to have
contynuaunce for ever, shall...immediatelie after the feast of

Easter next comminge, be adjudged and demed and allso be in the verie actuall and reall possession and seasone of our Soveraigne Lorde and his heires and Successors for ever; and in as large and ample manner and forme as the preists, wardens, masters, Ministers, Governors, Rulers or other Incumbents of them, or anny of them, at anny tyme within 5 yeres next before the begyninge of this present parlament had occupyed or enjoyed, or now hath occupyethe or enjoyethe the same;...

7. And furthermore...that the King...shall from the saide feast of Easter next comminge have and enjoye to him his heirs and successors for ever, all fraternityes brotherhedds and guyldes...other then suche corporacions guyldes fraternityes companies and felowshipps of misteryes or craftes [viz. as mentioned in § 6, namely Municipal Corporations, Craft Gilds and City Companies].

8. And allso be it ordeyned and enacted...that the King... maye directe his...Commission...to suche pursons as it shall please him...to enquyre...what mannors landes [etc.]...be geven to the King by this Acte; And allso that the same Commissyoners or twoo of them at the least, by vertewe of this Acte and of the Commissyon to them directed, shall have full power and aucthoritie to assigne and shall appoynte, in everye suche place where guylde fraternitye the Preist or Incumbent of anny Chauntrye in Esse the first daie of this present parlament by the foundacion ordynaunce [or] first Institucion therof shoulde or ought to have kepte a gramer scoole or a preacher, and so hath doon sithen the feaste of St Michell Tharchaungell last past, Landes tenements and other heredytaments of everye suche Chauntrye guylde and fraternitye to remayne and contynue in succession to a Scoole Maister or preacher for ever, for and towarde the kepinge of a Gramer Scoole or preaching and in suche manner and forme as the same Commyssyoners or twoo of them at the least shall assigne or appoynte [also to create vicars and assistants in colleges etc. which were parish churches]; as well to make ordynaunces and rules concerninge the service user

and demeanor of everye suche preist and Scoole Maister, as is aforesaide to be appoynted, as allso by what name or names he and theye shall from hensfoorth be named and called: to assigne...[also to grant pensions to the members of colleges and chantries suppressed; to continue payments out of them for the poor; and to appoint lands to gilds for piers, jetties, sea-walls, and harbours].

20. Provided allwayes...that this Acte...shall not in anny wise extende to anny College, Hostell or Hall being within either of the Universities of Cambrydge and Oxforde; nor to anny Chaunterye founded in anny of the Colleges Hostells or Halls being in the same Universities; nor to the Free Chappell of St George the Martyr scituate in the Castell of Wyndesor; nor to the Colledge called St Marye Colledge of Winchester besydes Winchester of the foundation of Bishopp Wikeham; nor to the College of Eton; nor to the parishe Churche commonlye called the Chappell in the Sea in Newton within the Isle of Elye in the Countye of Cambrydge;...nor to any Chappell made or ordeyned for the ease of the people dwelling distaunt from the parishe churche or suche lyke Chappell, wherunto no more landes or tenements then the churche yarde or a lytle Howse or close dothe belonge or pertaine; nor to anny Cathedrall Churche or Colledge where a Bishopp's Sea is within this Realme of Englande or Wales.

Schools Continuance Warrant for Cornwall.
1548.

[A. F. Leach, *English Schools at the Reformation*, p. 42. P. R. O. Grants for Schools, No. 12.]

Wee, Sir Walter Myldemay, Knight, and Robert Keylwey, Esquyer, Commyssioners, appoynted by the Kinges maiesties Commyssion, vnder the greate seale of England, bearyng date the 20th day of June last past, touchyng order to be taken for

the mayntenaunce and contynuaunce of Scoles and preachers, and of preestes and curates of necessitie for seruynge of cures and mynistracion of sacramentes, and for money and other thinges to be contynewed and paide to the poore, and for dyuerse other thinges appoynted to be done and executed by vertue of the same commyssion. To the Audytour and Receyvour of the Revenues of the court of The augmentacions and Revenues of the Kynges maiesties crowne in the Countie of Cornwall, and to either of them greatyng.

Forasmoche as it apperith by the certificate of the particuler surveyour of landes of the said court in the said countie

That a grammer scole hath been heretofore kept at Peryn, in the parishe of Glavias, with part of the revenues of the late colledge there, wiche scole is very mete and necessarie to be contynued.

And that a grammer scole hath been contynuallie kepte at saynt Mary Wike [etc.], with the reuenues of the late Chaunterie of Saynt John Baptist there, wiche scole is very necessary to contynue.

And that a grammer Scole hath been contynuallie kepte in the Borough of saltayshe in the said countie, which scole is very mete to contynue.

And that a grammer scole hath been contynually kept in Bodmyn in the said countie, which is very mete to be contynued, And that it is necessary to have a parsone to be assisttaunt to helpe to serve the cure in the parish church of Bodmyn in the said countie.

And that a grammer scole hath been contynually kept at Peryn in the said countie, And that John Arscot, scolemaster there, had for his wages yerelie £10 [graunted] to hym by the late Abbesse of syon by wryting vnder the Covent Seale of the late Monastery of Syon, which scole is very mete to be contynued....

Wee therefore the said commissioners by vertue and aucthoritie of the saide commission haue assigned and appointed that the said scole at Peryn aforesaid shall contynue, And that

the scolemaister there shall haue and enjoy £6. 18s. for his wages yerelie.

And that the said scole at saynt Mary Wike shall contynue, and that there shall be paid yerelie to the sustentacion and mayntenaunce of the same scole £17 13s. 3½d.

And that the said grammer scole at Saltaishe shall contynue, And that Androwe Furlong, scolemaster there, shall contynue in the Rome of Scolemaster there and shall haue for his wages yerelie, £7.

And that the said scole in Bodmyn shall contynue, And that Nicholas Taprell, scolemaster there shall contynue in the rome of scolemaister there, and shall assist the cure in Bodmyn aforesaid, And shall haue and enjoye the said some of £5 6s. 8d.

And that the said John Arscot shall teche scole as heretofore he hath vsed, and shall haue for his wages yerelie £10.

And we, the saide commyssioners in the Kynges maiesties behalf, by vertue of the saide commyssion, do requyre you, the saide Receyvour, that of suche the Kynges money and Revenues as from tyme to tyme shall be and remayne in your handes, you do content and pay yerelie from Easter last forthwarde the saide seuerall sommes of money and wages before mencioned to the persones before rehersed, and to suche other persone and persones as shall haue and enjoye the saide Romes and places of the same persones, to be paide wekelie, or quarterlie, or otherwise, as necessitie shall requyre, vnto suche tyme as further or other order shall be taken for the same.

And this warraunte shall be to you the saide Receyvour and Audytour sufficient discharge for the payment and allowaunce of the same accordynglie.

Given the xxth day of July in the seconde yere of the reigne of our soueraigne lord Edwarde the Sixt, by the grace of God [etc.].

Wa: Mildmay.
Robt Keylwey.

Re-foundation of Sherborne School. 1550.

[A. F. Leach, 'Sherborne School,' *Archaeol. Journal*, 1898, from Muniments of St John's Hospital, Sherborne, and of the School Governors.]

Mention of the School. 1437.

Visus computi Ricardi Rochell tam de diversis denariis per ipsum Ricardum receptis quam de diversis expensis...ad usum Domus Elemosinarie de Shirborn predicta anno regni Regis Henrici VI post conquestum sexto-decimo.

Idem respondet...

Chepstrett.

			s.	d.
Et de receptis de Rectore de la Grene	.	.	20	0
,, ,, ,, Waltero Weston	.	.	20	0
,, ,, ,, Matilda Meryett	.	.	.	8
,, ,, ,, Stephano Rochell	.	.	.	6
,, ,, ,, Magistro Scolarum	.	.	3	4

Compotus Ricardi Rochell, Magistri Domus Elemosinarie Sanctorum Johannis Baptiste, et Johannis Evangeliste ibidem, a festo S. Michaelis archangeli anno regni Regis Henrici VI post conquestum 16° usque in crastinum S. Johannis Baptiste anno regni ejusdem Domini Regis 17° ut pro 3 quarteriis anni.

Idem respondit...

  de £20 receptis de dono Johannis Fauntleroy.
 et ,, 100s. ,, ,, ,, Barett.
 ,, ,, 12d. ,, ,, ,, Bullock.
 ,, ,, 16d. ,, ,, Johanne Cardemaker.
 ,, ,, 20d. ,, ,, Roberti Potycary.
 . . . . .
 ,, ,, 3s. 4d. ,, ,, Thome Copeland, Magistri Scolarum de Shirbourne predicta.

Re-foundation of Sherborne School. 1550.

Mention of the School. 1437.

View of Richard Rochell's account as well of divers monies received by the same Richard as of divers necessary payments made by him to the use of the Almshouse of Sherborne aforesaid in the 16th year of King Henry the Sixth after the Conquest [1437].

The same answers...

Cheap Street.

		£	s.	d.
For receipts from the Rector of the Green	.	1	0	0
,,	Walter Weston	1	0	0
,,	Matilda Meryett			8
,,	Stephen Rochell			6
,,	The Schoolmaster		3	4

Account of Richard Rochell, master of the Almshouse of St John the Baptist and St John the Evangelist there, from Michaelmas 16 Henry the Sixth after the Conquest to the morrow of St John the Baptist in the 17th year of the same King as for three quarters of a year [29 Sept. 1437—24 June 1438].

He answers for...

£20 received of the gift of John Fauntleroy.				
£5	,,	,,	,,	John Barett.
1s.	,,	,,	,,	John Bullock.
1s. 4d.	,,	,,	,,	Jane Cardmaker.
1s. 8d.	,,	,,	,,	Robert Apothecary.
.	.	.	.	.
3s. 4d.	,,	,,	,,	Thomas Copeland, Master of the School of Sherborne aforesaid.

Thorncombe Exhibitions at Sherborne School in 1535.

[*Ib.* from *Val. Eccl.* I., 281–5, Rec. Com. 1810.]

Sherborne abbathia....Assignata ad officium Elimosinarii.

	£	s.	d.
Vale[n]t in redditibus assise terrarum et tenementorum in Shirborne per annum. . . .	7	1	2

Deductiones et allocationes.

Et in elemosina annuatim distributa de exitibus predictorum terrarum et tenementorum in Shirborne pro exhibitione trium scolarium in scola gramaticali apud Shirborne, ex fundatione Alfrici Thornecombe   78   0

Charter of Re-foundation. 1550.

[*Ib.* from Orig. Charter at Sherborne. Pat. 4 Edw. VI, pt ii. m.]

Edwardus Sextus Dei Gracia Anglie Francie et Hibernie Rex fidei Defensor, et in terra ecclesie Anglicane et Hibernice supremum caput, Omnibus ad quos presentes littere pervenerint, Salutem.

Sciatis quod nos, ad humilem peticionem tam inhabitancium ville de Shirborne in Comitatu Dorsettensi, quam aliorum quam plurimorum subditorum nostrorum tocius patrie ibidem vicine, nobis pro Scola Grammaticali ibidem erigenda et stabilienda pro institucione et instruccione puerorum et juvenum De gracia nostra speciali ac ex certa sciencia et mero motu nostris, necnon de avisamento consilii nostri, volumus concedimus et ordinamus, quod de cetero sit et erit una Scola Grammaticalis in dicta villa de Shirborne, que vocabitur LIBERA SCOLA GRAMMATICALIS REGIS EDWARDI SEXTI, pro educacione institucione et instruccione Puerorum et Juvenum in grammatica perpetuis temporibus futuris duratura; ac Scolam illam de uno Magistro seu Pedagogo et uno subpedagogo sive hipodidascalo pro perpetuo continuaturam erigimus, creamus, ordinamus et fundamus per presentes.

before the Dissolution

Thorncombe Exhibitions at Sherborne School in 1535.

The Monastery of the Blessed Mary the Virgin of Sherborne....Assigned to the Almoner's Office.

	£	s.	d.
Value in rents of assize of lands and tenements in Sherborne yearly	7	1	2

Deductions and allowances.

And in alms yearly distributed out of the issues of the aforesaid lands and tenements in Sherborne for the exhibition of three Scholars in the Grammar School at Sherborne, on the foundation of Alfric Thorncomb 3 18 0

Charter of Re-foundation. 1550.

Edward the Sixth, by the grace of God King of England, France and Ireland, Defender of the Faith, and on earth Supreme Head of the Church of England and of Ireland, To all to whom these present letters shall come, Health.

Know ye that we, at the humble petition as well of the inhabitants of the town of Sherborne in the county of Dorset as of very many other our subjects of the whole neighbouring country made to us for the erection and establishment of a Grammar School there for the education and instruction of boys and youths, of our special grace and of our certain knowledge and mere motion, also by the advice of our Council, will, grant and ordain that there may hereafter and shall be a Grammar School in the said town of Sherborne, which shall be called the Free Grammar School of King Edward the Sixth, to endure for all time to come for the education, institution and instruction of boys and youths in grammar; and that school to continue for ever of a Master or Teacher and a Sub-master or Under-teacher we erect, create, ordain and found by these presents.

Et ut intencio nostra predicta meliorem capiat effectum, et ut terre, tenementa, redditus, revenciones et alia ad sustentacionem scole predicte concedenda, assignanda et appunctuanda melius gubernentur, pro continuacione ejusdem, Volumus et ordinamus, quod de cetero imperpetuum sint et erunt infra villam et parochiam de Shirborne predicta viginti homines, de discretioribus et magis probioribus inhabitantibus earundem ville et parochie pro tempore existentibus, qui erunt et vocabuntur Gubernatores possessionum revencionum et bonorum dicte Scole, vulgariter vocate et vocande libere Scole Grammaticalis Regis Edwardi Sexti in Shirborne in comitatu Dorsettensi.

Et ideo sciatis quod nos assignavimus, eligimus [*sic*], nominavimus et constituimus, ac per presentes assignamus, eligimus, nominamus et constituimus dilectos nobis Nicholaum Serger, generosum [19 others named, being in fact the Master and Brethren, the Governing Body of St John's Hospital, Sherborne], inhabitantes dicte ville et parochie de Shirborne, fore et esse primos et modernos Gubernatores possessionum revencionum et bonorum dicte Libere Scole Grammaticalis Regis Edwardi Sexti in Shirborne in Comitatu Dorsettensi, ad idem officium bene et fideliter exercendum et occupandum a data presencium durante vita eorum.

Et quod iidem Gubernatores in re, facto et nomine, de cetero sint et erunt unum corpus corporatum et politiquum de se imperpetuum, per nomen 'Gubernatorum possessionum revencionum et bonorum libere Scole Grammaticalis Regis Edwardi Sexti in Shirborne in Comitatu Dorsettensi,' incorporatum et erectum. Ac ipsos Gubernatores [etc.] per presentes incorporamus, ac corpus corporatum et politiquum per idem nomen imperpetuum duraturum realiter et ad plenum creamus, erigimus, ordinamus, facimus et constituimus per presentes.

Et volumus et per presentes ordinamus et concedimus, quod iidem Gubernatores [etc.] habeant successionem perpetuam, et per idem nomen sint et erunt persone habiles et in lege capaces ad habendum et recipiendum de nobis

And that our intention aforesaid may take better effect and that lands, tenements, rents, revenues and other things to be granted, assigned and appointed for the maintenance of the school aforesaid may be better governed, for the continuance of the same, We will and ordain that henceforth for ever there may and shall be in the town and parish of Sherborne aforesaid 20 men of the discreeter and better inhabitants of the same town and parish for the time being, who shall be and shall be called 'Governors of the possessions, revenues and goods' of the said school, commonly called and to be called 'The Free Grammar School of King Edward the Sixth in Sherborne in the county of Dorset.'

And therefore know ye that we have assigned, elected, nominated and constituted, and by these presents assign, elect, name and constitute our beloved Nicholas Serger, gentleman [two others styled gentlemen, and 17 others named without any addition], inhabitants of the said town and parish of Sherborne, as about to be and to be the first and present 'Governors of the possessions, revenues and goods of the said Free Grammar School of King Edward the Sixth in Sherborne in the county of Dorset,' to exercise and occupy the same office well and faithfully from the date of these presents during their lives.

And that the same Governors may henceforth and shall be in deed, fact and name a body corporate and politic of themselves for ever, incorporated and erected by the name of 'The Governors of the possessions, revenues and goods of the Free Grammar School of King Edward the Sixth in Sherborne in the county of Dorset.' And the same as Governors of the possessions [etc. ut supra] we incorporate by these presents, and as a body corporate and politic to endure for ever by the same name we in deed and fully create, erect, ordain, make and constitute by these presents.

And we will and by these presents ordain and grant that the same Governors [etc.] may have perpetual succession and by the same name may and shall be persons able and capable in law to hold and take from us the lands, tenements, meadows,

terras, tenementa, prata, pasturas, redditus, reversiones, possessiones, revenciones et hereditamenta subscripta et inferius specificata, ac alia terras, tenementa, possessiones, revenciones et hereditamenta quecumque de nobis, sive de aliqua alia persona, seu aliis personis.

Et ordinamus et decernimus per presentes quod, quandocumque contigerit aliquem vel aliquos dictorum viginti Gubernatorum pro tempore existencium mori, seu alibi extra villam et parochiam de Shirborne predicta inhabitare ac cum familia sua decedere, quod tunc et tociens bene liceat et licebit aliis dictorum Gubernatorum superviventibus, et ibidem cum familiis commorantibus, vel majori parti eorundem, aliam idoneam personam vel alias idoneas personas de inhabitantibus ville et parochie de Shirborne predicta, in locum vel in locos sic morientis et moriencium, aut cum familia sua sicut prefertur decedentis vel decedencium, in dicto officio Gubernatoris successurum eligere et nominare; et hoc tociens quociens casus sic acciderit.

Et sciatis quod nos intencionem et prepositum nostrum in hac parte ad effectum deducere volentes, de gracia nostra speciali ac ex certa sciencia et mero motu nostris, necnon de avisamento consilii nostri, dedimus et concessimus, ac per presentes damus et concedimus prefatis modernis Gubernatoribus possessionum revencionum et bonorum dicte Libere Scole Grammaticalis de novo erecte in Shirborne predicta, totam nuper Cantariam de Martocke cum suis juribus et pertinenciis universis, in comitatu nostro Somersettensi, ac totam domum sive capitalem mansionem ejusdem nuper Cantarie, ac omnia domos, edificia [general words and names of tenants] dicte nuper Cantarie dudum spectancia et pertinencia, ac parcellam possessionum inde nuper existencia.

Necnon totam nuper Cantariam Sancte Katerine fundatam infra ecclesiam parochialem de Gyllingham in Comitatu nostro Dorsettensi, cum suis juribus et pertinenciis universis, ac totam domum [etc. as in the last chantry].

Ac eciam omnia mesuagia [etc.] nuper in tenura Thome

Lands of Dissolved Chantries 485

pastures, rents, reversions, possessions, revenues and hereditaments underwritten and specified below, and other lands, tenements, possessions, revenues and hereditaments whatsoever of us or of any other person or other persons.

And we ordain and decree by these presents that whenever it shall happen that any one or more of the said 20 Governors for the time being shall die, or live elsewhere out of the town and parish of Sherborne aforesaid and depart with their family, that then and so often it may and shall be lawful for the others of the said Governors surviving and living there with their families, or for the greater part of them, to elect and name another fit person or persons of the inhabitants of the town and parish of Sherborne aforesaid into the place or places of him or them so dying, or departing with their family as aforesaid, to succeed in the said office of Governor, and this as often as the case shall happen.

And know ye that we, wishing to bring to effect our intention and purpose in this behalf, of our special grace [etc. ut supra] have given and granted, and by these presents give and grant to the aforesaid present Governors of the possessions, revenues and goods of the said Free Grammar School newly erected in Sherborne aforesaid the whole of the late chantry of Martock with all its rights and appurtenances in our county of Somerset, and all the house or capital messuage of the same late chantry and all our houses [etc.] to the said late chantry formerly belonging and appertaining, and lately being parcel of the possessions thereof.

Also the whole late chantry of St Katharine founded in the parish church of Gillingham in our county of Dorset, with all its rights and appurtenances and all our house [etc.].

And also all messuages [etc.] late in the tenure of Thomas

Trenchard, militis, ac omnia alia mesuagia [etc.], situata, jacencia et existencia in Lychett Matravers et Sturmester Marshall in dicto comitatu Dorsettensi, nuper Cantarie vocate Gybbons Chauntrye in Lychett Matravers in dicto comitatu Dorsettensi dudum spectancia et pertinencia [etc.].

Ac eciam omnia alia mesuagia [etc.], dictis nuper cantariis sive earum alicui quoquomodo spectancia vel pertinencia, aut ut parcella possessionum, jurium, seu revencionum earundem, sive earum alicujus, antehac habita, cognita, accepta, usitata seu reputata existencia.

Ac totam nuper liberam Capellam de Thorneton, infra parochiam de Marnehull in dicto comitatu Dorsettensi [etc.].

Necnon omnes illas triginta acras...ac alia existencia in parochia de Symondesborough, in dicto comitatu nostro Dorsettensi, nuper Cantarie Sancte Katerine fundate infra ecclesiam parochialem de Ilmynster, in dicto comitatu nostro Somersettensi, dudum spectancia et pertinencia....

Necnon redditus et annualia proficua quecumque, reservata super quibuscumque dimissionibus et concessionibus in premissis, seu de aliqua inde parcella, quoquomodo factis adeo plene, libere et integre, ac in tam amplis modo et forma, prout aliqui Cantariste, Capellani aut aliqui alii Gubernatores vel ministri dictarum nuper Cantariarum et libere Capelle, habuerunt, tenuerunt vel gavisi fuerunt,.... Et adeo plene libere et integre, prout ea omnia et singula ad manus nostras racione vel pretextu cujusdam actus de diversis Cantariis, Gildis, fraternitatibus et liberis Capellis dissolvendis et determinandis, in parliamento nostro tento apud Westmonasterium, anno regni nostri primo, inter alia editi et provisi, seu quocumque alio modo, jure seu titulo devenerunt, seu devenire debuerunt, ac in manibus nostris jam existunt, seu existere debent vel deberent.

Que quidem mesuagia, terre, tenementa, redditus, reversiones, servicia, ac cetera omnia et singula premissa, modo extenduntur ad clarum annuum valorem viginti librarum, tresdecim solidorum et quatuor denariorum.

Trenchard, knight, and all other messuages [etc.] situate, lying and being in Lytchett Matravers and Sturminster-Marshall in the said county of Dorset, formerly belonging and appertaining to the late chantry called Gybbons chantry in Lytchett Matravers.

And also all other our messuages, [etc.] to the said late chantries or any of them any way belonging and appertaining, or before this, held, known, taken, used or reputed as being parcel of the possessions, rights or revenues of the same or of any of them.

And all the late free chapel of Thornton in the parish of Marnhull in the said county of Dorset [etc. as above].

Also all those our 30 acres...and other things being in the parish of Symondsbury in our said county of Dorset formerly belonging and appertaining to the late chantry of St Katharine founded in the parish church of Ilminster in our said county of Somerset...

Also all rents and annual profits whatsoever reserved on any leases or grants in the premises or any part thereof any way made as fully, freely and wholly and in as ample manner and form as any chantry priests, chaplains or any other Governors or ministers of the said late chantries or free chapel...had, held or enjoyed the same or any parcel thereof. And as fully, freely and wholly as they all and each came to our hands by reason or in title of a certain Act for the dissolution and putting an end to divers chantries, gilds, brotherhoods and free chapels passed and provided among others in our Parliament held at Westminster in the first year of our reign, or in any other manner, right or title and now are or ought to be or to have been in our hands.

Which messuages, lands, tenements, rents, reversions, services and all and singular the rest of the premises now extend to the clear yearly value of £20. 13s. 4d.

Habendum tenendum et gaudendum predicta omnia mesuagia [etc.], prefatis modernis Gubernatoribus possessionum revencionum et bonorum dicte Libere Scole de novo erecte, et successoribus suis imperpetuum Tenendum de nobis heredibus et successoribus nostris, ut de manerio nostro de Stalbrige in dicto comitatu nostro Dorsettensi, per fidelitatem tantum, in libero socagio Ac reddendo inde annuatim nobis, heredibus et successoribus nostris, tresdecim solidos et quatuor denarios legalis monete Anglie ad Curiam nostram Augmentationum et revencionum corone nostre, ad festum sancti Michaelis Archangeli singulis annis solvendos, pro omnibus reddititibus, serviciis et demandis quibuscumque.

[Grant of the rents as from Lady Day last past. Provision that the Governors may have a common seal and sue and be sued in their corporate name.]

Et ulterius de uberiori gracia nostra, ac ex certa sciencia et mero motu nostris, necnon de avisamento predicto, dedimus et concessimus, ac per presentes damus et concedimus prefatis modernis Gubernatoribus et successoribus suis, ac majori parti eorundem, plenam potestatem et auctoritatem nominandi et appunctuandi Pedagogum et Subpedagogum Scole predicte tociens quociens eadem Scola de pedagogo vel subpedagogo vacua fuerit; Et quod ipsi Gubernatores, cum advisamento Episcopi Bristollensis pro tempore existentis, de tempore in tempus, faciant et facere valeant et possint idonea et salubria statuta et ordinaciones in scriptis, concernencia et tangencia ordinacionem gubernacionem et direccionem Pedagogi et Subpedagogi ac Scolarium Scole predicte pro tempore existencium, ac stipendii et salarii eorundem Pedagogi et Subpedagogi, ac alia eandem Scolam, ac ordinacionem, gubernacionem, preservacionem et disposicionem reddituum et revencionum ad sustentacionem ejusdem Scole appunctuatorum et appunctuandorum, tangencia et concernencia Que quidem statuta et ordinaciones sic fienda volumus, concedimus et per presentes precipimus inviolabiliter observari de tempore in tempus imperpetuum.

To have, hold and enjoy all the aforesaid messuages [etc. as last above] to the aforesaid present Governors of the possessions, revenues and goods of the said Free School newly erected and their successors for ever To hold of us our heirs and successors as of our manor of Stalbridge in our said county of Dorset by fealty only, in free socage And rendering therefore yearly to us our heirs and successors 13*s*. 4*d*. of lawful money of England at our Court of the Augmentations and Revenues of our crown, to be paid at Michaelmas every year in place of all rents, services and demands whatsoever.

[Grant of the rents as from Lady Day last past. Provision that the Governors may have a common seal and sue and be sued in their corporate name.]

And further of our more ample grace, certain knowledge and mere motion, and also by the advice aforesaid, we have given and granted and by these presents give and grant to the aforesaid present Governors and their successors and the greater part of them full power and authority of nominating and appointing a Master and Under Master of the school aforesaid as often as the same school shall be void of a master or under master; And that the same Governors with the advice of the bishop of Bristol for the time being from time to time may make and shall have power to make fit and wholesome statutes and ordinances in writing concerning and touching the ordinance, governance, and direction of the Master and Under Master and scholars of the school aforesaid for the time being and of the stipend and salary of the same Master and Under Master and other things touching and concerning the same school and the ordering, governance, preservation and disposition of the rents and revenues appointed and to be appointed for the maintenance of the same school, Which statutes and ordinances so made we will, grant and by these presents command to be inviolably observed from time to time for ever.

Et ulterius de uberiori gracia nostra, et de avisamento predicto, dedimus et concessimus, ac per presentes damus et concedimus, prefatis modernis Gubernatoribus [etc.] et successoribus suis, licenciam specialem liberamque et licitam facultatem, potestatem et auctoritatem, habendi, recipiendi et perquirendi eis, et eorum successoribus imperpetuum, tam de nobis heredibus vel successoribus nostris, quam de aliis quibuscumque personis, et alia persona quacumque, maneria, messuagia, terras, tenementa, rectorias, decimas, aut alia hereditamenta quecumque, infra regnum Anglie, seu alibi infra dominaciones nostras, dummodo non excedant clarum annuum valorem viginti librarum, ultra dicta mesuagia, terras, tenementa et cetera premissa, prefatis Gubernatoribus et successoribus suis, ut prefertur, per nos in forma predicta concessa Statuto de terris et tenementis ad manum mortuam non ponendis, aut aliquo alio statuto, actu, ordinacione seu provisione, aut aliqua alia re, causa vel materia quacumque, in contrarium inde habito, facto, ordinato seu proviso in aliquo non obstante.

Et volumus ac per presentes concedimus prefatis modernis Gubernatoribus, quod habeant, et habebunt, has litteras nostras patentes sub magno sigillo nostro Anglie debite factas et sigillatas, absque fine seu feodo magno vel parvo nobis in Hanaperio nostro, seu alibi, ad usum nostrum, proinde quoquomodo reddendo, solvendo vel faciendo.

Eo quod expressa mencio de vero valore annuo, aut de certitudine premissorum, sive eorum alicujus, aut de aliis donis sive concessionibus per nos prefatis modernis Gubernatoribus et successoribus suis, ante hec tempora factis, in presentibus minime facta existit Aut aliquo statuto, actu, ordinacione, provisione, sive restriccione inde in contrarium facto, edito, ordinato sive proviso, aut aliqua alia re causa vel materia quacumque in aliquo non obstante.

In cujus rei testimonium has litteras nostras fieri fecimus patentes.

Teste me ipso apud Westmonasterium tercio decimo die Maii anno regni nostri quarto.

Per ipsum Regem et de data predicta, auctoritate parliamenti STANDYSSHE.

And further of our more ample grace, and by the advice aforesaid, we have given and granted and by these presents give and grant to the aforesaid present Governors of the possessions [etc.] and their successors special licence, free and lawful faculty, power and authority of having, taking and acquiring to them and their successors for ever, as well of us our heirs and successors as of any other persons or person whatsoever, manors, messuages, lands, tenements, rectories, tithes, or other hereditaments whatsoever in the kingdom of England, or elsewhere in our dominions, so long as they do not exceed the clear yearly value of £20, besides the said messuages, lands, tenements, and the rest of the premises granted by us in form aforesaid to the aforesaid Governors and their successors as aforesaid. Notwithstanding the statute against putting lands and tenements in mortmain or any other statute, act, ordinance or provision or any other thing, cause or matter whatsoever to the contrary had, done, ordained, or provided in any way.

And we will and by these presents grant to the aforesaid present Governors that they may and shall have these our letters patent duly made and sealed under our great seal of England without fine or fee, great or small, to be therefore rendered, paid or done to us in our Hanaper or elsewhere to our use in any way.

Notwithstanding the fact that express mention of the true yearly value or the certainty of the premises or any of them or of other gifts or grants by us to the aforesaid present Governors and their successors made before this is not made in these presents And notwithstanding any statute, act, ordinance, provision or restriction thereof to the contrary made, published, ordained or provided, or any other thing, cause or matter whatsoever in any way.

In witness whereof we have caused to be made these our letters patent.

Witness myself at Westminster the 13th day of May in the 4th year of our reign.

> By the King himself and of the date aforesaid by authority of Parliament STANDYSSHE.

Accounts of Governors of Sherborne School. 1553-61.

Shirborne Scole. *Anno Domini* 1553.

The accompte of George Swetnaham, Warden & Receptor of all the rents & Revenewys of the said Scole, from the Feast of Saynte Mighell th'archungell in the Sixte yere of the Reynge of Our late Soveraynge lorde Kynge Edwarde the Sixte, unto the said Feaste of Saynte Mighell in the Firste yere of the Reynge of our Soverayngne lady Marye, quene of Englonde, Fraunce & Irelonde &c.

Thaccompts of George Swetnaham and Jarveys Assheley
Annis 1553-1554.

	£	s.	d.
In primis, the said Accomptante accomptith of £13. 17s. 7d., by hym recevyd of John Yonge uppon the last accompte	13	17	7
Item of £7. 6s. 4d. of the rents assi[s]e in Bradforde Bryane & Barnardsley			
Item of 6s. 8d. for one messuage in Martocke			
Item of £6. 18s. 10d. for the rents of assi[s]e in Gyllyngham			
Item of 54s. for the Rente of Thorneton			
Item of 40s. for the Rente of Lychette matraverse			
Item of 40s. of the Rents of Symondsborugh			
	21	5	10
Item of 41s. 8d. in the full payment of the Fine of William Cowerde			
Item of 33s. 4d. in full payment of the fyne of Cristiane Kneplocke			

Fines and Court Fees

	£	s.	d.
Item of 10s. in the full payment of the fyne of William Asshecote			
Item of £3 in parte of payment of the fyne of John Barons			
Item of 20d. for the heryotte of William Clyffe			
	7	6	8
Summa totalis recepte	42	10	1

(1 b.) Whereof the said Accomptante praieth to be allowed of £20 paide to the Scole mayster & Ussher for their hole yeres wages . . . 20 0 0

Item for 2 yeres rente paid to the Quenys Hyghnes   26 8

,, for 2 acquytaunces for the same . . .   6

,, paid for the Steuerds Fee 13 4

,, for the rente of the Scole-house . . .   4

,, allowed for reparacions of the Ferme of Bradforde 6 4

,, paid to Baller for Sawyng of tymber in the parke for the Schole 3 4

,, for expences of the Courts this yere and for the recepte of the rents 11 2

,, for paper & parchement   4

Summa totalis allocationis . . . 23 2 0

Liberacio denariorum ad manus Jarvacii Assheley super compotum 19 8 1

       Et eligerunt in officium Gardiani Ricardum Coper.

[Delivery of cash to the hands of Gervase Ashley at the account 19 8 1

       And they elected Richard Cooper to the office of Warden.]

Cardinal Pole's Convocation Articles.
1 Jan. 1557–8.

[Wilkins, *Concilia*, IV. p. 158.]

De ecclesiis cathedralibus et aliis.

XXII. Ut in singulis praedictarum ecclesiarum sint sexaginta, vel plures pueri ex beneficiis appropriatis sustentandi, ibique grammaticam discant, qui clero postea inserviant.

Royal Injunctions. 1559.

[Wilkins, *Concilia*, IV. p. 182.]

Injunctions given by the Queen's Majesty, concerning both the clergy and laity of this realm, published A.D. 1559, being the first year of the reign of our Sovereign lady Queen Elizabeth.

The queen's most royal majesty, by the advice of her most honourable council, intending the advancement of the true honour of Almighty God, the suppression of superstition throughout all her highness's realms and dominions, and to plant true religion to the extirpation of all hypocrisie, enormities, and abuses (as to her duty appertaineth) doth minister unto her loving subjects these godly injunctions hereafter following.

XII. And, to the intent, that learned men may hereafter spring the more, for the execution of the premises, every parson, vicar, clerk, or beneficed man within this deanry having yearly to dispend in benefices and other promotions of the church £100, shall give £3. 6s. 8d. in exhibition to one scholar in either of the universities; and for as many £100 more as he may dispend, to so many scholars more shall give like exhibition in the University of Oxford or Cambridge, or

Cardinal Pole's Convocation Articles.
1 *Jan.* 1557–8.

Of cathedrals and other churches.

XXII. That in each of the said churches there shall be 60 or more boys maintained out of benefices appropriated for the purpose, to learn grammar there, and afterwards serve the clergy.

some grammar-school, which, after they have profited in good learning, may be partners of their patrons cure and charge, as well in preaching, as otherwise in executing of their offices, or may, when time shall be, otherwise profit the commonweal with their counsel and wisdom.

XXXIX. Item, that every schoolmaster and teacher shall teach the Grammar set forth by King Henry VIII of noble memory, and continued in the time of king Edward VI and none other.

XL. Item, that no man shall take upon him to teach, but such as shall be allowed by the ordinary, and found meet as well for his learning and dexterity in teaching, as for sober and honest conversation, and also for right understanding of God's true religion.

XLI. Item, that all teachers of children shall stir and move them to love and do reverence to God's true religion now truly set forth by public authority.

XLII. Item, that they shall accustom their scholars reverently to learn such sentences of scripture, as shall be most expedient to induce them to all godliness.

XLIII. Item, forasmuch as in these latter days many have been made priests, being children, and otherwise utterly unlearned, so that they could read ne say mattens or mass; the ordinaries shall not admit any such to any cure or spiritual function.

Statutes of Westminster School. 1560.

[Cath. Commission Report, 1854, p. (59), from Pat. 2 Eliz. pt xi.]

Elizabetha Dei gratia Angliae, Franciae, et Hiberniae Regina, Fidei Defensor etc., dilectis nobis in Christo Decano et Capitulo nostrae ecclesiae collegiatae beati Petri Westmonasteriensis, Salutem in Jesu Salvatore.

Proportio seu Distributio Collegii Beati Petri Westmonasteriensis ab illustrissima Regina Elizabetha fundati:

Decanus Collegii unus esto, qui sit presbyter et concionator.

Praebendarii duodecim. Iidem sint presbyteri et concionatores.

Lector theologiae unus.

Sint viginti novem ad sanctum Dei cultum pie et sacrosancte in ecclesia collegiata quotidie exequendum, quorum,

6. Presbyteri sex, ex quibus unus sit praecentor.
12. Clerici duodecim.
1. Unus sit choristarum doctor.
10. Decem pueri symphoniaci sive choristae.

Praeceptores duo ad erudiendam juventutem.

Discipuli grammatici quadraginta.

Pauperes duodecim.

CAP. 4. De duobus Praeceptoribus Puerorum, deque eorum officio.

Sint duo praeceptores, quorum alter archididascalus vocetur. Ille grammatices vel artium magister, hic baccalaureus artium ad minimum sit, si commode fieri potest. Horum gubernationi omnes discipuli subjecti sunto, utrique religiosi, docti, honesti, et laboriosi sint, ut pios, eruditos, ingenuos, et studiosos efficiant discipulos. Hos praeceptores eligent alternis vicibus decanus Ecclesiae Christi Oxonii et magister collegii Sanctae Trinitatis Cantabrigiae, cum consensu decani West-

Statutes of Westminster School. 1560.

Elizabeth, by the grace of God of England, France, and Ireland queen, defender of the faith, etc. to our beloved in Christ the Dean and Chapter of our collegiate church of the Blessed Peter of Westminster, Health in Jesu the Saviour.

The rate or distribution of the college of the Blessed Peter at Westminster, founded by the most illustrious Queen Elizabeth:

There shall be a Dean of the college, who shall be a priest and a preacher.

12 Prebendaries. They shall be priests and preachers.

A Reader of Theology.

There shall be 29 for the daily performance piously and holily of the holy worship of God in the said collegiate church, of whom

  6 shall be priests, and one of them Precentor.

  12 Clerks.

   1 Teacher of the choristers.

  10 Singing boys or choristers.

   2 Masters to educate the youth.

  40 Grammar scholars.

  12 Poor men.

CHAPTER 4. The two Masters of the Boys and their Duty.

There shall be two masters, one of whom shall be called Head Master. The one shall be a master of grammar or of arts, the other a bachelor of arts at least, if this can conveniently be done. All the scholars shall be under their government, both of them shall be religious, learned, honourable and painstaking, so that they may make their pupils pious, learned, gentlemanly and industrious. The Dean of Christ Church, Oxford, and the Master of Trinity College, Cambridge, shall in turn elect these masters, with the consent of the Dean

monasteriensis. Horum officium sit non solum grammaticam Latinam, Graecam, et Hebraicam literasque humaniores, poetas et oratores docere, et diligenter examinare, sed etiam puerorum mores instruere et corrigere, ut modeste se gerant tam in templo, schola, aula, et cubiculo, quam in omnibus progressibus et lusibus, ut facies, manus laventur, capita comantur, crines ac ungues abradantur, vestes lineae laneaeque, togae, caligae et calcei, munde nitide et honeste serventur, ne pediculi aut ullae sordes vel seipsos aut socios inficiant aut offendant, et ne unquam absque venia extra ambitum collegii exeant. Monitores varios e gravioribus discipulis praeterea constituant, qui reliquorum mores ubique inspiciant ac notant, ne quid uspiam indecori aut sordidi perpetretur. Si quis monitorum deliquerit, aut in officio negligenter se gesserit, aspere in aliorum exemplum vapulet.

CAP. 5. De Discipulorum duplici Electione.

Cum discipuli sunt numero 40, volumus ut in his eligendis praecipua ratio habeatur docilis ingenii, bonae indolis, doctrinae, virtutis et inopiae: et quo magis quisque ex eligendorum numero his rebus caeteros antecellat, eo magis (uti aequum est) praeferatur, et collegii choristae firmariorumque filii, si modo caetera respondeant, semper aliis praeferantur. Dies lunae post festum divi Petri et Pauli dies electionis esto. Electores sint decanus collegii nostri Westmonasteriensis, decanus Ecclesiae Christi Oxonie, et magister collegii Sanctae Trinitatis Cantabrigie, aut eorum vicarii. Hi tres alios tres examinatores singuli singulos et suo collegio artium magistros secum adjungant, et ludimagistrum scholae Westmonasteriensis. Hi tres praefecti, aut eorum vicarii, et tres examinatores cum ludimagistro die lunae proximo post festum divi Petri et Pauli, hora octava in aula, triclinio, aut aliquo idoneo loco intra collegium nostrum Westmonasteriense conveniant: quo tempore ludimagister discipulos nostros supremae classis doctrina praestantissimos coram adducet; his themata per examinatores

of Westminster. Their duty shall be not only to teach Latin, Greek and Hebrew Grammar, and the humanities, poets and orators, and diligently to examine in them, but also to build up and correct the boys' conduct, to see that they behave themselves properly in church, school, hall and chamber, as well as in all walks and games, that their faces and hands are washed, their heads combed, their hair and nails cut, their clothes both linen and woollen, gowns, stockings and shoes kept clean, neat, and like a gentleman's, and so that lice or other dirt may not infect or offend themselves or their companions, and that they never go out of the college precincts without leave. They shall further appoint various monitors from the gravest scholars to oversee and note the behaviour of the rest everywhere and prevent anything improper or dirty being done. If any monitor commits an offence or neglects to perform his duty he shall be severely flogged as an example to others.

CHAPTER 5. The twofold Election of Scholars.

The scholars being 40 in number, we will that in their election regard shall chiefly be had to their teachableness, the goodness of their disposition, their learning, good behaviour and poverty; and the more any of the candidates excels the rest in these respects, the more, as is right, he shall be preferred; and the choristers of the college and the sons of tenants of the college property, if they answer to the other requirements, shall always have the preference. Election day shall be Monday after St Peter and St Paul's day [29 June]. The electors shall be the Dean of our college of Westminster, the Dean of Christ Church, Oxford, and the Master of Trinity College, Cambridge, or their deputies. These three shall join with themselves three other examiners, each a master of arts of his own college, and the Schoolmaster of Westminster School. These three Heads, or their deputies, and three examiners with the Schoolmaster shall meet on Monday next after St Peter and St Paul's day, at 8 o'clock, in the hall, dining-room, or other suitable place within our college of Westminster, when the Schoolmaster shall bring before them the best-learned of our scholars of the highest form. They shall be set themes by the Examiners, on

tradentur, de quibus proximo die sequente hora secunda pomeridiana, tum carmine tum oratione soluta, quisque memoriter aut scripto de propositis thematibus quid sentiat coram electoribus in medium proferet. Interim diebus (viz. lunae et Martis) quicunque in nostros discipulos cooptari cupiunt a dictis examinatoribus examinabuntur, quid in grammatica, quid in literis humanioribus, quid scribendo possint. Et singuli nomina sua, parentelam, aetatem, comitatum, et oppidum in quo nati sunt, propria manu scribent. Et nec ante octavum annum quisquam admittatur in discipulum, nec post decimum octavum annum in schola nostra permaneat. His ita gestis die mercurii proximo sequente mane hora octava fiet electio eorum primum qui ad academias Cantabrigiae et Oxonii promovebuntur (juxta syngraphas inter haec tria regalia collegia hac de re conscriptas), deinde eorum qui in nostram scholam Westmonasteriensem sunt admittendi : solum autem tales in nostram scholam recipiendi sunt, qui ad minimum et memoriter octo partes grammaticae probe didicerint, et qui scribere saltem mediocriter noverint.

Modus autem Electionis esto.

[The Master of Trinity College, Cambridge, names those to be elected there, and if three Examiners or the two Deans agree he is elected. So with Christ Church and Westminster. Failing three, two suffice. The names of those elected are to be placed in order on three Indentures written by the Schoolmaster.]

Appendix pro Discipulorum Electione in Collegium
Westmonasterii.

Neminem in collegium nostrum qui in dicta schola nostra annum integrum ante tempus eleccionis educatus non fuerit, nec plures uno ex eodem comitatu in una eleccione eligi aut admitti volumus. Preterea nullus heres qui iam sit, aut qui futurus sit patre mortuo heres, cuius hereditas summam decem librarum excesserit in hunc numerum cooptetur. Electi autem quamprimum loca vacua fuerint [adepti?] suo ordine flexis

which at 2 p.m. next day each of them shall give out before the electors, in verse and prose, by heart or in writing, his sentiments on the themes set. Meanwhile, viz. on Monday and Tuesday, all who want to be elected among our scholars shall be examined by the said examiners on their proficiency in grammar, the humanities, and writing. And each of them shall write with his own hand his name, his parentage, age, and the county and town in which he was born. None shall be admitted a scholar before he is seven years old, nor remain in our school after he is 18. After this, on the Wednesday following, at 8 a.m., the Election shall take place, first of those who are to be promoted to the Universities of Cambridge and Oxford (in accordance with the agreements made as to this between the three royal colleges), and next of those who are to be admitted to our school of Westminster: such only are to be received into our school who have thoroughly learnt by heart at least the eight parts of speech and can know how to write at least moderately well.

This shall be the method of electing.

Appendix for the Election of Scholars to Westminister College.

We will that no one should be elected into our College who has not been educated in our said school for a whole year before the date of election, and not more than one shall be elected out of the same county in one election. Further, none shall be chosen into this number who is already heir, or who will be heir on his father's death, to an inheritance of more than £10 [a year]. Those elected shall as soon as there are vacant places be admitted in order kneeling, by the Dean or in

genibus a decano vel, eo absente, prodecano publice in aula, aut ante prandium, aut ante cenam, admittantur his verbis, Ego N. decanus, vel prodecanus, huius collegiate ecclesie admitto te N. in discipulum scholarem huius collegii, iuxta statuta eiusdem. In nomine Patris et Filii et Spiritus Sancti. Amen.

CAP. 6. De Pensionariis, Tutoribus et Pupillis.

Pensionarii ut studiorum socii in collegium recipiantur, sed ita ut nec moribus honestis, nec studiis desint; eisdem legibus teneantur, quibus discipuli, eadem ab his requirantur, eandem obedientiam praestent; sed ut neque munera, nec imperitia obsint, provideatur, ut neque decano plures quam sex, neque singulis praebendariis plures duobus, neque ludimagistro plures quatuor, neque hypodidascalo plures duobus pensionariis sint. Et ut hi solum in collegium admittantur qui prodecani unius praebendarii et ludimagistri judicio ad minimum octo orationis partes memoriter probe didicerint, et qui scribere saltem mediocriter noverint, et de quorum indole, honestis moribus, et in literis felici progressu bonam spem conceperint. Qui ita a prodecano alio praebendario et ludimagistro examinati sunt, hos solum consensu decani in collegium admitti volumus. Eundem modum in oppidanis, peregrinis, et aliis in scholam nostram recipiendis et admittendis observari volumus. Et ne nimio scholarium numero praeceptores onerentur, statuimus ne ex omni genere scholarium plures centum viginti, praeter choristas, unquam in scholam admittantur, aut in eadem esse permittantur.

CAP. 9. De Cultu Dei.

De Choristis et Choristarum Magistro.

Statuimus et ordinamus ut in ecclesia nostra praedicta sint decem choristae, pueri tenerae aetatis et vocibus sonoris ad cantandum, et ad artem musicam discendam, et etiam ad

his absence the Sub-dean, publicly in hall, either before dinner or before supper, in these words, 'I (Name), Dean, or Sub-dean, of this collegiate church, admit thee (Name) a pupil scholar of this College, according to the statutes of the same. In the name of the Father and the Son and the Holy Ghost. Amen.'

Chapter 6. Pensioners, Tutors and Wards.

Pensioners [paying scholars] may be received into college as companions in study on condition that they are not deficient in good character or in learning. They shall be bound by the same laws as the scholars, the same things shall be required of them, and they shall render the same obedience. But that neither money nor ignorance may be a difficulty, it is provided that the Dean may have no more than six, no Prebendary more than two, the Schoolmaster no more than four, and the Usher no more than two pensioners. And those only shall be admitted into college who in the judgment of the Sub-dean, a Prebendary and the Schoolmaster have thoroughly learnt by heart the eight parts of speech, and know how to write at least moderately well, and of whose disposition, good conduct, and happy progress in learning there is good hope. We will that those only who have been so examined shall, with the Dean's consent, be admitted to college. The same standard we will shall be observed in the reception and admission of town boys, strangers and others into our school. And to prevent the masters being overburdened by the number of scholars, we decree that not more than 120 of all kinds of scholars, besides the choristers, shall ever be admitted into the school or allowed to stay in it.

Chapter 9. Divine Worship.

The Choristers and the Choristers' Master.

We decree and ordain that there shall be in our church aforesaid 10 choristers, boys of tender age with clear voices, able to sing and learn the art of music and to play on musical

musica instrumenta pulsanda apti, qui choro inserviant, ministrent, et cantent. Ad hos praeclare instituendos, unus eligatur qui sit honestae famae, vitae probae, religionis sincerae, artis musicae peritus, et ad cantandum et musica instrumenta pulsanda exercitatus, qui pueris in praedictis scientiis et exercitiis docendis aliisque muniis in choro obeundis studiose vacabit. Hunc magistrum choristarum appellari volumus. Cui muneri doctores et baccalaureos musices aliis praeferendos censemus.

Volumus etiam quoties eum ab ecclesia nostra abesse contingat, alterum substituat a decano, vel eo absente prodecano approbandum. Prospiciat item puerorum saluti, quorum et in literis (donec ut in scholam nostram admittantur, apti censebuntur) et in morum modestia et in convictu educationem et liberalem institutionem illius fidei et industriae committimus. Quod si negligens et in docendo desidiosus, aut in salute puerorum et recta eorum educatione minime providus et circumspectus, et ideo non tolerandus inveniatur, post trinam admonitionem (si se non emendaverit) ab officio deponatur. Qui quidem choristarum magister ad officium suum per se fideliter obeundum juramento etiam adigetur. Choristae postquam octo orationis partes memoriter didicerint et scribere mediocriter noverint, ad scholam nostram ut melius in grammatica proficiant singulis diebus profestis accedant, ibique duabus ad minimum horis maneant, et a praeceptoribus instituantur.

De Pueris Grammaticis.

Pueri item grammatici quotidie mane hora 5ta priusquam cubiculum exeunt, vesperi autem hora octava antequam cubitum petant, in cubiculo, genibus flexis, matutinas et vespertinas preces invicem clare et religiose dicant...

instruments, who shall serve the choir, minister and sing. For their good instruction one shall be elected of good reputation, upright life, sincere religion, learned in music and skilled in singing and playing on musical instruments, and he shall diligently devote his time to teaching the boys the aforesaid sciences and exercises and in the performance of the other duties in choir. We will that he shall be called master of the choristers. We think that for this office doctors and bachelors of music should be preferred to others.

We will that whenever he shall be absent from our church he shall substitute another, to be approved by the Dean, or in his absence the Sub-dean. He shall also look after the boys' health, and we commit to his trust and care their education and liberal instruction in grammar (until they shall be thought fit to be admitted to our school) and in modesty of behaviour and manners. If he is negligent or idle in teaching or not prudent and careful of the boys' health or their right education, and therefore found intolerable, he shall, if after three warnings he does not amend, be put out from his office. The Choristers' Master shall be bound by oath faithfully to perform his duty in person. The choristers, after they have learnt the eight parts of speech by heart and know how to write fairly well, shall come to our school every week-day so as to become more proficient in grammar, and shall stay there for two hours at least and be instructed by the masters.

The Grammar Boys.

The grammar boys shall daily at 5 a.m., before they leave their chamber, and at 8 p.m. before they go to bed, kneeling in their chamber, clearly and devoutly say in turns morning and evening prayers...

[The prayers are set out in Latin. The General Confession, the Lord's Prayer, O come let us sing unto the Lord, the hymn 'Jam lucis orto sidere' etc., and the Graces before and after meals are also set out. They are the same as those in use at Winchester.]

CAP. 10. De Discipulorum Institutione et Ordine.

Discipuli omnes in uno aut duobus cubiculis bini in uno lecto pernoctent.

Hora 5ta unus ex cubiculi praepositis, qui omnes quatuor sunt numero, qui hoc muneris illa hebdomada obierit, Surgite intonet. Illi omnes statim consurgant fundentes, flexis genibus, matutinas preces, quas suis vicibus unusquisque ordiatur, ac caeteri omnes alternis versibus subsequantur, dicentes, Domine sancte Pater Omnipotens aeterne Deus, ut in cap. 10 de cultu Dei etc.

Finitis precibus lectos sternant. Inde unusquisque, quantum pulveris et sordium sub suo lecto est, in cubiculi medium proferat, quem deinde variis cubiculi locis conspersum, quatuor ex omni numero, ad hoc a praeposito designati, in unum acervum redigant, exportentque.

Tum omnes bini longo ordine lavatum manus descendant; a lavando reversi scholam ingrediantur, ac suum locum quisque capessat.

Preces in Schola dicendae.

Hora sexta ingrediatur praeceptor ac superiore scholae parte flexis genibus preces sequentes ordiatur; subsequantur discipuli alternis versibus Ps. 67....

His finitis praeceptor ad primam et infimam classem descendat, et aliquam orationis partem ac verbi suo ordine audiat. Progrediatur a prima classe ad secundam, a secunda ad tertiam, a tertia (si visum fuerit) ad quartam, quae in illius parte sedeat ad septimam usque horam; ibi si quid obscurius oriatur, examinandum.

Alter interim ex scholae praepositis, cuique ordini tam in archididascali quam in hypodidascali parte praepositos adiens, ab eis a matutinis precibus absentium nomina descripta auferat et hypodidascalo tradat. Alius item praepositus (qui solus semper hoc munus obit) singulorum manus et facies diligenter

CHAPTER 10. The Teaching and Ordering of the Scholars.

All the scholars shall spend the night in one or two chambers, two in a bed.

At 5 o'clock that one of the Monitors of Chamber (who shall be four in number) who shall be in course for that week, shall intone 'Get up.' They shall immediately all get up and, kneeling down, say Morning Prayers, which each shall begin in turn, and all the rest follow, in alternate verses, saying, 'O Lord, holy father, almighty, everlasting God,' as in Chapter 10 On Divine worship.

Prayers finished they shall make their beds. Then each shall take any dust or dirt there may be under his bed into the middle of the chamber, which, after being placed in various parts of the chamber, shall then be swept up into a heap by four boys, appointed by the Monitor, and carried out.

Then two and two in a long line they shall all go down to wash their hands; when they come back from washing they shall go into school and each take his place.

Prayers to be said in School.

At 6 o'clock the Master shall come in and, kneeling at the top of the school, begin the following prayers, the boys following in alternate verses. [Ps. 67 and responses after.]

Prayers finished, the Master shall go down to the First or lowest class and hear a part of speech and of a verb in its turn. He shall pass on from the First class to the Second, from the Second to the Third, from the Third, if he thinks fit, to the Fourth, which sits in his part of the school till 7 o'clock, to examine if any obscurity arises.

Meanwhile one of the Prefects of School goes to the head of each form in the Head Master's as well as in the Usher's part, and gets from them in writing the names of those absent from morning prayers and hands them to the Usher. Another Prefect (who always performs this duty by himself) carefully inspects each boy's hands and face, to see if they have come

intuitus, si qui forte illotis manibus ad scholam accesserunt, hos ille ingrediente archididascalo statim offerat. Hic ordo quotidie observetur.

Hora septima ordo quartus ab hypodidascalo ad archididascali partem se conferat. Ingrediatur scholam, huic omnes omnium ordinum praepositi suos post septimam absentes tradant. Ac unus etiam e scholae praepositis eorum nomina qui pridie post sextam et septimam vespertinam a schola abfuerant archididascalo suos, hypodidascalo item suos tradat. Inde omnes ordines quae sibi praelecta fuerant memoriter reddant, eo ordine ut custos semper incipiat, et caeteros recitantes diligenter observet.

Hora 8va archididascalus suis sententiam aliquam quartae classi vertendam, quintae variandam, sextae et septimae versibus concludendam proponat, cujus ab ore custos primus accepit, et primus vertit. Hypodidascalus item tertiae et secundae classi sententiam aliquam proponat vertendam, et primae quoque, sed eam brevissimam.

Vulgaria exhibita a singulis scribantur eodem mane, quae subsequente die et ordinate et memoriter recitent, ante horam nonam aut circiter. Primum superioris cujusque ordinis custos classi sibi proximae lectionem memoriter recitet et exponat. Deinde archididascalus suis, hypodidascalus item suis eandem praelegat.

In diebus Lunae et Mercurii quatuor superiores ordines de proposito illis themate soluta oratione scribant; ex secunda ordine, tertio et primo sibi quisque sententiam proponat et vertat.

In diebus Martis et Jovis superiores ordines themata sibi proposita carminibus concludant, reliqui duo soluta oratione eadem conscribant.

In diebus Lunae et Martis praelegat ludimagister:

Ordini
- 4°. Terentium, Salustium et Graecam grammaticam.
- 5°. Justinum, Ciceronem de Amicitia, et Isocratem.
- 6" et 7°. Caesaris Commentaria, Titum Livium, Demosthenem et Homerum.

with unwashed hands to school, and when the Head Master comes in immediately presents them to him. This order shall be kept every day.

At 7 o'clock the Fourth Form shall transfer itself from the Usher's part to the Head Master's. He shall come into school, and all the heads of each form shall after 7 o'clock hand him the names of their absents. And one of the Prefects of School shall hand the names of those who were absent from school after 6 and 7 o'clock in the evening on the day before to the Head Master and Usher respectively. Then all the classes shall say by heart what has been read to them in this order; viz. the Custos shall always begin and shall carefully observe the rest saying it afterwards.

At 8 o'clock the Head Master shall set some sentence to the Fourth Class to translate, to the Fifth to vary, and to the Sixth and Seventh to turn into verse. The Custos shall take it from his lips and translate it first. The Usher too shall set some sentence to the Third and Second Form to translate, and to the First also, but for them it shall be very short.

The vulguses shown up by each shall be written on the same morning, and next day they shall say it in order by heart, before or about 9 o'clock. The Custos of each of the upper forms shall first say by heart the lesson of the form next to him and explain it. Then the Head Master shall read the same lesson to his boys as the Usher to his.

On Mondays and Wednesdays the four highest forms shall write a prose on a theme set them; in the Second, Third, and First Form each shall set himself a sentence and translate it into Latin.

On Tuesdays and Thursdays the higher forms shall round off the themes set them in verse, the other two shall write them in prose.

On Mondays and Tuesdays the Schoolmaster shall read

To Form
{
Fourth, Terence, Sallust, and Greek Grammar.
Fifth, Justin, Cicero on Friendship, and Isocrates.
Sixth and Seventh, Caesar's Commentaries, Livy, Demosthenes and Homer.
}

Iisdem diebus praelegat praeceptor:

Ordini
- 3°. Terentium, Salustium.
- 2°. Terentium, aut Aesopi Fabulas.
- 1°. Ludovicum Vivem, aut Catonem.

In diebus Mercurii et Jovis praelegat ludimagister:
- 4°. Ovidium de Tristibus, Ciceronem de Officiis, et Luciani Dialogos Graecos.
- 5°. Ovidium Metamorphises, aut Plutarchum Graece.
- 6° et 7°. Virgilium et Homerum.

Iisdem diebus praelegat praeceptor:
- 3°. Ciceronis Epistolas per Sturmium selectas.
- 2°. Dialogos Sacros, Erasmi Colloquia.
- 1°. Ludovicum Vivem, Corderii Dialogos aut Confabulationes Pueriles.

Ex quibus lectionibus pueri excerpant flores, phrases, vel dicendi locutiones, item antitheta, epitheta, synonima, proverbia, similitudines, comparationes, historias, descriptiones temporis, loci, personarum, fabulas, dicteria, schemata, apothegmata.

Hora nona ubi suis praelegerint, detur discipulis spatium meditandi lectiones.

Illi vero ex utraque parte scholae erecte stantes praeeuntem aliquem pro arbitrio praepositi designatum sequantur.

Preces dicendae in Schola ante Prandium, ante Coenam, et ante Lusum....

Inde bini omnes ordine longo in aulam modeste procedant et ex utraque parte in aula erecti stent usque dum gratiae ante prandium agantur.

Tres aut plures e discipulis a ludimagistro assignati in medio aule ante mensam stent, quorum unus pro arbitrio Decani, prodecani aut ejus locum gerentis, aut ludimagistri gratias agere et mensam consecrare incipiat, et reliqui omnes tum praesentes uno ore respondeant ut supra cap. 10 De cultu Dei.

Finito prandio actisque gratiis ut praescribitur, discipuli eodem quo exibant modo, ad scholam revertantur. Idemque ordo quocunque incederint observetur.

On those days the Usher shall read

To Form
{ Third, Terence, Sallust.
Second, Terence or Aesop's Fables.
First, Ludovico Vives or Cato.

On Wednesdays and Thursdays the Schoolmaster shall read to the

>Fourth, Ovid's Tristia, Cicero on Duty, and Lucian's Dialogues in Greek.

>Fifth, Ovid's Metamorphoses, or Plutarch in Greek.

>Sixth and Seventh, Virgil and Homer.

On those days the Usher shall read to the

>Third, Sturmius' Select Epistles of Cicero.

>Second, Sacred Dialogues, Erasmus' Conversations.

>First, Ludovico Vives, Corderius' Dialogues, or Boys' Talks.

From these lessons the boys shall gather the flowers, phrases or idioms, also antitheses, epithets, synonyms, proverbs, similes, comparisons, stories, descriptions of seasons, places, persons, fables, sayings, figures of speech, apophthegms.

At 9, when they have read the lesson to their forms, an interval should be given to the pupils to think over the lessons. Then they, standing upright in either part of the school, shall follow one who leads, appointed at the discretion of the Monitor. The prayers to be said in school before dinner, supper and play....

Then two and two in a long line they shall go quietly to Hall and stand on either side of Hall till grace before meat is said.

Three or more of the scholars appointed by the Schoolmaster shall stand before the table in the middle of Hall, one of whom, at the selection of the Dean or Sub-dean or his vicegerent, or the School-master, shall begin to say grace and consecrate the table, and all the rest then present shall say the responses together as above in Chapter 10 Of Divine worship.

Dinner done and grace said as above-written the scholars shall return to school in the same way as they left it. And the same order shall be observed wherever they go.

Hora prima ingrediatur hypodidascalus, atque ea quae ante prandium quartae classi praelegerit archididascalus ab eadem tum sua parte inferiore usque ad primam sedente reposcet, et singulas orationis partes discutiat; eidem primo ingredienti, quatuor primorum ordinum praepositi, suorum nomina absentium exhibeant.

Hora 2da quarta classis in suam propriam sedem migret; jamque ingredienti magistro singulorum ordinum praepositi suos tradat absentes. Archididascalus quod spatii inter 2^{am} et 4^{am} datur, in quinto, sexto, septimoque ordine examinando insumat, et ex proposita lectione vulgaria ad linguae Latinae exercitationem condat, ita tamen ut dimidia hora ante quartam trium supremorum ordinum praepositi, sua et sociorum themata eidem tradant, quae examinabit diligenter.

Quoniam vero canendi peritia et usum plurimum valere deprehenditur ad claram et distinctam vocis elocutionem, volumus omnes scholae grammaticae discipulos binas horas singulis septimanis, vizt, feriis 3^a et 5ta inter 2^m et 3^m post meridiem, in arte musica collocare, in qua arte quo melius informentur volumus magistrum choristarum illos discipulos scholae grammaticae diligenter instruere et eundem magistrum a singulis eorum (exceptis illis qui antea choristae fuerunt) sex denarios singulis trimestribus a tutoribus percipere.

Hora 4ta, archididascalus, si velit, exeat, redeat ante 5^{tam}.

Hora 5ta vel ante, ingrediente archididascalo, exeat ad dimidium horae hypodidascalus. Quo tempore reddant ex his authoribus, quantum a magistro est constitutum, id rogante uno scholae praeposito.

Ordo
- 4^{tus}. Ex figuris in grammatica et carminum ratione.
- 5^{tus}. Valerium Maximum, Luciani Flores, Epistolas Ciceronis, Susenbrotum.
- 6^{tus}. Graecam:
- 7^{mus}. Hebraicam grammaticam cum praelectione Psalmorum in utroque idiomate, vizt Graeco et Hebraico.

Westminster School Time-Table, 1560

At 1 o'clock the Usher shall come in, and shall ask the Fourth Form, who are there until one, sitting in his part, what the Master read before dinner, and discuss each part of speech with them; the heads of the first four classes shall, when he comes in, show him the names of those absent.

At 2 o'clock the Fourth Form shall go to their own seats, and, the Master now coming in, the heads of each class shall hand him the names of those absent. The Head Master shall spend the time between 2 and 4 o'clock in examining the Fifth, Sixth and Seventh Forms, and shall make some vulguses out of the lesson set to exercise them in Latin, so however that half an hour before four the heads of the three upper forms shall bring up their own and the other boys' themes, which he shall examine carefully.

As a knowledge of singing is found to be of the greatest use for a clear and distinct elocution, we will that all the pupils in the Grammar School shall spend two hours each week, viz. from 2 to 3 p.m. on Wednesdays and Fridays, in the art of music, and for their better instruction in that art we will that the choristers' master shall carefully teach the pupils of the Grammar School, and the same master shall receive from each of them (except those who have been choristers) 6d. for each term from their tutors.

At 4 o'clock the Head Master may, if he wishes, go out of school, returning before 5 o'clock.

At 5 or before, when the Head Master comes into school, the Usher may go out for half an hour.

During this time they shall say out of these authors as much as the Master has set them, one of the Monitors of School asking for it;

Form Fourth: from figures of speech and the method of verse-making.

Form Fifth: Valerius Maximus, Flowers of Lucian, Cicero's Epistles, Susenbrotus.

Form Sixth, Greek; Seventh, Hebrew Grammar, with a lesson in the Psalms in both languages, viz. Greek and Hebrew.

Praeceptori {
  Suorum absentes exhibeantur.
  Tertii ordinis themata.
  Secundi sententiae quas quisque sibi proposuerit et in Latinum sermonem verterit.
}

Tum unusquisque quantum sibi ex regulis praescriptum erat memoriter dicat, tum etiam vulgaria, quo melius regulae grammatices intelligantur a pueris, conficiantur, ut inde Latinus sermo omni ratione familior fiat.

Hora 6ta, eodem exeant et revertantur ordine, quo ante prandium, eundemque in aula observent.

Hora 7ma, duo qui ex supremo ordine ad ceteras classes instruendas a ludimagistro designati sunt, suas provincias aggrediantur, et fidei suae commissos, in lectionibus exponendis et sententiis e vernaculo sermone in Latinum vertendis per dimidium horae spatium exerceant.

Item dictata eodem die a praeceptore recitent et ordinent.

Singularum classium praepositi hoc muneris subeant, ita ut scholae moderatores animadvertant in omnes ad perfectam in literis et morum compositionem.

Deinde precibus finitis, potum in aulam dimittantur.

Hora 8va semper cubitum eant, postquam preces supplices fuderint.

Preces Vespertinae in cubiculo dicendae priusquam Lectum petant.

[Prayers set out.]

Die Veneris Correctiones.

Diebus Veneris post lectionem, quam pridie habuerant, recitatam, qui grave aliquod crimen commiserunt, accusantur : aequum enim est malefactorum dignas dent poenas. Deinde singuli lectiones, quas illa hebdomada praelegerunt, magna cum diligentia recitent, ita ut partim ante prandium usque ad 11^m, partim a prima ad 2^{am} horam, nihilque eorum, quae per totam septimanam mane praelegerint omittatur.

Post 3^{am}, quicquid eadem hebdomada inter 4^m et 5^{am} didicerint doctoribus reddant.

To the Usher the absences of his forms shall be shown; the themes of the Third Form; and the Sentences of the Second Form which each has set himself and turned into Latin.

Then every boy shall say by heart such part of the rules as has been prescribed for him, then too vulguses shall be made by the boys so that they may better understand the rules of grammar, and so the Latin language become familiar in every way.

At 6 o'clock they shall go out and return in the same order as before dinner and observe the same order in Hall.

At 7 o'clock two of the highest form who have been appointed by the Schoolmaster to teach the rest of the forms shall get their subjects together and practise those committed to their charge for half-an-hour in explaining what has been read to them and in turning sentences from English into Latin. Also they shall read aloud and put in order what has been dictated that day by the Usher. The heads of each class shall perform this duty, but the Monitors of the School shall pay attention to all so as to render them perfect in learning and behaviour.

Then when prayers are over they shall be dismissed to Hall to drink.

At 8 o'clock they shall always go to bed, after they have said prayers.

Evening Prayers to be said in chamber before going to bed. [Prayers set out.]

Punishments on Friday.

On Fridays, after saying the lesson which they had set the day before, those who have committed any grave crime are accused; for it is right that they should pay the penalties of evil-doers. Then everyone is to repeat with the greatest diligence the lessons which have been read to them that week, partly before dinner up to 11, partly from 1 to 2, leaving out nothing of what they have read in the morning during the whole week.

After 3 they shall say to their teachers whatever they have learnt during the same week, between 4 and 5.

Ante 5^m praelegat ludimagister
- $4°$. Apothegmata, Epigram. { Martialis, Catulli, aut aliorum
- $5°$. Horatium
- 6to $7°$. Lucanum, Silium Italicum.

In horam 7^{am} diei sequentis magister thema aliquod proponat 6to et 7mo ordini versibus, 5to vero soluta oratione variandum. Ac in horam primam ejusdem diei pomeridianam ab eisdem rursus et 4to ordini soluta oratione fusius explicandum.

Ante 5^m praelegat praeceptor
- $3°$. Aesopi fabulas.
- $2°$. Aesopi fabulas.
- $1°$. Catonem.

Die Sabbati.

Hora 7ma reddant omnes ordines quae pridie praelecta fuerunt. Ludimagistro tradantur variationes. Praeceptor quae pridie praelegerat cuncta examinet.

Hora 1ma, quae illa hebdomada dictata sunt, pueros recitantes audiant.

Hora 2da, duo aut tres feria septima a ludimagistro assignati de proposito themate declament, idque publice in aula, coram universa collegii frequentia, pulsata prius campana, ad mandatum ludimagistri.

Quotidie observanda.

Ante 7^{am}, nemini nisi ad naturae requisita concedatur exeundi potestas, sed ne tum quidem pluribus quam tribus simul, idque cum fuste (quem in hunc usum habeant) egredi est permissum.

Custos in omnibus classibus is assignetur, vel qui Anglice loquitur, vel qui aliquam ex his quos didicerat regulam integram exceptis tribus verbis interroganti recitare non poterit, aut qui recte scribendi rationem negligens in orthographia ter peccaverit in suis chartariis.

Before 5 the master shall read to the

Fourth, Apophthegms, Epigrams of Martial, Catullus or others.

Fifth, Horace.

Sixth and Seventh, Lucan, Silius Italicus.

For 7 o'clock next day the Master shall set a theme for the Sixth and Seventh Form on which to do varyings in verse, for the Fifth in prose: and for 1 p.m. the same day to be explained again by them more at length, and to the Fourth in prose.

Before 5 the Usher shall read

To the Third and Second, Aesop's Fables, and to the First Cato.

Saturday.

At 7 all the Forms shall say what had been read to them the day before. Varyings shall be given up to the Schoolmaster. The Usher shall examine in all he read the day before.

At 1 they shall hear the boys say the dictation of the week.

At 2 on the 7th day, two or three appointed by the Schoolmaster, shall declaim on a set theme, publicly in Hall before the whole College, a bell being rung beforehand when the Master orders it.

Things to be observed every day.

Before 7 no leave out of school shall be given except as nature may require, and not even in that case to more than three at a time, and then it is allowed to go out with the club, which they use for the purpose.

That boy shall be made custos in each class who has spoken in English, or who cannot repeat one of the rules he has learnt without making more than three mistakes, or through neglect of writing perfectly has made three mistakes in spelling in his notes.

Diebus festis.

Ante meridiem, quandoque catechismo, nonnunquam Scripturis ediscendis detur opera ad unam minimum horam, post meridiem tres superiores ordines versibus, quartus et tertius soluta oratione Latine, secundus et primus Anglice concionis summam eodem die ante meridiem in ecclesia collegiata habitae scriptis ludimagistro exhibeant.

Moderatores e pueris.
- Scholae 4.
- Aulae 1.
- Templi 2.
- Cubiculi 4.
- Campi 4.
- Oppidanorum 2.

Immundorum et sordidorum puerorum, qui manus et faciem non lavant, et se nimis sordide adjiciunt, unus, qui etiam sit censor morum.

Statutum de Venia Ludendi.

Nunquam fas erit discipulis ludere absque decani, aut, eo absente, ejus vicemgerentis et ludimagistri venia, idque solum post meridiem, nec saepius quam semel in una hebdomada, ulla de causa: in qua autem hebdomada dies festus inciderit, in ea nulla ludendi venia detur.

De Comoediis et Ludis in Natali Domini Exhibendis.

Quo juventus majori cum fructu tempus Natalis Christi terat, et tum actioni tum pronunciationi decenti melius se assuescat: statuimus, ut singulis annis intra 12^m post festum Natalis Christi dies, vel postea arbitrio decani, ludimagister et praeceptor, simul Latine unam, magister choristarum Anglice alteram comoediam aut tragoediam a discipulis et choristis suis in aula privatim vel publice agendam, curent. Quod si non praestiterint singuli, quorum negligentia omittuntur decem solidis mulctentur.

Saints' Days.

Before midday, at least one hour shall be spent, sometimes in learning the catechism, sometimes in learning Scripture; in the afternoon the three highest forms shall show up to the Head Master in verse, the Fourth and Third in Latin prose, and the Second and First in English, a summary of the sermon preached the same day in the morning in the collegiate church.

Monitors of the boys: Four of School, one of Hall, two of church, four of chamber, four of playing field, two of town boys. One of the unclean and dirty boys, who do not wash their hands and faces, and make themselves too dirty; and he shall also be the censor of manners.

Statute as to Leave to Play.

The boys shall never play without the leave of the Dean, or in his absence of his vicegerent and the Schoolmaster, and then only in the afternoon, and not oftener than once a week for any reason; and in a week in which a Saint's day falls, no leave to play shall be given.

As to Comedies and Plays to be shown at Christmas.

That the youth may spend Christmas-tide with better result, and better become accustomed to proper action and pronunciation, we decree, that every year, within 12 days after Christmas day, or afterwards with the leave of the Dean, the Master and Usher together shall cause their pupils and the choristers to act, in private or public, a Latin comedy or tragedy in Hall, and the Choristers' Master an English one. And if they do not each do their part, the defaulter shall be fined 10 shillings.

Cap. 11. De commeatu in aula et stipendiis.

Decanus (si velit) in aula vel in conclavi aut coenaculo suo, mensam suo sumptu servet, nisi communi cum praebendariis residentibus mensa vivere dignetur......

Praebendarii quatuor suo ordine residentes simul in aula aut in conclavi, si decano visum sit, suis identidem sumptibus semper prandeant aut coenent. Quorum mensae alii etiam praebendarii praesentes, si velint, se adjungant....

In proxima mensa praeceptores grammatici (quos semper nisi aegrotaverint commensales esse volumus), sacellanii, clerici et generosi sedeant. Reliquas mensas occupent discipuli decente ordine, et pensionarii.... Absens suo commeatu semper careat, praesens pro dierum praesentiae ratione commeatum habeat....

De Stipendiis.

Stipendiorum pars debita in singulorum terminorum fine a thesaurario persolvatur.

Decanus collegii habeat pro annuo stipendio	c^{li}.
pro liberatura annua	iiij^{li}. xv$s$.
pro commeatu diario	vij$s$. viij$d$.
Prebendarii singuli pro annuo stipendio	vj^{li}. vj$s$. viij$d$.
pro liberatura annua	liij$s$. iiij$d$.
pro commeatu diario	xij$d$.

Chorus.

. . . .

Magister puerorum symphoniacorum pro stipendio	iiij^{li}.
pro liberatura	xxx$s$.
pro commeatu annuo	vj^{li}. xx$d$.
Pueri symphoniaci decem singuli pro liberatura	xij$s$. iiij$d$.
pro commeatu annuo	lx$s$. xd.

CHAPTER 11. Of Commons in Hall and Stipends.

The Dean shall keep his table at his own expense in Hall, if he wishes, or in the common room or his chamber, unless he prefers to live at a common table with the residentiary canons....

The four canons in residence in their turn shall always dine and sup together in Hall, or in the common room, if the Dean shall see fit. And the other prebendaries if present may join this table if they please....

At the second table the Grammar masters, who we will shall always be in commons, unless they are ill, the chaplains, clerks and gentlemen shall sit. The other tables shall be occupied by the scholars and pensioners in their proper order.... Anyone absent shall lose his allowance, and anyone present shall receive an allowance proportionate to the days he is there....

Of Stipends.

A due part of each stipend shall be paid by the Treasurer at the end of each term.

	£	s.	d.
The Dean of the college shall have for his yearly stipend	100	0	0
for his yearly livery	4	15	0
for his daily allowance 7s. 8d.	139	18	4
	244	13	4
Each Prebendary for his yearly stipend	6	6	8
,, ,, ,, ,, livery	2	13	4
,, ,, ,, daily allowance, 1s.	18	5	0
	27	5	0

The Choir.

	£	s.	d.
The Master of the singing boys for his stipend	4	0	0
for livery	1	10	0
for yearly allowance	6	1	8
	11	11	8
The ten singing boys each for livery	0	13	4
,, ,, ,, ,, for their yearly allowance	3	0	10
	3	14	2

Schola Grammaticalis.

Ludimagister pro stipendio annuo	xij^{li}.
pro liberatura annua	xxx$s$.
pro commeatu annuo.	vj^{li}. xx$d$.
Praeceptor pro stipendio	vij^{li}. vj$s$. viij$d$.
pro liberatura annua	xxiij$s$. iiij$d$.
pro commeatu annuo	vj^{li}. xx$d$.
Discipuli quadraginta singuli pro liberatura	xiij$s$. iiij$d$.
pro commeatu annuo	lx$s$. xd.

Appendix pro commeatu.

Praeter communem commeatum in singulas hebdomadas praescriptum in singulis Christi, Spiritus Sancti, Trinitatis, Purificacionis Mariae, et Petri Apostoli festis, tribuatur a collegio sacellanis, praeceptoribus, clericis, generosis et eis qui eo genere sunt, commeatus singulis iiij^d., discipulis autem et collegii famulis ij^d. Ita ut discipuli superiorum classium carmina componant, ceteri sentenciam aliquam sacram aut philosophicam describant, et scrinio aulae nominibus appositis affigant. In ceteris approbatis festis diebus, praeceptoribus et reliquis eius generis ij^d., discipulis vero et collegii famulis i^d.

CAP. 13. De exitu extra Collegii ambitum.

Praeceptores nonnisi gravissima de causa a Decano aut eo absente prodecano et praebendariis domi praesentibus approbanda unquam vel unum diem domo absint nec diutius quam ab eisdem praescriptum sit.

Discipuli autem nunquam a sociorum coetu discedant sub pena virgae nec collegii foribus exeant absque venia Prodecani et Ludimagistri, idque non sine comite modesto; qui si fuerint, acerbissime virga corrigantur. Si vero parentes aut amici suos e schola nostra ad unum diem vel plures justis de causis avocaverunt, et ita Decano vel Prodecano et Ludimagistro videbitur, tum discipuli prius nomina sua manu in

The Grammar School.

	£	s.	d.
The Schoolmaster for his yearly stipend	12	0	0
,, ,, ,, yearly livery	1	10	0
,, ,, ,, yearly allowance	6	1	8
	19	11	8
The Usher for his yearly stipend	7	6	8
,, ,, ,, ,, livery	1	3	4
,, ,, ,, ,, allowance	6	1	8
	14	11	8
Forty scholars each for their livery	0	13	4
,, ,, ,, ,, yearly allowance	3	0	10
	3	14	2

Appendix for Commons.

Besides the common allowance prescribed for each week the College shall provide on Christmas day, Whitsunday, Trinity Sunday, Purification of Mary [2 Feb.] and St Peter's day for the chaplains, masters, clerks, gentlemen and the like, 4^d for the commons of each, and 2^d for each boy and college servant. On condition that the boys of the higher forms compose verses while the rest write out some sacred or philosophical sentiment and hang them on the screen in Hall with their names affixed. On the other recognized feasts the masters and others of that order have 2^d, the boys and college servants 1^d.

CHAPTER 13. Going outside the College Precinct.

The masters shall never, not even for a day, be away from home except for the most urgent cause, to be approved by the Dean or in his absence the Sub-dean and prebendaries at home, and then no longer than has been directed by the same.

The boys shall never leave the company of their fellows on pain of the rod, and shall never go outside the College gate without leave from the Sub-dean and Schoolmaster, and then not without a companion of good character; and if they do they shall be severely beaten with the rod. But if parents or friends have summoned their boys from our school for one day or more for what shall appear to the Dean or Sub-dean and Schoolmaster reasonable excuse, the boys shall write their names

commentarios referant, et si pluribus quam viginti diebus in anno abfuerint, suum locum in collegio penitus amittant.

CAP. 14. De vitanda aeris contagione.

Tempus discedendi a collegio propter pestis aut aeris contagionem decanus et praebendarii praesentes dijudicent. Praeceptores cum discipulis in aedes ecclesiae Cheswici aedificatas quando et quoties decano videbitur, congregentur. Ibi preces, lectiones, caeteraque exercitia scholastica et commoda consueta habeant, eisdemque omnino legibus ibidem vivant ac si in collegio nostro Westmonasteriensi morarentur....

Unus de magistratibus prodecani arbitrio simul cum illis quasi moderator omnium rus eat, et unus e sacellanis, atque eisdem inserviat promus unus, cocus unus, lixa.

Recusant Schoolmasters. 1580.

The Council's letter to the Archbishop about those that fell off from the Church of England.

[Wilkins, *Concilia*, IV. p. 296.]

After our hearty commendations. Whereas the queen hath been informed that divers persons within the province of Canterbury, both of the common and better sort, who of late time have been conformable to the laws of this realm concerning religion, are now fallen away, and have withdrawn themselves from coming to church....

And for as much as a great deal of the corruption in religion, grown throughout the realm, proceedeth of lewd schoolmasters, that teach and instruct children, as well publicly as privately in men's houses, infecting eachwhere the youth, without regard had thereunto (a matter of no small moment, and chiefly to be lookt into by every bishop within his diocese) it is thought meet for redress thereof,

in their own hands in the Register, and if they stay away more than 20 days in a year shall wholly lose their place in college.

CHAPTER 14. Avoiding the Contagion of Air.

The time for going away from the college to avoid contagion of the plague or of the air shall be settled by the Dean and prebendaries in residence. The masters and boys shall meet at the house belonging to the church built at Chiswick when and as often as the Dean shall see fit. There they shall have their prayers, lessons, and the rest of the usual school exercises and advantages, and shall live altogether under the same rules as if they were staying in our college of Westminster....

[A clause follows absolutely prohibiting alienation of Chiswick manor.]

One of the officers, to be named by the Sub-dean, shall go into the country with them as governor of all, and one of the chaplains, and one butler, one cook and a scullion shall serve them.

that you cause all such schoolmasters, as have charge of children, and do instruct them either in public schools or in private houses, to be by the bishop of the diocese, or such as he shall appoint, examined touching their religion, and if any shall be found corrupt and unworthy, to be displaced, and proceeded withall, as other recusants, and fit and sound persons placed in their rooms.

And that certificate be made of the proceedings in the said Commission unto us of her majesty's privy council. From the court at Nonsuch 18 June M.DLXXX.

Articles, 21 June 1580.

IV. Item, what schoolmasters are within your parish, and what their names are, that teach publickly or privately within any man's house within your parish, of what state, calling, or condition soever he or they be, in whose house or houses any such schoolmaster or teacher is?

V. Item, whether any such schoolmaster, or schoolmasters, is reported, known or suspected to be backward in the religion now established by the laws of this realm, that are thought any way to be secret hinderers thereof?

Penalties on Recusant Schoolmasters. 1580.

[23 Eliz. c. 1, *Stat. of the Realm*, ed. 1819, IV. 656, S. 5.]

An Acte to reteine the Queenes Majestie's Subjectes in their due Obedience.

V. Penalty on Corporations employing Schoolmasters not resorting to Church £10; on Schoolmaster, Disability and Imprisonment.

And be yt further enacted, That yf any person or persons, Bodye Pollitike or Corporate, after the Feaste of Pentecost next cominge, shall kepe or mainteyne any Scholemaster, which shall not repayre to Churche as ys aforesaid, or be alowed by the Bisshopp or Ordinarye of the Diocesse where such Scholemaster shalbe so kept, shall forfaite and lose for everye moneth so keping him £10; Provided that no suche Ordinarye or their ministers shall take any thinge for the said Allowaunce; and suche Scholemaster or Teacher presuminge to teache contrarie to this Acte, and beinge therof lawfullye (convicted) shallbe disabled to be a Teacher of youth, and shall suffer ymprisonment without Baile or Maineprise for one yeare.

Bury St Edmunds Schule.

[Bury St Edmunds School Muniments.]

Ld Thresusor Burlyes letter concerninge unfitt schule maysters.
1581.

To my Loving Frend Mr Andrewes and the residue of the governors of hir Majesties free schoole in the town of Bury.

After my very hartie commendacions. Where by your foundacion of king Edward the vjth there was a grammar

schoole erected in the town of Bury for the instruction of yowth in lerning and good nurture, the which was also endowed by the said king with a competent revenue for the maintenaunce of the same, and certein persons apointed in the dotation to be governors of the Lands assigned for that use to see the same well and duely employed from tyme to tyme according to the said foundacion, the charge whereof for the present resteth uppon yow. Forasmuch as I am geven to understand that the schoolmaster there is a man not of so good choyce either for soundnes in religion or for maners and conversacion as was requisite for the good instruction and educacion of the youth by doctryne and example, I cannot but have a carefull regard thereof considering the same was founded by the said king hir Majesties brother, and thereuppon I am iustely moved to require yow to have dilligent care that if the said schoolmaster be of such sort as aforesaid (as I am credebly informed he is) yow wold seek meanes to be better provyded and furnished by some other more apt and sufficient person, as well for lerning and soundnes in relligion as in vertue and maners. [Similar charge as to two parsons.] And do therefore praie yow uppon receipt of these my Lettres to have conference with such as are wise and well disposed touching the contentes thereof and to advertise me your disposicions herein, and what yow shall intend to do for redresse and reformacion to be had in either of these two causes as nede shall be, perswading my self that if yow shall see the defectes in ech of thos places supplyed, yow cannot do a better act for the common benefitt of your town, and the countie adioyning, and shall thereby besides the commoditie and comfort to redound to your selves, geve a good example to other lyke places, whereof fewe I think in those partes shall be comparable with yow in those two respectes, if yow take the good order in ech of them that yow maie. And so I bidd yow hartely farewell.

I think good that you acquaint Mr Robert Jermin, Sir John Higham and other the gentlemen nere about yow that are Justices of peace within the town, with the contentes of this

my lettre to thintent yow might have there advice and assistance therein.

From the Court at St James this xxvij[th] of March 1581.

Your loving frend,

W. BURGHLEY.

Delyvered to me by Sir John Heigham's servant the 2 of Aprill. 1581.

Penalties for Unlicensed Schools. 1603–4.

[*Stat. of the Realm*, ed. 1819, IV, pt ii, S. 8.]

An Acte for the due Execution of the Statutes against Jesuits, Seminarie Preistes, Recusants etc., 1 Jas. I, c. 4.

VIII. Penalty on keeping School etc. without Licence 40s. per day.

And be it further enacted by the authoritie aforesaide That no person after the Feast of St. Michail Tharchangell next, shall keepe any Schoole or be a Schoole Master out of any the Universities or Colledges of this Realme, except it be in some publike or free Grammer Schoole, or in some such Noblemans or Noblewomans or Gentleman or Gentlewomans House as are not Recusants, or where the same Schoole Master shall be speciallie licensed thereunto by the Archbishop, Bishop or Guardian of the Spiritualities of that Diocesse, upon paine that aswell the Schoole Master as also the partie that shall retaine or maintaine any such Schoole Master contrarie to the true intent and meaninge of this Acte, shall forfeite each of them for every day so wittinglie offendinge 40s.

A Bishop prohibits any but Cathedral Grammar School at Exeter. 1624–5.

[*State Papers Dom.*, Jas. I, 1623–8. 184, No. 39.]

Your devoted the bishop of Exeter, beinge hindred by sicknes from makeinge my personall appearance before you this day, doth in all humblenes present unto you this

Bishop prohibits Town School at Exeter, 1624

narration of the difference betweene the citty of Exeter and Mr Perriman the Schoolemaster there, soe far as I have had anie hande or dealeinge therein between them.

It pleased your highnes to vouchsafe by your letters to referr unto me at my first cominge amongst them the heareinge and examineinge of a matter of which the Schoole master had exhibited a complainte unto your highnes....

Dureinge the late session of Parliament there came unto me 3 persons of quality (the Recorder of the City and 2 others) in the name of the Maior and his Bretheren with a request that I woulde allowe them to have in there City another Grammer Schoolemaster besides Mr. Perriman....

I, perceaivnge well that there mocion tended indirectly to the hinderance of Perriman and his Schoole, demaunded of them, first, Whether they had anie iust exception against him, either of insufficiencie or of negligence or of misdemeanor or of undue usage of his schollers And said that if they had anie such iust exception I would either reforme or remove him. They answered me that they had nothinge to say against him.

I secondly demaunded of them what cause they had to desire another Schoole Master with him, I sawe noe necessity thereof, for the Schoole house (built lately most at his owne chardge for perpetuity to the Citty) is soe spacious as it is able to receave and containe a hundreth more schollers than he hath, and he hath alsoe the helpe of Ushers under him sufficient to teach manie more.

I saw noe good thereby could com to the Citty but rather much inconvenience; for the indulgence of parents would, upon every slight occasion, remove there children from Schoole to Schoole, whereby the children would be hindred in their learneinge, and therefore consideringe these reasons and with all the well deservinge of the poore man for his 20 yeres paines and upwards taken amongst them, and alsoe how my predecessor had settled him in his place, inhibitinge anie others to teach Grammer there, save him aloane, I desired

them to rest contented, though I could not yeild unto there desire.

They replied that if I would not grant there desire they would seeke unto a higher power, where they did not doubt to obtaine it, and therein (as became me) I left them to there liberty.

This with my humble dutie remembred I testifie under my hande. Feb. 23, 1624.

Hoole's Grammar School Curriculum. 1637–60.

A NEW
DISCOVERY
of the old Art of
TEACHING SCHOOLE,
In four small
TREATISES.

1	concerning	A Petty-Schoole	In a
2		The Usher's Duty	Grammar
3		The Master's Method	Schoole.
4		Scholastick Discipline	

Showing how Children in their playing years may grammatically attain to a firm groundedness and exercise of the Latine, Greek and Hebrew Tongues.

Written about Twenty-three yeares ago, for the benefit of *Rotherham* School, where it was first used; and after 14 years' trial by diligent practise in London in many particulars enlarged, and now at last published for the general profit, especially of young Schoole-Masters. By *Charles Hoole,*

School Curriculum, 1637–60

Master of Arts, and Teacher of a Private Grammar School in Lothbury Gardens, London.

London: Printed by *J. T.*, for Andrew Crook, at the *Green Dragon*, in Paul's Churchyard, 1660.

The Usher's Duty, or a Plat-forme of Teaching Lilie's Grammar, by C. H.

. . . .

But because their wits are now ripened for the better understanding of Grammar, and it is necessary for them to be made wholly acquainted with it before they proceed to the exact reading of Authors, and making School-exercises, I would have them spend one quarter of a yeare chiefly in getting *Figurae* and *Prosodia* and making daily repetition of the whole Accidents and Common-Grammars, so that this third year will be well bestowed in teaching children of between nine and ten years of age the whole *Grammar*, and the right use of it, in a method answerable to their capacities, and not much differing from the common rode of teaching.

The Master's Method, or the Exercising of Scholars in Grammars, Authours, and Exercises; Greek, Latine, and Hebrew.

Chap. I.

p. 129. *How to make the Scholars of the fourth Form very perfect in the* Art of Grammar *and* Elements of Rhetorick; *and how to enter them upon Greek in an easy way. How to practise them* (as they read Terence *and* Ovid de Tristibus *and his* Metamorphosis, *and* Janua Latinae linguae *and* Sturmius, *and* Textor's Epistles) *in getting* Copy of words, *and learning their* Derivations *and* Differences, *and in* varying phrases. *How to show them the right way of* double translating *and* writing a most pure Latine style. *How to acquaint them with all sorts*

of English *and* Latine verses *and to make them to write* familiar *and* elegant Epistles, *either in English or Latine,* upon all occasions.

Chap. II.

p. 167. *How to teach Scholars in the fifth form to keep and improve the Latine and Greek Grammars, and Rhetorick, and how to acquaint them with an Oratory, stile and pronunciation. How to help them to translate Latine into Greek, and to make Greek verses as they read* Isocrates *and* Theognis. *How they may profit well in reading Virgil, and easily learn to make good Theams and elegant Verses with delight and certainty. And what Catechismes they may learn in Greek.*

V Form.

I have experienced it to be a most effectual mean to draw on my Scholars to emulate one another, who could make the best exercises of their own in the most Rhetoricall style, and have often seen the most bashfull and least promising boyes to outstrip their fellowes in pronouncing with a courage and comely gesture; and for bringing up this use first in my School I must here thank that modest and ingenious gentleman, Mr Edward Perkins, who was then my Usher, for advising me to set upon it. For I found nothing that I did formerly to put such a spirit into my Scholars, and make them like so many Nightingales, to contend who could most melodiously tune his voice and frame style to pronounce and imitate the prementioned orations....

On Tuesdaies and Thursdaies in the afternoons, after other tasks ended, to collect Short Histories out of Plutarch, &c.; Apologues out of Æsop, Hieroglyphicks out of Pierius and Causinus, Emblems and Symbols out of Alciat, Bega, Quarles, &c.; Ancient Laws and Customs out of Diodorus Siculus, &c. Witty Sentences out of Golden Grove, Moral Philosophie, &c. Rhetorical exornations out of Vossius,

School Curriculum, 1637–60

Farnabie, Butler, &c. Topical pieces out of Caussinus, &c. Descriptions of things natural and artificial out of Orbis Pictus, &c., which, together with all that can be got of this nature, should be laid up in the Schoole Library for Scholars to pick what they can......out of these they are to write on a Theme set.

Chapter III.

How to enter Scholars of the Sixth Forme in Hebrew; How to employ them in reading the best and most difficult Authours in Latine and Greeke, and how to acquaint them with all manner of Schoole Exercises, Latine, Greek or Hebrew.

p. 193. Though it be found a thing very rare, and is by some adjudged to be of little use for School boyes to make exercises in Hebrew; yet it is no small ornament and commendation to a Schoole (as Westminster Schoole at present can evidence) that Scholars are able to make orations and verses in Hebrew, Arabick or other Oriental Tongues, to the amazement of most of their hearers, who are angry at their own ignorance, because they know not well what is then said or written.

p. 202. The constant employment of this Sixth Form is:—

1. To read twelve verses out of the Greek Testament every morning before Parts.

2. To repeat Latine and Greek Grammar Parts and Elementa Rhetorices every Thursday morning.

3. To learn the Hebrew Tongue on Mondaies, Tuesdaies and Wednesdaies for morning Parts.

4. To read Hesiod, Homer, Pindar and Lycophron for forenoon lessons on Mondaies and Wednesdaies.

5. Zenophon, Sophocles, Euripides and Aristophanes on Tuesdaies and Thursdaies.

6. Laubegeois Breviarium Graecae linguae for afternoon Parts on Mondaies and Wednesdaies.

7. Lucian's Select Dialogues and Pontani Progymnasmata Latinitatis on Tuesday afternoons; and

8. Tullie's orations, Plinie's Panegyricos, Quintilian's Declamations on Thursdaye afternoons, and Goodwin's Antiquities at leisure times.

9. Their exercises for oratory should be to make Themes, Orations and Declamations, Latine, Greek and Hebrew; and for Poetry to make Verses upon such Themes as are appointed them every week.

10. And to exercise themselves in Anagrams, Epigrams, Epitaphs, Epithalamias, Eclogues and Acrosticks, English, Latine, Greek and Hebrew.

11. Their Catechismes are Nowell and Birket in Greek and the Church Catechisme in Hebrew.

So that in six, or at the most seven, yeares time (which children commonly squander away, if they be not continued at the Schoole after they can read English and write well) they may easily attaine to such knowledge in the Latine, Greek and Hebrew Tongues as is requisite to furnish them for future studies in the Universities, or to enable them for any ingenuous profession or employments which their friends shall think fit to put them upon in other places.

Advancement of Education during the Commonwealth and Protectorate. 1643–60.

[B. M. MS. 15669.]

27 July 1643.

A Committee to inquire into scandalous ministers though there be no malignancy.

Die Mercurii 18° Oct. 1643.

It is this day ordered by the Commons assembled in Parliament that the Committee for Plundered Ministers shall have power to enquire after malignant Schoolemasters.

Trial of Canterbury Schoolmaster. 1 July 1645.

[B. M. MS. 15669, f. 187.]

Canterbury: It is ordered that Mr Ludde Schoolemaster in Canterbury be referred unto the members of Parliament for the Citty of Canterbury Sir Richard Handres [two other knights, probably Deputy-Lieutenants of the county], John Lade Alderman of the citty [and four others named, the Parliamentary Committee], or any 5 or more of them, who are desired and hereby authorized to take the said Mr Ludd his defence to the articles examined and transmitted to this Committee against him and to call before them and examine such witnesses as hee shall produce for his defence, and to certify the same to the Committee for examination of Mr Ladd [*sic*].

A similar order is made on eight persons, three of whom are the same as in this order, on 25 Nov. 1645. On 14 March, 1645–6, 'the Committee of Parliament sitting at Canterbury' is desired to examine the complaints against him; and on 4 April 1646 the case is again returned to the Committee. Ludd kept his place.

Bury St Edmunds' Schoolmaster removed for Malignancy. 1645.

[Bury St Edmunds School Muniments.]

The order for Mr Stevens Removall from the Schoole.

To his much respected freind Mr John Woodward the elder this deliver.

By the Committee at Bury St. Edm., 29 Aug. 1645.

For as much as Tho Stephens clerke schule master of the free schule of Bury is a notorious malignant and hath oftentymes wytnessed his dissaffection to the Parlyment both by wordes and acions It is this day ordred that he shalbe removed from the sayd place of shoolemayster from and after the 14 of October 1645. And it is especially recom-

mended to Mr Alderman and the Governors of the sayd schoole to provide a godly able and well affected man agaynst that tyme to be shoolemaster of the sayd schoole in the roome of the sayd Mr Stephens whom they are desired to see removed at the day appoynted according to the intent of this order.

Examinatum per ED. BELAN, Registrary Committee Comitatus Suffolcie.

Augmentation to Colleges and Schools. St John's and Emanuell Colledges Cambridge. 4 Jan. 1650.

[Lambeth MS. Augmentation Books. 978, p. 32.]

Whereas the Committee for Reformacion of the Universities have by their order of the 26 of September last thought fitt to settle the yearely summe of £200 upon St Johns and Emanuell Colledges in Cambridge for an increase of maintenance to the respective Masterships thereof And the said Trustees are required to pay the same (by the said Order) unto Doctor John Arrowsmith, Master of St. Johns Colledge, and to Doctor Anthony Tuckney, Mr of Emanuell Colledge, and the same to commence from the 24 day of June last; soe that there became due unto the said doctors the 25 of December last one halfe years rent amounting to the summe of £100 It is therefore ordered that the Honourable the Committee for the publique Revenue be desired, and they are hereby desired, to cause to be issued out and paid (out of First Fruits and Tenthes paid into the Exchequer) unto the said Doctor Arrowsmith and Doctor Tuckney, or unto Mr Adoniram Byfeild (to their order), the said summe of £100 to them due as aforesaid.

Sarum Gramer Schole. 6 June 1651.

[*Ib.* 969, p. 137.]

Whereas Mr Arthur Warwicke, Scoole Master of the Gramer Schoole within the Close of Sarum, is lately

deceased and whereas the Scoole Master of the said Free Schoole was heretofore at the Provision Care and maintenance of the Deane and Chapter of Sarum which is now transferred and charged upon the said Trustees It is therefore ordered that Mr Thomas Garden bee and hee is hereby from hence forth setled and constituted Schoole Master of the said Schoole in the Roome and the Stead of the said Mr Warwicke and that hee shall take upon him the care and instruccion of the youth in good Literature and that hee shall have for his said service the house to the said Schoole Master belonging with the appurtenances and all sallaries stipends Fees and availes of and belonging to the Schoole Master of the said Freeschoole for the time being.

Sarum Schoole. 22 Aug. 1651.

[*Ib.* 969, p. 84.]

Whereas there is due and belonging to the Schoolemaster of the free schoole of the Close of Sarum for the time being the howse wherin the said Master liveth, to be repaired by the Comoners of the Deane and Chapter of the Cathedrall of Sarum, and alsoe the yearly stipend of £10 paiable quarterly by the said Deane and Chapter, of which stipend there became due unto Mr Arthur Warwick the then Master there the summe of 50*s*. for one quarters rent of the premisses ending the 25th of March last It is therefore ordered that Mr Lawrence Steele Treasurer doe forthwith pay unto the said Mr Warwick the said summe of 50*s*. due as abovesaid.

Sarum Schoole. 24 Dec. 1651.

[*Ib.*, p. 426.]

In pursuance of an Order of the Committee for Reformacion of the Universities of the 10th of Dec. instant It is ordered that the yearly summe of £30 be and the same is hereby graunted for increase of maintenance to the Master and Usher of the

Freeschoole of the Citty of Sarum in the County of Wilts vizt. to Mr John Hunt, the master of the said Schoole the yearly summe of £20, and to Mr Edward Hillary, the Usher thereof, the summe of £10 a yeare, the said yearly summes to be accompted from the 29th day of September last.

Caren, Pembrokeshire. 29 June 1652.

[Ib. 1006, p. 292.]

It is ordered that Mr Henry Williams be and is hereby authorized to keepe a free schoole in the parish of Caren for the fitting of youthes in the said parish and places adjacent for greater schooles And that he shall receive for his encouragement and maintenance the annuall summe of £20 out of the Treasury of the County of Pembrook to be paid him at the 25th of July and the 25th of December yearely. The first payment to begin on the 25th of July next And John Pryce Esq. Treasurer for Southwales is hereby authorized and enabled to pay and allow the same stipend notwithstanding any other order to the contrary at such times and seasons as the same shall grow due and payable.

Sunderland, Durham. 4 March 1652.

[Ib. 1006, p. 428.]

Whereas there is exceeding great want of a Schoolemaster in the part of Sunderland to teach children to write and instruct them in Arithmetique to fitt them for the sea or other necessary callings It is therefore ordered that the tythes of Suddicke of the present yearly value of £5. 6s. 8d. bee setled upon George Harison being a man well qualified and fitted for said purposes towardes his maintenance and encouragement in teaching children to write and instructing them in Arithmetique att Sunderland aforesaid.

Charity Schools. 1699–1718.

A Form of a Subscription for a Charity School.

Whereas Prophaness and Debauchery are greatly owing to a gross Ignorance of the Christian Religion, especially among the poorer sort; And whereas nothing is more likely to promote the practice of Christianity and Virtue, than an early and pious Education of Youth; And whereas many Poor People are desirous of having their Children Taught, but are not able to afford them a Christian and Useful Education; We whose Names are underwritten, do agree to pay Yearly, at Four equal Payments, (during Pleasure) the several and respective Sums of Money over against our Names respectively subscribed, for the setting up of a Charity-School in the Parish of   in the City of   or in the County of   for Teaching [Poor Boys, or Poor Girls, or] Poor children to Read and Instructing them in the Knowledge and Practice of the Christian Religion, as profess'd and taught in the Church of England; and for Learning them such other Things as are suitable to their Condition and Capacity. That is to say

£ s. d.

I A. B. do subscribe

In many Schools the Orders are to the effects following:

I. The master to be elected for this SCHOOL, shall be,

1. A member of the Church of England of a sober life and conversation, not under the Age of 25 years.

2. One that frequents the Holy Communion.

3. One that hath a good Government of himself and his Passions.

4. One of a Meek Temper and Humble Behaviour.

5. One of a good Genius for Teaching.

6. One who understands well the Grounds and Principles of the Christian Religion and is able to give a good account

thereof to the Minister of the Parish or Ordinary on Examination.

7. One who can Write a good Hand, and who understands the Grounds of Arithmetick.

8. One who keeps good order in his Family.

9. One who is approved by the Minister of the Parish (being a Subscriber) before he is presented to be Licensed by the Ordinary.

II. The following Orders shall be observed by the Master and Scholars.

1. The Master shall constantly attend his proper Business in the School during the Hours appointed for Teaching viz. from 7 to 11 in the Morning and from 1 to 5 in the Evening the Summer half year: And from 8 to 11 in the Morning and from 1 to 4 in the Evening the Winter half year; that he may improve the Children in good Learning to the utmost of his Power and prevent the Disorders that frequently happen for want of the Master's Presence and Care.

2. To the End the chief design of this School, which is for the Education of Poor Children in the Rules and Principles of the Christian Religion as professed and taught in the Church of England, may be the better promoted; The Master shall make it his chief Business to instruct the Children in the Principles thereof, as they are laid down in the Church catechism; which he shall first teach them to pronounce distinctly, and plainly; and then, in order to practice, shall explain it to the meanest capacity, by the help of *The whole Duty of Man*, or some good Exposition approved of by the Minister.

And this shall be done constantly twice a week; that everything in the Catechism may be the more perfectly repeated and understood. And the Master shall take particular care of the Manners and Behaviour of the Poor Children.

And by all proper methods shall discourage and correct the beginnings of Vice, and particularly, Lying, Swearing, Cursing,

taking God's name in vain, and the Prophanation of the Lord's Day etc....

3. The Master shall teach them the true spelling of Words, and Distinction of Syllables, with the Points and Stops, which is necessary to true and good Reading, and serves to make the Children more mindful of what they Read.

4. As soon as the Boys can read competently well, the Master shall teach them to write a fair legible Hand, with the Grounds of Arithmetick, to fit them for Services or Apprentices.

NOTE. The Girls learn to read etc. and generally to knit their Stockings and Gloves, to Mark, Sew, make and mend their Cloaths, several learn to write, and some to spin their Cloaths.

[5, 6. To provide for Church going on Sundays and Saints' days and twice daily Prayers in School from the Prayer-Book.]

7. [Names-calling at beginning of School]...Great Faults as Swearing, Stealing etc. shall be noted down in monthly or weekly bills to be laid before the Subscribers or Trustees every time they meet, in order to their correction or expulsion.

8. [Holidays.]

9. [Provides that the School is to be free, no charge whatever being made.]

10. [The children are to be sent to school clean.]

11. The Children shall wear their Caps, Bands, Cloaths, and other marks of Distinction every Day, whereby their Trustees and Benefactors may know them, and see what their Behaviour is abroad.

The ordinary charge of a School in London for Fifty Boys Cloath's comes to about £75 per annum, for which a School-Room, Books and Firing is provided, a Master paid, and to each Boy is given yearly Three Bands, one Cap, one Coat, one Pair of Stockings, and one Pair of Shoes.

[The cost for a school of 50 Girls is put at £60 a year to include]

Two Coifs, Two Bands, One Gown and Petticoat, one pair of knit Gloves, One Pair of Stockings, and Two Pair of Shoes.

Dissenters and Non-jurors prohibited from keeping Schools. 1713.

[13 Anne c. 7, *Stat. of the Realm*, ed. 1822, IX. 915, sec. 3.]

An Act to prevent the Growth of Schism and for the further security of the Churches of England and Ireland as by Law Established.

§ 3. And be it further enacted by the Authority aforesaid, That any person who shall have obtained a Lycence and subscribed the Declarations and taken and subscribed the Oaths as above appointed and shall at any time after during the time of his or their keeping any publick or private school or seminary, or instructing any youth as Tutor or Schoolmaster, knowingly or willingly resort to or be present at any Conventicle, Assembly, or Meeting, within England, Wales or Town of Berwick upon Tweed, for the exercise of religion in any other Manner than according to the Liturgy and Practice of the Church of England, or shall knowingly and wittingly be present at any meeting or Assembly for the exercise of religion, although the Liturgy be there used, when Her Majesty (whom God long preserve) and the Elector of Brunswick or such others as shall from time to time be lawfully appointed to be prayed for, shall not there be prayed for in express words according to the Liturgy of the Church of England...shall be liable to the Penalties in this Act and shall from thenceforth be incapable of keeping any publick or private School or Seminary or instructing any youth as tutor or Schoolmaster.

§ 4. ...if any person lycensed as aforesaid shall teach any other Catechism than the Catechism set forth in the Book of Common Prayer, the License of such person shall from thenceforth be void and such person shall be liable to the Penalties of this Act.

§ 5. ...it shall and may be lawful to and for the Bishop of

the Diocese or other proper Ordinary to cite any Person or Persons whatsoever keeping School or Seminary or teaching without Licence as aforesaid and to proceed against and punish such person or persons by Ecclesiastical Censure, subject to such Appeals as in Cases of ordinary jurisdiction....

§ 8. Provided always That this Act or anything therein contained shall not extend or be construed to extend to any Tutor teaching or instructing youth in any College or Hall within either of the Universities of that part of Great Britain called England, nor to any Tutor who shall be employed by any Nobleman or Noblewoman to teach his or her own children, grandchildren or great grandchildren only in his or her family; provided such Tutor so teaching in any Nobleman or Noblewoman's family do in every respect qualify himself according to this Act, except only in that of taking a Licence from the Bishop.

§ 10. ...if any person who shall have been convicted as aforesaid and thereby made incapable to teach or instruct any youth as aforesaid shall after such conviction conform to the Church of England for the space of one year without having been present at any Conventicle, Assembly or Meeting as aforesaid, and receive the Sacrament of the Lords Supper according to the Rites and Usage of the Church of England at least 3 times in that year, every such person or persons shall be again capable of having and using a License to teach School or to instruct youth as a Tutor or Schoolmaster, he or they also performing all that is made requisite thereunto by this Act.

§ 11. ...every such person so convicted and afterwards conforming in manner as aforesaid shall at the next term after his being admitted to or taking upon him to teach or instruct youth as aforesaid make oath in writing in some one of Her Majesties Courts at Westminster in publick and open Court, or at the next Quarter Sessions for that county or place where he shall reside, between the hours of 9 and 12 in the forenoon, that he hath conformed to the Church of England for the space of one year before such his admission without having been

present at any Conventicle Assembly or Meeting as aforesaid and that he hath received the Sacrament of the Lords Supper at least 3 times in the year which oath shall be there enrolled and kept upon Record.

§ 12. Provided always That this Act shall not extend or be construed to extend to any person who as a Tutor or Schoolmaster shall instruct youth in Reading, Writing, Arithmetick or any part of Mathematical Learning, only so far as such Mathematical Learning relates to Navigation or any Mechanical Art only and so as such Reading, Writing, Arithmetick or Mathematical Learning shall be taught in the English tongue only.

National Schools Trust Deed. 1870–1902.

I [A. B.] of [C.] under the authority of the Acts of the 5th and 8th years of the reign of Her Majesty for affording facilities for the Conveyance and Endowment of Sites for Schools do hereby freely and voluntarily and without valuable consideration grant and convey unto [X and Y] all that [land described] To hold the same unto and to the use of the said [X and Y] for the purposes of the said Acts, and upon trust to permit the said premises and all buildings thereon erected or to be erected to be for ever hereafter appropriated and used as and for a school for the education of children and adults or children only of the labouring manufacturing and other poorer classes in the Parish of [Z] and for no other purpose. And it is hereby declared that such school shall always be in union with and conducted according to the principles and in furtherance of the ends and designs of the National Society for promoting the Education of the Poor in the principles of the Established Church throughout England and Wales and subject to and in conformity with the declaration aforesaid such school and premises and the fund and endowments thereof in respect whereof no

other disposition shall be made by the donor shall be controlled and managed in manner following that is to say the principal officiating Minister for the time being of the said Parish shall have the superintendence of the religious and moral instruction of all the scholars attending such school subject to the provisions hereinafter contained and may use or direct the premises to be used for the purposes of a Sunday school under his exclusive control and management. But in all other respects the control and management of such school and premises and of the funds and endowments thereof and the selection appointment and dismissal of the schoolmaster and schoolmistress and their assistants (except when under the provisions hereinafter mentioned the dismissal of any master mistress or assistant shall be awarded by the Bishop of the Diocese or the Arbitrators as the case may be) shall be vested in and exercised by a Committee consisting of the principal officiating Minister for the time being of the said Parish his licensed Curate or Curates if the Minister shall appoint him or them to be a member or members of the said Committee and of [number] other persons of whom the following shall be first appointed That s to say [names] and such other persons continuing to be contributors in every year to the amount of twenty shillings each at the least to the funds of the said school and to be members of the Church of England as by law established and either to have a beneficial interest to the extent of a life estate at the least in real property situated in the said Parish or to be resident therein And any vacancy which shall occur in the number of the said other persons by death resignation incapacity or otherwise shall be filled up by the election of a person or persons qualified as aforesaid who shall be elected by the majority of votes of such of the contributors during the year current at the time of the election to the amount of ten shillings each at the least to the funds of the said school being members of the said Church of England....Provided that no election as aforesaid shall give or vest any right to or in any lay person to serve upon the Committee until after he shall have in the presence of the

Chairman at a meeting of the Committee made and signed in a book to be kept at the said school a declaration in the manner and form following that is to say 'I, A. B., do hereby solemnly and sincerely declare that I am a member of the Church of England as by law established' [do solemnly and sincerely declare that I am and have been for three years last past a communicant of the Church of England]... And it is hereby declared that no person shall be appointed or continue to be the master or mistress of the school who shall not be a member of the Church of England.

And it is further declared that all the provisions of the Elementary Education Act 1870 which constitute a public elementary school shall apply to the school to be constituted under this Deed. Provided that if the Committee of Management herein described pass a resolution at a Meeting composed of a majority of the Managers for the time being to repay any Grant made in aid of the establishment of the said school out of the Parliamentary Grant for Education and if the said Committee shall accordingly repay that amount to the Lords Commissioners of the Treasury for the time being the aforesaid declaration whereby this school shall be a public elementary school within the meaning of the Elementary Education Act 1870 shall forthwith become void and of no effect And the principal officiating Minister of the said Parish shall be Chairman of all meetings of the Committee when present thereat... And in case any difference shall arise between the Minister or Curate and the Committee of Management hereinbefore mentioned respecting the prayers to be used in the school not being the Sunday school or the religious instruction of the scholars attending the same or any regulation connected therewith or the exclusion of any book the use of which in the school may be objected to on religious grounds or the dismissal of any teacher from the school on account of his or her defective or unsound instruction of the children in religion the Minister or Curate or any member of the Committee may cause a written statement of the matter in difference to be

laid before the Bishop of the Diocese…and the decision of the Bishop in writing under his hand thereon when laid before the Committee shall be final and exclusive in the matter And the Committee of Management for the time being is hereby expressly required to take all such measures as may be necessary for immediately carrying the said decision into complete effect And in case any difference other than and except such difference as last described shall arise in the Committee of Management the minority thereof (being not fewer in number than one-third of the whole of the Committee) may make request in writing [to the President of the Council and the Bishop, each to appoint an arbitrator whose decision shall be final]. And the Committee may in the month of [M] in each year select and appoint a Committee of not more than [number] ladies being members of the said Church of England to assist them in the visitation and management of the girls and infant schools which Ladies Committee shall remain in office until the first day of the same month in the following year when such Committee may be renewed.… In witness whereof [etc.].

British School Trust Deed. 1870–1902.

[Formal parts as in National Society's Deed down to 'no other person.'] Which said school shall be conducted upon the principles of the British and Foreign School Society established in London and shall be under the general management of a Committee to be constituted as hereinafter mentioned that is to say such Committee shall consist of [names] until the month of [M] next and thenceforth of [number] persons being subscribers to the same school to the amount of [number of shillings] at least during the current year and such Committee shall be elected annually in the said month by the subscribers to the said school who shall have subscribed thereto the sum of   at least during the current year…

The said Committee at their first meeting shall elect a Chairman for the ensuing year who shall preside at each meeting of the said Committee and of the subscribers and such Committee shall subject to such principles as aforesaid appoint and at their discretion dismiss the Master and Mistress of the said school and shall admit and discharge all the scholars thereat and shall prescribe the terms of admission and the mode and times of payment.

[Proviso that Education Act 1870 shall apply and that if grants repaid deed shall be void.]

Scheme for Bradford Grammar School. 1871.

ENDOWED SCHOOLS COMMISSION.

Scheme for the management of the Free Grammar School of King Charles II at Bradford, in the County of York. Approved by Her Majesty in Council, 19 August, 1871.

Part I.—General Scope of Trust.

General object.

1. The object of this Foundation or Trust shall be:—

    (*a*) To supply a liberal education for boys,

    (*b*) To promote the education of girls,

by means of schools in Bradford.

And from the date of this scheme all the particulars which by the Endowed Schools Act, 1869, Sec. 46, are capable of being hereby repealed and abrogated, shall be repealed and abrogated.

Governing Body.

Part II.—Constitution of Governing Body and Management.

2. The Governing Body, hereafter called the Governors, shall, from and after the date of this Scheme, consist of not

more than 16 persons, nor less than 13, as herein-after provided. Of these, four shall be ex-officio Governors, four representative or elective, and the remainder coöptative.

3. The ex-officio Governors shall be:—
   The Vicar of Bradford,
   The Mayor of Bradford,
   The Chairman of the School Board of Bradford,
And the President of the Bradford Mechanics' Institute, if they will respectively undertake to act in the Trusts of this Scheme.

4. Of the Representative Governors two shall be elected by the Town Council of Bradford, and two by the School Board of Bradford. The first elections shall take place as soon after the date of this Scheme as can conveniently be managed.

5. The Representative Governors shall be elected to hold office for the term of five years, and shall then retire, but be re-eligible.

[6—10. Provisions as to election and admission of Governors.]

Religious opinions not to weigh in selection of Governors.

11. Religious opinions or attendance or non-attendance at any particular form of religious worship, shall not in any way affect the qualification of any person for being a Governor under this Scheme.

[12—26. Provisions as to management of meetings, property and business.]

Dissolution of existing Corporation.

27. From and after the date of this Scheme, the existing Corporation of the Governors of the Free Grammar School of King Charles II at Bradford, shall be dissolved, and, except as herein otherwise expressly provided, all property, rights and

powers vested in that Corporation shall be transferred to and vest in the Governors created by this Scheme.

Visitorial jurisdiction transferred to Crown.

28. From and after the date of this Scheme, all rights and powers reserved to, belonging to, or claimed by, or capable of being exercised by, the Archbishop of York, or any other person, as visitor of this Trust shall be transferred to Her Majesty, and all such rights and powers, and also any like rights and powers vested in Her Majesty on the 2nd day of August, 1869, shall be exercised only through and by the Charity Commissioners for England and Wales.

Jurisdiction of Ordinary abolished.

29. From and after the date of this Scheme, all jurisdiction of the Ordinary relating to or arising from the licensing of any Master under this Trust shall be abolished.

Part III.—The School and its Management.

Two branches of foundation.

30. This Foundation shall consist of two branches, one for the education of boys, the other for the education of girls.

Girls' School.

31. From and after the date of this Scheme, or within three years from such date, the Governors shall appropriate the annual sum of £200, and on the determination or failure of the pension hereafter contemplated for the present Schoolmaster or that assigned to the late Usher, the further annual sum of £50 for the establishment and maintenance of a girls' school, and such school shall be organised, supported, and managed in accordance with directions to be hereafter set forth in a supplementary Scheme.

Boys' School.

32. The boys' school shall be a day school, and shall be divided into two Departments, to be called respectively the Senior and Junior Departments. As soon as conveniently may be after the date of this Scheme, the Governors shall provide suitable accommodation for both Departments by erecting new buildings, or by enlarging, re-arranging, and adapting the present buildings in the way that shall appear most desirable. To this end they shall have power to raise, by sale or mortgage of the Trust property, as the Charity Commissioners shall direct, a sufficient sum of money not exceeding £4000. Until such new or remodelled buildings are ready for the reception of the scholars, the Governors shall hire or otherwise provide temporary accommodation for carrying on the school.

Masters not required to be in Holy Orders.

33. No person shall be disqualified for being a Master in the School by reason only of his not being, or not intending to be, in Holy Orders.

Head Master. Appointment.

34. The Head Master, who shall have control over both departments, and shall be responsible for the whole work of the boys' school, shall be appointed by the Governors at some meeting to be called for that purpose, as soon as conveniently may be after the occurrence of a vacancy, or after notice of an intended vacancy. The Master shall be a graduate of some University within the British Empire. In order to obtain the best candidates the Governors shall, for a sufficient time before making any appointment, give public notice of the vacancy, and invite competition by advertisements in newspapers or by such other methods as they may judge best calculated to secure the object.

Dismissal.

35. The Governors may dismiss the Head Master without assigning cause, after six calendar months' written notice, given to him in pursuance of a resolution passed at two consecutive meetings held at an interval of at least 14 days, and duly convened for that express purpose, such resolution being affirmed at each meeting by not less than two-thirds of the Governors present.

36. For urgent cause the Governors may by resolution passed at a special meeting duly convened for that express purpose, and affirmed by not less than two-thirds of the whole existing number of Governors, declare that the Head Master ought to be dismissed from his office, and in that case they may appoint another special meeting to be held within not less than a week of the former one, and may then by a similar resolution affirmed by as large a proportion of Governors, wholly and finally dismiss him. And if the Governors assembled at the first of such meetings think fit at once to suspend the Head Master from his office until the next meeting, they may do so by resolution affirmed by as large a proportion of Governors. Full notice and opportunity of defence at both meetings shall be given to the Head Master.

37. *Declaration to be signed by Head Master.*

[To do his duty and acquiesce if removed.]

38. *Head Master to reside in the house assigned to him in his official capacity.*

Head Master not to have other employment.

39. The Head Master shall give his personal attention to the duties of the School, and during his tenure of office he shall not accept or hold any benefice having the cure of souls, or any office or appointment which, in the opinion of the

Governors, may interfere with the proper performance of his duties as Head Master.

Masters not to receive other than authorised fees.

40. Neither the Head Master nor any Assistant Master shall receive or demand from any boy in the School, or from any person whomsoever on behalf of any such boy, any gratuity, fee, or payment, except such payments as are prescribed or authorised by this Scheme.

Jurisdiction of Governors over Scholastic arrangements.

41. Within the limits fixed by this Scheme the Governors shall prescribe the general subjects of instruction, the relative prominence and value to be assigned to each group of subjects, the division of the year into term and vacation, the payments of the scholars, and the number of holidays to be given in term. They shall take general supervision of the sanitary condition of the school buildings and arrangements. They shall determine what number of Assistant Masters shall be employed. They shall every year assign the amount which they think proper to be paid out of the income of the Trust for the purpose of maintaining Assistant Masters and a proper plant or apparatus for carrying on the instruction given in the School.

Governors to consult the Head Master.

42. Before making or altering any regulations under the last preceding clause the Governors shall consult the Head Master in such a manner as to give him full opportunity for the expression of his views.

Jurisdiction of Head Master over Scholastic arrangements.

43. Subject to the rules prescribed by or under the authority of this Scheme the Head Master shall have under

his control the choice of books, the methods of teaching, the arrangement of classes and school hours, and generally the whole internal organisation, management, and discipline of the School : Provided that if he expels a boy from the School, he shall forthwith make a full report of the case to the Governors.

Head Master to appoint and dismiss Assistant Masters, and to distribute fund assigned to Assistant Masters and plant.

44. The Head Master shall have the sole power of appointing and dismissing all Assistant Masters, and shall determine in what proportions the sum assigned by the Governors for the maintenance of Assistant Masters and of plant or apparatus shall be divided among the various persons and objects for the aggregate of which it is assigned. And the Governors shall pay the same accordingly, either through the hands of the Head Master or directly, as they think best. In the case of the Senior Master of the Junior Department his appointment or dismissal shall not be valid until it has been confirmed by the Governors.

45. The Head Master may from time to time submit proposals to the Governors for making or altering regulations as to any matter within their province, and the Governors shall consider such proposals and decide upon them.

Income of Head Master.

46. The Head Master shall receive a fixed stipend of £200 a year. He shall also receive payment according to the number of boys in the School; that is to say, such sum, calculated on such a scale, uniform or graduated, as may be agreed upon between himself and the Governors, being not less than £3 nor more than £6 yearly for each boy in the Senior Department, and not less than £1 nor more than £3 for each boy in the Junior Department. These payments shall be made terminally, and shall not be made for any boy who has not belonged to the School for the whole term.

Payments for entrance and tuition.

47. All boys, except such as herein-after provided, shall pay such entrance and tuition fees as the Governors shall fix from time to time, provided that no such entrance fee shall exceed £1 in the Junior and £2 in the Senior Department, and that no such tuition fee shall be less than £4 or more than £10 in the Junior, or less than £10 or more than £20 in the Senior Department. No extras of any kind shall be allowed without the sanction of the Governors.

48. *Payments to be made in advance.*

49. *Ages for Junior Department.* [8 to 15.]

50. *Ages for Senior Department.* [13 to 19.]

To whom School is open.

51. Subject to the provisions established by or under the authority of this Scheme, the School and all advantages of the School shall be open to all boys who are of good character, and of sufficient bodily health, and who are residing with their parents, guardians or next friends. No boy not so residing shall be admitted to the School unless he has previously obtained the express permission of the Governors. But the Governors may, if they think fit, arrange for the accommodation of daily or weekly boarders under the supervision of an Assistant Master or other person approved by them.

52. *Mode of Admission.*

53. *Register of applications* [to be kept by the Head Master].

54. *Entrance Examination* [to be held by the Head Master].

55. The examination for admission to the Junior Depart-

ment shall never fall below the following standard, that is to say :—

> Reading simple narrative;
> Writing text-hand;
> Easy sums in the first two rules of arithmetic.

56. The examination for admission to the Senior Department shall be graduated according to the age of the boy, but it shall never fall below the following standard, viz. :—

> Proficiency in reading and writing.
> Ability to write correctly from dictation.
> A sound elementary knowledge of arithmetic.
> A fair knowledge of English grammar, geography, the outlines of English history, and the Latin grammar, with ability to translate and parse simple Latin sentences.

The Governors may raise the minimum standard from time to time if they deem it advantageous to the School.

Provisions for special exemptions from religious instruction and worship.

57. The parent or guardian of or person liable to maintain or having the actual custody of any scholar may claim, by notice in writing addressed to the Head Master, the exemption of such scholar from attending prayer or religious worship, or from any lesson or series of lessons on a religious subject, and such scholar shall be exempted accordingly, and a scholar shall not by reason of any exemption from attending prayer or religious worship or from any lesson or series of lessons on a religious subject, be deprived of any advantage or emolument in this School or out of this Trust to which he would otherwise have been entitled. If any teacher in the course of other lessons at which any such scholar is in accordance with the ordinary rules of the School present, teaches systematically and persistently any particular religious doctrine, from the teaching of

which any exemption has been claimed, as in this clause before provided, the Governing Body shall, on complaint made in writing to them by the parent, guardian, or person liable to maintain or having the actual custody of such scholar, hear the complainant, and inquire into the circumstances, and if the complaint is judged to be reasonable, make all proper provisions for remedying the matter complained of.

Instruction: Religious.

58. The Governors and Head Master shall, within their respective departments, as herein-before defined, and subject to the provisions of this Scheme, make proper regulations for the religious instruction to be given in the School.

Secular.

59. The subjects of Secular Instruction shall be as follows:—

For the Junior Department.

In the Junior Department:—
  English language and literature.
  Arithmetic.
  Elements of Algebra and Geometry.
  English History.
  Geography.
  Some one branch of Natural Science.
  Latin.
  Some one modern European language.
  Drawing.
  Vocal Music.

For the Senior Department.

In the Senior Department:—
  English, Latin, French and German languages and literatures.

Arithmetic and Mathematics.
Geography.
At least one branch of Natural Science.
Ancient and Modern History.
Political Economy.
Drawing.
Vocal Music.

The boys shall be instructed in the foregoing subjects according to the classification and arrangements made by the Head Master. The Greek language and literature may be taught in the Senior Department if the Governors think fit, and under such arrangements as they may consider expedient.

60. *Annual Examination.*

[By Examiners appointed by Governors.]

Head Master's Annual Report.

61. The Head Master shall make an annual report to the Governors on the general condition of the School, and on any special occurrences during the year. He may also mention the names of any boys who in his judgment are worthy of praise or substantial reward, having regard both to proficiency and conduct.

Exhibitions at the School itself.

62. The Governors shall grant Exhibitions tenable at the School itself, and entitling the holders to exemption from the payment of tuition fees. All such exemptions shall be given as the reward of merit only, and shall be assigned—in the case of candidates for admission, on the result of an open competitive examination, to be conducted by an independent examiner under arrangements to be made by the Governors and Head Master—in the case of boys already attending the School, on the Reports of the Examiners and Head Master, and no exemption shall be granted to any such boy if the

Head Master reports that he is rendered undeserving of it by ill-conduct. The Governors may, under such conditions, exempt boys from the payment of the whole, or of one-half of the tuition fee, but such exemption shall in every case be liable to forfeiture in the event of misconduct or failure to maintain a reasonable standard of proficiency. Boys so exempted shall be called and ranked as Foundation Scholars. Not more than ten per cent. of the boys shall be wholly exempt, and no further exemption shall be allowed when the exemptions, total or partial, reach the proportion of one in every five boys in the School....The Governors may, if they think fit, restrict the competition for some portion of these Exhibitions to candidates who are being educated at the Public Elementary Schools within the school district of Bradford.

63. When the Funds admit, the Governors shall establish one or more Exhibitions, tenable for not more than four years at any such place of liberal, scientific, technical, or professional education or study as they may approve. Candidates shall be elected to these Exhibitions by the Governors on a consideration of the Reports of the Head Master and of the Examiners.

64. *Exhibitions not to be perverted from their proper purpose.*

Part IV.—Application of Income.

65. *Repair and Improvement Fund.* [A fund of £1000 to be formed.]

66—68. *Pensions.*

69. *Residue* [to go to improving the School or Girls' School].

Part V.—General.

Further Endowments.

70. The Governors may receive any additional donations or endowments...not calculated to give privileges to any boy or girl on any other ground than that of merit, and not otherwise inconsistent with or calculated to impede the due working of the provisions of this Scheme.

Charity Commissioners to decide doubtful questions.

71. If any doubt or question arises among the Governors as to the proper construction or application of any of the provisions of this Scheme, the Governors may apply to the Charity Commissioners for their opinion and advice thereon, which opinion and advice when given shall be binding on the Governors.

72. *Charity Commissioners to make new Schemes* [not inconsistent with the Endowed Schools Act].

Scheme to be printed and sold.

73. This Scheme shall be printed and a copy given to every person who shall become a Governor of the Trust, and to every Master or Assistant Master and Teacher appointed to the School, and copies shall be sold at a reasonable price to all persons who may wish to buy.

Date of Scheme.

74. The date of the Scheme shall be the day on which Her Majesty by Order in Council declares Her approbation of it.

We hereby signify our approval of this Scheme:

ARTHUR HOBHOUSE.
HUGH GEO. ROBINSON.

4th April, 1871.

Scheme for Andover Grammar School. 1909.

Scheme made by the Board of Education under the Charitable Trusts Acts, 1853 to 1894, for the alteration of the Scheme regulating the Andover Grammar School.

The Foundation.

1. In this Scheme the expression 'the Foundation' means the Andover Grammar School, in the Borough of

Andover, in the County of Southampton, so far as determined by an Order of the Charity Commissioners of 5 February 1904 to be held for educational purposes, which Foundation is now regulated by a Scheme made under the Endowed Schools Acts on 16 February 1903.

Repeal and Substitution.

2. The provisions of the Scheme of 16 February 1903 are hereby repealed so far as they relate to the Foundation, and the provisions of this Scheme are substituted therefor.

Title of Foundation.

3. The Foundation and its endowment (including the particulars specified in the Schedule to this Scheme) shall be administered under the name of the Andover Grammar School.

GOVERNORS.

Governing Body.

4—6. The Governing Body of the Foundation, in this Scheme called the Governors, shall, when complete, consist of 13 persons, being:

Ten Representative Governors, to be appointed:
Four by the Hampshire County Council,
Three by the Andover Town Council,
Two by the Trustees of the Andover Municipal Charities, and
One by the Warden and Fellows of Winchester College; and
Three Coöptative Governors, to be appointed by resolution of the Governors.

A Representative Governor need not be a member of the appointing body.

Every Governor to be appointed by the County Council shall be appointed for a term of office ending on the date of

the appointment of his successor, which may be made at any time after the ordinary day of retirement of County Councillors next after his appointment. The other Representative Governors shall be appointed each for a term of three years, and the Coöptative Governors each for a term of five years.

Additional Governors.

7. If an increase in the number of Representative Governors is required to comply with any conditions of a grant made by a Local Authority or by the Board of Education, or is considered desirable for any other reasons, additional Representative Governors may, with the consent of the Governors and the approval of the Board of Education (signified by writing under their seal), be appointed by a Local Authority.

[Cl. 8—16 relating to constitution of Governing Body, quorum, and management of property and business, are with verbal differences substantially the same as those in the Bradford Scheme; the management clauses now appearing in a Schedule.]

SCHOOL.

Day and Boarding School for Boys.

17. The School of the Foundation shall be a Day School, and, if the Governors think fit, a Boarding School, for boys, and shall be maintained in or near the Borough of Andover, in the present school buildings or in other suitable buildings provided by the Governors, as a Public Secondary School.

STAFF.

Head Master and Assistants.

18. There shall be a Head Master of the School, and such number of Assistant Masters as the Governors think fit.

Employment of Staff.

19. Every Master in the School shall be employed under a contract of service with the Governors, which shall, in the

case of appointments made after the date of this Scheme, be reduced to writing, and shall in any case be determinable only (except in the case of dismissal for misconduct or other good and urgent cause) upon a written notice given by or on behalf of the Governors or by the Master as the case may be, and taking effect in the case of the Head Master after the expiration of six months from the date of notice, and in other cases at the end of a school term and after the expiration of two months from the date of notice; but nothing in this clause shall—

(*a*) in the case of any person employed at the date of this Scheme, affect any special provisions as to notice contained in the Scheme under which he was appointed, or any special agreement as to notice in force at the date of this Scheme; or

(*b*) affect the special provisions of this Scheme as to the procedure to be followed by the Governors in the case of the dismissal of the Head Master.

20. *Masters need not be in Holy Orders.* [As in Bradford Scheme.]

Masters not to be Governors.

21. No Master in the School shall be a Governor.

Head Master—Appointment.

22. The Head Master shall be a graduate of a University in the United Kingdom or have such other equivalent qualification as may be approved by the Board of Education. He shall be appointed by the Governors after due public advertisement in newspapers and otherwise so as to secure the best candidates.

Dismissal of Head Master.

23. [A shortened form, identical in substance with cl. 35-6 of Bradford Scheme.]

24. *Head Master's Tenure and Official Residence.*

Head Master not to have other Employment.

25. The Head Master shall give his personal attention to the duties of the School. He shall not undertake any office or employment interfering with the proper performance of his duties as Head Master. He shall not hold any benefice having the cure of souls, nor during a school term perform for payment any ecclesiastical duty outside the School.

Income of Head Master.

26. Subject as in this Scheme provided, the Head Master shall receive a stipend in accordance with a rate or scale fixed by the Governors.

Assistant Masters.

27. The power of appointing and dismissing Assistant Masters in the School shall be exercised by the Head Master, after obtaining in every case the approval of the Governors, and every Assistant Master shall be dismissible at pleasure, either on notice given in accordance with the provisions of this Scheme, or, in the case of misconduct or other good and urgent cause, without notice.

An Assistant Master may at any time be suspended from duty by the Head Master and the Head Master shall in that case report the matter to the Governors.

Pensions or Insurance.

28. The Governors may contribute, or agree to contribute, while any Master is in their employment, towards yearly payments for securing on his behalf a pension or capital sum payable after that employment has ceased. The amount contributed by the Governors in respect of a Master in any year shall not exceed that contributed by the Master.

Organisation and Curriculum.

29—32. 29. *Jurisdiction of Governors over School Arrangements.* 30. *Views and Proposals of Head Master.* 31. *Jurisdiction of Head Master over School Arrangements.* 32. *Payments for School Objects.* Substantially identical with cl. 41—43 and second part of cl. 44 of Bradford Scheme.]

General Instruction.

33. Instruction shall be given in the School in such subjects proper to be taught in a Public Secondary School for boys as the Governors in consultation with the Head Master from time to time determine. Subject to the provisions of this Scheme, the course of instruction shall be according to the classification and arrangements made by the Head Master.

Religious Instruction.

34. Subject to the provisions of this Scheme, religious instruction in accordance with the principles of the Christian Faith shall be given in the School under regulations to be made by the Governors. No alteration in any such regulations shall take effect until the expiration of not less than one year after notice of the making of the alteration has been given by the Governors in such manner as they think best calculated to bring the matter within the knowledge of persons interested in the School.

Religious Exemptions.

35. [Identical with cl. 57 of Bradford Scheme.]

Examinations.

36. Once at least in every two years there shall be, at the cost of the Foundation, an examination of the whole of each of the upper forms of the School by, or under the direction of, a University or other examining body approved by the Board

of Education, with the assistance, if the Governors think fit, of any of the teaching staff of the School; and a report thereon shall be made to the Governors, who shall send copies of it to the Head Master and the County Council and two copies to the Board of Education. Provided that the Board may, either generally or in any particular year, dispense with that examination as regards any of the upper forms.

Once at least in every year there shall be an examination of the lower forms by the teaching staff of the School, and a report thereon shall be made to the Governors if they require it.

An examination may be partly in writing and partly oral, or, in the lower forms, wholly oral. If in any year the School as a whole is inspected by the Board of Education, the Board may dispense with any examination for that and the following year. The Board may decide which forms shall be considered to be 'upper' and 'lower' respectively for the purposes of this clause.

CONDITIONS OF ADMISSION.

37—41. 37. *To whom School is open.* 38. *Ages for School.* 39. *Application for Admission.* 40. *Register of Applications.* 41. *Entrance Examination.* [Substantially identical with cl. 49 to 54 of Bradford Scheme, except that the School is not divided into two departments and the leaving age is 18.]

Fees.

42. No fee, payment, or gratuity shall be received from or on behalf of any boy in the School, except in accordance with Rules for Payments, which shall be made by the Governors and shall among other things provide:

    (*a*) for the payment of such tuition fee, at the rate of not more than 12*l.* and not less than 6*l.* a year, as is prescribed in the rules; and

(b) in the case of any boarder, for the payment of a boarding fee, at the rate of not more than 40*l.* a year, in addition to the tuition fee.

The Rules for Payments shall be subject to the approval of the Board of Education signified by writing under their seal, and when so approved shall have effect accordingly.

FREE PLACES, MAINTENANCE ALLOWANCES, AND EXHIBITIONS.

Exemptions from Fees, and Foundation Scholars.

43. The Rules for Payments shall provide for total or partial exemptions from payment of tuition fees or entrance fees.

They shall among other things provide:

(a) that in every school year total exemptions from payment of tuition fees, to an extent of not less than 5 per cent. of the boys admitted to the School during the previous school year, shall be offered on admission to boys resident in the Borough of Andover, who are and have for not less than two years been in attendance at a Public Elementary School;

and may also provide:

(b) that any boys who are exempted from payment of tuition fees, and who by reason of their proficiency are deserving of the distinction, shall be called Foundation Scholars.

Maintenance Allowances.

44. The Governors may award to boys who are exempted from payment of tuition fees, and who, in the opinion of the Governors, are in need of financial assistance to enable them to enter or remain in the School, Maintenance Allowances each of a yearly value of not more than 10*l.* Any such Allowance may, at the discretion of the Governors, be paid to

the parent or guardian of the boy, or may be applied by them towards payments (other than tuition or entrance fees) under the Rules for Payments, or in providing the boy with travelling facilities or meals.

Leaving Exhibitions.

45. (*a*) The Governors may award Leaving Exhibitions, tenable at any University, Training College for pupils intending to enter the teaching profession, or other Institution of higher, including professional or technical, instruction.

(*b*) An Exhibition shall be either
   (i) a single payment, or
   (ii) a series of payments extending over not more than four years,

and in either case shall not exceed a total value of 200*l*.

(*c*) Exhibitions shall be awarded for merit only on the result of such examination as the Governors think fit, to boys who then are and have for not less than two years been in the School. Within the limits fixed by this Scheme the Exhibitions shall be freely and openly competed for, and shall be awarded under such rules and conditions as the Governors think fit, but so that as nearly as possible the same number may be awarded each year. Any Exhibition for which there is no duly qualified candidate, who on examination is adjudged worthy to take it, shall for that turn not be awarded.

Deprivation.

46. [Substantially identical with cl. 64 of Bradford Scheme.]

SPECIAL DEPARTMENTS.

Preparatory Department.

47. The Governors may, if they think fit, maintain in the School a Preparatory Department for the education of boys.

For this department the Governors may make such modifications as they think fit in the foregoing provisions relating to ages, instruction, and examination, and the Rules for Payments, and may prescribe such tuition fees as may be thought suitable.

Education of intending Elementary School Teachers.

48. The Governors may, with the approval in writing of the Board of Education, make special provision in or in connexion with the School for the education of boys who intend to qualify as teachers in Public Elementary Schools. For these boys, subject to the like approval, the Governors may make such modifications as they think fit in the foregoing provisions relating to ages, instruction, and examination, and the Rules for Payments may prescribe such tuition fees as may be thought suitable.

49—52.   TRANSITORY PROVISIONS.

53—56.   GENERAL PROVISIONS.

Interpretation.

57. The Interpretation Act, 1889, applies to the interpretation of this Scheme as it applies to an Act of Parliament.

58.   *Date of Scheme.*

MANAGEMENT RULES.

The Board of Education order that the foregoing Scheme be established.

Sealed this 30th day of November 1909.

INDEX

Abbot, John, xxxviii, 414
Acaster, College of, xli
Accounts of Almonry boys, Westminster, 306; building of Stratford-on-Avon School, 378; Governors of Sherborne School, 492; Merton College Grammar School boys, 210, 223, 298, 305
Adaliza, Queen, 56
Aeddi, Stephen, 4
Aelfric, Abbot of Evesham, xvi; Abp of Canterbury, xvi
Aelfric's Colloquy, xvii, 36-48; Grammar, xvii, 48
Aethelstan, priest, 33
Ailric, childemaister, 56
Albert, Abp of York, xiii, xiv, xlii, 10, 18
Albinus, 6
Alcimus, 16
Alcuin, xiii, xiv, 10-21, 278
Aldhelm, xii, xiv, 8, 16
Aldwincle School, xli, 434
Aldwincle, William, 434
Alexander III, Pope, 108, 118
Alexandria, schools of, ix, xvii
Alfred, King, xv, xix, 22, 24-35
Alfred's children, education of, 30; Palace School, 30-5
All Hallows Church, London, 419
All Souls College, Oxford, xxxix
Almonry Schools, xxxii; at St Albans, 296; Westminster, 306
Ambrose, Bishop, 16
Andover Grammar School scheme, li, 560
Apollonius of Alexandria, xvii
Apothecary, Robert, 478
Apprentices, Statute of, xxxviii, 386
April beard, William of the, 110

Arator, 16
Archididascalus, xliii, 456, 458, 464, 466, 468
Aristotle, xiv, 16
Arithmetic, xiii, xiv, xli, xlvii, xlix, 10, 136, 538
Arrowsmith, John, 536
Arscot, John, 476, 477
Arundel, Abp, xxxix, 394
Asser's *Life of Alfred*, xv, 24
Asshecote, William, 493
Assheley, Jarveys, 492, 493
Astronomy, xiv, 4, 12
Athanasius, 16
Athelard, Master, xviii, 54
Athens, schools of, ix
Augmentations to colleges and schools, 536-8
Augustine of Canterbury, ix, xi; of Hippo, ix, x, 16
Augustinian Canons, xxxiii
Aunger, Robert, 228

Bachelors at Beverley Grammar School, xxix, 294; Oxford, 192; St Albans Grammar School, xxix, xxx, 240, 244
Balsall, Thomas, 380
Balsham, Hugh of, xxviii, 224
Bardney, Abbot and Convent of, 146
Barett, John, 478
Barking, chapel of, 68
Barnby, William of, 289
Barnwell, schools at, xlvii
Barons, John, 493
Barton, Henry, 348
Barton (Lincs.) School, 280; Vicarage, 146
Basil, 16
Bata, Aelfric, 36

Bath, Simon, Bishop of, 96
Battes, William, 246
Beaumont, Aelma of, 88; Roger of, 88
Becket, Thomas à, xviii, xxiv, 84, 108
Bede, xiii, xiv, 16
Bede's *Ecclesiastical History*, ix, xii
Bedford School, xxii, 116
Beenly, John, 332, 336
Belan, Ed., 536
Bell, Rev. Andrew, l
Bellamy, Robert, xl, 436
Belmeis, Richard de, 80
Benedict XII, Pope, xxxiii, 288
Benedictine College at Cambridge, xxxiii; at Oxford, xxviii, 196; Monks, education of, 288
Bentworth, church of, 98
Berefield, John of, 218; William of, 218
Bereford, William of, 214
Berkeley, Katharine, Lady, xxxvi, 330; Sir Thomas of, 330
Berkhampstead School, xliv
Bertwald, 6
Bessils, P., 256
Beverley, Collegiate Church, xix; Grammar School, bachelors at, xxix, 294; choristers at, 270; master, 76; John of, 280
Bingham, William, xl, 402
Birchwood, Thomas of, 258
Birlingham, Richard, 310
Bishops, duty of, 20; power of, xlvi, 528
Black Death, the, xxxiv
Blois, Henry of, Bp of Winchester, xx, 108
Bloxham, John of, 328
Board of Education scheme, li, 560
Bodmin School, 476, 477
Boethius, 16
Bohun, Humfrey of, 94
Bokenhull, John, 306
Bologna University, xxiv; Professor of Oriental languages at, xxx, 268
Boniface, xi, xvii
Bonne Foy, Paul de, xxxi
Books, school, xi, xiv, xvi, xlii, 16, 30, 48, 192, 316, 420, 448-51,
466, 508, 512-16, 531-4; price of, 220, 222, 300
Bor, William, 258
Boreman, Richard, xlv
Borrowash, Henry, 392
Bosbury, John, 378
Boston (Lincs.) School, 280
Bourstead, Stephen of, 260
Boy-Bishop, xlvi
Brabazon, Richard, 348
Bracebridge, John, 388, 392
Bradford Grammar Schools, li, 548
Brasenose, Manciple of, 289
Brazier, John the, 376; William the, 376
Bridgenorth School, xxxviii, 439
Bridgys, William, 439
Bridport, Giles of, xxvii, 164
Bristol Cathedral, xliii; Kalendars' Gild at, 98; School, 98
British and Foreign School Society, xlix; Trust Deed, 547
Brown, Dr Carleton, xxxvii
Brownyng, Thomas, 450
Buckingham, John of, 328
Buckwell, John of, 266
Building lease for Giggleswick School, 441
Bullock, John, 478
Bund, Dean, 82
Burdon, John, 408
Burgh, Richard de, 230
Burghley, Lord Treasurer, xlvi, 526
Burnet, Walter, 330
Burton, Thomas of, 218
Bury, Richard of, 270
Bury St Edmunds School, xlvi, xlvii, xlviii, 128-33, 526; master, 535
Busby, Dr, xlvi
Byfeild, Adoniram, 536

Calne, Reginald of, 126
Cambridge, Grammar School, 210, 414; Mayor and bailiffs of, 152; Oxford students go to, 142; St John's Hospital, 222; Sheriff of, 148-53
Cambridge University, chancellor of, xxvi, xxix, 202; Clare Hall, xxxi, 403; Colleges excluded from Chantries Act, 475; Corpus Christi College, xxxi, xxxiv;

earliest mention of, 148; Emmanuel College, xlviii, 536; free lectures at, 436; God's House xxxiv, xli, 402; Gonville and Caius, xxxi; King's College, xxxv, 414; King's Hall, xxxi, xl, 436; Lady Margaret Professorships at, xl; Mathematical Professorships at, xlviii; Michael House, xxxi; origin of, xxv; Pembroke College, xxxi; Peterhouse, xxviii, 222; St John's College, xxviii, xlviii, 536; secession from, xxvi; Trinity College, xxxi, master of, 496, 498; Trinity Hall, xxxi

Campden, John of, 328
Cancerisio, Hugh of, 86
Candleshaw, Dean of, 282
Canterbury, Almonry School at, xxxii, 318; Augustine of, ix, xi; Church of, xi; Educational Canons of Convocation of, 444; St Martin's School, 260, 267
Canterbury Cathedral, Choristers, 454; Common Hall, 460; Ignorance of monks of, 444; Injunctions to, 471; livery of ministers of, 462; Oblates' and Novices' School, 60; Song School, xii, 6; stipends of ministers of, xxxiii, 444
Canterbury Cathedral Grammar School, xi, xii, xix, xxi, xliii, xlvii, 2; competition with, 260–7; curriculum of, 464; re-foundation of, 452; students in the Universities, 464; Usher, 252
Canterbury Cathedral Grammar Schoolmaster, xx, xxix, 471; appointment of, 238; jurisdiction of, 232, 252–67; trial of, 535
Canute, xviii, l, 52
Cardmaker, Jane, 478
Caren School, 538
Carlisle Cathedral, xliii
Carr, James, xlii, 441
Cassiodorus, 16
Cathedral Grammar Schools, xliii, 122, 142, 470, 494
Cathedrals of the New Foundation, 452
Caunton, Thomas, 378

Celestine, Pope, 168
Chamber, William, xli, 434
Chancellor, xix, xx; of Cambridge, xxvi, xxix, jurisdiction of, 202; of Oxford, xxix; of Salisbury, 72; jurisdiction of, 168; of St Paul's, 81, 90
Chantries Act, 472; exclusions from, 475
Chantries, dissolution of, xliv
Chantry, Aldwincle, 434; Gybbons, Lytchett Matravers, 486; Martock, Somerset, 484; St Katharine's, Gillingham, 484; St Katharine's, Ilminster, 486; St Mary's Chapel, Stamford, 236; priests ordered to teach, xliii, 446, 472; Schools, xxxvi, xli, 330, 434
Charity Commission, li
Charity Schools, xlix, 539–41
Charlemagne, xiii, xiv
Charlton, John, 400
Chaucer, xxxvi, 344–7
Cheminster, Thomas of, 266
Chester, Walter, Bishop of, 108
Chicheley, Abp, xxxvi
Choristers, xxxii; at Beverley Grammar School, 270; at Canterbury, 454
Choristers' School at Lincoln, 386
Christ Church, Hants, Dean and Chapter of, 74; School, 74
Christ's Hospital, xlvii
Christianity, coming of, ix
Chrysostom, 16
Cicero, xiv, 16, 451, 508, 512, 534
Cistercian college at Oxford, xxviii
Classics, episcopal attack on, 314
Clemens, 16
Clement V, xxx, 268
Clergy, education of, xxvi, 146, 154
Clopton, Thomas, 380
Clyffe, William, 493
Clyvedon, John of, 334
Codyngton, Peter of, 170
Colchester, William, 306
Colchirche, parish of, 419
Coleston, William of, 280
Colet, Dean, xxxvii, xxxviii, xlii
College, xxvi–xxviii, xxxiv, and *passim*
Collegiate Churches, Grammar

574 *Index*

Schools in, xviii, xix, xxi, 54, 66, 74, 76, 82, 86–9, 87, 116, 158, 185, 270, 272, 294, 404, 423–433, 496–523
Comminianus, 16
Commonwealth, education during, xlvii, 534
Cooper, Richard, 493
Copeland, Thomas, 478
Cornhill Grammar School, 396; William of, 140
Cornish, William, 312
Cornwall, John, xxxvi, 300, 343; Schools Continuance warrant for, 475
Corpus Iuris Canonici compiled, 108
Costentin, Nigel, 146
Cote, John, 419
Cotton, Richard, 238
Council, Lateran, xxv, 122; of 994(?), 36; Vienne, xxx, 268
Court of Arches, appeal from, 112
Coventry, Walter, Bishop of, 108
Cowerde, William, 492
Cowlay, Alice of, 200; Stephen of, 200
Cox, Henry, 408; Richard, schoolmaster, 450, scholar, 408
Cranley, Thomas of, 324
Cranmer, Thomas, Abp, 470
Cricklade, Robert of, xxiii, 102
Curriculum, School, xxix, li, 530; at Canterbury, 464; Eton, 450; Westminster, 508; Winchester, 448; York, xiv

Darley Abbey, 108
David, King of Scots, 92
Deans and Chapters, abolition of, xlvii
Dene, William, 408
Denifle, xxiii
Derby, Goda of, 110; Walkelin of, 110; School, xxii, 108, grant of house to, 110
Dereham, Elias of, 126, 154
Desiderius, Bishop of Vienne, x
Disputations in schools, 84
Disse, Walter of, 128; William of, 128
Dissenters prohibited from keeping school, 542

Dodkin, Roger, 212, 214; Thomas, 212, 214; William, 214
Dolling, Thomas, 302
Donatus, xvii, xxx, 16, 48, 192, 222
Dual School at Polesworth, xlviii
Dunstable School, xxii, 78, 92, 132
Dunwich School, xi, xii, 58
Durand, Master, 80
Durham, Randolph, Bishop of, 98; Almonry, 124; Cathedral Priory, xlii; College, xxxiii, xlviii; School, xliii, 124
Dustone, John of, 154

Eanbald, xiv, 14, 18
East Anglian Grammar School, 2
Easter, celebration of, 4, 12
Edgar, Canons of, xv, 34
Education; *see* Elementary, Free, Girls' and *passim*
Edward, son of Alfred, 30; VI, xliii, xliv, 472, 480, 482; injunctions of, 472
Edwin, King, 14
Edyngdon, William of, 318
Egbert, Abp of York, xiii, 10
Eleanor, Queen of Spain, 120
Elementary Schools, xlvi, xlix, l, 434
Elfthryth, 30
Elizabeth, Queen, xlv, xlvi, 494, 496
Ely, Archdeacon of, xxix, 202, 210
Endowed Schools Act, xx, li; Commission, xliv, scheme of, 548
Endowment of Bury St Edmunds School, 128; Derby School, 110; Eton College, 410; Merton College, 180; schoolmaster at Salisbury, 96; Sevenoaks School, 400; Sherborne School, 484–91; Stratford-on-Avon School, 380; Warwick School, 90; Winchester College, 322; Wotton-under-Edge School, 330; York School, 126, 128
Erasmus, xxxvii
Ernulf, Dean, 56
Erpwald, 2
Ethelbert, Abp, *see* Albert; Bishop, 20; King, xi
Ethelfleda, xix, 31
Ethelgifu, 30
Ethelwold, 48

Index

Eton College, xxxv, xxxix; excluded from Chantries Act, 475; Foundation Charter of, 404; grant of monopoly to, 412; Headmaster of, xlviii; time-table, 448

Eu, Henry, Count of, 68; Robert, Count of, xxi, 68

Eugenius, Pope, Canon of, xiv, 20

Euticus, 16

Everard, John, 252, 254, 258

Eversdone, Hugh of, 252

Evesham, John of, 408

Ewelme, Nicholas of, 194

Excommunication by schoolmaster, 252–61

Exeter, classics in diocese of, 314; College, see Oxford; Grammar School, xlvi, 528

Exhibitioners at Northampton, xxiv; Oxford, xxiv, 134, 136; Winchester, xxv, 140

Exhibitions at Durham School, 124; Sherborne School, 480; Universities or Grammar Schools, 472, 494; form of, 232; given by Canute, 52

Eye, priory of, 58

Fantosme, Jordan, 112

Farlington, Simon of, 124, 126

Farthinghoe School, xxxviii, 414

Fauntleroy, John, 478

Fees at Ipswich Grammar School, 422; Merton College School, 214–23, 300–5; for licence to teach, 118, 122, 138

Felix, Bishop, ix, xi, 2

Ferrers, Robert, Earl of, 110

Fitzrobert, William, 126

FitzStephen's *Life of Becket*, xxii, 82

Fleknore, Roger, 408

Flogging, xvii, 36, 46, 62

Forsham, H. of, 254

Fortunatus, 16

Fox, Richard, 380

Fray, John, 414

Free Schools, see Schools

Fretter, Richard the, 376

Friar, Chaucer's description of, 344

Fulgentius, 16

Furlong, Andrew, 477

Games in schools, 84

Garden, Thomas, 537

Gateshead Hospital, 124

Gebmund, 6

Geoffrey, Abbot, 78

Gerald of Wales, xxiv

Gerard, Abp, 70

Gerunds, 50

Giffard, Godfrey, Bp, 198; Sir John, 196

Giggleswick School, xlii, 441; boarder at, 443; inscription on, 443

Gild, Corpus Christi, Ipswich, 422; Holy Cross, Stratford-on-Avon, 376; Kalendars', Bristol, 98

Girls' education, xvii, xlviii

Glomery, master of, xxviii, xxix, 202, 210

Gloucester, Cathedral, xliii; College, xxxiii, 196–201; Gilbert, Earl of, 230; Humphrey, Duke of, 420; Milo of, 94; School, xxii, 76, grant of to Llanthony Abbey, 94

Gloves as fees, xxx, 294

Godstow, nuns of, xxiii

Gradone, Thomas, 302

Grammar, Aelfric's, 48; Donatus', xvii, xxx, 16, 48, 192; King Henry VIII's, 495; Lilie's, 531; Priscian's, xvii, 16, 48, 192

Grammar Schools, *passim*; churches to provide, 142; clergy ordered to attend, 146; six in Lincolnshire, 280; Act, li

Grantham School, 280; Thomas, 388

Gratian, Master, 108

Greek, learning, xii, xlii, 4, 6; teaching, 2

Green, Roger of the, 166; William, 314

Grefe, Gilbert, 408

Gregory, of Tours, x; the Great, Pope, x, xi, xiv, 6, 16; VII, Pope, 22; IX, Pope 152

Grimbold, 24

Grimsby School, 280

Grocers' Company, xxxviii, 398

Gryndour, Robert, xlii

Gunpowder Plot, xlvi

Gurney, William of, 280

Index

Gymming, 68

Hadrian, Abbot, xii, 2, 4, 6
Haeddi, Bp of Winchester, xiii, 8
Hales, Sir Christopher, 470
Hall, Richard, 252, 254
Handres, Sir Richard, 535
Hanley, John, 252
Harcourt, John of, 212, 214
Hardyng, Robert, 98
Harison, George, 538
Harold, Earl and King, xviii, 54
Haseley, Robert of, 98
Hastings, Collegiate church of, xxi; Grammar and Song Schools, 68
Haston, William, 408
Hatfield, Bishop, xxxiii
Hawvil, William of, 200
Hebrew, xlv, 512, 533; to be taught at Oxford, 268
Heigham, Ralf of, 166
Heighington, Robert of, 270; Walter of, 270
Helewyn, John, 408
Henley-in-Arden, xlvi
Henney, Robert of, 260, 264
Henry I, xix, 58, 74, 76, 88, 92; II, xviii, 94, 98, 110; IV, xxxvi, 372; VI, xxxix, 404; VII, xxxiii, 439; VIII, xliii, 452, 464
Henryson, William, 240, 246
Hereford, Robert, Bishop of, 94
Heriz, William of, 110
Hessle, John, 378
Hexham School, xiv, 20
Higden's *Polychronicon*, xxxvi, 340
Higham, Sir John, 527
Higham Ferrers School, xxxvi, xxxix, 348, 372
Hilarius, 16
Hillary, Edward, 538
Holtby, Sir John of, 166
Holy water carrying, 232
Honorius III, Pope, xxxiii, 144
Hoole, Charles, xlvi, xlviii
Hoole's School Curriculum, 530
Horncastle School, 280
Hospitals, xxii, 18; Gateshead, 124; St Anthony's, 417; St John's, Cambridge, 224; St John's, Sherborne, 482; St Thomas of Acres, 419

House, Walter, 396
Hugh, Dean of Hastings, 68
Hungary, Nicholas, clerk of, 134
Hunt, John, 538
Huntingdon, Earl of, 92; Priory, 92; School, xxii, 92; Walter, 348
Huntman, John, 388

Injunctions of Abp Parker, 471; Edward VI, 472; Elizabeth, 494
Innocent III, Pope, 142; IV, Pope, 136
Inns, *see* Hospitals
Ipswich School, xlii, 422
Ireland, xiii
Islipp, John, 440

James, Dr M. R., 403
Jekyll, John, 112
Jermin, Robert, 527
Jews, school for, 100
John, King, 94, 140
Jolyffe, Thomas, 380
Judith, xv
Juvencus, xiv, xlii, 16

Kent, William, 408
Keston, Roger, 396
Kette, John, 408
Keylwey, Robert, 475, 477
Kingston, Hugh of, 318; Public School, xxxii, l, 318
Kinoulton School, 234
Kneplocke, Christiane, 492

Lactantius, 6
Lacy, Hugh of, 96; Ilbert of, xxi, 66; Robert of, 68, 236
Lade, John, 535
Lancaster, Joseph, l
Laneham, William of, 126
Lanfranc, Abp, xx; constitutions of, xxi, 60
Langport, John of, 200
Langton, John, 414
Lateran Council, xxv, 122
Latham, Nicholas, xlvii
Latin, learning, x, xii, xiv, xvi, xvii, xxxviii, 2, 4, 6, 24, 38
Launceston School, xliv
Lavington, Thomas, 222
Lawrence, the priest, xi

Index

Leeds, William of, 342
Leicester, Robert of, 272; St John's Chapel, xxxix, 328; School, xxvi
Lemyng, Richard, 442
Leo, Pope, 16
Library at York School, 16
Licence to teach, xx, xxv, xlvi, xlix, 91, 236; Fees for, 118, 122, 138
Lichfield School, xiv
Lincoln, Anthony, Dean of, 282; Choristers' School, xxxviii, 386; Dean and Chapter of, xxxviii; Grammar School, xxvi, xxxviii, 386, 388; Robert of, xxvi, 414; Song Schools at, 236; Theology School at, 146
Liss Church, 96
Littlebury, Nicholas of, 212
Llanthony Abbey, 94
Lollard schools, xxxix, 328, 394
Lollards, Statute of, xxxix, 394; to be burnt for keeping schools, 374
London schools, xxii, 82; increase of, 416-20
Longsword, Maud, 200
Lovekin, Edward, 218
Lovetot, William of, 92
Lucan, xiv, 16
Lucius II, Pope, 100
Ludde, Mr, 535
Ludgershall, William of, 214
Ludus literarius, x
Luttrell, Robert, 236
Lycchefeld, William, 419
Lydford, John of, 328

Macclesfield Grammar School, xxxviii, 436
Madras system, 1
Maidstone, Richard of, 238
Maidulf, xiii
Makins, Richard, 218
Maldon, House of scholars at, 170
Malet, Hesilia, 60; Robert, 58; William, 60
Malham, John, 443; William, 443
Malling, Robert of, 260, 264
Malmesbury, xiii
Manchester School, xlii
Manumission of an Oxford M.A., 270

Margaret, Lady, xl
Maritime School, xlvii, 538
Marlborough School, xxvi, 152
Mathematics at Oxford, 136
Matilda, Queen, 88
Mean, Aylward, 98; Bristoic, 98
Mellent, Robert, Count of, 88
Mellitus, the monk, xi
Mercers' Company, xxxviii, 416
Mere, John of, 220
Merton, Canons of, 84; College, xxvii, xxxiv-xxxvi, 172-87; scholars of, xxvii, 170-9; Walter of, xxvii, 170
Merton College Grammar School, xxviii, 184; Accounts, 210-23, 298-305
Meryett, Matilda, 479
Mideford, John le Hay of, 246
Mildmay, Sir Walter, 475
Milton's *Tractate on Education*, xlviii
Moddyng, John, 408
Monasteries, dissolution of, xliii
Monastery not a church, 104; St Augustine's, Bristol, 100
Monastic control, xxii; education xxi, 288
Monks, Chaucer's description of, 344; colleges for, xxxiii, 196; contrasted with clerks, 104; education of Benedictine, 288; ignorance of Canterbury, 444; of Westminster to go to Oxford, 440
Monopoly of teaching, xx, xxii, xxix, xxxix, 91; grant of, to Eton, 412
Moody, Jane, 260
Morkyn, Walter, 332, 336
Morley, Adam of, 126
Morpeth School, xlv
Murder by Oxford student, xxv, 140
Musters, William de, 124
Muston, Robert of, 280

Nantes, Richard of, 252
National Schools Trust Deed, 544; Society, 1
Navarre, college of, xxxv; Joan of, xxxv
Neckham, Alexander, xxiv, 116, 134

Neell, John, 419
Nethersole, Sir Francis, xlviii
Newark Grammar School, xxvi, 156
Newborough, John, 310
New College, *see under* Oxford
Newland, xli
Newnham Priory, 116
Newport, John, 388
Newton, chapel in the Sea, 475
Niridanum, 2
Non-residence allowed to clergy, 144
Norman Conquest, xix
Northallerton Grammar and Song School, 342
Northampton, defence of, 160; exhibitioners at, xxiv, 120; School, xxvi, 120, 154; University, xxv, xxvi, 154, 158-63
Norton, Godfrey of, 232
Norwich Cathedral, xxi, xliii; School, 232
Nottingham School, 234
Nuns, learning of, xviii

Oblates, xxi, 60
Occhendon, William of, 86
Odiham Church, 96; John of, 218; Robert of, 216, 218
Offa, xiv
Oldham, Bishop, xlii
Olney, John, 304
Orchard, Robert, 372
Ordeals of fire and water, 58, 90
Ore, William of, 257
Oriental languages, xlvi, 512, 533; Professor of, xxxi, 268
Orosius, 16
Osred, King, 6
Otho, Cardinal Legate, xxvi
Oxford, Grammar School at, xxiv, 186; Mayor and bailiffs of, 152; St Frideswide's, 102; Sheriff of, 152
Oxford University, xxii, xxiii, xxiv, xxv; All Souls College, xxxix; beginnings of, 100; Benedictine College in, xxviii, 196; Brasenose College, 289; Chancellor of, xxvi, xxix; Christ Church, Dean of, 496, 498; Cistercian College in, xxviii; colleges excluded from Chantries Act, 475; curriculum in 1267, 190; excommunication on students, 154; Exeter College, xxxvi; exhibitioners, xxiv, 134, 136; lectures on Roman Law, 106; lectures on Theology, 100; Library, 420; Magdalen College, xxxv; mathematics at, 136; Merton College, xxviii, xxxiv, xxxv, xxxvi, 170-85; murder by student of, xxv, 140; New College, xxxiv, xxxv, 348-73; older than Paris, 278; Oriel College, xxxi; Professor of Oriental languages at, xxxi, 268; Queen's College, xxxi; Regulations for teaching Law, French and Letter-writing, 396; rights asked for from Pope, 276; scholars at defence of Northampton, 160; secessions from, xxv, xxvi, xxxiii, 140, 154, 282; Worcester College, xxviii, 198

Palace Schools, xiv, 30
Paris University, xxiii, xxiv, xxviii, 276, 294; College of Navarre, xxxv; Professor of Oriental languages at, xxxi, 268; Sorbonne, the, xxvi; student at, 116
Parker, Abp, 471
Parlour, John of the, 246
Partney School, 280, 282
Parts of speech, 50
Passevant, John, 250, 252
Paulinus, xii, 6, 16
Peacock, Reginald, xl
Peckham, Abp, xviii, 232, 256
Pencriche, Richard, 343
Pendock, William, 330
Penryn School, 476
Percyvale, Sir John, xxxviii, 436
Perkins, Edward, 532
Perriman, Mr, 529
Peter, Master, 56
Peterborough, Benedict, Abbot of, 102
Peterhouse, xxviii, 222
Petersfield, Adam of, 212, 214
Philippa, Queen, 282
Phocas, 16
Pigot, Walter, 280
Plautus, x
Plays at schools, xlvi, 78, 518

Plegmund, Abp, 24, 33
Pliny, xiv, 16
Ploughboy, work of, 40
Plumber, John, 252, 254
Plumpton, Roger of, 194
Pole, Convocation Articles of Cardinal, xlv, 494
Polesworth, xlviii
Pollard, Mr A. W., xliv
Pompeius, 16
Pontefract Castle, St Clement in, xxi, 66; School, 68
Popes: Alexander III, 108, 118; Benedict XII, xxxiii, 288; Celestine, 108; Clement V, xxx, 268; Eugenius, xiv, 20; Gregory, x, xi, xiv, 6, 16; Gregory VII, 22; Honorius III, xxxiii, 144; Innocent III, 142; Innocent IV, 136; John, 276, 278; Lucius II, 100
Portsmouth, William of, 212
Potter Hanworth, 146
Priests forbidden to teach, 439
Priscian, xvii, 16, 48, 192
Private Schools, xlviii
Probus, 16
Prosody, study of, xiii, 8
Prosper, 16
Pryce, John, 538
Public School at Kingston, xxxii, l, 318
Public Schools, l; Act, li; founded by Canute, 52
Pullein, Robert, *see* Robert the Chicken
Purley, John of, 218
Putta, 6

Rabanus Maurus, xiii
Randolph the grammarian, 68
Rank of a scholar, 54
Ranks, xviii, 52
Rashdall, Dr, xxiv
Raundes, Thomas, 348
Reading Abbey, 94; School, xxii, 94; University, xxv, 142
Redmere, Giles of, 280
Redvers, Baldwin of, 74; Richard of, 74
Redwald, 2
Reformation, the, xlii

Rewley Abbey, xxviii
Reynolds, Walter, Abp, 260
Rich, Lord, 470
Robert the Chicken, xxiii, 100
Rochell, Richard, 478; Stephen, 478
Rochester Mathematical School, xlvii; Song School, 6
Roger, Abp of York, 126
Roman Law, study of, xiii, 8, 106
Rome, schools of, ix
Romsey, Sir John of, 126
Rotherham, Abp, xli, 422; Jesus College, xxxv, xli, 422-33
Royal Lancasterian Institution, xlix

Sacraments not to be taught by Masters in Art or Grammar, 394
Safford, Hugh, 378
Saffron Walden, master at, xxxvii; School, xlv, 448
St Albans Almonry Boys, 296; School, xxii, xliv, 78, 116, 133; bachelors at, xxix, xxx, 240, 244; schoolmasters, 134; Statutes, 240, 253
St Andrew's, Holborn, 419
St Anthony's Hospital, 417
St Dunstan-in-the-East, 417
St Edmund of Abingdon, xxiv
St Jerome, x, xi, xvii, 16
St Lawrence, John of, 128
St Martin's-le-Grand School, 90, 92, 417
St Mary Axe, school in, xlviii
St Mary-le-Bow School, 90, 92, 238, 417
St Osmund, Institutions of, xix, 72
St Paul's School, xx, xxxvi, xxxviii, xlii, 417; Library, 80; master, xx, xxii, xxv, 80, 86, 90
St Peter's, Cornhill, 419
St Thomas of Acres Hospital, 419
Salamanca University, xxxi, 268
Salerno University, xxiv
Salisbury, John of, xx; Roger, Bp of, 94, 98
Salisbury School, xx, 72, 536; master, xx, 536-8; endowment of, 96
Salisbury University, xxv, xxvi, 154; College, xxvii, 164; scholars, jurisdiction over, 168

Saltash School, 476, 477
Samson, Abbot, l, 128
Say, Lord, xl, 420; William, xl, 218
Scales, Robert of, 128; Roger of, 130
Scawby, Hugh of, 146
Schalby, John of, 280
Scharle, R. of, 216
Scholar, rank of, 52; Oxford, Chaucer's description of, 345
Scholars, Bp of Ely's, 222; Merton, xxvii, 170-79; Valley, xxvii, 164
School, ABC, x; books, *see* Books; Dual, xlviii; Elementary and Grammar, xli; for Jews, 100; Grammar and Song, 342; Shakespeare's, xxxvii, 376; Song and Reading, Chaucer's description of, 346; Spelling and Reading, xli, 434
Schools, Almonry, xxxii, 296, 306; Boarding, xiv; British, 547; Cathedral, xliii, 470; Chantry, xxxvi, xli, 330, 434; Charity, xlix, 539; Continuance Warrant for, 475; dissenters prohibited from keeping, 542; Elementary, xlvi, l, 434; forbidden to be let, 96; Free, xxxviii, 122, 380; Grammar, ix, x, xi, xiv and *passim*; in churches, 36, 138; Lollard, xxxix, 328, 374, 394; Maritime, xlvii, 538; National, 544; Palace, xiv, 30; penalties for unlicensed, 528; plays at, xlvi, 78, 518; priests to keep, xxv, 140; Private, xlviii; Public, xxxii, l, 52, 318; Rhetoric, ix, x; Sites Act, l; Song, xii, xiv, xliii, 6, 236, 422; Theological, 142, 146; Writing, xiv, xli, 422
Schoolmaster, xix, xx; admission oath of, 210; Almonry, xxxii, 380; appointment of, 132, 238, 280, 342, 372, 537; called Chancellor, xxv; endowment of, 96; forbidden to be in holy orders, 400; in love, 76; jurisdiction of, 200, 232, 252-67; Mayor, 348, 471; Members of Gild, 378; monopoly of, xx, xxii, xxix; Papal delegate, 91, 152; precedence of, 392; recusant, 524, 526; removal of, 132, 535; trial of, 535
Secessions from Cambridge, *see under* Cambridge; Oxford, *see under* Oxford
Secular clergy, xxi
Sedulius, xiv, xlii, 16
Seliman, John, 434
Sentleger, Sir Anthony, 470
Serger, Nicholas, 482
Servius, 16
Sevenoaks Free Grammar School, xxxviii, 398
Sever, Henry, 408
Shakespeare's School, xxxvii, 376
Sherborne, John of, 212, 214; St John's Hospital, 482; School, xlv, 478-93
Sigebert, King of East English, ix, xi
Silsoe, William, 246
Singing master, 4
Singleton, xlviii
Smith, James, 443; Thomas the, 376; William, 328
Society for Promotion of Christian Knowledge, xlix
Song Schools, xii, xiv, xliii, 6, 236, 422
Sorbonne, College of the, xxvi; Robert of, xxvii
Southwell, Chapter of, 158; Grammar School, xxvi, 158
Stamford, Chantry in St Mary's Chapel, 236; College of Gilbertine Order of Sempringham at, 236; School, xliv; secession from Oxford to, xxxiii, 282
Statius, xiv, 16
Statute of Apprentices, xxxviii, 386; of Chantries, 472, 473; of Lollards, xxxix, 374, 394; of Recusants, 528
Statutes, College and School, xxix, xlv; Canterbury, 454; Merton College, 180-87; New College, 348, 373; Oxford, 186; St Albans Almonry, 296; St Albans Grammar, 240-53; Warwick, 272; Westminster, xlv, 496; Wotton-under-Edge, 324
Statutes, Papal, 288

Steele, Lawrence, 537
Stephen, King, 96, 108, 110
Stephens, Thomas, xlviii, 535
Stillingfleet, Bishop, xli
Stipends, xxxi: ministers in Cathedrals, 462; Rotherham College, 430; of Schoolmasters, Bodmin, 477; Caren, 538; Cornhill, 396; Farthinghoe, 416; Macclesfield, 439; Merton College, 214, 218, 220, 300, 302, 304; Penryn, 476; St Albans Almonry, 298; Saltash, 477; Sevenoaks, 400; Sherborne, 493; Stratford-on-Avon, 382; Sunderland, 538; Westminster Almonry, 306, 308, 312, 314; Westminster Choirmaster, 520; Choristers, 520; Dean of, 320; Prebendaries, 520; Scholars, 522; Schoolmasters, 522
Stock, William, 408
Stone, John, 332, 336
Stratford, John, 380
Stratford-on-Avon Gild, xxxvii, 376; School, xxxvii, 376, 378, 380
Suetonius, x
Sunderland School, xlvii, 538
Sutton, Richard, 438; Roger of, 270
Swanbury, Henry of, 210
Swetnaham, George, 492

Tanner, Thomas, 322
Taprell, Nicholas, 477
Tarsus, 2
Tebay, John, 414; Thomas, 414
Theobald, Abp, 108; of Étampes, xxiii, 102
Theodore, Abp, xii, xiii, 2, 4, 6
Theodulph of Orleans, xxv
Theological Schools, *see under* Schools
Theology, chair of, xxv; lectures in, 100
Thetford, Dean of, 82; School, xxii, 82
Thomas I, Abp, xix, 68, 70; II, Abp, 70
Thorncombe, Alfric, 480; Exhibitions, 480
Thornton Free Chapel, 486; William of, 236
Thurstan, Abp, 68, 102

Time-tables of Eton and Winchester, 448; Westminster, 508
Tobias, 6
Training College, xl, 402
Translation into French, xix, xxxvi, 340
Trenchard, Thomas, 486
Truro Grammar School, xliv
Trussel, William, 288
Tuckney, Dr Anthony, 536
Tully, *see* Cicero
Twichener, John, 450
Twyne, John, 471
Twyneham, *see* Christ Church, Hants

Universities, augmentation of, xlviii; commission, li; rise of, xxii, xxiii; Theology at, 144
University, Cambridge, *see under* Cambridge; Colleges, xxvi; Northampton, *see under* Northampton; Oxford, *see under* Oxford; Paris, *see under* Paris; Reading, *see* Reading; Salamanca, xxxi, 268; Salerno, xxiv; Salisbury, *see under* Salisbury
Upton, John of, 280, 282
Usher of Bury St Edmunds School, 130; Canterbury School, assault on, 252

Vacarius, xxiv, 106, 108
Valley Scholars, xxvii, 164
Veel, Peter of, 334
Vesey, John of, 230
Vicars ordered to attend school, 146, 154
Victorinus, 16
Vienne, Council of, xxx, 268
Virgil, xi, xiv, 16, 448, 451, 510, 532

Waerferth, Bp, 22
Wales, xlvii
Walkelin, Bp, xxi
Wallingford, John, 306; Thomas of, 210, 212
Waltham, College of Holy Cross, xviii, 54; Ralph of, 260
Walton, Margaret, 398, 400; Robert, 398
Ward, Thomas, 380

Warham, Abp, xxxiii, 444
Warren, Abbot, 132; John, Earl of, 288
Warwick, All Saints, xix, 58, 88; Grammar School, xxx, 272, master, xxxvii; Roger, Earl of, 88; St James's, 90; St Mary's, xix, 86, 88; St Nicholas, 90; schools at, xviii, 58, 86, 88; Song School, xxx, 272
Warwicke, Arthur, 536, 537
Watson, Idonea, 200; John, 200
Waytestathe, Richard, 328
Week St Mary, xliv, 476, 477
Werwulf, priest, 33
Westminster Almonry School Accounts, xxxi, 306; Council of, xxv, 138; Dean of, 498–505; Monks, 439; stipends and liveries, 520, 522; Synod at, 96
Westminster School, xliii, 496–525; play, xlvi, 518; statutes, xlv, 496; time-table, 508
Weston, Walter, 478
Whateley, George, xlvi
Whatvill, William of, 170
Wilfrid, Bishop, 4
Wilfrith, Bp of Worcester, 33
William I, 58, 66; II, 66
William, son of Mazel, 68
Williams, Henry, 538
Wimund, chaplain, 90
Winchelsea, Abp, 238
Winchester Cathedral, xxi
Winchester College, xvii, xxxiv, xliii; excluded from Chantries Act, 475; foundation deed of, 320; time-table, 448
Winchester Grammar School, xxxiv, 112; Exhibitioners at, xxv, 140
Winchester, William of, 86
Windsor, St George's, excluded from Chantries Act, 475
Winfrid, Abp, see Boniface
Wolsey, Cardinal, xlii
Wombe, Isabel, 228
Wood, Richard of the, 230
Woodward, John, 535
Worcester, Bishops of: Simon, 94; Thomas, 98; Wilfrith, 33
Worcester Cathedral, xxi; chamberlain of, xxxi
Worcester College, Oxford, xxviii, 198
Wotton-under-Edge School, xxxvi; foundation deed of, 330; statutes, 334
Wright, Mr T., 448
Writ for two schools in London, 416; of Henry I, xiv, 28
Writing Schools, *see under* Schools
Wulwin, 56
Wyard, Thomas, 304
Wycliffe, John, xl
Wykeham, William of, xvii, xxxiv, 320, 348
Wyle, Bp de la, xxvii
Wyncote, Robert, 378
Wyville, Dean of, 148

Yonge, John, 492
York, Cathedral, xix; Church of, xiii; Ralf of, 166; St Mary's Abbey Almonry School, xxxii; Separation of Grammar, Song and Writing Schools, 184; Song School, xii, 6; St Peter's School, xiv, xix, 10–19, 71, 126, Library, 16, master, xix, xxv